Impeachment of Richard M. Nixon
President of the United States

Report
of the
**Committee on the Judiciary
House of Representatives**
Peter W. Rodino, Jr., *Chairman*

GOVERNMENT REPRINTS PRESS
Washington, D.C.

COMMITTEE ON THE JUDICIARY
PETER W. RODINO, Jr., New Jersey, *Chairman*

HAROLD D. DONOHUE, Massachusetts	EDWARD HUTCHINSON, Michigan
JACK BROOKS, Texas	ROBERT McCLORY, Illinois
ROBERT W. KASTENMEIER, Wisconsin	HENRY P. SMITH III, New York
DON EDWARDS, California	CHARLES W. SANDMAN, Jr., New Jersey
WILLIAM L. HUNGATE, Missouri	TOM RAILSBACK, Illinois
JOHN CONYERS, Jr., Michigan	CHARLES E. WIGGINS, California
JOSHUA EILBERG, Pennsylvania	DAVID W. DENNIS, Indiana
JEROME R. WALDIE, California	HAMILTON FISH, Jr., New York
WALTER FLOWERS, Alabama	WILEY MAYNE, Iowa
JAMES R. MANN, South Carolina	LAWRENCE J. HOGAN, Maryland
PAUL S. SARBANES, Maryland	M. CALDWELL BUTLER, Virginia
JOHN F. SEIBERLING, Ohio	WILLIAM S. COHEN, Maine
GEORGE E. DANIELSON, California	TRENT LOTT, Mississippi
ROBERT F. DRINAN, Massachusetts	HAROLD V. FROEHLICH, Wisconsin
CHARLES B. RANGEL, New York	CARLOS J. MOORHEAD, California
BARBARA JORDAN, Texas	JOSEPH J. MARAZITI, New Jersey
RAY THORNTON, Arkansas	DELBERT L. LATTA, Ohio
ELIZABETH HOLTZMAN, New York	
WAYNE OWENS, Utah	
EDWARD MEZVINSKY, Iowa	

IMPEACHMENT INQUIRY STAFF
JOHN DOAR, *Special Counsel*
ALBERT E. JENNER, Jr., *Special Counsel to the Minority*
JOSEPH A. WOODS, Jr., *Senior Associate Special Counsel*
RICHARD CATES, *Senior Associate Special Counsel*
BERNARD W. NUSSBAUM, *Senior Associate Special Counsel*
ROBERT D. SACK, *Senior Associate Special Counsel*
ROBERT A. SHELTON, *Associate Special Counsel*
SAMUEL GARRISON III, *Deputy Minority Counsel*

FRED H. ALTSHULER, *Counsel*	ALAN MARER, *Counsel*
THOMAS BELL, *Counsel*	ROBERT P. MURPHY, *Counsel*
W. PAUL BISHOP, *Counsel*	JAMES B. F. OLIPHANT, *Counsel*
ROBERT L. BROWN, *Counsel*	RICHARD H. PORTER, *Counsel*
MICHAEL M. CONWAY, *Counsel*	GEORGE RAYBORN, *Counsel*
RUFUS CORMIER, *Special Assistant*	JAMES REUM, *Counsel*
E. LEE DALE, *Counsel*	HILLARY D. RODHAM, *Counsel*
JOHN B. DAVIDSON, *Counsel*	STEPHEN A. SHARP, *Counsel*
EVAN A. DAVIS, *Counsel*	JARED STAMELL, *Counsel*
CONSTANTINE J. GEKAS, *Counsel*	ROSCOE B. STAREK III, *Counsel*
RICHARD H. GILL, *Counsel*	GARY W. SUTTON, *Counsel*
DAGMAR HAMILTON, *Counsel*	EDWARD S. SZUKELEWICZ, *Counsel*
DAVID HANES, *Special Assistant*	THEODORE TETZLAFF, *Counsel*
JOHN E. KENNAHAN, *Counsel*	ROBERT J. TRAINOR, *Counsel*
TERRY R. KIRKPATRICK, *Counsel*	J. STEPHEN WALKER, *Counsel*
JOHN R. LABOVITZ, *Counsel*	BEN A. WALLIS, Jr., *Counsel*
LAWRENCE LUCCHINO, *Counsel*	WILLIAM WELD, *Counsel*
R. L. SMITH McKEITHEN, *Counsel*	WILLIAM A. WHITE, *Counsel*

COMMITTEE STAFF
JEROME F. ZEIFMAN, *General Counsel*
GARNER J. CLINE, *Associate General Counsel*
DANIEL L. COHEN, *Counsel*
FRANKLIN G. POLK, *Associate Counsel*

Impeachment of Richard M. Nixon President of the United States

© Ross & Perry, Inc. 2001 All rights reserved.

No claim to U.S. government work contained throughout this book.

Protected under the Berne Convention. Published 2001

Printed in The United States of America
Ross & Perry, Inc. Publishers
717 Second St., N.E., Suite 200
Washington, D.C. 20002
Telephone (202) 675-8300
Facsimile (202) 675-8400
info@RossPerry.com

SAN 253-8555

Government Reprints Press Edition 2001

Government Reprints Press is an Imprint of Ross & Perry, Inc.

Library of Congress Control Number: 2001095041
http://www.GPOreprints.com

ISBN 1-931641-30-7

⊗The paper used in this publication meets the requirements for permanence established by the American National Standard for Information Sciences "Permanence of Paper for Printed Library Materials" (ANSI Z39.48-1984).

All rights reserved. No copyrighted part of this publication may be reproduced, stored in a retrieval system, or transmitted, in any form or by any means, electronic, photocopying, recording, or otherwise, without the prior written permission of the publisher.

House Calendar No. 426

| 93D CONGRESS | HOUSE OF REPRESENTATIVES | REPORT |
| 2d Session | | No. 93-1305 |

IMPEACHMENT OF RICHARD M. NIXON, PRESIDENT OF THE UNITED STATES

AUGUST 20, 1974—Referred to the House Calendar and ordered to be printed

Mr. RODINO, from the Committee on the Judiciary, submitted the following

REPORT

together with

SUPPLEMENTAL, ADDITIONAL, SEPARATE, DISSENTING, MINORITY, INDIVIDUAL AND CONCURRING VIEWS

The Committee on the Judiciary, to whom was referred the consideration of recommendations concerning the exercise of the constitutional power to impeach Richard M. Nixon, President of the United States, having considered the same, reports thereon pursuant to H. Res. 803 as follows and recommends that the House exercise its constitutional power to impeach Richard M. Nixon, President of the United States, and that articles of impeachment be exhibited to the Senate as follows:

RESOLUTION

Impeaching Richard M. Nixon, President of the United States, of high crimes and misdemeanors.

Resolved, That Richard M. Nixon, President of the United States, is impeached for high crimes and misdemeanors, and that the following articles of impeachment be exhibited to the Senate:

Articles of impeachment exhibited by the House of Representatives of the United States of America in the name of itself and of all of the people of the United States of America, against Richard M. Nixon, President of the United States of America, in maintenance and support of its impeachment against him for high crimes and misdemeanors.

ARTICLE I

In his conduct of the office of President of the United States, Richard M. Nixon, in violation of his constitutional oath faithfully to execute the office of President of the United States and, to the best of his ability, preserve, protect, and defend the Constitution of the United States, and in violation of his constitutional duty to take care that the laws be faithfully executed, has prevented, obstructed, and impeded the administration of justice, in that:

On June 17, 1972, and prior thereto, agents of the Committee for the Re-election of the President committed unlawful entry of the headquarters of the Democratic National Committee in Washington, District of Columbia, for the purpose of securing political intelligence. Subsequent thereto, Richard M. Nixon, using the powers of his high office, engaged personally and through his subordinates and agents, in a course of conduct or plan designed to delay, impede, and obstruct the investigation of such unlawful entry; to cover up, conceal and protect those responsible; and to conceal the existence and scope of other unlawful covert activities.

The means used to implement this course of conduct or plan included one or more of the following:

(1) making or causing to be made false or misleading statements to lawfully authorized investigative officers and employees of the United States;

(2) withholding relevant and material evidence or information from lawfully authorized investigative officers and employees of the United States;

(3) approving, condoning, acquiescing in, and counseling witnesses with respect to the giving of false or misleading statements to lawfully authorized investigative officers and employees of the United States and false or misleading testimony in duly instituted judicial and congressional proceedings;

(4) interfering or endeavoring to interfere with the conduct of investigations by the Department of Justice of the United States, the Federal Bureau of Investigation, the Office of Watergate Special Prosecution Force, and Congressional Committees;

(5) approving, condoning, and acquiescing in, the surreptitious payment of substantial sums of money for the purpose of obtaining the silence or influencing the testimony of witnesses, potential witnesses or individuals who participated in such unlawful entry and other illegal activities;

(6) endeavoring to misuse the Central Intelligence Agency, an agency of the United States;

(7) disseminating information received from officers of the Department of Justice of the United States to subjects of investigations conducted by lawfully authorized investigative officers and employees of the United States, for the purpose of aiding and assisting such subjects in their attempts to avoid criminal liability;

(8) making false or misleading public statements for the purpose of deceiving the people of the United States into believing that a thorough and complete investigation had been conducted with respect to allegations of misconduct on the part of personnel of the executive branch of the United States and personnel of the Committee for the Re-election of the President, and that there was no involvement of such personnel in such misconduct; or

(9) endeavoring to cause prospective defendants, and individuals duly tried and convicted, to expect favored treatment and

consideration in return for their silence or false testimony, or rewarding individuals for their silence or false testimony.

In all of this, Richard M. Nixon has acted in a manner contrary to his trust as President and subversive of constitutional government, to the great prejudice of the cause of law and justice and to the manifest injury of the people of the United States.

Wherefore Richard M. Nixon, by such conduct, warrants impeachment and trial, and removal from office.

Article II

Using the powers of the office of President of the United States, Richard M. Nixon, in violation of his constitutional oath faithfully to execute the office of President of the United States and, to the best of his ability, preserve, protect, and defend the Constitution of the United States, and in disregard of his constitutional duty to take care that the laws be faithfully executed, has repeatedly engaged in conduct violating the constitutional rights of citizens, impairing the due and proper administration of justice and the conduct of lawful inquiries, or contravening the laws governing agencies of the executive branch and the purposes of these agencies.

This conduct has included one or more of the following:

(1) He has, acting personally and through his subordinates and agents, endeavored to obtain from the Internal Revenue Service, in violation of the constitutional rights of citizens, confidential information contained in income tax returns for purposes not authorized by law, and to cause, in violation of the constitutional rights of citizens, income tax audits or other income tax investigations to be initiated or conducted in a discriminatory manner.

(2) He misused the Federal Bureau of Investigation, the Secret Service, and other executive personnel, in violation or disregard of the constitutional rights of citizens, by directing or authorizing such agencies or personnel to conduct or continue electronic surveillance or other investigations for purposes unrelated to national security, the enforcement of laws, or any other lawful function of his office; he did direct, authorize, or permit the use of information obtained thereby for purposes unrelated to national security, the enforcement of laws, or any other lawful function of his office; and he did direct the concealment of certain records made by the Federal Bureau of Investigation of electronic surveillance.

(3) He has, acting personally and through his subordinates and agents, in violation or disregard of the constitutional rights of citizens, authorized and permitted to be maintained a secret investigative unit within the office of the President, financed in part with money derived from campaign contributions, which unlawfully utilized the resources of the Central Intelligence Agency, engaged in covert and unlawful activities, and attempted to prejudice the constitutional right of an accused to a fair trial.

(4) He has failed to take care that the laws were faithfully executed by failing to act when he knew or had reason to know that his close subordinates endeavored to impede and frustrate

lawful inquiries by duly constituted executive, judicial, and legislative entities concerning the unlawful entry into the headquarters of the Democratic National Committee, and the cover-up thereof, and concerning other unlawful activities, including those relating to the confirmation of Richard Kleindienst as Attorney General of the United States, the electronic surveillance of private citizens, the break-in into the offices of Dr. Lewis Fielding, and the campaign financing practices of the Committee to Re-elect the President.

(5) In disregard of the rule of law, he knowingly misused the executive power by interfering with agencies of the executive branch, including the Federal Bureau of Investigation, the Criminal Division, and the Office of Watergate Special Prosecution Force, of the Department of Justice, and the Central Intelligence Agency, in violation of his duty to take care that the laws be faithfully executed.

In all of this, Richard M. Nixon has acted in a manner contrary to his trust as President and subversive of constitutional government, to the great prejudice of the cause of law and justice and to the manifest injury of the people of the United States.

Wherefore Richard M. Nixon, by such conduct, warrants impeachment and trial, and removal from office.

Article III

In his conduct of the office of President of the United States, Richard M. Nixon, contrary to his oath faithfully to execute the office of President of the United States and, to the best of his ability, preserve, protect, and defend the Constitution of the United States, and in violation of his constitutional duty to take care that the laws be faithfully executed, has failed without lawful cause or excuse to produce papers and things as directed by duly authorized subpoenas issued by the Committee on the Judiciary of the House of Representatives on April 11, 1974, May 15, 1974, May 30, 1974, and June 24, 1974, and willfully disobeyed such subpoenas. The subpoenaed papers and things were deemed necessary by the Committee in order to resolve by direct evidence fundamental, factual questions relating to Presidential direction, knowledge, or approval of actions demonstrated by other evidence to be substantial grounds for impeachment of the President. In refusing to produce these papers and things, Richard M. Nixon, substituting his judgment as to what materials were necessary for the inquiry, interposed the powers of the Presidency against the lawful subpoenas of the House of Representatives, thereby assuming to himself functions and judgments necessary to the exercise of the sole power of impeachment vested by the Constitution in the House of Representatives.

In all of this, Richard M. Nixon has acted in a manner contrary to his trust as President and subversive of constitutional government, to the great prejudice of the cause of law and justice, and to the manifest injury of the people of the United States.

Wherefore Richard M. Nixon, by such conduct, warrants impeachment and trial, and removal from office.

CONTENTS

	Page
Committee Consideration	6
The Organization of the White House and Its Relationship to the Committee to the Committee for the Re-Election of the President	12

Article I:

Introduction	27
Adoption of a Political Intelligence Plan Including the Use of Electronic Surveillance	35
The Implementation of the Political Intelligence Plan	40
President Nixon's Response to the Arrests	42
Containment—July 1, 1972, to Election	55
Payments	66
Favored Treatment of Defendants and Prospective Defendants	75
Deception and Concealment	82
The President's Interference with the Department of Justice in March and April, 1973	98
The President's Interference with the Senate Select Committee on Presidential Campaign Activities	116
April 30, 1973 to the Present	121
Conclusion	133

Article II:

Introduction	139
Paragraph 1	141
Paragraph 2	146
Paragraph 3	157
Paragraph 4	171
Paragraph 5	177
Conclusion	180

Article III:

Introduction	187
The Committee Supoenas and the President's Response	191
Justification of the Committee's Subpoenas	197
Untrustworthiness of Edited Transcripts Produced by the President	203
The Claim of Executive Privilege	206
Conclusion	213

Other Matters:

Proposed Article on Concealment of Information about Bombing Operations in Cambodia	217
Proposed Article on Emoluments and Tax Evasion	220

Appendixes:

Appendix A—Analysis of the Technical Report on the 18½ Minute Gap	227
Appendix B—Subpoenas Issued to President Richard M. Nixon by the Committee on the Judiciary and Justification Memoranda	233
Supplemental, Additional, Separate, Dissenting, Minority, Individual and Concurring Views	281

COMMITTEE CONSIDERATION

The Constitution provides in Article I, Section 2, Clause 5, that "the House of Representatives shall have the sole power of impeachment." Article II, Section 4 provides, "The President, Vice President and all civil officers of the United States shall be removed from Office on Impeachment for, and Conviction of, Treason, Bribery, or other high Crimes and Misdemeanors."

Resolutions to impeach President Richard M. Nixon were introduced by members of the House in the last session of Congress and referred to the Committee on the Judiciary. On November 15, 1973, the House adopted H. Res. 702 to provide additional funds for the Committee for purposes of considering these resolutions. On December 20, 1973, special counsel was employed to assist the Committee in its inquiry.

On February 6, 1974, the Committee recommended that the House explicitly authorize the Committee's investigation to determine whether the House should exercise its constitutional power to impeach President Nixon.

On February 6, 1974, the House of Representatives, by a vote of 410 to 4, adopted H. Res. 803. That resolution authorized and directed the Committee on the Judiciary

> to investigate fully and completely whether sufficient grounds exist for the House of Representatives to exercise its constitutional power to impeach Richard M. Nixon, President of the United States of America. The Committee shall report to the House of Representatives such resolutions, articles of impeachment, or other recommendations as it deems proper.

As part of the resolution the Committee was granted the power of subpoena for its investigation. In its report to the House on H. Res. 803, the Committee had stated:

> The Committee's investigative authority is intended to be fully coextensive with the power of the House in an impeachment investigation—with respect to the persons who may be required to respond, the methods by which response may be required, and the types of information and materials required to be furnished and produced.

On February 21, 1974, the Committee received a report from its impeachment inquiry staff entitled, "Constitutional Grounds for Presidential Impeachment." The report reviewed the historical origins of impeachment, the intentions of the framers of the Constitution, and the American impeachment cases. The report also addressed the question whether grounds for impeachment, "high crimes and misdemeanors," must be crimes under the ordinary criminal statutes. The report concluded as follows:

> Impeachment is a constitutional remedy addressed to serious offenses against the system of government. The purpose of impeachment under the Constitution is indicated by the limited scope of the remedy (removal from office and possible disqualification from future office) and by the stated grounds for impeachment (treason, bribery and other high crimes and misdemeanors). It is not controlling

whether treason and bribery are criminal. More important, they are constitutional wrongs that subvert the structure of government, or undermine the integrity of office and even the Constitution itself, and thus are "high" offenses in the sense that word was used in English impeachments.

The framers of our Constitution consciously adopted a particular phrase from the English practice to help define the constitutional grounds for removal. The content of the phrase "high Crimes and Misdemeanors" for the framers is to be related to what the framers knew, on the whole, about the English practice—the broad sweep of English constitutional history and the vital role impeachment had played in the limitation of royal prerogative and the control of abuses of ministerial and judicial power.

Impeachment was not a remote subject for the framers. Even as they labored in Philadelphia, the impeachment trial of Warren Hastings, Governor-General of India, was pending in London, a fact to which George Mason made explicit reference in the Convention. Whatever may be said on the merits of Hastings' conduct, the charges against him exemplified the central aspect of impeachment—the parliamentary effort to reach grave abuses of governmental power.

The framers understood quite clearly that the constitutional system they were creating must include some ultimate check on the conduct of the executive, particularly as they came to reject the suggested plural executive. While insistent that balance between the executive and legislative branches be maintained so that the executive would not become the creature of the legislature, dismissible at its will, the framers also recognized that some means would be needed to deal with excesses by the executive. Impeachment was familiar to them. They understood its essential constitutional functions and perceived its adaptability to the American contest.

While it may be argued that some articles of impeachment have charged conduct that constituted crime and thus that criminality is an essential ingredient, or that some have charged conduct that was not criminal and thus that criminality is not essential, the fact remains that in the English practice and in several of the American impeachments the criminality issue was not raised at all. The emphasis has been on the significant effects of the conduct—undermining the integrity of office, disregard of constitutional duties and oath of office, arrogation of power, abuse of the governmental process, adverse impact on the system of government. Clearly, these effects can be brought about in ways not anticipated by the criminal law. Criminal standards and criminal courts were established to control individual conduct. Impeachment was evolved by Parliament to cope with both the inadequacy of criminal standards and the impotence of courts to deal with the conduct of great public figures. It would be anomalous if the framers, having barred criminal sanctions from the impeachment remedy and limited it to removal and possible disqualification from office, intended to restrict the grounds for impeachment to conduct that was criminal.

The longing for precise criteria is understandable; advance, precise definition of objective limits would seemingly serve both to direct future conduct and to inhibit arbitrary reaction to past conduct. In private affairs the objective is the control of personal behavior, in part through the punishment of misbehavior.

In general, advance definition of standards respecting private conduct works reasonably well. However, where the issue is presidential compliance with the constitutional requirements and limitations on the presidency, the crucial factor is not the intrinsic quality of behavior but the significance of its effect upon our constitutional system or the functioning of our government.

It is useful to note three major presidential duties of broad scope that are explicitly recited in the Constitution: "to take Care that the Laws be faithfully executed," to "faithfully execute the Office of President of the United States" and to "preserve, protect, and defend the Constitution of the United States" to the best of his ability. The first is directly imposed by the Constitution; the second and third are included in the constitutionally prescribed oath that the President is required to take before he enters upon the execution of his office and are, therefore, also expressly imposed by the Constitution.

The duty to take care is affirmative. So is the duty faithfully to execute the office. A President must carry out the obligations of his office diligently and in good faith. The elective character and political role of a President make it difficult to define faithful exercise of his powers in the abstract. A President must make policy and exercise discretion. This discretion necessarily is broad, especially in emergency situations, but the constitutional duties of a President impose limitations on its exercise.

The "take care" duty emphasizes the responsibility of a President for the overall conduct of the executive branch, which the Constitution vests in him alone. He must take care that the executive is so organized and operated that this duty is performed.

The duty of a President to "preserve, protect, and defend the Constitution" to the best of his ability includes the duty not to abuse his powers or transgress their limits—not to violate the rights of citizens, such as those guaranteed by the Bill of Rights, and not to act in derogation of powers vested elsewhere by the Constitution.

Not all presidential misconduct is sufficient to constitute grounds for impeachment. There is a further requirement—substantiality. In deciding whether this further requirement has been met, the facts must be considered as a whole in the context of the office, not in terms of separate or isolated events. Because impeachment of a President is a grave step for the nation, it is to be predicated only upon conduct seriously incompatible with either the constitutional form and principles of our government or the proper performance of constitutional duties of the presidential office.

On February 22, 1974, the full Committee on the Judiciary unanimously adopted a set of procedures governing confidentiality for the handling of material gathered in the course of its impeachment inquiry. The purpose and effect of these rules was that the Committee as a whole deferred, until the commencement of the initial presentation on May 9, its access to materials received by the impeachment inquiry staff. Only the Chairman and the Ranking Minority Member had access to, supervised and reviewed the assembly of evidentiary material and the preparation of transcripts of the President's recorded conversations.

In a status report to the Committee on March 1, 1974, the Inquiry staff reported on investigations in six principal areas:

A. Allegations concerning domestic surveillance activities conducted by or at the direction of the White House.

B. Allegations concerning intelligence activities conducted by or at the direction of the White House for the purpose of the Presidential election of 1972.

C. Allegations concerning the Watergate break-in and related activities, including alleged efforts by persons in the White House and others to "cover up" such activities and others.

D. Allegations concerning improprieties in connection with the personal finances of the President.

E. Allegations concerning efforts by the White House to use agencies of the executive branch for political purposes, and alleged White House involvement with election campaign contributions.

F. Allegations concerning other misconduct.

In anticipation of the presentation of evidentiary material by the Inquiry staff, the Committee on May 2, 1974, unanimously adopted a set of procedures for this presentation. These procedures were consistent with four general principles:

First, the Committee would receive from the staff and consider initially all reliable material which tended to establish the facts in issue. At the time that the evidentiary proceedings began, the Committee would give the President the opportunity to have his counsel present and to receive such documents and materials as the staff presented to the Committee Members for their consideration.

Second, during the presentation of this evidentiary material, whether in executive or in open session subject to the rules of the House, the Committee would give the President the opportunity to have his counsel present and to hear the presentation.

Third, at the end of this presentation, the Committee would give the President the opportunity to have his counsel make his position known, either orally or in writing, with respect to the evidentiary material received by the Committee.

At that time, President's counsel would be given the opportunity to recommend to the Committee names of witnesses to be called and to advise the Committee as to the witnesses' expected testimony.

Fourth, if and when witnesses were called, the Committee would give the President the opportunity to have his counsel ask such questions of the witnesses as the Committee deemed appropriate.

From May 9, 1974 through June 21, 1974, the Committee considered in executive session approximately six hundred fifty "statements of information" and more than 7,200 pages of supporting evidentiary material presented by the inquiry staff. The statements of information and supporting evidentiary material, furnished to each Member of the Committee in 36 notebooks, presented material on several subjects of the inquiry: the Watergate break-in and its aftermath, ITT, dairy price supports, domestic surveillance, abuse of the IRS, and the activities of the Special Prosecutor. The staff also presented to the Committee written reports on President Nixon's income taxes, presidential impoundment of funds appropriated by Congress, and the bombing of Cambodia.

In each notebook, a statement of information relating to a particular phase of the investigation was immediately followed by supporting evidentiary material, which included copies of documents and testimony (much of it already on public record), transcripts of presidential conversations, and affidavits. A deliberate and scrupulous abstention from conclusions, even by implication, was observed.

The Committee heard recordings of nineteen presidential conversations and dictabelt recollections. The presidential conversations were neither paraphrased nor summarized by the inquiry staff. Thus, no inferences or conclusions were drawn for the Committee. During the course of the hearings, Members of the Committee listened to each recording and simultaneously followed transcripts prepared by the inquiry staff.

On June 27 and 28, 1974, Mr. James St. Clair, Special Counsel to the President made a further presentation in a similar manner and form as the inquiry staff's initial presentation. The Committee voted to make public the initial presentation by the inquiry staff, including substantially all of the supporting materials presented at the hearings, as well as the President's response.

Between July 2, 1974, and July 17, 1974, after the initial presentation, the Committee heard testimony from nine witnesses, including all the witnesses proposed by the President's counsel. The witnesses were interrogated by counsel for the Committee, by Special counsel to the President pursuant to the rules of the Committee, and by Members of the Committee. The Committee then heard an oral summation by Mr. St. Clair and received a written brief in support of the President's position.

The Committee concluded its hearings on July 17, a week in advance of its public debate on whether or not to recommend to the House that it exercise its constitutional power of impeachment. In preparation for that debate the majority and minority members of the impeachment inquiry staff presented to the Committee "summaries of information."

On July 24, 25, 26, 27, 29, and 30, 1974, the Committee held its debate in open meetings, which were televised pursuant to H. Res. 1107, adopted by the House on July 22, 1974, permitting coverage of Committee meetings by electronic media. The Committee's meetings were conducted under procedures adopted on July 23, which provided both for general debate of no more than ten hours on a motion to recommend a resolution, together with articles of impeachment, impeaching Richard M. Nixon and for consideration of the articles after the conclusion of general debate. Each proposed article and additional articles were separately considered for amendment and immediately thereafter voted upon as amended for recommendation to the House. The procedures further provided:

> At conclusion of consideration of the articles for amendment and recommendation to the House, if any article has been agreed to, the original motion shall be considered as adopted and the Chairman shall report to the House said Resolution of impeachment together with such articles as have been agreed to or if articles are not agreed to, the Committee shall consider such resolutions or other recommendations as it deems proper.

On July 24, at the commencement of general debate, a resolution was offered including two articles of impeachment. On July 26, an amendment in the nature of a substitute was offered to Article I. In the course of the debate on this substitute, it was contended that the proposed article of impeachment was not sufficiently specific. Proponents of the substitute argued that it met the requirements of specificity under modern pleading practice in both criminal and civil litigation, which provide for notice pleading. They further argued that the President had notice of the charge, that his counsel had participated in the Committee's deliberations, and that the factual details would be provided in the Committee's report.

On July 27, the Committee agreed to the amendment in the nature of a substitute for Article I by a vote of 27 to 11. The Committee then adopted Article I, as amended, by a vote of 27 to 11. Article I, as adopted by the Committee charged that President Nixon, using the power of his high office, engaged, personally and through his subordinates and agents, in a course of conduct or plan designed to delay, impede, and obstruct the investigation of the unlawful entry into the headquarters of the Democratic National Committee in Washington, D.C., for the purpose of securing political intelligence; to cover up, conceal and protect those responsible; and to conceal the existence and scope of other unlawful covert activities.

On July 29, an amendment in the nature of a substitute was offered for Article II of the proposed resolution. After debate, the substitute was agreed to by a vote of 28 to 10. The Committee then adopted Article II, as amended, by a vote of 28 to 10. Article II, as amended, charged that President Nixon, using the power of the office of President of the United States, repeatedly engaged in conduct which violated the constitutional rights of citizens; which impaired the due and proper administration of justice and the conduct of lawful inquiries, or which contravened the laws governing agencies of the executive branch and the purposes of these agencies.

On July 30, an additional article was offered as an amendment to the resolution. After debate, this amendment was adopted by a vote of 21 to 17 and became Article III. Article III charged that President Nixon, by failing, without lawful cause or excuse and in willful disobedience of the subpoenas of the House, to produce papers and things that the Committee had subpoenaed in the course of it's impeachment inquiry, assumed to himself functions and judgments necessary to the exercise of the constitutional power of impeachment vested in the House. The subpoenaed papers and things had been deemed necessary by the Committee in order to resolve, by direct evidence, fundamental, factual questions related to presidential direction, knowledge, or appproval of actions demonstrated by other evidence to be substantial grounds for impeachment.

On July 30, the Committee considered an amendment to add a proposed Article, which charged that President Nixon authorized, ordered and ratified the concealment of information from the Congress and supplied to Congress false and misleading statements concerning the existence, scope and nature of American bombing operations in Cambodia. The proposed Article stated that these acts were in derogation of the powers of Congress to declare war, make appropriations, and raise and support armies. By a vote of 26 to 12, the amendment to add this Article was not agreed to.

Also on July 30, the Committee considered an amendment to add a proposed Article, charging that President Nixon knowingly and fraudulently failed to report income and claimed deductions that were not authorized by law on his Federal income tax returns for the years 1969 through 1972. In addition, the proposed Article charged that, in violation of Article II, Section 1 of the Constitution, President Nixon had unlawfully received emoluments, in excess of the compensation provided by law, in the form of government expenditures at his privately owned properties at San Clemente, California, and Key Biscayne, Florida. By a vote of 26 to 12, the amendment to add this article was not agreed to.

The Committee on the Judiciary based its decision to recommend that the House of Representatives exercise its constitutional power to impeach Richard M. Nixon, President of the United States, on evidence which is summarized in the following report.

THE ORGANIZATION OF THE WHITE HOUSE AND ITS RELATIONSHIP TO THE COMMITTEE FOR THE RE-ELECTION OF THE PRESIDENT

I

KEY ASSOCIATES OF THE PRESIDENT

On January 20, 1969, after taking his oath of office as President of the United States, Richard M. Nixon brought three key associates to the highest level of government, the office of the President. President Nixon appointed H. R. Haldeman White House Chief of Staff. He appointed John Ehrlichman Counsel to the President. He appointed John Mitchell Attorney General of the United States.

Haldeman's association with President Nixon began in 1956 when Haldeman was an advance man for then Vice President Nixon. In 1960 Haldeman was chief advance man and campaign tour manager for Richard Nixon's first Presidential campaign. In 1962 Haldeman managed Richard Nixon's unsuccessful campaign for Governor of California. In 1968 Haldeman was the chief of staff for the President's campaign. (Haldeman testimony, 7 SSC 2873)

The President and John Mitchell became law partners in New York City when their firms merged on January 1, 1967. In 1968 Mitchell was campaign director for the President's election campaign. (Mitchell testimony, 2 HJC 124–25, 192)

John Ehrlichman was recruited by Haldeman in late 1959 to work on President Nixon's 1960 campaign. During the 1960 Presidential campaign Ehrlichman took a leave of absence from his law firm to work as an advance man. Ehrlichman worked on Richard Nixon's 1962 campaign for Governor of California. Ehrlichman was the tour director of the President's 1968 Presidential campaign. (Ehrlichman testimony, 6 SSC 2514–15, 2522–24; Kalmbach testimony, 3 HJC 532)

II

WHITE HOUSE PERSONNEL

From January 21, 1969, through May 19, 1973, H. R. Haldeman was President Nixon's chief of staff. He was in charge of administering White House operations. He worked directly with the President in the planning of the President's daily schedule, provided the President with the information he requested from the members of his staff and the members of his administration, and relayed instructions from the President to other officers and members of the executive branch of the Government. Haldeman directed the activities of the President's Appointments Secretary and the White House Staff Secretary. He received copies of memorandums and letters written by senior staff members and assistants. He established, subject to the approval of the President, the White House budget. He had no independent schedule. His schedule was that of the President. He was at the call of the President at all times. During the reelection campaign, the President's campaign organization reported to Haldeman. The President announced Haldeman's resignation on April 30, 1973.

The following White House employees and other agents of the President reported to Haldeman:

(1) Lawrence M. Higby was Haldeman's personal aide and his chief administrative assistant throughout Haldeman's tenure at the White House. He had worked previously for Haldeman in private business and in the 1968 Presidential campaign. Higby supervised the flow of persons, papers, telephone calls, and correspondence to Haldeman, acted in Haldeman's name, and traveled with him. After Haldeman's resignation, Higby transferred to the Office of Management and Budget.

(2) In March 1971, after working for Herbert Klein, then director of communications for the executive branch, Gordon C. Strachan became Haldeman's principal political assistant. Strachan performed political assignments for Haldeman. He supervised the White House polling operation and reported on the activities of the Republican National Committee and the Committee for the Re-Election of the President (CRP). He regularly prepared political matters memorandums for Haldeman on the status of the 1972 election campaign, and often carried out decisions Haldeman made on the basis of the information they contained. After the 1972 election, Strachan was appointed as general counsel of the U.S. Information Agency.

(3) In January 1969, Alexander P. Butterfield was appointed deputy assistant to the President. Beginning in January 1970, Butterfield's office adjoined the President's. He had responsibility for the President's daily schedule. He oversaw the administration of the White House, including the office of the staff secretary. He reported directly to Haldeman and functioned as Haldeman's deputy in handling the actual flow of people and papers in and out of the President's office. In March 1973, Butterfield was appointed Administrator of the Federal Aviation Administration.

(4) Dwight L. Chapin had known Haldeman previously and had worked for the President at his law firm for 2 years before the 1968 election. In January 1969, Chapin joined the White House staff as a special assistant to the President and acted as the President's appointments secretary. Chapin had general planning responsibility for the President's schedule and travel. He reported directly to Haldeman and, at times, to the President. Two years later, Chapin was appointed deputy assistant to the President. He left the White House and entered private business in February 1973.

(5) In January 1969, Stephen B. Bull joined the White House staff and worked under Chapin in the scheduling office. In February 1973, he was appointed a special assistant to the President and assumed additional responsibilities for implementing the President's daily schedule.

(6) On January 20, 1969, Hugh W. Sloan, Jr., became a staff assistant to the President. He worked under Chapin on the planning of the

President's appointments and travel. He was also assigned certain special projects. Sloan left the White House in March 1971 to join the President's reelection campaign organization. He resigned as the treasurer of the Finance Committee to Re-Elect the President (FCRP) on July 11, 1972.

(7) In July 1970, John W. Dean was hired by Haldeman as counsel to the President. Dean had previously been an Associate Deputy Attorney General in the Justice Department. His duties in the White House included working with the Justice Department. The counsel's office advised the President on technical legal problems and prepared legal opinions on issues. Dean was also assigned by Haldeman to gather information on political matters of interest to the White House. Dean normally reported to Haldeman, but on certain domestic matters he reported to Ehrlichman. Dean resigned on April 30, 1973.

(8) In October 1970, Fred Fielding was hired as assistant to the counsel to the President. He became associate counsel in the spring of 1971. He was Dean's "principal deputy." Fielding was appointed deputy counsel in early 1973, and resigned from the President's staff on January 11, 1974.

(9) In January 1969, Herbert G. Klein was appointed to the newly created position of director of communications for the executive branch. His office handled many of the White House public relations and media activities. He and his assistants in the office of communications reported to Haldeman. Klein resigned from the White House on July 1, 1973.

(10) On October 7, 1969, Jeb Stuart Magruder was appointed special assistant to the President to work on Haldeman's staff. Later in 1969 Magruder was also named deputy director of communications. He held both positions until he resigned in May 1971 to work in the President's reelection campaign organization; he later became deputy campaign director of CRP. Magruder's responsibility at the White House was public relations. He organized letter writing programs, encouraged media coverage, and formed private committees to support administration positions.

(11) In December 1970, Herbert L. Porter came to the White House with the understanding that he would work in the reelection campaign. After doing advance work for about a month, Porter was offered a job by Magruder on Klein's staff. From January until May 1971 he worked as a staff assistant in the communications office, where he did public relations work, including scheduling speakers. Porter assumed scheduling responsibilities for the predecessor organization of CRP in May 1971.

(12) On November 6, 1969, Charles W. Colson was named special counsel to the President. Colson initiated, planned, and executed many White House public relations and media efforts. He was in charge of White House relations with "special interest groups" and coordinated fund raising for administration projects. Colson also organized political support for the President's policies. Generally, he reported to Haldeman, but he reported directly to the President on certain matters. On March 10, 1973, Colson resigned from the White House. (Colson testimony, 3 HJC 184–85)

(13) In September 1969, Frederick C. LaRue was appointed a special consultant to the President. He served without pay. LaRue

reported to Haldeman on the political projects he undertook for the White House. He resigned on February 15, 1972, to work in the President's re-election campaign and later became special assistant to CRP's campaign director.

(14) Herbert Kalmbach became the President's personal attorney in 1969. He had worked on President Nixon's 1962 campaign for Governor of California and had been associate finance chairman of the President's 1968 campaign. Kalmbach undertook various fundraising assignments on behalf of the President from 1969 through 1972. Kalmbach was not employed by the White House, although he acted at Haldeman's direction. (Kalmbach testimony, 3 HJC 529–30, 594, 660, 664)

In January 1969, John D. Ehrlichman was appointed counsel to the President. He reported primarily to Haldeman. On November 4, 1969, he became assistant to the President for Domestic Affairs and the President's chief assistant in the White House for all domestic matters. He advised the President on policy and communicated Presidential decisions to departments and agencies. On July 1, 1970, the Domestic Council was established in the Executive Office of the President as a separate entity with its own staff and budget. Ehrlichman was appointed Executive Director. On Jaunary 20, 1973, Ehrlichman resigned this position and on January 21 joined Haldeman as one of the four principal assistants to the President. He worked in that capacity until May 19, 1973. On April 30, 1973, the President announced Ehrlichman's resignation from the White House.

The following were among the members of the White House staff under Ehrlichman's supervision:

(1) In January 1969, Egil Krogh came to the White House as a staff assistant to Ehrlichman. He was deputy counsel to the President from May 1969 until November 1969, when he was appointed deputy assistant to the President for Domestic Affairs. In July 1970, he assumed the additional position of Assistant Director of the Domestic Council. Krogh reported to Ehrlichman, except on a few matters where he reported directly to the President. Krogh's responsibilities in domestic affairs focused on law enforcement, including work with the Federal Bureau of Investigation, drug enforcement programs, and internal security matters. In July 1971, pursuant to instructions from the President, Krogh organized the White House special investigations unit (the "Plumbers"). His work with the unit continued until December 1971. In January 1973 Krogh was appointed Under Secretary of Transportation.

(2) In 1969, David Young came to the White House as an administrative assistant to Henry Kissinger in the National Security Council (NSC). He was Kissinger's appointments secretary. In January 1971, Young became a special assistant, NSC, in charge of classification and declassification of documents. In July 1971, he was transferred to Ehrlichman's staff and assigned to work with Krogh on the White House special investigations unit. Young continued as an assistant to Krogh until January 1973, when he was appointed to a staff position on the Domestic Council. He left the White House in March 1973.

(3) G. Gordon Liddy became a member of the White House special investigations unit in July 1971. His appointment was authorized

by Ehrlichman and he was placed on the payroll of the Domestic Council. Liddy worked for Krogh until he resigned from the White House staff in mid-December 1971. He then became counsel to CRP and in March 1972 moved to a predecessor organization of FCRP. He was counsel to FCRP until June 28, 1972.

(4) In early July 1971, E. Howard Hunt started work as a White House consultant. He had been recommended by Colson and initially worked under Colson's supervision. In July 1971 Hunt was assigned with Ehrlichman's approval to the White House special investigations unit, where he worked under Krogh's direction. Hunt had spent 21 years with the Central Intelligence Agency.

(5) In late November 1968, Edward L. Morgan began working under Ehrlichman's supervision to coordinate some of the President's personal affairs. He worked as deputy counsel to the President, deputy assistant to the President for Domestic Affairs, and Assistant Director of the Domestic Council. Morgan left the White House in January 1973 and was appointed an Assistant Secretary of the Treasury.

(6) On April 8, 1969, John J. Caulfield, a former New York City police detective, was hired by Ehrlichman as a staff assistant to the counsel to the President. His duties were to act as liaison with Federal law enforcement agencies and to supervise White House investigations. Ehrlichman ordered the investigations Caulfield directed; later, when Dean became counsel to the President, Caulfield received assignments from both Ehrlichman and Dean. In March 1972 Caulfield left the White House to work for CRP. On April 28, 1972, he accepted a position in the Treasury Department. On July 1, 1972, Caulfield became the Acting Assistant Director for Enforcement of the Alcohol, Tobacco, and Firearms Division of the Internal Revenue Service.

(7) In July 1969, Anthony T. Ulasewiez, a retired New York City police detective, was authorized by Ehrlichman to work under Caulfield to carry out investigative tasks for the White House. Ulasewiez was not directly employed by the White House, but received investigative assignments through Caulfield, and reported to him. He was paid by Herbert Kalmbach, the President's personal lawyer, from July 1969 through 1972, and worked with Kalmbach from June 1972 through September 1972.

Rose Mary Woods has worked as President Nixon's personal secretary since 1951. She joined the White House staff as the President's personal secretary in January, 1969 and was promoted to executive assistant and personal secretary in June, 1973. (Rose Mary Woods testimony, *In re Grand Jury*, Misc. 47–73, November 8, 1973, 801, 812–13; Butterfield testimony, 1 HJC 63).

III

OTHER ADMINISTRATION OFFICIALS

On January 20, 1969 President Nixon appointed John Mitchell Attorney General of the United States. (Mitchell testimony, 2 HJC 124) In 1971 Mitchell began organizing the President's 1972 re-election campaign. Mitchell resigned as Attorney General on March 1, 1972, and officially became campaign director of the 1972 campaign on

April 9, 1972. (Mitchell testimony, 2 HJC 124-25) Mitchell resigned as campaign director on July 1, 1972, but continued to act as a consultant to CRP throughout the campaign and after the election. (Mitchell testimony, 2 HJC 125)

In February, 1969, Richard Kleindienst joined the Nixon Administration as Deputy Attorney General. (Kleindienst testimony, 9 SSC 3560) On February 15, 1972 the President nominated Kleindienst to be Attorney General to succeed John Mitchell, who was leaving the Department of Justice to become head of CRP. (Book V, 606-08) Kleindienst was confirmed by the Senate on June 8, 1972. (Kleindienst testimony, 9 SSC 3560) On April 30, 1973 the President announced Kleindienst's resignation as Attorney General.

In November, 1970, President Nixon appointed Robert Mardian Assistant Attorney General in charge of Internal Security Division of the Department of Justice. Mardian had previously served in the Nixon Administration as General Counsel for the Department of Health, Education and Welfare. From May, 1972 until June, 1972 Mardian was a political coordinator at the Committee for the Reelection of the President. After June 17, 1972 Mardian acted as a counsel to CRP for Watergate matters. (Mardian testimony, 6 SSC 2346-47; 6 Presidential Documents 1583).

Henry Petersen was a career employee of the Criminal Division of the Department of Justice. In January, 1972 the President appointed Petersen Assistant Attorney General in charge of the Criminal Division.

L. Patrick Gray was Acting Director of the Federal Bureau of Investigation from May 3, 1972 until he resigned that position on April 27, 1973. (Gray testimony, 9 SSC 3450, 3493) Gray had previously served as executive assistant to HEW Secretary Robert Finch, and in the Department of Justice as Assistant Attorney General, Civil Division. In February, 1972 the President nominated Gray to be Deputy Attorney General, but the nomination had not been acted upon by the Senate at the time of his appointment as acting Director of the FBI. (Gray testimony, 9 SSC 3473-75) On February 17, 1973 the President nominated Gray to be permanent Director of the FBI. On April 5, 1973 the President withdrew Mr. Gray's nomination. (9 Presidential Documents 335)

Richard Helms was the Director of the Central Intelligence Agency at the time Richard Nixon became President. Helms had been with the Agency since its inception in 1947 and became its Director on June 30, 1966. Helms left the CIA on February 2, 1973 after being appointed by the President as Ambassador to Iran (Helms testimony, 8 SSC 3232)

Vernon Walters, a lieutenant general in the U.S. Army, was appointed by the President to be Deputy Director of the CIA after General Cushman left the Agency. Walters began to serve in this capacity on May 2, 1972. General Walters had served as interpreter and aide to Richard Nixon when he toured South America as Vice President. (Walters testimony, 9 SSC 3403-04)

Maurice Stans was a principal fundraiser in President Nixon's 1968 campaign. (HJC. Background—White House/CRP 5) President Nixon appointed Stans Secretary of Commerce effective January 21, 1969. Stans served as Commerce Secretary until February 15, 1972, when he resigned to become Chairman of the Finance Committee to Re-elect the President. (Stans testimony, 2 SSC 695)

IV

OPERATION OF THE PRESIDENT'S STAFF

From January, 1970, until March, 1973, Alexander Butterfield was personal aide to the President. His office was next to the Oval Office of the President; his responsibilities were to insure the "smooth running of the President's official day." (Butterfield testimony, 1 HJC 9–10) He was in a uniquely well-suited position to know the manner in which the President's staff was organized and operated.

During his first term as President, according to testimony by Butterfield, President Nixon spent almost all of his working time with one of a handful of assistants: on all matters of policy, direction, politics, and strategy, with H. R. Haldeman; on most domestic matters, with John Ehrlichman; on political matters, with Charles Colson; and on foreign affairs, with Henry Kissinger. The vast majority of the President's time was spent with Haldeman, (Butterfield testimony, 1 HJC 14–16, 40) who, according to Butterfield, "was an extension of the President":

He [Haldeman] was far and away the closest person to the President. There was never any competition with regard to Mr. Haldeman's role.... He was an extension of the President .... (Butterfield testimony, 1 HJC 13)

Haldeman was the alter ego. Haldeman was almost the other President. I can't emphasize that enough. (Butterfield testimony, 1 HJC 66)

In his public statement of March 12, 1973 refusing to permit members of his personal staff to honor requests for Congressional appearances, the President himself said:

If the President is not subject to such questioning, it is equally appropriate that members of his staff not be so questioned, for their roles are in effect an extension of the Presidency. ("Presidential Statements," 3/12/73, 6)

In his testimony before the Committee, Butterfield drew an organizational chart of the White House staff showing the President's relationships to Haldeman and to other members of his staff. This diagram was made part of the record.

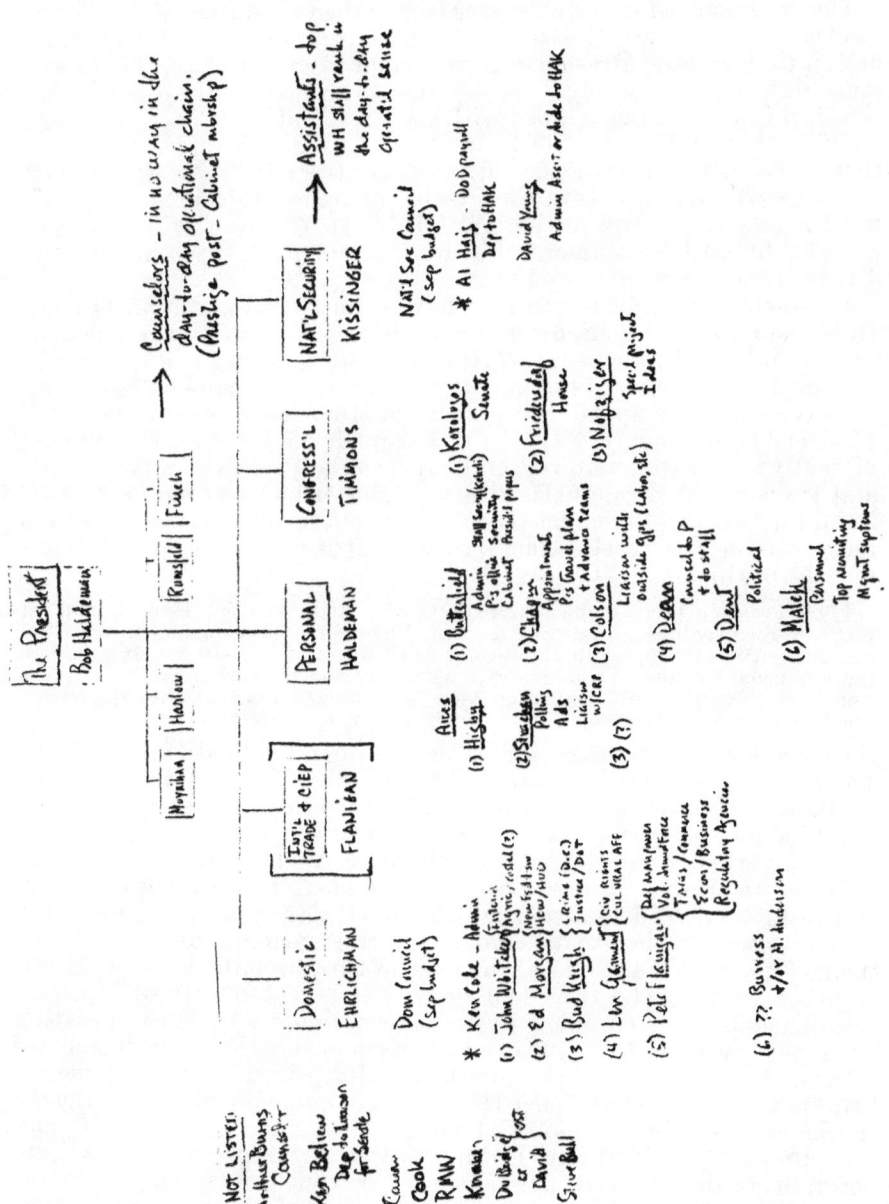

BUTTERFIELD EXHIBIT NO. 1

The testimony of other witnesses before the Committee, John Dean, Charles Colson, and Herbert Kalmbach, corroborates Butterfield's description of how President Nixon conducted his office. There are some differences, notably Colson's testimony as to the direct relationship Colson had developed with the President by 1972. But Colson testified that Haldeman had a practice of asking to screen anything that went to the President and obtained from the few senior staff members who had access to the President copies of documents sent to the President. (Colson testimony, 3 HJC 412) Colson acknowledged that he himself was answerable to Haldeman. (Colson testimony, 3 HJC 468)

President Nixon preferred to receive information and reports from Haldeman and to communicate his decisions through him. Haldeman had no independent schedule. (Haldeman testimony, 7 SSC 2871) He ordinarily spent several hours a day with the President— a "good six to seven times as much time with the President as anyone else." (Butterfield testimony, 1 HJC 40) Except for daily press summaries, virtually all written material addressed to the President was screened and transmitted through Haldeman. (Butterfield testimony, 1 HJC 36-37) When the President made a decision, he authorized one of his aides, almost always Haldeman, to see that it was carried out.[1] (Butterfield testimony, 1 HJC 42) Butterfield testified:

> [The President] communicated by telephone with a great many people at night, in the evenings, and during the day. But his normal communications, oral and in writing, were just to Haldeman, Ehrlichman and Kissinger. It would be quite unusual for him to communicate with anyone else—perhaps a few times to Colson during that 1972 campaign year. But almost always with Haldeman, almost always with Haldeman. (Butterfield testimony, 1 HJC 66)

The President's procedure for implementing a policy decision is illustrated in his approval, in 1970, of the Huston Plan for domestic surveillance and intelligence gathering. The President created an ad hoc intelligence committee consisting of representatives of the National Security Agency, the Defense Intelligence Agency, the CIA and the FBI. After the committee prepared a report, Tom Charles Huston, a Presidential staff assistant and White House representative to the committee, sent the report and a covering memorandum to Haldeman. (Book VII, 438-44) Haldeman in turn brought it to the President's attention. The President decided to accept certain of Huston's recommendations. Haldeman sent a memorandum to Huston stating that the President had approved the recommendations and instructed Huston to prepare and distribute a formal Presidential decision memorandum. (Book VII, 447-48) Huston prepared and distributed the decision memorandum. (Book VII, 454-61)

Butterfield testified that Haldeman was an "implementer." All important information in Haldeman's possession was relayed to the President; the President made all decisions of consequence. Butter-

---

[1] Haldeman had his own staff. Lawrence Higby, Haldeman's personal aide and chief administrative assistant, supervised the flow of persons, papers, telephone calls and correspondence to Haldeman. Gordon Strachan served as Haldeman's principal political assistant; he regularly prepared Political Matters Memoranda for Haldeman on the status of the 1972 election campaign. His principal assignment was to follow up on the details of Presidential decisions communicated to him by chief of staff Haldeman. Dwight Chapin acted as the President's Appointments Secretary and reported directly to Haldeman on matters concerning the President's schedule and travel. Bruce Kehrli, the White House Staff Secretary, who oversaw the day-to-day flow of papers within the White House, worked under Haldeman and Butterfield. (Butterfield testimony, 1 HJC 14-16)

field testified that it would have been "altogether out of character" for Haldeman to have decided anything more important than minor questions of staff management. He also testified:

Mr. JENNER. Was there any occasion during all of the time that you were at the White House that there came to your attention that Haldeman ever did anything without the knowledge of the President?
Mr. BUTTERFIELD. No, never.
Mr. JENNER. Dealing with White House affairs?
Mr. BUTTERFIELD. No; never, nothing unilaterally at all. He was essentially— I may have said this—but an implementer. Mr. Haldeman implemented the decisions of the President as did Mr. Ehrlichman but perhaps to a lesser extent. But Haldeman especially was an implementer, because the President ran his own personal affairs. He was not a decision maker. . . . I can hardly recall the decisions, any decisions that he made, unless that it was that the White House staff mess personnel would wear jackets or something along that line. He implemented the President's decisions. The President was the decision-maker. The President was 100 percent in charge. (Butterfield testimony 1 HJC 69–70; see also Haldeman testimony, 7 SSC 2872)

Mitchell's testimony was to the same effect in response to questions by Representative Thornton:

Mr. THORNTON. Did you ever check to determine whether or not the information relayed to you through Mr. Haldeman was a correct reflection of the President's instructions?
Mr. MITCHELL. There may have been occasions, Congressman, but I would have to say that in most all instances that I can recall, Mr. Haldeman's representations to me of the President's position were truthfully and fully stated.
Mr. THORNTON. Did you ever check with the President to determine whether information you had passed toward him through Mr. Haldeman had been received by him?
Mr. MITCHELL. No, I don't believe I did, but I think there again, the record of actions coming from such line of communication would indicate that they were fully and faithfully conveyed. (Mitchell testimony, 2 HJC 209–10)

V

THE RE-ELECTION CAMPAIGN

Haldeman's responsibility extended to the President's re-election campaign. During the summer and fall of 1971, Haldeman personally reviewed and supervised plans for the development of the re-election committee and the assignment of staff to it. He established rules and procedures for the transfer of employees from the White House staff to the re-election committee, waiver of these rules required his personal approval. (Political Matters Memorandum, 12/6/71, 5 [2]) In March, 1971, Hugh Sloan and Harry Flemming, members of Haldeman's staff, left the White House to become the first members of the staff of a predecessor of the Committee for the Re-Election of the President (CRP). (Butterfield testimony, 1 HJC 25; HJC, Background— White House/CRP 5) In May, 1971, Jeb Magruder (hired by Haldeman for his staff and then transferred by Haldeman to White House Communications Director Herbert Klein's office) transferred from the White House to become the acting campaign director of the CRP. (HJC, Background—White House/CRP 3)

---

[2] During 1971 and 1972 Strachan prepared 28 of these memoranda and sent them to Haldeman for review and decisions. The Committee has received 21 of these documents from the White House. Seven of the memoranda are published in the Statement of Information. The remainder currently are in the Committee's files.

By April, 1972, seventeen of the twenty-three senior CRP staff members were former members of the Administration or the White House staff. (Butterfield testimony, 1 HJC 53; HJC, Background—White House/CRP 5)

John Mitchell claimed to have been in charge of day-to-day operations of the campaign committee by mid-1971. He remained as Attorney General until March 1, 1972. Haldeman reviewed the hiring of key personnel (Political Matters Memoranda, 8/13/71, 4; 9/18/71, 3-4; 1/18/72, 4, and 1/7/72 attachment; Book VI, 899); reviewed proposed budgets for CRP departments and divisions (Political Matters Memoranda, 2/16/72, 78; 9/18/72, 4); gave the final approval to CRP advertising and campaign materials (Political Matters Memoranda, 2/16/72, 4; 9/18/72, 5; Haldeman testimony, 7 SSC 2878); supervised the expenditure of funds for polling (Political Matters Memoranda, 2/1/72, 1; 5/16/72, 2; Haldeman testimony, 7 SSC 2878); and reviewed CRP regional operations in key states. (Political Matters Memoranda, 5/16/72, 7; 12/6/71, 1; 1/18/72, 2-4; 7/29/72, 3; 8/11/72, 6)

Moreover, Haldeman and other members of the White House staff were active in formulating campaign strategy. A "political group," consisting of Haldeman, Ehrlichman, Clark MacGregor, Bryce Harlow, Charles Colson, Mitchell, and Harry Dent, met regularly at the White House to discuss the highest level decisions on campaign tactics and domestic policy. (HJC, Background—White House/CRP 6)

In addition, White House personnel handled other areas of the campaign. A White House group headed by Colson frequently prepared CRP press releases and speeches to be made by supporters of the President. (Political Matters Memoranda, 5/16/72, 5-6, and attachment; 3/3/72 attachment) Counsel to the President John Dean handled such legal matters for CRP as establishing finance committees (Political Matters Memorandum, 2/1/72, 1); preparing the defense to a law suit (Political Matters Memorandum, 11/16/71, 5); and transferring the Republican Convention site from San Diego to Miami Beach. (Political Matters Memorandum, 5/16/72, 5)

A copy of each document submitted to the CRP campaign director (first Mitchell and then MacGregor) was normally given to Haldeman's assistant, Gordon Strachan, who summarized the documents for Haldeman in "Political Matters Memoranda." (Political Matters Memorandum, 3/3/72, 5) The memoranda covered the entire range of activities in the campaign. Butterfield testified that Strachan's memoranda "would not go to the President under normal circumstances," but Haldeman "would relay the information when he spoke to the President next." (Butterfield testimony, 1 HJC 111) After reviewing the memoranda, Haldeman would write approvals, disapprovals and notations to Strachan, his deputy, with specific instructions for actions to be taken. Haldeman left no doubt that he was issuing directions and speaking for the President.[3]

---

[3] For example in item 14 of Magruder's Projects in a Political Matters Memorandum dated February 16, 1972, Strachan reported that Magruder and Colson were increasingly at odds about whether Muskie should be personally attacked for his war stand. Strachan reported that Magruder planned to seek authority from the Attorney General to be the only control with the spokesmen to the express exclusion of Colson. Haldeman replied, "This is *not* acceptable—Colson is acting under express instructions. Tell Magruder to talk to me if he has a problem. H" (Political Matters Memorandum, 2/16/72, 6; Book I, 89)

Strachan would then contact the appropriate CRP and White House personnel to carry out Haldeman's directions. (See Strachan's marginal notes, Political Matters Memoranda) Haldeman was regularly informed of even the most minor administrative decisions, including the rental of office space (Political Matters Memoranda, 6/29/72, 5; 11/16/71, 3; 12/16/71, 4); consideration of press requests for interviews with campaign staff (Political Matters Memoranda, 8/11/72, 6); and the development of CRP's field organizational plan. (Political Matters Memoranda, 2/1/72, 6; 7/29/72, 8) Haldeman met with Campaign Director Mitchell on a weekly basis to discuss such subjects as campaign financing, personnel and strategy.[4] (Mitchell testimony, 2 HJC 202) In February, 1972, Haldeman directed that $350,000 in campaign funds be placed under his control and Strachan picked up the cash from CRP prior to April 7, 1972. (Book I, 78, 84, 90)

The President was attentive to the operation of his re-election campaign. On April 30, 1973, the President said that in 1972, for the first time in his 27-year political career, he had left management of his campaign to others, concentrating instead on his duties as President. ("Presidential Statements," 4/30/73, 16) However, the transcript of a conversation on April 4, 1972, edited and released by the White House in June, 1974, shows that the President was fully aware of the detailed decisions of the campaign, and that he actively participated in them. For example, the President discussed with Haldeman and Mitchell details of a site for the 1972 convention: the President decided it would be changed to Miami Beach. The President also discussed the Wisconsin Democratic primary; the prospects for various Democratic Presidential candidates; a letter of support for the President from columnist William F. Buckley; the campaign of Representative Ashbrook for the Republican presidential nomination; various individuals and their duties in the President's re-election campaign; and the President's prospects and campaign organizations in Wisconsin, California, Illinois, Ohio, Pennsylvania, New York, New Jersey, Texas, Ohio, Michigan, Minnesota, Massachusetts and Vermont. (President's submission, Book I, 104-16) Similarly, the Political Matters Memoranda reveal that the President fully discussed campaign matters with Haldeman, Mitchell, Dent and Harlow. (Political Matters Memoranda, 10/27/71, 2; 6/6/72; 6/29/72; 9/18/72)

Butterfield testified that the President "made the big decisions," that "anything having to do with strategy would emanate from the President." (Butterfield testimony, 1 HJC 111) Butterfield testified that the Committee for the Re-election of the President "was pretty much an extension of the political White House." (Butterfield testimony, 1 HJC 52) The Political Matters Memoranda, transcripts of Presidential conversations, the structure of the campaign committee, and the mass of other evidence before the Committee fully corroborate this testimony.

On the basis of this evidence the Committee concluded that the President, acting primarily through Haldeman, controlled and directed the Committee for the Re-election of the President and its activities during the 1972 Presidential Campaign.

---

[4] Haldeman has testified that Mitchell also attended the regular morning White House staff meeting. (Haldeman testimony, 7 SSC 2878)

This conclusion is corroborated by evidence subsequently received by the Committee. In a White House edited transcript released August 5, 1974, reporting a conversation between the President and Haldeman on June 23, 1972, the President discussed detailed plans for the arrival and activities of his wife and daughters at the Republican National Convention, the use of media during the campaign, proposed photo opportunities for Republican and certain Democratic candidates with the President, campaign appearances by his daughters and a list of key fundraisers and supporters for the President to telephone. (WHT, June 23, 1972, 10:04–11:39 a.m., 19–30)

ARTICLE I

INTRODUCTION

Before entering on the execution of his office as President of the United States, Richard M. Nixon has twice taken, as required in Article II, Section 1, Clause 7 of the Constitution, the following oath:

I do solemnly swear that I will faithfully execute the Office of the President of the United States, and will to the best of my ability, preserve, protect and defend the Constitution of the United States.

Under the Constitution, the Executive power is vested in the President. In Article II, Section 3, the Constitution requires that the President "shall take care that the laws be faithfully executed."

On June 17, 1972, and prior thereto, agents of the Committee for the Re-Election of the President committed unlawful entry into the headquarters of the Democratic National Committee in Washington, D.C. for the purpose of securing political intelligence.

For more than two years, Richard M. Nixon continuously denied any personal or White House responsibility for the burglaries; he continuously denied any direction of or participation in a plan to cover up and conceal the identities of those who authorized the burglaries and the existence and scope of other unlawful and covert activities committed in the President's interest and on his behalf.

In the course of his public statements, from June 22, 1972, until August 5, 1974, the President repeated these denials which are detailed as follows:

On June 22, 1972, the President, in a news conference, said that his Press Secretary, Ronald Ziegler, had spoken "accurately" when Ziegler said, of the Watergate break-in, "The White House has no involvement whatever in this particular incident."

On August 29, 1972, in a news conference, in responding to a question about the Watergate case, the President said:

The other point that I should make is that these investigations, the investigation by the GAO, the investigation by the FBI, by the Department of Justice, have, at my direction had the total cooperation of the—not only the White House—but also of all agencies of the Government. In addition to that, within our own staff, under my direction, Counsel to the President, Mr. Dean, has conducted a complete investigation of all leads which might involve any present members of the White House Staff or anybody in the Government. I can say categorically that his investigation indicates that no one in the White House Staff, no one in this Administration, presently employed, was involved in this very bizarre incident.

. . . Before Mr. Mitchell left as campaign chairman he had employed a very good law firm with investigatory experience to look into the matter. Mr. MacGregor has continued that investigation and is continuing it now. I will say in that respect that anyone on the campaign committee, Mr. MacGregor has assured me, who does not cooperate with the investigation or anyone against whom charges are leveled where there is a prima facie case that those charges might indicate involvement will be discharged immediately. That, of course, will be true also of anybody in the Government. I think under these circumstances we are doing everything we can to take this incident and to investigate it and not to cover it up. . . . We have cooperated completely. We have indicated that we want all the facts brought out . . .

On March 2, 1973, in a news conference, the President said:

I will simply say with regard to the Watergate case what I have said previously, that the investigation conducted by Mr. Dean, the White House Counsel, in which, incidentally, he had access to the FBI records on this particular matter because I directed him to conduct this investigation, indicates that no one on the White House Staff, at the time he conducted the investigation—that was last July and August—was involved or had knowledge of the Watergate matter.

On March 12, 1973, the President, in a statement on executive privilege, said:

Thus, executive privilege will not be invoked until the compelling need for its exercise has been clearly demonstrated and the request has been approved first by the Attorney General and then by the President.

On March 15, 1973, the President, in a news conference, said:

We will cooperate; we will cooperate fully with the Senate, just as we did with the grand jury, as we did with the FBI, and as we did with the courts when they were conducting their investigations previously in what was called the Watergate matter.

On April 17, 1973, the President, in a press briefing, said:

On March 21, [1973], as a result of serious charges which came to my attention, some of which were publicly reported, I began intensive new inquiries into this whole matter.

As I have said before and I have said throughout the entire matter, all Government employees and especially White House Staff employees are expected fully to cooperate in this matter. I condemn any attempts to cover up in this case, no matter who is involved.

On April 30, 1973, the President, in an address to the nation, said that as soon as he learned about the June 17, 1972, break-in:

I immediately ordered an investigation by appropriate Government authorities. . . .

As the investigations went forward, I repeatedly asked those conducting the investigation whether there was any reason to believe that members of my Administration were in any way involved. I received repeated assurances that there were not. Because of these continuing reassurances, because I believed the reports I was getting, because I had faith in the persons from whom I was getting them, I discounted the stories in the press that appeared to implicate members of my Administration or other officials of the campaign committee.

Until March of this year, I remained convinced that the denials were true and that the charges of involvement by members of the White House Staff were false. The comments I made during this period, and the comments made by my Press Secretary in my behalf, were based on the information provided to us at that time we made those comments. However, new information then came to me which persuaded me that there was a real possibility that some of these charges were true, and suggesting further that there had been an effort to conceal the facts both from the public, from you, and from me . . .

The President continued:

I was determined that we should get to the bottom of the matter and that the truth should be fully brought out—no matter who was involved.

As the new Attorney General, I have today named Elliott Richardson . . . I have given him absolute authority to make all decisions bearing upon the prosecution of the Watergate case and related matters . . . We must maintain the integrity of the White House . . . There can be no whitewash at the White House.

On May 9, 1973, the President, in remarks at a Republican fundraising dinner, said:

In the American political process, one of the most difficult tasks of all comes when charges are made against high officials in an Administration. That is a very great test of an Administration, and many times, in the history of our country, Administrations have failed to meet the test of investigating those charges that might be embarrassing to the Administration because they were made against high officials in an Administration.

We have had such a situation. We have been confronted with it. We are dealing with it. And I will simply say to you tonight that this Nation, Republicans, Democrats, Independents, all Americans, can have confidence in the fact that the new nominee for Attorney General, Elliot Richardson, and the special prosecutor that he will appoint in this case, will have the total cooperation of the executive branch of this Government; they will get to the bottom of this thing; they will see to it that all of those who are guilty are prosecuted and are brought to justice. That is a pledge I make tonight and that I think the American people are entitled to. . . .

I can assure you that we will get to the bottom of this very deplorable incident.

On May 22, 1973, the President, in an address to the nation, said:

With regard to the specific allegations that have been made, I can and do state categorically:

1. I had no prior knowledge of the Watergate operation.
2. I took no part in, nor was I aware of, any subsequent efforts that may have been made to cover up Watergate.
3. At no time did I authorize any offer of executive clemency for the Watergate defendants, nor did I know of any such offer.
4. I did not know, until the time of my own investigation, of any effort to provide the Watergate defendants with funds.
5. At no time did I attempt, or did I authorize orders to attempt, to implicate the CIA in the Watergate matter. . . .

Within a few days . . . I was advised that there was a possibility of CIA involvement in some way. . . .

In addition, by this time, the name of Mr. Hunt had surfaced in connection with Watergate, and I was alerted to the fact that he had previously been a member of the Special Investigations Unit in the White House. Therefore, I was also concerned that the Watergate investigation might well lead to an inquiry into the activities of the Special Investigations Unit itself.

In this area, I felt it was important to avoid disclosure of the details of the national security matters with which the group was concerned. I knew that once the existence of the group became known, it would lead inexorably to a discussion of these matters, some of which remain, even today, highly sensitive. . . .

Therefore, I instructed Mr. Haldeman and Mr. Ehrlichman to ensure that the investigation of the break-in not expose either an unrelated covert operation of the CIA or the activities of the White House investigations unit—and to see that this was personally coordinated between General Walters, the Deputy Director of the CIA, and Mr. Gray of the FBI. It was certainly not my intent, nor my wish that the investigation of the Watergate break-in or of related acts be impeded in any way. . . .

At no time did I authorize or know about any offer of executive clemency for the Watergate defendants. Neither did I know until the time of my own investigation of any efforts to provide them with funds. . . .

With his selection of Archibald Cox—who served both President Kennedy and President Johnson as Solicitor General—as the special supervisory prosecutor for matters related to the case, Attorney General-designate Richardson has demonstrated his own determination to see the truth brought out. In this effort he has my full support. . . .

. . . [e]xecutive privilege will not be invoked as to any testimony concerning possible criminal conduct or discussions of possible criminal conduct, in the matters presently under investigation, including the Watergate affair and the alleged cover-up.

On July 23, 1973, in a letter he sent to Senator Ervin and made public, the President wrote:

Accordingly, the tapes, which have been under my sole personal control, will remain so. . . .

On May 22nd I described my knowledge of the Watergate matter and its aftermath in categorical and unambiguous terms that I know to be true.

On August 15, 1973, the President spoke to the nation over radio-television as follows:

On May 22, I stated in very specific terms—and I state again to every one of you listening tonight these facts—I had no prior knowledge of the Watergate break-in; I neither took part in nor knew about any of the subsequent coverup activities . . .

That was and that is the simple truth. . . .

From the time when the break-in occurred, I pressed repeatedly to know the facts, and particularly whether there was any involvement of anyone in the White House. I considered two things essential:

First, that the investigation should be thorough and aboveboard; and second, that if there were any higher involvement, we should get the facts out first. . . .

. . . Throughout the summer of 1972, I continued to press the question, and I continued to get the same answer: I was told again and again that there was no indication that any persons were involved other than the seven who were known to have planned and carried out the operation, and who were subsequently indicted and convicted. . . .

On September 15, the day the seven were indicted, I met with John Dean, the White House Counsel. He gave me no reason whatever to believe that any others were guilty; I assumed that the indictments of only the seven by the grand jury confirmed the reports he had been giving to that effect throughout the summer. . . .

It was not until March 21 of this year that I received new information from the White House Counsel that led me to conclude that the reports I had been getting for over 9 months were not true. On that day, I launched an intensive effort of my own to get the facts and to get the facts out. Whatever the facts might be, I wanted the White House to be the first to make them public. . . .

I turned over all the information I had to the head of that department, Assistant Attorney General Henry Petersen, . . . I ordered all members of the Administration to testify fully before the grand jury.

Far from trying to hide the facts, my effort throughout has been to discover the facts—and to lay those facts before the appropriate law enforcement authorities so that justice could be done and the guilty dealt with.

In the written statement which accompanied his August 15, 1973 address, the President said:

. . . I stated categorically that I had no prior knowledge of the Watergate operation and that I neither knew of nor took part in any subsequent efforts to cover it up. I also stated that I would not invoke executive privilege as to testimony by present and former members of my White House Staff with respect to possible criminal acts then under investigation. . . .

Those indictments also seemed to me to confirm the validity of the reports that Mr. Dean had been providing to me, through other members of the White House Staff—and on which I had based my August 29 statement that no one then employed at the White House was involved. It was in that context that I met with Mr. Dean on September 15, and he gave me no reason at that meeting to believe any others were involved.

Not only was I unaware of any coverup, but at that time, and until March 21, I was unaware that there was anything to cover up. . . .

. . . At that time [February and March, 1973], on a number of occasions, I urged my staff to get all the facts out, because I was confident that full disclosure of the facts would show that persons in the White House and at the Committee for the Re-election of the President were the victims of unjustified innuendos in the press.

. . . I was told then that funds had been raised for payments to the defendants with the knowledge and approval of persons both on the White House Staff and at the Re-election Committee. But I was only told that the money had been used for attorneys' fees and family support, not that it had been paid to procure silence from the recipients. I was also told that a member of my staff had talked to one of the defendants about clemency, but not that offers of clemency had been made. I was told that one of the defendants was currently attempting to blackmail the White House by demanding payment of $120,000 as the price of not talking about other activities, unrelated to Watergate in which he had engaged. These allegations were made in general terms, they were portrayed to me as being based in part on supposition, and they were largely unsupported in details or evidence.

These allegations were very troubling, and they gave a new dimension to the Watergate matter. They also reinforced my determination that the full facts must be made available to the grand jury or to the Senate Committee. If anything illegal had happened, I wanted it to be dealt with appropriately according to the law. If anyone at the White House or high up in my campaign had been involved in wrongdoing of any kind, I wanted the White House to take the lead in making that known.

When I received this disturbing information on March 21, I immediately began new inquiries into the case and an examination of the best means to give to the grand jury or Senate Committee what we then knew and what we might later learn. On March 21, I arranged to meet the following day with Messrs. Haldeman, Ehrlichman, Dean and Mitchell to discuss the appropriate method to get the facts out. On March 23, I sent Mr. Dean to Camp David, where he was instructed to write a complete report on all that he knew of the entire Watergate matter. . . . I instructed Mr. Ehrlichman to conduct an independent inquiry and bring all the facts to me. On April 14, Mr. Ehrlichman gave me his findings, and I directed that he report them to the Attorney General immediately. . . .

My consistent position from the beginning has been to get out the facts about Watergate, not to cover them up.

On May 22 I said that at no time did I authorize any offer of executive clemency for the Watergate defendants, nor did I know of any such offer. I reaffirm that statement.

. . . Even if others, from their own standpoint, may have been thinking about how to cover up an illegal act, from my standpoint I was concerned with how to uncover the illegal acts. It is my responsibility under the Constitution to see that the laws are faithfully executed, and in pursuing the facts about Watergate I was doing precisely that.

On August 22, 1973, the President, in a news conference, said:

In June, I, of course, talked to Mr. MacGregor first of all, who was the new chairman of the committee. He told me that he would conduct a thorough investigation as far as his entire committee staff was concerned. . . .

Mr. Dean, as White House Counsel, therefore sat in on the FBI interrogations of the members of the White House Staff because what I wanted to know was whether any member of the White House Staff was in any way involved. If he was involved, he would be fired. And when we met on September 15, and again throughout our discussions in the month of March, Mr. Dean insisted that there was not—and I use his words—"a scintilla of evidence" indicating that anyone on the White House Staff was involved in the planning of the Watergate break-in. . . .

. . . [I] should also point out that as far as my own activities were concerned, I was not leaving it just to them. I met at great length with Mr. Ehrlichman, Mr. Haldeman, Mr. Dean and Mr. Mitchell on the 22d. I discussed the whole matter with them. I kept pressing for the view that I had had throughout, that we must get this story out, get the truth out, whatever and whoever it is going to hurt. . . .

. . . Mr. Haldeman has testified to that, and his statement is accurate. Basically, what Mr. Dean was concerned about on March 21 was not so much the raising of money for the defendants, but the raising of money for the defendants for the purpose of keeping them still—in other words, so-called hush money. The one would be legal—in other words, raising a defense fund for any group, any individual, as you know, is perfectly legal and it is done all the time. But if you raise funds for the purpose of keeping an individual from talking, that is obstruction of justice. . . .

. . . And so, that was why I concluded, as Mr. Haldeman recalls perhaps, and did testify very effectively, one, when I said, "John, it is wrong, it won't work. We can't give clemency and we have got to get this story out. And therefore, I direct you, and I direct Haldeman, and I direct Ehrlichman, and I direct Mitchell to get together tomorrow and then meet with me as to how we get this story out."

On September 5, 1973, in a news conference, the President said:

... As a matter of fact, the only time I listened to the tapes, to certain tapes—and I didn't listen to all of them, of course—was on June 4. There is nothing whatever in the tapes that is inconsistent with the statement that I made on May 22 or of the statement that I made to you ladies and gentlemen in answer to several questions, rather searching questions I might say, and very polite questions 2 weeks ago, for the most part, and finally nothing that differs whatever from the statement that I made on the 15th of August.

On October 26, 1973, in a news conference, the President said:

... [W]e have decided that next week the Acting Attorney General, Mr. Bork, will appoint a new special prosecutor for what is called the Watergate matter. The special prosecutor will have independence. He will have total cooperation from the executive branch, ... And I can assure you ladies and gentlemen, and all of our listeners tonight, that I have no greater interest than to see that the new special prosecutor has the cooperation from the executive branch and the independence that he needs to bring about that conclusion.

On March 6, 1974, at a press conference, the President said:

At all times it had been my goal to have a complete disclosure of this whole situation because, as you know, I have said there can be no cloud over the White House. I want that cloud removed. That is one of the reasons we have cooperated as we have with the Special Prosecutor. We will also cooperate with the Rodino committee.

The President also said that after a March 22, 1973, meeting with John Mitchell, H. R. Haldeman, John Ehrlichman and John Dean, "the policy was one of full disclosure, and that was the decision that was made at the conclusion of the meeting."

On March 19, 1974, in a question-and-answer session before the National Association of Broadcasters in Houston, Texas, the President said:

... It should not have been covered up, and I have done the very best that I can over the past year to see that it is uncovered. I have cooperated completely with not only the grand jury but also with other investigative agencies and have waived executive privilege perhaps further than I should. ...

On April 29, 1974, the President, in a nationally broadcast address, said:

I have asked for this time tonight in order to announce my answer to the House Judiciary Committee's subpoena for additional Watergate tapes, and to tell you something about the actions I shall be taking tomorrow—about what I hope they will mean to you and about the very difficult choices that were presented to me.

These actions will at last, once and for all, show that what I knew and what I did with regard to the Watergate break-in and coverup were just as I have described them to you from the very beginning.

... For 9 months—until March 1973—I was assured by those charged with conducting and monitoring the investigations that no one in the White House was involved.

In these folders that you see over here on my left are more than 1,200 pages of transcripts of private conversations I participated in between September 15, 1972, and April 27 of 1973, with my principal aides and associates with regard to Watergate. They include all the relevant portions of all the subpoenaed conversations that were recorded, that is, all portions that relate to the question of what I knew about Watergate or the coverup and what I did about it.

In these transcripts, portions not relevant to my knowledge or actions with regard to Watergate are not included, but everything that is relevant is included—the rough as well as the smooth, the strategy sessions, the exploration of alternatives, the weighing of human and political costs.

As far as what the President personally knew and did with regard to Watergate and the coverup is concerned, these materials—together with those already made available—will tell it all.

... in the context of the current impeachment climate, I believe all the American people, as well as their Representatives in Congress, are entitled to have not only the facts but also the evidence that demonstrates those facts.

I want there to be no question remaining about the fact that the President has nothing to hide in this matter.

The basic question at issue today is whether the President personally acted improperly in the Watergate matter. Month after month of rumor, insinuation, and charges by just one Watergate witness—John Dean—suggested that the President did act improperly.

This sparked the demands for an impeachment inquiry. This is the question that must be answered. And this is the question that will be answered by these transcripts that I have ordered published tomorrow.

His [John Dean's] revelations to me on March 21 were a sharp surprise, even though the report he gave to me was far from complete, especially since he did not reveal at that time the extent of his own criminal involvement.

I was particularly concerned by his report that one of the Watergate defendants, Howard Hunt, was threatening blackmail unless he and his lawyer were immediately given $120,000 for legal fees and family support, and that he was attempting to blackmail the White House, not by threatening exposure on the Watergate matter, but by threatening to reveal activities that would expose extremely sensitive, highly secret national security matters that he had worked on before Watergate.

I probed, questioned, tried to learn all Mr. Dean knew about who was involved, what was involved. I asked more than 150 questions of Mr. Dean in the course of that conversation. . . .

Whatever the potential for misinterpretation there may be as a result of the different options that were discussed at different times during the meeting, my conclusion at the end of the meeting was clear. And my actions and reactions as demonstrated on the tapes that follow that date show clearly that I did not intend the further payments to Hunt or anyone else be made. These are some of the actions that I took in the weeks that followed in my effort to find the truth, to carry out my responsibilities to enforce the law.

I made clear that there was to be no coverup. . . .

To anyone who reads his way through this mass of materials I have provided, it will be totally abundantly clear that as far as the President's role with regard to Watergate is concerned, the entire story is there.

On May 22, 1974, in a letter, dated May 15, 1974, sent to Chairman Rodino, in response to two subpoenas of the House of Representatives, the President wrote:

... I submitted transcripts not only of all the recorded Presidential conversations that took place that were called for in the subpoena, but also a number of additional Presidential conversations that had not been subpoenaed. I did this so that the record of my knowledge and actions in the Watergate matter would be fully disclosed, once and for all. . . .

The Committee has the full story of Watergate, in so far as it relates to Presidential knowledge and Presidential actions.

On July 27, 1974, the Committee on the Judiciary decided that since June 17, 1972, Richard M. Nixon, using the power of his high office, engaged, personally and through his subordinates and agents, in a course of conduct or plan designed to delay, impede and obstruct the investigation of the unlawful entry into the headquarters of the Democratic National Committee; cover-up; conceal; and protect those responsible and to conceal the existence and scope of the unlawful and covert activities.

This report is based on the evidence available to the Committee at the time of its decision. It contains clear and convincing evidence that the President caused action—not only by his own subordinates but by agencies of the United States, including the Department of Justice, the Federal Bureau of Investigation, and the Central Intelligence Agency—to cover up the Watergate break-in. This concealment required perjury, destruction of evidence, obstruction of justice—all of which are crimes. It included false and misleading public statements as part of a deliberate, contrived, continued deception of the American people.

On August 5, 1974, the President submitted to the Committee on the Judiciary three additional edited White House transcripts of Presidential conversations, which only confirms the clear and convincing evidence, that from the beginning, the President, knowingly directed the cover-up of the Watergate burglary.

The evidence on which the Committee based its decision on Article I is summarized in the following sections.

ADOPTION OF A POLITICAL INTELLIGENCE PLAN INCLUDING THE USE OF ELECTRONIC SURVEILLANCE

I

INTRODUCTION

To conduct his 1972 re-election campaign, President Nixon authorized the establishment of the Committee for the Re-election of the President (CRP). (IIJC, Background—White House/CRP 11)

On or about May 27 and June 17, 1972, agents of CRP broke into the Democratic National Committee (DNC) headquarters at the Watergate for the purpose of obtaining political intelligence for use in the President's campaign. They acted according to an approved program, which had specifically contemplated illegal electronic surveillance. Gordon Liddy was responsible for carrying out the program; E. Howard Hunt was his chief assistant. Liddy, a former FBI agent, had first worked for the Nixon administration in the Alcohol, Tobacco and Firearms Division of the Treasury Department. Hunt had been an employee of the CIA. Before they were transferred to CRP, both men had been employed in a secret White House unit, established by the President, that engaged in illegal covert activity under the supervision of Assistant to the President John Ehrlichman.

II

PRIOR COVERT ACTIVITIES

Beginning in May, 1969, the White House conducted covert intelligence gathering, not for reasons of national security, but for political purposes. In May, 1969, President Nixon ordered the FBI to engage in electronic surveillance of at least seventeen persons, including four newsmen and three White House subordinates whose jobs were unrelated to national security. (Book VII, 142–47, 153) Taps were maintained on the telephones of two employees of the National Security Council after they had left the government to work for a Democratic presidential candidate, although a review over a reasonable period would have shown neither was discussing classified materials. One tap remained for 18 months after Assistant FBI Director William Sullivan had specifically recommended its termination. (Book VII, 212–13, 220–21, 326)

Written summaries of the results of this surveillance were originally sent to the President, Haldeman, Kissinger and Ehrlichman; later, at the President's direction, they were sent only to Haldeman. (Book VII, 205, 370) It is undisputed that information forwarded by FBI Director Hoover to President Nixon was used by Haldeman in January, 1970, to take steps to deal with a proposed magazine article critical of the President's Vietnam policy. (Book VII, 360–68)

At the President's direction, the FBI records of surveillance were kept outside of normal FBI files. (Book VII, 182-90) In July, 1971, the President ordered that the records be moved from FBI headquarters. (Book VII, 767) In August, 1971, Assistant Attorney General Robert Mardian handed the records to an official at the Oval Office in the White House whom, in an FBI interview, he declined to name. (Book VII, 2063) Subsequently, Ehrlichman placed the surveillance records in his safe. On April 30, 1973, President Nixon ordered that the FBI records be removed from Ehrlichman's safe and placed among the President's papers. (Book VII, 782)

During the same period, White House personnel also engaged directly in illegal surveillance for political purposes. In 1969, Counsel to the President John Ehrlichman hired Anthony Ulasewicz, a retired police detective, to conduct investigations under the supervision of John Caulfield, a subordinate to Ehrlichman. (Book VII, 336-44) In June, 1969, Caulfield, at Ehrlichman's direction initiated a wiretap on the residence telephone of newspaper columnist Joseph Kraft. (Book VII, 314-15) Ehrlichman discussed this wiretap with the President (Book VII, 323) During the next three years, Caulfield and Ulasewicz, under Ehrlichman's or Dean's direction, conducted a number of covert inquiries concerning political opponents of the President. (Book VII, 342, 346-47)

Following the publication of the Pentagon Papers in June, 1971, the President created a special investigations unit which engaged in covert and unlawful activities. (Book VII, 620-23, 651) This organization (dubbed "the Plumbers" by its members) was based in the White House, under the immediate supervision of John Ehrlichman. Howard Hunt and Gordon Liddy worked in the unit. (Book VII, 651) The Plumbers acquired from the FBI information about the Pentagon Papers investigation (Book VII, 952-53), twice requested the CIA to prepare psychological profiles of Daniel Ellsberg (Book VII, 898-99, 1401-03), and formulated a plan to acquire derogatory information about Ellsberg to leak to the press for political purposes. (Book VII, 1126-28) In August, 1971, after obtaining Ehrlichman's approval for a covert operation, provided it was not traceable, Plumbers co-directors Egil Krogh and David Young authorized Hunt and Liddy to undertake an operation to gain access to Ellsberg's psychiatric records. (Book VII, 1240-44) On September 3, 1971, a team consisting of Bernard Barker, Felipe DeDiego and Eugenio Martinez (all of whom subsequently participated in one of the Watergate break-ins), acting under the direction and immediate supervision of Hunt and Liddy, illegally broke into the office of Dr. Lewis Fielding, Ellsberg's psychiatrist. (Book VII, 1281-87)

The President's closest personal staff, particularly Ehrlichman and Colson, authorized Hunt to perform other covert activities for political purposes. With disguise and credentials obtained on Ehrlichman's authority from the CIA, Hunt interviewed Clifton DeMotte to obtain derogatory information about the Kennedys (Book VII, 853); and with diplomatic cables obtained on Young's authority from the State Department, Hunt fabricated cables purporting to implicate the Kennedy Administration in the assassination of Vietnamese President Diem. (Book VII, 1031-34, 1046-47) During 1971, Ehrlichman authorized Liddy to place an unspecified number of wiretaps on other persons. (Book VII, 828)

III

DEVELOPMENT OF POLITICAL INTELLIGENCE CAPABILITY

Preparations began in the White House to develop a political intelligence capability.

On August 10, 1971, Chief of Staff Haldeman gave instructions that Gordon Strachan, Patrick Buchanan, Dwight Chapin and Ron Walker should develop recommendations for "political intelligence and covert activities" in connection with the President's re-election campaign in 1972. (Political Matters Memorandum, 8/13/71, 2) At around the same time, White House staff assistant John Caulfield submitted to Counsel to the President John Dean a political intelligence proposal. It was called Operation Sandwedge, which was to include electronic surveillance operations and "black bag" capability. (Book VII, 1341, 1352-53)

Dean completed a planning study of Operation Sandwedge and other "covert" intelligence activities in early October, 1971, and discussed the proposal with Mitchell. (Book VII, 1349) After Attorney General Mitchell did not make the "hard decisions" about Sandwedge and other covert activities which were required to make the plan operational, Haldeman instructed Strachan to arrange a meeting between Mitchell and Haldeman. (Book VII, 1363-64)

Accordingly, in November, 1971, Haldeman and Mitchell met to discuss Sandwedge. (Political Matters Memorandum, 10/27/71, attachment) Magruder and Strachan were present. Strachan had prepared for Haldeman's use at this meeting a detailed agenda, called a talking paper, that noted that Sandwedge "has received an initial 50," and asked, "are we really developing the capability needed?" (Political Matters Memorandum, 10/27/71, attachment) The talking paper also listed topics for discussion between Haldeman and Mitchell when Magruder and Strachan were to be absent. One topic was: "Who should we designate to increase the surveillance of EMK [Senator Edward M. Kennedy] from periodic to constant?" and "Is there any other candidate or group, such as Common Cause, about whom we should obtain damaging information?" (Political Matters Memorandum, 10/27/71, attachment) In the copy of the October 27, 1971, talking paper provided by the White House to the Committee, the bottom of the page had been cut off, effectively deleting a portion of a paragraph that begins, "From Campaign funds I need 800-300 for surveillance. . . ." (Political Matters Memorandum, 10/27/71, attachment)

By November, 1971, Sandwedge had been rejected. Dean was told by Mitchell and Ehrlichman to find someone other than Caulfield to manage the campaign intelligence operation. Dean suggested Liddy. In explaining this to the President on March 21, 1973, Dean told the President that Liddy was a lawyer with an intelligence background with the FBI. Dean knew that Liddy had done some "extremely sensitive things for the White House while he had been at the White House, and he had apparently done them well uh going into Ellsberg's doctor's office," to which the President replied, "Oh yeah." Krogh had recommended Liddy as "a hell of a good man." (HJCT 81-82) Dean introduced Liddy to Mitchell, who believed him qualified to be counsel to CRP. (Mitchell testimony, 2 HJC 125) Thereafter, Liddy was transferred from the White House to CRP to put together an intelligence operation. (HCJT 82)

In Strachan's December 2, 1971 Political Matters Memorandum to Haldeman, Strachan noted that instead of Sandwedge, Liddy, "who has been working with Bud Krogh" (co-director of the Plumbers unit), would handle political intelligence as well as legal matters, and would work with Dean on the "political enemies" project. (Book I, 34) On December 8, 1971, Haldeman approved in writing Liddy's transfer to CRP. In spite of a policy that there were to be no salary increases for White House staff transferring to CRP, Haldeman authorized a salary increase of $4,000 for Liddy. (Book I, 49-50) Haldeman later acknowledged to the President that Operation Sandwedge had been "the grandfather" of the Liddy Plan. (WHT 526)

From this evidence it is clear that Haldeman and Mitchell had decided to set up a political intelligence gathering unit for the purpose of securing political intelligence on potential opponents of President Nixon.

IV

Liddy's Proposals

In late January, 1972, after consultation with Howard Hunt, his associate in the Plumbers unit, CRP Counsel Liddy proposed a $1 million intelligence program to Mitchell, Magruder and Dean at a meeting in Attorney General Mitchell's office. (Book I, 58-60; Hunt testimony, 9 SSC 3708) The proposal included mugging, kidnapping, prostitutes, and electronic surveillance. (Book I, 59) At the close of the meeting, Mitchell directed Liddy to prepare a revised and more realistic proposal. (Book I, 57, 60) Mitchell has denied this (Book I, 58), but the fact is that, in February, 1972, Liddy returned to Attorney General Mitchell's office with a $500,000 intelligence program, which he presented to Mitchell, Magruder and Dean. The plan specifically envisioned electronic surveillance of the DNC headquarters. (Book I, 66-67) Counsel to the President Dean reported this meeting to Haldeman. Dean expressed his opposition to a political intelligence operation that included illegal activities like burglary and wiretapping of the DNC. Although Haldeman told Dean he agreed that the White House should have nothing to do with such activities, Haldeman did not order that the proposal be abandoned. (Book I, 66, 73-75)

Sometime in February or March, 1972, Liddy and Hunt met with Special Counsel to the President Charles Colson at the White House. (Book I, 105, 110-11) Colson, who was a friend of Hunt's and had recommended him for employment by the White House after Colson had discussed the political possibilities of the Ellsberg case with the President in late June, 1971, was aware that Liddy and Hunt had taken part in the Plumbers operations, including the Fielding break-in. (Book I, 113; Colson testimony, 3 HJC 197-99, 205-06, 236-37) During this meeting, Colson called Magruder, the CRP chief of staff, and told him to resolve whatever it was Hunt and Liddy wanted to do and to be sure he had an opportunity to listen to their plans. (Book I, 105; Colson testimony, 3 HJC 244-49) Magruder has testified that Colson told him to "get off the stick" and get Liddy's plans approved, and that information was needed, particularly about Democratic National Committee Chairman Lawrence O'Brien. (Book I, 113)

V

ADOPTION OF THE PLAN

On March 30, 1972, in Key Biscayne, Florida, the Liddy Plan was reviewed in a meeting among Mitchell, Magruder and Fred LaRue. (LaRue testimony, 1 HJC 180-83) They considered the proposal for electronic surveillance and, according to Magruder, approved its revised budget of either $250,000 or $300,000. (Book I, 116-20, 129, 148, 182) After the meeting, Magruder instructed his assistant, Robert Reisner, who was at CRP headquarters in Washington, to tell Liddy that his proposal had been approved. Reisner telephoned Liddy, who had become general counsel to the Finance Committee to Re-elect the President (FCRP), and conveyed Magruder's message that the plan had been approved and that Liddy was to get started in the next two weeks. (Book I, 49-50, 136-46)

In a Political Matters Memorandum dated March 31, 1972, Strachan told Haldeman that Magruder reported CRP now had a "sophisticated political intelligence gathering system including a budget of [$]300 [,000]." (Book I, 148, 150-53) A talking paper which Strachan had prepared for a meeting between Haldeman and Mitchell on April 4, 1972, included a question on the "adequacy of the political intelligence system." (Book I, 162-64)

Strachan has testified that three days after the June 17, 1972 Watergate break-in, Haldeman ordered him to destroy both the March 31, 1972 Political Matters Memorandum and the April 4, 1972 talking paper. (Book I, 165-66)

Although Liddy's involvement in the break-in was known by the President, Mitchell, and other high CRP and White House officials shortly after the break-in (WHT, June 23, 1972, 10:04-11:39 a.m., 6; Book II, 91, 93-97, 145-46), Liddy was not discharged as counsel to FCRP until eleven days afterward. (Book II, 478-82)

This, and evidence of cover-up activity after the break-in discussed in the following sections, along with the direct evidence regarding Haldeman's and Mitchell's planning activities prior to the break-in, support the conclusion that the Watergate break-in was pursuant to a program of unlawful electronic surveillance approved in advance by Mitchell, in which Haldeman concurred, and aimed at political opponents of the President for the political benefit of the President.

THE IMPLEMENTATION OF THE POLITICAL INTELLIGENCE PLAN

The implementation of the plan to gather political intelligence for use in the President's re-election campaign began in April, 1972. (Book I, 172–75) Prior to June, 1972, with the approval of John Mitchell, FCRP Treasurer Hugh Sloan disbursed approximately $199,000 in cash to Liddy.[1] (Book I, 178–79) Of this sum James McCord, CRP Security Director, spent approximately $65,000 on electronic monitoring equipment and for related purposes. (Book I, 190)

The first break-in at the Democratic National Committee (DNC) occurred on or about May 27, 1972. (Book I, 216–17) During the first or second week in June, 1972, Deputy Campaign Director Magruder received transcripts, on paper labeled "Gemstone," of conversations intercepted at the DNC Headquarters. (Book I, 234–35) There is evidence that these transcripts were shown to Mitchell. (Book I, 235) Magruder's assistant, Robert Reisner, testified that Magruder once asked him to place a group of the Gemstone papers in the file labeled "Mr. Mitchell's file," the file used by Magruder in regular daily meetings with Mitchell. (Book I, 237–38) Magruder also received prints of documents photographed during the first entry into the DNC headquarters.[2] (Book I, 234)

The White House received reports obtained from the break-in and bugging. Magruder forwarded the information to Strachan in Haldeman's office. (Book I, 165–66, 168–69)

In his March 13, 1973 meeting with Dean, the President described the Watergate operation as "a dry hole, huh?" Dean responded, "That's right." (HJCT 72) Later in the same conversation, Dean said he thought there were "some people who saw the fruits of it," but added that that was "another story." Dean was talking about the criminal conspiracy to enter the DNC offices. (HJCT 74)

After the burglars first broke into and bugged the DNC headquarters, they began getting information, which was in turn relayed to Haldeman's office. At one point Haldeman gave instructions to change their political surveillance capabilities from Muskie to McGovern; he sent the instructions to Liddy through Strachan. Liddy started to make arrangements for the electronic surveillance of the McGovern operation. In a conversation on the morning of March 21, 1973, John Dean reported to the President:

> DEAN. . . . The information was coming over here to Strachan. Some of it was given to Haldeman, uh, there is no doubt about it. Uh—
> PRESIDENT. Did he know what it was coming from?
> DEAN. I don't really know if he would.

---

[1] Sloan testified that when he asked Stans the purpose for which the money would be spent, Stans, who had discussed the matter with Mitchell, said, "I do not want to know and you don't want to know." (Book I, 179)

[2] Shortly after the June 17, 1972 break-in, Reisner, at Magruder's direction, removed the Gemstone files and other politically compromising documents from the CRP files. These documents were delivered to Magruder who destroyed them. (Book I, 236, 239–40)

PRESIDENT. Not necessarily.
DEAN. Not necessarily. That's not necessarily. Uh—
PRESIDENT. Strachan knew what it was from.
DEAN. Strachan knew what it was from. No doubt about it, and whether Strachan—I have never come to press these people on these points because it,
PRESIDENT. Yeah.
DEAN. it hurts them to, to give up that next inch, so I had to piece things together. All right, so Strachan was aware of receiving information, reporting to Bob. At one point Bob even gave instructions to change their capabilities from Muskie to McGovern, and had passed this back through Strachan to Magruder and, apparently to Liddy. And Liddy was starting to make arrangements to go in and bug the, uh, uh, McGovern operation. They had done prelim—
PRESIDENT. They had never bugged Muskie, though, did they?
DEAN. No, they hadn't but they had a, they had, uh, they'd
PRESIDENT. (Unintelligible)
DEAN. infiltrated it by a, a, they had
PRESIDENT. A secretary.[3]
DEAN. a secretary and a chauffeur. Nothing illegal about that. (HJCT 85)

On April 14, 1973, Haldeman told the President that Strachan, at some time, had stopped reading the DNC wiretap reports, which had been made available to him.

E The one copy that Magruder had had pictures of the kinds of papers that you'd find around with campaign headquarters. He sent a synopses of the pictures to Mitchell. He thought it was so bad he picked up the phone and called Liddy and chewed him out. He called 'em "(expletive deleted)" "I [Magruder] told Strachan that the synopses were here. He may have come over and read them." and as I [Ehrlichman] pressed him on that he got less and less sure of that. He says, "I [Magruder] told him they were there."
H Strachan says, "I stopped reading the synopses, and they were—we had 'em here." (WHT 586)

On April 14, 1973, the President asked Haldeman what he would say if Magruder testified that the DNC wiretap reports had come to Haldeman's office. Haldeman responded, "This doesn't ever have to come out." (WHT 520–21)

Thus the Liddy Plan was implemented under Mitchell's direction with Haldeman's concurrence to provide political intelligence information for the President's benefit in his re-election campaign.

---

[3] In the edited White House transcript, it is Dean who first says "a secretary." (WHT 180)

PRESIDENT NIXON'S RESPONSE TO THE ARRESTS

I

INITIAL RESPONSE

At 2:00 a.m. on June 17, 1972, five of Liddy's men, including CRP Security Director McCord, made the second entry into the DNC offices. They were found there and arrested. (Book II, 72–74) They had on their persons fifteen $100 bills. In their hotel room police found additional $100 bills, a check drawn by Hunt, and a notebook that contained Hunt's White House telephone number. (Book II, 84–85) Hunt and Liddy were elsewhere, in the Watergate Hotel. Upon discovering the arrests of the others, they left. (Book II, 72–76) Hunt went to his office in the Executive Office Building (EOB), placed a briefcase containing electronic equipment in his safe and removed from the safe $10,000 in cash that Liddy had previously given to him to be used in case of need. Hunt gave the money that morning to Douglas Caddy, a Washington attorney. (Book II, 76–77)

At the time of the break-in, the President was in Key Biscayne with Haldeman and Presidential Press Secretary Ronald Ziegler. (Book II, 127)

John Mitchell, Robert Mardian, Jeb Magruder, and Fred LaRue, all top officials in CRP, were in Los Angeles working on the President's re-election campaign. On the morning of June 17, 1972, Liddy telephoned Magruder in California and asked him to call back on a secure phone. (Book II, 106) At the time, Magruder was eating breakfast with LaRue. Before going to a pay telephone to return Liddy's long distance call, Magruder remarked to LaRue, "I think last night is when they were going into the DNC." Magruder then called Liddy who informed him of the break-in and the arrests of the burglars, including McCord, the CRP Security Director. (LaRue testimony, 1 HJC 185) Magruder immediately relayed Liddy's report to LaRue, who informed Mitchell. (Book II, 106)

When LaRue told Mitchell that McCord, the CRP Security Director, was one of the five persons arrested, Mitchell asked LaRue to get more information. (Book II, 108) Mardian was ordered to return to Washington. (LaRue testimony, 1 HJC 194) Mitchell's aides prepared a press release falsely stating that the arrested men had not been operating on behalf of or with the consent of CRP. (LaRue testimony, 1 HJC 188–90, 212–14) Mitchell made a decision to issue that press release that said:

> We have just learned from news reports that a man identified as employed by our campaign committee was one of five persons arrested at the Democratic National Committee headquarters in Washington, D.C. early Saturday morning.
> The person involved is the proprietor of a private security agency who was employed by our Committee months ago to assist with the installation of our security system.
> He has, as we understand it, a number of business clients and interests and we have no knowledge of those relationships.

We want to emphasize that this man and the other people involved were not operating either in our behalf or with our consent.

I am surprised and dismayed at these reports.

At this time, we are experiencing our own security problems at the Committee for the Re-election of the President. Our problems are not as dramatic as the events of Saturday morning—but nonetheless of a serious nature to us. We do not know as of this moment whether our security problems are related to the events of Saturday morning at the Democratic headquarters or not.

There is no place in our campaign or in the electoral process for this type of activity and we will not permit nor condone it. (LaRue Exhibit No. 2, 1 HJC 212; Mitchell testimony, 2 HJC 150–51)

On June 17, 1972, Mitchell also directed Liddy to contact Attorney General Kleindienst. (LaRue testimony, 1 HJC 187) Liddy met with Kleindienst at the Burning Tree Country Club near Washington, D.C., and told him that some of the people arrested were White House or CRP employees. Liddy told Kleindienst that Mitchell wanted a report on the break-in. Kleindienst refused to discuss the matter and ordered Liddy off the premises. (Book II, 108, 111–12)

On the afternoon of June 17, the Secret Service contacted John Ehrlichman, who was in Washington, to inform him that the District of Columbia police had found the White House telephone number of Howard Hunt in the burglars' hotel room. (Book II, 118, 494) Ehrlichman knew of Hunt's participation in the burglary of Ellsberg's psychiatrist's office and of other covert operations Hunt had performed for the White House. (Book VII, 728, 1220)[1]

Upon learning that evidence now linked Hunt with those arrested inside the DNC offices, Ehrlichman immediately called Colson, whom he knew to have been Hunt's sponsor at the White House. (Book II, 118; Book VII, 677) Colson, who had recommended Hunt for his White House position (Book VII, 676) knew of Hunt's previous covert activities undertaken with Ehrlichman's authorization: on September 9, 1971, shortly after a meeting with the President, Ehrlichman had told Colson of Hunt's and Liddy's break-in into Dr. Fielding's office and instructed him not to talk about the matter. (Colson testimony, 3 HJC 236) In March, 1972, Colson himself had instructed Hunt to interview Dita Beard in Denver, following publication of her memorandum about the settlement of ITT antitrust litigation. (Colson testimony, HJC 250–51)

On the afternoon of the Watergate break-in, Ehrlichman and Colson talked about how to handle records of Hunt's employment at the White House; and about Douglas Caddy, the lawyer Hunt had hired following the arrests. (Book II, 118–20; Colson testimony, 3 HJC 257–58)

In the late afternoon of June 17, 1972, the day of the Watergate break-in, Ehrlichman telephoned Ziegler in Key Biscayne and told him about the documents that linked Hunt to the Watergate burglars. (Book II, 118) It is not known what information Ziegler conveyed to the President. The next day, June 18, 1972, Ehrlichman

---

[1] On July 7, 1971, when Hunt was first hired as a consultant to the the White House, Ehrlichman called the CIA and said :

"I want to alert you that an old acquaintance, Howard Hunt, has been asked by the President to do some special consultant work on security problems. He may be contacting you sometime in the future for some assistance. I wanted you to know that he was in fact doing some things for the President. He is a long-time acquaintance with the people here. He may want some help on computer runs and other things. You should consider he has pretty much carte blanche." (Book II, 467)

placed another call to Key Biscayne, this time to Haldeman. He reported McCord's and Hunt's involvement in the break-in and the problems it created for CRP and the White House. (Book II, 130) It is not known what information Haldeman passed on to the President. Haldeman knew that an investigation might reveal that Mitchell, with Haldeman's concurrence, had authorized a plan to place the President's political opponents under electronic surveillance; that funds for the operation were campaign funds supplied by CRP; and Ehrlichman knew that the participants in the Watergate break-in had previously engaged in illegal covert activities on behalf of the President, under Ehrlichman's supervision.

After this telephone conversation, Haldeman called Magruder in California and discussed the arrests. Haldeman directed Magruder to go to Washington to meet with Dean, Strachan and Sloan in order to determine exactly what had happened and the source of the money found on the arrested persons. (Book II, 126; Mitchell testimony, 2 HJC 153) Magruder told Mitchell of Haldeman's order, and the instruction that Mardian should return immediately to Washington was reversed. (LaRue testimony, 1 HJC 194) Later the same day Haldeman, in a telephone conversation with Colson, inquired about Hunt's employment status at the White House. (Colson testimony, 3 HJC 258-59)

On June 18, 1972, the President also called Colson from Key Biscayne. He told Colson he had been so angry about the involvement of McCord in the Watergate break-in that he had thrown an ash tray across the room. (Colson testimony, 3 HJC 259) [2]

That day, John Dean, counsel to the President, returned to California from a trip to the Far East. He was told by White House aide Fred Fielding to cancel his plans to stay in California, and to return to Washington, which he did. (Book II, 144)

On June 18, President Nixon put John Ehrlichman in charge of the Watergate matter; Ehrlichman assigned Dean to work on it. (Book II, 132; "Presidential Statements," 8/22/73, 46; Dean testimony, 2 HJC 223-24) On June 19, Dean met with Liddy, who told Dean that the break-in was a CRP operation. Dean reported this conversation to Ehrlichman.[3] (Dean testimony, 3 HJC 224)

On June 19, 1972, Ehrlichman, Colson and Dean met. (Book II, 145-46; Colson testimony, 3 HJC 260-61, 66) Their discussion of the break-in concerned the fact that White House records did not reflect any termination of Hunt's status as a consultant; they also discussed the contents of Hunt's safe in the EOB. (Book II, 146, 190) Ehrlichman and Colson directed Dean to take possession of the contents of Hunt's safe. Ehrlichman ordered that Hunt's safe in the EOB be drilled open. This was done and its contents were delivered to Dean. (Book II, 190; Colson testimony, 3 HJC 264-65) The safe contained, among other things, State Department cables Hunt had fabricated;

---

[2] Representative Thornton explained the significance of this occurrence during the general debate: ". . . [w]hat that outburst of anger also indicates, at least to me, was a revelation, as of that moment, at the start, that [the President's] own men were involved in a stupid and criminal act, which had the potential of terrible embarrassment to him." (HJC debates, July 25, 1974, TR. 288)

[3] Liddy nevertheless continued to serve as general counsel to FCRP until June 28, 1972, when he was discharged by Stans for refusing to be interviewed by the FBI. (Book II, 478-82)

materials related to the Plumbers; McCord's briefcase filled with electronic equipment, which Hunt had placed in the safe immediately after the arrests; and two notebooks. (Book II, 76, 163. 425)

Late on June 19, 1972, Magruder, Mitchell, Mardian and LaRue, who had returned to Washington, met in Mitchell's apartment. Dean later joined the meeting. They discussed the break-in and the need for a statement from CRP denying any responsibility for the burglary. (Book II, 224; Mitchell testimony, 2 HJC 154–55, 159) Magruder was directed at that meeting to destroy documents related to the political surveillance operation. (LaRue testimony, 1 HJC 196–97; Book II, 225–26)

II
JUNE 19, 1972–JUNE 29, 1972

On June 19, 1972, at about noon, the President telephoned Colson. They talked for approximately one hour about the break-in. (Book II, 156, 158–59) Colson told the President that Administration officials in Washington were holding a meeting to determine how they should react. (Colson testimony, 3 HJC 264)

Later on June 19, 1972, the President and Haldeman returned from Key Biscayne. (Book II, 240)

The next morning, June 20, 1972, at 9:00 a.m., Haldeman met in Ehrlichman's office—which was located one floor above the Oval Office (Butterfield testimony, 1 HJC 24)—with Ehrlichman and Mitchell, both of whom knew that the DNC break-in was a CRP operation carried out under the direction of Liddy. (Book II, 108, 153, 240) Dean, who also knew that the DNC break-in was a CRP operation, and Attorney General Kleindienst (Book II, 112. 144) jointed this meeting about 9:45 and 9:55 a.m. respectively. (Book II, 240) The previous day, Kleindienst had requested that Gray arrange for a briefing on the FBI investigation, because Kleindienst had to brief the President that day or the next. (Book II, 137) At the meeting, on the morning of June 20, Kleindienst, Haldeman, Ehrlichman, Mitchell and Dean discussed the Watergate break-in. (Book II, 240–41)

On that same morning at 9:00 a.m. the President arrived in his Oval Office. While this meeting on Watergate took place one floor above among the President's chief of staff, his chief domestic adviser, his counsel, his Attorney General, and his campaign director, the President remained alone in the Oval Office (with the exception of a three-minute meeting with Butterfield from 9:01 to 9:04 a.m. The President left the Oval Office at 10:20 a.m., and went to his EOB office. (Book II, 243)

At his EOB office, the President met with Ehrlichman from 10:25 until 11:20 a.m. (Book II, 243) The President did not discuss Watergate with Ehrlichman, even though the President had given Ehrlichman the highest level responsibility for investigation of the Watergate matter. (*In re Grand Jury*, Misc. 47–73. order, 12/19/73; Book II, 238; "Presidential Statements." 8/22/73, 45–46)

Starting at 11:26 a.m.. during a meeting which lasted one hour and 19 minutes, the President did discuss Watergate with Haldeman. Haldeman—who by this time had been fully briefed and who, according to Strachan, that day instructed Strachan to destroy documents related to the Liddy Plan and other compromising documents—met with the President. (Book II, 243, 265) At this meeting, the President issued certain directives about the Watergate break-in. (Book II, 249–50) A portion of the notes taken by Haldeman during the meeting read:

> be sure EOB office is thoroly ckd re bugs at all times—etc. what is our counter attack? PR offensive to top this . . . hit the opposition w/ their activities Pt out libertarians have created public callousness. Do they justify this less than stealing Pentagon papers, Anderson file etc. we shld be on the attack for diversion (Book II, 246–48)

In July, 1973, the tape recording of this June 20, 1972 meeting between the President and Haldeman was subpoenaed by the Special Prosecutor. The subpoena was resisted by the President on the grounds of executive privilege (Book II, 258) but upheld by the Court of Appeals. (Book IX, 748, 750–54) On November 26, 1973, when the President's lawyer finally produced the recording, it contained an eighteen and one-half minute erasure. The erasure obliterated that portion of the conversation which, according to Haldeman's notes, referred to Watergate. (Book II, 249–50) The obliteration was, in fact, caused by repeated manual erasures, which were made on the tape recorder used by the President's personal secretary Rose Mary Woods. (See Appendix A)

Although the President had six other conversations with Haldeman and Colson that day,[4] the President did not meet with his Attorney General Kleindienst, his FBI Director Gray or his Campaign Director Mitchell. (Book II, 243–44)

On the morning of June 20, 1972, Magruder, as instructed by Haldeman, met with Sloan and determined that the source of the money found on the persons arrested was the Finance Committee to Re-Elect the President (FCRP), an arm of CRP. (Book II, 126)

On June 20, 1972, in spite of the fact that he was aware of the CRP responsibility for the Watergate break-in, Mitchell issued a prepared statement denying any legal, moral or ethical accountability on the part of the CRP. (Book II, 303) That evening, the President telephoned Mitchell. They discussed the break-in. (Book II, 310) On July 23, 1973, the tape of that telephone call was subpoenaed by the Special Prosecutor. (Book IX, 415–16) On October 30, 1973, the President responded that the conversation had not been recorded. (Book IX, 836) The President did provide a dictabelt recording of his recollections of that day (Book II, 309), which included the following account of his conversation with Mitchell:

> Paragraph. I also talked to John Mitchell in—late in the day and tried to cheer him up a bit. He is terribly chagrined that, uh, the activities of anybody attached to his committee should, uh, have, uh, been handled in such a manner, and he said that he only regretted that he had not policed all the people more effectively on a—in his own organization—(42 second silence) (unintelligible) (Book II, 310)

The President issued no order to discharge Gordon Liddy, Counsel to FCRP. Mitchell knew that Liddy was responsible for the burglary—

---

[4] On May 15, 1974, the House Judiciary Committee subpoenaed the tape recordings and other materials related to conversations between the President and Haldeman on June 20, 1972 from 4:35 to 5:25 p.m.; from 7:52 to 7:59 p.m.; and from 8:42 to 8:50 p.m.; and between the President and Colson from 2:20 to 3:30 p.m.; from 8:04 to 8:21 p.m.; and from 11:33 p.m. to 12:05 a.m., June 21, 1972. The President refused to produce these recordings.

he had authorized the Liddy Plan and had been told by Mardian and LaRue that Liddy had planned and participated in the break-in. (Book II, 280) Haldeman knew—he had approved Liddy's transfer to CRP for intelligence-gathering purposes, (Book I, 49) and on June 20 had directed Strachan to destroy documents that contained discussions about the fruits of Liddy's activities. (Book II, 262–63) Dean knew—Liddy told him the whole story on June 19. (Book II, 145) Ehrlichman knew—Dean had told him on June 19 of Liddy's confession (Book II, 145–46) because as Ehrlichman later said: "Well, the only reason to tell me was not for me as me but because I was one of the two conduits that he [Dean] had to the Boss." (WHT 1172) Colson knew—Colson had telephoned Magruder prior to March 30 in the presence of Liddy and Hunt and urged Magruder to see to it that Liddy's political intelligence gathering proposal was considered.[5] Colson also knew of Hunt's role in the break-in. (Book I, 113; HJCT 84)

On June 22, 1972, the President—who had been with Haldeman in Key Biscayne when the news of the break-in first appeared; who had remained there with Haldeman on June 17, 18 and 19; who had discussed Watergate with Colson on June 19 and with Haldeman and Mitchell on June 20—held a news conference. He was asked if he had ordered any sort of investigation to determine the truth of the charges "that the people who bugged [DNC] headquarters had a direct link to the White House." The President replied:

> Mr. Ziegler and also Mr. Mitchell, speaking for the campaign committee, have responded to questions on this in great detail. They have stated my position and have also stated the facts accurately.
>
> This kind of activity, as Mr. Ziegler had indicated, has no place whatever in our electoral process, or in our governmental process. And, as Mr. Ziegler has stated, the White House has had no involvement whatever in this particular incident.
>
> As far as the matter now is concerned, it is under investigation, as it should be, by the proper legal authorities, by the District of Columbia police, and by the FBI. I will not comment on those matters, particularly since possible criminal charges are involved. (Book II, 352–53)

When the President issued this statement, he knew or should have known that Howard Hunt, Gordon Liddy and other CRP personnel were responsible for the burglary, and that some of these persons had previously engaged in covert activities, as members of the Plumbers unit, on the President's behalf.

By June 21, 1972, the decision had been made to prevent further Watergate disclosures and the President's closest subordinates and agents were beginnning to carry out this decision. The President had placed Ehrlichman in charge. Ehrlichman had assigned Dean to monitor the FBI investigation. Ehrlichman called Gray and told him that Dean was conducting an inquiry into the Watergate matter for the White House. He instructed Gray to work closely with Dean. (Book II, 314)

The identification of Hunt as a suspect in the Watergate burglary created a risk that a direct link to the White House might be established. After discussions between Colson and White House Staff Sec-

---

[5] McCord, CRP security head who was arrested at the break-in and therefore exposed, was immediately discharged and Mitchell disclaimed CRP responsibility for his activities.

retary Bruce Kehrli, Ehrlichman and Colson decided that White House records should state that Hunt's status as a White House consultant had been terminated as of April 1, 1972.[6] (Book II, 168-69) On or about June 21, 1972, Colson's office forwarded to Kehrli a memorandum which was dated March 30, 1972 and which expressed a desire to assist Hunt on an annuity problem "and then totally drop him as a consultant so that 1701 [CRP] can pick him up and use him." Within a week after June 19, 1972, Kehrli circled the reference to dropping Hunt as a consultant and wrote at the bottom of the memorandum: "OK—Drop as of April 1, 1972 BAK." Kehrli was also told by Colson to remove Hunt's name from the White House phone directory; on Kehrli's instructions, the name was removed. (Kehrli affidavit, 2-4; Colson testimony, 3 HJC 262-63; Book II, 184)

The money found on those arrested created for the President another risk of disclosure and another danger to his re-election campaign. The risk was that it could be traced back to the Campaign Committee—exposing the Committee's responsibility for the burglary and also exposing illegal corporate campaign contributions.

Because of this risk, Haldeman, on June 18, 1972, the day after the break-in, directed Magruder to return from California to Washington, and talk to Sloan, Dean and Strachan about the source of the money. (Book II, 126) Liddy, who was also aware of the risk, shredded the $100 bills in his possession immediately after the break-in. (Book II, 289)

The money was part of the sum of five campaign contribution checks totalling $114,000. Four of the five checks were drawn on a Mexican bank by Manuel Ogarrio, a Mexican attorney. The fifth check was signed by Kenneth Dahlberg, a Minnesota businessman. FCRP Treasurer Hugh Sloan had given the checks to Gordon Liddy sometime in April to convert into cash. Liddy in turn had given the checks to Bernard Barker, one of those later arrested at Watergate. Barker had deposited the checks in his Florida bank account. Barker gave the cash to Liddy, who transmitted it to Sloan. Later, when Sloan gave Liddy cash, he apparently gave him some of the same bills which Liddy had obtained for FCRP. (Book II, 96-97, 339, 370-71)

It is standard practice for banks to record the serial numbers of cash paid out in large transactions. Thus, the FBI probably could trace the $100 bills back to the bank that supplied the cash and to the five checks deposited in the bank account of Bernard Barker. (Book II, 339) Dahlberg and Ogarrio could tell the FBI that the checks bearing their names were delivered to the President's re-election campaign; Dahlberg had in fact handed his check personally to Stans. (Book II, 366-67) Ogarrio could also tell the FBI that he had covered his checks by charging a fee to Gulf Resources & Chemical Corporation.

The risk that the CRP link would be uncovered became imminent on June 21 and 22, 1972, when Gray informed Dean that the $100 bills had already been traced by the FBI to Barker's bank account in

---

[6] Butterfield testified that shortly after the Watergate break-in he was told by Kehrli that Hunt was then a White House consultant, but that at Haldeman's direction Hunt was not listed on the employment rolls. (Butterfield testimony, 1 HJC 55-57) Kehrli states he does not recall this conversation. (Kehrli affidavit, 3) Colson has testified he told Kehrli on June 19, 1972 to make White House records reflect Hunt's termination as of March 31, 1972. (Colson testimony, 3 HJC 262-63)

Florida, that Dahlberg and Ogarrio had been identified, and that the Bureau intended to interview them. (Book II, 339) On June 23, 1972, Dean reported to Haldeman the information given to him by Gray; Haldeman immediately reported to the President.[7] (Book II, 356)

At the time that the Committee on the Judiciary voted on Article I, it was undisputed that on June 23, 1972 the President directed Haldeman and Ehrlichman to meet with Helms and Walters, to express White House concern that the FBI investigation might expose unrelated covert CIA operations or the activities of the White House Special Investigations Unit, and to ask that Walters meet with Gray to communicate these concerns to him. (Book II, 358–59)[8]

On the afternoon of June 23, 1972, Ehrlichman and Haldeman met with Helms and Walters. (Book II, 356–57) Helms assured Haldeman that there was no CIA involvement in the Watergate break-in, and told him that he had given a similar assurance to acting FBI Director Gray. (Book II, 383–84) In reply, Haldeman said that the FBI investigation was leading to important people; and that it was the President's wish, because an FBI investigation in Mexico might uncover CIA activities or assets, that Walters suggest to Gray that it was not desirable to pursue the inquiry, especially into Mexico. (Book II, 380, 385–86) Ehrlichman said that the Mexican checks, traced to the Florida bank account, were mentioned as an example of the type of thing about which the President was concerned. (Book II, 392)

While the meeting among Haldeman, Ehrlichman, Helms and Walters was going on, Dean telephoned Gray and told him to expect a call from Walters. (Book II, 400) After the meeting, Walters told Gray that the FBI investigation should not be pursued into Mexico or beyond the five persons already in custody. (Book II, 402–04) Gray agreed to hold in abeyance the planned interview of Ogarrio, although he said the FBI would continue to try to locate and interview Dahlberg. (Book II, 400–01) On June 23, 1972, Stans asked Dahlberg to fly from Minneapolis to Washington and they met later that day at the CRP offices. (Book II, 368, 406–07)

On June 23, 1972, Walters determined that no CIA sources would be jeopardized by an FBI investigation in Mexico. (Book II, 410–11) On June 26, 1972, he so informed Dean, whom Ehrlichman had designated as liaison to the White House. (Book II, 411–12) On June 27, 1972, Helms notified Gray that the CIA had no interest in Ogarrio. (Book II, 447) Helms and Gray set up a meeting for the following day; Gray reported the meeting planned for June 28 to Dean. (Book II, 447, 453–54) In preparation for the meeting Helms had told the CIA employees who were to attend the meeting that the CIA still adhered to its request that the FBI not expand its investigation beyond those already arrested or directly under suspicion. (Book II, 459) On the morning of June 28, 1972, Ehrlichman telephoned Gray and instructed him to cancel his meeting with Helms, saying only that the meeting was not necessary. (Book II, 454) Gray called Helms and

---

[7] On May 15, 1974, the House Judiciary Committee subpoenaed the tape recordings and other materials related to this and other conversations between the President and Haldeman on June 23, 1972. The President did not produce these recordings prior to the conclusion of the Committee's inquiry.

[8] After the Committee voted on the recommended articles, the President released three edited transcripts of the June 23, 1972, conversations with Haldeman. Material from these transcripts appears at the end of this section.

cancelled the meeting and Helms reported that the CIA had no interest in Dahlberg. At Helms' request Gray cancelled interviews of two CIA employees (Book II, 454, 459) who, in 1971, had furnished Hunt with information, with disguises and with alias identification cards in connection with his covert activities. (Book II, 460–66)

On June 28, 1972, Dean asked Walters whether the CIA could stop the FBI investigation at the five suspects already in custody. He pointed out that the FBI had leads to Dahlberg and Ogarrio. Walters said he could not think of a way the CIA could help the White House. (Book II, 440–41) On the evening of June 28, 1972, Dean called Gray and urged that, for reasons of national security, Ogarrio and Dahlberg not be interviewed.

On June 28, 1972, Dean and Ehrlichman gave to Gray those contents of Hunt's safe that had been withheld from FBI agents on the previous day, with the exception of two notebooks. (Book II, 503)

On the morning of June 29, 1972, Gray retracted an order of the previous day to interview Ogarrio and instructed the FBI's Minneapolis Field Division to make no further attempts to interview Dahlberg. (Book II, 474–75)

III

KALMBACH FUND-RAISING ASSIGNMENT

These activities of Haldeman, Ehrlichman, Dean, Helms, Walters and Gray impeded the FBI's Watergate investigation. In addition, there were other problems. The defendants were in jail and needed money for bail, for attorneys' fees and for other support. Mitchell decided CRP could not provide bail. (Book III, 99) Dean asked Walters if the CIA would pay bail and support money, and was told it would not. (Book II, 433)

On June 28, 1972, Ehrlichman and Haldeman agreed that Dean should direct Kalmbach, the President's personal attorney and a longtime high-level fundraiser for the President, to handle the raising of money for the Watergate defendants. (Book III, 149–53, 277–79; Book IV, 536; WHT 493–96) That night, at Dean's request, Kalmbach flew to Washington. (Book III, 152–54) The following morning he met with Dean and agreed to undertake the assignment. (Book III, 154–55; Kalmbach testimony, 3 ILJC 535–37) On June 29, 1972, Kalmbach obtained $75,000 in cash from Stans. On the following day, Kalmbach delivered it to Anthony Ulasewicz, who had previously engaged in surveillance and other activities under Ehrlichman's direction. Ulasewicz was instructed to make clandestine payments for the benefit of those who had participated in the break-in. (Book III, 167–69; Book VII, 336–337; Kalmbach testimony, 3 ILJC 538–41)

IV

MITCHELL'S RESIGNATION AS CRP DIRECTOR

As of June 30, 1972, the risks of further disclosure with respect to the connection between the White House or CRP and the break-in were contained, at least temporarily. Cash was in hand to be distributed to the persons arrested; the cash found on the persons arrested had not yet been traced to CRP. By June 28, 1972, Gray had stopped the FBI's efforts to trace the money found on those arrested. Neither Hunt nor Liddy had been charged with involvement in the break-in.

On June 30, 1972, the President met with Haldeman and Mitchell to discuss Mitchell's resignation as Director of CRP. (Book II, 515-16) Mitchell had approved Liddy's intelligence activities. (Book I, 116) Following Liddy's call to Magruder on the morning of June 17, 1972 (Book II, 106), Mitchell had been kept fully informed of developments. At the time of this June 30, 1972 meeting, Haldeman knew of CRP and White House involvement in the political intelligence gathering program and in the Watergate break-in itself. Since October 7, 1971, Haldeman knew that "Operation Sandwedge", which contemplated a "black bag" capability and electronic surveillance, was once under study by Attorney General Mitchell and John Dean. (Book VII, 1341-42, 1363-64) Haldeman knew that on December 2, 1971, Operation Sandwedge had been scrapped, and that Liddy had been hired "instead" by CRP to handle political intelligence. (Political Matters Memorandum, 12/2/71, 3) Haldeman knew that, in February, 1972, Liddy had made two presentations to Mitchell, Magruder and Dean, and that Liddy's plans had contemplated the use of electronic surveillance and illegal entries into such targeted facilities as the DNC headquarters. (Book I, 66) At the end of March, 1972, Haldeman knew that a sophisticated political intelligence gathering system with a budget of $300,000 had been approved by CRP. (Book I, 148) Haldeman knew that he had directed Liddy to change his "capabilities" from Muskie to McGovern. (Book I, 192-93) Haldeman knew, shortly after the break-in, that McCord and Hunt had been involved in CRP's intelligence gathering activities. (Book II, 130) On June 18, 1972, Haldeman knew of the possibility that the money found on the five persons arrested in the DNC offices was CRP money. (Book II, 126-27) On June 20, 1972, Haldeman knew that he had instructed his assistant Strachan to destroy documents. (Book II, 265) On June 23, 1972, Haldeman knew that the FBI had uncovered five checks totalling $114,000 and one bearing the names of Dahlberg and Ogarrio which had passed through the bank account of Watergate conspirator Bernard Barker. (Book II, 339-41) On June 23, 1972, Haldeman knew that he had instructed Walters to inform Gray that the FBI investigation should not be pursued into Mexico. On June 28, 1972, Haldeman knew that he and Ehrlichman had approved Dean's use of Kalmbach to raise and covertly distribute cash for those involved in Watergate. (Book III, 149-53, 277-79; Book IV, 536; WHT 493-96)

One of the subjects of the June 30, 1972, discussion among the President, Haldeman and Mitchell was Mitchell's resignation as head of CRP:

HALDEMAN. Well, there maybe is another facet. The longer you wait the more risk each hour brings. You run the risk of more stuff, valid or invalid, surfacing on the Watergate caper—type of thing—
MITCHELL. You couldn't possibly do it if you got into a—
HALDEMAN. —the potential problem and then you are stuck—
PRESIDENT. Yes, that's the other thing, if something does come out, but we won't—we hope nothing will. It may not. But there is always the risk.

HALDEMAN. As of now there is no problem there. As, as of any moment in the future there is at least a potential problem.

PRESIDENT. Well, I'd cut the loss fast. I'd cut it fast. If we're going to do it I'd cut it fast. That's my view, generally speaking. And I wouldn't—and I don't think, though, as a matter of fact, I don't think the story, if we, if you put it in human terms—I think the story is, you're positive rather than negative, because as I said as I was preparing to answer for this press conference, I just wrote it out, as I usually do, one way—terribly sensitive [unintelligible]. A hell of a lot of people will like that answer. They would. And it'd make anybody else who asked any other question on it look like a selfish son-of-a-bitch, which I thoroughly intended them to look like.

*   *   *   *   *   *   *

MITCHELL. [Unintelligible] Westchester Country Club with all the sympathy in the world.

PRESIDENT. That's great. That's great.

MITCHELL. [Unintelligible] don't let—

HALDEMAN. You taking this route—people won't expect you to—be a surprise.

PRESIDENT. No, if it's a surprise. Otherwise, you're right. It will be tied right to Watergate. [Unintelligible]—tighter if you wait too long, till it simmers down.

HALDEMAN. You can't if other stuff develops on Watergate. The problem is, it's always potentially the same thing.

PRESIDENT. Well if it does, don't just hard-line.

HALDEMAN. [Unintelligible] That's right. In other words, it'd be hard to hard-line Mitchell's departure under—

PRESIDENT. That's right. You can't do it. I just want it to be handled in a way Martha's not hurt.

MITCHELL. Yeah, okay. (Book II, 515–16)

On July 1, 1972, Mitchell resigned as director of the President's re-election campaign organization. Mitchell wrote to the President that he could no longer remain as campaign manager "and still meet the one obligation which must come first: the happiness and welfare of my wife and daughter. They have patiently put up with my long absences for some four years, and the moment has come when I must devote more time to them." As the President had suggested on the previous day, the story was put in "human terms." (Book II, 514)

However the story was put, all the prior circumstances since June 17, 1972, provided substantial proof that President Nixon decided shortly after learning of the Watergate break-in that his subordinates should take action designed to delay, impede, and obstruct the investigation of the Watergate break-in, to cover-up, conceal and protect those responsible, and to conceal the existence and scope of other unlawful covert activities.

On August 5, 1974, President Nixon publicly released and delivered to the Committee on the Judiciary [9] after the Committee had concluded its vote, edited transcripts of three of his conversations of June 23, 1972, with H. R. Haldeman. At their morning meeting, the President

---

[9] On August 5, 1974, James St. Clair, Special Counsel to the President, wrote John Doar, Special Counsel to the Judiciary Committee, as follows:

At the direction of the President, I am forwarding to you herewith transcripts of three additional recorded Presidential conversations between the President and H. R. Haldeman on June 23, 1972, for submission to the members of the Committee on the Judiciary as a supplement to the President's *Submission of Recorded Presidential Conversations* dated April 30, 1974.

These conversations first came to my attention a few days ago and I believe they are necessary to more accurately and completely describe the events involving the relationship between the FBI Watergate investigation and the CIA in 1972 than has been previously furnished the Committee.

Copies of the Transcripts were immediately distributed to each member of the Committee.

directed Haldeman to direct the CIA to impede the FBI investigation, which had begun to trace money in the possession of the burglars to CRP.

H . Now, on the investigation, you know the Democratic break-in thing, we're back in the problem area because the FBI is not under control, because Gray doesn't exactly know how to control it and they have—their investigation is now leading into some productive areas—because they've been able to trace the money—not through the money itself—but through the bank sources—the banker. And, and it goes in some directions we don't want it to go. Ah. also there have been some things—like an informant came in off the street to the FBI in Miami who was a photographer or has a friend who is a photographer who developed some films through this guy Barker and the films had pictures of Democratic National Committee letterhead documents and things. So it's things like that that are filtering in. Mitchell came up with yesterday, and John Dean analyzed very carefully last night and concludes, concurs now with Mitchell's recommendation that the only way to solve this, and we're set up beautifully to do it, ah, in that and that—the only network that paid any attention to it last night was NBC—they did a massive story on the Cuban thing.
P That's right.
H That the way to handle this now is for us to have Walters call Pat Gray and just say, "Stay to hell out of this—this is ah, business here we don't want you to go any further on it." That's not an unusual development, and ah, that would take care of it.
P What about Pat Gray—you mean Pat Gray doesn't want to?
H Pat does want to. He doesn't know how to, and he doesn't have . . . any basis for doing it. Given this, he will then have the basis. He'll call Mark Felt in . . .
P Yeah.
H He'll call him and say, "We've got the signal from across the river to put the hold on this." And that will fit rather well because the FBI agents who are working the case, at this point, feel that's what it is. . . .
H And you seem to think the thing to do is get them to stop?
P Right, fine. (WHT, June 23, 1972, 10:04–11:39 a.m., 2–5)

The President asked Haldeman if Mitchell knew in advance about the Watergate burglaries. Haldeman said he thought so. The President then asked, "Is it Liddy?" (WHT, June 23, 1972, 10:04 to 11:39 a.m., 6) Since Haldeman had not mentioned Liddy and since the President had said he did not learn of the Fielding break-in (in which Liddy was involved) until March 17 of the following year, the question clearly indicates that the President must have known about Liddy before the conversation of June 23, 1972.

The President told Haldeman what to say to the CIA officials. He said to tell them that it involved Hunt and that it would be detrimental for them to go further.

In the early afternoon, the President repeated his instructions to Haldeman to have the CIA limit the investigation because Hunt knew too much.

P O.K., just postpone (scratching noises) (unintelligible) Just say (unintelligible) very bad to have this fellow Hunt, ah, he knows too damned much, if he was involved—you happen to know that? If it gets out that this is all involved, the Cuban thing it would be a fiasco. It would make the CIA look bad, it's going to make Hunt look bad, and it is likely to blow the whole Bay of Pigs thing which we think would be very unfortunate—both for CIA, and for the country, at this time, and for American foreign policy. Just tell him to lay off. Don't you? (WHT, June 23, 1972, 1:04–1:13 p.m., 1)

At 2:20 p.m. Haldeman reported to the President that Gray had suspicions that the break-in might be a CIA operation; that Walters "was very happy to be helpful" in limiting the FBI investigations; and that Walters would call Gray about it.

H . . . He [Walters] said, he said we'll be very happy to be helpful [unintelligible] handle anything you want. I would like to know the reason for being helpful, and I made it clear to him he wasn't going to get explicit [unintelligible] generality, and he said fine. And Walters [unintelligible]. Walters is going to make a call to Gray. That's the way we put it and that's the way it was left. (WHT, June 23, 1972, 2:20–2:45 p.m., 2–3)

The President, on June 23, 1973, thus accepted Mitchell's recommendation, delivered by Haldeman, that the FBI investigation into Watergate be limited by a false claim of CIA involvement.

The President directed Haldeman to set this part of the coverup in motion, on the President's behalf:

P . . . I'm not going to get that involved. I'm [unintelligble].
H No, sir, we don't want you to.
P You call them in. (WHT, June 23, 1972, 10:04–11:39 a.m., 7)

CONTAINMENT—JULY 1, 1972, TO ELECTION

I

Presidential Plan for Containment

From late June, 1972, until after the Presidential election in November, President Nixon through his close subordinates engaged in a plan of containment and concealment which prevented disclosures that might have resulted in the indictment of high CRP and White House officials; that might have exposed Hunt and Liddy's prior illegal covert activities for the White House; and that might have put the outcome of the November election in jeopardy. Two of the President's men, John Dean, Counsel to the President, a subordinate, and Herbert Kalmbach, personal attorney to the President, an agent, who had been assigned to carry out the cover-up, carried out their assignment. They did so with the full support of the power and authority of the President of the United States.

Tape recordings of Presidential conversations in the possession of the Committee establish that implementation of the plan prior to the election had the full approval of the President. On June 30, 1972, the President told Haldeman and Mitchell that there was a risk of further Watergate disclosures and that his desire was to "cut the loss." Haldeman said, "As of now there is no problem there"; but, "As, as of any moment in the future, there is, there is at least a potential problem." (Book II, 514) On September 15, 1972, after Dean had said that he could conceive of all kinds of unfortunate complications (Dean's term was "you can spin out horribles"), the President told him and Haldeman, "You really can't just sit and worry yourself about it all the time (thinking the worst may happen) ... you just try to button it up as well as you can and hope for the best." (HJCT 13–14) On the morning of March 21, 1973, Dean told the President regarding his investigation after the break-in, "I was under pretty clear instructions [laughs] not to really to investigate this, that this was something that just could have been disastrous on the election if it had—all hell had broken loose, and I worked on a theory of containment." The President replied, "Sure." (HJCT 88) During the same conversation, Dean said of the cover-up, "We were able to hold it for a long time." The President's reply was, "Yeah, I know." (HJCT 101–02) Dean said that some bad judgments, some necessary judgments had been made before the election, but that at the time, in view of the election, there was no way.

The President said, "We're all in on it." [1] (HJCT 104) The Presi-

---
[1] The words "We're all in on it" do not appear in the edited White House transcript. (WHT 207)

dent told Dean, "[Y]ou had the right plan, let me say, I have no doubts about the right plan before the election.[2] And you handled it just right. You contained it. Now after the election we've got to have another plan, because we can't have, for four years, we can't have this thing—you're going to be eaten away. We can't do it." (HJCT 129–30) On the evening of March 21, 1973, the President told Colson that Dean was only doing what he had to do, what anyone would have done under the circumstances. (Colson testimony, 3 HJC 334) And on March 22, 1973, the President told Mitchell, "the whole theory has been containment, as you know, John." (HJCT 183) [3]

Much of the evidence for the period July 1, 1972 to March 21, 1973 concerns actions by the President's subordinates and agents. Of necessity, every President must rely on subordinates to carry out his instructions.

Whether or not the President knew about the details of the means used by his subordinates to carry out the cover up, evidence of these actions was relevant in determining the degree to which the President was responsible for them. The issue, whether his subordinates and agents were acting in accordance with his plan and on his behalf, generally turn in large part on circumstantial evidence. Since concealment, duplicity, dissembling and secrecy are fundamental elements of a successful cover-up of illegal activity, this is a case in part of circumstantial evidence. It is common that offenses of this type must be proved in this way.

As the cover up continued, more and more direct evidence accumulated to establish the President either actually knew what his men were doing, or ratified or condoned their actions.

II

IMPLEMENTATION OF CONTAINMENT PLAN

Beginning in June, Kalmbach secured the funds required for payments to the Watergate defendants. The cash was paid clandestinely. By the middle of September, when he withdrew from any further assignment relating to making payments to the defendants, Kalmbach had delivered approximately $190,000 in cash to the defendants or their attorneys. (Book III, 378–79, 381; Kalmbach testimony, 3 HJC 557–58) Dean or LaRue consulted with Kalmbach on each of the deliveries. (Book III, 229; Kalmbach testimony, 3 HJC 542) Dean reported the payments to Haldeman and Ehrlichman. (Book III, 202) During the latter part of July, Kalmbach, who had been requested to seek sources of funds outside CRP, became concerned about the secrecy of the activity. Kalmbach sought and obtained assurances from Ehrlichman that Dean had the authority to pursue the payments project and that it was vital for Kalmbach to continue working on it. (Kalmbach testimony, 3 HJC 547–49; Book III, 268–69, 277)

Investigations by federal agencies were hampered by the President's key political associates. In June, 1972, Ehrlichman assigned Dean to

---

[2] In the edited White House transcript, the President said ". . . And then, once you decide on the right plan, you say, 'John,' you say, 'no doubts about the right plan before the election. You handled it right. You contained it.'" instead of the above quoted material. (WHT 248)

[3] This material does not appear in the edited White House transcript. (WHT 310)

monitor the FBI investigation for the White House. (Book II, 314–15; Dean testimony, 2 HJC 226–27) Dean obtained reports on the results of the FBI investigation and tried to enlist the CIA to narrow the scope of the FBI investigation. (Book II, 315, 392–95) Dean regularly obtained information from Gray and from FBI reports, which he showed to CRP officials and attorneys. (Book II, 558; O'Brien testimony, 1 HJC 167) He sat in on several FBI interviews of White House personnel—a procedure that Ehrlichman arranged with Gray. (Book II, 314–15) Thus, Dean was able to anticipate the leads the FBI would follow and coach those persons who had knowledge of the facts within CRP and the White House. (Book II, 484) Instead of having White House staff members Colson, Krogh, Young, Chapin and Strachan appear before the Watergate Grand Jury, Dean arranged with Assistant Attorney General Petersen to have their depositions taken outside the presence of the Grand Jury. (Book II, 565) On July 5, 1972, when Mitchell was interviewed by the FBI, he falsely denied knowledge of any information related to the break-in. Mitchell had been told by Mardian and LaRue of Liddy's involvement in the break-in, but he has testified that he was not, under any circumstances, volunteering information. (Book III, 240)

On July 19 and 20, 1972, Porter and Magruder falsely told FBI agents that the funds obtained by Liddy from CRP were for legal intelligence gathering activities. (Book III, 242–43, 247–48) At the Senate Select Committee on Presidential Campaign Activities (SSC) hearings, Porter testified that when Magruder asked him to lie to prevent embarrassment to the President, Haldeman and Mitchell, Magruder said that Porter's name had come up as a person who could be counted on. (Book III, 160) On August 10, 1972, Porter testified falsely before the Watergate Grand Jury as to the purpose for which CRP funds were disbursed to Liddy. (Book III, 293, 296) On August 18, 1972, Magruder, after rehearsing with Dean his false story about the Liddy money, testified falsely before the Watergate Grand Jury. (Book III, 300) On or about August 28, 1972, Krogh, Ehrlichman's assistant who had been a co-director of the Plumbers unit, testified falsely before the Watergate Grand Jury as to prior activities of Liddy and Hunt. (Book III, 312–15, 322–23, 324–25) He said that the only travel Hunt had ever done for the White House was a trip to Texas and that the only reason Liddy had ever traveled to California was to contact customs officials. Krogh knew that Hunt and Liddy had, in fact, traveled to California to break into Dr. Fielding's office. (Book VII, 1310–12) On September 12 or 13, 1972, Magruder met with Mitchell and Dean to plan a false story regarding the meetings among Mitchell, Magruder, Dean and Liddy in early 1972, in which political intelligence and electronic surveillance were discussed; Magruder thereafter testified falsely about the meetings before the Watergate Grand Jury. He said that one of the meetings listed in his calendar had been cancelled and that the purpose of the other was to discuss Liddy's duties as General Counsel. (Book III, 344, 351–52)

The President decided that former Commerce Secretary, then Chairman of FCRP, Maurice Stans should not appear personally before the Grand Jury. He assigned Ehrlichman to see that Stans need not appear. (Book II, 567) In July, 1972, Stans asked Dean to make arrangements with Henry Petersen to have his deposition taken outside of the Grand Jury. Dean and then Ehrlichman contacted Petersen. Petersen insisted that Stans testify before the Grand Jury. Finally, Ehrlichman telephoned Kleindienst. Petersen subsequently agreed to take Stans' deposition in his office, in lieu of a scheduled Grand Jury appearance. (Book II, 565, 567–69, 571) in spite of the fact that Kleindienst told Ehrlichman that Ehrlichman was lucky Petersen had not filed an obstruction of justice complaint. (Book II, 564–65)

III

Gray's Warning

Shortly after July 1, 1972, the FBI had a break in the case. Alfred Baldwin, a CRP employee recruited by McCord, had monitored the intercepted conversations at the DNC. At the time of the break-in Baldwin was across the street from Watergate at the Howard Johnson Motel. He was not arrested. On July 5, Baldwin stepped forward and identified Hunt as one of the Watergate burglars. (Baldwin testimony, 1 SSC 389–90)

On the morning of July 6, 1972, Gray met with Walters. (Book II, 529) The two men discussed the danger to the President from the efforts by his White House staff to suppress the FBI investigation and interfere with the CIA. They discussed the need to raise the matter with the President. (Book II, 526–27, 528–29, 551) After Walters left, Gray called Clark MacGregor, the new chairman of CRP, who was with the Presidential party in California. (Book II, 551; Gray testimony, 9 SSC 3462)

Gray told MacGregor that both he and Walters were concerned about the misuse of the CIA and FBI by White House staff members. Gray asked MacGregor to inform the President that the FBI and CIA had been injured by the conduct of members of the White House staff and that the same persons were hurting the President.[4]

Thirty-seven minutes after Gray's conversation with MacGregor, Gray received a telephone call from the President. (Book II, 524, 544) The President began the conversation by saying how pleased he was with the way the FBI had handled an attempted skyjacking in San Francisco. (Book II, 550) Gray thanked the President. The President did not raise the subject of Watergate, nor the serious allegation Gray had just made to MacGregor. Gray then warned the President that both he and General Walters thought people on the President's staff were trying to "mortally wound" the President by manipulation of the FBI and CIA; Gray told the President that he had just spoken to MacGregor and "asked him to speak to you about this." In response to Gray's warnings the President said only: "Pat, you just continue to conduct your aggressive and thorough investigation."[5] The President asked no questions about what facts

---

[4] MacGregor has testified that Gray called him on the night of July 5, 1972, but that Gray did not give him any message to pass to the President or discuss interference with the FBI's Watergate investigation. (Book II, 533–34) On the other hand, Ehrlichman testified that the President mentioned to him that MacGregor had received a telephone call from Gray, had told the President about it and that the President had immediately called Gray. (Book II, 548)

[5] The President has stated that Gray warned that the matter of Watergate might lead higher. (Book II, 550, 553)

Gray had to support his serious charges; the President asked for no names. There is no evidence that the President pursued the matter. (Book II, 552-53; Gray testimony, 9 SSC 3462)

On July 8, 1972, two days after the President's telephone conversation with Gray, Ehrlichman and the President, while walking on a beach at San Clemente, discussed the possibility of clemency for the Watergate defendants. Ehrlichman has said that he told the President that "presidential pardons or something of that kind would inevitably be a question that he would have to confront by reason of the political aspect of this." (Book III, 182-83) The President's response, according to Ehrlichman and to the President's public statement, was that no one in the White House should "get into this whole area of clemency with anybody involved in this case and surely not make any assurances to anyone." (Book III, 189) At the time of this conversation, Ehrlichman knew that Liddy and Hunt and two of the Cubans arrested at the Watergate had been involved in the break-in of Ellsberg's psychiatrist's office. The President has said that he did not learn of that break-in until more than eight months later, on March 17, 1973. ("Presidential Statements," 8/15/73, 42)

IV

PRESIDENTIAL STATEMENT OF AUGUST 29, 1972

In August, 1972, the President discussed with Ehrlichman the issuance of public statements on Watergate. (Book II, 588) At that time Ehrlichman knew the details of CRP and White House involvement in the Watergate break-in (Book II, 152-53); Erhlichman and Dean had concealed certain of the contents of Hunt's safe outside the normal channels of the law by delivering them personally to Acting FBI Director Gray with instructions that they never see the light of day. (Book II, 503) Ehrlichman had agreed to the use of Kalmbach to make secret payments to the defendants. Ehrlichman knew of the actual payments to the defendants. (Book III, 150-51, 269) And Ehrlichman knew of the President's instructions to use the CIA to narrow and thwart the FBI investigation. (Book II, 382-84)

On August 29, 1972, the President held a news conference. He discussed various pending investigative proceedings in connection with Watergate—including those of the FBI, the Department of Justice, the House Banking and Currency Committee and the GAO—in suggesting that the appointment of a special prosecutor would serve no useful purpose. He said:

> In addition to that, within our own staff, under my direction, Counsel to the President, Mr. Dean has conducted a complete investigation of all leads which might involve any present members of the White House Staff or anybody in the Government. I can say categorically that his investigation indicates that no one in the White House Staff, no one in this Administration, presently employed, was involved in this very bizarre incident.

With respect to the involvement of CRP, the President said,

> Before Mr. Mitchell left as campaign chairman he had employed a very good law firm with investigatory experience to look into this matter. Mr. MacGregor

has continued that investigation and is continuing it now. I will say in that respect that anyone on the campaign committee, Mr. MacGregor has assured me, who does not cooperate with the investigation . . . will be discharged immediately. (Book II, 589)

With respect to his efforts, and those of his aides in the investigation, the President said:

I think under these circumstances we are doing everything we can to take this incident and to investigate it and not to cover it up. What really hurts in matters of this sort is not the fact that they occur, because overzealous people in campaigns do things that are wrong. What really hurts is if you try to cover it up. I would say that here we are, with control of the agencies of the Government and presumably with control of the investigatory agencies of the Government with the exception of the GAO, which is independent. We have cooperated completely. We have indicated that we want all the facts brought out and that as far as any people who are guilty are concerned, they should be prosecuted. ("Presidential Statements," 8/29/72, 3)

In fact, Dean had conducted no investigation. He had been acting to narrow and frustrate investigation by the FBI. He had reached no conclusion that no one in the White House had been involved in Watergate. He had made no report of such an investigation. (Book II, 590–91) MacGregor had received only periodic briefings on matters related to Watergate. Their primary purpose was not to report on CRP involvement in the break-in, but to determine CRP's status in the pending civil suits initiated by the DNC. MacGregor has denied that he ever gave assurance to the President that anyone who did not cooperate with the investigation would be discharged. (MacGregor testimony, 12 SSC 4924)

The President and his staff had not "cooperated completely" with the investigatory agencies. The evidence, rather, shows clearly and convincingly that the President and his closest aides acted to obstruct and impede the investigations.

The President's statements on August 29 themselves were designed to delay, impede and obstruct the investigation of the Watergate break-in; to cover-up, conceal, and protect those responsible and to conceal the existence and scope of other unlawful covert activities.

V

SEPTEMBER 15, 1972 MEETING

On September 15, 1972, Liddy, Hunt and the five persons arrested in the DNC Watergate offices on June 17 were indicted for burglary, unlawful entry for the purpose of intercepting oral and wire communications, and conspiracy, all felonies. No other CRP or White House officials were charged with or named as having been involved in the break-in. (Book III, 360–61)

On that same day, John Dean was summoned to see the President. (Dean testimony, 2 HJC 228) Prior to this meeting Dean had been in the President's presence only three times that year: for three minutes on April 13, 1972 when the President signed his tax return, for five minutes on May 1, 1972 when photos were taken in the Rose Garden for National Secretaries Week, and for twenty-three minutes on August 14, 1972 when the President and Mrs. Nixon executed legal documents. (Book III, 598–99)

At the time of this conversation, it is undisputed that the President knew, and had known since a few days after the break-in, that Howard Hunt's name had "surfaced" in connection with Watergate and that Hunt had previously been a member of the White House Special Investigations Unit. ("Presidential Statements," 5/22/73, 24) The President had discussed Watergate with Haldeman and Mitchell, who were fully apprised of CRP and White House connections with the Watergate break-in. The President refused to comply with subpoenas from the Committee requiring tape recordings of six conversations between the President and Haldeman or Colson on June 20; it is undisputed that on June 20 he had instructed Haldeman to be on the attack for diversion. (Book II, 246) On June 20 he had been told by Mitchell with reference to Watergate that Mitchell regretted not keeping better control over the men. (Book II, 310) On June 23 he had instructed Haldeman to direct the CIA to request the FBI to curtail its investigation of the break-in. (WHT, June 23, 1972. 10:04–11:39 a.m., 3–7, 16–17) He had arranged, authorized and publicly advanced the misleading explanation for Mitchell's resignation from CRP on June 30. (Book II, 514–16) On July 6 he had received Gray's warning of White House interference with the FBI's Watergate investigation. (Book II, 524, 551–53) On July 8, more than two months before the return of indictments of Hunt and Liddy and six months before the trial, he had discussed executive clemency with Ehrlichman. (Book III, 182–83) He had arranged for Stans to testify before the prosecutors rather than the Grand Jury. (Book II, 567) On August 29 he had made an untrue public statement about Dean's "complete investigation" of the Watergate matter. (Book II, 589) These facts about the extent of the President's knowledge at the time of his September 15, 1972 meeting with Dean are undisputed.

Prior to Dean's arrival at the September 15, 1972 meeting, Haldeman told the President that Dean was "one of the quiet guys that gets a lot done," the type of person who "enables other people to gain ground while he's making sure that you don't fall through the holes." Haldeman continued, "Between times, he's doing, he's moving ruthlessly on the investigation of McGovern people, Kennedy stuff, and all that too." (HJCT 1) When Dean entered the room, the President asked him about the events of the day:

PRESIDENT. Well, you had quite a day today, didn't you? You got, uh, Watergate, uh, on, the, way, huh?
DEAN. Quite a three months.[6]
HALDEMAN. How did it all end up?
DEAN. Uh, I think we can say "Well" at this point. The, uh, the press is playing it just as we expect.
HALDEMAN. Whitewash?
DEAN. No, not yet; the, the story right now—
PRESIDENT. It's a big story.
DEAN. Yeah.
PRESIDENT. [Unintelligible]
HALDEMAN. Five indicted—
DEAN. Plus,
HALDEMAN. They're building up the fact that one of—
DEAN. plus two White House aides.

---

[6] In the edited White House transcript the words "We tried" appear instead of "Quite a three months." (WHT 55)

HALDEMAN. Plus, plus the White House former guy and all that. That's good. That, that takes the edge off whitewash really—which—that was the thing Mitchell kept saying that,
PRESIDENT. Yeah.
HALDEMAN. that to those in the country, Liddy and, uh, Hunt are big men.
DEAN. That's right.
PRESIDENT. Yeah. They're White House aides.[7] (HJCT 2)

The President asked how MacGregor handled himself. Dean responded that MacGregor had made a good statement about the Grand Jury indictment, and he had said it was time to realize that some apologies may be due. (HJCT 2) The President replied, "[J]ust remember all the trouble they gave us on this. We'll have a chance to get back at them one day." (HJCT 3)

Then the President, his Chief of Staff, and his Counsel talked about the pending civil litigation regarding the Watergate break-in, including Stans' libel action. Dean explained that the federal prosecutor of the Watergate defendants said that the civil cases made it difficult to draw criminal indictments because the prosecutors did not want to come out with indictments when civil cases tended to approach matters differently. (HJCT 6)

In the course of the September 15 meeting, the President talked briefly on the telephone with Clark MacGregor, telling him that Watergate "is just, uh, you know, one of those side issues and a month later everybody looks back and wonders what the hell the shouting was about." (HJCT 7) Then the conversation returned to the indictments handed down that day:

DEAN. Three months ago I would have had trouble predicting where we'd be today. I think that I can say that fifty-four days from now that, uh, not a thing will come crashing down to our, our surprise.

*   *   *   *   *   *   *

PRESIDENT. Well, the whole thing is a can of worms. As you know, a lot of this stuff went on. And, uh, and, uh, and the people who worked [unintelligible] awfully embarrassing. And, uh, and, the, uh, but the, but the way you, you've handled it, it seems to me, has been very skillful, because you—putting your fingers in the dikes every time that leaks have sprung here and sprung there. [Unintelligible] having people straighten the [unintelligible]. The Grand Jury is dismissed now? (HJCT 7)

Dean spoke of problems that might lie ahead, remarking that some bitterness and internal dissension existed in CRP. (HJCT 9) The President stated:

PRESIDENT. They should just, uh, just behave and, and, recognize this, this is, again, this is war. We're getting a few shots and it'll be over. And, we'll give them a few shots. It'll be over. Don't worry [Unintelligible] I wouldn't want to be on the other side right now. Would you? (HJCT 9)

In a discussion on ways to get even with those who had made an issue of Watergate, the President said, "I want the most, I want the most comprehensive notes on all of those that have tried to do us in. Because they didn't have to do it .... I mean if ... they had a very close election everybody on the other side would understand this game. But now they are doing this quite deliberately and they are asking for it and they are going to get it." (HJCT 10)

---

[7] The words "Yeah. They're White House aides." do not appear in the edited White House transcript. (WHT 55)

Dean then turned to the Patman (House Banking and Currency Committee) hearings. He identified the hearings as another potential problem "now that the indictments are down." He was uncertain of success in "turning that off." (HJCT 11) The conversation continued:

DEAN. . . . We've got a plan whereby Rothblatt and Bittman, who are counsel for the five men who were, or actually a total of seven, that were indicted today, are going to go up and visit every member and say, "If you commence hearings you are going to jeopardize the civil rights of these individuals in the worst way, and they'll never get a fair trial," and the like, and try to talk to members on, on that level. Uh—
PRESIDENT. Why not ask that they request to be heard by, by the Committee and explain it publicly?
DEAN. How could they—They've planned that what they're going to say is, "If you do commence with these hearings, we plan to publicly come up and say what you're doing to the rights of individuals." Something to that effect.
PRESIDENT. As a matter of fact they could even make a motion in court to get the thing dismissed.

And the discussion of the "plan" involving Rothblatt and Bittman, counsel for the Watergate burglars, continued further:

HALDEMAN. Well, going the other way, the dismissal of the, of the, of the indictment—[8]
PRESIDENT. How about trying to get the criminal cases, criminal charges dismissed on the grounds that there, well, you know—
HALDEMAN. The civil rights type stuff. (HJCT 11–12)

Dean said that he was having civil rights groups contacted for the purpose of putting pressure on Patman and suggested that Stans see Congressman Ford and brief him on Stans' difficulties with the law suits. They could also look at the campaign spending reports of every member of the Patman Committee. (HJCT 12–13)

The three men spoke of how to influence the minority members of the Committee to oppose the hearings. Both Secretary Connally and Congressman Gerald Ford were mentioned as liaison people. (HJCT 12–13) The President continued to stress the importance of cutting off the Patman hearings, which Dean said was a forum over which they would have the least control.

PRESIDENT. Gerry has really got to lead on this. He's got to be really be [unintelligible]
HALDEMAN. Gerry should, damn it. This is exactly the thing he was talking about, that the reason they are staying in is so that they can
PRESIDENT. That's right.
HALDEMAN. run investigations.
PRESIDENT. Well, the point is that they ought to raise hell about this, uh, this—these hearings are jeopardizing the—I don't know that they're, that the, the, counsel calling on the members of the Committee will do much good. I was. I—it may be all right but—I was thinking that they really ought to blunderbuss in the public arena. It ought to be publicized.
DEAN. Right.
HALDEMAN. Good.
DEAN. Right.
PRESIDENT. That's what this is, public relations.
DEAN. That's, that's all it is, particularly if Patman pulls the strings off, uh—[9] That's the last forum that, uh, uh, it looks like it could be a problem where you just have the least control the way it stands right now. Kennedy has also suggested he may call hearings of his Administrative Practices and Procedure Sub-

---
[8] This passage does not appear in the edited White House transcript. (WHT 68)
[9] The passage beginning "It ought to be publicized . . ." and ending ". . . if Patman pulls the strings off, uh . . ." does not appear in the edited White House transcript. (WHT 69)

committee. Uh, as, as this case has been all along, you can spin out horribles that, uh, you, you can conceive of, and so we just don't do that. I stopped doing that about, uh, two months ago.
PRESIDENT. Yeah.
DEAN. We just take one at a time and you deal with it based on—
PRESIDENT. And you really can't just sit and worry yourself
DEAN. No.
PRESIDENT. about it all the time, thinking, "The worst may happen," but it may not. So you just try to button it up as well as you can and hope for the best. And,
DEAN. Well if Bob—
PRESIDENT. and remember that basically the damn thing is just one of those unfortunate things and, we're trying to cut our losses.
DEAN. Well, certainly that's right and certainly it had no effect on you. That's the, the good thing.
HALDEMAN It really hasn't.
PRESIDENT. [Unintelligible.]
HALDEMAN. No, it hasn't. It has been kept away from the White House almost completely [10] and from the President totally. The only tie to the White House has been the Colson effort they keep trying to haul in. (HJCT 13–14)

There is no evidence to suggest that any member of the Patman Committee knew or should have known that the President was attempting to interfere with this congressional investigation. But that is not the point. The point is that the President attempted to block the investigation in order to avoid the risk of disclosure of who was responsible for the Watergate break-ins, illegal campaign contributions, unlawful use of campaign funds, and the illegal prior White House activities of Hunt and Liddy.

The President elaborated on how the plan must be carried out. He explained that a Congressman had to know that it came from the top but that the President could not talk to him himself. (HJCT 15–16)

PRESIDENT. I think maybe that's the thing to do [unintelligible]. This is, this is big, big play. I'm getting into this thing.[11] So that he—he's got to know that it comes from the top.
HALDEMAN. Yeah.
PRESIDENT. That's what he's got to know,
DEAN. Right.
PRESIDENT. and if he [unintelligible] and we're not going to—I can't talk to him myself—and that he's got to get at this and screw this thing up while he can, right?
DEAN. Well, if we let that slide up there with the Patman Committee [12] it'd be just, you know, just a tragedy to let Patman [13] have a field day up there.
PRESIDENT. What's the first move? When does he call his wit—,witnesses? (HJCT 16)

Dean also reported that Congressman Garry Brown had written a letter to Kleindienst saying that the Committee hearings were going to jeopardize the criminal cases against the Watergate defendants. The President approved of this. Dean told the President, "we can keep them well briefed on the moves if they'll, if they'll move when we provide them with the strategy." (HJCT 16) Dean reported that they would use the Stans libel suit and the abuse of process suit to take depositions of DNC officials.

---

[10] The words "almost completely" do not appear in the edited White House transcript. (WHT 70)
[11] The words "I'm getting into this thing." do not appear in the edited White House transcript. (WHT 72)
[12] The words "with the Patman Committee" do not appear in the edited White House transcript. (WHT 72)
[13] In the edited White House transcript "Them" appears instead of "Patman." (WHT 72)

HALDEMAN. We can take depositions on both of those?
DEAN. Absolutely.
PRESIDENT. Hell yes.
HALDEMAN. [Laughs] (HJCT 18)

After the September 15, 1972 meeting, and a consultation with Haldeman, Dean took the necessary steps to implement the President's decision to stop the Patman hearings. (Dean testimony, 3 SSC 960–62) He contacted Assistant Attorney General Henry Petersen and urged Petersen to respond to Congressman Brown's letter of September 8, 1972 to Kleindienst. Petersen wrote to Chairman Patman and stated that the proposed hearings could prejudice the rights of the seven Watergate defendants. (Dean testimony, 3 SSC 961, 1194–99) On October 2, 1972, the same day the Petersen letter was sent to the Committee, the Committee released the names of the persons it expected to call to testify during its hearings. The list included the names of Magruder, Sloan, Caulfield, Mitchell, Stans, Dean, Mardian, LaRue, Porter and MacGregor. (Dean testimony, 3 SSC 961, 1190–93) The next day, the House Committee on Banking and Currency voted 20 to 15 to withhold from its Chairman, Congressman Wright Patman, the power to issue subpoenas for the purpose of investigating the financing of the Watergate break-in. (Dean testimony, 3 SSC 962) Unknown to the Congress, the efforts of the President, through Dean, his counsel, had effectively cut off the investigation.

All of this was part of the President's plan to delay, impede, and obstruct the investigation of the Watergate break-in, to cover up, conceal and protect those responsible, and to conceal the existence and scope of other unlawful covert activities. Through the election the plan worked, but then it faced new threats, one of which was Hunt's demands for money. Although a program of payments had commenced shortly after the break-in, Hunt's demands escalated as his trial approached.

PAYMENTS

I

PAYMENTS PRIOR TO ELECTION

Before the Watergate break-in, Gordon Liddy had given Howard Hunt $10,000 to use in case of need. Hunt had placed the money in a safe in his EOB office. Immediately after the arrests at the Watergate, Hunt went to his office and withdrew the money. In the early morning hours following the break-in, Hunt delivered the money on behalf of those arrested to Douglas Caddy, an attorney who had agreed to represent the Watergate defendants. (Book II, 76-77)

On June 20 or 21, 1972, Liddy told LaRue and Mardian that promises of bail money, support and legal assistance had been made to the defendants, and that Hunt felt it was CRP's obligation to provide bail money to get the five men out of jail. Liddy also told LaRue and Mardian of his and Hunt's prior involvement in the Fielding break-in, and of Hunt's interview with Dita Beard, in the ITT matter. (LaRue testimony, 1 HJC 197; Book III, 91, 93-95) Mardian and LaRue reported to Mitchell on Liddy's request for money. (Book III. 98-99; Mitchell testimony, 4 SSC 1673) They also transmitted to Mitchell Liddy's statement that he, Hunt and two of those arrested had also participated in the Fielding break-in. (Book III, 98-99, 102) Mitchell told Mardian that no bail money would be forthcoming. (Book III, 99)

Between June 26 and 28, 1972, after discussions with Mitchell and Ehrlichman, Dean met twice with CIA Deputy Director Walters, to ask that the CIA provide bail and salaries for the arrested men. Walters rejected this request. (Book III, 125, 137-38)

On June 28, 1972, Haldeman and Ehrlichman directed Dean to contact Herbert Kalmbach, President Nixon's personal attorney and political fundraiser, to ask Kalmbach to raise funds for the Watergate defendants. (Book III, 149, 152; WHT 494-96) Kalmbach flew to Washington that night; the following morning he met with Dean (Book III, 152, 154-55) and LaRue (Book III, 176-77, 179-80) to discuss procedures for making payments. Kalmbach thereafter transferred to Anthony Ulasewicz campaign donations he had received in cash from CRP officials. Stans (Book III, 167) and LaRue, (Book III, 257-58) and from a private contributor. Kalmbach had told the private contributor that he could not reveal the use intended for the contribution. (Book III, 282-83, 286-87)

Between July 7, 1972 and September 19, 1972, Kalmbach directed Ulasewicz to make payments totalling $187,500 for the Watergate defendants. (Book III, 208-17, 259-60, 284-85, 378-79) Ulasewicz made the deliveries by sealing cash in unmarked envelopes and leaving the envelopes at various drops such as airport lockers. (Book III, 222-28) In communicating with each other, Ulasewicz, Kalmbach, LaRue and the recipients of the payments used aliases. (Book III, 173, 176–77, 225–26, 229) Soon Kalmbach became concerned about the covert assignment. On July 26, 1972, he met with Ehrlichman, who assured him that they, while the money payments were necessary and legally proper, they had to be kept secret. (Book III, 268–70)

In September, 1972, Kalmbach told Dean and LaRue that he could "do no more." Kalmbach transferred the remainder of the funds to LaRue, met with Dean and LaRue in Dean's office to report on the total payments, and then put his notes of the payments in Dean's ash tray and burned them. (Book III, 378–82)

II

PAYMENTS FOR HUNT PRIOR TO MARCH 21, 1973

Gordon Liddy and Howard Hunt were involved in both the Fielding and the Watergate break-ins. They knew the identity of White House and CRP officials who had authorized those activities. Liddy remained silent. From the outset, Hunt made demands for others and for himself. (Book III, 88–95) During the summer and fall of 1972, prior to the November election, Hunt received payments amounting to over $200,000 for other defendants and for himself. (Book III, 218–19, 223, 233, 383, 386–89)

Shortly after the November, 1972 election, Hunt telephoned Colson. (Book III, 411) Hunt told Colson that "commitments that were made to all of us at the onset have not been kept," and that ". . . the people who were paralyzed initially by this within the White House could now start to give some creative thinking to the affair and some affirmative action for Christ sake." (Book III, 408) Hunt continued:

> . . . we're protecting the guys who are really responsible, but now that's . . . and of course that's a continuing requirement, but at the same time, this is a two way street and as I said before, we think that now is the time when a move should be made and surely the cheapest commodity available is money. (Book III, 409)

Colson tape-recorded this conversation and gave it to Dean. (Book III, 417) Dean testified that he played the recording for Haldeman and Ehrlichman. On their instructions,[1] Dean flew to New York and played the recording for Mitchell. (Book III, 418–19) Mitchell confirmed this, describing the tape as a lot of self-serving statements by Colson. (Mitchell testimony, 2 HJC 134–35)

In late November, 1972, Dean reported to Haldeman the need for additional funds to pay the defendants. At that time, Haldeman had control of a cash fund of $328,000, the remainder of $350,000 in campaign funds which he had ordered placed under his control in February, 1972. (Book I, 78, 84) Strachan had picked up the cash from CRP and on April 7, 1972, on Haldeman's instructions, relayed through Strachan, Butterfield had delivered the cash to a personal friend of his for safekeeping. (Book I, 97; Butterfield testmony, 1 HJC 53–54) After Dean informed Haldeman of CRP's need for

---

[1] On May 30, 1974, the House Judiciary Committee subpoenaed the tape recording and other materials related to this meeting among Dean, Haldeman and Ehrlichman. The President refused to produce this recording.

money for the Watergate defendants. Haldeman approved the transfer of the fund. (Book III, 430–35) In late November, 1972, Butterfield picked up the cash and delivered it to Strachan. (Butterfield testimony, 1 HJC 55) On Haldeman's orders, in December Strachan delivered between $40,000 and $70,000 to LaRue, who handled the cash with rubber gloves and refused to furnish Strachan with a receipt. Shortly thereafter, LaRue delivered $40,000 in cash to Hunt's attorney. (Book III, 436–48) In January, 1973, Hunt made additional demands for money. (Book III, 458) At Haldeman's direction, Strachan delivered the remainder of the funds to LaRue. As before, LaRue would not give him a receipt. (Book III, 437–41; LaRue testimony, 1 HJC 220–24)

Prior to March 21, 1973, LaRue disbursed $132,000 from the fund for the defendants, including $100,000 to Hunt's attorney, William Bittman. (Book III, 436–38, 500, 518–19; LaRue testimony, 1 HJC 203–04)

On February 28, 1973, the President acknowledged to Dean his knowledge of Kalmbach's role in providing money to Hunt. Dean told the President that the Senate Select Committee had subpoenaed Kalmbach's records, but that Kalmbach was "hunkered down" and "ready to handle it." The President replied that "it'll be hard for him, he—, 'cause it'll, it'll get out about Hunt." [2] (HJCT 43) The only connection between Kalmbach and Hunt was the clandestine payments.

On March 16, 1973, Hunt met with Colson's law partner, David Shapiro. (Book III, 925) Hunt told Shapiro that if certain financial commitments that had been made to him were broken the Republicans would lose the 1974 election, and probably the 1976 election as well; but if the commitments were met none of his men would "blow." Shapiro's memorandum of the meeting reads:

Hunt stated that several persons should be terribly concerned were he to testify before the Ervin Committee (where he said he presently proposed to invoke the 5th Amendment). These persons he identified as John Dean, Bud Krogh, Pat Gray, John Mitchell and one or two others whom I can't remember (I did not take notes). Hunt said he knew he was risking the possibility of an obstruction of justice charge when he convinced those who pleaded guilty to do so, but is also convinced that if the commitments made to him are kept, no one in his "operation" will "blow." (Colson Exhibit No. 19, 3 HJC 327)

On March 19, 1973, Shapiro met with Colson and related the substance of his March 16 conversation with Hunt. Shapiro advised Colson not to tell anyone at the White House about Hunt's message because he might "unwittingly become a party to an obstruction of justice." (Colson testimony, 3 HJC 331) Colson, former Special Counsel to the President, and his close political associate and friend, said he had a telephone conversation with the President on March 19, but did not tell the President about this. (Colson testimony, 3 HJC 332)

On either March 16 or 19, 1973, Hunt told Paul O'Brien, an attorney for CRP, that he required $130,000 before being sentenced. Hunt said he had done "seamy things" for the White House and that if he were not paid he might have to reconsider his options. (Book III, 902–04, 906–07, 910–13; O'Brien testimony, 1 HJC 125) O'Brien conveyed Hunt's message to Dean. (Book III, 947) Dean told O'Brien that both

---

[2] The words "he—, cause it'll, it'll get out about Hunt" do not appear in the edited White House transcript. (WHT 106)

of them were being used as conduits in an obstruction of justice, that he, Dean, was tired of being caught in the middle, and that he had no intention of being so used. (O'Brien testimony, 1 HJC 128) Dean added that he was out of the money business, that it was time to end it all and that it had gotten to the point where he could not live with it. (Dean testimony, 2 HJC 239) At 3:30 p.m. on March 20, 1973, Dean and Ehrlichman discussed Hunt's demand for money and the possibility that Hunt would reveal the activities of the Plumbers, and tell some seamy things about Ehrlichman, if the money were not paid. (Book III, 952–53, 963) Ehrlichman then left Dean in order to see the President. From 4:26 to 5:39 p.m. the President and Ehrlichman met.[3] Later that afternoon, Ehrlichman told Krogh, who had been co-chairman of the Plumbers, that Hunt was asking for a great deal of money, and that if it were not paid Hunt might blow the lid off and tell all he knew. (Book III, 960–62) On the same afternoon, Dean also discussed Hunt's demand with Krogh and with Richard Moore.[4] (Book III, 960, 966, 968)

On the evening of March 20, 1973, the President telephoned Dean.[5] (WHT 161) Dean told the President he had spoken with Ehrlichman that afternoon, before Ehrlichman met with the President. Dean said, "I think that one thing that we have to continue to do, and particularly right now, is to examine the broadest, broadest implications of this whole thing, and, you know, maybe about 30 minutes of just my recitation to you of facts so that you operate from the same facts that everybody else has." (WHT 163) The President agreed to meet with Dean the following morning. (WHT 164)

III

March 21, 1973, Morning Meeting

On the morning of March 21, 1973, Dean met with the President for almost two hours. (HJCT 79) Dean told the President about payments to the Watergate burglars. (HJCT 89–92, 94–95) He said that the payments had been made for purposes of "containment," (HJCT 88) that this activity constituted an obstruction of justice, and that, in addition to Dean, the President's Chief of Staff Haldeman, Domestic Advisor Ehrlichman, and Campaign Director Mitchell were all involved. (HJCT 90)

The President did not express either surprise or shock. He did not condemn the payments or the involvement of his closest aides. He did not direct that the activity be stopped. He did not report it to the proper investigative agencies. He showed concern about criminal

---

[3] On May 30, 1974, the House Judiciary Committee subpoenaed the tape recording and other materials related to this conversation. The President refused to produce this recording.

[4] Dean has testified that he also spoke with LaRue on March 20 or March 21, prior to his morning meeting with the President or on both days. Dean testified that he told LaRue that he was out of the money business and would have nothing more to do with Hunt's money demands and that LaRue should call Mitchell to find out what to do about Hunt's demand. (Dean testimony, 2 HJC 250, 260–62) LaRue has testified that he had a telephone conversation with Dean regarding Hunt's demand on the morning of March 21, 1973. (LaRue testimony, 1 HJC 230)

[5] On April 11, 1974, the House Judiciary Committee subpoenaed the tape recording and other materials related to this conversation. The President refused to produce this recording. The President submitted an edited transcript.

liability of the White House personnel. He indicated familiarity with the payment scheme, and an awareness of some details—such as the use of a Cuban Committee: [6]

DEAN. Uh, Liddy said, said that, you know, if they all got counsel instantly and said that, you know, "We'll, we'll ride this thing out." All right, then they started making demands. "We've got to have attorneys' fees. Uh, we don't have any money ourselves, and if—you are asking us to take this through the election." All right, so arrangements were made through Mitchell, uh, initiating it. in discussions that—I was present—that these guys had to be taken care of. Their attorneys' fees had to be done. Kalmbach was brought in. Uh, Kalmbach raised some cash. Uh, they were obv—, uh, you know.

PRESIDENT. They put that under the cover of a Cuban Committee or [unintelligible]

DEAN. Yeah, they, they had a Cuban Committee and they had—some of it was given to Hunt's lawyer, who in turn passed it out. This, you know, when Hunt's wife was flying to Chicago with ten thousand, she was actually, I understand after the fact now, was going to pass that money to, uh, one of the Cubans—to meet him in Chicago and pass it to somebody there.

PRESIDENT. [Unintelligible]. Maybe—Well, whether it's maybe too late to do anything about it, but I would certainly keep that, [laughs] that cover for whatever it's worth.

DEAN. I'll—
PRESIDENT. Keep the Committee.[7]
DEAN. Af—, after, well, that, that, that's
PRESIDENT. [Unintelligible]
DEAN. the most troublesome post-thing, uh, because (1) Bob is involved in that; John is involved in that; I am involved in that; Mitchell is involved in that. And that's an obstruction of justice.
PRESIDENT. In other words the fact that, uh, that you're, you're, you're taking care of witnesses.
DEAN. That's right. Uh,
PRESIDENT. How was Bob involved?
DEAN. well, th—, they ran out of money over there. Bob had three hundred and fifty thousand dollars in a safe over here that was really set aside for polling purposes. Uh, and there was no other source of money, so they came over here and said, "You all have got to give us some money."
PRESIDENT. Right.
DEAN. I had to go to Bob and say, "Bob, you know, you've got to have some—they need some money over there." He said, "What for?" And so I had to tell him what it was for 'cause he wasn't about to just send money over there willy-nilly. And, uh, John was involved in those discussions, and we decided, you know, that, you know, that there was no price too high to pay to let this thing blow up in front of the election.
PRESIDENT. I think you should handle that one pretty fast.
DEAN. Oh, I think—
PRESIDENT. That issue, I mean.
DEAN. I think we can.
PRESIDENT. So that the three-fifty went back to him. All it did was— [8]
DEAN. That's right. I think we can too.
PRESIDENT. Who else [unintelligible]?
DEAN. But, now, here, here's what's happening right now.
PRESIDENT. Yeah. (HJCT 89–91)

Dean then turned to the crisis precipitated by Hunt's demands. Dean explained that these demands, and possibly others, could amount to a million dollars over the next two years. The President said that $1 million could be gotten and said it could be obtained in cash.

---

[6] The President was familiar with the use of Thomas Pappas. Ehrlichman had suggested to LaRue that Pappas, a long-time supporter of the President, be contacted to see if he would be of any assistance in connection with raising the money. (Book III. 958) LaRue's use of Pappas was brought out in the March 21 conversation. The President said that he already knew about this. (HJCT 94) See p. 54 below.
[7] This line does not appear in the edited White House transcript. (WHT 187)
[8] This line does not appear in the edited White House transcript. (WHT 188)

The problem was exactly how to avoid disclosure of the source of the money and its use. The President considered various possibilities:

DEAN. . . . Now, where, where are the soft spots on this? Well, first of all, there's the, there's the problem of the continued blackmail
PRESIDENT. Right.
DEAN. which will not only go on now, it'll go on when these people are in prison, and it will compound the obstruction of justice situation. It'll cost money. It's dangerous. Nobody, nothing—people around here are not pros at this sort of thing. This is the sort of thing Mafia people can do: washing money, getting clean money, and things like that, uh—we're—We just don't know about those things, because we're not used to, you know—we are not criminals and not used to dealing in that business. It's, uh, it's, uh—
PRESIDENT. That's right.
DEAN. It's a tough thing to know how to do.
PRESIDENT. Maybe we can't even do that.

*   *   *   *   *   *   *

PRESIDENT. Let me say, there shouldn't be a lot of people running around getting money. We should set up a little—[9]
DEAN. Well, he's got one person doing it who I am not sure is—
PRESIDENT. Who is that?
DEAN. He's got Fred LaRue, uh, doing it. Now Fred started out going out trying to
PRESIDENT. No.
DEAN. solicit money from all kinds of people. Now I learned about that, and I said,
PRESIDENT. No.
DEAN. "My God."
PRESIDENT. No.
DEAN. "It's just awful. Don't do it."
PRESIDENT. Yeah.
DEAN. Uh, people are going to ask what the money is for. He's working—He's apparently talked to Tom Pappas.
PRESIDENT. I know.
DEAN. And Pappas has, uh, agreed to come up with a sizeable amount, I gather, from, from
PRESIDENT. Yeah.
DEAN. Mitchell.[10]
PRESIDENT. Yeah. Well, what do you need, then? You need, uh, you don't need a million right away, but you need a million. Is that right?
DEAN. That's right.
PRESIDENT. You need a million in cash, don't you? If you want to put that through, would you put that through, uh—this is thinking out loud here for a moment—would you put that through the Cuban Committee?
DEAN. Um, no.
PRESIDENT. Or would you just do this through a [unintelligible][11] that it's going to be, uh, well, it's cash money, and so forth. How, if that ever comes out, are you going to handle it? Is the Cuban Committee an obstruction of justice, if they want to help?
DEAN. Well, they've got a pr—, they've got priests, and they—
PRESIDENT. Would you like to put, I mean, would that, would that give a little bit of a cover, for example?
DEAN. That would give some for the Cubans and possibly Hunt.
PRESIDENT. Yeah.
DEAN. Uh, then you've got Liddy, and McCord is not, not accepting any money. So, he's, he is not a bought man right now.
PRESIDENT. Okay. (HJCT 93–95)

This discussion primarily concerned payments over the long term. There remained the immediate demand by Hunt for approximately

---

[9] "We should set up a little—" does not appear in the edited White House transcript. (WHT 194)
[10] This line does not appear in the edited White House transcript. (WHT 194)
[11] This line does not appear in the edited White House transcript. (WHT 195)

$120,000. The President said that Hunt's demands should be met. At the very least, he reasoned, the payment would buy time.

PRESIDENT. Well, your, your major, your major guy to keep under control is Hunt.
DEAN. That's right.
PRESIDENT. I think. Because he knows
DEAN. He knows so much.
PRESIDENT. about a lot of other things.[12]
DEAN. He knows so much. Right. Uh, he could sink Chuck Colson. Apparently, apparently, he is quite distressed with Colson. He thinks Colson has abandoned him. Uh, Colson was to meet with him when he was out there, after, now he had left the White House. He met with him through his lawyer. Hunt raised the question: he wanted money. Colson's lawyer told him that Colson wasn't doing anything with money, and Hunt took offense with that immediately, that, uh, uh, that Colson had abandoned him. Uh—
PRESIDENT. Don't you, just looking at the immediate problem, don't you have to have—handle Hunt's financial situation
DEAN. I, I think that's,
PRESIDENT. damn soon?
DEAN. that is, uh, I talked to Mitchell about that last night,
PRESIDENT. Mitchell.
DEAN. and, and, uh, I told—
PRESIDENT. Might as well. May have the rule you've got to keep the cap on the bottle that much,
DEAN. That's right; that's right.
PRESIDENT. in order to have any options.
DEAN. That's right.
PRESIDENT. Either that or let it all blow right now.
DEAN. Well that, you know, that's the, that's the question. Uh—
PRESIDENT. Now, go ahead. The others. You've got Hunt; (HJCT 96)

* * * * * * *

PRESIDENT. But at the moment, don't you agree that you'd better get the Hunt thing? I mean, that's worth it, at the moment.[13]
DEAN. That, that's worth buying time on, right.
PRESIDENT. And that's buying time on, I agree. (HJCT 105)

The President instructed Dean to summon Haldeman, Ehrlichman, and Mitchell to meet for a discussion of a strategy to carve matters away from the President. The President then called Haldeman into the meeting. When Haldeman entered the Oval Office, the President repeated his authorization of immediate payment to Hunt. The President said, "His price is pretty high, but at least, uh, we should buy the time on that, uh, as I, as I pointed out to John." [14] (HJCT 109) The President instructed Dean and Haldeman to lie about the arrangements for payment to the defendants.

PRESIDENT. As far as what happened up to this time, our cover there is just going to be the Cuban Committee did this for them up through the election.[15]
DEAN. Well, yeah. We can put that together. That isn't, of course, quite the way it happened, but, uh—
PRESIDENT. I know, but it's the way it's going to have to happen. (HJCT 119)

The President then returned to Hunt's demand:

PRESIDENT. that's why your, for your immediate thing you've got no choice with Hunt but the hundred and twenty or whatever it is. Right?

---
[12] In place of "Because he knows about a lot of other things," the edited White House transcript reads, "Does he know a lot?" (WHT 196)
[13] In place of, "I mean, that's worth it, at the moment," the edited White House transcript reads, ". . . that's where that —" (WHT 209)
[14] In place of, "we should buy the time on that" the edited White House transcript reads, "we can buy time on that." (WHT 215)
[15] Instead of ". . . our cover is just going to be . . . ," the edited White House transcript reads ". . . these fellows . . . are covered on their situation, because. . . ." (WHT 231)

DEAN. That's right.
PRESIDENT. Would you agree that that's a buy time thing, you better damn well get that done, but fast?[16]
DEAN. I think he ought to be given some signal, anyway, to, to—
PRESIDENT. Yes.
DEAN. Yeah—You know.
PRESIDENT. Well for Christ's sakes get it in a, in a way that, uh—Who's, who's going to talk to him? Colson? He's the one who's supposed to know him.
DEAN. Well, Colson doesn't have any money though. That's the thing. That's been our, one of the real problems. They have, uh, been unable to raise any money. A million dollars in cash, or, or the like has been a very difficult problem as we discussed before. (HJCT 121–22)

After discussing how Hunt could incriminate Mitchell, Ehrlichman and Krogh, the President again returned to Hunt's demand:

PRESIDENT. That's right. Try to look around the track. We have no choice on Hunt but to try to keep him—
DEAN. Right now, we have no choice. (HJCT 125)

IV

MARCH 21, 1973, PAYMENTS FOR HUNT

On the afternoon of March 21, 1973, the President met with Dean, Haldeman and Ehrlichman. (HJCT 131) The President asked what was being done about Hunt's demand. Dean said Mitchell and LaRue would be able to do something. The President remarked that it was going to be a "long road." (HJCT 133) That evening the President asked Colson what he thought about the million dollars Bittman had demanded. (Colson testimony, 3 HJC 334)

On March 21, 1973, Dean told LaRue by telephone that he was out of the money business and to talk to Mitchell.[17] LaRue telephoned Mitchell, who authorized the payment to Hunt. Late that evening, LaRue arranged the delivery of $75,000 to Bittman. (Book III, 1193–97, 1199–1201)

President Nixon, knowing that Hunt had made threats to break his silence in order to secure money, encouraged the payment to Hunt and took no steps to stop the payment from being made.

On the next day, March 22, 1973, Mitchell told Haldeman, Ehrlichman and Dean that Hunt was not a "problem any longer." (Book III, 1255–57, 1269) Later that day, Ehrlichman told Krogh that Hunt was stable and would not disclose matters. (Book III, 1278–79) That afternoon, the President met for more than 90 minutes with Mitchell, Haldeman, Ehrlichman and Dean. Hunt's demand for money was never discussed and the President did not attempt to determine whether anything had been done to deal with the problem that had occupied so much of his time the previous day. (HJCT 147–86)

On March 27, 1973, the President and Haldeman talked about payments to Hunt. "Hunt is at the Grand Jury today," Haldeman said. "We don't know how far he is going to go. The danger area for him is on the money, that he was given money. He is reported by O'Brien, who

---

[16] Instead of "... buy time ...," the edited White House transcript reads, "... prime ..." and leaves out "but fast." (WHT 234)
[17] Dean testified that his conversation with LaRue occurred prior to his morning meeting with the President on March 21, 1973. (Dean testimony, 2 HJC 250, 260) LaRue testified that to his best recollection, Dean's telephone call was in the morning. (LaRue testimony, 1 HJC 237)

has been talking to his lawyer, Bittman, not to be as desperate today as he was yesterday but to still be on the brink, or at least shaky. What's made him shaky is that he's seen McCord bouncing out there and probably walking out scot free." (WHT 326–27) On April 16, 1973, the President and Dean again discussed the Hunt demand. Dean said that Mitchell had told him, Haldeman and Ehrlichman, on March 22, 1973, that the problem with Hunt had been solved. The President expressed his satisfaction it had been solved "at the Mitchell level." He also said, "I am planning to assume some culpability on that [unintelligible]." [18] (HJCT 194–95)

On April 8, 1973, Dean, and on April 13, 1973, Magruder, began meeting with the prosecutors. (Book IV, 538, 610) On the afternoon of April 17, 1973, Haldeman pointed out to the President that one problem was that people would say the President should have told Dean on March 21, 1973, not that the blackmail was too costly, but that it was wrong.[19] (WHT 1035)

In mid-April, 1973, the President tried to diminish the significance of his March 21 conversation with Dean. He tried to make the payments appear innocent and within the law. On April 14, 1973, the President instructed Haldeman and Ehrlichman to agree on the story that payments were made, not "to obstruct justice," but to "help" the defendants.[20]

This evidence clearly establishes that pursuant to the President's plan of concealment, surreptitious payments of substantial sums of money were made to the Watergate defendants for the purpose of obtaining their silence and influencing their testimony. The evidence also clearly establishes that when the President learned that Hunt was going to talk unless paid a substantial sum of money, and that Mitchell and LaRue were in a position to do something about Hunt's demand he approved of the payment to Hunt rather than taking steps to stop it from being made.

---

[18] The edited White House transcript reads, "That assumes culpability on that, doesn't it?" (WHT 798)
[19] On April 11, 1974, the House Judiciary Committee subpoenaed the tape recording and other materials related to this conversation. The President refused to produce this recording. The President submitted an edited transcript.
[20] On April 11, 1974, the House Judiciary Committee subpoenaed the tape recording and other materials related to this conversation. The President refused to produce this recording. The President submitted an edited transcript.

FAVORED TREATMENT OF DEFENDANTS AND PROSPECTIVE DEFENDANTS

I

Discussions of Clemency for Hunt

On July 8, 1972, while walking on a beach at San Clemente, the President and Ehrlichman discussed possible clemency for the Watergate defendants. Ehrlichman has said that he told the President that "presidential pardons or something of that kind inevitably would be a question that he would have to confront by reason of the obvious political aspect of this." (Book III, 182-83) The President's response, according to Ehrlichman and the President's own public statement, was that no one in the White House should "get into this whole area of clemency with anybody involved in this case and surely not make any assurances to anyone." (Book III, 189, 195) At the time of this conversation, Ehrlichman knew that Liddy and Hunt and three of those arrested at the Watergate had been involved in the break-in of Ellsberg's psychiatrist's office. The President has said that he did not learn of that break-in until more than eight months later, or 'Iarch 17, 1973.[1] (Book VII, 1877)

On December 31, 1972, Hunt wrote to Charles Colson, Special Counsel to the President, complaining about his "abandonment by friends on whom I had in good faith relied" and suggesting that he was close to breaking down. (Book III, 458) Hunt's trial was scheduled to begin on January 8, 1973. (*United States* v. *Liddy*, CR 1827-72, docket) Colson forwarded Hunt's letter to Dean with a note, "Now what the hell do I do." (Book III, 457)

On January 3, 1973, Colson, Dean and Ehrlichman discussed the need to reassure Hunt about the amount of time he would have to spend in jail. (Book III, 460; Colson Exhibit No. 17, 3 HJC 307) Subsequently, on April 14, 1973, Ehrlichman reported his conversation with Colson to the President. "[Colson] said, 'What can I tell [Hunt] about clemency.' And I said 'Under no circumstances should this ever be raised with the President.' "[2] (WHT 421)

Later on January 3, and again on the following day, Colson met with Bittman, Hunt's attorney. Bittman discussed Hunt's family problems since December 8, 1972, when Hunt's wife had died. He said that because of his children Hunt was very worried that Judge Sirica

---

[1] The President's awareness of Hunt's previous activity is shown in his instructions to Haldeman on June 23, 1972, with respect to the investigation:
"Of course, this Hunt, that will uncover a lot of things. You open that scab there's a hell of a lot of things and we just feel that it would be very detrimental to have this thing go any further." (WHT, June 23, 1972, 10:04-11:39 a.m., 6)
[2] On April 11, 1974, the House Judiciary Committee subpoenaed the tape recording and other materials related to this conversation. The President refused to produce this recording. The President submitted an edited transcript.

(75)

would give him a long jail sentence. (Bittman testimony, 2 HJC 20–24; Colson testimony, 3 HJC 302–04, 313–15; Colson Exhibit No. 17, 3 HJC 308) According to Colson, Bittman said he thought Hunt might be able to survive the prospect of a reasonable term, perhaps a year. Bittman also mentioned that he understood Dean and Mitchell had discussed plans for electronic surveillance prior to Watergate. (Colson Exhibit No. 17, 3 HJC 308–09) Colson assured Bittman of his friendship for Hunt, of his understanding of Hunt's need to be out of jail, and of his willingness to do whatever he could to assist Hunt. Colson has said:

> In addition, I may well have told Bittman that I had made "people" aware that, if it were necessary, I was going to come back to the White House to speak for Hunt. Indeed, since I wanted to do all I could to comfort Hunt, it is most probable that I did say this. I do not know how Bittman evaluated my position and influence at the White House, but despite my insistence that I could do no more than try to help Hunt as a friend, Bittman might have inferred that if Hunt received an unreasonably long sentence, my willingness to go to bat for Hunt would result in Hunt's sentence being reduced by executive action of some sort. (Colson Exhibit No. 17, 3 HJC 311)

On January 3, 1973, Colson reported to Ehrlichman and Dean on his conversation with Bittman, and said he wanted to speak to the President regarding Hunt. (Colson Exhibit No. 17, 3 HJC 310; Book III, 461) Dean testified that Colson told him on January 5, 1973, that he had given assurances of clemency to Bittman and he had spoken with the President about clemency for Hunt. (Dean testimony, 2 HJC 286–87; Book III, 461) The President told Haldeman and Ehrlichman on April 14, 1973, that he had had a conversation with Colson about clemency for Hunt.[3]

On January 9, 1973, Hunt withdrew a motion, which he had filed on October 11, 1972, for the return of items that had been recovered from his EOB office and that had not been inventoried by the FBI. (*United States* v. *Liddy*, motion, January 9, 1973; Book II, 425) Among the documents encompassed by the motion were two notebooks that had been taken from Hunt's safe and kept by Dean. (Book II, 425; Dean testimony, 2 HJC 236) On December 22, 1972, Petersen had questioned Dean about the notebooks and told him he would be called as a witness in the hearing on Hunt's motion. (Petersen testimony, 3 HJC 75–76; Book II, 422–23, 425) In January, 1973, Dean shredded the notebooks. (Dean testimony, 2 HJC 287–88) Colson was also a potential witness. During Bittman's meeting with Colson on January 3, 1973, Bittman had discussed Colson's prospective testimony. (Bittman testimony, 2 HJC 21–22; Book III, 472–74) The withdrawal of the motion made it unnecessary for Dean and Colson to appear as witnesses. (Petersen testimony, 3 HJC 76) It also avoided the possible disclosure of such compromising documents in Hunt's safe as fabricated State Department cables and documents related to the Plumbers. Two days after the withdrawal of his motion, Hunt pleaded guilty to charges arising out of the Watergate break-in. (Book III, 484)

---

[3] On May 30, 1974, the House Judiciary Committee subpoenaed the tape recording and other materials related to the two conversations Charles Colson had with the President on January 5, 1973. The President refused to produce these recordings.

II

President's Recollection of Clemency Discussions

On February 28, March 21 and April 14, 1973, the President spoke of his recollection of a discussion of clemency for Hunt. On February 28, 1973, speaking to Dean about the Watergate defendants' expectations of clemency, the President asked, "What the hell do they expect, though? Do they expect that they will get clemency within a reasonable time?" Dean said that he thought they did. The President asked whether clemency could be granted "in six months." Dean replied that it could not because, "This thing may become so political." (HJCT 40) There was no specific mention of Colson's assurances to Hunt. The President did allude to Hunt's personal situation, and to the death of his wife. (HJCT 40)

On March 21, 1973, after Hunt had increased his demands for money (Book III, 968), Dean told the President that Caulfield had spoken about commutation with McCord. Dean added, "as you know Colson has talked to, indirectly to Hunt about commutation." Dean said these "commitments" were problems because they were the sort of thing the Senate would be looking for, but that he did not think the Senate could find them. The President agreed that it would be "pretty hard as far as the witnesses are concerned." (HJCT 91)

After Haldeman joined the meeting, the President said, "You know Colson has gone around on this clemency thing with Hunt and the rest." Dean added, "Hunt is now talking in terms of being out by Christmas." The discussion continued:

HALDEMAN. By Christmas of this year?
DEAN. Yeah.
HALDEMAN. See that, that really, that's very believable 'cause Colson,
PRESIDENT. Do you think Colson could have told him—[4]
HALDEMAN. Colson is an, is an—that's, that's your fatal flaw, really, in Chuck, is he is an operator in expediency, and he will pay at the time and where he is
PRESIDENT. Yeah.
HALDEMAN. whatever he has to, to accomplish what he's there to do.
DEAN. Right. (HJCT 115–16)

The President acknowledged that he had discussed clemency for Hunt:

Great sadness. The basis, as a matter of fact [clears throat] there was some discussion over there with somebody about, uh, Hunt's problems after his wife died and I said, of course, commutation could be considered on the basis of his wife, and that is the only discussion I ever had in that light. (HJCT 93)[5]

On April 14, 1973, the President acknowledged that, contrary to Ehrlichman's direction, Colson had in fact raised with him the question of clemency in a tangential way. The President said: "As I remember a conversation this day was about five thirty or six o'clock that Colson only dropped it in sort of parenthetically, said I had a little problem today, talking about Hunt, and said I sought to reassure him, you know, and so forth. And I said, Well. Told me about Hunt's wife. I said it was a terrible thing and I said obviously we will do just, we

---

[4] This line does not appear in the edited White House transcript. (WHT 226)
[5] On May 30, 1974, the House Judiciary Committee subpoenaed the tape recording and other materials related to a Presidential conversation about granting clemency to Hunt on the basis of his wife's death. The President refused to produce this recording.

will take that into consideration. That was the total of the conversation." [6] (WHT 419)

In the conversations on March 21 the President acknowledged his predicament on the issue of clemency for Hunt; the President feared that any action that seemed to Hunt a repudiation of assurance of clemency would lead Hunt to "blow the whistle." (HJCT 125) On the other hand, the President was aware that clemency for Hunt by Christmas, 1973, would be politically impossible because it would require direct and public action by the President. (HJCT 103–04, 115)

On the afternoon of March 21, 1973, when the President met with Haldeman, Ehrlichman and Dean, he continued to assess the risk Hunt posed to the cover-up. The President asked what should be done about Hunt. He agreed with Ehrlichman's answer that "Hunt's interests lie in getting a pardon if he can." The President said that "He's got to get that by Christmas time," [7] and Ehrlichman suggested that Hunt's "indirect contacts with John" about it "contemplate that, that, that's already understood."

PRESIDENT. I know.
HALDEMAN. That's right.
EHRLICHMAN. They think that that's already understood.
PRESIDENT. Yeah. (HJCT 133)

Although the President knew Hunt was relying on a belief he would get a pardon, the President did not authorize or intimate to anyone to tell Hunt that a pardon would not be possible.

In a meeting on March 27, 1973, with Haldeman, Ehrlichman and Ziegler, the President again discussed the issue of clemency for the Watergate defendants after the 1974 elections. The President considered appointing a "super panel" of distinguished citizens to study the Watergate case. Haldeman said that the idea had the advantage that it would drag out the investigation until after the 1974 elections, when the President could pardon everyone, and the "potential ultimate penalty anybody would get hit in this process could be about two years." [8] (WHT 338–42)

III

MITCHELL, MAGRUDER AND DEAN

The President considered clemency not only for the seven Watergate burglars, but also for three of his closest associates, Mitchell, Magruder and Dean, who were involved in the cover-up.

By the middle of April, 1973, the President knew that the cover-up was threatened by Magruder and Dean, who were talking to the pros-

---

[6] On April 11, 1974, the House Judiciary Committee subpoenaed the tape recording and other materials related to this conversation on April 14, 1973. The President refused to produce this recording. The President submitted an edited transcript. Colson testified before the Committee that he recalled his conversation with the President as follows: "I was going to say someday I may want to come talk to you about Hunt. Half way through that sentence the President interrupted and he said, he said oh, I just can't believe, Chuck, in the circumstances you have just described, with his wife in that shape and his kids, he said, I just can't believe that he will go to jail. He said I just can't believe any judge would do that. I just am sure he won't, and don't worry about it, and relax and don't let it get you down." (Colson testimony, 3 HJC 318)
[7] This statement was attributed to Dean in the edited White House transcript. (WHT 133)
[8] On April 11, 1974, the House Judiciary Committee subpoenaed the tape recording and other materials related to this conversation. The President refused to produce this recording. The President submitted an edited transcript.

ecutors. (Book IV, 538–39, 610) On April 14, 1973, the President directed Haldeman and Ehrlichman to imply to Magruder, and also to Mitchell who had been implicated by Magruder, the President's assurances of clemency. The President carefully explained how he wanted Haldeman and Ehrlichman to handle these assurances.[9] (WHT 408–514)

The President instructed Ehrlichman to tell Mitchell and Magruder that the President did not regard it as in his interests for them to remain silent; that the President held great affection for them and their families. The President set the language for Ehrlichman to use to get the clemency across to Magruder:

> Lovely wife and all the rest, it just breaks your heart. And say this, this is a very painful message for me to bring—I've been asked to give you, but I must do it and it is that: Put it right out that way. Also, I would first put that in so that he knows I have personal affection. That's the way the so-called clemency's got to be handled. Do you see, John? (WHT 503)

Ehrlichman said he understood. Haldeman told Ehrlichman to "[d]o the same thing with Mitchell," although the President also said that Mitchell would put on "the damnest defense" and never go to prison. (WHT 503) The President then asked Ehrlichman how to handle the "problem of clemency" for people like Hunt. Haldeman replied, "Well, you don't handle it at all. That's Colson's, cause that's where it comes from." (WHT 485) Ehrlichman immediately carried out the President's instructions.

Ehrlichman met with Mitchell at 1:40 p.m., April 14, 1973. (Book IV, 718) He reported to the President that he had spoken to Mitchell and that Mitchell "appreciated the message of the good feeling between you and him." The President responded, "He got that, huh?"[10] (WHT 524) The President added that there could be clemency at the proper time; but that they all knew that, for the moment, it was ridiculous to talk about it. (WHT 544)

As Ehrlichman left the Oval Office for his meeting with Magruder (Book IV, 801) the President said:

P Be sure to convey my warm sentiments.
E Right. (WHT 578)

On the evening of April 14, 1973, the President telephoned Ehrlichman. (Book IV, 854) They discussed how Ehrlichman might divert Dean from implicating Haldeman and Ehrlichman. Ehrlichman said he would see Dean the next day. The President told Ehrlichman to remind Dean indirectly that only one man, the President, had the power to pardon him, and keep him from disbarment as a lawyer, if things should go wrong:

E I am going to try to get him around a bit. It is going to be delicate.
P Get him around in what way?
E Well to get off the passing the buck business.
P John that's—
E It is a little touchy and I don't know how far I can go.

---

[9] On April 11, 1974, the House Judiciary Committee subpoenaed the tape recording and other materials related to this conversation. The President refused to produce this recording. The President submitted an edited transcript.
[10] On April 11, 1974, the House Judiciary Committee subpoenaed the tape recording and other materials related to this conversation. The President refused to produce this recording. The President submitted an edited transcript.

P John, that is not going to help you. Look he has to look down the road to one point that there is only one man who could restore him to the ability to practice law in case things go wrong. He's got to have that in the back of his mind. . . . He's got to know that will happen. You don't tell him, but you know and I know that with him and Mitchell there isn't going to be any damn question, because they got a bad rap.[11] (WHT 663–64)

Later in the conversation the President directed Ehrlichman to tell Dean that the President thought Dean has "carried a tremendous load" and that the President's affection and loyalty remained undiminished. (WHT 667)

IV

April 16, 1973, Meeting

On April 16, 1973, after Dean had begun meeting with the prosecutors, the President and Dean discussed potential charges of obstruction of justice against members of the President's White House staff. (Book IV, 1143) The President tried to make the Hunt clemency assurance the responsibility solely of Mitchell. Dean, however, corrected him.

DEAN. It's, uh, it's, uh, all the obstruction is technical stuff that mounts up.
PRESIDENT. Yeah. Well, you take, for example, the clemency stuff. That's solely Mitchell, apparently, and Colson's talk with, uh, Bittman where he says, "I'll do everything I can because as a, as a friend—"
DEAN. No, that was with Ehrlichman.
PRESIDENT. Huh?
DEAN. That was Ehrlichman.
PRESIDENT. Ehrlichman with who?
DEAN. Ehrlichman and Colson and I sat up there, and Colson presented his story to Ehrlichman
PRESIDENT. I know.[12]
DEAN. regarding it and, and then John gave Chuck very clear instructions on going back and telling him that it, you know, "Give him the inference he's got clemency but don't give him any commitment."
PRESIDENT. No commitment?
DEAN. Right.
PRESIDENT. Now that's all right. But first, if an individual, if it's no commitment—I've got a right to sit here—Take a fellow like Hunt or, uh, or, or a Cuban whose wife is sick and something—that's what clemency's about.
DEAN. That's right.
PRESIDENT. Correct?
DEAN. That's right.
PRESIDENT. But, uh, but John specifically said, "No commitment," did he? He—
DEAN. Yeah.
PRESIDENT. No commitment. Then, then Colson then went on to, apparently—
DEAN. I don't know how Colson delivered it, uh—
PRESIDENT. Apparently to Bittman—
DEAN. for—
PRESIDENT. Bittman. Is that your understanding?
DEAN. Yes, but I don't know what his, you know, specific—
PRESIDENT. Where did this business of the Christmas thing get out, John? What the hell was that?
DEAN. Well, that's, a, that's a—
PRESIDENT. That must have been Mitchell, huh?
DEAN. No, that was Chuck, again. I think that, uh—
PRESIDENT. That they all, that they'd all be out by Christmas?

---

[11] On April 11, 1974, the House Judiciary Committee subpoenaed the tape recording and other materials related to this conversation. The President refused to produce this recording. The President submitted an edited transcript.
[12] The President's "I know" does not appear in the edited White House transcript. (WHT 811)

DEAN. No, I think he said something to the effect that Christmas is the time that clemency generally occurs.
PRESIDENT. Oh, yeah.
DEAN. Uh—
PRESIDENT. Well, that doesn't—I, I, I don't think that is going to hurt him.
DEAN. No.
PRESIDENT. Do you?
DEAN. No.
PRESIDENT. "Clemency," he says—One [unintelligible] he's a friend of Hunt's. I'm just trying to put the best face on it. If it's the wrong—if it is—I've got to know.
DEAN. Well, one, one of the things I think you have to be very careful, and this is why Petersen will be very good, is, if you take a set of facts and let the prosecutors who have no—they'll be making, making no PR judgments.
PRESIDENT. Yeah.
DEAN. But they'll give you the raw facts as they relate to the law, uh, and it's later you've got to decide, you know, what public face will be put on it. In other words, they'll—If their

Dean suggested that Petersen might be able to advise whether the attempt to silence Hunt by offering clemency was lawful. (HJCT 204–06)

In a meeting with Petersen, just three hours after this meeting with Dean, (Book IV, 1230) the President asked whether the prosecutors had anything on Colson. Petersen said that there were allegations, but nothing specific.[15] (WHT 872–75) The President neither posed a hypothetical question to determine the legality of Colson's conduct, as Dean had suggested, nor informed Petersen of Colson's conversation with Bittman.

Thereafter, the President made repeated statements on the clemency issue to the public. On May 22, 1973, the President said:

At no time did I authorize any offer of executive clemency for the Watergate defendants, nor did I know of any such offer. ("Presidential Statements," 5/22/73, 21)

On August 15, 1973, the President said:

... under no circumstances could executive clemency be considered for those who participated in the Watergate break-in. I maintained that position throughout. ("Presidential Statements," 8/15/73, 42)

And on November 17, 1973, the President said:

Two, that I never authorized the offer of clemency to anybody and; as a matter of fact, turned it down whenever it was suggested. It was not recommended by any member of my staff but it was, on occasion, suggested as a result of news reports that clemency might become a factor. ("Presidential Statements," 11/17/73, 64)

These statements are contradicted by the transcripts of the President's own words.

This evidence establishes that the President personally and through his subordinates and agents endeavored to cause prospective defendants and those duly tried and convicted, to expect favored treatment and consideration in return for their silence or false testimony.

---
[15] On April 11, 1974, the House Judiciary Committee subpoenaed the tape recording and other materials related to this conversation. The President refused to produce this recording. The President submitted an edited transcript.

DECEPTION AND CONCEALMENT

I

FALSE REPRESENTATIONS ABOUT OFFICIAL INVESTIGATIONS

In his public statements, as part of the continuing cover-up the President repeatedly said that he had ordered, and even personally undertaken, thorough investigations of the Watergate matter, and that those investigations determined that no one from the White House was involved. The President said he had ordered three investigations by his immediate staff: two in August, 1972, and March, 1973, by Dean; and one in April, 1973, by Ehrlichman. He said his intention was to get to the bottom of the matter, and get the truth out. However, clear and convincing evidence indicates that this was not the case.

A. THE AUGUST 1972 DEAN INVESTIGATION

On August 29, 1972, at a news conference, President Nixon said that in addition to investigations into Watergate by the Department of Justice, the FBI, the GAO and the Banking and Currency Committee, John Dean had conducted an investigation under the direction of the President:

> In addition to that, within our own staff, under my direction, Counsel to the President, Mr. Dean, has conducted a complete investigation of all leads which might involve any present members of the White House Staff or anybody in the Government. I can say categorically that his investigation indicates that no one in the White House Staff, no one in this Administration, presently employed, was involved in this very bizarre incident. . . .
> I think under these circumstances we are doing everything we can to take this incident and to investigate it and not to cover it up. ("Presidential Statements," 8/29/72, 3)

At the time President Nixon made those statements he knew that Dean had not made or reported any such investigation. According to White House records, the President had not met or spoken with Dean since before the break-in. Dean testified that he first heard of his "complete" investigation in the President's announcement. (Dean testimony, 2 HJC 252; Book II, 590–92) No independent evidence exists that such an investigation was ever completed or undertaken.

On September 15, 1972, more than two weeks after the August 29, 1972 press conference, the President and Dean first discussed Watergate. (Book II, 598; Dean testimony, 2 HJC 228) Before Dean entered the room, Haldeman told the President it had been "a good move . . . bringing Dean in;" that Dean, while "he'll never again gain any ground for us . . . enables other people to gain ground while he's making sure that you don't fall through the holes." (HJCT 1) When Dean joined the meeting, the President referred to the Watergate matter as a "can of worms," and congratulated Dean for "putting your fingers in the dikes every time that leaks have sprung there."

(HJCT 7) The President also said, "So you just try to button it up as well as you can and hope for the best." (HJCT 13-14)

In his March 21, 1973, morning meeting with Dean the President confirmed that, in the summer of 1972, Dean was directed to help with the cover-up, not to conduct a "complete investigation."

DEAN. ... Now, [sighs], what, what has happened post-June 17? Well, it was, I was under pretty clear instructions [laughs] not to really to investigate this, that this was something that just could have been disastrous on the election if it had—all hell had broken loose, and I worked on a theory of containment
PRESIDENT. Sure.
DEAN. to try to hold it right where it was.
PRESIDENT. Right. (HJCT 88)

Later in the conversation, the President said "you had the right plan let me say, I have no doubts about the right plan before the election. And you handled it just right. You contained it." (HJCT 129)

B. THE MARCH 1973 DEAN REPORT

In a public statement on August 15, 1973, President Nixon said: "On March 23, [1973], I sent Mr. Dean to Camp David, where he was instructed to write a complete report on all he knew of the entire Watergate matter." ("Presidential Statements, 8/15/73, 41-42)

The "report" that President Nixon had, in fact, requested Dean to make in March, 1973, was one intended to mislead official investigators and to conceal the President's complicity in the cover-up. In a March 20, 1973, telephone conversation,[1] the President told Dean to "make it very incomplete."

P But you could say, "I have this and this is that." Fine. See what I am getting at is that, if apart from a statement to the Committee or anything else, if you could just make a statement to me that we can use. You know, for internal purposes and to answer questions, etc.
D As we did when you, back in August, made the statement that—
P That's right.
D And all the things—
P You've got to have something where it doesn't appear that I am doing this in, you know, just in a—saying to hell with the Congress and to hell with the people, we are not going to tell you anything because of Executive Privilege. That, they don't understand. But if you say, "No, we are willing to cooperate," and you've made a complete statement, but make it very incomplete. See, that is what I mean. I don't want a, too much in chapter and verse as you did in your letter,[2] I just want just a general—
D An all around statement.
P That's right. Try just something general. Like "I have checked into this matter; I can categorically, based on my investigation, the following: Haldeman is not involved in this, that and the other thing. Mr. Colson did not do this; Mr. so and so did not do this. Mr. Blank did not do this." Right down the line, taking the most glaring things. If there are any further questions, please let me know. See?
D Uh, huh. I think we can do that. (WHT 167-68)

On the afternoon of March 21, 1973, after Dean had discussed with the President the involvement of White House staff in perjury (HJCT

---

[1] On April 11, 1974, the House Judiciary Committee subpoenaed the tape recording and other materials related to this conversation. The President refused to produce this recording. The President submitted an edited transcript.
[2] Dean had drafted a letter to Senattor Eastland, Chairman of the Senate Judiciary Committee, in connection with hearings on the nomination of L. Patrick Gray to be Director of the FBI.

81), payments to the defendants (HJCT 96), "promises" of executive clemency for Hunt (HJCT 103-04) and the potential criminal liability of Haldeman, Ehrlichman, Colson, Dean, Magruder, Mitchell, Strachan, Krogh and Chapin, (HJCT 88-89, 95-96, 100) the President met with Ehrlichman, Haldeman and Dean. The President repeated his instructions about the "report."

> PRESIDENT. ... Uh, if you as the White House Counsel, John, uh, on direction—uh, I ask for a, a written report, which I think, uh, that—which is very general, understand. Understand, [laughs] I don't want to get all that God damned specific.[3] I'm thinking now in far more general terms, having in mind the fact that the problem with a specific report is that, uh, this proves this one and that one that one, and you just prove something that you didn't do at all. But if you make it rather general in terms of my—your investigation indicates that this man did not do it, this man did not do it, this man did do that. . . . (HJCT 136)

Ehrlichman spoke of the advantage to the President of having a written report on which he could later rely if additional facts came out.

> Well, but doesn't it give, doesn't it permit the President to clean it out at such time as it does come up? By saying, "Indeed, I relied on it. And now this, this later thing turns up, and I don't condone that. And if I'd known about that before, obviously, I wouldn't have done it. And I'm going to move on it now." (HJCT 140)

On March 22, 1973, Ehrlichman repeated this point at a meeting of the President, Haldeman, Mitchell, and Dean:

> [A]ssuming that some corner of this thing comes unstuck at some time, you're then in a position to say, "Look, that document I published [Dean Report] is the document I relied on. . . . (HJCT 159)

The President also discussed using the Dean report if White House aides were called to testify before the Grand Jury or Senate Select Committee.

> PRESIDENT. Well, they go in—do both: Appear before the Grand Jury and the Committee?
> DEAN. Sure.
> EHRLICHMAN. You have to bottom your defense, your position on the report.
> PRESIDENT. That's right.
> EHRLICHMAN. And the report says, "Nobody was involved." (HJCT 172)

The President's public statements regarding a Dean "report" were in every case, as revealed by the transcripts, part of the continuing cover-up.

C. THE EHRLICHMAN REPORT

At a press conference on September 5, 1973, President Nixon said that when he realized that John Dean would not be able to complete his report at Camp David, he assigned John Ehrlichman to conduct a "thorough investigation" to get all the facts out:

> The investigation, up to that time, had been conducted by Mr. Dean. . . . When he was unable to write a report, I turned to Mr. Ehrlichman. Mr. Ehrlichman did talk to the Attorney General . . . on . . . I think it was the 27th of March. The Attorney General was quite aware of that and Mr. Ehrlichman, in addition, questioned all of the major figures involved and reported to me on the 14th of April, and then, at my suggestion—direction, turned over his report to the Attorney General on the 15th of April. An investigation was conducted in the most thorough way. ("Presidential Statements," 9/5/73, 52)

---

[3] The sentence "Understand, [laughs] I don't want to get all that God damned specific." does not appear in the White House transcript. (WHT 257)

The "report" Ehrlichman had been asked to prepare in April, 1973, was part of a "scenario" designed to prevent disclosure of the President's complicity in the cover-up and to explain the President's lack of response to Dean's information of March 21, 1973. The President also wanted the "report" to give him credit for disclosing facts about to be revealed by potential defendants (La Rue, Dean, Magruder) to the United States attorneys and the grand jury, in spite of his own attempts to prevent those disclosures. Since Dean had told the President on March 21, 1973, of Ehrlichman's complicity in an obstruction of justice, and of his potential criminal liability for the break-in at the office of Ellsberg's psychiatrist, (HJCT 90–92) the fact that the President appointed Ehrlichman to make an "investigation" is, in itself, evidence of the President's direction of, and complicity in, the cover-up.

By mid-April, 1973, Magruder and Dean were meeting with United States attorneys. (Book IV, 538, 610) On April 14, 1973 the President met with Haldeman and Ehrlichman at 8:55 a.m.[4] (Book IV, 662) Ehrlichman told the President that Colson had reported that, since there was no longer any point in remaining silent, Hunt had decided to testify; and that Hunt's testimony would lead to the indictment of Magruder and Mitchell. (WHT 409–10) Ehrlichman suggested that the President could put pressure on Mitchell to accept full responsibility for the Watergate affair by telling Mitchell that Ehrlichman's "report", which was never prepared, already showed his guilt.

E I'm essentially convinced that Mitchell will understand this thing.
P Right.
E And that if he goes in it redounds to the Administration's advantage. If he doesn't then we're—
P How does it redound to our advantage?
E That you have a report from me based on three weeks' work; that when you got it, you immediately acted to call Mitchell in as the provable wrongdoer, and you say, "My God, I've got a report here. And it's clear from this report that you are guilty as hell. Now, John, for (expletive deleted) sake go on in there and do what you should. And let's get this thing cleared up and get it off the country's back and move on." And—
H Plus the other side of this is that that's the only way to beat it now. (WHT 439–40)

The President's hope was that this scheme to "nail" Mitchell, the "big fish" (WHT 670–71), the "big Enchilada" (WHT 347), would "take a lot of the fire out of this thing on the coverup" (WRT 756) and that, as Ehrlichman told the President, the prosecutors "would certainly be diverted." (WHT 457)

At 2:24 p.m. on April 14, the President met with Haldeman and Ehrlichman.[5] (Book IV, 779) Ehrlichman said that he saw no purpose in seeing Magruder. Haldeman added that "Magruder is already going to do what John is going to tell him to do. . . ." The President reminded Haldeman and Ehrlichman, however, that, "Our purpose, as I understood it—what I mean Bob, was for making a record." (WHT 537)

---

[4] On April 11, 1974, the House Judiciary Committee subpoenaed the tape recording and other materials related to this conversation. The President refused to produce this recording. The President submitted an edited transcript.
[5] On April 11, 1974, the House Judiciary Committee subpoenaed the tape recording and and other materials related to this conversation. The President refused to produce this recording. The President submitted an edited transcript.

Later in the conversation there was a discussion of what the scope of the Ehrlichman report should be:

E Well, I didn't go into White House involvement. I assume that—
P No. I (unintelligible)
E That what you needed to know from me, and this would be what I would say, "What the President needed to know was the truth or falsity of charges that were leaking out with regard to—Committee for the Re-election personnel and any connections to the White House that might exist. That was the area of inquiry rather than whether anybody in the White House was involved."
P (Unintelligible) trying to get you out there in a way that you didn't have to go into all that stuff, you see. (WHT 564–65)

Two days later, on April 16, 1973, after the President had learned the substance of Dean's disclosure to the prosecutors (Petersen testimony, 3 HJC 81–82), the President directed Ehrlichman to prepare "a scenario with regard to the President's role. . . ." "Otherwise," Ehrlichman said, "the Justice Department will, of course, crack this whole thing." [6] (WHT 782–83)

From 10:00 to 10:40 a.m. on April 16, the President met with Dean. (Book IV, 1143) The President asked Dean to think about how to handle things "[so] that the President is in front. . . ." Dean agreed to give the President some notes. The President said, "The record. Here's what I've done. Here's what I've done, and what you think the President ought to do and when—you see what I mean?" (HJCT 207)

In another meeting with Ehrlichman and Haldeman at 10:50 a.m.,[7] (Book IV, 1204) the President asked how the "scenario" had worked out. Haldeman replied:

H Well, it works out very good. You became aware sometime ago that this thing did not parse out the way it was supposed to and that there were some discrepancies between what you had been told by Dean in the report that there was nobody in the White House involved, which may still be true.
P Incidentally, I don't think it will gain us anything by dumping on the Dean Report as such.
E No.
P What I mean is I would say I was not satisfied that the Dean Report was complete and also I thought it was my obligation to go beyond that to people other than the White House.
E Ron has an interesting point. Remember you had John Dean go to Camp David to write it up. He came down and said, "I can't."
P Right.
E That is the tip off and right then you started to move.
P That's right. He said he could not write it.
H Then you realized that there was more to this than you had been led to believe. (unintelligible)
P How do I get credit for getting Magruder to the stand?
E Well it is very simple. You took Dean off of the case right then.
H Two weeks ago, the end of March.
P That's right.
E The end of March. Remember that letter you signed to me?
P Uh, huh.
E 30th of March.
P I signed it. Yes.

---

[6] On April 11, 1974, the House Judiciary Committee subpoenaed the tape recording and other materials related to this conversation. The President refused to produce this recording. The President submitted an edited transcript.
[7] On April 11, 1974, the House Judiciary Committee subpoenaed the tape recording and other materials related to this conversation. The President refused to produce this recording. The President submitted an edited transcript.

E Yes sir, and it says Dean is off of it. I want you to get into it. Find out what the facts are. Be prepared to—

Ehrlichman suggested that the President say that after Dean was taken off, "we started digging into it," "[y]ou began to move," and that it all "culminated last week." The "culmination" was to be when Mitchell, Magruder and Strachan were "brought in."

E In your decision that Mitchell should be brought down here; Magruder should be brought in; Strachan should be brought in.
P Shall I say that we brought them all in?
E I don't think you can. I don't think you can.
H I wouldn't name them by name. Just say I brought a group of people in.
E Personally come to the White House.
P I will not tell you who because I don't want to prejudice their rights before (unintelligible)

Ehrlichman continued:

E I had this report and I tried all day long to get the Attorney General who was at the golf course and got him as soon as he got home for—
P Do we want to put this report out sometime?
E I am not sure you do, as such.
P I would say it was just a written report.
E The thing that I have—
P The thing they will ask is what have you got here?
H It was not a formal report. It was a set of notes.
P Handwritten notes?
E Yeah. There are seven pages, or eight pages. Plus all my notes of my interviews. (WHT 820-25)

Ehrlichman later testified that he had not conducted an investigation. (Ehrlichman testimony, 7 SSC 2713–14) He delivered to the SSC some notes of interviews but nothing that could constitute a report. (Ehrlichman testimony, 7 SSC 2915–43) No letter from the President saying "Dean is off of it," as suggested in the "scenario" to the President on April 16, 1973, has ever been produced. There is no evidence that any such letter existed. Ehrlichman said he had interviewed Paul O'Brien on April 5, 1973 (Book IV, 509, 518); Kalmbach on April 6, 1973 (Book IV, 534, 536), Dean on April 8, 1973 (Book IV, 540); Strachan on April 12, 1973 (Book IV, 550–51); Colson on April 13, 1973 (Book IV, 595–96); Mitchell and Magruder on April 14, 1973 (Book IV, 718–19); and Strachan on April 5, 1973 (Book IV, 897; Ehrlichman testimony, 7 SSC 2727). The meeting with O'Brien was at O'Brien's request. O'Brien originally had requested a meeting with Haldeman to request that the civil suits by the DNC and common cause against CRP be settled and that O'Brien be permitted to confer with the Senate Select Committee. (O'Brien testimony, 1 HJC 132, 134–36; Book IV, 512) Ehrlichman's notes of the meeting contain the entries "Must close ranks—JNM [Mitchell] will tough it out" and "H must bring Jeb [Magruder] up short—shut up, stop seeing people." (Book IV, 527, 532), Ehrlichman's notes of his meeting with Kalmbach say that Kalmbach was worried about the effect that his testimony about raising money for the Watergate defendants would have upon his reputation and his family; and that Kalmbach thought Dean told him Ehrlichman and Haldeman had approved his raising these funds. (Kalmbach testimony, 3 HJC 564; Book IV, 536) The edited White House transcript of Ehrlichman's April 8, 1973, account to the President of his meeting with Dean and Haldeman shows that the meeting consisted of a discussion of strategy. (WHT 401–07)

The meeting with Strachan, which Haldeman attended, was about Strachan's concern that he had committed perjury in his grand jury testimony of the day before. (Book IV, 550-51) On April 12, 1973, the President asked Colson what he thought the President should do about Watergate. (Colson testimony, 3 HJC 341) The edited White House transcript of Ehrlichman's April 14, 1973, account of his meeting with Colson shows that the meeting consisted of a discussion of strategy.[8] (WHT 409-14) In his conversation of April 14, 1973, with Mitchell, Ehrlichman did not seek to elicit facts. (Book IV, 725-68) On April 14, 1973, after he was informed that Magruder was about to meet with the prosecutors, the President instructed Ehrlichman to meet with Magruder just "for making a record" for which the President hoped to get credit.[9] (WHT 537) Ehrlichman met with Strachan. (Book IV, 891-95, WHT 646-47)

Ehrlichman never mentioned his assignment to Acting FBI Director Gray. (Book IV, 1) Although they spoke at least twice in early April, Ehrlichman did not discuss his inquiry with Attorney General Kleindienst until April 14, 1973. (Book IV, 215) On April 14, 1973, when Ehrlichman did speak with Kleindienst, he said he had very little to add to what Magruder had already given the United States Attorney. (WHT 632) He said that Magruder had implicated people up and down in CRP. When Kleindienst asked whom Magruder had implicated besides Mitchell, Ehrlichman answered Dean, LaRue, Mardian and Porter. He did not mention Colson or Strachan. Ehrlichman's notes of his meeting with Magruder read: "Strachan primary contact, copies of bud. [budget] talked to JSM [Magruder]"; "all nervous—Mag., Mitch, Strachan"; "Strachan informed—orally, Liddy's project, He had budget, '6 bugs @' etc"; "Strachan saw synopses"; "CC [Colson] called—never said wiretap—projects"; "CC Needed info on L. O'Brien"; "CC—Had to get O'B." (Book IV, 803-09)

II

Perjury by White House and CRP Officials

To continue the cover-up, White House and CRP officials lied under oath. Some witnesses told untrue stories. Others untruthfully said they could not recall certain facts.[10]

The first distinct phase in which the President, his White House staff and CRP officials, including Porter and Mitchell, Strachan, and Magruder, made false and misleading statements to further the cover-up was from June, 1972, to March, 1973. It is uncontested that on March 13 the President was informed of Strachan's perjury and on March 21 of Magruder's and Porter's perjury. Magruder's untruth-

---

[8] On April 11, 1974, the House Judiciary Committee subpoenaed the tape recording and other materials related to this conversation. The President refused to produce this recording. The President submitted an edited transcript.
[9] On April 11, 1974, the House Judiciary Committee subpoenaed the tape recording and other materials related to this conversation. The President refused to produce this recording. The President submitted an edited transcript.
[10] Ehrlichman and Chapin have been convicted of perjury. Krogh, Magruder, and Porter pleaded guilty to conspiracy charges which included their perjury among the overt acts. Mitchell, Haldeman and Strachan have been indicted for perjury and are awaiting trial. Haldeman, Ehrlichman and Mitchell testified, in response to questions, they could not recall 206, 136 and 255 times respectively, according to transcripts in the Committee's files.

ful testimony provided an innocent explanation for the commitment of $250,000 of CRP money to the Liddy Plan. (Book III, 246–51, 298) Porter's untruthful testimony corroborated Magruder's story. (Book III, 236–41, 292–93) Strachan's false statements concealed the involvement of Haldeman and the White House in the Liddy Plan. (*United States* v. *Mitchell*, CR 74–110, indictment, 44–50, "Criminal Cases," 146–52; Book IV, 551)

The second phase of false statements to further the cover-up began near the end of March, 1973, with the reconvening of the Watergate Grand Jury.

Some of this testimony was given at the direction of the President. On March 21, 1973, the President told Dean and Haldeman "[j]ust be damned sure you say I don't ... remember; I can't recall, I can't give any honest, an answer to that that I can recall. But that's it."[11] (HJCT 120)

There is no evidence that when the President learned of perjury, false statements or failure to recall, or other false statements, on the part of his staff, he condemned such conduct, instructed that it be stopped, dismissed the responsible members of his staff, or reported his discoveries to an appropriate authority. The evidence before the Committee shows, on the contrary, that the President directed this conduct, condoned it, approved it, rewarded it, and in some instances specifically instructed witnesses on how to mislead investigators.

1. Strachan

From the time of the break-in, Strachan, who was Haldeman's liaison with CRP (Butterfield testimony, 1 HJC 15), could link Haldeman with approval of the Liddy Plan. (Book I, 164–66) On March 13, 1973, Dean informed the President that Strachan had falsely denied White House involvement soon after the break-in, and that Strachan planned to stonewall again:

DEAN. Well, Chapin didn't know anything about the Watergate, and—
PRESIDENT. You don't think so?
DEAN. No. Absolutely not.
PRESIDENT. Did Strachan?
DEAN. Yes.
PRESIDENT. He knew?
DEAN. Yes.
PRESIDENT. About the Watergate?
DEAN. Yes.
PRESIDENT. Well, then, Bob knew.[12] He probably told Bob, then. He may not have. He may not have.
DEAN. He was, he was judicious in what he, in what he relayed, and, uh, but Strachan is as tough as nails. I—
PRESIDENT. What'll he say? Just go in and say he didn't know?
DEAN. He'll go in and stonewall it and say, "I don't know anything about what you are talking about." He has already done it twice, as you know, in interviews.[13]
PRESIDENT. Yeah, I guess he should, shouldn't he, in the interests of—Why? I suppose we can't call that justice, can we? We can't call it [unintelligible]
DEAN. Well, it, it—
PRESIDENT. The point is, how do you justify that?

---

[11] In the White House transcript, the President says, "But you can say I don't remember. You can say I can't recall. I can't give any answer to that that I can recall." (WHT 235)
[12] The words "Bob knew" do not appear in the edited White House transcript. (WHT 146)
[13] The word "as" does not appear in the edited White House transcript.

DEAN. It's a, it's a personal loyalty with him. He doesn't want it any other way. He didn't have to be told. He didn't have to be asked. It just is something that he found is the way he wanted to handle the situation.
PRESIDENT. But he knew? He knew about Watergate? Strachan did?
DEAN. Uh huh.
PRESIDENT. I'll be damned. Well, that's the problem in Bob's case, isn't it. It's not Chapin then, but Strachan. 'Cause Strachan worked for him.
DEAN. Uh huh. They would have one hell of a time proving that Strachan had knowledge of it, though.
PRESIDENT. Who knew better? Magruder?
DEAN. Well, Magruder and Liddy.
PRESIDENT. Ah—I see. The other weak link for Bob is Magruder, too. He having hired him and so forth. (HJCT 70–71)

2. *Magruder and Porter*

An explanation was necessary for CRP's payment of $250,000 to Liddy. Magruder invented the story that the Liddy Plan contemplated only legitimate intelligence activities. (Book III, 298–99) He enlisted his assistant Porter to corroborate this untruthful testimony. (Book III, 292) Magruder worked on his false story with Dean and discussed it with Mitchell. (Book III, 299) Magruder and Porter lied to the FBI in July 1972, and committed perjury before the Grand Jury in August 1972, and at the trial of the Watergate defendants in January 1973. (Book III, 292–94, 506)

Whether or not the President knew of Magruder's perjury before March 21, 1973, there is no doubt that on that date Dean told the President that Magruder and Porter had committed perjury:

PRESIDENT. Liddy told you he was planning—where'd he learn there was such a plan—from whom?
DEAN. Beg your pardon?
PRESIDENT. Where did he learn of the plans to bug Larry O'Brien's suite?
DEAN. From Magruder, after the, long after the fact.
PRESIDENT. Oh, Magruder, he knows.
DEAN. Yeah. Magruder is totally knowledgeable on the whole thing.
PRESIDENT. Yeah.
DEAN. All right, now, we've gone through the trial. We've—I don't know if Mitchell has perjured himself in the Grand Jury or not. I've never—
PRESIDENT. Who?
DEAN. Mitchell. I don't know how much knowledge he actually had. I know that Magruder has perjured himself in the Grand Jury. I know that Porter has perjured himself, uh, in the Grand Jury.
PRESIDENT. Porter [unintelligible]
DEAN. He is one of Magruder's deputies.
PRESIDENT. Yeah
DEAN. Uh, that they set up this scenario which they ran by me. They said, "How about this?" I said, "I don't know. I, you know, if, if this is what you are going to hang on, fine." Uh, that they—
PRESIDENT. What did they say before the Grand Jury?
DEAN. They said, they said, as they said before the trial and the Grand Jury, that, that, uh, Liddy had come over as, as a counsel
PRESIDENT. Yeah.
DEAN. and we knew he had these capacities to,
PRESIDENT. Yeah.
DEAN. you know.
PRESIDENT. Yeah.
DEAN. to do legitimate intelligence. We had no idea what he was doing.
PRESIDENT. Yeah.
DEAN. He was given an authorization of $250,000
PRESIDENT. Right.
DEAN. to collect information, because our surrogates were out on the road. They had no protection. We had information that there were going to be demonstrations against them, that, uh, uh, we had to have a plan to get information as to what liabilities they were going to be confronted with

PRESIDENT. Right.
DEAN. and Liddy was charged with doing this. We had no knowledge that he was going to bug the DNC. Uh—[14]
PRESIDENT. Well, the point is, that's not true.
DEAN. That's right.
PRESIDENT. Magruder did know that—
DEAN. Magruder specifically instructed him to go back in the DNC.
PRESIDENT. He did?
DEAN. Yes.
PRESIDENT. You know that? Yeah. I see. Okay. (HJCT 86–87)

The President did not act on this information, did not pursue it, did not convey it to the Department of Justice.

In January, 1973, Magruder, before testifying at the Watergate trial, told Haldeman that he would commit perjury. (Book III, 515) On February 14, 1973, after the trial, Magruder met with Haldeman to discuss his future employment. (Book III, 566–67) On February 19, 1973, Dean prepared a talking paper for a meeting at which Haldeman would discuss with the President Magruder's possible appointment to an Administration job. (Book III, 570–71) Dean noted that Hugh Sloan, whom Magruder had unsuccessfully importuned to commit perjury, would testify against Magruder before the Senate if Magruder were appointed to any position for which Senate confirmation was required. (Book III, 561) The talking paper reads:

(3) What to do with Magruder
—Jeb wants to return to White House (Bicentennial project).
—May be vulnerable (Sloan) until Senate hearings are completed.
—Jeb personally is prepared to withstand confirmation hearings. (Book III, 574–75)

After meeting with the President,[15] Haldeman told Magruder he could not have a White House job, but offered him the highest paying available position which did not require Senate confirmation: a $36,000 per year job in the Department of Commerce. (Book III, 567, 572–73, 577–78) Haldeman believed this was the kind of decision to be checked with the President. (Book III, 569) Magruder did not lose his position on March 21, 1973, when Dean told the President that Magruder had committed perjury. (HJCT 87; Book IV, 565, 1626) Magruder resigned on April 26, 1973, two weeks after he had come forward and confessed to the United States Attorney.

III

STATEMENTS TO COVER UP THE COVER-UP

In late March, 1973, the President was told by his assistants that the cover-up was threatened from various directions. On March 21, 1973, there was Hunt's immediate demand, which the President believed could be satisfied in cash. (HJCT 118) But there was also Hunt's expectation of clemency, which Dean advised the President would be politically impossible to fulfill: the President agreed. (HJCT 103–04) On April 14, 1973, the President, Haldeman and Ehrlichman discussed

---
[14] In the edited White House transcript there is a question mark after this sentence.
[15] On April 11, 1974, the House Judiciary Committee subpoenaed the tape recording and other materials related to this conversation. The President stated that no such recorded conversation could be located.

their anxiety that Hunt had changed his mind and would talk to the prosecutors about payments and offers of clemency. (WHT 541-619) Another threat to the cover-up was McCord's letter to Judge Sirica and the decision to reconvene the Grand Jury. (Book IV, 220-24, 336) A third threat was posed by potential disclosures on the part of key subordinates involved in the Watergate cover-up. (HJCT 134)

Faced with a disintegrating situation, the President, after March 21, 1973, assumed an operational role in the detailed management of the cover-up. He knew of the previous untruthful testimony of his aides and of his own false public statements. He issued direct instruction for his subordinates to give false and misleading testimony. The President knew that his agents had instructed and were continuing to instruct witnesses on how to testify to protect the cover-up; the President himself so instructed witnesses. On April 15, 1973, the President learned from Ehrlichman that Mardian had worked with witnesses on false testimony for their appearances before the Grand Jury.

P Well, is there anything wrong with that?
E Yeah, well there's something wrong with—
P He was not their attorney is the problem?
E Well, no the problem—the problem is he asked them to say things that weren't true. (WHT 687-88) [16]

1. *Magruder*

On March 23, 1973, Judge Sirica read in open court a letter from James McCord charging that witnesses had committed perjury in his trial, and that more people than the seven original defendants were involved in Watergate. (Book IV, 220-24) In meetings with Haldeman and Ehrlichman, the President developed a strategy to implicate Mitchell and to conceal the complicity of the President and his closest White House aides. The President reasoned that, in exchange for a promise of immunity, Magruder would limit his disclosure to his own complicity and Mitchell's. At the March 27, 1973 meeting the President took part in the following discussion with Haldeman and Ehrlichman:

H Let's go another one. So you persuade Magruder that his present approach is (a) not true; I think you can probably persuade him of that; and (b) not desirable to take. So he then says, in despair, "Heck, what do I do? Here's McCord out here accusing me. McCord has flatly accused me of perjury—He's flatly accused Dean of complicity." Dean is going to go, and Magruder knows of the fact that Dean wasn't involved, so he knows that when Dean goes down, Dean can testify as an honest man.

* * * * * *

P What would you advise him [Magruder] to do?
H I would advise him to go down and clean it up.
P And say I lied?
H I would advise him to seek immunity and do it.
P Do you think he can get immunity?
H Absolutely.
P Then what would he say?
E He would say, "I thought I was helping. It is obvious that there is no profit in this route. I did it on my own motive. Nobody asked me to do it. I just did it

---

[16] On April 11, 1974, the House Judiciary Committee subpoenaed the tape recording and other materials related to this conversation. The President refused to produce this recording. The President submitted an edited transcript.

because I thought it was the best thing to do. Everybody stands on it. I was wrong to do it." That's basically it.

H Magruder's viewpoint that to be ruined that way which isn't really being ruined is infinitely preferable to going to jail. Going to jail for Jeb will be a very, very, very difficult job.

E (unintelligble) he says he is a very unusual person. The question now is whether the U.S. Attorney will grant immunity under the circumstances.

H Well he would if he thought he was going to get Mitchell.

E Yeah, that's right.

H The interesting thing would be to watch Mitchell's face at the time I recommend to Magruder that he go in and ask for immunity and confess.[17] (WHT 350–52)

On April 13, 1973 Magruder started talking to the prosecutors. (Book IV, 610–11) Haldeman's principal assistant, Lawrence Higby, called Magruder and confronted him with reports that he had implicated Haldeman in the Watergate break-in. (Book IV, 613–16) Higby recorded the conversation. He told Magruder that it was not in Magruder's long or short range interest to blame the White House. Higby said he could not believe Magruder would implicate Haldeman, who "has brought you here." (Book IV, 619, 624) Magruder said that Strachan had not specifically told him that Haldeman wanted the Liddy Plan approved. (Book IV, 625–27) On the morning of April 14, 1973, Haldeman reported this conversation to the President. Haldeman said that Higby had handled it skillfully and that the recording made by Higby "beats the socks off" Magruder if he ever "gets off the reservation." (WHT 415–16) The President had known as early as March 21, 1973, that he could not count on Magruder. (Book III, 1245–46; HJCT 120, 140–41)[18] On April 14, 1973, the President concurred when Ehrlichman described Magruder as an "emotional fellow ready to crack."[19] (WHT 417) The President instructed Ehrlichman to meet with Magruder for the purpose of making a record.(WHT 478, 500, 537) Later that day, Haldeman said in the presence of the President, that Magruder should be asked to repeat what he told Higby and that Ehrlichman should say, "Good."[20] (WHT 537)

2. Strachan

If Magruder were to admit having committed perjury and were to cooperate fully with the United States Attorney, Strachan's prior knowledge of the DNC bugging would be revealed, and this would implicate Haldeman. At an afternoon meeting on April 14, 1973, the President and Haldeman discussed what Strachan's strategy before the Grand Jury should be.

H I don't think Magruder knows about the aftermath.
P Where does he [Magruder] get to Gordon Strachan?

[17] On April 11, 1974, the House Judiciary Committee subpoenaed the tape recording and other materials related to the conversation. The President refused to produce this recording. The President submitted an edited transcript.
[18] In his dictated recollections on March 21, the President said Magruder would "bring Haldeman down" and was "a rather weak man, who had all the appearances of character, but who really lacks it when the, uh, chips are down." (Book III, 1245–46)
[19] On April 11, 1974, the House Judiciary Committee subpoenaed the tape recording and other materials related to this conversation. The President refused to produce this recording. The President submitted an edited transcript.
[20] On April 11, 1974, the House Judiciary Committee subpoenaed the tape recording and other materials related to this conversation. The President refused to produce this recording. The President submitted an edited transcript.

H He says he gets Gordon on—
P Sending material to him—

* * * * * * *

P He will testify that he sent materials to the White House?
H If he is asked, he will, yes.
P He'll be asked—is that something he will say he sent to the White House. What would Strachan say?
H Strachan has no problem with that. He will say that after the fact there are materials that I can now surmise were what he is referring to but they were not at the time identified in any way as being the result of wiretaps and I did not know they were. They were amongst tons of stuff. Jeb makes the point. He said, I am sure Gordon never sent them to Bob because they were all trash. There was nothing in them. He said the tragedy of this whole thing is that it produced nothing.
P Who else did he send reports to—Mitchell?
H I don't know. The th'ng I got before was that he sent them either to— that one went to him and one went to Strachan.
P What our problem there is if they claim that the reports came to the White House—basically to your office—what will you say then?
H They can. This doesn't ever have to come out.[21] (WHT 520–21; see also WHT 537, 592)

Haldeman explained that even if the question were asked before the Grand Jury, Grand Jury proceedings are secret. (WHT 521) On the night of April 14, 1973, the President telephoned Haldeman. He told Haldeman that before Strachan appeared before the Grand Jury he should be told what Magruder had told the United States Attorneys. The President asked Haldeman if Strachan were smart enough to testify in a way that did not indicate that he knew what Magruder had said. The President also said that Strachan has to be prepared and that Ehrlichman should speak to Strachan and "put him through a little wringer." [22] The President said Ehrlichman should be the one to do it because he was conducting an investigation for the President. (WHT 639–41, 646–47) On the afternoon of April 16, 1973, Ehrlichman told the President that Strachan had stonewalled, that although the prosecutors "really worked him over" and "[d]espite considerable fencing, he refused to discuss the matter and was excused by the prosecutors." [23] (WHT 933)

3. *Haldeman*

On April 25, 1973, the President directed Haldeman to listen to the taped conversation of the March 21, 1973 morning meeting among the President, Dean and Haldeman. (Book IX, 108–11) Haldeman requested and received twenty-two tapes of Presidential conversations held in February, March and April, 1973. (Book IX, 114–15, 123–25) On the afternoon of April 25, 1973, Haldeman listened to the March 21 morning conversation, made twenty pages of detailed notes, and reported to the President on the contents of the tape. (Book IX, 116) The President ordered Haldeman to listen to the March 21 tape again.

---

[21] On April 11, 1974, the House Judiciary Committee subpoenaed the tape recording and other materials related to this conversation. The President refused to produce this recording. The President submitted an edited transcript.
[22] On April 11, 1974, the House Judiciary Committee subpoenaed the tape recording and other materials related to this conversation. The President refused to produce this recording. The President submitted an edited transcript.
[23] On April 11, 1974, the House Judiciary Committee subpoenaed the tape recording and other materials related to this conversation. The President refused to produce this recording. The President submitted an edited transcript.

On April 26, 1973, Haldeman again listened to the March 21 tape and reported to the President. On April 26, 1973, the President and Haldeman met for approximately five hours, beginning at 3:59 p.m., and concluding at 9:03 p.m. (Book IX, 126)[24]

On June 4, 1973, the President told Alexander Haig and Ziegler that Haldeman could "handle" the March 21 conversation. (Book IX, 177–78, 193)

PRESIDENT. . . . . Well, as I told you, we do know we have one problem: It's that damn conversation of March twenty-first due to the fact that, uh, for the reasons [unintelligible]. But I think we can handle that.
HAIG. I think we ca—, can. That's, that's the—
PRESIDENT. Bob can handle it. He'll get up there and say that—Bob will say, "I was there; the President said—".

*   *   *   *   *   *   *

PRESIDENT. Okay. The twenty-first and the twenty-second. Uh, uh, twenty—twenty-first I've got to Bob already. The twenty-second [unintelligible].
ZIEGLER. [Unintelligible]
PRESIDENT. Well—no, if you can—I don't think you can. He's, he's got it all in our file and I don't—let's just forget it. I think after the twenty-first we forgot what the hell—What do you think? (Book IX, 177–78, 193)

Haldeman subsequently testified before the SSC about the meeting of March 21, 1973, specifically citing the following statement:

(a) That the President said, "[T]here is no problem in raising a million dollars, we can do that, but it would be wrong." (Book IX, 440)
(b) That "There was a reference to his [Dean's] feeling that Magruder had known about the Watergate planning and break-in ahead of it, in other words, that he was aware of what had gone on at Watergate. I don't believe that there was any reference to Magruder committing perjury." (Haldeman testimony, 8 SSC, 3144)

On August 22, 1973, the President said that Haldeman's testimony regarding the President's statements during the conversation was accurate. ("Presidential Statements," 8/22/73, 49)

4. Ehrlichman

On April 17, 1973, the President met with Haldeman and Ehrlichman and Secretary of State Rogers. (Book IV, 1423) After a brief discussion of Haldeman's and Ehrlichman's future,[25] the President spoke of his former personal attorney, Herbert Kalmbach, saying that it was "terribly important that poor Kalmbach get through this thing." (WHT 1201) The President asked if Dean had called Kalmbach about fundraising. Haldeman replied that Dean had. Ehrlichman said that Dean had told Kalmbach what the money was to be used for. The President suggested that Ehrlichman testify otherwise.

E Dean told me that he told him what it was for. I don't believe him. Herb said that he just followed instructions, that he just went ahead and did it and sent the money back and—
P They said they need it for?

---

[24] On May 30, 1974, the House Judiciary Committee subpoenaed the tape recording and other materials related to this conversation. The President refused to produce this recording.
[25] On April 11, 1974, the House Judiciary Committee subpoenaed the tape recording and other materials related to this conversation. The President refused to produce this recording. The President submitted an edited transcript.

E I don't even know if they told him what for. It was an emergency and they needed this money and I don't know whether he can get away with that or if it's more specific than that.
P You can corroborate then Herb on that one.
E I can if Dean is the accuser. I can.
P If Dean is the accuser, you can say that he told you on such and such a date that he did not tell Herb Kalmbach what the money was for. (WHT 1201)

5. Colson

On April 14, 1973, Ehrlichman reported to the President about his conversation with Magruder, in which Magruder had told Ehrlichman what he was telling the prosecutors. (WHT 582–87) [26] The President, concerned that Colson would be called before the Grand Jury (WHT 602), instructed Ehrlichman to warn Colson about what Magruder had told the prosecutors.

P We'll see. We'll see. Do your other business, etc. John, [Dean] too, I wonder if we shouldn't reconsider, if you shouldn't, I mean you have to consider this—rather than having Colson go in there completely blind, give him at least a touch up—or do you think that is too dangerous.
E Say that again—I didn't quite hear it.
P Colson—rather than just saying nothing to him, if it isn't just as well to say—look you should know that Magruder is going to testify, etc., or is that dangerous according to Kleindeinst?
E I'm not so sure. I have to call him anyway tomorrow. He has an urgent call in for me. Ah, I don't think I want to say anything at all to him about John. John, incidentally, I understand, was on CBS News and just hardlined them.
P Oh, I agree on John.
E Yeah
P On Magruder that is what I meant.
E Well, I can say something very brief. I don't need to indicate that he said anything to me.
P Yeah, that you understand that he has talked. I mean, not to the Grand Jury but to—
E Yeah, I think I could safely go that far.
P And say that he should know that before he goes, and be prepared.
E Friday—I will call him in the morning.
P Let me put it this way: I do think we owe it to Chuck to at least—
E Sure
P So that he doesn't, I mean, go in there and well frankly on a perjury rap—
E I understand. I don't think he is in any danger on that but—
P Why wouldn't he be in any danger, because he's got his story and knows pretty well what he is going to say?
E Yeah, I think he is pretty pat, but I will talk to him in the morning and give him a cautionary note anyway. (WHT 650–51) [27]

III

April 30, 1973 Statement

On April 30, 1973, the President addressed the nation about the Watergate investigation.

Last June 17, while I was in Florida trying to get a few days rest after my visit to Moscow, I first learned from news reports of the Watergate break-in. I was appalled at this senseless, illegal action, and I was shocked to learn that

---

[26] On April 11, 1974, the House Judiciary Committee subpoenaed the tape recording and other materials related to this conversation. The President refused to produce this recording. The President submitted an edited transcript.
[27] On April 11, 1974, the House Judiciary Committee subpoenaed the tape recording and other materials related to this conversation. The President refused to produce this recording. The President submitted an edited transcript.

employees of the Re-election Committee were apparently among those guilty. I immediately ordered an investigation by appropriate Government authorities. On September 15, as you will recall, indictments were brought against seven defendants in the case.

As the investigations went forward, I repeatedly asked those conducting the investigation whether there was any reason to believe that members of my Adminstration were in any way involved. I received repeated assurances that there were not. Because of these continuing reassurances, because I believed the reports I was getting, because I had faith in the persons from whom I was getting them, I discounted the stories in the press that appeared to implicate members of my Administration or other officials of the campaign committee.

Until March of this year, I remained convinced that the denials were true and that the charges of involvement by members of the White House staff were false. The comments I made during this period, and the comments made by my Press Secretary in my behalf, were based on the information provided to us at the time we made those comments. However, new information then came to me which persuaded me that there was a real possibility that some of these charges were true, and suggesting further that there had been an effort to conceal the facts both from the public, from you, and from me.

As a result, on March 21, I personally assumed the responsibility for coordinating intensive new inquiries into the matter, and I personally ordered those conducting the investigations to get all the facts and to report them directly to me, right here in this office.

I again ordered that all persons in the Government or at the Re-election Committee should cooperate fully with the FBI, the prosecutors, and the grand jury. I also ordered that anyone who refused to cooperate in telling the truth would be asked to resign from government service. And, with ground rules adopted that would preserve the basic constitutional separation of powers between the Congress and the Presidency, I directed that members of the White House Staff should appear and testify voluntarily under oath before the Senate committee which was investigating Watergate.

I was determined that we should get to the bottom of the matter, and that the truth should be fully brought out—no matter who was involved. ("Presidential Statements," 4/30/73, 14-15)

This statement, like the President's statement on August 29, 1972, that "we are doing everything we can to investigate this incident and not cover up," was false. The evidence set forth in this section compelled the Committee to conclude that both before and after March 21, 1973, the cover-up was sustained by false public statements by the President assuring that the White House or CRP were not involved, as well as, by false statements and testimony by the President's close subordinates, which the President condoned and encouraged and in some instances directed, coached and personally helped to fabricate.

THE PRESIDENT'S INTERFERENCE WITH THE DEPARTMENT OF JUSTICE INVESTIGATION IN MARCH AND APRIL 1973

I

THE NEW PLAN AFTER MARCH 21, 1973

On the morning of March 21, 1973, Counsel to the President John Dean told the President that there was a "cancer" close to the Presidency, which, Dean said, was growing daily. Dean warned that the White House was being blackmailed; and that even people who had not yet committed perjury would soon have to perjure themselves to protect other people. Dean said there was no assurance that the problems could be contained. (HJCT 81) He spoke of the adoption of the Liddy Plan. He said that in February, 1972, Liddy and Hunt had gone to Colson; that Colson had called Magruder and told him either to "fish or cut bait"; that Colson had "had a damn good idea" what Liddy and Hunt were talking about. Dean said Colson would deny it and probably get away with it unless Hunt talked. The President acknowledged the problem of criminal liability in the White House.

Dean said that when the Liddy Plan had gotten under way Strachan had started pushing Magruder for information. Magruder had taken that as a signal, and had told Mitchell that the White House was anxiously pushing the plan. Dean said that Haldeman had once instructed Liddy to change his "capability" from Muskie to McGovern. (HJCT 84–85)

Dean said that in June, 1972, when he had called Liddy to find out what happened, Liddy had told him that no one in the White House was involved. Liddy said he had been pushed without mercy by Magruder to get more information. Dean said that Magruder had said, "The White House is not happy with what we're getting." (HJCT 86)

Dean then spoke of the cover-up. Dean said that Magruder and Porter had prepared with him a false story about the purpose of the money spent on the Liddy Plan, and then perjured themselves before the Grand Jury. (HJCT 87) Dean said he had worked on a theory of "containment" and the President responded, "Sure." (HJCT 88) Dean said that Colson had told the FBI he had no knowledge concerning the break-in; and that Strachan had been coached before his FBI interview. Dean said Liddy had gone to Attorney General Kleindienst and asked him "to get my men out of jail," but that "this has never come up." (HJCT 89)

Dean spoke about payments to the defendants, who had made demands. He said that arrangements had been made through Mitchell to take care of the demands; that Kalmbach had been used and had raised some cash. The President interrupted by asking if that had been put under the cover of a Cuban Committee. He instructed Dean to keep "that cover for whatever it's worth." Dean said Haldeman, Ehrlichman, Mitchell and Dean were involved in the payments and "that's an obstruction of justice" (HJCT 90), but that they had all decided that there was no price too high to pay to keep the thing from blowing up before the election. When, after the election, they had still needed money, Dean said, Haldeman had released his $350,000 fund with full knowledge of the purpose for which it was to be used. (HJCT 90)

Dean spoke of clemency. He said that Colson had talked indirectly to Hunt about commutation and that these "promises" and "commitments" were problems. (HJCT 91) Dean reviewed other potential problems, "soft spots." One was the "continued blackmail," particularly by Hunt, who was now demanding $120,000. Dean said Hunt had threatened to put Ehrlichman in jail for his involvement in the Ellsberg break-in (HJCT 92), and that Hunt "could sink Chuck Colson." (HJCT 96). The President said that the major guy to keep under control was Hunt because he knew about a lot of other things. Another potential problem was the number of people who knew. Dean said that the Cubans Hunt used in the Watergate were the same Cubans used in the Ellsberg break-in. Dean said that the lawyers for the defendants knew, and that some wives knew. (HJCT 92–93) Dean said that Krogh had been forced to commit perjury and that he had been haunted by it (HJCT 95), and that Kalmbach might find himself in a perjury situation. (HJCT 97)

After Dean had said all this, the President suggested that it could come down to a criminal case against Haldeman, Dean, Mitchell and Ehrlichman. The President considered steps "to contain it again." (HJCT 100)

At that point Dean said he was not comfortable. The President said, "You used to feel comfortable." Dean said that they had been able "to hold it for a long time," and the President replied, "Yeah, I know." (HJCT 101–02) The President raised the possibility of asking for another grand jury. Dean said some people would have to go to jail and he was bothered about the obstruction of justice. The President said he thought that "could be cut off at the pass." He explained that sometimes "it's well to give them something and then they don't want the bigger fish." (HJCT 102–03)

The President and Dean continued to explore ways of avoiding criminal liability for anyone at the White House. Dean told the President that he had been a conduit for information on taking care of people who are guilty of crimes. (HJCT 102) The President said, "You mean the blackmail," and Dean said, "Right."

When Dean said that before the election there had been some bad judgments, some necessary judgments, but that, faced with the election, there was no way, the President agreed. (HJCT 104)

When the President and Dean returned to the subject of potential criminal liability—and talked about Ehrlichman's risk (HJCT 105), Dean said, "I don't have a plan of how to solve it but we should think in terms of how to cut our losses." (HJCT 105) The President instructed (1) to stabilize Hunt for the short term; and (2) to get Mitchell down to meet with Haldeman, Ehrlichman and Dean, to discuss the most dangerous problems for the President, *e.g.*, criminal liability of his close subordinates.

Dean told the President that the Grand Jury would reconvene during the next week, and that a lot of these people could be indicted. The President said that if they indicted Bob and the rest "you'd never recover from that" and it would be "better to fight it out instead." (HJCT 106)

Then the President asked how soon a meeting with Mitchell could be arranged. Dean said that Bob and John had not wanted to talk to Mitchell. The President then called Haldeman into the meeting. (HJCT 107)

After Haldeman had entered the room, the President instructed him to call Mitchell to Washington to discuss with Haldeman, Ehrlichman and Dean ways of avoiding criminal liability for members of the White House staff. The President was concerned because, as he said, "Bob, let's face it, too many people know." (HJCT 109)

The President directed that Colson be kept out of the strategy meeting. "Colson must be damn sure I don't know anything," the President said. Then he added, in the face of all that Dean had just told him, "and I don't." (HJCT 110) The President's denial of knowledge which the transcript of the conversation itself establishes that he already possessed occurs repeatedly in the transcript of March 21, 1973:

DEAN. Well, I know he [Colson] used, uh,
PRESIDENT. Hunt to go out there?
DEAN. Hunt.
PRESIDENT. I knew about that.
DEAN. Yeah.
PRESIDENT. I did know about it. Uh, I knew that there was, there was something going on there,
DEAN. Right.
PRESIDENT. but I didn't know it was Hunt. (HJCT 100-01)

At the very beginning of Dean's account, on March 21, 1973, of what he knew of the Watergate break-in and cover-up, when Dean said, "I have the impression that you don't know everything I know," the President interrupted him with the words, "That's right." If the President did not already know what Dean was about to tell him, the reply is inexplicable.

There was a discussion of a new grand jury. The President said a grand jury would give a reason not to have to go before the Senate Select Committee (SSC) and it would look like the President was cooperating. Dean said the problem was that there was no control. (HJCT 120-24) At the end of the conversation, the President said it was necessary to have a new plan.[1]

As the President continued to discuss alternatives out of an impossible situation, the President directed Haldeman to have Mitchell come to the White House by the next day. Haldeman said the erosion was now going to the President, and "that is the thing we've got to turn off, at whatever the cost. We've got to figure out where to turn it off at the lowest cost we can, but at whatever costs it takes." (HPCT 130)

On the afternoon of March 21, 1973, the President again met with Haldeman, Ehrlichman and Dean to continue to discuss Watergate strategy. When the President again suggested the option of various

---

[1] The President's March 21 dictabelt conclusively shows that the President was not concerned with getting out the facts or that he had any doubts about what the true facts were. (There is a 59 second gap at the end of the President's dictation before he starts on another subject.)

witnesses going before the grand jury without immunity, Ehrlichman replied that such a course of action could lead to very drastic results, ". . . there are awful opportunities for indictment, and, uh So, uh, . . . you end up with people in and out of the White House indicted for various, for various offenses." (HJCT 131–32)

On the following day, March 22, 1973,[2] Mitchell came to Washington. The President, Mitchell, Haldeman, Ehrlichman and Dean met and discussed how to avoid criminal liability, how "to protect our people if we can." The President decided on a strategy of continued concealment which Ehrlichman called a "modified limited hang out." (HJCT 179) The President told Mitchell:

PRESIDENT. Then he can go over there as soon [unintelligible] this. But, uh, the, uh, the one thing I don't want to do is to—Now let me make this clear. I, I, I thought it was, uh, very, uh, very cruel thing as it turned out—although at the time I had to tell [unintelligible]—what happened to Adams. I don't want it to happen with Watergate—the Watergate matter. I think he made a, made a mistake, but he shouldn't have been sacked, he shouldn't have been—And, uh, for that reason, I am perfectly willing to—I don't give a shit what happens. I want you all to stonewall it, let them plead the Fifth Amendment, cover-up or anything else, if it'll save it—save the plan. That's the whole point. On the other hand, uh, uh, I would prefer, as I said to you, that you do it the other way. And I would particularly prefer to do it that other way if it's going to come out that way anyway. And that my view, that, uh, with the number of jackass people that they've got that they can call, they're going to—The story they get out through leaks, charges, and so forth, and innuendos, will be a hell of a lot worse than the story they're going to get out by just letting it out there.
MITCHELL. Well——
PRESIDENT. I don't know. But that's, uh, you know, up to this point, the whole theory has been containment, as you know, John.
MITCHELL. Yeah.
PRESIDENT. And now, now we're shifting. As far as I'm concerned, actually from a personal standpoint, if you weren't making a personal sacrifice—it's unfair—Haldeman and Dean. That's what Eisenhower—that's all he cared about. He only cared about—Christ, "Be sure he was clean." Both in the fund thing and the Adams thing. But I don't look at it that way. And I just—That's the thing I am really concerned with. We're going to protect our people, if we can.[3] (HJCT 183)

In the course of that meeting the President telephoned Attorney General Kleindienst. (HJCT 153–54) He called not to give the Attorney General the information he had received as to the potential criminal liability of his associates, but to instruct Kleindienst to contact Senator Howard Baker, the ranking minority member of the SSC.[4] He asked Kleindienst to be "our Baker handholder," to "baby-sit him, starting in like, like in about ten minutes." (HJCT 154)

II

SUBSTANCE OF THE NEW PLAN

During the rest of March and throughout April the President assumed active command of the cover-up. He, himself, acted time and

---
[2] On May 30, 1974, the House Judiciary Committee subpoenaed the tape recording and other materials related to a conversation between the President and Haldeman from 9:00 to 10:35 a.m., March 22, 1973. The President refused to produce this recording. The President submitted a two and one-half page edited transcript.
[3] This entire passage does not appear in the White House transcript.
[4] The President also spoke to Kleindienst on March 23 and March 25, 1973. There is no evidence that the President made disclosure to the Attorney General during the course of those conversations.

time again to protect his principal assistants who were the subjects of criminal and congressional Watergate investigations. On March 26, 1973, Watergate Grand Jury proceedings were reopened. (Book IV, 336) In April Magruder and Dean began talking to the prosecutors. During the same period, other political associates and White House subordinates were called before the SSC. The President realized that some disclosures were unavoidable but he tried to monitor, control and distribute information so that these investigations would not result in criminal liability for Haldeman and Ehrlichman, or others members of his personal staff.

III

McCord Letter

On March 23, 1973, Judge Sirica read in open court a letter written by James McCord. The letter charged that political pressures to plead guilty and remain silent had been applied to the defendants in the Watergate trial; that perjury had occurred during the trials and that others involved in the Watergate operation were not identified by those testifying. (Book IV, 221–25) On the afternoon of March 23, 1973, the President telephoned Acting FBI Director Gray (Book IV, 242) and told him that he knew the beating Gray was taking during his confirmation hearings and he believed it to be unfair. He reminded Gray that he had told him to conduct a "thorough and aggressive investigation." (Book IV, 245) He did not tell Gray any of the facts that he knew about the responsibility for the Watergate burglary and its subsequent cover-up nor did he tell his FBI Director what Dean had told him on March 21, 1973.

On the morning of March 26, 1973, the *Los Angeles Times* published a story that McCord had told investigators for the Senate Select Committee that Dean and Magruder had prior knowledge of the Watergate break-in. (Book IV, 313) On this morning Haldeman called Dean and asked him his reaction to an announcement that the President was requesting that Dean appear before the Grand Jury without immunity. Dean replied that he would have no problem appearing before the Grand Jury but told Haldeman that his testimony regarding the Liddy Plan meetings would conflict with Magruder's and that there were other areas of concern, including payments to the defendants, the $350,000 White House fund, the Hunt threat, and Colson's talk about helping Hunt. (Book IV, 317–18) Following this telephone call, the President met with Haldeman. The President then decided to drop his plan to announce that Dean would appear before the Grand Jury. (Book IV, 315, 318) Later that day, Ronald Ziegler, at the instruction of the President, announced publicly that the President had "absolute and total confidence in Dean." (Book IV, 325)

On March 27, 1973, the day after the Watergate Grand Jury was reconvened, the President met for two hours with Haldeman, Ehrlichman, and Ziegler.[5] The President directed Ehrlichman to tell Kleindienst that no White House personnel had prior knowledge of the

---

[5] On April 11, 1974, the House Judiciary Committee subpoenaed the tape recording and other materials related to this conversation. The President refused to produce this recording. The President submitted an edited transcript.

break-in, but that a serious question had been raised about Mitchell. He also devised a scheme for Ehrlichman to request that Kleindienst pass on to Ehrlichman information from the Grand Jury, not on the basis of a request from the White House, but on the basis of an obligation Kleindienst owed to Mitchell:

E   I will see Kleindienst. That settled——
P   You'll see Kleindienst? When?
E   This afternoon at three o'clock.
P   Three o'clock, and then I think, when—huh?
H   Should I also see Kleindienst? Should I, or should John be the only one?
P   John, you do it.
H   That's what Mitchell was asking. Mitchell is very distressed that Kleindienst isn't stepping up to his job as the contact with the Committee, getting Baker programmed and all that (A), and (B) that he isn't getting—see Dean, Dean got turned off by the Grand Jury. Dean is not getting the information from Silbert on those things said at the Grand Jury. And Mitchell finds that absolutely incompetent and says it is Kleindienst's responsibility. He is supposed to be sending us——
P   Ask Kleindienst, John, put it on the basis that you're not asking nor in effect is the White House asking; that John Mitchell says you've got to have this information from the Grand Jury at this time and you owe it to him. Put it right on that basis, now, so that everybody can't then say the White House raised hell about this, because we are not raising hell. Kleindienst shouldn't— where are you going to see him there or here?
E   In my office
P   Have a session with him about how much you want to tell him about everything.
E   Ah——
P   I think you've got to say, "Look, Dick, let me tell you, Dean was not involved—had no prior knowledge—Haldeman had no prior knowledge: you Ehrlichman, had none; and Colson had none. Now unless—all the papers writing about the President's men and if you have any information to the contrary you want to know. You've got to know it but you've go to say too that there is serious question here being raised about Mitchell. Right? That's about it isn't it? (WHT 366–67)

Later in the meeting, the President said that Kleindienst was worried about furnishing "Grand Jury things" to the White House (WHT 370–71) and that Ehrlichman should tell Kleindienst that the President wanted Grand Jury information to determine whether any White House people were involved: "Not to protect anybody, but to find out what the hell they are saying." (WHT 371) The President then suggested that Ehrlichman request a daily flow of information: "What have you today? Get every day so that we can move one step ahead here. We want to move." (WHT 371)

Ehrlichman telephoned Kleindienst the next day. He relayed the President's message that White House staff members had no prior knowledge of the break-in, but that serious questions were being raised with regard to Mitchell. (Book IV, 413–15) Ehrlichman told Kleindienst that the President wanted to know any evidence or inference from evidence about Mitchell's involvement. (Book IV, 414) When Ehrlichman passed on to Kleindienst what he termed the "best information that the President had, and has. . . ." (Book IV, 413) He did not disclose the information that the President had received on March 21 from Dean; he had clearly not been instructed by the President to do so. (Book IV, 409–21; WHT 366–67) In fact, the clear implication of the President's instruction was to deny any White House involvement in the Watergate matter.

IV

INSTRUCTIONS TO EHRLICHMAN REGARDING DEAN'S ROLE

Late in the afternoon on April 14, 1973 Ehrlichman reported to the President on the substance of Magruder's interview that day with the prosecutors.[6] That evening the President discussed with Haldeman and Ehrlichman how to prepare Strachan and Colson for their appearances before the Grand Jury (See Deception and Concealment, pp. 93–96.)

During a telephone conservation with Ehrlichman on the night of April 14, 1973, the President told Ehrlichman to attempt to persuade Dean, who the President knew was talking with the prosecutors, to continue to play an active role in the formulation of White House strategy regarding Watergate. The President directed Ehrlichman to approach Dean in the following manner:

> Well, you start with the proposition, Dean, the President thinks you have carried a tremedous load, and his affection and loyalty to you is just undiminished. . . . And now, let's see where the hell we go. . . . We can't get the President involved in this. His people, that is one thing. We don't want to cover up, but there are ways. And then he's got to say, for example? You start with him certainly on the business of obstruction of justice. . . . Look, John—we need a plan here. And so that LaRue, Mardian, and the others—I mean, (WHT 667)

Ehrlichman said that he was not sure that he could go that far with Dean, but the President responded, "No. He can make the plan up." Ehrlichman indicated that he would "sound it out." (WHT 667)

V

APRIL 15, 1973 MEETINGS WITH KLEINDIENST AND PETERSEN

From approximately 1:00 to 5:00 a.m. on the morning of April 15, 1973, the Watergate prosecutors met with Attorney General Kleindienst to apprise him of the new information they had received from Dean and Magruder. Later that day, the Attorney General met with the President in the President's EOB office from 1:12 to 2:22 p.m. (Book IV, 931) Kleindienst reported to the President on the evidence then in the possession of the prosecutors against Mitchell, Dean, Haldeman, Ehrlichman, Magruder, Colson and others. (WHT 696–746) Kleindienst has testified that the President appeared dumbfounded and upset when he was told that Administration officials were implicated in the Watergate matter. (Book IV, 926) The President did not tell Kleindienst that he had previously received this information from John Dean. (Book IV, 928)

The President asked about the evidence against Haldeman and Ehrlichman and took notes on Kleindienst's reply. (WHT 720–23; Book IV, 929) The President's notes on Kleindienst's reply included the following:

E (Conditional Statements)
Dean—
Deep Six documents

---

[6] On April 11, 1974, the House Judiciary Committee subpoenaed the tape recording and other materials related to this conversation. The President stated that the conversation was not recorded.

```
Get Hunt out of country
Haldeman—
Strachan—
will give testimony—H had papers indicating Liddy was in eavesdropping.
$350,000—to LaRue.
```

*   *   *   *   *   *   *

```
What will LaRue say he got the 350 for?
Gray—documents (Book IV, 929)
```

The President and his Attorney General also discussed payments to the defendants and the motive necessary to establish criminal liability. Kleindienst explained in detail to the President that the payment of money to witnesses or defendants for the purpose of keeping them silent was an obstruction of justice. (WHT 704–08)

Later that day, from 4:00 to 5:00 p.m., Petersen and Kleindienst met with the President in the President's EOB office.[7] (Book IV, 976) Petersen reported on the information the prosecutors had received from Dean and Magruder. (Book IV, 979–80) His report included: information respecting Mitchell's approval of the $300,000 budget for the Liddy "Gemstone" operation; the receipt by Strachan of budget information for "Gemstone" and summaries of intercepted conversations for delivery to Haldeman (Book IV, 993); the prosecutors' belief that if they could develop Strachan as a witness, "school was going to be out as far as Haldeman was concerned" (Book IV, 982); Ehrlichman's instructions, through Dean, that Hunt should leave the country; Ehrlichman's direction to Dean to "deep six" certain materials recovered from Hunt's EOB office (Book IV, 992); and Dean's delivery of certain politically embarrassing material from Hunt's EOB office to Acting FBI Director Gray personally. (Petersen testimony, 3 HJC 82)

Petersen recommended that Haldeman and Ehrlichman be relieved of their responsibilities and that the President request their resignations. (Petersen testimony, 3 HJC 82) The President demurred. The President did not disclose to Petersen the factual information that Dean had discussed with the President on March 21, 1973. (Petersen testimony, 3 HJC 103, 153) He did not tell Petersen that Dean had confessed to obstructing justice and had charged Haldeman and Ehrlichman with complicity in that crime.

On April 15, 1973, after receiving Petersen's report, the President met twice with Haldeman and Ehrlichman in his EOB office that evening.[8] (Book IV, 1062) At the second meeting, the President discussed with Haldeman and Ehrlichman information he had received from the Attorney General and Assistant Attorney General Petersen that afternoon. Ehrlichman testified that during their meeting the President requested that he telephone Patrick Gray and discuss with him the issue of documents taken from Hunt's White House safe and given by Dean to Gray in Ehrlichman's presence in June 1972. During

---

[7] On April 11, 1974, the House Judiciary Committee subpoenaed the tape recording and other materials related to this conversation. The President stated that the conversation was not recorded.

[8] On April 11, 1974, the House Judiciary Committee subpoenaed the tape recording and other materials related to these conversations. The President stated that these conversations were not recorded.

the course of this meeting, Ehrlichman did so. (Book IV, 1063–64, 1078)

VI
April 16, 1973, Meeting With Petersen

On April 16, 1973, from 1:39 to 3:25 p.m., the President met with Henry Petersen. (Book IV, 1230)[9] The President promised to treat as confidential any information disclosed to him by Petersen. The President emphasized that ". . . you're talking only to me . . . and there's not going to be anybody else on the White House staff. In other words, I am acting counsel and everything else." The President suggested that the only exception might be Dick Moore. (WHT 847) When Petersen expressed some reservation about information being disclosed to Moore, (WHT 847–48) the President said, ". . . let's just . . . better keep it with me then." (WHT 849)

At this meeting Petersen supplied the President with a memorandum the President had requested on the previous day summarizing the existing evidence that implicated Haldeman, Ehrlichman and Strachan. The memorandum indicated that the prosecutors had information (1) that Ehrlichman had told Dean to "deep six" certain materials and had issued an instruction that Liddy tell Hunt to leave the country; (2) that Strachan had received Gemstone information and summaries of intercepted conversations for delivery to Haldeman and that Haldeman had failed to issue instructions to discontinue the surveillance program; (3) that Strachan had refused to answer questions about the allegations involving Haldeman. (Book IV, 1225–26) Petersen also informed the President about the Grand Jury's not believing Magruder's testimony in the summer of 1972 (WHT 869–70); Gray's denial that he had received documents from Hunt's safe; the implication of Ehrlichman by his "deep six" statement (WHT 862); the limited nature and scope of Strachan's prior Grand Jury testimony (WHT 867); and Ehrlichman's request to the CIA for assistance to Hunt. (WHT 883–84)

Early in the meeting, the President described to Petersen what actions he had taken almost a month earlier on the Watergate matter. His account followed the "scenario" Ehrlichman had suggested that morning. (See Deception and Concealment, p. 86–87.)

—a month ago I got Dean in and said (inaudible) a report (inaudible) Camp David and write a report. The report was not frankly accurate. Well it was accurate but it was not full. And he tells me the reason it wasn't full, was that he didn't know. Whether that is true or not I don't know. Although it wasn't I'm told. But I am satisfied with it and I think I've read enough in the (inaudible) (inaudible) papers up here. So then I put Ehrlichman to work on it. (WHT 860)

What the President told Petersen was not true. The President did not tell Petersen that one reason Dean did not complete a full report was that his assignment was to write a misleading report—one that

---
[9] On April 11, 1974, the House Judiciary Committee subpoenaed the tape recording and other materials related to this conversation. The President refused to produce this recording. The President submitted an edited transcript.

would minimize the involvement of White House personnel in the Watergate matter. (See Deception and Concealment, p. 83–84.)

Later in this meeting on April 16, the President and Petersen discussed the possibility that if Strachan's and Dean's testimony established that Haldeman was informed of the Liddy Plan after the second planning meeting, Haldeman might be considered responsible for the break-in for his alleged failure to issue an order to stop the surveillance operation. (WHT 920–21) When Petersen told the President that the question of Haldeman's liability depended on who had authority to act with respect to budget proposals for the Liddy Plan (WHT 921), the President said:

    P   Haldeman (inaudible)
    HP He did not have any authority?
    P   No, sir . . . none, none—all Mitchell—campaign funds. He had no authority whatever. I wouldn't let him (inaudible). (WHT 922)

What the President said was at least misleading. The White House Political Matters Memoranda establish that Haldeman did possess and exercise authority over the use of campaign funds. (Political Matters Memoranda, 10/7/71, Book VII, 1359–61; 2/1/72, Book I, 78–79; 2/16/72, Book VI, 908–09; 5/16/72, 1–2; 9/18/72, 1, and attachment.)

At the opening of a meeting with Ehrlichman and Ziegler that began two minutes after Petersen's departure,[10] (Book IV, 1254) the President informed Ehrlichman that Petersen had told him that Gray had denied personally receiving documents from Hunt's safe. The President and Ehrlichman then discussed Ehrlichman's recollections of the facts related to this incident. (WHT 929–30) The President told Ehrlichman that he had discussed with Petersen the June 19, 1972 incidents in which Ehrlichman was alleged to have issued instructions to Hunt to leave the country and to Dean to "deep six" certain materials. (WHT 935) The President next reported to Ehrlichman that Petersen had told him that Magruder had not yet gotten a deal; and that Dean and his lawyers were threatening to try the Administration and the President if Dean did not get immunity. (WHT 938) The President relayed to Ehrlichman Petersen's views about Haldeman's vulnerability with respect to criminal liability. (WHT 938–41)

On the following day, Ehrlichman took steps to gather information about the events Dean had been discussing with the prosecutors. He telephoned Ken Clawson and questioned him about the events of the meeting on June 19, 1972 (Book IV, 1321–22); Clawson responded that "If you want me to be forthwith and straightforward with you, I'll recollect anything that you want." Ehrlichman then recited Dean's allegations. (Book IV, 1322) Clawson told Ehrlichman that he did not recall the deep six instruction or the instruction for Hunt to leave the country. (Book IV, 1322–23)

On the same day, Ehrlichman telephoned Colson. He relayed to him the information that Dean had not been given immunity; that the "grapevine" had it that Colson would be summoned to the Grand Jury that day and would be asked about the meeting of June 19, 1972. (Book IV, 1326–29) Ehrlichman then gave Colson Dean's version of

---

[10] On April 11, 1974, the House Judiciary Committee subpoenaed the tape recording and other materials related to this conversation. The President refused to produce this recording. The President submitted an edited transcript.

the events of that day. Colson said that he would deny Dean's allegation. (Book IV, 1327–29) Later in the call, Colson told Ehrlichman that, "There are a couple of things that you and I need to do to protect each other's flank here. . . . But—Listen, we'll talk about that." Ehrlichman responded, "All right . . . fair enough." (Book IV, 1329–30) As the call ended, Colson also made it clear that he felt they should act against Dean: "Let's get it, uh, clearly understood that that son-of-a-bitch doesn't get immunity. I want to nail him." Ehrlichman responded that he was doing his best, to which Colson added, "No. I want to nail him. I'll take immunity first." (Book IV, 1330)

VII

April 16, 1973, Telephone Conversation With Petersen

On April 16, 1973 from 8:58 to 9:14 p.m. the President spoke by telephone with Petersen.[11] (Book IV, 1306) He asked Petersen if there were any developments he "should know about," and he reassured Petersen that ". . . of course, as you know, anything you tell me, as I think I told you earlier, will not be passed on . . . [b]ecause I know the rules of the Grand Jury." (WHT 966) Petersen told the President that Fred LaRue had confessed to the prosecutors to participating in the crime of obstruction of justice; that he had attended a third planning meeting regarding the Liddy Plan with Mitchell (WHT 967); and that LaRue had told Mitchell it was all over. (WHT 968) Petersen described LaRue as "rather pitiful." (WHT 966)

Petersen then reported additional details regarding Ehrlichman's involvement: that Liddy had admitted to Dean on June 19, 1972 that he had been present at the Watergate break-in and Dean had then reported to Ehrlichman (WHT 968); and that Colson and Dean were together with Ehrlichman when Ehrlichman advised Hunt to get out of town. (WHT 969)

With respect to payments to the Watergate defendants, Petersen reported that he had been informed that Mitchell had requested that Dean approach Kalmbach to raise funds, and Dean had contacted Haldeman and Haldeman had authorized the use of Kalmbach. (WHT 969, 975–76) Petersen told the President that Kalmbach would be called before the Grand Jury regarding the details of the fund-raising operation. (WHT 969) They also discussed the prosecutors' interest in the details of the transfer from Haldeman to LaRue of the $350,000 White House fund that was used for payments to the defendants. (WHT 976)

On the following morning, April 17, 1973, the President met with Haldeman.[12] (Book IV, 1312) Early in the meeting, the President passed on the disclosures Dean had made to the prosecutors regarding Dean's meeting with Liddy on June 19, 1972. (WHT 982) The President also told Haldeman that the money issue was critical: "Another

---

[11] On April 11, 1974, the House Judiciary Committee subpoenaed the tape recording and other materials related to this conversation. The President refused to produce this recording. The President submitted an edited transcript.

[12] On April 11, 1974, the House Judiciary Committee subpoenaed the tape recording and other materials related to this conversation. The President refused to produce this recording. He submitted an edited transcript. The President did not interpose such a claim with respect to this portion of the conversation.

thing, if you could get John and yourself to sit down and do some hard thinking about what kind of strategy you are going to have with the money. You know what I mean." This comment is followed by a deletion of "material unrelated to President's action." [13] (WHT 983) Following the deletion, the transcript shows that the President instructed Haldeman to call Kalmbach to find out what Kalmbach was going to say Dean had told him regarding the purpose of the fund-raising. In addition, the President instructed Haldeman:

> Well, be sure that Kalmbach is at least aware of this, that LaRue has talked very freely. He is a broken man. (WHT 983)[14]

At 12:35 p.m. on April 17, 1973,[15] the President met with Haldeman, Ehrlichman and Ziegler. (Book IV, 1347) At this meeting, he again relayed information relating to the Watergate investigation. The President and Haldeman discussed Petersen's opinion, that while the prosecutors had a case on Ehrlichman, the Grand Jury testimony of Strachan and Kalmbach would be crucial to proof of Haldeman's criminal liability. The President returned to the problem presented by the funds paid to the defendants—the issue which Petersen had informed him was then being explored by the Grand Jury. The President encouraged Haldeman and Ehrlichman to deal with the problem: "Have you given any thought to what the line ought to be—I don't mean a lie—but a line, on raising the money for these defendants?" (WHT 994) He advised Haldeman that, "you see, you can't go in there and say I didn't know what in the hell he wanted the $250 for." (WHT 995)

Later in the meeting, the President discussed with Haldeman and Ehrlichman the man Petersen had identified as critical to the issue of Haldeman's liability, Gordon Strachan. The President said, "Strachan has got to be worked out," (WHT 1011-12) and then proceeded to discuss with Haldeman the facts about which Strachan could testify. At this point, the President told Haldeman that Petersen believed that Strachan had received material clearly identifiable as telephone tap information. (WHT 1012) After a brief discussion of the issue, the President closed this discussion by saying, ". . . I want you to know what he's [Petersen] told me." (WHT 1013)

VIII

April 17, 1973, Meeting With Petersen

Shortly after his meeting with Haldeman, Ehrlichman and Ziegler, the President met with Petersen from 2:46 to 3:49 p.m.[16] (Book IV,

---

[13] In response to the Supreme Court decision in *United States* v. *Nixon*, the President produced in the District Court for examination by Judge Sirica a tape recording of this conversation. The decision permitted the President to interpose claims of privilege with respect to parts of the conversation not related to Watergate, but the President made no such claim with respect to this portion of the conversation.
[14] When the President was told at a later meeting on April 17 that Dean had told Ehrlichman that he had revealed to Kalmbach the purpose of the payments, he suggested that Ehrlichman could falsely state that Dean had told Ehrlichman he did not tell Kalmbach the purpose of the payments. (WHT 1201)
[15] On April 11, 1974, the House Judiciary Committee subpoenaed the tape recording and other materials related to this conversation. The President refused to produce this recording. He submitted an edited transcript.
[16] On April 11, 1974, the House Judiciary Committee subpoenaed the tape recording and other materials related to this conversation. The President refused to produce this recording. He submitted an edited transcript.

1397) The President opened the discussion by asking if there were anything new that he should know; he also cautioned Petersen that he did not want to be told anything out of the Grand Jury, unless Petersen thought the President needed to know it. (WHT 1060) Later in the meeting, they discussed the status of Haldeman and Ehrlichman if Magruder were indicted. Petersen suggested the government might name everybody but Haldeman and Ehrlichman as unindicted co-conspirators in order "to give you time and room to maneuver with respect to the two of them." (WHT 1088)

Petersen reported that LaRue had broken down and cried like a baby when testifying about John Mitchell (WHT 1095); that in all probability there was not enough evidence to implicate Strachan as a principal, that at this point he was a fringe character (WHT 1091–92); that the case against Ehrlichman and Colson was more tangential than that against Haldeman (WHT 1081); and that Hunt had testified in the Grand Jury that Liddy had told him that "his principals" (who remained unidentified) had said Hunt should leave the country. (WHT 1083) Petersen also reported that Gray had admitted that Dean had turned over documents from Hunt's safe in Ehrlichman's presence (WHT 1097–98); and that Magruder was naming Haldeman and Ehrlichman not by first-hand knowledge, but by hearsay. (WHT 1105–06)

One minute after the end of this meeting with Petersen, the President met again with Haldeman, Ehrlichman and Ziegler.[17] (Book IV, 1413) The President relayed the information that Petersen had talked to Gray and that Gray admitted receiving and destroying the Hunt files. (WHT 1116) The President then told Haldeman and Ehrlichman about his conversation with Petersen regarding the possibility of their being named as unindicted co-conspirators in an indictment of Magruder. The President detailed the nature of this discussion:

P Here's the situation, basically, (unintelligible) They're going to haul him [Magruder] in court, have him plead guilty, put a statement out because Sirica always questions the witnesses who plead guilty. They are going to make it as broad as they can and as narrow as they can at the same time. By being as broad as they can, they are going to say that he has named certain people and they are going to name a group of people that is nonindictable co-conspirators. They're going to include everybody on that list. I said, "Is Dean going to be on that list?" He said, "Yes." He said, "Frankly (unintelligible) not include Haldeman and Ehrlichman, which give you an option." I said, "Are you telling me that if Haldeman and Ehrlichman decide to take leave, that you will not then proceed with the prosecution." "No," he said, "I don't mean that." He said, "What I mean is that they are not going to appear on that list and that (unintelligible) Grand Jury and make case there (unintelligible). So there's the—
E Well, whether we take leave or not doesn't effect the list that they read off.
P Yes. Yes.
E Oh, it does? Yes, it does. They will put us on the list if we don't take leave?
P Yes, because otherwise, he says, he says Sirica is going to question Magruder and he's going to question (unintelligible) and it appears (unintelligible). If he does that, then it will appear that the Justice Department again is covering up. (WHT 1116–17)

Between April 17 and April 25, 1973, Petersen reported to the President that lie detector tests had been administered to Magruder and

---

[17] On April 11, 1974, the House Judiciary Committee subpoenaed the tape recording and other materials related to this conversation. The President refused to produce this recording. He submitted an edited transcript.

to Strachan. Strachan contradicted Magruder's testimony that Magruder had given Strachan the Liddy Plan budget and summaries of intercepted communications for delivery to Haldeman. Strachan failed his test; Magruder passed his; and Petersen advised the President of these facts. (Petersen testimony, 3 HJC 102) In spite of the fact that the President knew who was telling the truth, he did not help Assistant Attorney General Petersen form a judgment as to the credibility of Magruder or Strachan.

IX

IMMUNITY FOR DEAN

During the course of the Grand Jury investigation the President tried to persuade Petersen to refuse to grant immunity to Dean. On April 15, 1973, Petersen told the President that Dean was attempting to provide enough evidence to secure immunity from prosecution. (Petersen testimony, 3 HJC 82) The President was aware that Dean possessed information that could implicate Haldeman, Ehrlichman, Colson, and possibly the President himself in the Watergate matter. On April 14, Dean told Haldeman and Ehrlichman that the prosecutors had told his lawyers that they were targets of the Grand Jury and that in Dean's opinion they could be indicted on obstruction of justice charges. (Book IV, 699–701) On the same day, the President said to Haldeman and Ehrlichman that they should find out about Dean: ". . . To find out—let me put it this way. You've got to find out what the hell he is going to say. (unintelligible) which is frightening to me, (unintelligible)" (WHT 540)

Under the immunity statutes, the power to obtain a court order of immunity is given to United States Attorneys acting with the approval of the Attorney General, the Deputy Attorney General or designated Assistant Attorney General. (18 U.S.C. § 6003) The President does not have the power to grant immunity. Although the President issued no order to Petersen about immunity for Dean, the President discouraged its use. Without immunity, Dean was less likely to testify.

After Petersen told the President that Dean was seeking immunity, the President closely followed the status of Dean's negotiations with the prosecutors. At a meeting with Petersen on April 16, 1973, the President asked about the deal with Dean.

Petersen told the President that while there was no deal with Dean, Dean's counsel wanted one. Petersen said he was considering granting immunity to Dean if he could provide evidence that could be used to convict higher-ups. (WHT 885–90) The President was told that Dean's negotiation tactics could present an important threat not only to Haldeman and Ehrlichman, but also to the President. (WHT 925–26)

On April 17, 1973, the President discussed with Haldeman the threat that Dean's efforts to secure immunity presented: "Dean is trying to tell enough to get immunity and that is frankly what it is Bob." Haldeman responded, "That is the real problem we've got. . . ."[18]

---

[18] On April 11, 1974, the House Judiciary Committee subpoenaed the tape recording and other materials related to this conversation. The President refused to produce this recording. He submitted an edited transcript.

(WHT 986–87) At a meeting later in the day, Ehrlichman relayed to the President Colson's recommendation that denying immunity to Dean would discourage him from providing harmful information to the prosecution. Ehrlichman stated further that:

Colson argues that if he is not given immunity, then he has even more incentive to go light on his own malfactions and he will have to climb up and he will have to defend himself. (WHT 987–88)

Later in the meeting, the President acknowledged that "Petersen's the guy that can give immunity. . . ." and "Dean is the guy that he's got to use for the purpose of making the case." (WHT 993–94)

After discussing Colson's recommendation, the President, Haldeman and Ehrlichman considered the matters about which Dean might testify. They expressed concern that Dean could disclose facts relating to the Ellsberg break-in; "the ITT thing" (WHT 1029) ; and Dean's conversation with the President on March 21, 1973 regarding the payment to Hunt. (WHT 991, 1031–34) The meeting ended with the President deciding to get Petersen in to tell him that the President did not want anybody on the White House staff to be given immunity. (WHT 1051–52, 1056)

Later in the afternoon of April 17, 1973, the President met with Petersen. The President warned Petersen that any immunity grant to Dean would be interpreted as a "straight deal" (WHT 1078) on Petersen's part to conceal the fact that Petersen had provided Dean with Grand Jury information during the summer of 1972. The President stated that while he did not care whether Petersen immunized Strachan or other "second people" (WHT 1077), he did not want Petersen giving immunity to Dean. (WHT 1077–79) Near the end of the meeting, Petersen objected to the President's proposed public statement opposing grants of immunity to Administration officials, and reminded the President that he felt it was a terribly important tool for the prosecutors to have available. (WHT 1101–02)

Within an hour, the President issued a public announcement on Watergate, including the statement that the President felt that no individual holding a position of major importance in the Administration should be granted immunity. (Book IV, 1420) Two days later the President met with the attorneys for Haldeman and Ehrlichman. (Book IV, 1513, 1515) The President described Dean as a "loose cannon" and told them that he had put out his statement on immunity because the prosecutors were at that point hung up on the question of giving immunity to Dean. (WHT 1239–40)

On April 18, 1973, the President called Petersen.[19] (Book IV, 1471) Petersen has testified that the President "was rather angry" (Book IV, 1474) and chewed Petersen out for having granted immunity to Dean. (Petersen testimony, 3 HJC 98, 176) Petersen denied that Dean had been granted immunity and told the President he would check with the prosecutors and call the President back.[20] In this second call, Petersen assured the President that Dean had not been given immunity. When Petersen reported this denial, the President said he had a

---

[19] On April 11, 1974, the House Judiciary Committee subpoenaed the tape recording and other materials related to this conversation. The President refused to produce this recording. He submitted an edited transcript. Petersen has testified that the edited transcript is not fully accurate. (Petersen testimony, 3 HJC 176–78)

[20] On April 30, 1974, the House Judiciary Committee subpoenaed the tape recording and other materials related to this conversation. The President denied that the conversation was recorded.

tape to prove his contention. (Book IV, 1474–75; Peterson testimony, 3 HJC 97)

By the end of April, the prosecutors' negotiations with Dean for immunity were broken off, and Dean did not receive immunity from prosecution. (Petersen testimony, 3 HJC 117)

X

OTHER CONTACTS WITH PETERSEN PRIOR TO APRIL 27, 1973

From April 18, 1973 through April 30, 1973, the date of Haldeman's and Ehrlichman's resignations, the President continued his series of meetings and telephone calls with Petersen.[21] (Book IV, 1532–34) During a telephone conversation on the evening of April 18, 1973, Petersen informed the President that the Department of Justice had received information that Hunt and Liddy had broken into the offices of Daniel Ellsberg's psychiatrist.[22] The President told Petersen that [23] that was a national security matter and that Petersen should stay away from it. (Book VII, 1959–62; 1956–66) The President did not disclose to Petersen on March 17, 1973 that Dean had told him that Hunt and Liddy had broken into Dr. Fielding's office (WHT 157–58); that on March 21, 1973 Dean had told him that Ehrlichman had potential criminal liability for the conspiracy to burglarize the Fielding office (HJCT 105); or that on the afternoon of March 21, 1973 Ehrlichman had told him that the Fielding break-in was an illegal search and seizure that might be sufficient at least for a mistrial in the Ellsberg prosecution. (HJCT 139; Petersen testimony, 3 HJC 153)

At many of the meetings with Petersen during this period the President continued to seek information on the progress of the Watergate investigation and on the evidence that was being accumulated against Haldeman and Ehrlichman. (Book IV, 1535–41) During this period, the President also met frequently with Haldeman and Ehrlichman.[24] (Book IV, 1469–70, 1558; Meetings and Conversations between the President and John Ehrlichman, April 18–29, 1973)

The President knew by this time that Haldeman was a prime suspect of the Grand Jury investigation. On April 15, 1973, Petersen had recommended to the President that Haldeman be dismissed because of his alleged involvement in various Watergate-related matters (Petersen testimony, 3 HJC 82); from that date Petersen had kept the President informed about the evidence against Haldeman. On April 17, 1973, Petersen also told the President that the evidence on Haldeman, Ehrlichman and Colson indicated that Haldeman was the most directly involved.[25] (WHT 1080) By April 25, 1973, the President was aware

---

[21] On May 30 and June 24, 1974, the House Judiciary Committee subpoenaed the tape recording and other materials related to the April 19, 1973 conversation. The President refused to produce this recording.

[22] On April 11, 1974, the House Judiciary Committee subpoenaed the tape recording and other materials related to this conversation. The President responded that the conversation was not recorded.

[23] Petersen testified "that could have referred either to knowledge of the break-in or to knowledge of the report to the prosecutors." (Petersen testimony, 3 HJC 163)

[24] On May 30, 1974, the House Judiciary Committee subpoenaed the tape recording and other materials related to 19 such conversations. The President refused to produce these recordings. (Book IX, 1060–64)

[25] On April 11, 1974, the House Judiciary Committee subpoenaed the tape recording and other materials related to this conversation. The President refused to produce this recording. He submitted an edited transcript.

that the issue of the payments to the Watergate defendants and Haldeman's role in this and other matters were being investigated by the Grand Jury. (WHT 994–95)

On April 25, 1973, the President directed Haldeman to listen to the tape of the March 21 conversation with Dean. (Book IX, 108, 114) Dean had been speaking to the prosecutors during April; Haldeman in listening to the tapes would be able to prepare a strategy for meeting whatever disclosures Dean might make.

On April 25, 1973, pursuant to the President's direction, Haldeman requested and received twenty-two tapes of Presidential conversations during February, March and April 1973. (Book IX, 108, 114–15, 123) On the afternoon of April 25, 1973, Haldeman listened to the March 21, 1973 morning conversation. In listening to the recording of this meeting, Haldeman made twenty pages of detailed notes on its contents. (Book IX, 116) At 4:40 p.m. on April 25, 1973, Haldeman met with the President and reported to him on the contents of the tape. (Book IV, 1558, 1562) The President instructed Haldeman to listen to the March 21 tape again. (Book IX, 118, 126)

The meeting between the President and Haldeman on April 25, 1973 ended at 5:35 p.m. (Book IV, 1558) Two minutes later, at 5:37 p.m., Petersen entered and met with the President for more than an hour. (Book IV, 1618) The President did not inform Petersen of the taping system, the contents of the March 21, 1973 tape, or of the fact that Haldeman had been directed to listen to it and had done so that very day. (Petersen testimony, 3 HJC 102)

On April 26, 1973, Haldeman again received the group of tapes, including the March 21 tape. (Book IV, 1560, 1563) He listened again to the March 21 tape and reported to the President. (Book IX, 119–21) On April 26, 1973, Haldeman and the President met for more than five hours.[26] (Book IX, 126) Haldeman's review and his meeting with the President also were not reported to Petersen.

XI

April 27, 1973, Meetings With Petersen

On April 27, 1973, the President met twice with Petersen. (Book IV, 1633) They discussed the Grand Jury investigation and the President's concern about rumors that Dean was implicating the President in the Watergate matter. (WHT 1257–93) Petersen assured the President that he had told the prosecutors that they had no mandate to investigate the President. (WHT 1259) In this context, and one day after discussing with Haldeman the contents of the March 21 tape, the President made the following statement to Petersen about his conversation with Dean about the payment to Hunt:

> . . . let me tell you the only conversations we ever had with him, was that famous March 21st conversation I told you about, where he told me about Bittman coming to him. No, the Bittman request for $120,000 for Hunt. And I then finally began to get at them. I explored with him thoroughly, "Now what the hell is this for?" He said, "It's because he's blackmailing Ehrlichman."

---

[26] On May 30, 1974, the House Judiciary Committee subpoenaed the tape recordings and other materials related to the conversations of April 25, 1973 and April 26, 1973. The President refused to produce these recordings. (Book IX, 1036, 1060–64)

Remember I said that's what it's about. And Hunt is going to recall the seamy side of it. And I asked him, "Well how would you get it? How would you get it to them?" so forth. But my purpose was to find out what the hell had been going on before. And believe me, nothing was approved. I mean as far as I'm concerned—as far as I'm concerned turned it off totally. (WHT 1259)

At his second meeting with Petersen on April 27, 1973, the President provided Petersen with another version of the events occurring on March 21 and March 22, 1973:

Dean. You will get Dean in there. Suppose he starts trying to impeach the President, the words of the President of the United States and says, "Well, I have information to the effect that I once discussed with the President the question of how the possibility, of the problem," of this damn Bittman stuff I spoke to you about last time. Henry, it won't stand up for five minutes because, nothing was done, and fortunately I had Haldeman at that conversation and he was there and I said, "Look, I tried to give you this, this, this, this, and this." And I said, "When you finally get it out, it won't work. Because, I said, "First, you can't get clemency to Hunt." I mean, I was trying to get it out. To try to see what that Dean had been doing. I said, "First you can't give him clemency." Somebody has thrown out something to the effect that Dean reported that Hunt had an idea that he was going to get clemency around Christmas. I said, "Are you kidding? You can't get clemency for Hunt. You couldn't even think about it until, you know, '75 or something like that." Which you could, then because of the fact, that you could get to the—ah—But nevertheless, I said you couldn't give clemency. I said, "The second point to remember is 'How are you going to get the money for them?' If you could do it, I mean you are talking about a million dollars." I asked him—well, I gave him several ways. I said, "You couldn't put it through a Cuban Committee could you?" I asked him, because to me he was sounding so damned ridiculous. I said, "Well under the circumstances," I said, "There isn't a damn thing we can do." I said, "It looks to me like the problem is John Mitchell." Mitchell came down the next day and we talked about executive privilege. Nothing else. Now, that's the total story. And—so Dean—I just want you to be sure that if Dean ever raises the thing, you've got the whole thing. You've got that whole thing. Now kick him straight —." (WHT 1278-79)

XII

Conclusion

After March 21, 1973, the President acted to avoid the indictment of Haldeman, Ehrlichman and others at the White House by concealing what he knew about their involvement in Watergate and the cover-up, by personally misleading Attorney General Kleindienst and Assistant Attorney General Petersen, by personally obtaining information from Petersen in order to convey that information to subjects of investigation, by personally planning false and misleading explanations for Haldeman and Ehrlichman, by personally urging Petersen not to grant immunity to Dean in order to make it more difficult for the Department of Justice to build a case against Haldeman and Ehrlichman, by personally directing the coaching of witnesses corruptly using information in preparing a defense strategy, and by personally instructing witnesses to give untrue testimony.

THE PRESIDENT'S INTERFERENCE WITH THE SENATE SELECT COMMITTEE ON PRESIDENTIAL CAMPAIGN ACTIVITIES

I

INTRODUCTION

The President's strategy in March and April, 1973, was not only directed at blocking the investigation by the Department of Justice, but also at narrowing and thwarting the hearings of the Senate Select Committee on Presidential Campaign Activities (SSC).

II

POLICY TOWARD SSC PRIOR TO MARCH 21, 1973

On February 7, 1973, the SSC was established by unanimous vote of the Senate to investigate 1972 Presidential campaign fundraising practices, the Watergate break-in and the concealment of evidence relating to the break-in. (Book III, 522-25).

On February 10 and 11, 1973, Haldeman, Ehrlichman, Dean and Special Counsel to the President Richard Moore met at La Costa, California to discuss strategy to deal with the proposed SSC hearings. The President wanted to know what strategy should be adopted on executive privilege and other similar matters. The meetings lasted between 8 and 14 hours. (Book III, 536) The President decided that CRP rather than the White House would take primary responsibility for the defense on Watergate-related matters and that John Mitchell should be asked to coordinate activities. (Book III, 546) They discussed possible dilatory tactics with respect to the SSC hearings, such as monetary assistance to the attorneys for the Watergate defendants in seeking judicial delay of the hearings. They agreed Moore would go to New York to speak to Mitchell about the group's discussions and Mitchell's role in preparing for the hearings. (Book III, 539-40)

On February 28, 1973, the Senate Judiciary Committee opened its hearings on the nomination of L. Patrick Gray to be FBI Director. The Gray hearings focused on the initial FBI investigation of Watergate and especially upon the actions of Gray and Dean. During the hearings, committee members discussed Dean's being called to explain his receipt and use of FBI files during the investigation.

Prior to February 27, 1973, and again in the first week of March, Dean explained to Ehrlichman that the President would not be able to assert executive privilege with respect to Dean because Dean had so little personal contact with him. (Book III, 598-604, 610-11) On February 27, the President met with Dean and directed him to assume responsibility for Watergate-related matters. (Book III, 600, 608) On February 28, 1973, the President instructed Dean that his staff would not testify before the SSC or the Senate Judiciary Committee, but would answer written interrogatories. The President directed Dean to tell Attorney General Kleindienst, who was to meet with Senator Ervin, about the President's policy as to executive privilege. The President said ". . . our position is written interrogatories, which they will never probably accept, but it may give us a position, I mean it'd be reasonable in the public mind." (HJCT 20) The President told Dean to tell Attorney General Kleindienst, "you keep it at your level; don't say the President told you to say. . . . [T]his is the position, Dick, you should take." (HJCT 26)

In a March 2, 1973 news conference the President stated that Dean's investigation showed that no member of the White House staff had knowledge of or was involved in Watergate. (Book III, 745) The President asserted executive privilege for Dean and said that he would not allow Dean to testify before any congressional committee. When asked if he would change that position in light of allegations of illegality and impropriety against Dean, the President said he would answer that question when the issue arose. The President also promised to provide a statement on executive privilege. (Book III, 746)

The President and Dean met nineteen times in March, at the President's request; they had not met at all in the months from December, 1972 to February 27, 1973, had never before met alone, and had been together on only nine occasions since January, 1972. (Book III, 969–75)

On March 6 and 7 the President and Dean discussed executive privilege guidelines that would cover former as well as present White House personnel. (Book III, 756, 761) On March 10 the President told Dean the statement on executive privilege should be released before Dean was called as a witness by the Senate Judiciary Committee so that it would not appear to be issued in response to the Gray hearings. (Book III, 786–87, 791)

On March 12, 1973, the President issued his policy statement on executive privilege. The statement said that executive privilege would not be used to prevent disclosure of embarassing information and would be invoked only in "the most compelling circumstances where disclosure would harm the public interest . . . ." (Book III, 796)

On March 13, 1973, the President, Haldeman and Dean discussed listing Colson and Chapin, both of whom had left the White House, as private "consultants" to the President so that they could continue to claim executive privilege with respect to the future communications with the White House regarding Watergate:

HALDEMAN. Say, did you raise the question with the President on, on, uh, Colson as a consultant?
DEAN. No, I didn't.
HALDEMAN. Was that somebody [unintelligible]?
DEAN. It was—the thought was—
PRESIDENT. [Unintelligible]
DEAN. well [unintelligible] it's a consultant without doing any consulting— Yeah.
HALDEMAN. He wanted it [unintelligible]
DEAN. He wants it for continued protection on, uh—
HALDEMAN. Solely for the purpose of, of executive privilege protection. So that—
DEAN. One of those things that's kept down in the personnel office, and nothing's done on it.
PRESIDENT. What happens to Chapin?
DEAN. Well, Chapin doesn't have quite the same problems appearing that Colson will.

HALDEMAN. Yeah but—you have the same, you, you have the same problems as Chapin appearing versus Colson.

PRESIDENT. Well, can't—That would be such an obvious fraud to have both of them as consultants, that that won't work. I think he's right. Uh, you'd have to leave Chapin—

HALDEMAN. Well, you can't make Chapin a consultant, I—we've already said he's not.

PRESIDENT. Yeah.

DEAN. Yeah. (HJCT 47)[1]

Haldeman suggested that the consulting agreement be back dated to the previous Saturday, so that Colson's relationship with the President would be continuous. (HJCT 48)

On March 13, 1973, during his meeting with the President, Dean discussed his role in the cover-up (HJCT 50–51); the perjury of Strachan, Magruder, and Porter (HJCT 67, 71); Segretti's activities and their supervision by Chapin (HJCT 50, 74–75); Colson's relationship with Hunt (HJCT 70–71); and Kalmbach's fundraising and campaign contributions activities. (HJCT 50) On March 15, the President reiterated his refusal to allow Dean to testify at the Gray hearings, claiming there was "a double privilege, the lawyer-client relationship, as well as the Presidential privilege." (Book III, 899)

On March 20, 1973, the President asked Dean to prepare a general statement about the involvement of White House staff members in Watergate. The President wanted to refute charges that executive privilege was part of the cover-up. The President explained to Dean:

> You've got to have something where it doesn't appear that I am doing this in, you know, just in a—saying to hell with the Congress and to hell with the people, we are not going to tell you anything because of Executive Privilege. That, they don't understand. But if you say, "No, we are willing to cooperate," and you've made a complete statement, but make it very incomplete. (WHT 168; Book III, 987)

On the afternoon of March 21, 1973, the President held another extensive discussion of using the report to be drafted by Dean to mislead and divert the SSC's inquiry into the Watergate matter. (HJCT 132, 136–39, 143–44) The Dean report was to describe generally the White House investigation of Watergate and to minimize the involvement of White House personnel. (See Deception and Concealment, p. 82.) At the afternoon meeting on March 21, Ehrlichman said that the Dean report might have the effect of reducing the scope of the SSC inquiry.

> ... the big danger in the Ervin hearings, as I see it, is that they will, they will run out, uh, leads into areas that, that it would be better not to have to get into. But, uh, if, uh, Baker, you know, under his direction—Uh, and if you could put out a basic document that would, uh, define a limited set of issues, uh, even if you, you don't try to concentrate on target, you just might have something. . . . (HJCT 132)

III

POLICY AFTER MARCH 21, 1973

On March 22, 1973, Mitchell came to Washington for a meeting with the President, Haldeman, Ehrlichman and Dean to develop a

---

[1] Colson testified that sometime around March 8 or 9, 1973, he discussed with Dean and Haldeman the possibility of being retained as a White House consultant. He further testified that he signed a consulting agreement either at the time he left the White House (March 10, 1973) or shortly thereafter. (Colson testimony, 3 HJC 322)

new strategy to keep criminal liability away from the President's closest subordinates, as well as to use executive privilege and the Dean report. (Book III, 1267–75) At the March 22 meeting there was a discussion of revised strategy that Ehrlichman called a "modified limited hang out." (HJCT 179) This combined providing the Dean report to the committee with a limited waiver of executive privilege to allow certain White House aides, specifically Colson, Haldeman and Ehrlichman, to appear before the SSC, preferably in private sessions. Mitchell argued, however, against permitting Dean to testify. (HJCT 16) Haldeman said that the President's previous position on executive privilege looked like "the only active step you've [the President] taken to cover up the Watergate all along," and that "the guy sitting at home who watches John Chancellor" wonders "What the hell's he covering up? If he's got no problem why doesn't he let them go and talk?" (HJCT 164–65)

After deciding to adopt a limited waiver of executive privilege as part of the "modified limited hang out" strategy, the President discussed ways to use executive privilege to negotiate with the committee for a compromise on conditions governing staff appearances and the bounds of the committee's investigation. Ehrlichman suggested turning the Dean report over to the committee as a quid pro quo for an agreement "on how witnesses will be treated up there." (HJCT 161) The report, if limited to the conclusion that no one in the White House was involved in Watergate, could also be used to support an argument for limiting the committee's inquiry. The President indicated that he wanted such a report forwarded to the SSC, and he indicated that the report could be billed as all the information the White House then possessed:

> This is everything we know, Mr. Senator .... This is everything we know; I know nothing more. This is the whole purpose, and that's that. If you need any further information, my, our counsel will furnish it, uh, that is not in here .... (HJCT 181)

The President stressed the importance of testimony being taken in executive session so that the claim of executive privilege to a particular question would not create the unfavorable impression often associated with a Fifth Amendment plea. (HJCT 182)

On the evening of April 14, the President talked to Ehrlichman, who suggested that if Mitchell were indicted, Mitchell's lawyers would fight to delay the SSC. (WHT 655–57) The President suggested that would leave the committee "hanging for a while," and that if hearings were delayed it might be possible to "get off the damn executive privilege" and put the President "in the position of being as forthcoming as we can." (WHT 657–58)

On April 17, 1973, the President stated publicly that the White House and the SSC had decided on ground rules that would permit the appearance of White House aides in public session. (Book IV, 1420) Shortly after the President acknowledged the certainty of appearances at public hearings by former and present aides, he asked Haldeman to listen to certain recordings of Presidential conversations to confirm what transpired during the President's March 21 meeting with Dean. (Book IV, 1567)

IV

HALDEMAN'S TESTIMONY

The President was particularly concerned about the charges expected to be made against him by Dean. On April 25, 1973, Haldeman, at the President's direction, listened to the tape of the March 21, 1973 morning meeting among the President, Dean and Haldeman. (Book IV, 1567, 1569) He made twenty pages of notes from the tape and immediately reported to the President. During this meeting, the President decided that Haldeman should listen again to the March 21 tape to determine answers to certain points of doubt raised by the tape. Haldeman listened to the tape again and reported to the President. (Book IX, 109–21) On April 26, 1973, Haldeman and the President met for approximately five hours.[2] (Book IV, 1558)

On June 4, 1973, the President listened to tape recordings of certain of his conversations in February and March, 1973. (Book IX, 170–72) During the day the President spoke with Haig and Ziegler about their March 21 conversation. The President said:

PRESIDENT. . . . Well, as I told you, we do know we have one problem: It's that damn conversation of March twenty-first due to the fact that, uh, for the reasons [unintelligible]. But I think we can handle that.
HAIG. I think we ca—, can. That's, that's the—
PRESIDENT. Bob can handle it. He'll get up there and say that—Bob will say, "I was there; the President said—". (Book IX, 177–78)

Haldeman appeared before the SSC on July 30, 31, and August 1, 1973. (Book IX, 434–35) He testified about the substance of the President's March 21 morning meeting with Dean. He testified

(a) That the President said, "[T]here is no problem in raising $1 million, we can do that, but it would be wrong." (Book IX, 436–37, 440)

(b) That "There was a reference to his [Dean's] feeling that Magruder had known about the Watergate planning and break-in ahead of it, in other words, that he was aware of what had gone on at Watergate. I don't believe that there was any reference to Magruder committing perjury." (Haldeman testimony, 8 SSC 3144)

Later, the President himself said that Haldeman had testified accurately.

V

CONCLUSION

President Nixon's attempts to cover up the facts of Watergate included an effort to narrow and divert the SSC's investigation. The President directed the preparation of an "incomplete" Dean report to mislead the committee and narrow its inquiry. He attempted to extend executive privilege to former aides and attempted to invoke the doctrine to prevent their testimony. After hearings began, false testimony was given to prevent the truth from emerging, testimony that the President himself confirmed.

---

[2] On May 30, 1974, the House Judiciary Committee subpoenaed the tape recording and other materials related to the conversations of April 25 and 26, 1973. The President refused to produce these recordings.

APRIL 30, 1973 TO THE PRESENT

I

Pledge of Cooperation

On April 30, 1973, the President accepted the resignations of Haldeman, Ehrlichman and Kleindienst. He requested and received the resignation of Dean. (Book IX, 132) In his public statement announcing these resignations, the President described Haldeman and Ehrlichman as two of the finest public servants it had been his privilege to know. (Book IX, 134) The President told the American people that he wanted them to know beyond a shadow of a doubt that during his term as President, justice would be pursued fairly, fully and impartially, no matter who was involved. The President pledged to the American people that he would do everything in his power to insure that the guilty were brought to justice. (Book IX, 135) The President said that he had given Attorney General designate Elliot Richardson absolute authority to make all decisions bearing upon the prosecution of the Watergate case, and related matters. (Book IX, 134-35) On May 9, 1973, the President reiterated that both his nominee for Attorney General and the Special Prosecutor that Richardson would appoint, in this case, would have the total cooperation of the executive branch of this government. (Book IX, 141)

On May 21, 1973, Richardson appeared with Special Prosecutor designate Archibald Cox before the Senate Judiciary Committee. In response to requests by Senators on the Committee for assurances with respect to the Special Prosecutor's authority, Richardson submitted to the Committee a statement of the duties, authority, and responsibilities the Special Prosecutor would have. The statement, which incorporated the views of Members of the Senate Committee, provided the Special Prosecutor with jurisdiction over offenses arising out of the unauthorized entry into the DNC headquarters at the Watergate, offenses arising out of the 1972 Presidential election, allegations involving the President, members of the White House staff or Presidential appointees and other matters which the Special Prosecutor consented to have assigned by the Attorney General. The guidelines also provided that the Special Prosecutor would have full authority for determining whether to contest the assertion of executive privilege, or any other testimonial privilege and that he would not be removed except for "extraordinary improprieties." The guidelines later were published as a formal Department of Justice regulation. (Book IX, 150)

On May 22, 1973, the President stated publicly that Richardson had demonstrated his own determination to see the truth brought out: "In this effort he had my full support." The President also said that executive privilege would not be invoked as to any testimony concerning possible criminal conduct or discussions of possible criminal conduct, in the matters presently under investigation, including the Watergate affair and the alleged cover-up. (Book IX, 153) In spite of these statements, on May 25, 1973, just before Richardson was sworn in as Attorney General, the President mentioned privately to Richardson that the waiver of executive privilege extended to testimony but not to documents. (Book IX, 157) This reservation had not been raised nor alluded to in any way during the Senate Judiciary Committee hearings on Richardson's nomination.

II

REFUSAL TO PROVIDE DOCUMENTS

Beginning in April, 1973, documents necessary to the Watergate and related investigations were transferred to rooms in the EOB to which all investigators were denied access. (Book IX, 163, 258–59) On April 30, 1973, the day he resigned, Ehrlichman instructed David Young to make sure that all papers involving the Plumbers were put in the President's files, where all investigators would be denied access to them. Ehrlichman told Young that, before he left, Ehrlichman himself would be putting some papers in the President's files. (Book IX, 128–29) Other White House aides including Haldeman, Dean, Strachan, and Buchanan had their records transferred to the President's files as well.

On June 11 and June 21, 1973, the Special Prosecutor wrote to J. Fred Buzhardt, the President's Counsel, requesting an inventory of the files of Haldeman, Ehrlichman, Mitchell, LaRue, Liddy, Colson, Chapin, Strachan, Dean, Hunt, Krogh and Young, and other files related to the Watergate investigation. Buzhardt informed Cox that the President would review the request and would decide upon it and other requests from the Special Prosecutor. After many weeks, Cox was told that the President had denied his request for an inventory. (Book IX, 258, 260–61) Those documents which were turned over to Cox were not delivered until after a long delay. Certain White House logs and diaries requested by Cox on June 13, 1973, were not delivered for more than five months. The White House file on ITT, originally requested on June 21, 1973, was not produced until August. (Book IX, 592–93, 884)

On August 23, 1973, Cox requested from the White House certain records concerning the Pentagon Papers and the Fielding break-in. (Book IX, 504–07) On October 4, 1973, Cox repeated the request. (Book IX, 508–10) On August 27, 1973, Cox requested White House records on the electronic surveillance of Joseph Kraft. (Book IX, 518) None of these documents was produced while Cox was Special Prosecutor. (Book IX, 302, 511)

In September, 1973, prior to his appearance before the Senate Select Committee and the Watergate Grand Jury, Special Assistant to the President Patrick Buchanan was instructed by White House counsel not to take certain documents from the White House, but to transfer them to the President's files, to which all investigators have been denied access. (Book IX, 600–02)

III

CONCEALMENT OF THE TAPING SYSTEM

Evidence bearing on the truth or falsity of allegations of criminal misconduct may be contained in recordings of conversations between the President and his staff. The President attempted to conceal the existence of these recordings (Book IX, 179-80, 246) and, once their existence became known, refused to make them available to the Special Prosecutor. (Book IX, 408, 426) The President discharged Cox for insisting on the right to obtain them through judicial process.

Before the existence of the White House taping system was disclosed, Special Prosecutor Cox was advised that the President had a tape of his April 15, 1973, meeting with John Dean. On June 11, 1973, Cox requested access to that tape. On June 16, Buzhardt, after speaking with the President about Cox's request, informed Cox that the tape in question was a dictabelt recording of the President's recollections of the events of April 15, 1973, and that it would not be produced. (Book IX, 246-47, 253) On June 20, 1973, Cox wrote to Buzhardt stating that, on April 18, 1973, when Henry Petersen was in charge of the Watergate investigation, the President had offered the tape to him. (Book IX, 244-45, 248-49) Buzhardt never told Cox that all conversations in the Oval Office, the President's EOB office, and from certain telephones were recorded.

On July 16, 1973, ten weeks after Cox's first request for the April 15 tape, Alexander Butterfield publicly disclosed before the Senate Select Committee the existence of the White House taping system. (Book IX, 380-81) Two days later, the President ordered the taping system disconnected, and custody of the tapes transferred from the Secret Service to a White House aide. (Book IX, 385-86) On July 18, 1973, Special Prosecutor Cox requested tapes of eight Presidential conversations. (Book IX, 389-92) On July 20, 1973, Cox wrote Buzhardt to ask that all necessary steps be taken to insure the integrity of the tapes, that custody of the tapes be limited and that access to them be documented. (Book IX, 394) On July 25, 1973, Buzhardt replied in writing:

> . . . I am glad to be able to assure you that the tapes you referred to therein are being preserved intact. The President has sole personal control of those tapes and they are being adequately protected under secure conditions.

The President confirmed this in a letter to Senator Sam Ervin, on July 23, 1973. ("Presidential Statements," 7/23/73, 29)

IV

The Discharge of Special Prosecutor Cox

On July 23, 1973, when the President refused Cox's request for tapes, the Special Prosecutor issued a subpoena for recordings of nine Presidential conversations. (Book IX, 408-10, 414-16) On August 29, 1973, Judge Sirica ordered the production of these recordings for *in camera* review. (Book IX, 586) On October 12, 1973, the United States Court of Appeals dismissed the President's appeal and upheld Judge Sirica's order. (Book IX, 748)

Rather than comply with the court order, the President set in motion a chain of events that culminated one week later in the discharge of Cox. On October 17, 1973, at the President's direction, Attorney General Richardson relayed to Cox a White House proposal whereby, in lieu of the *in camera* inspection of the recordings required by the Court's decision, Senator John Stennis would verify White House transcripts of the tapes. (Book IX, 762, 766–67) Richardson told Cox that the question of other tapes and documents would be left open for later discussions. The next day, Cox replied that the President's proposal was not, in essence, unacceptable. (Book IX, 767) The President, through Special Counsel Charles Alan Wright, ordered Cox, as an added condition of the proposal, to refrain from going to court for additional tapes and presidential documents. (Book IX, 791–92, 795) Richardson wrote the President that while he had thought the initial proposal reasonable, he did not endorse the new condition. (Book IX, 812–13)

On the evening of October 19, 1973, the President issued a statement ordering Cox to agree to the proposal and to desist from issuing subpoenas for tapes and documents. (Book IX, 800) On October 20, 1973, Cox said that his responsibilities as Special Prosecutor compelled him to refuse to obey that order. (Archibald Cox Press Conference, October 20, 1973, 3–4, 6–7, 16–17) The President then instructed Richardson to discharge Cox. Richardson refused and resigned. When the President gave the same instruction to Deputy Attorney General Ruckelshaus, Ruckelshaus also refused and resigned. (Book IX, 817, 819) The President then directed Solicitor General Robert Bork to fire Cox, and Bork did so. Later that night, White House Press Secretary Ziegler announced that the office of Special Prosecutor had been abolished. (Book IX, 823–25)

There is evidence that the President's decision to discharge Cox was made several months before October 20, 1973. On June 27, 1973, the Special Prosecutor formally requested that the President furnish a detailed narrative statement covering the conversations and incidents described by Dean before the Senate Select Committee. Cox noted that the President had been named as someone with information about the involvement of a number of persons in a major conspiracy to obstruct justice. He suggested that the President attach copies of all relevant transcripts and other papers or memoranda to his narrative. (Book IX, 318–19) On July 3, 1973, General Alexander Haig, who had replaced Haldeman as the President's Chief of Staff, called Richardson, in connection with a news story that Cox was investigating expenditures at the Western White House at San Clemente, and told Richardson that it could not be part of the Special Prosecutor's responsibility to investigate the President and that the President might discharge Cox. (Book IX, 331) On July 23, 1973, Haig again complained about various activities of the Special Prosecutor. Haig said that the President wanted a "tight line drawn with no further mistakes," and that "if Cox does not agree, we will get rid of Cox." (Book IX, 331–32) On July 15, 1973, Buzhardt, responding to Cox's request of June 27, 1973, said that, at an appropriate time, the President intended publicly to address the subjects, being considered by the SSC, including Dean's testimony. In his public statement of August 15, 1973, the President said that the record before the SSC was lengthy, the facts complicated, the evidence confusing and that he had on May 22, 1973 issued a detailed statement addressing the charges that had been made against the President and that he would not deal with the various charges in detail. ("Presidential Statements," 8/15/73, 33) In an affidavit submitted to the House Judiciary Committee, Richardson has said that, when he met with the President in late September or early October 1973, "[a]fter we finished our discussion about Mr. Agnew, and as we were walking toward the door, the President said in substance, 'Now that we have disposed of that matter, we can go ahead and get rid of Cox.' " (Book IX, 159)

After the President discharged Cox, resolutions called for the President's impeachment were introduced in the House. Bills calling for the creation of an independent investigatory agency were introduced in the House and Senate. (Cong. Record, October 23, 1973, H9356; Cong. Record, October 24, 1973, H9397; Cong. Record, October 23, 1973, S19439, S19443-44, S19454, H9354, H9355; and Cong. Record, October 24, 1973, H9396) Under tremendous public pressure the President surrendered to the court some subpoenaed tapes and offered explanations for the absence of others. (Book IX, 1230, 673, 677, 878) The President then authorized the appointment of another Special Prosecutor. (Book IX, 833)

V

REFUSAL TO COOPERATE WITH SPECIAL PROSECUTOR JAWORSKI

On October 26, 1973, the President announced he had decided that Acting Attorney General Bork would appoint a new Special Prosecutor. The President stated that the Special Prosecutor would have independence. He would have total cooperation from the executive branch. The President added that it was time for those who were guilty to be prosecuted, and for those who were innocent to be cleared. (Book IX, 883) On November 1, 1973, Acting Attorney General Robert Bork named Leon Jaworski Special Prosecutor. (Book IX, 847)

On February 14, 1974, Jaworski wrote to Chairman Eastland of the Senate Judiciary Committee that, on February 4, Special Counsel to the President James St. Clair had informed Jaworski that the President would not comply with the Special Prosecutor's outstanding requests. Jaworski also said that St. Clair had informed him that the President refused to reconsider his decision to terminate cooperation with the Watergate investigation and would not produce any tape recordings of Presidential conversations related to the Watergate break-in and cover-up. The President had also refused to cooperate with the investigation of political contributions by dairy interests or the investigation of the Plumbers. (Book IX, 936-38, 945)

VI

TAPES LITIGATION

On April 16, 1974, Jaworski, joined by defendants Colson and Mardian, moved that a trial subpoena be issued in *United States* v. *Mitchell* directing the President to produce tapes and documents relating to specific conversations between the President and the defendants and potential witnesses. On April 18, 1974, Judge Sirica granted the motion. (Book IX, 988-89) Judge Sirica denied the President's motion to quash the subpoena. The President appealed to the Court of Appeals. Because of the public importance of the issues presented and the need for their prompt resolution, the Supreme Court of the United States granted the Specal Prosecutor's petition for certiorari before judgment. On July 24, 1974, the Court ordered the President to turn over the subpoenaed tapes and documents to Judge Sirica for an *in camera* inspection. The Court stated that neither the doctrine of separation of powers, nor the need for confidentiality of high level communications, without more, could sustain an absolute, unqualified presidential privilege of immunity from judicial process under all circumstances. The Court further stated that the President's generalized assertion of privilege must yield to the demonstrated, specific need for evidence in a pending criminal trial. (*United States* v. *Nixon*, "Criminal Cases," 162–63, 182, 189)

On May 28, 1974, Jaworski asked Judge Sirica to turn over to the Special Prosecutor a portion of the tape of a September 15, 1972 meeting among the President, Haldeman and Dean. Both Haldeman and Dean had testified that the discussion concerned IRS treatment of opponents of the White House. (*In re Grand Jury*, Misc. 47–73, Affidavit, May 28, 1974) Judge Sirica ruled against the President's claim of privilege on June 12, 1974, and the President appealed. (*In re Grand Jury*, Misc. 47–73, Order, June 12, 1974, and Notice of Appeal, June 14, 1974) The appeal is pending. Judge Sirica denied the request of counsel for the Committee and the letter request of Chairman Rodino that Committee counsel be permitted to listen to the portions the September 15 tape in question and that the transcript of the conversation which he had ordered delivered to the Special Prosecutor also be delivered to the Committee.

VII

Altered and Missing Evidence

A. 18½ Minute Gap on June 20, 1972 Tape

After the Court of Appeals, in *Nixon* v. *Sirica*, required the President to surrender the tapes that Cox had subpoenaed, the President informed Judge Sirica that some of the material was unavailable—specifically, that there was an 18½ minute gap on the June 20, 1972 conversation between Haldeman and the President, and that there was no April 15, 1973 tape of his conversation with John Dean and there was no June 20, 1972 tape of the telephone conversation between the President and Mitchell. (Book IX, 836, 869, 871)

On August 6, 1974, the President's special counsel St. Clair told Chief Judge Sirica that a conversation between the President and Charles Colson, also on June 20, 1972, had never existed.

The erased meeting between the President and Haldeman occurred approximately one hour after Haldeman had been briefed on Watergate by Ehrlichman, Mitchell, and Dean, all of whom knew of the White House and CRP involvement. Kleindienst, who arrived 55 minutes after that briefing meeting had begun, had been told by Liddy that those involved in the break-in were White House or CRP employees. Haldeman's notes show that Buzhardt has acknowledged that the only erased portion of the tape was the conversation dealing with Watergate. (Book II, 108, 112, 153, 237–38, 240–43, 246, 249–50) It is a fair inference that the erased conversation of June 20, 1972, contained evidence showing what the President knew of the involvement of his closest advisors shortly after the Watergate break-in.

There is no record that the tape in question was ever taken out of the tape vault until the weekend of September 28, 1973, when it was delivered by the President's Special Assistant Stephen Bull to the President's personal secretary Rose Mary Woods. (*In re Grand Jury*, Misc. 47–73, Exhibits 7, 7(a), 112 and 113) From October 1, 1973, when the Uher 5000 tape recorder was delivered to Miss Woods, until November 13–14, 1973, when the 18½ minute gap was discovered, the Uher 5000 tape recorder and the June 20, 1972 EOB tape were in the possession of Miss Woods, where the President also had access to them. (Rose Mary Woods testimony, *In re Grand Jury*, Misc. 47–73, November 26, 1973, 1214–16; November 28, 1973, 1432–33)

On November 21, 1973, the Court and the Special Prosecutor were informed of the gap. (J. Fred Buzhardt testimony, *In re GrandJury*, Misc. 47–73, November 29, 1973, 1614–15, 1617) Judge Sirica appointed an advisory panel of experts nominated jointly by the President's Counsel and the Special Prosecutor to examine various tape recordings, including the June 20, 1972 EOB tape, and to report on their findings. (Book IX, 870–71) The panel unanimously concluded that: (i) the erasing and rerecording which produced the buzz on the tape were done on the original tape; (ii) the Uher 5000 recorder machine used by Rose Mary Woods probably produced the buzz; (iii) the erasures and buzz recordings were done in at least five to nine separate and contiguous segments and required hand operation of the controls of the Uher 5000 recorder; and (iv) the manually erased portion of the tape originally contained speech, which, because of the manual erasures and rerecordings, could not be covered. (An analysis of this report is set forth in Appendix A.)

B. *April 15, 1973 Tape and Dictabelt*

The President said that, because the tape on the recorder in the White House taping system at his Executive Office Building office ran out, the April 15, 1973 tape never existed. He has also said that the dictabelt of his recollections of the day (referred to by Buzhardt in his June 16, 1973 letter to Cox) could not be located.[2] (Book IX, 860) Among the conversations that would have been recorded on the evening of April 15, 1973 was a meeting between the President and Dean. Dean testified, prior to the disclosure of the taping system, that he thought the President might have recorded that conversation. His suspicion was aroused because the President asked leading questions, went to the corner of the room, and said in a low voice that he had been foolish to discuss Hunt's clemency with Colson and that he had been joking when he said one million dollars for the Watergate defendants could be raised. (Book IV, 1044–46)

---

[2] On November 12, 1973, the President announced that he would supply the tapes of two conversations with Dean on April 16, 1973 in lieu of the April 15 conversation. The President stated that the substance of the conversations on April 16 was similar to the matters discussed on April 15 as reflected in the President's notes of the meeting. ("Presidential Statements," 11/12/73, 61)

On April 18, 1973, the President told Petersen, with reference to the substance of his April 15, 1973 meeting with Dean, that he had it on tape. (Book IV, 1474-75) On June 4, 1973, the President listened to tape recordings of certain of his conversations in February and March 1973. (Book IX, 170, 172) When his aide, Stephen Bull, asked which additional tapes he wanted, the President said:

PRESIDENT. March twenty-first. I don't need April, I don't need April fifteen. I need the sixteenth. [Unintelligible] correct. There were two on April sixteenth. I just want the second [unintelligible]. You can skip the—April fifteen.
BULL. And March twenty-first.
PRESIDENT. March twenty-first, that's right, I have those. (Book IX, 183)

In the summer of 1973, during an interview with the Senate Select Committee staff, White House assistant Stephen Bull stated that in late June, 1973, Haig called him to request that the April 15 tape of the President's conversation with Dean be flown to the President at San Clemente. Bull said that since there were no further courier flights to San Clemente that night, Haig instructed Bull to arrange for the Secret Service to play the tape for Buzhardt, so that Buzhrardt could brief the President by telephone on its contents. (Book IX, 298-99, 308-09) Later Bull testified at hearings regarding the missing Presidential tapes that he had only guessed at the date of the conversation, and that the President must have been referring to the tape of a March 20 telephone call.[3] (Book IX, 311-12)

C. June 20, 1972 Dictabelt and March 21, 1973 Cassette Gaps

In addition to the erased June 20, 1972 tape and the missing April 15, 1973 tape and dictabelt, both of which were in the sole personal custody of the President, other dictabelts contain gaps. There is a 42-second gap in the dictabelt on which the President dictated his recollections of a June 20, 1972 conversation with Mitchell. (Book II, 310) There is a 57-second gap in a cassette on which the President dictated his recollections of his March 21, 1973 conversation with Dean. (Book III, 1249)

D. Other Unrecorded Conversations

After the Supreme Court's decision in *United States* v. *Nixon*, the President informed Judge Sirica that some of the subpoenaed conversations were not available. Specifically, the President stated that six subpoenaed telephone conversations were placed from or received in the residence portion of the White House on a telephone not connected to the recording system; that the tape ran out after the first fourteen minutes of the telephone conversation between the President and Colson from 7:53 to 8:24 p.m. on March 21, 1973; and that he had been unable to find tape recordings covering three subpoenaed meetings. (*United States* v. *Mitchell*, Cr. No. 74-110, Analysis and Particularized Claims of Executive Privilege for Subpoenaed Recorded Presidential Conversations, August 6, 1974, 2; August 9, 1974, 2)

E. Inaccuracies in Presidential Transcripts

On April 29, 1973, when the President announced that he was providing approximately 1,200 pages of transcripts of private conver-

---

[3] Buzhardt has testified that the taped conversation he listened to in June was a telephone conversation between the President and Dean which took place on March 20, 1973. (Book IX, 297)

sations in which he participated to the House Judiciary Committee, he stated that these materials, together with those already made available, will tell it all—that they included all conversations or parts thereof all the portions that related to the question of what the President knew about Watergate or the cover-up and what he did about it. (Book IX, 993, 999)

The House Judiciary Committee has been able to compare eight of the edited White House transcripts with the transcripts prepared by its staff from the tapes which the President has turned over to the Committee and from tapes in the possession of Judge Sirica. ("Comparison of White House and Judiciary Committee Transcripts of Eight Recorded Presidential Conversations") The comparison shows significant omissions, misattributions of statements, additions, paraphrases, and other signs of editorial intervention in all eight transcripts. Presidential remarks are often entirely omitted from the White House version, or significantly reworded, or attributed to another speaker.

The House Judiciary Committee transcript of the March 22, 1973 conversation among the President, Haldeman, Ehrlichman, Mitchell and Dean shows that the participants continued to talk about Watergate following the point in the discussion at which the White House transcript ends. The White House transcript does not acknowledge this omission. In a portion of a discussion with Mitchell omitted from the White House version, the President said:

> I am perfectly willing to—I don't give a shit what happens. I want you all to stonewall it, let them plead the Fifth Amendment, cover-up or anything else, if it'll save it—save the plan. That's the whole point. On the other hand, uh, uh, I would prefer, as I said to you, that you do it the other way. And I would particularly prefer to do it that other way if it's going to come out that way anyway.
>
> * * * * * * *
>
> ... [U]p to this point, the whole theory has been containment, as you know, John.
>
> * * * * * * *
>
> ... That's the thing I am really concerned with. We're going to protect our people, if we can. (HJCT 183)

At another point in the Committee transcript of the March 22 conversation, the President talked about getting "on with the cover up plan." The Committee and White House versions of the passage in which that occurs is set forth below:

WHITE HOUSE TRANSCRIPT, p. 290	HOUSE JUDICIARY COMMITTEE TRANSCRIPT, p. 164
PRESIDENT. If I am not mistaken, you thought we ought to draw a line here.	PRESIDENT. If I am not mistaken, you thought we ought to draw the line where we did [unintelligible].
* * *	* * *
P Well all John Mitchell is arguing then, is that now we use flexibility in order to get off the coverup line.	PRESIDENT. But now—what—all that John Mitchell is arguing, then, is that now we, we use flexibility. DEAN. That's correct. PRESIDENT. In order to get on with the coverup plan.

In the March 21, 1973 afternoon meeting among the President, Dean, Haldeman and Ehrlichman, the White House version of the transcript attributes to Dean a comment about clemency by the President.

WHITE HOUSE TRANSCRIPT, p. 252	HOUSE JUDICIARY COMMITTEE TRANSCRIPT, p. 133
E Well, my view is that Hunt's interests lie in getting a pardon if he can. That ought to be somehow or another one of the options that he is most particularly concerned about. Now, his indirect contacts with John don't contemplate that at all—(inaudible)	EHRLICHMAN. Well, my, my view is that, that, uh, Hunt's interests lie in getting a pardon if he can. That ought to be, somehow or another, one of the options that he is most particularly concerned about. Uh, his his indirect contacts with John don't contemplate that at all. Well, maybe they, maybe they contemplate it—but they say there's going [unintelligible] PRESIDENT. I know.
* * * *	* * *
D He's got to get that by Christmas, I understand. E That's right....	PRESIDENT. I mean he's got to get that by Christmas time. Dean. That's right....

In response to the Committee's subpoena of a forty-five minute conversation between the President and Dean on March 17, 1973, the President supplied the Committee with a three-page transcript that deals only with Segretti and the Fielding break-in. (WHT 157–60) On June 4, 1973, however, the President described the March 17 conversation to Ziegler:

[...] then he said—started talking about Magruder, you know: "Jeb's good, but if he sees himself sinking he'll drag everything with him."

* * * * * * *

.... And he said that he'd seen [....] Liddy right after it happened. And he said, "No one in the White House except possibly Strachan's involved with, or knew about it." He said, "Magruder had pushed him without mercy."
.... I said, "You know, the thing here is that Magruder [...] put the heat on, and Sloan starts pissing on Haldeman." I said, "That couldn't be [...]" I said, "We've, we've got to cut that off. We can't have that go to Haldeman."

* * * * * * *

.... And I said, well, looking to the future, I mean, here are the problems. We got this guy, this guy and this guy." And I said, "Magruder can be one, one guy—and that's going to bring it right up home.

That'll bring it right up to the, to the White House, to the President." And I said, "We've got to cut that back. That ought to be cut out." (Book IX, 209–11) [4]

In response to a subpoena of his telephone conversation on the afternoon of April 18, 1973, with Assistant Attorney General Henry Petersen, the President has provided the Committee with a five-page edited White House transcript. (WHT 1203–07) The transcript is not in accord with Petersen's recollection of that conversation. (Petersen testimony, 3 HJC 146) In response to a subpoena of the recording of a March 22, 1973, conversation, the President submitted an edited transcript, with the heading: "Appendix 8. Meeting: The President, Haldeman, Ehrlichman, Dean and Mitchell, EOB Office, March 22,

---

[4] On July 31, 1974, the President submitted to Judge Sirica, pursuant to the Supreme Court's order in *United States* v. *Nixon*, particularized claims of executive privilege as to certain taped conversations that were ordered turned over to the Special Prosecution Force. There is no claim that any portion of the one hour and fifteen minute conversation is not relevant to the subject matter before the Court. (*United States* v. *Mitchell*, Cr. No. 74–110, Analysis and Particularized Claims of Executive Privilege for Subpoened Recorded Presidential Conversations, July 31. 1974, 1)

1973. (1:57–3:43 p.m.)" Although both White House logs and the transcript itself indicate that the conversation lasted until 3:43, the last line of the transcript begins "It is 3:16." The President's transcript does not acknowledge or account for this apparent omission of 27 minutes.

In response to a subpoena of the recording of an April 16, 1973, conversation with Ehrlichman and Petersen, the President submitted an edited transcript, which included an inadvertent repetition of a single conversation in two separate sections of the transcript. The two versions of the single conversation differ from one another in a manner which indicates not simple misunderstanding of sounds, but direct editorial intervention.

In response to a subpoena of the recording of a March 27, 1973, conversation with Haldeman, Ehrlichman and Ziegler, which lasted 140 minutes, the President submitted an edited transcript of 70 pages, with 8 deletions (of unspecified duration) characterized as "Material Unrelated to Presidential Action."

In response to a subpoena of the recording of an April 17, 1973, conversation with Haldeman, Ehrlichman and Ziegler, which lasted 45 minutes, the President submitted an edited transcript of 19 pages, with no acknowledged deletions.

These and other substantive, chronological and typographical anomalies and discrepancies, including inexplicable non-sequiturs, indicate that the edited White House version of the 35 Presidential conversations of which the Committee does not have its own transcripts are even less accurate than the eight conversations of which it does.

On August 5, 1974, the President released edited transcripts of three of his conversations of June 23, 1973, which the Committee had subpoened. The first conversation lasted 95 minutes; the President submitted a transcript of 34 pages, two of which were misnumbered; a section of the conversation was transcribed twice, verbatim. The second conversation lasted nine minutes. The President submitted an edited transcript of one page. These transcripts confirm the Committee's conclusion that the edited White House transcripts reflect extensive editorial intervention.

F. Ehrlichman's Notes

On June 24, 1974, the Committee issued a subpoena for copies of certain of John Ehrlichman's notes, which were impounded in the White House. On July 12, 1974, the President said he would furnish those copies of Ehrlichman's notes which the President previously had turned over to Ehrlichman and the Special Prosecutor pursuant to a subpoena authorized by Judge Gesell and only after Judge Gesell had denied the President's motion to quash that subpoena.

On Monday, July 15, 1974, Mr. St. Clair, the President's counsel, delivered a package of materials to Mr. Doar, Special Counsel to the House Judiciary Committee. Mr. St. Clair also submitted a letter to Chairman Rodino dated July 12, 1974, in which it was stated that the materials furnished were "those parts of John Ehrlichman's notes . . . that were furnished to Mr. Ehrlichman pursuant to his subpoena."

At about the same time, Mr. St. Clair apparently had requested that the Office of the Special Prosecutor deliver to him a copy of the set of Ehrlichman notes of his meetings with the President that had been filed with the Court in response to the Ehrlichman subpoena, and furnished to the Special Prosecutor contemporaneously. Because of a misunderstanding on the part of the Special Prosecutor's office as to St. Clair's request, the Special Prosecutor delivered the set of notes to Doar rather than St. Clair, together with a forwarding letter to Doar, a copy of which was sent to St. Clair. Upon receipt of the letter, St. Clair requested Doar to return the notes, but later modified that request to seek a copy of what had been delivered to Doar.

A comparison of the Ehrlichman notes furnished to the Judiciary Committee by the President with the Ehrlichman notes received by the Judiciary Committee from the Special Prosecutor shows that substantial relevant portions were deleted by masking all or a portion of pages in the version supplied to the Committee. Notes covering eleven meetings between the President and Ehrlichman were not included in the materials furnished by the President to the Committee in response to its subpoena. The omissions were as follows: one meeting on June 19, 1971; three meetings on June 23, 1971; one meeting on June 29, 1971; two meetings on July 1, 1971; one meeting on July 2, 1971; one meeting on July 6, 1971; one meeting on August 12, 1971 and one meeting on January 5, 1972. The Special Prosecutor's submission contains Ehrlichman's notes as to each of those meetings. The notes cover some forty-two pages.

The first page of the Special Prosecutor's material contains an Ehrlichman handwritten identification and explanation of the eleven "shorthand symbols" employed by Ehrlichman in making his notes. Neither that page nor that explanatory material is included in the President's submission to the Judiciary Committee in response to the Committee's subpoena.

The Ehrlichman notes, as delivered by the Special Prosecutor but omitted in the submission by the President, contain information relating to the President's dealings with Mr. Ehrlichman and other close aides, cabinet officers and other officers of government directly and through aides. The materials contain precise directions to be carried out by Ehrlichman and others. Among deletions in the President's submission to the committee were references to the Ellsberg case pending before Judge Matthew Byrne and accounts of efforts, directed by the President, to discredit Ellsberg in the media while the case was pending.

CONCLUSION

After the Committee on the Judiciary had debated whether or not it should recommend Article I to the House of Representatives, 27 of the 38 Members of the Committee found that the evidence before it could only lead to one conclusion: that Richard M. Nixon, using the powers of his high office, engaged, personally and through his subordinates and agents, in a course of conduct or plan designed to delay, impede, and obstruct the investigation of the unlawful entry, on June 17, 1972, into the headquarters of the Democratic National Committee; to cover up, conceal and protect those responsible; and to conceal the existence and scope of other unlawful covert activities.

This finding is the only one that can explain the President's involvement in a pattern of undisputed acts that occurred after the break-in and that cannot otherwise be rationally explained.

1. The President's decision on June 20, 1972, not to meet with his Attorney General, his chief of staff, his counsel, his campaign director, and his assistant John Ehrlichman, whom he had put in charge of the investigation—when the subject of their meeting was the Watergate matter.

2. The erasure of that portion of the recording of the President's conversation with Haldeman, on June 20, 1972, which dealt with Watergate—when the President stated that the tapes had been under his "sole and personal control."

3. The President's public denial on June 22, 1972, of the involvement of members of the Committee for the Re-election of the President or of the White House staff in the Watergate burglary, in spite of having discussed Watergate, on or before June 22, 1972, with Haldeman, Colson, and Mitchell—all persons aware of that involvement.

4. The President's directive to Haldeman on June 23, 1972 to have the CIA request the FBI to curtail its Watergate investigation.

5. The President's refusal, on July 6, 1972, to inquire and inform himself what Patrick Gray, Acting Director of the FBI, meant by his warning that some of the President's aides were "trying to mortally wound" him.

6. The President's discussion with Ehrlichman on July 8, 1972, of clemency for the Watergate burglars, more than two months before the return of any indictments.

7. The President's public statement on August 29, 1972, a statement later shown to be untrue, that an investigation by John Dean "indicates that no one in the White House staff, no one in the Administration, presently employed, was involved in this very bizarre incident."

8. The President's statement to Dean on September 15, 1972, the day that the Watergate indictments were returned without naming high CRP and White House officials, that Dean had handled his work skillfully, "putting your fingers in the dike every time that leaks have sprung here and sprung there," and that "you just try to button it up as well as you can and hope for the best."

9. The President's discussion with Colson in January, 1973 of clemency for Hunt.

10. The President's discussion with Dean on February 28, 1973, of Kalmbach's upcoming testimony before the Senate Select Committee, in which the President said that it would be hard for Kalmbach because "it'll get out about Hunt," and the deletion of that phrase from the edited White House transcript.

11. The President's appointment in March, 1973, of Jeb Stuart Magruder to a high government position when Magruder had previously perjured himself before the Watergate Grand Jury in order to conceal CRP involvement.

12. The President's inaction in response to Dean's report of March 13, 1973, that Mitchell and Haldeman knew about Liddy's operation at CRP, that Sloan has a compulsion to "cleanse his soul by confession," that Stans and Kalmbach were trying to get him to "settle down," and that Strachan had lied about his prior knowledge of Watergate out of personal loyalty; and the President's reply to Dean that Strachan was the problem "in Bob's case."

13. The President's discussion on March 13, 1973, of a plan to limit future Watergate investigations by making Colson a White House "consultant without doing any consulting," in order to bring him under the doctrine of executive privilege.

14. The omission of the discussion related to Watergate from the edited White House transcript, submitted to the Committee on the Judiciary, of the President's March 17, 1973, conversation with Dean, especially in light of the fact that the President had listened to the conversation on June 4, 1973.

15. The President's instruction to Dean on the evening of March 20, 1973, to make his report on Watergate "very incomplete," and his subsequent public statements misrepresenting the nature of that instruction.

16. The President's instruction to Haldeman on the morning of March 21, 1973, that Hunt's price was pretty high, but that they should buy the time on it.

17. The President's March 21st statement to Dean that he had "handled it just right," and "contained it;" and the deletion of the above comments from the edited White House transcripts.

18. The President's instruction to Dean on March 21, 1973, to state falsely that payments to the Watergate defendants had been made through a Cuban Committee.

19. The President's refusal to inform officials of the Department of Justice that on March 21, 1973, Dean had confessed to obstruction of justice and had said that Haldeman, Ehrlichman, and Mitchell were also involved in that crime.

20. The President's approval on March 22, 1973, of a shift in his position on executive privilege "in order to get on with the cover up plan," and the discrepancy, in that phrase, in the edited White House transcript.

21. The President's instruction to Ronald Ziegler on March 26, 1973, to state publicly that the President had "absolute and total confidence" in Dean.

22. The President's action, in April, 1973, in conveying to Haldeman, Ehrlichman, Colson and Kalmbach information furnished to the President by Assistant Attorney General Petersen after the President had assured Petersen that he would not do so.

23. The President's discussions, in April, 1973, of the manner in which witnesses should give false and misleading statements.

24. The President's directions, in April, 1973, with respect to offering assurances of clemency to Mitchell, Magruder and Dean.

25. The President's lack of full disclosure and misleading statements to Assistant Attorney General Henry Petersen between April 15 and April 27, 1973, when Petersen reported directly to the President about the Watergate investigation.

26. The President's instruction to Ehrlichman on April 17, 1973, to give false testimony concerning Kalmbach's knowledge of the purpose of the payments to the Watergate defendants.

27. The President's decision to give Haldeman on April 25 and 26, 1973, access to tape recordings of Presidential conversations, after Assistant Attorney General Petersen had repeatedly warned the President that Haldeman was a suspect in the Watergate investigation.

28. The President's refusal to disclose the existence of the White House taping system.

29. The President's statement to Richardson on May 25, 1973, that his waiver of executive privilege, announced publicly on May 22, 1973, did not extend to documents.

30. The refusal of the President to cooperate with Special Prosecutor Cox; the President's instruction to Special Prosecutor Cox not to seek additional evidence in the courts and his firing of Cox when Cox refused to comply with that directive.

31. The submission by the President to the Committee on April 30, 1974, and the simultaneous release to the public of transcripts of 43 Presidential conversations and statements, which are characterized by omissions of words and passages, misattributions of statements, additions, paraphrases, distortions, non-sequiturs, deletions of sections as "Material Unrelated to Presidential Action," and other signs of editorial intervention; the President's authorization of his counsel to characterize these transcripts as "accurate;" and the President's public statement that the transcripts contained "the whole story" of the Watergate matter.

32. The President's refusal in April, May, and June 1974, to comply with the subpoenas of the Committee issued in connection with its impeachment inquiry.

In addition to this evidence, there was before the Committee the following evidence:

1. Beginning immediately after June 17, 1972, the involvement of each of the President's top aides and political associates, Haldeman, Mitchell, Ehrlichman, Colson, Dean, LaRue, Mardian, Magruder, in the Watergate coverup.

2. The clandestine payment by Kalmbach and LaRue of more than $400,000 to the Watergate defendants.

3. The attempts by Ehrlichman and Dean to interfere with the FBI investigation.

4. The perjury of Magruder, Porter, Mitchell, Krogh, Strachan, Haldeman and Ehrlichman.

Finally, there was before the Committee a record of public statements by the President between June 22, 1972, and June 9, 1974, deliberately contrived to deceive the courts, the Department of Justice, the Congress and the American people.

President Nixon's course of conduct following the Watergate break-in, as described in Article I, caused action not only by his subordinates but by the agencies of the United States, including the Department of Justice, the FBI, and the CIA. It required perjury, destruction of evidence, obstruction of justice, all crimes. But, most important, it required deliberate, contrived, and continuing deception of the American people.

President Nixon's actions resulted in manifest injury to the confidence of the nation and great prejudice to the cause of law and justice, and was subversive of constitutional government. His actions were contrary to his trust as President and unmindful of the solemn duties of his high office. It was this serious violation of Richard M. Nixon's constitutional obligations as President, and not the fact that violations of Federal criminal statutes occurred, that lies at the heart of Article I.

The Committee finds, based upon of clear and convincing evidence, that this conduct, detailed in the foregoing pages of this report, constitutes "high crimes and misdemeanors" as that term is used in Article II, Section 4 of the Constitution. Therefore, the Committee recommends that the House of Representatives exercise its constitutional power to impeach Richard M. Nixon.

On August 5, 1974, nine days after the Committee had voted on Article I, President Nixon released to the public and submitted to the Committee on the Judiciary three additional edited White House transcripts of Presidential conversations that took place on June 23, 1972, six days following the DNC break-in. Judge Sirica had that day released to the Special Prosecutor transcripts of those conversations pursuant to the mandate of the United States Supreme Court. The Committee had subpoenaed the tape recordings of those conversations, but the President had refused to honor the subpoena.

These transcripts conclusively confirm the finding that the Committee had already made, on the basis of clear and convincing evidence, that from shortly after the break-in on June 17, 1972, Richard M. Nixon, acting personally and through his subordinates and agents, made it his plan to and did direct his subordinates to engage in a course of conduct designed to delay, impede and obstruct investigation of the unlawful entry of the headquarters of the Democratic National Committee; to cover up, conceal and protect those responsible; and to conceal the existence and scope of other unlawful covert activities.

ARTICLE II

INTRODUCTION

On July 29 the Committee adopted Article II, as amended, by a vote of 28 to 10. The Article provides:

Using the powers of the office of President of the United States, Richard M. Nixon, in violation of his constitutional oath faithfully to execute the office of President of the United States and, to the best of his ability, preserve, protect, and defend the Constitution of the United States, and in disregard of his constitutional duty to take care that the laws be faithfully executed, has repeatedly engaged in conduct violating the constitutional rights of citizens, impairing the due and proper administration of justice and the conduct of lawful inquiries, or contravening the laws governing agencies of the executive branch and the purposes of these agencies.

Article II charges that Richard M. Nixon, in violation of his constitutional duty to take care that the laws be faithfully executed and his oath of office as President, seriously abused powers that only a President possesses. He engaged in conduct that violated the constitutional rights of citizens, that interfered with investigations by federal authorities and congressional committees, and that contravened the laws governing agencies of the executive branch of the federal government. This conduct, undertaken for his own personal political advantage and not in furtherance of any valid national policy objective, is seriously incompatible with our system of constitutional government.[1]

Five instances of abuse of the powers of the office of President are specifically listed in Article II. Each involves repeated misuse of the powers of the office, and each focuses on improprieties by the President that served no valid national policy objective. Each of them individually and all of them together support the ground of impeachment charged in Article II—that Richard M. Nixon, using the power of his office, repeatedly engaged in conduct violating the constitutional rights of citizens, impairing the due and proper administration of justice and the conduct of lawful inquiries, or contravening the laws governing agencies of the executive branch and the purposes of these agencies.

Richard M. Nixon violated the constitutional rights of citizens by directing or authorizing his subordinates to interfere with the impartial and nonpolitical administration of the internal revenue laws. He violated the constitutional rights of citizens by directing or authorizing unlawful electronic surveillance and investigations of citizens and the use of information obtained from the surveillance for his own political advantage. He violated the constitutional rights of citizens by

---

[1] In some of the instances in which Richard M. Nixon abused the powers of his office, his unlawful or improper objective was not achieved. But this does not make the abuse of power any less serious, nor diminish the applicability of the impeachment remedy. The principle was stated by Supreme Court Justice William Johnson in 1808: "If an officer attempt an act inconsistent with the duties of his station, it is presumed that the failure of the attempt would not exempt him from liability to impeachment. Should a President head a conspiracy for the usurpation of absolute power, it is hoped that no one will contend that defeating his machinations would restore him to innocence." *Gilchrist v. Collector of Charleston*, 10 F. Cas. 355, 365 (No. 5, 420) (C.C.D.S.C. 1808).

permitting a secret investigative unit within the office of the President to engage in unlawful and covert activities for his political purposes. Once these and other unlawful and improper activities on his behalf were suspected, and after he knew or had reason to know that his close subordinates were interfering with lawful investigations into them, he failed to perform his duty to see that the criminal laws were enforced against these subordinates. And he used his executive power to interfere with the lawful operations of agencies of the executive branch, including the Department of Justice and the Central Intelligence Agency, in order to assist in these activities, as well as to conceal the truth about his misconduct and that of his subordinates and agents.

ARTICLE II, PARAGRAPH (1)

(1) HE HAS, ACTING PERSONALLY AND THROUGH HIS SUBORDINATES AND AGENTS, ENDEAVORED TO OBTAIN FROM THE INTERNAL REVENUE SERVICE, IN VIOLATION OF THE CONSTITUTIONAL RIGHTS OF CITIZENS, CONFIDENTIAL INFORMATION CONTAINED IN INCOME TAX RETURNS FOR PURPOSES NOT AUTHORIZED BY LAW, AND TO CAUSE, IN VIOLATION OF THE CONSTITUTIONAL RIGHTS OF CITIZENS, INCOME TAX AUDITS OR OTHER INCOME TAX INVESTIGATIONS TO BE INITIATED OR CONDUCTED IN A DISCRIMINATORY MANNER

The Committee finds clear and convincing evidence that a course of conduct was carried out by Richard M. Nixon's close subordinates, with his knowledge, approval, and encouragement, to violate the constitutional rights of citizens—their right to privacy with respect to the use of confidential information acquired by the Internal Revenue Service; their right to have the tax laws of the United States applied with an even hand; and their right to engage in political activity in opposition to the President. This conduct involved an attempt to interfere with the lawful administration of the Internal Revenue Service and the proper conduct of tax inquiries by misusing confidential IRS information and the powers of investigation of the IRS for the political benefit of the President. In approving and encouraging this activity, he failed to take care that the laws be faithfully executed and violated his constitutional oath faithfully to execute the office of President and to preserve, protect, and defend the Constitution.

I

WALLACE INVESTIGATION

On various occasions, President Nixon's subordinates acting under his authority and in order to serve his political interests sought and obtained information from the Internal Revenue Service about tax investigations of citizens. The first instance of which the Committee has evidence involves Governor George Wallace. In the spring of 1970, Wallace was running against Albert Brewer in the Alabama primary for the Democratic party's gubernatorial nomination. A Wallace defeat was considered helpful to the President because it would lessen Wallace's prospects in the 1972 presidential election. Four hundred thousand dollars in campaign funds remaining from the President's 1968 campaign was secretly contributed to the Brewer primary campaign. (Kalmbach testimony, 3 HJC 565, 664–66)

IRS information about Wallace was also used to try to defeat Wallace in the Alabama gubernatorial primary. In early 1970 Haldeman learned, apparently from an IRS sensitive case report,[1] about an

---

[1] Sensitive case reports are used by the IRS to inform the Secretary of the Treasury, the IRS Commissioner and, at their discretion, other Administration officials of the existence of proceedings or investigations involving prominent individuals.

investigation of George Wallace and his brother Gerald. Haldeman directed Clark Mollenhoff, special councel to the President, to obtain a report of the IRS investigation. (Book VIII, 38) According to Mollenhoff:

> I initially questioned Mr. Haldeman's instruction, but upon his assurance that the report was to be obtained at the request of the President, I requested the report of IRS Commissioner [Randolph] Thrower. (Book VIII, 38)

Mollenhoff obtained the IRS report on the Wallace investigation from Commissioner Thrower. (Book VIII, 38, 41) On March 21, 1970, Mollenhoff delivered it to Haldeman on his assurance that it was for the President. (Book VIII, 36, 38)

Material contained in the report was later transmitted to columnist Jack Anderson. Portions of it adverse to George Wallace were published nationally on April 13, 1970, several weeks before the primary election. (Book VIII, 37, 39, 41)

After the publication, Commissioner Thrower and the Chief Counsel of the IRS met with Ehrlichman and Haldeman and discussed the seriousness of the leak and the fact that an unauthorized disclosure constituted a criminal act.[2] Haldeman and Ehrlichman assured Thrower that they would take steps to prevent a recurrence. (Book VIII, 42)

II

INFORMATION AND AUDITS

In the fall of 1971, John Dean's assistant, John Caulfield, sought and obtained information from the IRS on the financial status and charitable contributions of Lawrence Goldberg in order to assess Goldberg's suitability for a position at the Committee to Re-elect the President. (Book VIII, 138–42) Confidential IRS material was also obtained about a journalist investigating the affairs of a campaign fundraiser and about various prominent entertainers. (Book VIII, 156–60, 211)

At Haldeman's request, and under Dean's direction, attempts were made to have tax audits conducted on various other persons. There is no evidence that these audits were in fact undertaken. (Book VIII, 176–80)

III

O'BRIEN INVESTIGATION

During the spring or summer of 1972, John Ehrlichman learned from an IRS sensitive case report that an investigation of Howard Hughes' business interests was under way. The report reflected a connection between the Hughes matters being investigated and the personal finances of Democratic National Committee Chairman Lawrence O'Brien. (Book VIII, 223–24) Ehrlichman sought and obtained information about O'Brien's tax returns from Assistant to the Com-

---

[2] 26 U.S.C. § 7213 provides in part that it "shall be unlawful for any officer or employee of the United States to divulge . . . to any person the amount or source of income, profits, losses, expenditures, or any particular thereof, set forth or disclosed in any income return." This section makes such activity a misdemeanor and requires the discharge of the guilty officer or employee. The IRS considers data obtained in an IRS investigation to be income return information. IRS Reg. § 301.6103(a)–1(a)(3)(i)(b).

missioner Roger Barth. (Roger Barth testimony, SSC Executive Session, June 6, 1974, 3-6) Ehrlichman also told Treasury Secretary Shultz that the Internal Revenue Service should interview O'Brien. The IRS policy then in effect was that audits and interviews, absent statute of limitations and other compelling considerations, would not be conducted during an election year with respect to candidates or others in politically sensitive positions. Book VIII, 219-20) Since the 1972 election campaign was in progress, the IRS would not have interviewed O'Brien until after election day, November 7, but because of Ehrlichman's demands the IRS had a conference with O'Brien in mid-August. (Book VIII, 219-21) According to Walters:

IRS interviewed Mr. O'Brien on or about August 17, 1972. Mr. O'Brien was cooperative although the interview was limited timewise, and Mr. O'Brien suggested that any further interview be postponed until after the election. My recollection is that IRS furnished a copy of the Conference Report to Secretary Shultz. A short time thereafter, Secretary Shultz informed me that Mr. Ehrlichman was not satisfied and that he needed further information about the matter. I advised the Secretary that IRS had checked the filing of returns and the examination status of those returns (closed) and that there was nothing else IRS could do.

On or about August 29, 1972, at the request of Secretary Shultz, I went to his office with Roger Barth so that we could conclude review of the O'Brien matter and dispose of it. Secretary Shultz, Mr. Barth and I discussed the matter and agreed that IRS could do no more. We then jointly telephoned Mr. Ehrlichman. Secretary Shultz informed Mr. Ehrlichman of that; I stated that IRS had verified that Mr. O'Brien had filed returns, that those returns reflected large amounts of income, that IRS already had examined and closed the returns, and that we (Shultz, Walters and Barth) all agreed that there was nothing further for IRS to do. Mr. Ehrlichman indicated disappointment, and said to me "I'm goddamn tired of your foot dragging tactics." I was offended and very upset but decided to make no response to that statement. Following the telephone conversation, I told Secretary Shultz that he could have my job any time he wanted it. (Book VIII, 234-35)

In early September, Ehrlichman telephoned Kalmbach and told him that O'Brien had IRS problems. He gave Kalmbach figures on O'Brien's allegedly unreported income and asked Kalmbach to plant the information with Las Vegas newspaperman Hank Greenspun, a friend of Kalmbach. Kalmbach refused to do so, despite subsequent requests by Ehrlichman and Mitchell. (Kalmbach testimony, 3 HJC 615-17)[3]

IV

McGOVERN SUPPORTERS

On September 11, 1972, Dean, at the direction of Ehrlichman, gave to IRS Commissioner Walters a list, which had been compiled by CRP campaign aide Murray Chotiner, of the names of 575 members of George McGovern's staff and contributors to his campaign. Dean asked

---

[3] According to an affidavit of SSC Minority Counsel Fred Thompson, he was informed by Special Counsel to the President J. Fred Buzhardt that John Dean reported to the President on the IRS investigation of O'Brien on September 15, 1972. (Book VIII, 337-39) In a staff interview, Dean said he did not recall discussing O'Brien's taxes with the President. On June 12, 1974, Judge Sirica held that the conversation from 6:00 to 6:13 p.m. on September 15, 1972, is relevant to the Watergate Special Prosecutor's investigation of alleged abuse of the IRS and ordered that this portion of the tape be turned over to the Special Prosecutor. The President has appealed Judge Sirica's order. Judge Cirica ruled that he was without judicial power, because of restrictions in an earlier Court of Appeals mandate, *Nixon v. Sirica*, to deliver a copy of this tape or transcript to the Committee. On June 24, 1974, the Committee subpoenaed the tape recording and materials related to this 13-minute conversation from the President.

that the IRS investigate or develop information about the people on the list. (Dean testimony, 2 HJC 229) According to Walters:

> Mr. Dean stated that he had not been asked by the President to have this done and that he did not know whether the President had asked that any of this activity be undertaken. Mr. Dean expressed the hope that the IRS could do this in such a manner that would "not cause ripples." He indicated that he was not yet under pressure with respect to this matter.
> I advised Mr. Dean that compliance with the request would be disastrous for the IRS and for the Administration and would make the Watergate affair look like a 'Sunday School picnic' . . . . I advised him that I would discuss the matter with Secretary Shultz, and that I would recommend to Secretary Shultz that we do nothing on the request. (Book VIII, 239)

Two days later, Walters and Shultz discussed the list and agreed to do nothing about Dean's request. (Book VIII, 275-76)

During his appearance before the Committee, Dean was asked by Representative Railsback about his instructions for giving the list of McGovern supporters to Walters.

> Mr. RAILSBACK. Were you instructed to tell Mr. Walters on September 11 that the President himself had not authorized [the request]?
> Mr. DEAN. I was instructed to not use the President's name, that is correct.
> Mr. RAILSBACK. And who instructed you?
> Mr. DEAN. Well, that was very clear in my discussions with Mr. Ehrlichman. (Dean testimony, 2 HJC 301)

On September 15, 1972, the President and Haldeman met and discussed the activities of John Dean. Dean was about to join the meeting. Haldeman explained what Dean had been doing:

> HALDEMAN. Between times, [Dean's] doing, he's moving ruthlessly on the investigation of McGovern people, Kennedy stuff, and all that too. I just don't know how much progress he's making, 'cause I—
> PRESIDENT. The problem is that's kind of hard to find.
> HALDEMAN. Chuck, Chuck has gone through, you know, has worked on the list, and Dean's working the, the thing through IRS and, uh, in some cases, I think some other [unintelligible] things. He's—He turned out to be tougher than I thought he would, which is what
> PRESIDENT. Yeah. (HJCT 1)

After Dean joined the meeting, the President, Haldeman and Dean discussed using federal agencies to attack the President's political opponents. (HJCT 10, 15) They spoke of the reluctance of the the IRS to follow up on White House complaints.[4] (Book VIII, 333) Dean testified before the Committee about this portion of the September 15, 1972, conversation:

> I am not sure how directly or specifically it came up, but there was a, indeed, a rather extended discussion with the President on the use of IRS. He made some rather specific comments to me, which in turn resulted in me going back to Mr. Walters again.
> . . . [A]s I recall the conversation, we were talking about the problems of having IRS conduct audits, and I told him that we hadn't been very successful at this because Mr. Walters had told me that he just didn't want to do it. I did not—I did not push him. As far as I was concerned I was off the hook. I had done what I had been asked, and I related this to the President. (Dean testimony, 2 HJC 229)

---

[4] This segment of the conversation was obtained accidentally when the September 15, 1972 tape was rerecorded for the Committee at the White House. On June 24, 1974, the Committee subpoenaed the tape recording and materials related to the conversation among the President, Haldeman and Dean from 6:00 to 6:13 p.m., and between the President and Haldeman from 4:43 to 5:27 p.m. The President refused to submit these recordings.

Dean also testified that the President said that if Dean had any problem with Shultz or the IRS, Dean should tell the President, who would straighten it out. (Dean testimony, 2 HJC 229) Dean testified that it was his impression that the September 15 meeting was not the first time the President had been advised of the requested audits of McGovern supporters (Dean testimony, 2 HJC 301); and that, after September 15, he believed his authority with respect to approaches to the IRS came directly from the President. (Dean testimony, 2 HJC 250)

As a result of his conversation with the President, Dean again contacted Commissioner Walters on September 25, 1972. (Dean testimony, 2 HJC 229, 350) According to Commissioner Walters:

> [Dean] inquired as to what progress I had made with respect to the list. I told him that no progress had been made. He asked if it might be possible to develop information on fifty-sixty-seventy of the names. I again told him that, although I would consider the matter with Secretary Shultz, any activity of this type would be inviting disaster. (Book VIII, 354)

Walters again discussed the matter with Schultz and they decided to do nothing with respect to Dean's demand. (Book VIII, 280–85, 354)

V

IRS SOURCES

On March 13, 1973, the President, Haldeman and Dean discussed the President's "project to take the offensive" with respect to the Senate Watergate hearings. The President mentioned the difficulty of obtaining information about contributions to the McGovern campaign. The President asked Dean, "Do you need any IRS [unintelligible] stuff?" Dean answered:

> [T]here is no need at this hour for anything from IRS, and we have a couple of sources over there that I can go to. I don't have to fool around with Johnnie Walters or anybody, we can get right in and get what we need. (HJCT 50)

ARTICLE II, PARAGRAPH (2)

(2) HE MISUSED THE FEDERAL BUREAU OF INVESTIGATION, THE SECRET SERVICE, AND OTHER EXECUTIVE PERSONNEL, IN VIOLATION OR DISREGARD OF THE CONSTITUTIONAL RIGHTS OF CITIZENS, BY DIRECTING OR AUTHORIZING SUCH AGENCIES OR PERSONNEL TO CONDUCT OR CONTINUE ELECTRONIC SURVEILLANCE OR OTHER INVESTIGATIONS FOR PURPOSES UNRELATED TO NATIONAL SECURITY, THE ENFORCEMENT OF LAWS, OR ANY OTHER LAWFUL FUNCTION OF HIS OFFICE; HE DID DIRECT, AUTHORIZE, OR PERMIT THE USE OF INFORMATION OBTAINED THEREBY FOR PURPOSES UNRELATED TO NATIONAL SECURITY, THE ENFORCEMENT OF LAWS OR ANY OTHER LAWFUL FUNCTION OF HIS OFFICE; AND HE DID DIRECT THE CONCEALMENT OF CERTAIN RECORDS MADE BY THE FEDERAL BUREAU OF INVESTIGATION OF ELECTRONIC SURVEILLANCE

The Committee finds clear and convincing evidence that Richard M. Nixon violated his constitutional oath and his constitutional duty to take care that the laws be faithfully executed by directing or authorizing executive agencies and personnel to institute or continue unlawful electronic surveillance and investigations, in violation or disregard of the constitutional rights of citizens. The surveillance and investigations served no lawful purpose of his office; they had no national security objective, although he falsely used a national security pretext to attempt to justify them. Information obtained from this surveillance was used by his subordinates, with his authorization or permission, for his political advantage; and the FBI records of electronic surveillance were concealed at his direction.

I

THE FBI WIRETAPS

In the spring of 1969, the President authorized the FBI to install wiretaps on the home telephones of a number of government employees and newsmen.[1] (Book VII, 147) This decision was made about the time of the appearance of an article by William Beecher in *The New York Times* which disclosed the bombing of Cambodia by the United States Air Force. (Book VII, 148–49) It was not known whether Beecher's article was based on classified information leaked from the National Security Council (NSC). (Book VII, 143–45, 299–300)

The President's orders were transmitted to the FBI by Colonel Alexander Haig. Haig told FBI officials that the directive to install wiretaps came on the highest authority, instructed the FBI not to maintain regular records of the wiretaps in the indices kept by the

---

[1] Letter, President Nixon to Senate Foreign Relations Committee, 7/12/74.

FBI for all of its other wiretaps and assured the Bureau that these surveillances would be necessary for only a few days. (Book VII, 189–90) Between May 12 and June 4, 1969, FBI wiretaps were installed on the telephones of five NSC staff members, two newsmen and one employee of the Department of Defense. (Book VII, 204–05)

One of the five NSC employees whose telephones were tapped was Morton Halperin (designated "N" in the Committee's statement of information).[2] The wiretap of Halperin's telephone was installed on May 9, 1969.[3] (Memorandum from Director, FBI to Attorney General, June 24, 1974; letter from Deputy Attorney General Silberman to Senator J. W. Fulbright, June 18, 1974) On July 8, 1969, Assistant FBI Director William Sullivan, who had day-to-day responsibility for the wiretaps, reported to Hoover that "nothing" of significance from the standpoint of the leak in question "has come to light" from the Halperin tap. Sullivan told Hoover that he had suggested to Colonel Haig that some of this coverage be removed. (Book VII, 326) The Halperin wiretap, however, remained in place.

On September 19, 1969, Halperin resigned from the staff of the NSC; he remained an NSC consultant until May, 1970. At the beginning of 1970, he became a consultant to Senator Edmund Muskie. (Book VII, 212–13, 329–30) Although Halperin, for more than a year, had no access to national security information, and despite Sullivan's assurance to Hoover that the tap had revealed no leaks, there is no evidence of any check to find grounds for continuing the tap on Halperin; the tap was not removed until February 10, 1971. (Book VII, 331–33) Between May 12, 1969 and May 11, 1970, the President received 14 summary letter reports regarding the Halperin wiretap. In May, 1969, Assistant to the President Henry Kissinger received copies of these letters and three additional summaries. (Book VII, 372–73) After Halperin terminated his relationship with the NSC, summaries were sent only to Haldeman, who received, in all, eighteen summary letters regarding Halperin. (Book VII, 370) The summaries included reports on the political activities of Senator Muskie. (Book VII, 229)

Haig requested the wiretap of another consultant to Senator Muskie's campaign, who had been employed by the NSC. (Book VII, 197, 212–13) The wiretap was installed at the time that he announced his resignation from the NSC, which occurred in June, 1970. The tap lasted from May 13, 1970, until February 10, 1971, the same date Halperin's tap was removed. (Book VII, 205) The summaries from this wiretap were sent only to Haldeman; they included information on the Muskie political campaign; they contained no discussion of classified matters. (Book VII, 228)

On February 28, 1973, in a conversation with John Dean, the President revealed that he was aware that there had been wiretaps on Muskie aides. While discussing the wiretap program, he asked Dean, "Didn't Muskie do anything bad on there?" (HJCT 37) The word "there" referred to the taps.

The President's policy of using the FBI to conduct electronic surveillance for purposes unrelated to national security, or any other

---

[2] Halperin's identity was disclosed in documents filed in *Halperin v. Kissinger*. The other subjects of the tap are not identified by name in this report.
[3] The Attorney General did not sign the authorization for the wiretap until three days after the tap was installed. (Book VII, 192–93)

proper purpose, was also carried out in the placing of taps on three White House employees working solely on domestic matters. On July 23, 1969, Attorney General Mitchell directed the FBI to initiate a wiretap (and also 24 hour-a-day physical surveillance) on an assistant to Ehrlichman, then Counsel to the President. (Book VII, 269–70) Mitchell told the FBI that this surveillance was at the express direction of the President. (Book VII, 269) This assistant had responsibilities with regard to domestic matters only. The reports, which were sent to Ehrlichman, contained information only about personal matters and domestic politics. (Book VII, 280) On August 4, 1969, Haig directed the FBI to tap the telephone of a White House speech writer, who had been overheard (in the course of a previously initiated White House tap on a newsman) agreeing to furnish the newsman with background information on a speech by the President on revenue sharing and welfare reform. (Book VII, 267; FBI memorandum W. C. Sullivan to C. D. DeLoach, 8/1/69)

In December, 1970, at Haldeman's direction, the home phone of a third member of the White House staff, who was not involved in national security, was tapped. (Book VII, 205, 268) After the FBI had delivered the first two daily reports on this employee, who was the son-in-law of a prominent Republican, Lawrence Higby, Haldeman's principal aide, called the FBI and ordered that FBI tap reports include only pertinent material. Six later reports were limited to political activities of the White House employee's father-in-law, general political matters, and the White House employee's personal affairs.[4] (Book VII, 274, 282)

On September 10, 1969, Attorney General Mitchell directed the FBI to install a wiretap on a network television reporter and to place him under 24-hour-a-day surveillance. Mitchell said that the President had expressly ordered this surveillance, and that the President had studied the FBI file on the reporter. The FBI installed the wiretap, but persuaded Mitchell not to order physical surveillance. (Book VII, 243–44) On October 9, 1969, the FBI reported to the Attorney General that conversations overheard on the reporter's telephone related primarily to family matters or matters of employment. The reporter had no known connection with any classified material. Hoover requested that the tap be discontinued. The tap continued for another month. (Book VII, 205, 254, 257)

In October and December, 1970, Haldeman directed that the FBI tap the telephones of two White House employees, one of whom was an NSC employee whose previous telephone tap had been discontinued. (Book VII, 204, 207) Haldeman claimed no national security justification for the tap; he said the employee was "a bad apple." (Book VII, 198–99)

The President's program to use the FBI to tap White House employees and newsmen ended February 10, 1971, when FBI Director Hoover, who was about to testify before a subcommittee of the House Appropriations Committee, insisted that all the remaining taps be

---

[4] Secretary Kissinger testified that, while he was familiar with the name of the speech writer, he had never even heard of the assistant to Ehrlichman or the son-in-law of the politician. He said he did not know that any of these three taps was installed. (Book VII, 261–66)

terminated.[5] From May, 1969, until February, 1971, the President caused the FBI to tap the telephones of at least 17 persons.[6] (Book VII, 204–05) None was reported to have made unauthorized disclosures. (Book VII, 233, 237)

At the time of these wiretaps it was the policy of the Department of Justice to review wiretaps every ninety days to determine whether probable cause existed for the wiretap to be continued on grounds of national security. The Department did not review any of the 17 taps.[7] (Book VII, 175, 178) The taps violated other Department of Justice criteria for permitting wiretaps without obtaining judicial warrants.[8]

On December 29, 1969, Hoover sent to the President a wiretap summary disclosing that former Secretary of Defense Clark Clifford planned to write a magazine article critical of the President's Vietnam policy. (Book VII, 360–61) In response to that information, Haldeman directed Magruder to find methods of "pre-action," and wrote, ". . . the key now is now to lay the ground work and be ready to go—

---

[5] According to a report by Senators Sparkman and Case to the Senate Foreign Relations Committee on the 1969–71 wiretaps, William Ruckelshaus stated that it was Hoover's practice to discontinue wiretaps shortly before congressional appearances of his so that he could report minimum taps in effect if he were questioned. (Book VII, 569–70)

[6] The reports of the wiretaps were sent during 1969 and 1970 to the President (34), Kissinger (37) and Ehrlichman (15). From May 14, 1970, to February 11, 1971, at the President's direction, the reports were sent only to Haldeman. From July, 1969, until the termination of the wiretap on February 11, 1971, Haldeman received a total of 52 wiretap reports.

[7] The Justice Department's ninety-day review period stemmed from holdings by the Supreme Court which placed strict limits on the duration of wiretaps on a single showing of probable cause. In *Katz v. United States*, 389 U.S. 347 (1967), the Supreme Court held that wiretaps are governed by the Fourth Amendment, which protects the rights of citizens to be secure in their homes, papers, and effects against unreasonable searches and seizures. This Amendment generally requires that all searches be pursuant to warrant, with the exception of a narrow group of cases, confined to very special circumstances. The Supreme Court has held that even in the case of wiretaps installed pursuant to warrants, the duration of those taps must be strictly limited. In *Berger v. New York*, 388 U.S. 41 (1967), the Supreme Court considered a New York State wiretap statute that permitted taps pursuant to warrants for an initial period of sixty days. The Court held that this period was too long without a new showing of probable cause for the issuance of the warrant:

[A]uthorization of eavesdropping for a two month period is the equivalent of a series of intrusions, searches and seizures pursuant to a single showing of probable cause . . . . Moreover, the statute permits, and there were authorized here, extensions of the original two-month period—presumably for two months each—on a mere showing that such extension is "in the public interest." . . . This we believe insufficient without a showing of probable cause for the continuance of the eavesdrop. (388 U.S. at 59)

Partly in response to the Supreme Court's decision in *Berger*, Congress enacted 18 U.S.C. § 2518(5) as a part of the Omnibus Crime Control and Safe Streets Act of 1968. That section provides that each wiretap authorization shall automatically terminate as soon as the objective of the authorization has been achieved, and that in no case may any authorization exceed 30 days. The courts have strictly applied the 30-day limit and have frequently limited the duration further on the basis of the Fourth Amendment. See, e.g., *United States v. Cafero*, 473 F. 2d 489 (3d Cir., 1973); *United States v. Focarile*, 340 F. Supp. 1033 (D. Md., 1972)

[8] In a report to Attorney General Richardson in 1973, Deputy Attorney General Olson stated:

". . . Up until the decision in the *Keith* case, [*United States v. United States District Court*, 407 U.S. 297 (1972)] it was necessary for the proposed surveillance to satisfy one or more of the following criteria:

(1) That it is necessary to protect the nation against actual or potential attack or any other hostile action of a foreign power.
(2) That it is necessary to obtain foreign intelligence information deemed essential to the security of the United States.
(3) That it is necessary to protect national security information against foreign intelligence activities.
(4) That it is necessary to protect the United States against the overthrow of the Government by force or other unlawful means.
(5) That it is necessary to protect the United States against a clear or present danger to the structure or the existence of its Government.

After the *Keith* decision, only the first three criteria (dealing with the foreign aspects of national security) have been taken into consideration. These criteria reflect the standards enunciated in 18 U.S.C. § 2511(3), as part of the Omnibus Crime Control and Safe Streets Act of 1968. In those cases where a determination is made that one or more of the appropriate standards is met, a written authorization or a reauthorization for a specified period not to exceed three months is executed by the Attorney General."

as well as to take all possible preliminary steps." Haldeman directed Magruder, "Let's get going." (Book VII, 365, 368) Magruder showed the memo and letter to Butterfield and asked for advice. Butterfield wrote a memo suggesting how Magruder should proceed to undercut Clifford. (Book VII, 362–63) When Ehrlichman saw the letter from Hoover, he wrote Haldeman that the information about Clifford was "the kind of early warning we need more of." He said, "Your game planners are now in an excellent position to map anticipatory action." (Book VII, 366)

In his public statement of May 22, 1973, the President said of the wiretaps:

> They produced important leads that made it possible to tighten the security of highly sensitive materials. I authorized this entire program. Each individual tap was undertaken in accordance with procedures legal at the time and in accord with longstanding precedent. ("Presidential Statements," May 22, 1973, 22)

Evidence before the Committee shows, on the contrary, that some of the taps were not legal, that they did not concern national security, but that they were installed for political purposes, in the President's interest and on his behalf. The President also privately admitted that the taps were very unproductive and were useless in determining the source of leaks. (HJCT 37).

II

JOSEPH KRAFT WIRETAP AND SURVEILLANCE

In June, 1969, John Ehrlichman directed his assistant, John Caulfield, to use private employees to install a wiretap at the home of a newspaper columnist, Joseph Kraft. John Ragan, a security consultant to the Republican National Committee, installed the wiretap, which remained in place for one week. (Book VII, 314–18)

The President discussed the Kraft tap with Ehrlichman. Although Ehrlichman has testified that the wiretap was authorized for a national security purpose (Book VII, 323), there is no evidence of this in FBI records or in any other evidence before the Committee. The Attorney General did not sign an FBI authorization for the Kraft wiretap. It was not authorized by court order. (Book VII, 356)

After the tap was installed, Ehrlichman told Caulfield that the FBI had been persuaded to take over the surveillance of Kraft. In June, 1969, Assistant FBI Director Sullivan traveled to a foreign country where Kraft was staying and arranged for microphone coverage of Kraft's hotel room by local authorities. From November 5 to December 12, 1969, at the direction of Attorney General Mitchell, the FBI conducted spot physical surveillance of Kraft in Washington, D.C. In July and November, 1969, the FBI sent reports on the coverage of Kraft to Ehrlichman. (Book VII, 315, 356–57)

III

DANIEL SCHORR FBI INVESTIGATION

In August, 1971, Daniel Schorr, a television commentator for the Columbia Broadcasting System, was invited to the White House to meet with the President's staff assistants to discuss an unfavorable analysis he had made of a presidential speech. (Book VII, 1113)

Shortly thereafter, Haldeman instructed his chief aide, Higby, to obtain an FBI background report on Schorr. (Book VII, 1120) The FBI conducted an extensive investigation of Schorr, interviewing twenty-five people in seven hours, including Schorr's friends and employers, and members of his family. (Book VII, 1113, 1115, 1120) When press reports revealed that the investigation had taken place, the President's aides fabricated and released to the press the explanation that Schorr was being considered for an appointment as an assistant to the Chairman of the Council on Environmental Quality. (Book VII, 1119) The President knew that Schorr had never been considered for any government position. The President approved the cover story. (Colson testimony, 3 HJC 238–39) Haldeman has testified that, although he could not remember why the investigation was requested, Schorr was not being considered for federal employment. (Book VII, 1120)

IV

THE DONALD NIXON SURVEILLANCE AND WIRETAP

In 1969, Haldeman and Ehrlichman asked the Central Intelligence Agency to conduct physical surveillance of Donald Nixon, the President's brother, who was moving to Las Vegas. Haldeman was reported to have feared that Donald Nixon would come into contact with criminal elements. (Report of CIA Inspector General and Deputy Director Robert Cushman, 6/29/73) The CIA, which has no jurisdiction to engage in domestic law enforcement or internal security activities, refused.[9]

In late 1970, the Secret Service [10] installed a wiretap on Donald Nixon's home telephone. The President has not claimed that the Secret Service was performing the function (which is within its jurisdiction) of protecting the President and his immediate family. The President said that the wiretap was installed to monitor conversations in which persons might try to cause his brother to exert "improper influence," particularly if such persons were in a foreign country. The President has said that his brother learned of the wiretap during its existence.[11] The Secret Service has no legal jurisdiction to wiretap for such purposes. (Book VII, 522)

V

THE HUSTON PLAN

On June 5, 1970, the President appointed an ad hoc committee of the Directors of the FBI, CIA, National Security Agency, and Defense Intelligence Agency to study domestic intelligence operations.

---

[9] 50 U.S.C. § 403(d)(3) defines the jurisdiction of the CIA as follows:
"(3) to correlate and evaluate intelligence relating to the national security, and provide for the appropriate dissemination of such intelligence within the Government using where appropriate existing agencies and facilities: Provided, That the Agency shall have no police, subpoena, law-enforcement powers, or internal-security functions: Provided further, That the departments and other agencies of the Government shall continue to collect, evaluate, correlate, and disseminate departmental intelligence; And provided further, That the Director of Central Intelligence shall be responsible for protecting intelligence sources and methods from unauthorized disclosure."

[10] The Secret Service's jurisdiction is confined to enforcement of the laws against counterfeiting; to protect the physical safety of the President and his immediate family, and to related matters. (18 U.S.C. § 3056).

[11] Under 18 U.S.C. § 2511(2)(6), consensual wiretaps are lawful only when consent is obtained in advance of the installation of the tap.

(Book VII, 377) On June 25 the ad hoc committee submitted an analysis by the intelligence agencies of the nature and extent of threats to internal security from dissident groups and other sources, and set forth proposals for loosening existing legal restraints on domestic intelligence-gathering procedures. The report noted that the FBI objected to relaxation of these restraints. (Book VII, 384-431)

During the first week of July, 1970, Tom Charles Huston, a White House staff assistant, submitted the ad hoc committee's report and wrote a memorandum to Haldeman recommending that the President adopt its proposals. Surreptitious entries, electronic surveillance and covert mail covers (described in the Huston Memorandum as "surreptitious screening," including opening and examining first class mail) were among the proposals in the report. Huston acknowledged the illegality of the techniques, but sought to justify them. (Book VII, 438-42) His defense of "surreptitious entries" was as follows:

> Use of this technique is clearly illegal: It amounts to burglary. It is also highly risky and could result in great embarrassment if exposed. However, it is also the most fruitful tool and can produce the type of intelligence which cannot be obtained in any other fashion.
>
> The FBI, in Mr. Hoover's younger days, used to conduct such operations with great success and with no exposure. (Book VII, 440)

On July 14, 1970, Haldeman wrote to Huston, in a memorandum: "The recommendations you have proposed as a result of the review have been approved by the President." (Book VII, 447) Huston, on Haldeman's instructions, prepared and distributed a formal decision memorandum (Book VII, 499) advising the members of the ad hoc committee that the President ordered:

> [1.] *Electronic Surveillance and Penetrations.* The intelligence community is directed to intensify coverage of individuals and groups in the United States who pose a major threat to the internal security. . . .
>
> [2.] *Mail Coverage.* Restrictions on legal coverage are to be removed. Restrictions on covert coverage are to be relaxed to permit use of this technique on selected targets of priority foreign intelligence and internal security interest.
>
> [3.] *Surreptitious Entry.* Restraints on the use of surreptitious entry are to be removed. . . . (Book VII, 454)

FBI Director Hoover and Attorney General Mitchell opposed the decision. (Book VII, 464) Mitchell informed the President and Haldeman of his opposition. (Book VII, 465) On July 27 or 28, 1970, on Haldeman's instructions, Huston recalled the decision memorandum.[12] (Book VII, 470-74)

VI

Concealment of Records of the 1969-1971 FBI Wiretaps

In conducting wiretaps, the FBI maintains a central file and indices of records of the taps so that the names of persons overheard are re-

---

[12] In addition to the options relating to relaxation of restraints on intelligence gathering methods, the Huston Plan recommended the formation of an Intelligence Evaluation Committee (IEC) to coordinate the work of the several intelligence agencies. The Huston Plan was a response only to domestic security threats, but the IEC was to include personnel from DIA, NSA and CIA as well as the FBI. Although the Huston Plan was recalled, the IEC was established in late 1970 and continued in effect through 1973. The agencies provided and evaluated intelligence information. The existence of the IEC was concealed under the cover of an existing unit called the Inter-Divisional Information Unit (IDIU). The cover was recommended by Dean in a memorandum to Mitchell on September 18, 1970. Dean described the IEC as both an operational and evaluation unit. (Book VII, 488-497) The IEC furnished the White House with information on all types of demonstrations that might have an impact on the President's reelection campaign. (Dean testimony, 2 HJC 347-48)

trievable if production should be required during a criminal prosecution.[13] The FBI was expressly ordered by Haig not to maintain records of the wiretaps initiated under the President's 1969 authorization, and was told that it would be desirable to have the matter handled without going to the Department of Justice. (Book VII, 189) The FBI nevertheless maintained unindexed logs and records of these taps and kept them in the office of Assistant Director William Sullivan. (Book VII, 182–83, 186)

On June 13, 1971, *The New York Times* published the first of the Pentagon Papers. On June 28, 1971, Daniel Ellsberg was indicted in connection with their release. (Book VII, 593, 616–17) On July 2, the Internal Security Division of the Department of Justice, which had responsibility for the Ellsberg prosecution, asked the FBI to review its files to determine if Ellsberg had been overheard on any wiretaps. (Book VII, 686–87)

Shortly after the Internal Security Division had requested the FBI check of its files, Sullivan informed Assistant Attorney General Robert Mardian, the head of the Internal Security Division, that Sullivan had custody of the files and logs of the 1969–1971 wiretaps, that he expected to be forced out of the FBI by Director Hoover and that he wanted to turn the wiretap records over to Mardian. According to Mardian, Sullivan said he feared Hoover would use the wiretap material to pressure the President to retain him as Director of the FBI. (Book VII, 757, 766–67)

Mardian sought advice from Attorney General Mitchell and then, on July 11, 1971, was contacted by either Haldeman or Ehrlichman, who instructed him to fly to San Clemente to discuss the matter with the President. (Book VII, 758, 767) John Ehrlichman's notes of a July 10 meeting with the President include: "Re: Grand Jury [14]—Don't worry re taps on discover—re WHs." Mardian arrived in San Clemente on July 11, 1971, and met with the President and Ehrlichman the next day. (Book VII, 806) The President directed Mardian to obtain the logs and files from Sullivan, to deliver them to the White House, and check with Kissinger, Haig and Haldeman to make sure all reports sent to them were accounted for. (Book VII, 2061) The FBI report of an interview of Mardian states:

He [Mardian] said the following morning after his arrival in San Clemente, California, [i.e., on July 12] he went directly to the Western White House and spoke with the President of the United States, Mr. Nixon. He said he received at that time two instructions—one was to get the FBI material from Mr. W. C. Sullivan and deliver it to the White House, and the second was to check to see if all the material the White House had in Washington, D.C., matched the material supplied by Mr. Sullivan.... (Book VII, 2060–61)

---

[13] Under the rule of *Alderman* v. *United States*, 394 U.S. 169 (1969), the Government is required to produce all materials generated by wiretaps for inspection by defendants in criminal cases.

[14] The Los Angeles Grand Jury that had indicted Ellsberg on June 28 continued in session, and eventually issued a superseding indictment. In addition, a Grand Jury in Boston was investigating the Pentagon Papers matter. Ehrlichman's notes of a meeting with the President on July 6, 1961 reflect a reference to the Boston Grand Jury. (Ehrlichman's notes, item 12, 39). On July 15, 1974, the House Judiciary Committee received a copy of certain of John Ehrlichman's handwritten notes taken during meetings with the President. The President had produced those notes pursuant to a subpoena issued in *United States* v. *Ehrlichman*, Cr. 74–110 (D. D.C.). They relate to discussions by the President about the Pentagon Papers disclosure and related matters. The 174 pages of notes received are contained in an appendix to the Committee's statement of informatieon.

In early August, after checking with Kissinger, Haig and Haldeman, as ordered by the President, Mardian delivered the wiretap files to someone in the Oval Office of the White House. He has refused to say to whom he actually delivered them. (Book VII, 2063) The FBI report of an interview of Mardian says:

> He [Mardian] said when he went to the White House he went directly to Dr. Kissinger's office. Dr. Kissinger and General Haig were present....
>
> Mr. Mardian said that in Dr. Kissinger's and General Haig's presence he opened the bag and removed a group of papers from the bag "clipped together" with a sheet of paper on top which had the chronological listing of summaries of wiretap information that had been previously furnished by the FBI to the White House. He said that he and Dr. Kissinger checked by date and satisfied themselves that Dr. Kissinger's material matched with the cover sheet which Mr. Mardian was using....
>
> He said that after he and Dr. Kissinger and General Haig were satisfied that the material in Dr. Henry Kissinger's office matched the itemized list, he walked into Mr. Haldeman's office. He said, again this point is not completely clear in his mind but he had the distinct impression that he left the check list with Mr. Haldeman to check against the summaries that Haldeman had in his possession in his own office.
>
> He said that as a result of Mr. Haldeman's check, as best he can recall, two of the summaries which were sent to the White House did not check against the list. He said his memory could be at fault and that, in effect, it could have been two that were in Dr. Kissinger's possession; however, he feels that the two missing summaries were missing from the summaries which Mr. Haldeman checked against the itemized list.
>
> After Mr. Haldeman completed his check, Mr. Mardian said he retrieved the bag with all its contents and walked into the Oval Room of the White House and left the bag. He was specifically asked to whom he gave the bag. He said he preferred not to answer because of the President's order concerning employees talking about national security information. Mr. Mardian was specifically asked "Did you give the bag to Mr. Nixon, the President of the United States?" He sat back in his chair, shrugged his shoulders, hesitated and said, "I cannot answer that question...." (Book VII, 2062–63)

The President directed Ehrlichman to take possession of the files. Ehrlichman placed them in a filing cabinet in his office, where they remained until his resignation on April 30, 1973. Ehrlichman then removed the documents from his office and turned them over to the President as Presidential papers. (Book VII, 782)

The concealment of the logs, together with the decision not to have the 1969–71 wiretaps indexed, were among the factors ultimately leading to the dismissal of the Ellsberg case in the spring of 1973. On January 24, 1972, when Judge Byrne, the trial judge in the case, directed the prosecution to disclose any electronic surveillance or overhearing of Halperin or Ellsberg, the government prosecutor in charge of the case filed affidavits denying that there had been electronic surveillance or overhearing of Ellsberg. (Book VII, 1504–11) In fact, Halperin's telephone had been tapped for 21 months and Ellsberg had been overheard on the tap 15 times. (Book VII, 681)

On February 22 or 23, 1973, the White House press office learned of a forthcoming *Time* magazine article that would disclose the existence of wiretaps on newsmen and White House employees including Halperin. (Book VII, 1742) Disclosure of this tap would show that the Government's affidavits in the trial were false, and would enable Ellsberg and his attorneys to ascertain that, contrary to the government's affidavit, Ellsberg had been overheard on a wiretap. John Dean investigated the *Time* story by contacting Assistant FBI Director

Mark Felt, Sullivan and Mardian. Each confirmed the existence of the wiretaps, and Mardian said that the files had been delivered to Ehrlichman. Ehrlichman told Dean that he had the files, but nevertheless directed Dean to have Presidential Press Secretary Ronald Ziegler publicly deny the *Time* story. (Book VII, 1743)

The *Time* article was published on February 26, 1973. It reported the existence of the FBI taps on newsmen and White House employees. The White House press office issued a denial. (Book VII, 1747–48) Two days later, on February 28, Dean reported to the President on the *Time* story and his meeting with Sullivan about the wiretaps. Dean told the President that the White House was stonewalling totally on the wiretap story. The President replied, "Oh, absolutely." (HJCT 36)

The following day, March 1, 1973, Acting FBI Director L. Patrick Gray publicly testified about the wiretaps. The Senate Judiciary Committee was holding hearings on Gray's nomination to be Director of the FBI. He testified that FBI records did not reveal any taps of newsmen or White House employees and that, as a result of the White House denial of their existence, he had not investigated the matter further. (Book VII, 1756) Gray testified that: (1) Mr. Hoover would not do something like this in the first place; (2) When Gray came into the Federal Bureau of Investigation on May 3, the very first thing that he had said was that he would not permit any wiretaps that were not in accordance with law; (3) If these acts [the wiretaps] had occurred, it was a felony; no question about it, certainly; (4) It was a crime; and (5) He did not check with the White House because the White House had already issued a denial. (Book VII, 1756–1759)

The White House continued to deny the existence of the wiretaps until May, 1973. During this period the continuing Ellsberg trial was the subject of the President's attention. On April 5, 1973, Ehrlichman, on behalf of the President, asked Judge Byrne if he were interested in the position of Director of the FBI. (Book VII, 1881–82) In addition, on April 18, 1973, in a telephone conversation,[15] Assistant Attorney General Henry Petersen told the President that he had received information that Hunt and Liddy and others were responsible for a break-in at the office of Dr. Ellsberg's psychiatrist. The President, according to Petersen, replied angrily that he knew about that. "Stay out of that. That's national security matter. Your mandate is Watergate." (Petersen testimony, 3 HJC 98) On April 25, 1973, Attorney General Kleindienst showed the President Justice Department memoranda, concerning the break-in of Dr. Ellsberg's psychiatrist.[16] Kleindienst insisted to the President that this information should be disclosed to the court in the Ellsberg case. The President, authorized the disclosure. (Book VII, 1984)

On May 9, 1973, after another news article about the wiretaps, an FBI agent told Acting FBI Director William Ruckelshaus that he recalled hearing Ellsberg on a wiretap three years earlier. (Book VII,

---

[15] On April 11, 1974, the House Judiciary Committee subpoenaed the tape recording and other materials related to this conversation. The President stated that the telephone call was from Camp David and was not recorded.
[16] On June 24, 1974, the House Judiciary Committee subpoenated the tape recording and other materials related to this conversation. The President refused to produce this recording.

2047–49) Ruckelshaus immediately reported this information to Assistant Attorney General Henry Petersen who forwarded it to Judge Byrne on May 10. Petersen also told Judge Byrne that the logs could not be located and that there were no records of the date, duration, or nature of the wiretap. (Book VII, 2051–54) Judge Byrne ordered an immediate investigation. On the same day, the FBI interviewed Mardian, who revealed that he had delivered the records to the White House. (Book VII, 2061–63) Ehrlichman could not be located until the following day. Two hours before Ehrlichman was interviewed, Judge Byrne dismissed all charges against Ellsberg and his co-defendant, on the basis of misconduct by the Government. He stressed the failure of the Government to produce the wiretap records as one ground for dismissal. (Book VII, 2079)

ARTICLE II, PARAGRAPH (3)

(3) HE HAS, ACTING PERSONALLY AND THROUGH HIS SUBORDINATES AND AGENTS, IN VIOLATION OR DISREGARD OF THE CONSTITUTIONAL RIGHTS OF CITIZENS, AUTHORIZED AND PERMITTED TO BE MAINTAINED A SECRET INVESTIGATIVE UNIT WITHIN THE OFFICE OF THE PRESIDENT, FINANCED IN PART WITH MONEY DERIVED FROM CAMPAIGN CONTRIBUTIONS, WHICH UNLAWFULLY UTILIZED THE RESOURCES OF THE CENTRAL INTELLIGENCE AGENCY, ENGAGED IN COVERT AND UNLAWFUL ACTIVITIES, AND ATTEMPTED TO PREJUDICE THE CONSTITUTIONAL RIGHT OF AN ACCUSED TO A FAIR TRIAL

The Committee finds clear and convincing evidence that Richard M. Nixon established a secret investigative unit in the White House to engage in covert activities. This unit engaged in unlawful activities that violated the constitutional rights of citizens, including the fourth amendment right of Dr. Lewis Fielding and the right of Daniel Ellsberg to a fair trial. The unit used the resources of the CIA unlawfully to assist in its operations and used campaign contributions to partially finance its unlawful activities. Although Richard M. Nixon later asserted that the activities of the unit were undertaken for national security purposes, the Committee finds that its unlawful activities served no such objective. Richard M. Nixon, without regard for law, permitted the unit to engage in these unlawful activities, and by so doing violated his constitutional oath and his duty to take care that the laws be faithfully executed.

I

THE CREATION AND PURPOSES OF THE SPECIAL INVESTIGATIONS UNIT

The creation of the special investigations unit (the Plumbers) referred to in paragraph (3) of Article II resulted from the publication of the Pentagon Papers, portions of which first appeared in *The New York Times* on June 13, 1971. (Book VII, 593) The President viewed the publication of the Pentagon Papers primarily as a political opportunity rather than a threat to national security.

Ehrlichman's handwritten notes [1] of a meeting with the President on June 17, 1971, under the designation π (Ehrlichman's symbol for the President), read: "Win PR, not just court case." (Ehrlichman notes, Item 1, p. 3) The notes, taken four days after the Pentagon Papers were first published, indicate that Daniel Ellsberg had been

---

[1] On July 15, 1974, the House Judiciary Committee received a copy of certain of John Ehrlichman's handwritten notes taken during meetings with the President. Those notes were produced pursuant to a subpoena issued in *U.S. v. Ehrlichman*, CR 74-116 (D.D.C.) and relate to discussions by the President about the Pentagon Papers disclosure and related matters. The 174 pages of notes received are being printed by the Committee as a separate volume of evidence.

identified as the source of the disclosure. Although the President's National Security Adviser, Henry Kissinger, was present at this June 17 meeting, Ehrlichman's notes do not reflect a discussion by Kissinger or anyone else of a fear that Ellsberg would disclose other classified material. (Ehrlichman notes, pp. 3–5)[2] Ehrlichman's notes of a meeting two days later state: "Win the case but the NB [important] thing is to get the public view right. Hang it all on LBJ." (Ehrlichman notes, p. 7).

On June 25, 1971, Colson wrote in a memorandum to Haldeman that it was important to keep the Pentagon Papers issue alive because of its value in evidencing the poor judgment of prior Democratic administrations, thus working to the disadvantage of most Democratic candidates. Colson's memoradum recommended encouraging Congressional hearings with respect to the Pentagon Papers because an analysis of the origins of U.S. involvement in Vietnam would hurt the Democrats.[3] (Book VII, 664–72) Once again there was no mention of any effect of the disclosure of the Pentagon Papers on national security.

Colson wrote:

> There is another opportunity in this whole episode. That is the prosecution of Ellsberg. It would indeed arouse the heartland which is at present not very excited over the whole issue.
>
> * * * * * *
>
> The Ellsberg case, if pressed hard by us, will of course keep the issue alive.
>
> * * * * * *
>
> In short, I think it is very clear that there are profound political implications, that this offers us opportunities in ways we perhaps did not initially appreciate, that we can turn what appeared to be an issue that would impair Presidential credibility into one that we can use by effective contrast to improve the credibility of this Administration; and further, that it is a tailor-made issue for causing deep and lasting divisions within the Democratic ranks.
>
> For this reason, I feel that we must not move precipitously or worry about tomorrow's headlines. We must keep our eye on the real target: to discredit the Democrats, to keep them fighting and to keep ourselves above it so that we do not appear to be either covering up or exploiting. (Book VII, 670, 671, 673)

This memorandum was delivered to the President; he discussed aspects of it with Colson on the day it was written. (Colson testimony, 3 HJC 197) On the morning of July 1, 1971, the President met with Haldeman and Colson and discussed the Ellsberg trial.[4] Ehrlichman joined the meeting a half hour after it began. His notes indicate that they were advised to read the chapter about Alger Hiss in the Presi-

---

[2] Although there is evidence that a portion of the Pentagon Papers was delivered to the Soviet Embassy on June 17, 1971, this was later repudiated by Krogh and Young (Book VII, 633, 637, 1392) there is no evidence in Ehrlichman's notes that he discussed this matter with the President. There is evidence that Ellsberg was not suspected or investigated by the Plumbers for this delivery. (Colson testimony, 3 HJC 512) A memorandum from Krogh and Young to Ehrlichman dated November 1, 1971, stated that one of the problems with the Ellsberg prosecution was the fact that Ellsberg gave the papers to the press and not to a foreign power. (Book VII, 1392)

[3] Throughout the summer of 1971 and into September, Colson continued to encourage congressional hearings. (Book VII, 835–36, 841, 1066–69) Colson testified that it was the President's wish that hearings be held as a method of publicly airing the facts. (Colson testimony, 3 HJC 197–98) Ehrlichman's notes of meetings with the President also reflect several discussions of congressional hearings. (Ehrlichman notes, Items 5–7, p. 16, 18–21, 36–37, 56–57, 59) Hunt was instructed to select the politically damaging material from the Pentagon Papers. (Book VII, 1218) Hunt also fabricated State Department cables purporting to show President Kennedy as responsible for the assassination of Diem. These cables were shown to a Life magazine writer in connection with Colson's efforts in September, 1971 to publish a major expose of the Diem coup and to revitalize interest in a Congressional investigation of the origins of the Vietnam War. (Book VII, 1031, 1035–39, 1042–51, 1068–75)

[4] On June 24, 1974, the House Judiciary Committee subpoenaed the tape recording and other materials related to the conversation among the President, Haldeman, Colson and Ehrlichman on July 1, 1971. The President refused to produce these materials, other than the edited Ehrlichman notes.

dent's book, "*Six Crises*," and quote the President as saying the Hiss case "was won in the press." (Ehrlichman notes, Item 6, p. 26) The notes then state: "Leak stuff out—this is the way we win." (Ehrlichman notes, Item 8, p. 27)[5]

Also on July 1, Colson telephoned Howard Hunt. The following exchange took place:

C One question that occurs to me. This thing could go one of two ways. Ellsberg could be turned into a martyr of the new left (he probably will be anyway), or it could be another Alger Hiss case, where the guy is exposed, other people were operating with him, and this may be the way to really carry it out; we might be able to put this bastard into a helluva situation and discredit the new left.
H It would [sic] a marvelous way if we could do it, but of course, you've got the *Times* and the *Post* and the *Monitor* and all sorts of things.
C They've got to print the news, you know, if this thing really turns into a sensational case.
H Well, you of course, you're in a much better spot to see how the Administration stands to gain from it and at this point, I would be willing to set aside my personal yen for vengeance to make sure that the Administration profits from this. Now it's turned out, I gather from noonday news reports, it's become apparent that JFK was the guy who slid us into this thing back in May or so of 1961.
C Hell, you know that from where you were.
H I knew that, yes, but it had never surfaced before.
C Let me ask you this, Howard, this question. Do you think with the right resources employed that this thing could be turned into a major public case against Ellsberg and co-conspirators?
H Yes, I do, but you've established a qualification here that I don't know whether it can be met.
C What's that?
H Well, with the proper resources.
C Well, I think the resources are there.
H Well, I would say so absolutely.
C Then your answer would be he should go down the line to nail the guy cold?
H Go down the line to nail the guy cold, yes . . . (Book VII, 700–01)

Colson sent a transcript of this conversation to Haldeman on July 2. The transmittal memorandum noted that Hunt had information from his CIA involvement in the Bay of Pigs that would destroy President Kennedy. (Book VII, 699)

The President discussed the Ellsberg matter again with Haldeman, Ehrlichman, and Mitchell on July 6, 1971. Ehrlichman's notes include: "π [President] to JM: must be tried in the paper. Not Ellsberg (since already indicted). Get conspiracy smoked out thru the papers. Hiss and Bentley cracked that way." During the same conversation, Ehrlichman wrote: "π leak the (e) [evidence] of guilt." (Ehrlichman notes, Items 7, 15, p. 38, 40) Ehrlichman's notes of a meeting with the President on July 10, 1971, stated: "Goal—Do to McNam., Bundy, JFK elite the same destructive job that was done on Herbert Hoover years ago." (Ehrlichman notes, Item 12, p. 52)

II

STAFFING THE PLUMBERS

Around June 25, 1971, the President directed Colson, Haldeman and Ehrlichman to try to find a person, preferably from the White House

---

[5] On the afternoon of July 1, 1971, the President and Ehrlichman met with a national security study group regarding declassification of documents. The notes of that meeting contain the following references: "Espionage not involved in Ellsberg case" and "Don't think in terms of spies." (Ehrlichman notes, Items 29 and 30, p. 32–33)

staff, to assume responsibility for all aspects of the Pentagon Papers disclosure, including coordination of the ongoing investigations by other Federal agencies and the handling of the prospective congressional investigations. (Colson testimony, 3 HJC 198) Colson prepared a memorandum for Haldeman dated July 2, 1971, which named several candidates, including Hunt and Buchanan, a White House speech writer. (Book VII, 678) Colson also sent Haldeman a transcript of the telephone conversation between Colson and Hunt. (Book VII, 699-702)

Buchanan, the first choice of Haldeman and Ehrlichman, declined the offer. (Book VII, 704-06) On July 8, 1971, Buchanan, sent a memorandum to Ehrlichman setting out his contrary views on the Ellsberg project.

> Having considered the matter until the early hours, my view is that there are some dividends to be derived from Project Ellsburg [sic]—but none to justify the magnitude of the investment recommended.
>
> At the very best, let us assume we can demonstrate, after three months investigation, that Ellsburg [sic] stole the documents, worked hand-in-glove with ex-NSC types, collaborated with leftist writers Neil Sheehan and Fox Butterfield, got together a conspiracy to drop the documents at set times to left-wing papers, all timed to undercut McGovern-Hatfield opposition—what have we accomplished?
>
> What benefit would be derived to the President and his political fortunes in 1972—and what damage visited upon his major political adversaries on the other side of the aisle. . . .
>
> This is not to argue that the effort is not worth-while—but that simply we ought not now to start investing major personnel resources in the kind of covert operation not likely to yield any major political dividends to the President. (Book VII, 708-09)

Hunt was hired, effective July 6, 1971, to work on the Pentagon Papers project. (Book VII, 715-16, 721) Colson had known Hunt socially for several years and was aware of his background with the CIA. (Book VII, 677)

Ehrlichman's notes of his meeting with the President on July 6, 1971, state: "π: put on a non[legal] team on the conspiracy?" (Ehrlichman's notes, Item 11, p. 39)

On July 7, 1971, after being introduced to Hunt by Colson, (Book VII, 718-19) Ehrlichman called CIA Deputy Director Robert Cushman and said:

> I want to alert you that an old acquaintance, Howard Hunt, has been asked by the President to do some special consultant work on security problems. He may be contacting you sometime in the future for some assistance. I wanted you to know that he was in fact doing some things for the President. He is a longtime acquaintance with the people here. He may want some help on computer runs and other things. You should consider he has pretty much carte blanche. (Book VII, 728)

This call was transcribed by Cushman's secretary. (Book VII, 729-31) The President and Ehrlichman met on July 9, 1971, and Ehrlichman's notes state: "Dave Young to a special project." (Ehrlichman's notes, Item 36, p. 48)

On July 12 in San Clemente the President met with Assistant Attorney General Mardian, chief of the Internal Security Division. According to Ehrlichman's affidavit in *United States* v. *Ehrlichman*, the President received a report on the status of the investigation of the Pentagon Papers. The President was not satisfied with the progress and insisted upon an early designation of a man to be in charge of the White House effort.[6] Ehrlichman summoned David Young and Egil Krogh to San Clemente, and on July 17, 1971, he assigned them to be cochairmen of a unit to coordinate the Ellsberg-Pentagon Papers investigations. (Book VII, 806–07)

Ehrlichman called Colson from San Clemente on the weekend of July 17 and asked Colson to assign Hunt to work for Krogh. On July 22, 1971, Hunt was assigned to the unit in a meeting with Colson and Krogh. (Colson testimony, 3 HJC 206–07) Gordon Liddy, who had prior investigative experience with the FBI and the Department of Treasury, was also hired to work with the unit. (Book VII, 816–20)

In a discussion with Krogh and Ehrlichman on July 24, 1971, the day after the publication of a story disclosing the American negotiating position in the Strategic Arms Limitation talks, the President said:

> This does affect the national security—this particular one. This isn't like the Pentagon Papers. (Book VII, 885)

III

ACTIVITIES OF THE PLUMBERS

A. *Publicly Discrediting Ellsberg*

After the establishment of the unit headed by Krogh and Young, the President assigned Colson the task of publicly disseminating derogatory material collected by the Plumbers. The President also assigned Colson the task of insuring that Congressional hearings were held as a method of bringing out information that would discredit Ellsberg. (Book VII, 830–42; Colson testimony, 3 HJC 197–98)

The President directed Colson to release information concerning alleged ties of Ellsberg's lawyer. Leonard Boudin, with the Communist Party (Book VII, 1139–41) and also to release personal information about Ellsberg himself. On June 3, 1974, Colson pleaded guilty to a criminal information that read in part:

> On or about June 28, 1971, and for a period of time thereafter, in the District of Columbia and elsewhere, CHARLES W. COLSON, the DEFENDANT, unlawfully, willfully and knowingly did corruptly endeavor to influence, obstruct and impede the due administration of justice in connection with the criminal trial of Daniel Ellsberg under indictment in the case of *United States* v. *Russo*, Criminal Case No. 9373, United States District Court, Central District of California, by devising and implementing a scheme to defame and destroy the public image and credibility of Daniel Ellsberg and those engaged in the legal defense of Daniel Ellsberg, with the intent to influence, obstruct, and impede the conduct and outcome of the criminal prosecution then being conducted in the United States District Court for the Central District of California. (Book VII, 918–23)

Concerning the President's role in these activities, Colson stated in court:

> [T]he President on numerous occasions urged me to disseminate damaging information about Daniel Ellsberg, including information about Ellsberg's attor-

---

[6] Ehrlichman's notes of the July 12, 1971 meeting between the President and Mardian contain no reference to the President's dissatisfaction with the investigation or his insistence that someone should be placed in charge of a White House effort. (Ehrlichman notes, pp. 53–58) In fact, the notes state, "FBI going all out now." (Ehrlichman notes, Item 12, p. 57)

ney and others with whom Ellsberg had been in close contact. I endeavored to do so—and willingly. (Colson testimony, *United States v. Colson*, June 21, 1974, 5–6) Colson testified before the House Judiciary Committee that his notes of a meeting with the President in mid-August reflect a discussion of material about Boudin and his alleged ties to the Communist Party. (Colson testimony, 3 HJC 223) Krogh and Young advised Ehrlichman by memorandum dated August 19, 1971, that the President was after Colson to get something out on Ellsberg and that Hunt was preparing an article about Boudin. (Book VII, 1127) On August 24, Ehrlichman forwarded the article to Colson, who gave it to a journalist. (Book VII, 1128–40, 1144)

B. *Use of the CIA for Technical Assistance and Psychological Profile*

The President authorized enlisting the aid of the CIA in the activities of the Plumbers. Ehrlichman's only contacts with the CIA were at the direction of the President. (Book VII, 734–38) This conclusion is based on Ehrlichman's sworn testimony and he also testified that he called CIA Deputy Director Cushman on July 7, 1971, and on behalf of the President requested assistance for Hunt.

Hunt began receiving assistance from the CIA on July 22, 1971 when he met with Cushman and requested alias identification and disguise materials. Although this assistance was beyond the statutory jurisdiction of the CIA,[7] the materials were provided to Hunt the next day. (Book VII, 844–58)

The CIA disguise and false identification were used by Hunt in (1) an interview of Clifton DeMotte who allegedly had information derogatory to Senator Kennedy and members of the Kennedy political group (Book VII, 853), (2) the reconnaissance and subsequent break-in of Dr. Fielding's office in Los Angeles, (3) the interview of ITT lobbyist Dita Beard in Denver in March 1972, and (4) the break-in of the Democratic National Committee Headquarters in June 1972. (House Armed Services Committee Report No. 93–25, October 29, 1973, 3) At Hunt's request the CIA also provided him with a tape recorder in a typewriter carrying case; (Book VII, 1226–27) and before Hunt and Liddy went to Los Angeles for their reconnaissance of the office of Ellsberg's psychiatrist the CIA provided Liddy with false identification, disguise material and a camera concealed in a tobacco pouch. Upon their return from Los Angeles, the CIA developed the film of the photographs of the psychiatrist's office. (Book VII, 1152–65)

Hunt also requested a CIA secretary, credit cards, and an office in New York City with a backstopped phone. The CIA refused these requests, and Cushman called Ehrlichman on August 27, 1971, and obtained Ehrlichman's permission not to fill Hunt's latest requests. (Book VII, 1226–27, 1231–38) An internal CIA memorandum stated that Hunt's requests drew the Agency further into the sensitive area of domestic operations against Americans. (Book VII, 1230)

In addition to this type of assistance, Young also requested a psychological profile of Ellsberg from the CIA. (Book VII, 898) Hunt,

---

[7] The CIA's jurisdiction is limited by a provision in the National Security Act of 1947, as amended, which states: "[T]he agency shall have no police, subpoena, law-enforcement powers, or internal-security functions. . . ." 50 U.S.C. § 403(d)(3).

in a memorandum to Colson dated July 28, 1971, entitled *Neutralization of Ellsberg*, recommended the development of a psychological profile as part of a file of derogatory information. The memorandum stated that the file would be a basic tool essential in determining how to destroy Ellsberg's public image and credibility. (Book VII, 914) Hunt told the CIA psychiatrist that the profile would be useful in trying Ellsberg in the press. (Book VII, 1083–84, 1087)

The request for a psychological profile was made directly to Helms, the CIA Director. Young stressed to Helms the high level of White House interest in the project. (Book VII, 898–903) On August 12 he told the psychiatrist who directed its preparation that the President was aware of the study. (Book VII, 1083, 1090–93) The profile, the only one known to have ever been prepared by the CIA on an American civilian (Book VII, 899), had been delivered to the White House the previous day. (Book VII, 1008–09, 1011–19)

The Plumbers were not satisfied with the profile and on August 12, 1971, requested the CIA to prepare an expanded psychological profile on Ellsberg. CIA staff members believed that the profile was beyond the Agency's jurisdiction and had suspicions as to the use that might be made of it. (Book VII, 1408–11) The staff psychiatrist who directed the effort concluded that the purpose was to defame or manipulate Ellsberg. (Book VII, 1400–07)

Despite the reluctance of the CIA, a second profile was prepared by the Agency in early November, 1971. Helms directed that it be delivered to the White House. He sent a separate letter to David Young expressing the CIA's pleasure in being of assistance but impressing upon Young the importance of concealing the CIA's involvement. (Book VII, 1412–20)

C. The Fielding Break-in

The July 28, 1971 memorandum from Hunt to Colson entitled *Neutralization of Ellsberg* recommended obtaining Ellsberg's psychiatric records from his former psychiatrist for use in destroying Ellsberg's image and credibility. (Book VII, 914) The Plumbers had been informed by the FBI that on July 20 and 26, 1971, the psychiatrist, Dr. Lewis Fielding, had refused to be interviewed. (Book VII, 975, 983, 987–90) On or about August 5, Krogh and Young complained to Ehrlichman that the FBI would not cooperate fully in the Ellsberg investigation. (Book VII, 983, 1000) Krogh recommended that Hunt and Liddy be sent to California to complete the Ellsberg investigation. (Book VII, 983–84) Ehrlichman has stated that between July 26 and August 5, 1971, he discussed with the President his conversations with Krogh, and the President told Ehrlichman that Krogh should do whatever he considered necessary. Ehrlichman passed this instruction on to Krogh. (Book VII, 1000–01) Ehrlichman has also testified that the President approved the recommendation that the unit become operational and approved a trip by Hunt and Liddy to California to get "some facts which Krog felt he badly needed." (Book VII, 993, 997–98, 1001, 1166)

In April, 1973, the President reaffirmed the fact that he had authorized operations against Dr. Fielding. In a telephone conversation on

April 18, 1973, Henry Petersen advised the President that the Justice Department had learned of the Fielding break-in. (Book VII, 1956-57) Ehrlichman has stated in an affidavit that he was present during the call and that immediately after the President hung up he told Ehrlichman that the break-in was in furtherance of national security and fully justified under the circumstances. (Book VII, 810) Colson testified before the Committee that on April 19, 1973, Ehrlichman told him about the Petersen call. Ehrlichman told Colson that the President had informed Petersen that the President approved the Ellsberg operation in advance after consultation with Hoover and that Petersen was to stay out of it. (Colson testimony, 3 HJC 237)

On August 11, 1971, Krogh and Young submitted a memorandum to Ehrlichman informing him of the delivery of the CIA psychological profile and of their dissatisfaction with it. (Book VII, 1023) The memorandum also said:

> In this connection we would recommend that a covert operation be undertaken to examine all the files still held by Ellsberg's psychoanalyst covering the two-year period in which he was undergoing analysis.

Ehrlichman initialed the line "approve" and wrote, "if done under your assurance that it is not traceable." (Book VII, 1024)

Young sent a memorandum to Ehrlichman on August 26, 1971, entitled, *Status of Information Which Can Be Fed Into Congressional Investigation of Pentagon Papers Affair.* (Book VII, 1215) The memorandum asked how quickly the Administration wanted to bring about a change in Ellsberg's image and contained the following footnote:

> [I]t is important to point out that with the recent article on Ellsberg's lawyer, Boudin, we have already started on a negative press image for Ellsberg. If the present Hunt/Liddy Project #1 is successful, it will be absolutely essential to have an overall game plan developed for its use in conjunction with the Congressional investigation. In this connection, I believe that the point of Buchanan's memorandum on attacking Ellsberg through the press should be borne in mind; namely that the situation being attacked is too big to be undermined by planted leaks among the friendly press.
> If there is to be any damaging of Ellsberg's image and those associated with him, it will therefore be necessary to fold in the press planting with the Congressional investigation. I mentioned these points to Colson earlier this week, and his reply was that we should just leave it to him and he would take care of getting the information out. I believe, however, that in order to orchestrate this whole operation we have to be aware of precisely what Colson wants to do. (Book VII, 1219)

Hunt and Liddy, equipped with alias identification, disguise materials and a camera provided by the CIA, made a reconnaissance trip to California on August 25, 1971 to inspect Dr. Fielding's office. The CIA later developed the photographs taken there. (Book VII, 1152, 1157-60, 1165-67) Krogh and Young have testified that on or about August 30, 1971, after Hunt and Liddy reported that their reconnaissance satisfied them that an entry operation was feasible, they called Ehrlichman and told him that they believed an operation that could not be traceable to the White House was possible and that Ehrlichman gave his approval. (Book VII, 1240-44)

The break-in of Dr. Fielding's office was executed on September 3, 1971, by a team under the immediate and close direction of Hunt and Liddy. (Book VII, 1276, 1281-92) There is a conflict between the testimony of Dr. Fielding and the burglars as to whether the burglary yielded any information about Ellsberg. (Book VII, 1276, 1289–91, 1293–97)

The break-in violated Dr. Fielding's right under the Fourth Amendment of the Constitution to be secure in his person, house, papers and effects, against unreasonable searches and seizures. Krogh pleaded guilty to conspiracy to violate the civil rights of Dr. Fielding (18 U.S.C. § 241); [8] Ehrlichman, Liddy and two of the members of the team that performed the break-in were convicted on July 12, 1974 of conspiring to violate Dr. Fielding's civil rights.[8a] The President in his public statements has stated that the break-in was illegal, unauthorized and completely deplorable. ("Presidential Statements," 8/22/73, 47)

Hunt and Liddy reported the results of the operation against Dr. Fielding's office to Krogh and Young on the afternoon of September 7, 1971. (Book VII, 1302–06) Ehrlichman's logs show that at 10:45 on the morning of September 8, 1971, Krogh and Young met with Ehrlichman. (Book VII, 1336) Ehrlichman has testified that he discussed the break-in with Krogh and Young. (Book VII, 1334) At 3:26 on the afternoon of September 8, Ehrlichman met with the President. (Book VII, 1335) Ehrlichman informed Colson on September 9 that Hunt and Liddy had attempted to get Ellsberg's psychiatric records but failed. (Colson testimony, 3 HJC 236; (book VII, 1335) On September 10, 1971, Ehrlichman met with the President from 3:08 to 3:51 p.m.,[9] and then met with Krogh and Young at 4:00 p.m. The President called Colson immediately following his meeting with Ehrlichman on September 10. (Book VII, 1335, 1337)

D. Financing

Part of the financing for the Fielding break-in was arranged by Colson, who borrowed $5,000 in cash from Joseph Baroody, a Washington public relations man. Baroody brought the money to Krogh at the White House. (Book VII, 1266–67) Krogh, in turn, gave the money to Liddy on September 1, 1971, immediately before Liddy and Hunt left for Los Angeles. (Book VII, 1257–59) In order to repay Baroody, Colson called George Webster, a Washington attorney, and asked if there were any campaign committees available to receive a contribution. Webster advised Colson of the existence of a committee called "People United for Good Government." Colson solicited the Associated Milk Producers, Inc. to make a $5,000 contribution to that committee. Colson instructed Webster to cash the check and hold the money for Baroody, who later picked it up at Webster's office. (Book VII, 1269–74)

E. Other Activities

The Plumbers were instructed to investigate the source of the July 23, 1971 disclosure in a newspaper article of the American negotiating position in the SALT talks. In a meeting with Ehrlichman

---

[8] *United States* v. *Krogh*, Information and Docket (Book VII, 1608–13).
[8a] Transcript of Proceedings, *United States* v. *Ehrlichman*, July 12, 1974.
[9] On June 24, 1974, the House Judiciary Committee subpoenaed the tape recordings and other materials related to these conversations between the President and Ehrlichman. The President refused to produce the recordings or other materials.

and Krogh on July 24, 1971, the President instructed Krogh to conduct polygraph examinations of Defense Department and State Department personnel. (Book VII, 864–66, 868–70) The tape recording of that conversation suggests that the President believed that the disclosure affected national security because it interfered with current negotiations. (Book VII, 885) Krogh contacted the CIA and obtained personnel and equipment to conduct the polygraph examinations. (Book VII, 895) In an interview, Donald Stewart, a Defense Department investigator, stated that the FBI became involved in the investigation and that the source of the leak was not discovered.[10] William Beecher, the journalist who wrote the article, was subsequently appointed Deputy Assistant Secretary of Defense for Public Affairs. (Book VII, 891–92)

On December 13 and 14, 1971, articles by Jack Anderson appeared in *The Washington Post* disclosing the American position in the India-Pakistan War.[11] (Book VII, 1430–31) Krogh refused to authorize wiretaps in connection with this investigation and for that reason was removed from the unit. (Book VII, 1432) Young worked alone on this assignment. The Defense Department conducted the investigation and copies of investigative reports were sent to Young at the White House. (Book VII, 1422–29) The FBI placed wiretaps on persons suspected of the disclosure. (Book VII, 1438–40) During the course of the investigation it was discovered that Yeoman Charles Radford, one of the persons suspected, had been furnishing documents from Kissinger and the National Security Council to the Joint Chiefs of Staff. (Book VII, 1423–24, 1426)

IV

CONCEALMENT OF THE PLUMBERS' ACTIVITIES

Following the Watergate break-in the President initiated a policy of preventing federal investigations from uncovering the Plumbers' activities. The President said on May 22, 1973, that his concern that activities of the Plumbers might be exposed was one reason for ordering Haldeman and Ehrlichman to insure that the Watergate investigations did not lead to their disclosure. ("Presidential Statements," 5/22/73, 24)[12]

On March 17, 1973, John Dean reported to the President that Hunt and Liddy had broken into the office of Ellsberg's former psychiatrist.[13] (WHT 157–60) Neither Dean nor the President said that the break-in was related to national security.

---

[10] In a memorandum to Ehrlichman dated August 13, 1971, Krogh and Young reported that the investigation of the SALT disclosure had unsatisfactory results. (President's Submission, Book IV, 134)

[11] Ehrlichman's notes of meetings with the President on December 23, 1971 and January 5, 1972 contain references to this incident (Ehrlichman's notes pp. 125–30). At one point the notes state, "We'll prosecute Anderson, et al after the election." (Ehrlichman's notes, Item 8, p. 129)

[12] On August 5, 1974, the President made public transcripts of conversations with H. R. Haldeman on June 23, 1972. During the course of the meeting between the President and Haldeman at 10:04 a.m. on June 23 the President said,

"Of course, this Hunt, that will uncover a lot of things. You open that scab there's a hell of a lot of things and we just feel that it would be very detrimental to have this thing go any further. This involves these Cubans, Hunt, and a lot of hanky-panky that we have nothing to do with ourselves. Well, what the hell, did Mitchell know about this?"

[13] On April 11, 1974, the House Judiciary Committee subpoenaed the tape recording and other materials related to this conversation. The President refused to produce this recording. The President submitted an edited transcript of four pages.

On the morning of March 21, Dean and the President discussed Hunt's blackmail threat. Dean told the President that Hunt threatened to bring Ehrlichman to his knees and to put Ehrlichman and Krogh in jail for the seamy things Hunt did at their direction, including the Fielding break-in. Dean reviewed for the President the soft points including the fact that Hunt and Liddy knew that the authorization for the break-in came from the White House. The President said, "I don't know what the hell we did that for." Dean said, "I don't either." (HJCT 92) Dean advised the President that Ehrlichman was criminally liable for the conspiracy to burglarize the doctor's office. (HJCT 104-05) Dean started to tell the President about something in the files that would reveal the break-in and the President interrupted and said, "Oh, I saw that. The picture." [14] (HJCT 105) This was a reference to the photograph of Liddy in front of Dr. Fielding's office which the Justice Department had obtained from the CIA. Dean responded, "Yeah, the picture. That, see, that's not all that buried. . . ." (HJCT 105)

Haldeman joined the meeting (HJCT 1081) and the conversation returned to a discussion of the Fielding break-in and how they could prevent its disclosure. A national security theory was developed:

PRESIDENT. . . . You see, John is concerned, as you know, Bob, about, uh, Ehrlichman which, uh, worries me a great deal because it's, a, uh,[15] it—and it, and this is why the Hunt problem is so serious, uh, because, uh, it had nothing to do with the campaign.
DEAN. Right, it, uh—
PRESIDENT. Properly, it has to do with the Ellsberg thing. I don't know what the hell, uh—
HALDEMAN. But why—
PRESIDENT. Yeah. Why—I don't know.
HALDEMAN. What I was going to say is—
PRESIDENT. What is the answer on that? How do you keep that out? I don't know. Well, we can't keep it out if Hunt—if—You see the point is, it is irrelevant. Once it has gotten to this point—
DEAN. You might, you might put it on a national security ground, basis, which it really, it was.
HALDEMAN. It absolutely was.
DEAN. And just say that, uh,
PRESIDENT. Yeah.
DEAN. that this is not, you know, this was—
PRESIDENT. Not paid with CIA funds.
DEAN. Uh—
PRESIDENT. No, seriously. National security. We had to get information for national security grounds.
DEAN. Well, then the question is, why didn't the CIA do it or why didn't the FBI do it?
PRESIDENT. Because they were—We had to do it, we had to do it on a confidential basis.
HALDEMAN. Because we were checking them?
PRESIDENT. Neither could be trusted.
HALDEMAN. Well, I think
PRESIDENT. That's the way I view it.
HALDEMAN. That has never been proven. There was reason to question their
PRESIDENT. Yeah.
HALDEMAN. position.

---

[14] In the edited White House transcript, the President says, "Oh, I thought of it." (WHT 208)
[15] ". . . worries me a great deal . . ." reads ". . . worries him a great deal . . ." in the edited White House transcript. (WHT 220)

PRESIDENT. You see really, with the Bundy thing and everything coming out, the whole thing was national security.

DEAN. I think we can probably get, get by on that. (HJCT 112)

Dean told the President of Krogh's perjury in denying that he knew anything about Hunt and Liddy's travels. Dean said that Krogh was willing to take responsibility for authorizing the break-in. (HJCT 95) The President asked what would happen if they did not meet Hunt's demands and Hunt "blew the whistle." (HJCT 125)

DEAN. Krogh, Krogh could go down in smoke. Uh—

PRESIDENT. Because Krogh, uh—Where could anybody—But on the other hand, Krogh just says he, uh, uh, Krogh says this is a national security matter. Is that what he says? Yeah, he said that.

DEAN. Yeah, but that won't sell, ultimately, in a criminal situation. It may be mitigating on sentences but it won't, uh, the main matter—

HALDEMAN. Well, then that—

PRESIDENT. That's right. Try to look around the track. We have no choice on Hunt but to try to keep him—(HJCT 125)

In a meeting that afternoon Ehrlichman said that if he were questioned about the Fielding break-in he would say that Hunt was conducting an investigation on Ellsberg. He added, "Now, I suppose that lets Ellsberg out, that's an illegal search and seizure that may be sufficient at least for a mistrial. . . ." The President asked if the case was close to completion and Ehrlichman said, "Oh, it'll go on a while yet." Haldeman asked if Ellsberg would be entitled to a mistrial after a conviction and Ehrlichman said, "Yeah, sure." (HJCT 139)[16]

On March 27, 1973, the President and Ehrlichman discussed whether it would be necessary for Krogh to take responsibiilty for the Fielding break-in. Ehrlichman said he did not believe it would be necessary because if it came to light he would "put the national security tent over this whole operation." The President agreed with Ehrlichman's recommendation to "just hard line it." [17] (WHT 334-37)

In April, the President actively participated in an effort to conceal the break-in under a national security tent. In a conversation with Attorney General Kleindienst on April 15, 1973, the President told Kleindienst that the "deep six thing" related to some of Hunt's operations in the White House on national security matters and had nothing to do with Watergate.[18] (WTH 721-23) On April 16, Henry Petersen told the President that the Department of Justice had information that Hunt had received alias documentation and a camera from the CIA. The President told Petersen that such action was perfectly proper because Hunt was conducting an investigation in the national security area for the White House.[19] (WHT 883-84)

In a meeting on April 17, 1973, the President told Haldeman and Ehrlichman that he had instructed Dean not to discuss with the

[16] The President later directed John Ehrlichman to contact Judge Matthew Byrne, the presiding judge in the Ellsberg trial. On April 5 and 7, 1973 Ehrlichman met with Judge Byrne and informed him that the President was considering appointing Judge Byrne to the directorship of the FBI. At the meeting on April 5, 1973 at San Clemente the President also met briefly with Judge Byrne. (Book VII, 1874–75, 1893, 1895)

[17] On April 11, 1974, the House Judiciary Committee subpoenaed the tape recording and other materials related to this conversation. The President refused to produce this recording. The President submitted an edited transcript.

[18] On April 11, 1974, the House Judiciary Committee subpoenaed the tape recording and other materials related to this conversation. The President refused to produce this recording. The President submitted an edited transcript.

[19] On April 11, 1974, the House Judiciary Committee subpoenaed the tape recording and other materials related to this conversation. The President refused to produce this recording. The President submitted an edited transcript.

United States attorney certain areas, including the Fielding break-in, because they were national security and privileged. The President said that Dean had agreed. He also said that it would be necessary to instruct Petersen that these were matters of national security and were subject to executive privilege and that Petersen should be instructed to pass the word down to the prosecutors.[20] (WHT 1028-30)

On April 18, 1973, Henry Petersen called the President and advised him that the Justice Department had learned that Hunt and Liddy burglarized the office of Ellsberg's psychiatrist.[21] The President told Petersen to stay out of it because it was national security and Petersen's mandate was Watergate. (Petersen testimony, 3 HJC 98; Book VII, 1956-66) The President issued this order although he had been told on March 21 that the Fielding break-in created criminal liability for Ehrlichman (HJCT 104-05); that national security would be mitigating upon the sentences but not a defense to the break-in (HJCT 125) and that it was an unreasonable search and seizure that would result in a dismissal of the Ellsberg case. (HJCT 139)

On April 25, 1973, Attorney General Kleindienst told the President that he knew of the Fielding break-in and recommended that the break-in be revealed to Judge Byrne, who was presiding at Ellsberg's trial. Kleindienst described the President as being upset at that meeting, but agreeing that the information about the break-in should be transmitted to Judge Byrne. (Book VII, 1984-85) On April 26, memoranda regarding the break-in were filed *in camera* with Judge Byrne. (Book VII, 1996) He later reconvened court and asked the government's position as to turning the materials over to the defendants. (Book VII, 1998-2004) The next morning Judge Byrne was informed that the Department of Justice did not want the contents of the *in camera* filing disclosed to the defense. Judge Byrne nevertheless ordered the information to be supplied to the defense and made a statement from the bench revealing the break-in and ordering an investigation. (Book VII, 2005-13)

On the afternoon of April 27, 1973, the President and Ehrlichman discussed the fact that the news of the Fielding break-in was public. The notes state, "[President] to HP [Henry Petersen] from CD [Camp David] re this—Review of what was said:" The remainder of the page was masked. (Ehrlichman notes, 159) Later that afternoon the President and Ehrlichman met and discussed the Fielding break-in. The notes of that meeting state, "Make an affidavit. Say they exceeded their auth[ority], a critical nat'l security pro[ject]. Then resign." (Ehrlichman's notes, Item 5, 172) This is a reference to Egil Krogh who later filed an affidavit in the Ellsberg trial and resigned. The notes further state, "In March learned things—Only when A/G [Attorney General] confirmed it. I acted instantly," (Ehrlichman notes, Item 7, 173) and "as soon as it came to my attn [atten-

---

[20] On April 11, 1974, the House Judiciary Committee subpoenaed the tape recording and other materials related to this conversation. The President refused to produce this recording. The President submitted an edited transcript.

[21] On April 11, 1974, the House Judiciary Committee subpoenaed the tape recording and other materials related to this conversation. The President has stated that the telephone conversation was not recorded. Ehrlichman's notes of a meeting with the President on April 27, 1973 state, "π [President] to HP [Henry Petersen] from CD Camp David re this—review of what was said—" the remainder of the notes have been masked (Ehrlichman notes, 159).

tion] is NB [important] point Relayed instantly—to Calif.", and "ph [phone] call to HP [Henry Petersen] April 18—confused by a month." (Ehrlichman notes, Items 9, 10, 173) The notes of that meeting also state, "By all means get it to Prosec[utor] or Dean will hold it over your head." (Ehrlichman notes, Item 7, 173) The final reference in the notes reads, "Did I know about it sooner? (no(d) by E-no sound) If so, it made no impression, ets." (Ehrlichman notes, Item 13, 174)

The President met with Henry Petersen on the evening of April 27, 1973. (Book IV, 1633) Petersen told the President of Dean's threat to tie in the President, not in Watergate but in other things. (WHT 1265)

> HP That was one of the reasons that was so important to disclose that because they could have hung that over our heads, you see and—
> P You remember my call from Camp David. I said, "Don't go into the national security stuff." I didn't mean—
> HP Oh, I understand.
> P 'cause I remember I think we discussed that silly damned thing. I had heard about it, just heard about. You told me that. That's it, you told me. (WHT 1266–67)

Ehrlichman met with Young on April 30, 1973. According to Young's testimony, Ehrlichman told him not to address the question of whether Ehrlichman had discussed the Fielding break-in with the President. (Book VII, 2029, 2034) On May 2, 1973, Ehrlichman had at least three telephone conversations with Krogh which Ehrlichman recorded. The first recorded conversation included the following discussion:

> E The feeling is that you ought to be relieved of any executive privilege obligation in order to make an affidavit and that you should try and make clear to [Acting Attorney General] Elliot [Richardson] today by phone or in person that it was not known to our principal down here until he was informed by the Justice Department. Now I don't know how you can say. You can say I told you that, I guess. But that's his story.
> K to our principal until he was informed (as in writing it down while repeating)
> E Right
> K And that would have been? Say this last weekend?
> E No, it would have been either late March or April, but Kleindienst would know. Because he got it from Kleindienst and Petersen apparently. Now, he would like a call back through me after you have successfully reached Elliot. And he says that he's got to ask for your resignation. At the same time he thinks that probably you're going to have an easier time of it if perhaps over the weekend or something of that kind it could be affected (Ehrlichman notes, 161)

In the third recorded telephone conversation, Krogh and Ehrlichman said,

> K You know, John he's [the President's] on thin ice himself.
> E On this national security thing?
> K Yeah. He's on darn thin ice and one of the things that is very clear—yesterday—after listening to him which I thought was an unpersuasive speech, and is that if it comes out that he was told about this, about the same time he was told about everything else assuming that he did not know long in advance and I think he did but that's something else again. And he has decided not to investigate it vigorously, he's in a helluva spot. (Ehrlichman notes, 168)

On May 11, 1973, Judge Byrne dismissed the criminal charges against Ellsberg and his co-defendant because of governmental misconduct, including the Fielding break-in. (Book VII, 2076–81)

ARTICLE II, PARAGRAPH (4)

(4) HE HAS FAILED TO TAKE CARE THAT THE LAWS WERE FAITHFULLY EXECUTED BY FAILING TO ACT WHEN HE KNEW OR HAD REASON TO KNOW THAT HIS CLOSE SUBORDINATES ENDEAVORED TO IMPEDE AND FRUSTRATE LAWFUL INQUIRIES BY DULY CONSTITUTED EXECUTIVE, JUDICIAL, AND LEGISLATIVE ENTITIES CONCERNING THE UNLAWFUL ENTRY INTO THE HEADQUARTERS OF THE DEMOCRATIC NATIONAL COMMITTEE, AND THE COVER-UP THEREOF, AND CONCERNING OTHER UNLAWFUL ACTIVITIES INCLUDING THOSE RELATING TO THE CONFIRMATION OF RICHARD KLEINDIENST AS ATTORNEY GENERAL OF THE UNITED STATES, THE ELECTRONIC SURVEILLANCE OF PRIVATE CITIZENS, THE BREAK-IN INTO THE OFFICES OF DR. LEWIS FIELDING, AND THE CAMPAIGN FINANCING PRACTICES OF THE COMMITTEE TO RE-ELECT THE PRESIDENT

The President's duty to take care that the laws be faithfully executed imposes an affirmative obligation upon him to take reasonable steps to insure that his close subordinates, who serve at his pleasure and rely on his authority in the conduct of their positions, do not interfere with the proper functioning of government. This obligation must be reasonably construed, especially in the context of a presidential impeachment. The President cannot personally attend to the faithful enforcement of each provision of the Federal criminal code against every violator, nor can he supervise the activities of even his closest subordinates in every particular.

The premise of Paragraph (4) is that the President, when he has actual knowledge or reason to know of activities by his close subordinates, conducted for his benefit and on his behalf, to obstruct investigations into wrongful and criminal conduct within his administration, is constitutionally obligated to take all necessary steps to stop these activities. In this connection, Representative McClory stated, "There is a clear violation of the President's responsibility when he permits multiple acts of wrongdoing by large numbers of those who surround him in possession of [great] responsibility and influence in the White House." (HJC Debates, July 29, 1974, TR. 816)

Richard M. Nixon has recognized this presidential responsibility. On March 21, 1973, John Dean told the President that he would be hurt the most by disclosures of what his subordinates had been doing with respect to Watergate. The President agreed: "First, because I am expected to know this, and I am supposed to, supposed to check these things." (HJCT 101) The Committee finds clear and convincing evidence that Richard M. Nixon failed to fulfill this responsibility and that he failed to exercise his authority when he should have done so in order to prevent his close subordinates from interfering with investigations into criminal or improper conduct carried on in his behalf.[1]

I

ELECTRONIC SURVEILLANCE AND THE FIELDING BREAK-IN— OBSTRUCTION OF THE ELLSBERG TRIAL

The Committee found clear and convincing evidence that the President failed to act, contrary to his constitutional duty to take care that the laws be faithfully executed, with respect to activities by his close subordinates, for his benefit and on his behalf, which interfered with the Ellsberg trial. Among the activities of his subordinates (previously reviewed in connection with Paragraphs (2) and (3) of this Article) are the following:

1. Ehrlichman's concealment of the wiretap files and logs, which interfered with the Ellsberg trial.

2. Patrick Gray's misleading testimony before the Senate Judiciary Committee in its hearings on his nomination to be Director of the FBI, suggestion that there had been no FBI wiretaps of newsmen and White House personnel.

3. Concealment of the Fielding break-in, which interfered with the Ellsberg trial. The President was told of the break-in on March 17, 1973 by Dean and on March 21 by Ehrlichman, but he did not act on these disclosures. On April 18 he directed Petersen to stay away from the break-in on the pretext that it was a national security matter.

II

OBSTRUCTION OF WATERGATE INQUIRIES

The Watergate break-in and cover-up involved the President's closest subordinates. It is clear that both the break-in and the cover-up were carried out for the President's benefit. On numerous occasions the President was told of their unlawful attempts and actions to impede and frustrate investigations aimed at uncovering the facts of the Watergate matter. The President repeatedly failed to remedy or prevent unlawful acts of obstruction by these subordinates. The instances are fully reviewed in connection with Article I. For example:

1. The President's failure to act to prevent obstruction of the investigation after Haldeman told him on June 30, 1972 that as of the moment there was no problem, but that there were risks for the future—informing the President of a policy of concealment and cover-up.

---

[1] Like Article I, Paragraph (4) focuses on interference with the due administration of justice. However, Paragraph (4) differs from Article I in two important respects:

First, Article I charges that the President engaged in a course of conduct or plan to obstruct justice. By contrast, Paragraph (4) relates to obstruction of justice by the President's close subordinates for his benefit and a failure by the President to supervise these subordinates so as to stop their misconduct.

Second, Paragraph (4) reaches not only the Watergate cover-up, but also interference with lawful inquiries into other matters. Specifically, it reaches interference with lawful inquiries into the ITT settlement (the Kleindienst confirmation hearings), the Ellsberg trial (by concealing the wiretaps and by authorizing and then concealing the Fielding break-in), and lawful inquiries into illegal campaign financing practices of the Committee for the Re-election of the President.

2. The President's failure to respond to the warning by Acting FBI Director Gray on July 6, 1972, that the President's close subordinates were trying to mortally wound him.

3. The President's failure to act in response to Ehrlichman's raising the question on July 8, 1972, of executive clemency for those involved in Watergate, though Ehrlichman raised the issue two months before an indictment was returned and six months before trial.

4. The President's praise of John Dean on September 15, 1972, after Dean told him seven people had been indicted, including two former White House aides. The President told Dean that a lot of this stuff went on and that Dean had been very skillful, putting his fingers in the dikes every time leaks had sprung here and sprung there.

5. The President's failure to act on March 13, 1973, when Dean told him that Strachan had knowledge before June 17, 1972 of the electronic surveillance at the headquarters of the Democratic National Committee and that Strachan had stonewalled FBI investigations and would continue to do so in the future.

6. The President's failure to act on March 21, 1973, when Dean confessed his own involvement in obstructing the Watergate investigation and told the President that Haldeman, Ehrlichman and Mitchell had also been involved in the obstruction of justice and that Porter and Magruder had committed perjury.

7. The President's failure to act when Haldeman and Ehrlichman told him that they had known of the payments to Watergate defendants in the summer of 1972 and had referred Dean to Kalmbach to arrange these payments.

8. The President's failure to disclose the information he had about the obstruction of justice by his subordinates when he met with Kleindienst and Petersen on April 15, 1973, and with Petersen during the following weeks.

9. The President's failure to reveal information about the unlawful obstruction of justice by his subordinates that he learned of, by his own admission, on and after March 21, 1973.

10. The President's endeavor to conceal the existence of the White House taping system and his refusal to comply with requests by the Special Prosecutor for access to relevant and material tapes and documents.

11. The President's failure to report to the authorities Haldeman's false testimony about the March 21, 1973, conversation before the Senate Select Committee on Presidential Campaign Activities.

III

OBSTRUCTION OF INQUIRIES INTO CAMPAIGN FINANCING PRACTICES AND USE OF CAMPAIGN FUNDS

The President learned in June and September, 1972, and in February, March and April, 1973, that the Committee for the Re-Election of the President had engaged in unlawful campaign financing practices and his aides were endeavoring to obstruct lawful investigations into these practices and the use of campaign funds. As demonstrated by the following examples, the President took no action to inform authorities of his subordinates' conduct:

1. The President failed to inform the authorities when Dean explained to the President on March 13, 1973, the method used by Allen and Ogarrio to make illegal campaign contributions.

2. The President failed to stop plans to interfere with the proposed hearings of the House Banking and Currency Committee (the Patman Committee) on campaign financing practices of the Committee to Re-elect the President, which Dean discussed with the President on September 15, 1972.

3. The President failed to report Herbert Kalmbach's use of $75,000 in campaign funds received from Stans and Haldeman's use of $350,000 in surplus cash campaign contributions to make payments or have payments made to Watergate defendants.

4. The campaign activities of Donald Segretti were the subject of specific inquiry by the Watergate Grand Jury and FBI in August, 1972, and again by the Watergate Grand Jury in April, 1973. On February 28, March 2, 13 and 14, 1973, the President discussed with Dean the extent of White House involvement with Segretti, who had been recruited by Chapin and Strachan to disrupt campaigns of Democratic presidential candidates, had been paid $45,000 for salary and expenses by Kalmbach pursuant to Haldeman's authorization, and had committed repeated violations of federal campaign laws in fulfilling his assignment. On March 21, 1973, Dean warned the President that Chapin could be charged with a felony for violating the civil rights statute in connection with Segretti's activities. On April 14, 1973, the President, Haldeman and Ehrlichman discussed Haldeman's involvement with Segretti, the White House having been informed by Chapin that Haldeman's name had been mentioned in connection with the hiring of Segretti during Chapin's April 11 appearance before the Grand Jury.

IV

Kleindienst Confirmation Hearings

During the hearings before the Senate Committee on the Judiciary on Richard Kleindienst's nomination to be Attorney General in 1972, both Kleindienst and former Attorney General John Mitchell gave false testimony regarding the President's involvement in the ITT antitrust cases. Clearly, Kleindienst and Mitchell were protecting the President. The President followed Kleindienst's confirmation hearings closely, but took no steps to correct the false testimony and continued to endorse Kleindienst's appointment. Because the President's conduct in the Kleindienst matter has not previously been discussed in this Report, the facts are summarized here.

On February 15, 1972, the President nominated Deputy Attorney General Richard Kleindienst to succeed John Mitchell as Attorney General of the United States. Beginning on February 29, 1972, columns by Jack Anderson were published which alleged that a pledge by the International Telephone and Telegraph Corporation of financial support for the 1972 Republican National Convention was connected with the settlement by the Department of Justice of three antitrust suits against ITT, and that Mitchell and Kleindienst were involved. (Book V, 634–36, 640) Kleindienst requested that his confirmation hearings before the Senate Judiciary Committee, which had approved his nomination, be resumed to investigate the charges. On March 2, 1972, the Committee's hearings were reconvened. (Book V, 678–79)

During the course of the resumed Kleindienst confirmation hearings both Mitchell and Kleindienst repeatedly gave false testimony with respect to the role of the President in the ITT cases. On March 2, 1972, and again on the following day, Kleindienst testified that he had not received directions from the White House about the handling of the ITT cases. (Book V, 680, 732) In fact, on April 19, 1971, the President had ordered Kleindienst to drop an appeal in the ITT-Grinnell case.[2] (Book V, 312, 315–16) On March 3, 1972, when asked why an extension of time to appeal the *ITT-Grinnell* case was obtained, Kleindienst testified, "I do not recollect why that extension was asked." (Book V, 734) In fact, the extension had been obtained because of the President's order. Four days later, on March 7, 1972, Kleindienst read a prepared statement describing in detail circumstances surrounding the request for an extension. He did not mention the President's telephone call ordering that the appeal be dropped. (Book V, 753–54) Again on March 8, 1972, Kleindienst denied having received directions from the White House about the handling of the ITT cases. (Book V, 765)

On March 14, 1972, John Mitchell appeared before the Senate Judiciary Committee. (Book V, 772) Mitchell twice testified that there had been no communication between the President and him with respect to the ITT antitrust litigation or any other antitrust litigation. (Book V, 772–74) In fact, Mitchell had met with the President on April 21, 1971, and persuaded the President to rescind his order not to appeal the *ITT-Grinnell* case. (Book V, 372–76)

The President took a direct interest in the Kleindienst confirmation hearings. In early March, 1972, he established a White House task force to monitor the hearings. Colson kept the President informed on the work of the task force. (Colson testimony, HJC 381–82, 400; Book V, 765) On the evening of March 14, the day Mitchell testified falsely that he and the President had not communicated regarding the ITT litigation, the President had a telephone conversation with Mitchell. (Book V, 775)

On March 24, 1972, the President held his only press conference during the period of the resumed Kleindienst confirmation hearings. He said:

. . . as far as the [Senate Judiciary Committee] hearings are concerned, there is nothing that has happened in the hearings to date that has in one way shaken my confidence in Mr. Kleindienst as an able, honest man, fully qualified to be Attorney General of the United States. (Book V, 801; 8 Presidential Documents 674)

During late March, 1972, the President was urged to withdraw the Kleindienst nomination by Colson and Clark MacGregor. The President on March 27, 1972, discussed with Colson, and on March 28, 1972,

---

[2] During the April 19 conversation the President brusquely ordered that the appeal be dropped and demanded that Antitrust Division Chief Richard McLaren be dismissed if this was not done. (Book V, 315–16) Colson has testified that in March, 1972, Haldeman, who did not witness the April 19, 1971 conversation, assured the President that he spoke to Kleindienst about policy and not about the ITT cases. (Colson testimony, 3 HJC 383)

discussed with Colson, Haldeman and MacGregor, whether the Kleindienst nomination should be withdrawn. On March 29, 1972, Haldeman told Colson and MacGregor that the President was going to meet with Kleindienst to determine whether his nomination should be withdrawn. (Colson testimony, 3 HJC 384–85)

On the morning of March 30, 1972, Haldeman told White House aides Colson and MacGregor that the President had met with Kleindienst and talked with Mitchell by telephone the day before, and had decided not to withdraw Kleindienst's nomination. (Colson testimony, 3 HJC 392–95, 397; Book V, 805–09) Colson wrote a memorandum to Haldeman stating his opposition to continuing the Kleindienst nomination. (Book V, 803–05) His reasons included the possibility that documents Colson had reviewed would be revealed and reflect that the President had discussions with Mitchell about an ITT case in 1971, thereby contradicting statements made by Mitchell under oath during the Kleindienst hearings. The President said he would read the memorandum, and Colson testified that assuming normal White House practice was followed, the President received the memorandum. (Colson testimony, 3 HJC 397)

On April 27, 1972, Kleindienst again testified that no one in the White House had called him and instructed him on the handling of the ITT cases. (Book V, 852) On June 8, 1972, Kleindienst's nomination was confirmed. (Book V, 903) At his swearing-in ceremonies on June 12, 1972, the President expressed his great confidence in Kleindienst's honesty, integrity and devotion to law. He said that the Senate confirmation proceedings had in no way reduced that confidence. (Book V, 904)

At no time did the President act to correct the false testimony of his Attorney General designate. Instead, he permitted Kleindienst's nomination to be confirmed and appointed him Attorney General. The Committee finds that the President knew or had reason to know that Kleindienst testified falsely before the Senate Judiciary Committee. This conclusion is supported by the facts that: (1) Colson's March 30, 1972, memorandum to Haldeman reported that certain documents contradicted Mitchell's sworn testimony with respect to, among other things, the President's involvement in the ITT cases; (2) the Kleindienst confirmation hearings received extensive press coverage; (3) a White House task force monitored the hearings and the President was kept informed of its work; (4) the President and senior members of his staff maintained a keen interest in the progress of the hearings; and (5) the President has failed to comply with the Committee's subpoena for tape recordings and other material related to Presidential conversations during the hearings.

ARTICLE II, PARAGRAPH (5)

(5) IN DISREGARD OF THE RULE OF LAW, HE KNOWINGLY MISUSED THE EXECUTIVE POWER BY INTERFERING WITH AGENCIES OF THE EXECUTIVE BRANCH, INCLUDING THE FEDERAL BUREAU OF INVESTIGATION, THE CRIMINAL DIVISION, AND THE OFFICE OF WATERGATE SPECIAL PROSECUTION FORCE, OF THE DEPARTMENT OF JUSTICE, AND THE CENTRAL INTELLIGENCE AGENCY, IN VIOLATION OF HIS DUTY TO TAKE CARE THAT THE LAWS BE FAITHFULLY EXECUTED

This Paragraph is based upon a fundamental constitutional principle governing the President's conduct in exercising his control over the agencies and institutions of the executive branch and discharging his responsibilities with respect to them. The principle is that he is accountable, through impeachment, for violating his constitutional duties by knowingly and repeatedly abusing the executive power, systematically and over a considerable period of time, in a manner that demonstrates a disregard of the rule of law, to direct agencies to engage in activities that are contrary to law or in derogation of their purposes and functions. In Paragraph (5) the principle is applied to the President's interference with and abuse of the Federal Bureau of Investigation, the Criminal Division of the Department of Justice, the Watergate Special Prosecution Force, the Central Intelligence Agency, and their officers and agents. The faithful administration of each of these agencies of government is vital to the protection of the rights of citizens and to the maintenance of their confidence in the integrity of their government. The Committee finds clear and convincing evidence that Richard M. Nixon knowingly disregarded laws and regulations and constitutional tenets that govern the administration of these agencies, and sought to have them serve his personal, political objectives.

In so doing, he violated his constitutional duty "to take Care that the Laws be faithfully executed," and his constitutional oath that he would faithfully execute the office of President and, to the best of his ability, preserve, protect and defend the Constitution.

Paragraph (5) addresses the President's abuse of the FBI and the CIA to aid in violations of the constitutional rights of citizens, conduct also covered in Paragraphs (2) and (3) of this Article. In addition, Paragraph (5) covers other abuse of these executive agencies contrary to law, specifically including the improper use of the executive power by Richard M. Nixon to impede and obstruct lawful investigations into criminal conduct involving close subordinates and agents within his administration.

Some of the evidence of misuse of executive agencies to obstruct investigations is also applicable to and supportive of a portion of Article I, which is addressed to the President's direction of and participation in a plan or course of conduct to interfere with lawful inquiries into the Watergate break-in and its aftermath. Although there are facts common to this Paragraph and parts of Article I, these facts are conceptually part of two different patterns of conduct—one of interference with lawful inquiries into the Watergate matter, the other of knowing abuse of executive agencies in disregard of the rule of law for personal political advantage. Unlike Article I, Paragraph (5) does not require proof that the interference was part of a plan or course of conduct conceived by the President and executed by his subordinates at his direction; it is sufficient for Paragraph (5) that the President acted knowingly. Moreover, Paragraph (5) focuses on the abuse by Richard M. Nixon of the powers of the Presidency to interfere with executive agencies. By contrast, Article I, which focuses upon the President's interference with lawful inquiries into the Watergate matter, encompasses a variety of means, not simply those involving the use of the President's power over executive agencies.

Among the important incidents supportive of Paragraph (5) (previously discussed in other portions of this report) are the following:

1. The President interfered with both the CIA and the FBI by directing his principal aides, Haldeman and Ehrlichman (and, through them, Dean), to have the CIA delay or prevent FBI investigation of the source of the funds recovered from those apprehended at the Watergate break-in, in order to prevent the FBI from discovering that those funds were political contributions obtained from the Committee to Re-elect the President and that CRP personnel were involved in devising and executing the break-in in furtherance of the President's re-election campaign, as well as from discovering other unlawful covert activities.

2. The President improperly used his office to interfere with the Department of Justice investigation of the Watergate break-in and cover-up by obtaining information from Assistant Attorney General Henry Petersen, which the President passed on to targets of the investigation, and by making false or misleading representations to Petersen, including his failure to disclose to Petersen his knowledge of criminal conduct as part of the cover-up.

3. The President interfered with the Office of the Watergate Special Prosecution Force by withholding and concealing evidence, and by discharging Special Prosecutor Cox and attempting to abolish the office of Special Prosecutor for the purpose of impeding and circumscribing its investigation and functions.

4. The President interfered with the proper functioning of the CIA by authorizing his subordinates to request CIA assistance for Howard Hunt and for the activities of the secret investigative unit in the office of the President (the Plumbers) directed at discrediting a defendant in a criminal trial and interfering with his right to a fair trial.

5. The President interfered with the proper functioning of the FBI by directing it to undertake unlawful surveillance of newsmen and White House personnel for his own political purposes, and by ordering that normal indices of the records of this surveillance not be maintained and later that the records be concealed at the White House. As a result of this concealment, the due and proper administration of justice was impeded and the criminal prosecution of Ells-

berg, who had been on trial for many months, was dismissed on the grounds of governmental misconduct.

6. The President interfered with the Department of Justice when he instructed Petersen not to investigate the Fielding break-in on the pretext that it involved national security, when he knew the Fielding break-in was not a national security matter.

CONCLUSION

In recommending Article II to the House, the Committee finds clear and convincing evidence that Richard M. Nixon, contrary to his trust as President and unmindful of the solemn duties of his high office, has repeatedly used his power as President to violate the Constitution and the law of the land.

In so doing, he has failed in the obligation that every citizen has to live under the law. But he has done more, for it is the duty of the President not merely to live by the law but to see that law faithfully applied. Richard M. Nixon has repeatedly and willfully failed to perform that duty. He has failed to perform it by authorizing and directing actions that violated or disregarded the rights of citizens and that corrupted and attempted to corrupt the lawful functioning of executive agencies. He has failed to perform it by condoning and ratifying, rather than acting to stop, actions by his subordinates that interfered with lawful investigations and impeded the enforcement of the laws.

Article II, section 3 of the Constitution requires that the President "shall take Care that the Laws be faithfully executed." Justice Felix Frankfurter described this provision as "the embracing function of the President"; [1] President Benjamin Harrison called it "the central idea of the office." "[I]n a republic," Harrison wrote, "the thing to be executed is the law, not the will of the ruler as in despotic governments. The President cannot go beyond the law, and he cannot stop short of it." [2]

The conduct of Richard M. Nixon has constituted a repeated and continuing abuse of the powers of the Presidency in disregard of the fundamental principle of the rule of law in our system of government. This abuse of the powers of the President was carried out by Richard M. Nixon, acting personally and through his subordinates, for his own political advantage, not for any legitimate governmental purpose and without due consideration for the national good.

The rule of law needs no defense by the Committee. Reverence for the laws, said Abraham Lincoln, should "become the political religion of the nation." [3] Said Theodore Roosevelt, "No man is above the law and no man is below it; nor do we ask any man's permission when we require him to obey it." [4]

It is a basic principle of our government that "we submit ourselves to rulers only if [they are] under rules." [5] "Decency, security, and lib-

---

[1] *Youngstown Sheet and Tube Co. v. Sawyer,* 343 U.S. 579, 610 (1952) (concurring opinion).
[2] B. Harrison, *This Country of Ours* 98-99 (1897).
[3] "Address Before the Young Men's Lyceum of Springfield, Illinois," January 27, 1837, in 1 *Complete Works of Abraham Lincoln* 43 (J. Nicolay and J. Hay eds., 1894).
[4] "Third Annual Message to Congress," December 7, 1903, in 9 *Messages and Papers of the Presidents* 6860 (J. Richardson ed. 1911).
[5] *Youngstown Sheet and Tube Co. v. Sawyer,* 343 U.S. 579, 646 (1952) (Jackson, J., concurring).

erty alike demand that government officials shall be subjected to the same rules of conduct that are commands to the citizen," wrote Justice Louis Brandeis.[6] The Supreme Court has said:

> No man in this country is so high that he is above the law. No officer of the law may set that law at defiance with impunity. All the officers of the government, from the highest to the lowest, are creatures of the law, and are bound to obey it.
> It is the only supreme power in our system of government, and every man who by accepting office participates in its functions is only the more strongly bound to submit to that supremacy, and to observe the limitations upon the exercise of the authority which it gives.[7]

Our nation owes its strength, its stability, and its endurance to this principle.

In asserting the supremacy of the rule of law among the principles of our government, the Committee is enunciating no new standard of Presidential conduct. The possibility that Presidents have violated this standard in the past does not diminish its current—and future—applicability. Repeated abuse of power by one who holds the highest public office requires prompt and decisive remedial action, for it is in the nature of abuses of power that if they go unchecked they will become overbearing, depriving the people and their representatives of the strength of will or the wherewithal to resist.

Our Constitution provides for a responsible Chief Executive, accountable for his acts. The framers hoped, in the words of Elbridge Gerry, that "the maxim would never be adopted here that the chief Magistrate could do no wrong."[8] They provided for a single executive because, as Alexander Hamilton wrote, "the executive power is more easily confined when it is one" and "there should be a single object for the ... watchfulness of the people."[9]

The President, said James Wilson, one of the principal authors of the Constitution, "is the dignified, but accountable magistrate of a free and great people."[10] Wilson said, "The executive power is better to be trusted when it has no screen. ... [W]e have a responsibility in the person of our President; ... he cannot roll upon any other person the weight of his criminality...."[11] As both Wilson and Hamilton pointed out, the President should not be able to hide behind his counsellors; he must ultimately be accountable for their acts on his behalf. James Iredell of North Carolina, a leading proponent of the proposed Constitution and later a Supreme Court Justice, said that the President "is of a very different nature from a monarch. He is to be ... personally responsible for any abuse of the great trust reposed in him."[12]

---

[6] *Olmstead* v. *United States*, 277 U.S. 438, 485 (1928) (dissenting opinion) Justice Brandeis went on to say: "In a government of laws, existence of the government will be imperilled if it fails to observe the law scrupulously. Our government is the potent, the omnipresent teacher. For good or for ill, it teaches the whole people by its example. Crime is contagious. If the government becomes a lawbreaker, it breeds contempt for law; it invites every man to become a law unto himself; it invites anarchy. To declare that in the administration of the criminal law the end justifies the means—to declare that the government may commit crimes in order to secure the conviction of a private citizen—would bring a terrible retribution."
[7] *United States* v. *Lee*, 106 U.S. 196, 220 (1882).
[8] 1 *The Records of the Federal Convention* 66 (M. Farrand ed. 1911) (brackets in original omitted).
[9] *The Federalist* No. 70, at 460 (Modern Library ed.).
[10] Wilson, *Lectures on Law*, in 1 *The Works of James Wilson* 319 (R. McCloskey ed. 1967).
[11] 2 J. Elliot, *The Debates in the Several State Conventions on the Adoption of the Federal Constitution* 480 (reprint of 2d ed.).
[12] 4 *Id.* 74.

In considering this Article the Committee has relied on evidence of acts directly attributable to Richard M. Nixon himself. He has repeatedly attempted to conceal his accountability for these acts and attempted to deceive and mislead the American people about his own responsibility. He governed behind closed doors, directing the operation of the executive branch through close subordinates, and sought to conceal his knowledge of what they did illegally on his behalf. Although the Committee finds it unnecessary in this case to take any position on whether the President should be held accountable, through exercise of the power of impeachment, for the actions of his immediate subordinates, undertaken on his behalf, when his personal authorization and knowledge of them cannot be proved, it is appropriate to call attention to the dangers inherent in the performance of the highest public office in the land in an air of secrecy and concealment.

The abuse of a President's powers poses a serious threat to the lawful and proper functioning of the government and the people's confidence in it. For just such Presidential misconduct the impeachment power was included in the Constitution. The impeachment provision, wrote Justice Joseph Story in 1833, "holds out a deep and immediate responsibility, as a check upon arbitrary power; and compels the chief magistrate, as well as the humblest citizen, to bend to the majesty of the law." [13] And Chancellor James Kent wrote in 1826:

> If . . . neither the sense of duty, the force of public opinion, nor the transitory nature of the seat, are sufficient to secure a faithful exercise of the executive trust, but the President will use the authority of his station to violate the Constitution or law of the land, the House of Representatives can arrest him in his career, by resorting to the power of impeachment.[14]

The Committee has concluded that, to perform its constitutional duty, it must approve this Article of Impeachment and recommend it to the House. If we had been unwilling to carry out the principle that all those who govern, including ourselves, are accountable to the law and the Constitution, we would have failed in our responsibility as representatives of the people, elected under the Constitution. If we had not been prepared to apply the principle of Presidential accountability embodied in the impeachment clause of the Constitution, but had instead condoned the conduct of Richard M. Nixon, then another President, perhaps with a different political philosophy, might have used this illegitimate power for further encroachments on the rights of citizens and further usurpations of the power of other branches of our government. By adopting this Article, the Committee seeks to prevent the recurrence of any such abuse of Presidential power.

The Committee finds that, in the performance of his duties as President, Richard M. Nixon on many occasions has acted to the detriment of justice, right, and the public good, in violation of his constitutional duty to see to the faithful execution of the laws. This conduct has demonstrated a contempt for the rule of law; it has posed a threat to our democratic republic. The Committee finds that this conduct constitutes "high crimes and misdemeanors" within the meaning of the Constitution, that it warrants his impeachment by the House, and that it requires that he be put to trial in the Senate.

---

[13] 1 J. Story, *Commentaries on the Constitution of the United States* § 813 at 564 (3d ed. 1858).
[14] 1 J. Kent, *Commentaries on American Law* 289 (6th ed. 1848).

In recommending Article II to the House, the Committee finds clear and convincing evidence that Richard M. Nixon has not faithfully executed the executive trust, but has repeatedly used his authority as President to violate the Constitution and the law of the land. In so doing, he violated the obligation that every citizen has to live under the law. But he did more, for it is the duty of the President not merely to live by the law but to see that law faithfully applied. Richard M. Nixon repeatedly and willfully failed to perform that duty. He failed to perform it by authorizing and directing actions that violated the rights of citizens and that interfered with the functioning of executive agencies. And he failed to perform it by condoning and ratifying, rather than acting to stop, actions by his subordinates interfering with the enforcement of the laws.

ARTICLE III

INTRODUCTION

On February 6, 1974, the House of Representatives adopted H. Res. 803, authorizing and directing the Committee on the Judiciary to investigate whether sufficient grounds exist to impeach President Richard M. Nixon. This resolution authorized the Committee "to require ... by subpoena or otherwise ... production of such things ... as deemed necessary to such investigation."

On February 25, 1974, Special Counsel to the Committee wrote to the President's counsel requesting tape recordings of designated presidential conversations and related documents. Some of these items had previously been provided by the President to the Special Prosecutor; others had not. In response to this request, the President agreed to produce only those materials he had previously given to the Special Prosecutor.

By subsequent letters and, ultimately, by service of eight subpoenas upon the President, the Committee sought:

    (1) tape recordings, notes and other writings relating to 147 specified conversations;

    (2) a list of the President's meetings and telephone conversations known as "daily diaries," for five special periods in 1971, 1972 and 1973;

    (3) papers and memoranda relating to the Watergate break-in and its aftermath and to the activities of the White House special investigative unit (the Plumbers), prepared by, sent to, received by or at any time contained in the files of seven named former members of the President's staff; and

    (4) copies of the President's daily news summaries, for a 3½ month period in 1972, that contain his handwritten notes pertaining to the hearings before the Senate Judiciary Committee on Richard Kleindienst's nomination to be Attorney General and matters involving ITT antitrust litigation.

The President was informed that the materials demanded by these eight subpoenas were necessary for the Committee's inquiry into the Watergate matter, domestic surveillance, the relationship between a governmental milk price support decision and campaign contributions by certain dairy cooperatives, the conduct of ITT antitrust litigation and alleged perjured testimony by administration officials during the Kleindienst confirmation hearings, and the alleged misuse of the Internal Revenue Service.

In response to these subpoenas the President produced:

    (1) edited transcripts of all or part of 33 subpoenaed conversations and 6 conversations that had not been subpoenaed, all but one of which related to the Watergate matter;

    (2) edited copies of notes made by John Ehrlichman during meetings with the President, which had been previously furnished

to Ehrlichman and the Special Prosecutor in connection with the trial *United States* v. *Ehrlichman,* and

(3) copies of certain White House news summaries, containing no handwritten notes by the President.

The Committee did not receive a single tape recording of any of the 147 subpoenaed conversations. Nor, apart from the edited notes of Ehrlichman and the copies of news summaries, did the Committee receive any of the other papers or things sought by its subpoenas.

Shortly after the President's response, the Committee informed the President that his submissions were not considered compliance with its subpoenas and that his refusal to comply might be regarded as a ground for impeachment.

At the conclusion of its inquiry, the Committee approved by a vote of 21-17 the following Article of Impeachment:

ARTICLE III

In his conduct of the office of President of the United States, Richard M. Nixon, contrary to his oath faithfully to execute the office of President of the United States, and to the best of his ability, preserve, protect, and defend the Constitution of the United States, and in violation of his constitutional duty to take care that the laws be faithfully executed, has failed without lawful cause or excuse to produce papers and things as directed by duly authorized subpoenas issued by the Committee on the Judiciary of the House of Representatives on April 11, 1974, May 15, 1974, May 30, 1974, and June 24, 1974, and willfully disobeyed such subpoenas. The subpoenaed papers and things were deemed necessary by the committee in order to resolve by direct evidence fundamental, factual questions relating to presidential direction, knowledge or approval of actions demonstrated by other evidence to be substantial grounds for impeachment of the President. In refusing to produce these papers and things, Richard M. Nixon, substituting his judgment as to what materials were necessary for the inquiry, interposed the powers of the presidency against the lawful subpoenas of the House of Representatives, thereby assuming to himself functions and judgments necessary to the exercise of the sole power of impeachment vested by the Constitution in the House of Representatives.

In all of this, Richard M. Nixon has acted in a manner contrary to his trust as President and subversive of constitutional government, to the great prejudice of the cause of law and justice, and to the manifest injury of the people of the United States.

Wherefore, Richard M. Nixon by such conduct, warrants impeachment and trial, and removal from office.

The refusal of the President to comply with the subpoenas was an interference by him with the efforts of the Committee and the House of Representatives to fulfill their constitutional responsibilities. It was, as Article III states, an effort to interpose "the powers of the presidency against the lawful subpoenas of the House of Representatives, thereby assuming to himself functions and judgments necessary to this exercise of the sole power of impeachment vested by the Constitution in the House of Representatives."

Evidence of the President's refusal to comply with the Committee's subpoenas seeking evidence with respect to the Watergate matter could be introduced as proof of the allegations in paragraph 4 of Article I—which charges interference with investigations by Congressional Committees as one of the means used to obstruct justice in the Watergate matter. But the refusal by the President to comply with subpoenas issued after the Committee was satisfied there was other evidence pointing to the existence of impeachable offenses, is a grave interference with the efforts of the Committee and the House to fulfill their constitutional responsibilities. regardless of whether it is part of a course of conduct or plan to obstruct justice. Only Article III is concerned with enforcing general standards requiring Presidential compliance with subpoenas in impeachment inquiries.

The Committee has been able to conduct an investigation and determine that grounds for impeachment exist—even in the face of the President's refusal to comply. But this does not mean that the refusal was without practical import. The Committee had enough evidence to recommend the adoption of two other articles. but it does not and did not have at the time it deliberated and voted—despite the President's contentions to the contrary—the "full story." Had it received the evidence sought by the subpoenas. the Committee might have recommended articles structured differently or possibly ones covering other matters.[1] Article III states, the evidence sought was "deemed necessary by the Committee in order to resolve by direct evidence fundamental, factual questions relating to presidential direction. knowledge or approval of actions demonstrated by other evidence to be substantial grounds for impeachment of the President." It is the defiance of the Committee's subpoenas under these circumstances that gave rise to the impeachable offense charged by Article III.

The President's statement on August 5, 1974, that he would transmit to the Senate certain material subpoenaed by the Committee, did not lessen the need for Article III. The President said on August 5 that he would supply to the Senate, for an impeachment trial, those portions of recordings of 64 conversations that Judge Sirica decides should be produced for the Special Prosecutor for use in the Watergate criminal trial. This assurance did not remove the interference with the exercise of their responsibilities by the Committee and the House charged in Article III.

Article III charges the President with interfering with the discharge of the Committee's responsibility to investigate fully and completely whether sufficient grounds exist to impeach him. The Committee's duty is different from the duty of a prosecutor, a grand jury, or a trial jury, whose task it is to determine whether specific criminal statutes have been violated. What may be relevant or necessary for the Watergate criminal trial would not necessarily coincide with what is relevant and necessary for this inquiry. And. in any event, it is for the Committee—not a trial judge in a criminal case—to determine what is relevant and necessary to the Committee's inquiry. Thus, even if the President had, on August 5, 1974, consented to deliver to the House the portions of the 64 recordings that Judge Sirica eventually found relevant and necessary to the Watergate criminal trial, the President's refusal to comply with the Committee's subpoenas would nonetheless constitute an interference with the duty of this Committee.

Similarly, the President's willingness to furnish to the Senate some

---

[1] The Committee's inquiry into the relationship between the contributions by certain dairy cooperatives and the decision in 1971 to raise milk price supports is one instance in which the Committee was unable to make a final determination because of the President's noncompliance with its subpoenas. The evidence before the Committee provided some support for the suspicion that the President's conduct in this matter may have been grounds for his impeachment, but without the subpoenaed materials the Committee lacked the evidence to determine whether there was basis for such a charge.

material that was sought by the Committee's subpoenas does not remove the obstruction of the constitutional process. In the first place, the President's assurance related only to a portion of the material sought by the Committee. But more fundamentally, providing material to the Senate did not eliminate the interference with this Committee's responsibilities because the duty of the Committee differs also from that of the Senate. The responsibility of the Senate is to determine whether the evidence is sufficient to remove the President on the basis of specific articles of impeachment previously transmitted to it by the House. The duty of the Committee is to investigate first and then to recommend to the House whether there is sufficient evidence to transmit articles of impeachment to the Senate. In order for this Committee and the House to be able to perform their responsibilities, it is not sufficient for the President to meet the demands of other bodies seeking evidence for other purposes; the demands of the Committee and House must also be met.

Rather than removing the need for Article III, the events of August 5 underscore its importance. On that day, the President not only made the statement concerning transmittal of materials to the Senate, but also released edited transcripts of three conversations that took place on June 23, 1972 between himself and Haldeman. These conversations were requested by the Committee by letter dated April 19, 1974 and subpoenaed on May 15, 1974. The President, by letter dated May 22, 1974, refused to comply with the subpoena stating that "the Committee has the full story of Watergate, insofar as it relates to Presidential knowledge and Presidential actions."

There is no question that the three June 23, 1972 conversations bear significantly upon presidential knowledge and presidential actions. There is also no question that, prior to sending his May 22, 1974 letter defying the Committee's subpoena, the President listened to recordings of two of these conversations. Both of these facts were admitted in his August 5 statement. Yet the President did not make the June 23 conversations available until after the Committee had completed its deliberations, and then only as a consequence of the Supreme Court decision in *United States* v. *Nixon* directing that the conversations be produced for the Watergate criminal trial. The President's defiance of the Committee forced it to deliberate and make judgments on a record that the President now acknowledges was "incomplete." His actions demonstrate the need to ensure that a standard be established barring such conduct in impeachment inquiries. That is the function of Article III.

THE COMMITTEE'S SUBPOENAS AND THE PRESIDENT'S RESPONSE

A. THE FEBRUARY 25, 1974 LETTER

On February 25, 1974, at the direction of the Committee's Chairman and Ranking Minority Member, Special Counsel John Doar wrote to the President's Special Counsel, James D. St. Clair. On behalf of the Committee, Mr. Doar requested (1) certain materials previously furnished by the President to the Special Prosecutor, including 19 tape recordings of presidential conversations and recollections, and (2) all tape recordings, notes and other writings relating to 42 specifically identified presidential conversations, which had not previously been provided to the Special Prosecutor.

No response to the Committee's request had been made by March 1, 1974. On that day the Federal grand jury investigating the Watergate matter delivered a report and supporting materials to Chief Judge John Sirica for submission to the Committee. These materials included 12 recordings of presidential conversations and recollections pertinent to the Watergate matter, together with related documentary materials. On March 6, 1974, Judge Sirica held a hearing to determine whether the Grand Jury report and supporting materials should be delivered to the Committee. Mr. St. Clair stated during this hearing, and confirmed by letter of the same date to Mr. Doar, that the President would furnish to the Committee all material he had previously furnished to the Special Prosecutor.

Between March 8 and March 22, the President delivered to the Committee the materials he had produced for the Special Prosecutor. These materials included the 12 recordings related to the Watergate matter, and 7 recordings relating to the ITT, dairy, and Plumbers matters. Also included were approximately 700 pages of documents pertaining to these areas.[1] On March 26, the grand jury report and accompanying materials were delivered to the Committee.

After several meetings between Mr. Doar, the Minority Counsel, Albert Jenner, and Mr. St. Clair, Mr. Doar wrote Mr. St. Clair on April 4, reiterating the Committee's request for the 42 presidential conversations first specified in Mr. Doar's February 25 letter. On April 9, Mr. St. Clair responded that a review of the materials was underway which would probably be completed by the end of the Congressional Easter recess. Mr. St. Clair made no commitment to produce any material at the completion of the review. Accordingly, on April 11, 1974 the Committee, by a vote of 33 to 3, authorized the issuance of its first subpoena directed to the President.

---

[1] A number of the documents were duplicates.

B. THE FOUR WATERGATE SUBPOENAS

(1) April 11, 1974

The subpoena authorized on April 11, 1974 demanded the production of all tapes, dictabelts or other electronic recordings and transcripts, memoranda, notes or other writings relating to 42 specified conversations. Six of these conversations took place in February and March 1973; the other 36 were in April. They involved the President and Haldeman, Ehrlichman, Dean, Kleindienst and Henry Petersen. The return date for the subpoena was originally April 25, but was extended to April 30 at the President's request. In a television address to the Nation on the evening of April 29, the President announced that he would deliver transcripts of certain conversations to the Committee rather than the tapes themselves.

The following day, the President released to the public and delivered to the Committee edited transcripts of 31 of the 42 subpoenaed conversations. The President said that five of the 11 other subpoenaed conversations had not been recorded because the tape had run out. These conversations had taken place on April 15, 1973 in the President's office in the Executive Office Building. Four of the eleven were telephone calls and the President said they were not recorded because they were made on a telephone not connected to the taping system. The President said that the two remaining conversations, those in February, 1973, which were specified by subject matter rather than by precise time or date, either did not take place or could not be located. In addition to the edited transcripts of 31 conversations, the President produced edited transcripts of seven conversations between March 27 and April 27, 1973 that had not been subpoenaed. The President was a participant in four of these conversations. The President did not produce any notes or other writings relating to the 42 conversations as required by the April 11 subpoena.

The President stated in his April 30 submission to the Committee that he would permit the Chairman and Ranking Minority Member—without staff assistance—to listen to the subpoenaed tapes at the White House for the purpose of verifying the edited transcripts. He also stated that he would respond under oath to written interrogatories and that he would be willing to meet with the Chairman and Ranking Minority Member at the White House and submit to questioning by them.

On May 1, Chairman Rodino stated to the Committee that the procedure suggested by the President for reviewing the subpoenaed tape recordings to determine the relevance and accuracy of the edited transcripts was not compliance with the Committee's subpoena. The Chairman explained:

> The subpoena issued by the Committee required materials covered by it to be delivered to the Committee in order that they be available for the Committee's deliberations. There was good reason for this. It is not simply a question of the accuracy of transcripts or even of the relevancy of omissions, although both factors are obviously critical. The procedures followed by the Committee must be such that all Committee members—each of whom has to exercise personal judgments on this matter of enormous importance to the nation—and ultimately all members of the House of Representatives, are satisfied that they have had full and fair opportunity to judge for themselves all the evidence. It is therefore mandatory that the Committee not depart from the ordinary and expected process

in the way the President suggested, or in any other manner that might suggest the intrusion of secret accommodations, or raise new questions about the thoroughness, fairness and objectivity of the Committee's work.

That same day, the Committee, pursuant to a 20 to 18 vote, formally advised the President by letter that he had failed to comply with its subpoena.

(2) May 15, 1974

On May 9, the Committee's inquiry staff began its initial presentations on information on the Watergate matter. On May 15, after requests by letter dated April 19 for specified tapes and documents were not met, the Committee authorized the issuance of two additional subpoenas to the President. The first subpoena, approved by a vote of 37 to 1, demanded the production of tape recordings and materials relating to 11 presidential conversations referred to in the staff presentations to the Committee. These conversations occurred on April 4, 1972, June 20, 1972 and June 23, 1972 and involved the President and Haldeman, Mitchell and Colson. The second subpoena issued on May 15 sought lists (known as "daily diaries") of the President's meetings and telephone calls in four specified periods: April through July 1972; February through April 1973; July 12 through July 31, 1973; and October 1973.[2]

By a letter to Chairman Rodino dated May 22, the President declined to furnish any of the materials required by the Committee's two May 15 subpoenas. The President wrote:

> On April 30, 1974, in response to a subpoena of the House of Representatives dated April 11, 1974, I submitted transcripts not only of all the recorded Presidential conversations that took place that were called for in the subpoena, but also of a number of additional Presidential conversations that had not been subpoenaed. I did this so that the record of my knowledge and actions in the Watergate matter would be fully disclosed, once and for all.
>
> Even while my response to this original subpoena was being prepared, on April 19, 1974, my counsel received a request from the Judiciary Committee's counsel for the production of tapes of more than 140 additional Presidential conversations—of which 76 were alleged to relate to Watergate—together with a request for additional Presidential diaries for extended periods of time in 1972 and 1973.
>
> The subpoenas dated May 15 call for the tapes of the first 11 of the conversions that were requested on April 19, and for all of the diaries that were requested on April 19. My counsel has informed me that the intention of the Committee is to also issue a series of subpoenas covering all 76 of the conversations requested on April 19 that are thought to relate to Watergate. It is obvious that the subpoenaed diaries are intended to be used to identify even more Presidential conversations, as a basis for yet additional subpoenas.
>
> Thus, it is clear that the continued succession of demands for additional Presidential conversations has become a never-ending process, and that to continue providing these conversations in response to the constantly escalating requests would constitute such a massive invasion into the confidentiality of Presidential conversations that the institution of the Presidency itself would be fatally compromised.
>
> The Committee has the full story of Watergate, in so far as it relates to Presidential knowledge and Presidential actions. Production of these additional

---

[2] Each of the time periods included in the second May 30 subpoena was approved by separate votes. The period April through July 1972 (prior to and shortly after the Watergate break-in) was approved 36 to 2; February through April 1973 (during which the Watergate cover-up began to unravel) by a vote of 32 to 6; July 12 through July 31, 1973 (shortly before and after the disclosure of the White House taping system) by a vote of 29 to 9; and October 1973 (the month Special Prosecutor Cox was dismissed) by a vote of 32 to 6.

conversations would merely prolong the inquiry without yielding significant additional evidence. More fundamentally, continuing ad infinitum the process of yielding up additional conversations in response to an endless series of demands would fatally weaken this office not only in this Administration but for future Presidencies as well.

Accordingly, I respectfully decline to produce the tapes of Presidential conversations and Presidential diaries referred to in your request of April 19, 1974, that are called for in part in the subpoenas dated May 15, 1974, and those allegedly dealing with Watergate that may be called for in such further subpoenas as may hereafter be issued.

(3) May 30, 1974

On May 30, at the conclusion of the staff's presentation on the Watergate affair, the Committee authorized the issuance of a fourth subpoena by a vote of 37 to 1. This subpoena called for tape recordings and other materials relating to 45 specified conversations between November 15, 1972 and June 4, 1973 involving the President and Haldeman, Ehrlichman, Colson, Dean, Petersen and the attorneys for Haldeman, and Ehrlichman. The subpoena also sought all papers relating to Watergate and its aftermath prepared by, sent to, received by or at any time contained in the files of five former White House employees—Haldeman, Ehrlichman, Colson, Dean, and Gordon Strachan.

Also on May 30, the Committee, by a vote of 28 to 10, approved the text of a response by Chairman Rodino to the President's letter of May 22. Chairman Rodino's response stated in part:

> The Committee on the Judiciary regards your refusal to comply with its lawful subpoenas as a grave matter. Under the Constitution it is not within the power of the President to conduct an inquiry into his own impeachment, to determine which evidence, and what version or portion of that evidence, is relevant and necessary to such an inquiry. These are matters which, under the Constitution, the House has the sole power to determine.
>
> In metting their constitutional responsibility, Committee members will be free to consider whether your refusals warrant the drawing of adverse inferences concerning the substance of the materials, and whether your refusals in and of themselves might constitute a ground for impeachment.

On June 9, the President answered Chairman Rodino's May 30 letter. He wrote that his decision not to comply with any further Watergate subpoenas was based on the principle of the separation of powers. He also stated that:

> the voluminous body of materials that the Committee already has—and which I have voluntarily provided, partly in response to Committee requests and partly in an effort to round out the record—does give the full story of Watergate, insofar as it relates to Presidential knowledge and Presidential actions. The way to resolve whatever ambiguities the Committee may feel still exist is not to pursue the chimera of additional evidence from additional tapes, but rather to call live witnesses who can place the existing evidence in perspective, and subject them to cross-examination under oath. Simply multiplying the tapes and transcripts would extend the proceedings interminably, while adding nothing substantial to the evidence the Committee already has.

On June 10, Mr. St. Clair wrote Chairman Rodino with specific reference to the May 30 subpoena. He stated that the President would not furnish the materials called for in that subpoena.

C. THE ITT, DOMESTIC SURVEILLANCE, DAIRY AND IRS SUBPOENAS

By June 24, the staff had completed the initial presentation on the conduct of ITT antitrust litigation and the subsequent Kleindienst confirmation hearings, domestic surveillance, the alleged relationship between governmental decisions affecting the dairy industry and campaign contributions, and alleged misuse of the IRS. On that day, the Committee authorized the issuance of four subpoenas to the President requiring the production of evidence in each of these areas. Earlier requests by letter for this evidence had been denied.[3]

(1) The ITT Subpoena

The subpoena respecting the ITT matter and the Kleindienst confirmation hearings was authorized by a vote of 34 to 4. It required production of tape recordings and other materials relating to 19 specified conversations involving the President, Haldeman, Ehrlichman, Colson and Mitchell during the period March 6 through April 5, 1972. It also sought the President's daily news summaries for the period February 22 through June 9, 1972, containing his handwritten notations on items relating to the ITT matter and the Kleindienst confirmation hearings.

By letter dated July 12, 1974 from Mr. St. Clair to Chairman Rodino, the President declined to produce any recordings of conversations or materials related to the conversations. He agreed to and did produce copies of parts of White House news summaries, but not the original pages or copies containing his handwritten notes. Mr. St. Clair wrote that there were no notes by the President on his own copies "which related to Mr. Kleindienst's testimony that there was no White House pressure concerning the settlement of the ITT antitrust case." Mr. St. Clair advised the Chairman and Ranking Minority Member that they could verify this fact by examining the President's copy of the news summaries.

(2) The Domestic Surveillance Subpoena

The subpoena pertaining to the Committee's inquiry into domestic surveillance was authorized by voice vote. It required production of:

(1) recordings of 10 conversations during the period June 23, 1971 through April 25, 1973, in which the President and Haldeman, Colson, Ehrlichman, Petersen and Kleindienst participated;

(2) all memoranda, correspondence, papers and things relating to the White House special investigation unit (the "Plumbers") prepared by, sent to, received by or at any time contained in the files of Colson, Haldeman, Ehrlichman, Egil Krogh, and David Young, including all of Ehrlichman's handwritten notes produced by the White House pursuant to an order by Judge Gerhard Gesell in *United States* v. *Ehrlichman;* and

(3) Ehrlichman's handwritten notes of a meeting of July 12, 1971 among the President, Ehrlichman and Robert Mardian.

On July 12, 1974, the President declined to produce the 10 recordings or any of the other documents sought, except for those portions of Ehrlichman's notes that had previously been made available to Ehrlichman and the Special Prosecutor for the trial of *United States* v. *Ehrlichman.*

---

[3] The President, in response to a letter dated April 19, 1974, from Mr. Doar to Mr. St. Clair requesting recordings and other materials relating to conversations for the Committees inquiry into the ITT antitrust litigation and the Kleindienst confirmation hearings, did produce an edited transcript of a conversation on April 4, 1972 among the President, Haldeman and Mitchell. He did not produce any of the other materials sought by the April 19 letter.

(3) The Dairy Subpoena

The subpoena respecting the dairy matter, authorized by a vote of 34 to 4, sought: (1) recordings and other materials relating to 18 conversations between March 19 through March 25, 1971, involving the President, Ehrlichman, Colson and John Connally; and (2) a list of Presidential meetings and telephone calls for that seven-day period. On July 12, 1974 the President declined to produce any recordings or other material sought by this subpoena.

(4) The IRS Subpoena

The subpoena in connection with the Committee's investigation into the alleged misuse of the IRS was authorized by a voice vote. It sought recordings of and materials related to two conversations involving the President, Haldeman and Dean on September 15, 1972. On July 12, 1974 the President declined to produce any of the recordings or materials sought by this subpoena.

D. Summary

In response to its initial request by letter of February 25, 1974, the Committee received from the President 19 tape recordings and documents relating to the Watergate, ITT, dairy, and Plumbers matters. All these recordings and documents had previously been furnished to the Special Prosecutor. Twelve of the recordings and related documents—those pertaining to the Watergate matter—were part of the Grand Jury submission to the Committee, which had been announced on March 1, 1974 before Mr. St. Clair responded to the Committee's February 25 letter. Thus, the 12 Watergate recordings and related materials would have been obtained by the Committee regardless of the President's response.

In response to eight subpoenas issued between April 11 and June 24, 1974 seeking recordings and materials relating to 147 conversations and various documents, the Committee received 33 edited transcripts of subpoenaed conversations,[4] edited notes previously turned over to the Special Prosecutor and Ehrlichman in connection with his trial, and news summaries without the President's notations. Apart from the recordings and documents, furnished to the Special Prosecutor, the Committee did not receive any tape recordings, or any notes, memoranda, or other writings relating to any Presidential conversations. The Committee did not receive any of the lists of the President's meetings and calls it subpoenaed, nor (apart from a portion of Ehrlichmans' edited notes) any subpoenaed documents from the files of specified White House employees relating to the Watergate matters or the activities of the Plumbers.

---

[4] Since the delivery of the 31 edited transcripts on April 30, the President delivered to the Committee edited transcripts for all or part of two additional subpoenaed conversations: one, as previously indicated, which took place on April 4, 1972 (among the President, Haldeman and Mitchell), and the other, a 2½ page excerpt from a 1 hour and 24 minute conversation on March 22, 1973, between the President and Haldeman, which excerpt was given to the Committee on July 18, 1974, during Mr. St. Clair's closing argument. The total of 33 edited transcripts does not include the edited transcripts delivered to the Committee on August 5, 1974, of three June 23, 1972, conversations between the President and Haldeman.

JUSTIFICATION OF THE COMMITTEE'S SUBPOENAS

Before the issuance of any subpoenas, the Impeachment Inquiry Staff submitted to the Committee detailed memoranda specifically justifying the request for each of the items sought. These memoranda accompanied each of the subpoenas, and are included in this report as Appendix B. They evidence the orderly procedures adhered to by the Committee. They also show the basis for the Committee's judgment as stated in Article III, that the "subpoenaed papers and things were . . . necessary . . . to resolve by direct evidence fundamental, factual questions relating to presidential direction, knowledge or approval of actions demonstrated by other evidence to be substantial grounds for impeachment of the President."

A. WATERGATE

The subpoenas issued on April 11, May 15 and May 30 covered 98 Watergate-related conversations. The Special Prosecutor subpoenaed 63 of these 98 conversations for use in the trial of *United States* v. *Mitchell* (the prosecution arising out of the Watergate cover-up). After the Special Prosecutor demonstrated to the District Court, and ultimately to the Supreme Court, that the material sought from the President was "essential to the justice of the [pending criminal] case," [1] the President was ordered by the Supreme Court on July 24, 1974, to produce the tape recordings of those conversations for *in camera* inspection by the District Court.

The 98 conversations sought by the Committee may be divided into two periods: those that occurred on or prior to March 21, 1973, and those that took place after that date. The justifications for each group will be examined separately. But it should first be emphasized that apart from one conversation that occurred on April 4, 1972 (among the President, Haldeman and Mitchell) the President has never claimed to the Committee that any of the 98 subpoenaed conversations is unrelated to the Watergate break-in and its aftermath.[2]

(1) *Pre-March 21, 1973*

The President repeatedly stated publicly that it was not until March 21, 1973 that facts were brought to his attention respecting the break-in and Watergate cover-up. ("Presidential Statements," 8/15/73, 49; 4/17/73, 12) To investigate this contention the Committee by subpoena sought recordings and other materials relating to 33 specified conversations that took place on or prior to March 21, 1973. In response, the President produced only edited transcripts of three

---

[1] *United States* v. *Nixon*, Slip opinion at 28 (July 24, 1974).
[2] The President, after the Supreme Court decision in *United States* v. *Nixon* informed Judge Sirica when turning over conversations subpoenaed by the Special Prosecutor that a January 5, 1973 conversation between the President and Colson and a March 21, 1973 conversation between the President and Ehrlichman did not relate to Watergate. These two conversations were among the 98 subpoenaed by the Committee.

conversations: a meeting on April 4, 1972, between the President, Haldeman and Mitchell; a telephone call on March 20, 1973, between the President and Dean; and a meeting on March 17, 1973, between the President and Dean (for which the President produced a 4-page edited portion of a 45-minute conversation). The President refused to produce any materials with respect to the other 30 subpoenaed conversations on or before March 21.

Among the Presidential conversations sought in the pre-March 21 period were 9 that occurred within six days following the break-in on June 17, 1972. Six of these conversations took place on June 20 and 23 with Haldeman; the other three were with Colson and occurred on June 20. During this period shortly after the break-in, the Watergate cover-up plan was first conceived and put into motion. These conversations bear upon the President's role in directing that cover-up.

June 20, 1972 was the first day that the President was in Washington following the Watergate break-in. (Book II, 156, 243) Haldeman, after being briefed on the Watergate matter by Kleindienst, Dean, Gray, Ehrlichman and others, (Book II, 240) reported to the President between 11:26 a.m. and 12:45 p.m. (Book II, 243) The portion of that discussion dealing with the Watergate break-in is unavailable because 18½ minutes of the tape recording of the conversation have been manually erased. (See Appendix A) Haldeman conferred with the President three additional times on June 20. The Committee subpoenaed those conversations. (Book II, 245) Colson also spoke with the President on June 20. (Book II, 243) Colson's three June 20 conversations with the President were also subpoenaed.

Three other subpoenaed conversations in the period shortly after the break-in took place on June 23, 1972. They were between the President and Haldeman. On that day the President instructed Haldeman and Ehrlichman to have the CIA ask the FBI to circumscribe the Watergate investigation. (Book II, 356–57, 359) The Committee subpoenaed the three June 23 conversations between the President and Haldeman because they were critical in resolving what the President knew when he ordered that the CIA be used to limit the FBI investigation and his reason for that order. The Committee was proved correct in assessing the need for the June 23 conversations when the President ultimately released transcripts of those conversations on August 5, 1974.[3]

Among the other subpoenaed conversations that occurred prior to March 21, 1973 were four discussions between the President and Colson in January and February, 1973. They are relevant to whether or not assurances of executive clemency to Howard Hunt were authorized by the President and to determine the President's knowledge of actions by White House and CRP personnel respecting the Watergate matter. The President's own statements, as reflected in the tape recording of the morning meeting with Dean of March 21, 1973 and the edited transcript of a conversation of April 14, 1973, and Colson's testimony before the Committee, demonstrate that discussions took place in

---

[3] The conversations between the President and Haldeman on June 23, 1972 lasted 95 minutes, 9 minutes and 25 minutes. The edited transcript released by the President for these conversations were 34 pages, 1 page and 11 pages, respectively.

January and February, 1973, between the President and Colson concerning these matters. (HJCT 93, 115–16; WHT 418–19; "Presidential Statements," 5/22/73, 21; Colson testimony, 3 HJC 317–18)

Additional conversations on or before March 21 that were subpoenaed are discussions in February, 1973, between the President and Haldeman concerning the possible appointment of Magruder to a government position at a time when Haldeman knew that Magruder had committed perjury, and between the President, Haldeman and Ehrlichman concerning the assignment of Dean to work directly with the President on Watergate.

Finally, the Committee subpoenaed recordings of meetings and calls between the President and Dean in February and March, 1973 in the course of which there were discussions of the Watergate matter; between the President and Haldeman and the President and Ehrlichman on March 20, the day Ehrlichman learned from Dean of Hunt's demands for $120,000 (Book III, 952–56), and between the President and Ehrlichman on the morning of March 21 immediately before the President's meeting with Dean at which Hunt's demand and the Watergate cover-up were discussed. These conversations bear directly upon the knowledge or lack of knowledge of, or action or inaction by, the President or any of his senior administration officials with respect to the investigation of the Watergate break-in.

(2) Post-March 21, 1973

The Committee sought 65 conversations in the period subsequent to March 21. Fifty-one of these conversations involved the President and his aides, Haldeman, Ehrlichman, Colson and Dean, and the attorneys for Haldeman and Ehrlichman. The other 14 conversations took place between the President and Justice Department officials, Henry Petersen and Richard Kleindienst. The bulk of the edited transcripts produced by the President—some 30 in number—are of Presidential conversations during this post-March 21 period.

It is evident from those edited transcripts that during this period there were repeated discussions of the Watergate matter among the President, Haldeman and Ehrlichman. They discussed the effect of statements being made by Dean, Magruder and others to the Watergate prosecutors, the facts being developed by the Justice Department, the course of action to be adopted in the face of the continuing Justice Department, Grand Jury and Senate Select Committee investigations, and the need to contact others and inform them of the results of the investigation so that they could be prepared when questioned.

Among the conversations subpoenaed in the post-March 21 period were six conversations on April 25 and 26 between the President and Haldeman; one of these lasted almost six hours. Although the President had repeatedly been informed by Henry Petersen that Haldeman was a prime subject of the Department of Justice's investigation, Haldeman, on April 25 and 26, at the President's direction, listened to the March 21 tape, made notes and reported to him. (Book IX, 116, 119–21; Book IV, 1560) Subsequently, on June 4, 1973, the President told Ronald Ziegler and Alexander Haig that, while the March 21 conversation was a problem, Haldeman could handle it. (Book IX, 177–78, 193) The President also spoke to Haldeman twice by telephone on June 4. (Book IX, 237–38) The Committee subpoenaed these telephone conversations.

Subsequently, in July, 1973, Haldeman testified about the March 21 meeting before the Senate Select Committee on Presidential Campaign Activities. (Book IX, 439–41) Two months after that testimony, the President (who had stated publicly that Haldeman testified accurately) was required to furnish the tape recording of the March 21 conversation to the Special Prosecutor. Haldeman was thereafter indicted for perjury respecting his testimony about that conversation.

The remaining group of post-March 21 conversations cover 14 discussions between the President and Kleindienst, and the President and Petersen. The edited transcripts produced by the President respecting a number of these conversations clearly indicate that they bear upon the extent to which the President informed the Justice Department officials of facts within his knowledge, including facts conveyed to him by Dean and others concerning the Watergate break-in and subsequent events. They are also relevant to determining the information that the President learned from Petersen and Kleindienst, and (when considered together with the President's conversations with Haldeman and Ehrlichman) the uses to which the President put that information. In sum, the 14 conversations were subpoenaed to help ascertain whether the President was seeking to discover the truth or to cover-up for himself and his closest aides.

B. IRS

The subpoena issued on June 24, 1974 in connection with the Committee's investigation of alleged abuse of the IRS sought recordings and documents related to two conversations: one between the President and Haldeman on September 15, 1972, from 4:43 to 5:27 p.m., and another among the President, Dean and Haldeman on that same day from 6:00 to 6:13 p.m. The Committee had at that time a tape of a portion of a conversation on September 15 between the President and Haldeman from approximately 5:17 to 5:27 p.m.[4] and among the President, Dean and Haldeman from 5:27 to 6:00 p.m. Segments of the taped conversation that the Committee possesses, an affidavit by Special Prosecutor Jaworski seeking the portion of the conversation from 6:00 to 6:13 p.m. on the ground that it relates to alleged abuse of the IRS, the decision of Judge Sirica (after listening to the conversation) ordering that it be turned over to the Special Prosecutor, and the testimony of John Dean before the Committee, (Dean testimony, 2 HJC 228–29; HJCT 1–18) all demonstrate that the two conversations sought by the Committee in its June 24 subpoena bear on the President's actions in connection with the use of the Internal Revenue Service to harass or obtain information about political enemies.

---

[4] The White House staff in re-recording for the Committee a portion of a conversation among the President, Haldeman and Dean on September 15, 1972, from 5:27 to 6:00 p.m., inadvertently recorded approximately ten minutes of additional conversation between the President and Haldeman prior to 5:27 p.m. This additional ten minutes proved to be relevant to the Committee's inquiry into both the Watergate matter and alleged abuse of the IRS.

C. Domestic Surveillance

Five of the ten subpoenaed conversations in the domestic surveillance area relate to the issue of the President's knowledge of the break-in by the Plumbers into the office of Dr. Fielding. On September 7, 1971, shortly after the break-in, Egil Krogh and David Young, who headed the White House Plumbers unit, reported to Ehrlichman on the results of the break-in. (Book VII, 1310–17) The Committee subpoenaed three conversations between the President and Ehrlichman between September 7 and September 10, 1971—two of which occurred immediately before and after Ehrlichman's meetings with Krogh and Young at which the break-in was discussed.

The Committee also subpoenaed five conversations between the President and Colson that took place between June 23 and September 10, 1971. It was Colson who had arranged for the delivery of funds that were used to finance the break-in of Dr. Fielding's office. (Book VII, 1248–49) During this period the events also occurred that ultimately resulted in Colson's pleading guilty to having endeavored to obstruct justice in connection with the trial of Daniel Ellsberg. Colson has stated that he discussed with the President the release of derogatory information about Ellsberg and his attorney. ("Criminal Case," 22–23)

Finally, with respect to domestic surveillance, the Committee subpoenaed documents from the files of Haldeman, Ehrlichman, Colson, Krogh and Young relating to the origin and activities of the White House Plumbers unit. These documents were necessary for a thorough investigation by the Committee of domestic surveillance activities. The President refused to produce any of the documents from the files of his aides except for a portion of the edited Ehrlichman notes of meetings and conversations with the President which had previously been turned over to Ehrlichman and the Special Prosecutor for use in the trial in *United States* v. *Ehrlichman.*

D. Dairy

In this area of its inquiry, the Committee was investigating the relationship between political contributions by certain dairy cooperatives and governmental decisions affecting the dairy industry. On March 12, 1971, the Secretary of Agriculture announced his decision not to raise milk price supports. (Book VI, 392–93) On March 25, 1971, that decision was reversed. (Book VI 768–69) The 18 conversations sought by the Committee's subpoena of June 24, 1974, all occurred during the six-day period from March 19 to March 25, 1971. They were conversations: (1) between the President and Ehrlichman who, as the President's principal advisor in domestic affairs, participated in the White House review of the initial decision not to raise price supports (Book VII, 382, 628–71); (2) between the President and Secretary of the Treasury John Connally, who was present at discussions with the President respecting the milk price support issue;[5] and (3) between the President and Colson, who was one of the President's chief political advisors, the White House liaison with

---

[5] On July 29, 1974, Connally was indicted for accepting money to influence the decision respecting milk price supports.

the dairy industry, and the person to whom the dairy industry initially made a $2,000,000 campaign pledge in 1970. (Book VI, 154–55)

The failure of the President to produce the recordings of these conversations—or even a listing of Presidential meetings and telephone calls between March 19 and March 25, 1971—seriously frustrated this area of the Committee's inquiry. Because of the President's defiance of its subpoenas, the Committee was unable to make a determination as to the President's knowledge or lack of knowledge of, or involvement or lack of involvement in, alleged bribery in connection with the increase of milk price supports in, March 1971.

E. ITT AND KLEINDIENST CONFIRMATION HEARINGS

The Committee, as part of its inquiry, sought to determine the President's knowledge or lack of knowledge respecting alleged false testimony by John Mitchell and Richard Kleindienst about the ITT antitrust case during the hearings before the Senate Select Committee on Kleindienst's nomination to be Attorney General. These hearings took place in March and April, 1972.

The 19 conversations for which recordings and related materials were subpoenaed by the Committee for this phase of its inquiry took place between March 6 and April 5, 1972, while the Kleindienst confirmation hearings were in progress. It is undisputed that Kleindienst failed to fully and completely answer questions at the hearings; he has pleaded guilty to such a charge in the United States District Court for the District of Columbia. (Book V, 966–70) A major issue for the Committee was the President's knowledge of his conduct. The recordings which the Committee sought but did not obtain would have shed light on this question, for the conversations involve the President and Haldeman, Ehrlichman, Colson and Mitchell, all of whom played roles in connection with Kleindienst's confirmation hearings.

UNTRUSTWORTHINESS OF EDITED TRANSCRIPTS PRODUCED BY THE PRESIDENT

In response to the Committee's eight subpoenas for recordings and materials related to 147 conversations, the President has produced edited transcripts of 33 conversations. Upon examination, it was found that in numerous instances the transcripts were untrustworthy.

The Committee was able to determine the unreliability of the transcripts because, in addition to releasing edited transcripts of tape recordings that the Committee did not have, the President released to the public eight edited transcripts of tape recordings that the Committee did have: namely, recordings of conversations primarily between the President and John Dean on September 15, 1972, February 28, 1973, March 13, 1973, March 21, 1973 (two conversations), March 22, 1973 and April 16, 1973 (two conversations).

The Committee's Impeachment Inquiry Staff carefully prepared its own transcripts of each of these eight conversations. The Committee's transcripts were then compared with the edited transcripts of the eight conversations made public by the White House on April 30, 1974. The eight White House edited transcripts were inaccurate and incomplete in numerous respects.[1] Statements were omitted that were on the tape recordings; statements were added that were not on the recordings; statements were attributed to one speaker when they were made by another; statements were denominated as unintelligible when they were not; and statements were inaccurately transcribed, some in a manner that seriously misrepresented the substance and tone of the actual conservation.

A prime example is in the March 22, 1973 conversation among the President, Haldeman, Ehrlichman, Mitchell and Dean, in which approximately 20 minutes of conversation were omitted from the edited White House transcript without notice of a deletion. The omitted material included the following exchange:

PRESIDENT. . . . But, uh, the, uh, the one thing I don't want to do is to—Now let me make this clear. I, I, I thought it was, uh, very, uh, very cruel thing as it turned out—although at the time I had to tell [unintelligible]—what happened to Adams. I don't want it to happen with Watergate—-the Watergate matter. I think he made a, made a mistake, but he shouldn't have been sacked, he shouldn't have been—And, uh, for that reason, I am perfectly willing to—I don't give a shit what happens. I want you all to stonewall it, let them plead the Fifth Amendment, cover-up or anything else, if it'll save it—save the plan. That's the whole point. On the other hand, uh, uh, I would prefer, as I said to you, that you do it

---

[1] The Committee's staff has prepared a detailed written comparison of the Committee's transcripts and the White House edited transcripts. That document has been published as a separate Committee print. It contains comparisons of 65 passages in the edited transcripts of the 8 conversations the President delivered to the Committee and released to the public on April 30, 1974 and the same passages as transcribed by the Committee's inquiry staff. It does not purport to reflect all the differences between the two sets of transcripts. It does demonstrate beyond question that in numerous instances the White House edited transcripts do not accurately portray the substance or the tone of the conversations.

the other way. And I would particularly prefer to do it that other way if it's going to come out that way anyway. And that my view, that, uh, with the number of jackass people that they've got that they can call, they're going to—The story they get out through leaks, charges, and so forth, and innuendos, will be a hell of a lot worse than the story they're going to get out by just letting it out there.

MITCHELL. Well—

PRESIDENT. I don't know. But that's, uh, you know, up to this point, the whole theory has been containment, as you know, John.

MITCHELL. Yeah.

PRESIDENT. And now, now we're shifting. As far as I'm concerned, actually from a personal standpoint, if you weren't making a personal sacrifice—it's unfair—Haldeman and Dean. That's what Eisenhower—that's all he cared about. He only cared about—Christ, "Be sure he was clean." Both in the fund thing and the Adams thing. But I don't look at it that way. And I just—That's the thing I am really concerned with. We're going to protect our people, if we can. [HJCT 183]

There are other bases for distrusting the accuracy and completeness of the White House transcripts. The notation "Material Unrelated to Presidential Actions Deleted" appears at a number of places in the transcripts. No explanation has ever been given to the Committee by the President or his counsel as to what this notation means or why this material was deleted. Some of the notations appear at places in the edited transcripts where, considering what precedes and follows the excision, it is difficult to believe that the omitted conversation is not relevant.

It can be demonstrated, that at least to some extent, this disbelief is warranted. As a result of the Supreme Court decision on July 24, 1974, in *United States* v. *Nixon*, the White House turned over to the District Court tapes of 20 conversations for which edited transcripts had been made public on April 30. Under the Supreme Court decision, the White House is entitled to interpose in the District Court claims of privilege with respect to any portions of the conversations not relevant to the Watergate matter. The White House did not interpose any claim of privilege with respect to at least seven instances in these 20 conversations where the notation "Material Unrelated to Presidential Actions Deleted" had been used in the edited transcripts delivered to the Committee.

Other evidence continues to emerge that the edited transcipts supplied by the President were incomplete and that portions of conversations were omitted. For example, as a result of the Supreme Court decision, the White House was compelled to inform Judge Sirica that the tape of an April 17, 1973 conversation between the President, Haldeman and Ehrlichman from 3:50 to 4:35 p.m. contained a gap of approximately 5 minutes. The edited transcript of that conversation delivered to the Committee contains no indication that there is any such gap.

The March 17, 1973 conversation between the President and John Dean (which was sought by the Committee in its April 11 subpoena) lasted approximately 45 minutes. The President on April 30, 1974 provided the Committee with a 4-page edited transcript relating only to the Fielding break-in. There was no discussion of the Watergate matter reflected in that transcript. However, a description of that March 17 conversation supplied in June, 1973, by J. Fred Buzhardt, a White House counsel, to minority staff members of the Senate Select

Committee on Presidential Campaign Activities, reflected that there was extensive discussion of the Watergate matter during that conversation. Furthermore, the Committee has in its possession a June 4, 1973 tape recording that includes a conversation between the President and Ronald Ziegler. In the course of that conversation, the President—who had just listened to a tape of the March 17 conversation—described it to Ziegler. The President stated that on March 17, he discussed the Watergate matter with Dean and that after it was stated that Magruder had "put the heat on" and Sloan started blaming Haldeman, the President told Dean that "we've got to cut that off. We can't have that go to Haldeman."

Moreover, on July 31, 1974, a tape recording of the entire March 17, 1973 conversation was delivered to Judge Sirica as a result of the decision in *United States* v. *Nixon*. No claim of privilege was made by the White House with respect to any portion of that conversation. Thus, the White House has acknowledged that the major portions of that 45-minute conversation that are not reflected in the 4-page edited transcript supplied to the Committee on April 30, 1974, are in fact relevant to the Watergate matter. Yet, despite the Committee's April 11, 1974 subpoena, the President did not produce the remainder of the March 17 conversation.

There are other circumstances that raise questions about the reliability of the White House edited transcripts. For example, in response to a subpoena of the recording of a March 27, 1973, conversation with Haldeman, Ehrlichman and Ziegler which lasted 140 minutes, the President submitted an edited transcript of only 70 pages, with 8 deletions (of unspecified duration) characterized as "Material Unrelated to Presidential Actions." In response to a subpoena of the recording of an April 17, 1973, conversation with Haldeman, Ehrlichman and Ziegler, which lasted 45 minutes, the President submitted an edited transcript of only 19 pages, with no acknowledged deletions.

In sum, not only has the President failed to comply with the terms of the Committee's subpoenas—not only has the Committee failed to receive a single recording in response—but the minimal submission that the President has made, the 33 edited transcripts, has proven to be untrustworthy. These edited transcripts do not accurately and completely reflect the conversations that they purport to transcribe.

THE CLAIM OF EXECUTIVE PRIVILEGE

As early as 1796, it was stated on the floor of the House that the power of impeachment "certainly implied a right to inspect every paper and transaction in any department, otherwise the power of impeachment could never be exercised with any effect."[2] Similarly, in *Kilbourn* v. *Thompson*, 103 U.S. 168, 190 (1881), the Supreme Court stated:

> The House of Representatives has the sole right to impeach officers of the government, and the Senate to try them. Where the question of such impeachment is before either body acting in its appropriate sphere on that subject, we see no reason to doubt the right to compel the attendance of witnesses and their answers to proper questions, in the same manner and by the use of the same means, that courts of justice can in like cases.

Throughout our history this power of inquiry has been recognized as essential to the impeachment power.

Before the current inquiry, sixty-nine Federal officials had been the subject of impeachment investigations. With the possible exception of one minor official who invoked the privilege against self-incrimination,[3] not one of them challenged the power of the committee conducting the impeachment investigation to compel the production of evidence it deemed necessary.

In 1867 the Committee on the Judiciary conducted the initial inquiry concerning the impeachment of President Andrew Johnson. Hearings were held over a period of eleven months. Records were requested and obtained from a number of executive departments and from the Executive Mansion itself. Cabinet officers and Presidential aides were questioned in detail about cabinet meetings and private conversations with the President. The Comitee examined the circumstances leading to a number of presidential decisions, including the prosecution of Jefferson Davis, presidential pardons, the issuance of executive orders, the conduct of Reconstruction and the vetoing of legislation.[4]

---

[2] 5 *Annals of Congress* 601 (1796).
In 1848, in a dispute with President Tyler about the production of documents (which he ultimately provided), for a legislative investigation, a House Committee said:
"The House of Representatives has the sole power of impeachment. The President himself in the discharge of his most independent functions, is subject to the exercise of this power— a power which implied the right of inquiry on the part of the House to the fullest and most unlimited extent. . . . If the House possess the power to impeach, it must likewise possess all the incidents of that power—the power to compel the attendance of all witnesses and the production of all such papers as may be considered necessary to prove the charges on which the impeachment is founded. If it did not, the power of impeachment conferred upon it by the Constitution would be nugatory. It could not exercise it with effect."
H. Rep. No. 271, 27th Cong., 3d Sess., 4–6. Excerpts from this report are printed in 3 *Hind's Precedents of the House of Representatives*, § 1885 at 181–86 (1907) (hereinafter cited as *Hind's Precedents*).

[3] In 1879, a House committee reported articles of impeachment against George Seward, former consul general of Shanghai. One article alleged that Seward had concealed and refused to deliver certain records to the Committee. H. Rep. No. 134, 45th Cong., 3d Sess. (1879). The House adjourned without acting on this recommendation. Another committee of the House considered the separate question of whether Seward was in contempt of the House. It refused to recommend a contempt citation finding that he had validly invoked the privilege against self-incrimination. See H. Rep. No. 141, 45th Cong., 3d Sess. (1879) ; also printed in 3 *Hind's Precedents* § 1699 at 56–70.

[4] See, generally, Reports of Committees, Impeachment Investigation, 40th Cong., 1st Sess. 183–578 (1867).

One witness in the hearings, Jeremiah Black, an adviser to President Johnson who later served as one of his counsel in his impeachment trial, did protest against being asked to disclose a conversation between himself and the President regarding the preparation of a veto message. Black recognized, however, that he was bound to disclose the conversation if the Committee pressed the issue (which it did) and he acknowledged that "a witness sworn to testify before any tribunal is bound in conscience to answer a question which that tribunal declares he ought to answer; that he is himself not the judge of what he ought to answer and what he ought not." [5] Black and other witnesses answered detailed questions on the opinions of the President, statements made by the President, and advice given to the President. There is no evidence that Johnson ever asserted any privilege to prevent disclosure of presidential conversations to the Committee, or failed to comply with any of the Committee's requests.[6]

This uniform historical practice has been acknowledged in the statements of various Presidents.[7] The clearest instance is that of James Polk. He protested a legislative investigation being conducted by a House committee, but, in his message to the House, Polk "cheerfully admitted" the right of the House to investigate the conduct of all government officers with a view to the exercise of its impeachment power. "In such a case," he wrote:

> the safety of the Republic would be the supreme law, and the power of the House in the pursuit of this object would penetrate into the most secret recesses of the Executive Departments. It could command the attendance of any and every agent of the Government, and compel them to produce all papers, public or private, official or unofficial, and to testify on oath to all facts within their knowledge . . . . If the House of Representatives, as the grand inquest of the nation, should at any time have reason to believe that there has been malversation in office by an improper use of application of the public money by a public officer, and should think proper to institute an inquiry into the matter, all the archives and papers of the Executive Departments, public or private, would be subject to the inspection and control of a committee of their body and every facility in the power of the Executive be afforded to enable them to prosecute the investigation.[8]

It is against this historical background that President Nixon refused to comply with the Committee's subpoenas. He invoked a claim of "executive privilege" and said it was based on two grounds: (1) the need to preserve the separation of powers, and (2) the need to protect the confidentiality of Presidential conversations. In his letter of June 9, 1974 to Chairman Rodino, the President wrote that his refusal to comply with further Committee subpoenas was based in part on his study to "preserv[e] the principle of the separation of powers—and

---

[5] *Id.* at 27.
[6] There is evidence of President Johnson's views concerning the investigation, which relates to whether his personal bank records should be produced for the Committee. The cashier of the bank, who was reluctant to produce the records "upon the general principle of never imparting any information to outsiders in regard to the business of our customers." had told President Johnson of the request. The cashier reported to the Committee that the President made no objection to the production of the records:

"He smiled, and said he had no earthly objection to have any of his transactions looked into; that he had done nothing clandestinely, and desired me to show them anything I had relating to his transactions." *Id.* at 182–83.
[7] See, e.g., statements by Buchanan (5 Richardson, *Messages and Papers of Presidents* 615 (1896) (hereinafter cited as *Richardson*)); Grant (7 *Richardson* at 362); Cleveland (*Id.* at 4964); and Theodore Roosevelt (*The Letters of Archie Butt, Military Aide to President Roosevelt* 305 (Abbot ed.)).
[8] H.R. Jour., 29th Cong., 1st Sess., 693 (1846); 4 *Richardson*, 434–35 (1896).

of the executive as a co-equal branch." And in his May 22, 1974 letter, the President wrote that providing recorded conversations in response to the Committee's subpoenas would constitute "such a massive invasion into the confidentiality of Presidential conversations that the institution of the Presidency itself would be fatally compromised."

A similar claim of executive privilege was advanced by the President in the criminal proceedings arising out of the Watergate cover-up. On October 12, 1973, the Court of Appeals for the District of Columbia in *Nixon* v. *Sirica* rejected that claim; the President decided not to seek Supreme Court review of that decision. On July 24, 1974, the Supreme Court in *United States* v. *Nixon* also rejected this claim. The Court unanimously held: (1) if the President invokes executive privilege as a bar to producing evidence in a criminal prosecution, it is ultimately for the courts and not the President to determine the application of that privilege; and (2) the generalized assertion of privilege would not prevail when weighed against the "legitimate needs of the judicial process."

Both of these holdings confirm the rejection by this Committee of the claim of executive privilege interposed by the President to its subpoenas.

A. THE MERITS OF THE CLAIM

The Supreme Court in *United States* v. *Nixon* held that the interest in preserving separation of powers was not a sufficient basis for sustaining the claim of executive privilege when it was interposed as a basis for withholding relevant and necessary information from a criminal prosecution. The Court stated that the separation of powers must not be permitted to interfere with "the primary constitutional duty of the Judicial Branch to do justice in criminal prosecutions." The Court added that to permit such interference

would plainly conflict with the function of the courts under Art. III. In designing the structure of our Government and dividing and allocating the sovereign power among three coequal branches, the Framers of the Constitution sought to provirde a comprehensive system, but the separate powers were not intended to operate with absolute independence. (Slip Opinion at 22)

It is even clearer that the doctrine of separation of powers cannot justify the withholding of information from an impeachment inquiry. The very purpose of such an inquiry is to permit the legislative branch, acting on behalf of the people, to curb the excesses of another branch, in this instance the Executive.

The records of the Constitutional Convention establish that the impeachment process was considered by the Framers almost exclusively in terms of the removal of the executive; and that it was written into the Constitution despite repeated arguments by its opponents that it would violate the separation of powers and make the President overly dependent on Congress. Charles Pinckney asserted in the major debate on impeachment of the executive that, if the legislature had the power, they would hold impeachment "as a rod over the Executive and by that means effectually destroy his independence." Rufus King argued that impeachment by the legislature violated the separation of powers and would be "destructive of [the executive's] independence and of the principles of the Constitution." These arguments were decisely rejected by the Constitutional Convention, which voted eight states to two to make the executive impeachable by the legislature. This was done because, as George Mason stated, "No point is of more importance than that the right of impeachment should be continued." [9]

Alexander Hamilton confirmed that the doctrine of separation of powers was never intended to act as a limitation on the exercise of the impeachment power. He wrote in *The Federalist* that the "true meaning" of separation of powers is "entirely compatible with a partial intermixture" of departments for special purposes. This "partial intermixture," he wrote, "is even, in some cases, not only proper but necessary to the mutual defense of the several members of the government against each other." According to Hamilton, the "powers relating to impeachment" are such a case—"an essential check" in the hands of the legislature "upon the encroachment of the executive." [10]

President Nixon also stated that in invoking "executive privilege" he was relying on the need to protect the confidentiality of Presidential conversations. The Supreme Court in *United States* v. *Nixon* stated that despite the absence of an explicit reference in the Constitution to a presidential privilege of confidentiality, "to the extent this interest relates to the effective discharge of a President's powers, it is constitutionally based." (Slip Opinion at 26) Nonetheless, the Court concluded that:

[W]hen the ground for asserting privilege as to subpoenaed materials sought for use in a criminal trial is based only on the generalized interest in confidentiality, it cannot prevail over the fundamental demands of due process of law in the fair administration of criminal justice. The generalized assertion of privilege must yield to the demonstrated, specific need for evidence in a pending criminal trial. (Slip Opinion at 28).

In the Committee's impeachment inquiry the President has similarly asserted only a generalized interest in confidentiality, and the Committee (which has subpoenaed, among other items, the same conversations as the Special Prosecutor) has clearly and overwhelmingly demonstrated a specific need for the evidence sought. If a generalized Presidential interest in confidentiality cannot prevail over "the fundamental demand of due process of law in the fair administration of justice," neither can it be permitted to prevail over the fundamental need to obtain all the relevant facts in the impeachment process. Whatever the limits of legislative power in other contexts—and whatever need may otherwise exist for preserving the confidentiality of Presidential conversations—in the context of an impeachment proceeding the balance was struck in favor of the power of inquiry when the impeachment provision was written into the Constitution. And this is particularly true when, as in this case, the power to compel the production of evidence from the President was exercised by the Com-

---

[9] 2. *The Records of the Federal Convention* 63–69 (M. Farrand ed. 1911). The constitutional exception to the President's pardon power, that it should not extend to cases of impeachment, provides additional support for the argument that he cannot seek to impede the House in the exercise of its sole power to impeach. Justice Story wrote, "The power of impeachment will generally be applied to persons holding high office under the government; and it is of great consequence, that the President should not have the power of preventing a thorough investigation of their conduct, or of securing them against the disgrace of a public conviction by impeachment, if they should deserve it. The Constitution has, therefore, wisely interposed this check upon his power, so that he cannot, by any corrupt coalition with favorites, or dependents in high offices, screen them from punishment." 2 J. Story, *Commentaries on the Constitution of the United States* § 1501 at 363 (3rd ed. 1858) (hereinafter cited as *Story*). See also, 1 Kent, *Commentaries on American Law*, Lect. XIII at 184 (6th ed. 1848).

[10] "The Federalist," No. 66 at 429–30 (Modern Lib. ed.).

mittee only after it had other evidence pointing to the existence of grounds for impeachment.

The President's statements that the institution of the Presidency is threatened when he is required to comply with a subpoena in an impeachment inquiry exaggerate both the likelihood of such an inquiry and the threat to confidentiality from it. Only two Presidents (including President Nixon) out of thirty-seven have ever been the subject of impeachment investigations. It can scarcely be contended that the far-reaching inquiry into the deliberations between President Andrew Johnson and his cabinet appointees and aides resulted in any impediment of the communications between Presidents and their advisors. There is no more reason to believe that this impeachment inquiry will have that effect.

For these reasons, the Committee concluded that the President's unprecedented claim of executive privilege in an impeachment inquiry was without merit.

B. THE INAPPROPRIATENESS OF SEEKING JUDICIAL ENFORCEMENT OF THE COMMITTEE SUBPOENAS

The Committee concluded that it would be inappropriate to seek the aid of the courts to enforce its subpoenas against the President.[11] This conclusion is based on the constitutional provision vesting the power of impeachment solely in the House of Representatives and the express denial by the Framers of the Constitution of any role for the courts in the impeachment process.

The initial proposals considered by the Constitutional Convention in 1787 called for the national judiciary to try impeachments of national officers. Late in the Convention, this arrangement was altered, to provide for trial in the Senate. James Madison argued for trial by a tribunal of which the Supreme Court formed at least a part, contending that trial by the Senate, upon an impeachment by the House of Representatives, made the President "improperly dependent" on the legislature. Madison's position, however, was decisively rejected by the Convention.[12] In support of the Convention's decision to exclude the Supreme Court from the trial of impeachments, Justice Joseph Story wrote that political representatives, not judges, must control the impeachment process, both to assure its proper functioning and to protect the courts. He noted:

> Whatever shall have a tendency to secure in tribunals of justice, a spirit of moderation and exclusive devotion to juridicial duties is of inestimable value. What can more surely advance this object than the exemption of them from all participation in, and control over, the acts of political men in their official duties.[13]

The Committee's determination not to seek to involve the judiciary reflected not only an intent to preserve the constitutional structure, but also the high probability that the courts would decline to rule on the

---

[11] The President has also expressly disclaimed any interest in involving the courts in the impeachment process. During the oral argument in *United States v. Nixon*, Mr. St. Clair, the President's attorney, stated that "under the Constitution, as we view it, only the legislature has the right to conduct impeachment proceedings. The courts have been, from the history involved and from the language of the provisions, excluded from that function." Oral Argument on Behalf of the President by James D. St. Clair, *United States v. Nixon*, Transcript at 49 (July 8, 1974).
[12] *The Records of the Federal Convention*, 550–53 (M. Farrand ed. 1911).
[13] 1 *Story* § 764–66 at 532–33.

merits of the case because it is nonjusticiable—that is, not "the kind of controversy courts traditionally resolve." [14]

As the Supreme Court said in *Marbury* v. *Madison*, 5 U.S. (1 Cranch) 137, 177 (1803), and most recently reaffirmed in *United States* v. *Nixon*, Slip opinion at 18, "it is emphatically the province and the duty of the judicial department to say what the law is." In *Marbury* v. *Madison*, however, Chief Justice Marshall also said:

> The province of the court is, solely, to decide on the rights of individuals, not to inquire how the executive or executive officers perform duties in which they have a discretion. Questions in their nature political, or which are, by the constitution and laws, submitted to the executive, can never be made in this court. (5 U.S. (1 Cranch) at 170.)

The impeachment power is explicitly vested in the House of Representatives by the Constitution; its use necessarily involves the exercise of discretion by the House. While it is true that the courts may on occasion act as an umpire between Congress and the President, there are also many issues where the courts will decline to intervene because the question is one that has been constitutionally submitted to another branch.[15]

The applicable criteria of nonjusticiability—the "political question" doctrine—were stated by the Supreme Court in *Baker* v. *Carr*, 360 U.S. 186, 217 (1962):

> [A] textually demonstrable constitutional commitment of the issue to a coordinate political department; or a lack of judicially discoverable and manageable standards for resolving it, or the impossibility of deciding without an initial policy determination of a kind clearly for nonjudicial discretion; or the impossibility of a court's undertaking independent resolution without expressing lack of the respect due coordinate branches of the government; or an unusual need for unquestioning adherence to a political decision already made; or the potentiality of embarrassment from multifarious pronouncements by various departments on one question.

Litigation on the Committee's subpoenas would appear to be nonjusticiable on the basis of at least three of the criteria enumerated in *Baker* v. *Carr*. First, there is no question that there is a "textually demonstrable constitutional commitment of the issue"—the extent of the power of inquiry in an impeachment proceeding—to the House of Representatives. Second, if a court were to resolve the question independently, it could not escape "expressing lack of the respect due [a] coordinate [branch] of government." Third, there is a significant "potentiality of embarrassment from multifarious pronouncements by various departments on one question."

---

[14] *United States* v. *Nixon*. Slip Opinion at 12. It is also questionable whether the courts would have subject matter jurisdiction over a suit by the Committee to enforce its subpoenas again the President. Existing statutes governing he jurisdiction of the federal courts provide at most an uncertain basis for litigation of this type. The Senate Select Committee on Presidential Campaign Activities, which subpoenaed tape recordings from the President for its legislative inquiry, required special legislation providing jurisdiction for court adjudication of its subpoenas. Pub. L. No. 93-190 (1973); *Senate Select Committee* v. *Nixon*, 366 F. Supp. 51 (D.D.C. 1973). Thus, in order to seek a court adjudication of its subpoenas, the Committee might well have needed affirmative legislative action by the Senate, as well as the House—including, if necessary, a two-thirds vote of each to override a presidential veto. Furthermore, the constitutionality of such legislation could be questioned, since it might be thought to impinge upon the impeachment power vested solely in the House.

[15] In *United States* v. *Nixon*, the Court recognized that powers vested in one branch of government cannot be shared with another: "[T]he 'judicial power of the United States' vested in the federal courts by Art. III, § 1 can no more be shared with the Executive Branch than the Chief Executive, for example, can share with the Judiciary the veto power, or the Congress share with the Judiciary the power to override a presidential veto." Slip opinion at 19.

In deciding upon the validity of subpoenas in an impeachment inquiry, the court would necessarily have to determine whether the subpoenaed material was reasonably relevant to the inquiry. This, in turn, would lead it to pass, at least implicitly, on the scope of constitutional grounds for impeachment. While it may be argued that any judicial determination of the scope of impeachable offenses would not be binding upon either the House or the Senate in deciding whether to impeach or convict after trial, there is an obvious potential for conflict between "various departments on one question." Inevitably, there would be a serious impairment of the confidence of the people in the legitimacy of the impeachment process if the court's definition varied from those adopted by the House or the Senate in any significant respect.

The courts, moreover, do not have adequate means for enforcing a decision with respect to the validity of the subpoenas. The usual means of court enforcement, contempt, would be unavailing against a defiant President. The court would have to rely on impeachment to deal with noncompliance with its order requiring the President to surrender material in accordance with the subpoenas.

An asserted advantage of a court decision affirming the validity of of the subpoenas is that it would be an independent determination by an entity with no interest in the proceedings. But the impeachment process itself provides an opportunity for such a determination—initially by the House in deciding whether to prosecute the Article of Impeachment, and, ultimately, by the Senate, the tribunal for an impeachment trial. Neither the Committee nor the House would be the final judge of the validity of the Committee's subpoenas. Whether noncompliance with the subpoenas is a ground for impeachment would ultimately be adjudicated in the Senate.

Unless noncompliance is a ground for impeachment, there is no practical way to compel the President to produce the evidence that is necessary for an impeachment inquiry into his conduct, nor any means of assuring that the extent of the House's power of inquiry in an impeachment proceeding may be adjudicated and clarified. In the unique case of subpoenas directed to an incumbent President, a House adjudication of contempt would be an empty and inappropriate formality.[16] As the Supreme Court said in *United States* v. *Nixon*, in refusing to require a contempt citation against the President before the matter could be appealed, "the typical contempt avenue . . . is peculiarly inappropriate due to the unique setting in which the question arises." (Slip opinion at 12) No typical contempt sanction could be applied to the President to coerce compliance. In the final analysis, reliance would have to be placed on the impeachment power.

---

[16] The President was put on notice of the possible consequences of his failure to comply with Committee subpoenas by letter from Chairman Rodino dated May 30, 1972 (approved by a vote of 28 to 10). And he responded at length—by letter dated June 9, 1974—setting forth his justifications for failing to comply. In addition, the President would have an opportunity to be heard in defense in the Senate trial before the imposition of any sanction (in the case of impeachment, removal from office upon conviction). This procedure fully meets the due process requirements for legislative contempt proceedings, which consist of "reasonable notice of a charge of an opportunity to be heard in defense before punishment. . . ." *Groppi* v. *Leslie*, 404 U.S. 496, 502 (1972).

CONCLUSION

The undisputed facts, historic precedent, and applicable legal principles support the Committee's recommendation of Article III. There can be no question that in refusing to comply with limited, narrowly drawn subpoenas—issued only after the Committee was satisfied that there was other evidence pointing to the existence of impeachable offenses—the President interfered with the exercise of the House's function as the "Grand Inquest of the Nation." Unless the defiance of the Committee's subpoenas under these circumstances is considered grounds for impeachment, it is difficult to conceive of any President acknowledging that he is obligated to supply the relevant evidence necessary for Congress to exercise its constitutional responsibility in an impeachment proceeding. If this were to occur, the impeachment power would be drained of its vitality. Article III, therefore, seeks to preserve the integrity of the impeachment processs itself and the ability of Congress to act as the ultimate safeguard against improper presidential conduct.

OTHER MATTERS

PROPOSED ARTICLE ON CONCEALMENT OF INFORMATION ABOUT BOMBING OPERATIONS IN CAMBODIA

On July 30, 1974, the Committee considered a proposed Article of Impeachment dealing with the unauthorized bombing of Cambodia and the concealment from the Congress of that bombing:

In his conduct of the office of President of the United States, Richard M. Nixon, in violation of his constitutional oath faithfully to execute the office of President of the United States and, to the best of his ability, preserve, protect, and defend the Constitution of the United States, and in disregard of his constitutional duty to take care that the laws be faithfully executed, on and subsequent to March 17, 1969, authorized, ordered, and ratified the concealment from the Congress of the facts and the submission to the Congress of false and misleading statements concerning the existence, scope and nature of American bombing operations in Cambodia in derogation of the power of the Congress to declare war, to make appropriations and to raise and support armies, and by such conduct warrants impeachment and trial and removal from office.

The Committee, by a vote of 26-12, decided not to report the proposed Article to the House.

The article charged that the President had concealed the bombing in Cambodia from the Congress and that he had submitted, personally and through his aides, false and misleading statements to the Congress concerning that bombing. The investigation of those allegations centered upon the initial decision to bomb Cambodia; the type, scope, extent and nature of the bombing missions; the reporting and recording system used internally within the military and the Administration; and the statements made by Administration officials to Congress and to the public both during the military operation and after it had ceased.[1]

On February 11, 1969, the President received the initial request to institute the bombing from his military advisors. On March 17, 1969, after a series of National Security Council meetings, the President approved the request and directed that the operation be undertaken under tight security.

On March 18, 1969, the bombing of Cambodia commenced with B-52 strikes under the code name MENU OPERATION. These strikes continued until May 26, 1970, almost one month after the American incursion into Cambodia. The operational reports prepared after each mission stated that these strikes had taken place in South Vietnam rather than in Cambodia.

Between April 24 and May 24, 1970, American planes conducted tactical air strikes in Cambodia under the code name "regular" PATIO. No operational reports were made with respect to these

---

[1] The detailed findings of the Inquiry Staff concerning the bombing of Cambodia are compiled in Book XI of the Statement of Information. The findings were based upon an examination of all available sources of material, including Congressional testimony, classified documents made available by Congressional Committees, and reports of public statements by the President, civilian and military officials of the Department of Defense, and State Department officials. Some classified documents were not made available to the Committee.

strikes. Similarly, prior to June 30, 1970, an unspecified number of tactical air strikes occurred in various parts of Cambodia. Again no regular reports were prepared.

On May 14, 1970, a one day series of "special" PATIO sorties were conducted, operational reports stated that the strikes had occurred in Laos rather than Cambodia. The tactical air sorties with the code name "regular" FREEDOM DEAL were accurately reported as having occurred in Cambodia. A series of tactical air bombing missions in Cambodia called "special" FREEDOM DEAL occurred outside the boundaries designated for FREEDOM DEAL bombing, although the operational reports indicated otherwise.

On July 1, 1973, Congress enacted P.L. 93-50 and P.L. 93-52 providing for the cessation of all bombing in Cambodia by August 15, 1973. At that time the bombing had not been formally acknowledged by the President or his representatives.

Later, during the Senate Armed Services Committee hearings on the Cambodian bombing, military and Administration officials explained that the bombing was not publicized because of the delicate diplomatic and military situation in Southeast Asia prior to the American incursion into Cambodia. They stated that it was their understanding that Cambodia's ruler, Prince Sihanouk, had privately agreed to the bombing of Cambodia prior to his overthrow. It was further stated that certain Members of Congress had been informed of the military action and that this constituted sufficient notice to Congress of the President's military decision. Finally, the submission of false data to Congress was said to have resulted from the highly classified nature of the accurate bombing statistics.

The Committee considered the views of the supporters of this proposed Article of Impeachment that the President's conduct constituted ground for impeachment because the Constitution vests the power to make war in Congress and implicitly prohibits the Executive from waging an undeclared war. Stating that impeachment is a process for redefining the powers of the President, the supporters argued that the President, by issuing false and misleading statements, failed to provide Congress with complete and accurate information and thereby prevented Congress from responsibly exercising its powers to declare war, to raise and support armies, and to make appropriations. They stated that informing a few selected members of the Congress about the Cambodian bombing did not constitute the constitutionally required notice, particularly inasmuch as the President's contemporaneous public statements were contrary to the facts and the selected Members were committed to a course of action involving war that did not represent the views of a substantial portion of American citizens. The supporters also stated that Congress had not ratified the President's conduct through inaction or by its 1973 limitation on bombing because Congress did not know of the bombing until after it voted the authorization. Finally, they asserted that the technicalities or merits of the war in Southeast Asia, the acquiescence or protests of Prince Sihanouk, and the arguably similar conduct of past Presidents were irrelevant to the question of President Nixon's constitutional accountability in usurping Congress' war-making and appropriations powers.

The Committee did not agree to the article for a variety of reasons. The two principal arguments in opposition to it were that President Nixon was performing his constitutional duty in ordering the bombing and that Congress had been given sufficient notice of the bombing. Several Members stated that the President as Commander-in-Chief was acting to protect American troops and that other Presidents had engaged in similar military activities without prior Congressional consent.[2] Examining the bombing of Cambodia from the perspective of Congressional responsibility, the opponents of the Article concluded that, even if President Nixon usurped Congressional power, Congress shared the blame through acquiescence or ratification of his actions. They stated that the President had provided sufficient notice of the military actions to Congress by informing key Members. Finally, they said that the passage of the War Powers Resolution in 1973 mooted the question raised by the Article.

---

[2] Representative Seiberling also stated that because of the President's decision not to declassify certain materials, such evidence could not be made public or be discussed during the Committee's debate. Representative Seiberling said that this prevented the public use of certain documents which tied the President into acts of concealment. He stated that this was one of the reasons he opposed the Article. The classified materials which were not publicly disclosed are listed on pages 122–23 of Book XI of the "Statement of Information." (HJC Debates, 7/30/74, TR. 1225–26).

PROPOSED ARTICLE ON EMOLUMENTS AND TAX EVASION

On July 30, 1974, the Committee considered the following proposed Article:

In his conduct of the office of President of the United States, Richard M. Nixon, in violation of his constitutional oath faithfully to execute the office of the President of the United States, and, to the best of his ability, preserve, protect and defend the Constitution of the United States, and in violation of his constitutional duty to take care that the laws be faithfully executed, did receive emoluments from the United States in excess of the compensation provided by law pursuant to Article II, Section 1, of the Constitution, and did willfully attempt to evade the payment of a portion of Federal income taxes due and owing by him for the years 1969, 1970, 1971, and 1972, in that:

(1) He, during the period for which he has been elected President, unlawfully received compensation in the form of government expenditures at and on his privately-owned properties located in or near San Clemente, California, and Key Biscayne, Florida.

(2) He knowingly and fraudulently failed to report certain income and claimed deductions in the years 1969, 1970, 1971, and 1972 on his Federal income tax returns which were not authorized by law, including deductions for a gift of papers to the United States valued at approximately $576,000.

In all of this, Richard M. Nixon has acted in a manner contrary to his trust as President and subversive of constitutional government, to the great prejudice of the cause of law and justice and to the manifest injury of the people of the United States.

After debate, by a vote of 26 to 12, the Committee decided not to report the Article to the House.

This Article was based upon allegations in two areas. The expenditure of federal funds on the President's privately-owned properties at San Clemente, California, and Key Biscayne, Florida, was alleged to constitute a violation of Article II, Section 1, Clause 7, of the Constitution. That clause reads, "The President shall, at stated Times, receive for his Services, a Compensation, which shall neither be increased nor diminished during the Period for which he shall have been elected, and he shall not receive within that Period any other Emolument from the United States, or any of them." The second allegation is that the President knowingly and fraudulently failed to report certain income and claimed certain improper deductions on his federal income tax returns.

A. EXPENDITURE OF FEDERAL FUNDS ON THE PRESIDENT'S PROPERTIES

Several investigations have been undertaken with regard to the amount and propriety of Federal expenditures at or near the President's properties in San Clemente, California and Key Biscayne, Florida. The House Committee on Government Operations found that a total of $17 million had been spent by the Federal Government in connection with the President's properties, including personnel costs, communication costs, and amounts expended on adjacent Federal facilities. (Book XII, 95) The staff of the Joint Committee on Internal Revenue Taxation found that the President realized more than $92,000 in personal income from government expenditures on his properties in the years 1969 through 1972. (Book XII, 95) The Internal Revenue Service concluded that the President realized more than $67,000 in personal income from government expenditures on his properties in those years. (Book XII, 95)

The federal expenditures at San Clemente which were found to be primarily for the President's personal benefit included payments for such items as a sewer system, a heating system, a fireplace exhaust fan, enlargement of den windows, refurbishing or construction of outbuildings, paving, and boundary and structural surveys. (Book XII, 101) Expenditures brought into question at Key Biscayne included expenditures for such items as the reconstruction of a shuffleboard court and the building of a fence and hedge system. (Book XII, 157) The Government also made significant expenditures for landscape construction and maintenance on both properties. (Book XII, 101, 157)

The proponents of this section of the Article argued that the President, personally and through his agents, supervised the planning and execution of non-protective government expenditures at his private homes for his personal enrichment. The opponents maintained that a majority of the questionable expenditures were made pursuant to a Secret Service request, that there was no direct evidence of the President's awareness at the time of the expenditures that payment for these items were made out of public rather than personal funds, and that this section of the Article did not rise to the level of an impeachable offense.

B. Internal Revenue Code Violations

In examining the President's income tax returns for the years 1969 through 1972, the Internal Revenue Service found that his reported income should have been increased by more than $230,000 and that deductions claimed in excess of $565,000 should be disallowed, for a total error in reported taxable income of more than $796,000. (Book X, 410–11) The staff of the Joint Committee on Internal Revenue Taxation determined that the President's improper deductions and unreported income for that period totaled more than $960,000. (Joint Committee Report, 7) Central to the tax section of the proposed Article was the charitable deduction claimed by the President for the years 1969–1972 for a gift of his private papers claimed to have been made to the Government in 1969 which was allegedly worth $576,000. (Book X, 348)

Both the IRS and the Joint Committee staff disallowed this deduction as not having been made on or before July 25, 1969, the last day on which a gift of such papers could entitle the donor to a tax deduction. (Joint Committee Report, 5; Book X, 410–11) While the papers allegedly donated were physically delivered to the National Archives on March 27, 1969, they were part of a larger mass of papers, and the selection of the papers given was not completed until March 27, 1970. (Book X, 11–12) The President's attorneys argued that in February 1969, the President told an aide that he wanted to make a gift (Book X, 464–65), but no contemporary record of this instruction was produced. A deed of gift, signed not by President Nixon but by a White House attorney who had no written authority to sign on behalf of the President (Book X, 129), was not delivered to the Archives until April 1970, although on its face it appears to have been executed on April 21, 1969. (Book X, 326) The IRS and Joint Committee staff investigations established that the deed was actually executed on April 10, 1970, and backdated to the 1969 date (before the deduction cut-off date of July 25, 1969). (Book X, 14–15) It was found that through the end of 1969, the National Archives, the donee, thought that no gift had been made. (Book X, 282, 284) Finally, even though the deed contained restrictions limiting access to the papers, the President's 1969 tax return stated that the gift was made without restrictions. (Joint Committee Report, A–297–98; Book X, 348)

The IRS assessed a five percent negligence penalty against the President. (Book X, 409) An internal IRS memorandum recommending against the assertion of a fraud penalty stated that as of late March 1974 there was not sufficient evidence available to assert such a penalty. (Book X, 387) On April 2, 1974 IRS Commissioner Alexander wrote to Special Prosecutor Jaworski recommending a grand jury investigation into possible violations of law arising out of the preparation of the President's 1969 income tax return. Commissioner Alexander stated that the IRS was unable to complete its processing of the matter because of the lack of cooperation of some of the witnesses and because of many inconsistencies in the testimony of individuals to the IRS. (Book X, 404) The Joint Committee staff report did not address the question of fraud. (Joint Committee Report, 4)

The Joint Committee staff did submit questions to the President concerning the gift-of-papers deduction and other tax matters. (Book X, 416–22) The President did not answer the questions.

The proponents of this Article argued that the President knew that no gift of papers had been made by July 25, 1969, and that the deduction was improper. They noted that it was contrary to rational tax planning for such a large gift to be made so early in the year. They pointed to the President's personal involvement in a similar gift in 1968, and memoranda and incidents in 1969 which showed his interest in his personal financial affairs in general and the gift-of-papers deduction in particular. They referred to the opinion of an expert on criminal tax fraud matters that if this were the case of an ordinary taxpayer, the case would be referred to a grand jury for prosecution. It was argued that the President took advantage of his office in claiming this unlawful deduction, knowing that the tax return of a President would receive only cursory examination by the IRS.

The opponents of the tax fraud section stated that the President had not knowingly underpaid his taxes, but relied on attorneys and agents; that the IRS failure to assess a fraud penalty was dispositive; and that even if fraud were shown, the offense of tax evasion did not rise to the level of an impeachable offense. Some who voted against the Article were of the opinion that the evidence before the Committee did not satisfy the standard of "clear and convincing proof" which some Members thought applicable.

Some of the Members who opposed the proposed Article argued that there was no clear and convincing evidence that the President had committed tax fraud and stated that the President had not knowingly underpaid his taxes, but rather relied on attorneys and agents. Opponents of the proposed Article also asserted that an impeachment inquiry in the House and trial in the Senate are inappropriate forums to determine the President's culpability for tax fraud, and that this kind of offense can be properly redressed through the ordinary processes of the criminal law. Finally they argued that even if tax fraud were proved, it was not the type of abuse of power at which the remedy of impeachment is directed.

APPENDIXES

APPENDIX A

Analysis of the Technical Report on the 18½ Minute Gap

On November 21, 1973, Chief Judge Sirica was informed by the President's counsel that the tape of a June 20, 1972 conversation between the President and Haldeman contained an 18½ minute buzz which obliterated the recorded conversation. Subsequently, Judge Sirica asked a panel of six technical experts, previously appointed by the Judge and endorsed by the Special Prosecutor and the counsel for the President, to determine and report on the nature and cause of the obliteration of that tape recording that had been supoenaed by the Watergate Grand Jury. (Book IX, 871) On January 15, 1974, the panel reported the conclusions of its study to Judge Sirica (Book IX, 926–28) and on May 31, 1974 the panel's final report on the EOB tape of June 20, 1972 was submitted to the Court. The key conclusions of the panel were:

    (1) The Uher 5000 tape recorder used by the President's secretary, Rose Mary Woods, to transcribe tapes of Presidential conversations probably produced the 18½ minute erasure and buzz.

    (2) The 18½ minutes of erasure and buzz were accomplished by at least five, and perhaps as many as nine, contiguous and separate operations.

    (3) Erasure and recording of each segment of erasure and buzz required manual operation of keyboard controls on the Uher 5000 recorder. (May 1974 Tape Report, 35–36)

The Uher 5000 tape recorder, as it true of the Sony 800B tape recorder used to record the Presidential conversation, has two magnetic "heads," an erase head and a record head. (The record head performs both recording and playback functions.) When the "playback" button on the tape recorder is depressed, the erase head is inactive while the record head is activated to pick up electronic signals from the magnetic tape as the tape is drawn across it. The machine then translates the electronic signals into sound. When the "record" button is depressed, both the erase head and the record head are activated. The tape is drawn first over the erase head where the tape is cleansed of prior magnetic signals and then over the record head where new magnetic signals, representing the sounds being recorded, are imparted to the tape. To erase a tape, the "record" button is depressed but no new sounds are introduced into the recording machine; the tape passes over the erase head and is erased, and then over the activated but silent record head.

The Uher 5000 machine may be used in conjunction with a foot pedal. The pedal is capable only of moving the tape forward at recording speed or backward at the higher rewind speed. The foot pedal cannot, in effect, depress the "playback" or "record" button; it cannot activate or deactivate either the erase head or the record head. (Thomas Stockham testimony, *In re Grand Jury*, Misc. 47–73, 1/15/74, 16)

Whenever the record head is activated by depression of the "record" button, it leaves a distinctive "record-head-on" mark on the tape. (Richard Bolt testimony, *In re Grand Jury*, Misc. 47-73. 1/15/74, 2172) When the "record" button is released, and the erase and record heads are deactivated, the electronic pulses dying on those heads leave distinctive "erase-head-off" and "record-head-off" marks, respectively, on the tape. (Thomas Stockham testimony, *In re Grand Jury*, Misc. 47-73, 1/15/74, 12-13) The "record-head-on," "erase-head-off" and "record-head-off" marks vary from one type of machine to another, and may be used to help identify the machine on which tapes were recorded or erased.

The panel was able to identify five clear sets of "on" and "off" markings which enabled it to determine that erasure of 18½ minutes of the June 20 conversation was accomplished in at least five different segments. (Richard Bolt testimony, *In re Grand Jury*, Misc. 47-73, 1/15/74, 8)

When a segment of erasure is completed, and the machine is reversed and restarted, the "on" and "off" markings of previous erasures may themselves be erased. The panel found four additional markings that might have been part of segments of erasure where the matching "on" or "off" markings themselves had been erased; the panel could not be sure whether these marks were evidence of additional segments of erasure. (Thomas Stockham testimony, *In re Grand Jury*, Misc. 47-73, 1/15/74, 21-22)

The Advisory Panel conducted the following tests and analyses on the June 20 tape in reaching its conclusions:

1. Critical Listening

The panel played 67 minutes of the evidence tape, including the 18½ minute buzz, through high quality back-play equipment. Their expertise enabled them to identify and clarify significant acoustic phenomena on the tape. (May, 1974 Tape Report, 8)

2. Magnetic Marks

The tape was treated with a liquid that "developed" the tape, that is, rendered visible the magnetic patterns and markings on the tape, such as "record-head-on," "record-head-off," "erase-head-off," and "K-1-pulse" (see below) marks. (May, 1974 Tape Report, 8-11)

3. Wave Forms

When the electrical output of a recorded tape is fed into an oscilloscope, each signal on the tape produces a distinctive wave form. Wave form analysis enabled the panel to make a detailed study of the significant events on the June 20 tape. The panel scrutinized the wave forms of the events that occurred during the 18½ minute erasure and buzz, and found that the wave form analysis corroborated the conclusions drawn from examination of the magnetic marks. (May, 1974 Tape Report, 11-13)

4. Spectra of Speech and Buzz

Through spectral analysis (analyzing the component frequencies and amplitudes of sound signals), the panel was able to study the differences, similarites, and time of the signals. Through use of a chart of the spectral analysis of the 18½ minute buzz (a spectrogram), the panel was able to examine "windows" (tiny fragments) of original speech, to conclude that the 60 cycles per second power line hum was the source of the buzzing sound, and to corroborate the evidence of stops and starts indicated by the magnetic marks. (May, 1974 Tape Report, 13–16)

5. Phase Continuity and Speed Constancy

There is a discernible wave pattern in the power line hum on all recorded tape; this wave pattern will be of a continuous nature until the recording is stopped. Each uninterrupted portion is called a phase. The panel could determine where the recording mode has been stopped and restarted by noting the phase discontinuities. The phase discontinuities on the June 20 tape corroborated the "stop" and "start" conclusions drawn by the panel from their study of the magnetic marks and wave forms. (May, 1974 Tape Report, 16–18, 43)

6. Flutter Spectra

The mechanical irregularities in the rotating elements of every tape recorder are unique to that machine. These irregularities produce additional tones known as "flutter sidebands," distinct from the machine's original or "pure" tone.

The degree of "flutter" can be plotted, and this phenomenon will aid in the identification of a particular tape recorder.

The panel used this test to determine which machine was responsible for recording the 18½ minute buzz on the tape. (May, 1974 Tape Report, 18–20)

7. Search for Physical Splices

The panel studied the June 20 tape with an instrument (an accelerometer) that could measure and detect any variances in tape thickness. The panel concluded as a result of their studies that the tape contained no physical splices. (May, 1974 Tape Report, Technical Note 13.1)

8. The K–1 Switch

As further proof that the erasure was caused by manipulation of the keyboard, the panel studied evidence of K–1 pulses on the tape.

The K–1 switch is an internal mechanical switch. This switch only opens and closes as a result of pushing certain keys on the keyboard. It cannot be actuated by a malfunction in the electronics of the recorder. It cannot be actuated by the foot pedal. (May, 1974 Tape Report, 45) The switch opens and closes as a result of a physical latching and unlatching action that only occurs when one of the keys is pressed down manually. There are four keys that can close this switch: the recording key, the rewind key, the start key, and the forward key. (May, 1974 Tape Report, Technical Note 8.3)

K–1 switch activity is reflected on the tape by K–1 pulses. Because of the many other larger transient pulses that are generated by other electro-mechanical activity, K–1 pulses are difficult to discern. However, where a K–1 pulse is unambiguously identified, it is an unmistakable sign of manual activity of the keyboard. The expert panel was able to identify six distinct K–1 pulses. (May, 1974 Tape Report, Technical Notes 8.3–8.5)

ALTERNATE HYPOTHESES

A number of alternative hypotheses to the conclusions reached by the expert panel were considered and rejected by the panel in arriving at its conclusion, including the following:

Hypothesis No. 1

That the 18½ minute gap was produced on the June 20, 1972 tape at the same time that the tape was originally recorded. This hypothesis failed because the June 20, 1972 original tape was recorded on a Sony 800B tape recorder. The experts determined that the 18½ minute gap was produced by a Uher 5000 tape recorder. (May, 1974 Tape Report, Technical Notes 9.1–9.2)

Hypothesis No. 2

That the 18½ minute obliteration was caused by setting the Uher tape recorder in the record mode and operating it in fast rewind. This hypothesis was rejected because if the tape had been erased in rewind the obliterated section would have had an audible tone of 500 cycles when played back at its usual operating speed of 24 millimeters per second. However, the frequency that is on the 18½ minute gap is the normal 60-cycle frequency. This shows that the tape was erased at its standard operating speed of 24 millimeters per second. Additionally, if the 18½ minute buzz had been recorded in rewind, there would have been no record and erase-head-off marks left on the tape. More than 20 such marks were found in the obliterated section. (May, 1974 Tape Report, Technical Note 9.2)

Hypothesis No. 3

The tape was erased through use of the foot pedal. This hypothesis was rejected because of the record and erase head signatures that were found on the tape; signatures that cannot be made by the foot pedal. Second, a distinctive set of magnetic marks is made by the Uher tape recorder when stopped and restarted by the foot pedal. None of these marks was found on the 18 minute buzz section. Furthermore, six K–1 pulses were found in the obliterated section. K–1 pulses also cannot be made by the foot pedal. (May, 1974 Tape Report, Technical Notes 9.2–9.3)

Hypothesis No. 4

The distinctive magnetic marks found on the 18½ minute gap came from a power supply failure within the Uher 5000 machine, *i.e.*, a defective diode caused the power supply to sputter on and off, thus putting the distinctive marks on the tape while the tape was still moving. The experts rejected this hypothesis because they were able to determine that the wave forms that would have been produced by this sort of activity were not present on the evidence tape. Furthermore, if this "sputter" activity had taken place, there would be no phase discontinuity following the record-head-on marks. The evidence tape shows phase discontinuity and erase head signatures associated with the record-head-on marks. Additionally, there are K–1 pulses found on the tape that could only be caused manually. (May, 1974 Tape Report, Technical Notes 9.3–9.5)

Hypothesis No. 5

Voltage irregularities on the AC power line working in conjunction with the failing diode of the bridge rectifier caused the distinctive magnetic marks. A voltage drop sufficient to put these marks in the tape would have caused a drop in motor speed with a resulting differential in tone frequency. There was no evidence of this on the evidence tape. Moreover, a drop in voltage could not cause the recording of K-1 pulses. (May, 1974 Tape Report, Technical Notes 9.6–9.8)

THE STANFORD RESEARCH INSTITUTE REPORT OF MAY 31, 1974

Dr. Michael Hecker of the Stanford Research Institute conducted experiments for the Special Counsel to the President with regard to the June 20, 1972 tape. It should be noted that while Dr. Hecker reviewed experiments and held a number of conferences with the expert panel, he never studied the June 20, 1972 tape directly. (SRI Report) Dr. Hecker reviewed the findings of the expert panel and stated that he agreed with the panel's approach and agreed with the panel's expertise. Dr. Hecker stated further that he was in substantial agreement with the panel's final report. (SRI Report 3) The Stanford Research Institute found evidence that there had been manual manipulation of the keyboard controls of the Uher 5000 tape recorder in order to cause some portions of the 18½ minute gap. The Stanford Research Institute studied and rejected all the alternative hypotheses that were considered by the panel. (SRI Report, 4)

Dr. Hecker was less willing to commit himself to a finding of at least five manual erasures than the expert panel had been. (Michael Hecker testimony. *In re Grand Jury*, Misc. 47–73, 5/13/74, 18–19; SRI Report, 3) The panel rejected the hypothesis that any of the magnetic marks suggesting manual operation could have been caused by a malfunctioning machine. (SRI Report, 3–4) Dr. Hecker was of the opinion that it was wrong to rule out conclusively the chance that the malfunctioning machine could have caused some of the indicia of manual operation. (SRI Report, 4; Michael Hecker testimony, *In re Grand Jury*, Misc. 47–73, 5/13/74, 18–19) Dr. Hecker stated that because the machine had broken down once during testing; and after a defective diode bridge rectifier was replaced, the distinctive buzz could no longer be reproduced. Dr. Hecker did not state that any of the indicia of manual operation were caused by the defect on the machine; he merely said that, in his opinion, this possibility could not be ruled out completely. (SRI Report, 4–5) However, Dr. Hecker remained convinced that some of the marks of the operations were caused by manual manipulation of the keyboard controls. Dr. Hecker stated that he was absolutely sure that three events associated with the 18½ minute gap were caused by manual operation of the keyboard controls and that he was practically certain that two other marks had been caused by manual operation of the keyboard controls. He testified on May 13, 1974 that he was willing to agree with the panel that at least five of the events on the 18½ minute buzz had been caused by manual operation of the machine. (Michael Hecker testimony, *In re Grand Jury*, Misc. 47–73, 5/13/74, 18–21)[1]

---

[1] The Court received two reports obtained by Miss Woods' attorney that questioned the conclusions of the Panel, whose conclusions in substance had been confirmed by the Stanford Research Institute, expert for the counsel to the President. The Committee staff has obtained copies of these reports. The organizations submitting the reports are Home Service, Inc., a Magnavox sales and service center in Cleveland Heights, Ohio, dated May 24, 1974, and Dektor Counterintelligence and Security, Inc. in Springfield, Virginia, dated May 30, 1974. Neither organization examined the evidence tape or Uher 5000 recorder, or reviewed the experiments with the expert panel.

APPENDIX B

SUBPOENAS ISSUED TO PRESIDENT RICHARD M. NIXON BY THE COMMITTEE ON THE JUDICIARY AND JUSTIFICATION MEMORANDA

	Page
April 11, 1974	234
Schedule	235
Justification	237
May 15, 1974 (President's Daily Diaries)	244
Schedule	245
May 15, 1974 (Presidential Conversations)	246
Schedule	247
Justification	247
May 30, 1974	250
Schedule	251
Justification	253
June 24, 1974 (ITT)	261
Schedule	262
Justification	263
June 24, 1974 (1971 Milk Price Support Decision)	268
Schedule	269
Justification	269
June 24, 1974 (IRS)	271
Schedule	272
Justification	272
June 24, 1974 (Domestic Surveillance)	274
Schedule	275
Justification	275

COPY

BY AUTHORITY OF THE HOUSE OF REPRESENTATIVES OF THE CONGRESS OF THE UNITED STATES OF AMERICA

To **Benjamin Marshall, or his duly authorized representative:**

You are hereby commanded to summon **Richard M. Nixon, President of the United States of America, or any subordinate officer, official or employee with custody or control of the things described in the attached schedule,**

to be and appear before the **Committee on the Judiciary** ~~Committee~~ of the House of Representatives of the United States, of which the Hon. **Peter W. Rodino, Jr.** is chairman, **and to bring with him the things specified in the schedule attached hereto and made a part hereof,**

in their chamber in the city of Washington, on **or before April 25, 1974**, at the hour of **10:00 A.M.**, then and there to **produce and deliver said things to said Committee, or their duly authorized representative, in connection with the Committee's investigation authorized and directed by H. Res. 803, adopted February 6, 1974.**

Herein fail not, and make return of this summons.

Witness my hand and the seal of the House of Representatives of the United States, at the city of Washington, this **11th** day of **April**, 19**74**.

Peter W. Rodino, Jr. *Chairman.*

Attest:

[signature] *Clerk.*

On behalf of Richard M. Nixon, President of the United States of America, I accept service on April 11, 1974, of the original subpoena, of which the foregoing is a copy.

[signature]

JAMES D. ST. CLAIR
Special Counsel to the President

SCHEDULE OF THINGS REQUIRED TO BE PRODUCED PURSUANT TO SUBPOENA DATED APRIL 11, 1974

All tapes, dictabelts or other electronic recordings, transcripts, memoranda, notes or other writings or things relating to the following conversations:

1. Certain conversations between the President and Mr. Haldeman or Mr. Ehrlichman or Mr. Dean in February, March and April, 1973, as follows:

(a) Conversations between the President and Mr. Haldeman on or about February 20, 1973, that concern the possible appointment of Mr. Magruder to a government position;

(b) Conversations between the President, Mr. Haldeman and Mr. Ehrlichman on or about February 27, 1973, that concern the assignment of Mr. Dean to work directly with the President on Watergate and Watergate-related matters;

(c) Conversations between the President and Mr. Dean on March 17, 1973, from 1:25 to 2:10 p.m. and March 20, 1973, from 7:29 to 7:43 p.m.

(d) Conversations between the President and Mr. Ehrlichman on March 27, 1973 from 11:10 a.m. to 1:30 p.m., and on March ? 1973, from 12:02 to 12:18 p.m.; and

(e) Conversations between the President and Mr. Haldeman and the President and Mr. Ehrlichman during the period April 14 through 17, 1973, as follows:

April 14

8:55 to 11:31 a.m.	Meeting among the President, Mr. Ehrlichman and Mr. Haldeman
1:55 to 2:13 p.m.	Meeting between the President and Mr. Haldeman
2:24 to 3:55 p.m.	Meeting among the President, Mr. Ehrlichman and Mr. Haldeman
5:15 to 6:45 p.m.	Meeting among the President, Mr. Ehrlichman and Mr. Haldeman
11:02 to 11:16 p.m.	Telephone conversation between the President and Mr. Haldeman
11:22 to 11:53 p.m.	Telephone conversation between the President and Mr. Ehrlichman

April 15

10:35 to 11:15 a.m.	Meeting between the President and Mr. Ehrlichman
2:24 to 3:30 p.m.	Meeting between the President and Mr. Ehrlichman
3:27 to 3:44 p.m.	Telephone conversation between the President and Mr. Haldeman
7:50 to 9:15 p.m.	Meeting among the President, Mr. Haldeman and Mr. Ehrlichman
10:16 to 11:15 p.m.	Meeting among the President, Mr. Ehrlichman and Mr. Haldeman

April 16

12:08 to 12:23 a.m	Telephone conversation between the President and Mr. Haldeman
8:18 to 8:22 a.m	Telephone conversation between the President and Mr. Ehrlichman
9:50 to 9:59 a.m	Meeting among the President, Mr. Haldeman and Mr. Ehrlichman
10:50 to 11:04 a.m	Meeting among the President, Mr. Haldeman and Mr. Ehrlichman
12:00 to 12:31 p.m	Meeting among the President, Mr. Ehrlichman and Mr. Haldeman
3:27 to 4:02 p.m	Meeting between the President and Mr. Ehrlichman (Mr. Ziegler present from 3:35–4:04 p.m.)
9:27 to 9:49 p.m	Telephone conversation between the President and Mr. Ehrlichman

April 17

9:47 to 9:59 a.m	Meeting between the President and Mr. Haldeman
12:35 to 2:30 p.m	Meeting among the President, Mr. Haldeman and Mr. Ehrlichman (Mr. Ziegler present from 2:10–2:17 p.m.)
2:39 to 2:40 p.m	Telephone conversation between the President and Mr. Ehrlichman
3:50 to 4:35 p.m	Meeting among the President, Mr. Haldeman and Mr. Ehrlichman
5:50 to 7:14 p.m	Meeting among the President, Mr. Haldeman and Mr. Ehrlichman (Mr. Rogers present from 5:20–6:19 p.m.)

2. Conversations between the President and Mr. Kleindienst and the President and Mr. Petersen during the period from April 15 through 18, 1973, as follows:

April 15

10:13 to 10:15	Telephone conversation between the President and Mr. Kleindienst
1:12 to 2:22 p.m	Meeting between the President and Mr. Kleindienst
3:48 to 3:49 p.m	Telephone conversation between the President and Mr. Kleindienst
4:00 to 5:15 p.m	Meeting among the President, Mr. Kleindienst and Mr. Petersen
8:14 to 8:18 p.m	Telephone conversation between the President and Mr. Petersen
8:25 to 8:26 p.m	Telephone conversation between the President and Mr. Petersen
9:39 to 9:41 p.m	Telephone conversation between the President and Mr. Petersen
11:45 to 11:53 p.m	Telephone conversation between the President and Mr. Petersen

April 16

1:39 to 3:25 p.m	Meeting between the President and Mr. Petersen (Mr. Ziegler present from 2:25–2:52 p.m.)
8:58 to 9:14 p.m	Telephone conversation between the President and Mr. Petersen

April 17

2:46 to 3:49 p.m	Meeting between the President and Mr. Petersen

April 18

2:50 to 2:56 p.m_____ Telephone conversation between the President and Mr. Petersen
6:28 to 6:37 p.m_____ Telephone conversation between the President and Mr. Petersen

Memorandum to Committee on the Judiciary Respecting Conversations Requested on February 25, 1974

The following sets forth the facts and bases underlying the requests for the conversations specified in the letter of February 25, 1974 from Mr. Doar to Mr. St. Clair:

(1) Conversations between the President and Mr. Haldeman on or about February 20, 1973, that concern the possible appointment of Mr. Magruder to a government position.

Jeb Magruder was deputy director of the Committee to Re-elect the President and participated in meetings at which plans for the electronic surveillance of the President's political opponents were discussed (Magruder, 2 SSC p. 787-790). Mr. Magruder has testified that he committed perjury before the grand jury investigating the break-in at the Democratic National Committee Headquarters and at the trial of the seven defendants in *United States* v. *Liddy, et al.* (Magruder, 2 SSC p. 805). Mr. Magruder has testified that he informed Mr. Haldeman in mid-January, 1973 that he was going to commit perjury during the trial (Magruder, 2 SSC p. 832). Mr. Haldeman does not recollect this discussion but does state that he met with Mr. Magruder on February 14, 1973 and on March 2, 1973 about Mr. Magruder's future (Haldeman, 7 SSC p. 2886-87).

Mr. Dean testified that in January and February of 1973 there were discussions about a job for Mr. Magruder (Dean, 3 SSC p. 990). Hugh Sloan, the former treasurer of the President's Campaign Finance Committee, testified he told Mr. Dean that if Mr. Magruder (who Sloan testified made efforts to persuade him to commit perjury) (Sloan, 2 SSC p. 543, 581, 583) were given an appointment requiring Senate confirmation, Mr. Sloan would voluntarily seek out the Senate Committee and testify against Mr. Magruder (Sloan, 2 SSC p. 591). Mr. Dean has further testified that on or about February 19, 1973 he was asked by Mr. Haldeman to prepare an agenda of topics which the President could use as a basis for a meeting with Mr. Haldeman (Dean, 3 SSC p. 987). That agenda raised as a topic the question of a White House position for Mr. Magruder. The agenda stated that Mr. Magruder "[m]ay be vulnerable (Sloan) until Senate Hearings are completed." (Exhibit 34-34, 3 SSC p. 1243) Mr. Dean has testified that on or about February 20, 1973, Mr. Haldeman met with the President to discuss the topics covered by the memorandum (Dean, 3 SSC p. 988).

Mr. Haldeman testified that at the time he received the agenda he had already told Magruder that a White House job would not be possible "but I think the point here was to check that decision with the President to be sure he concurred." (Haldeman, 7 SSC p. 2891). In March 1973, Mr. Magruder was appointed to a $36,000 a year government post which did not require Senate confirmation (Magruder, 2 SSC p. 831; Haldeman, 7 SSC p. 2887).

(2) Conversations between the President, Mr. Haldeman and Mr. Ehrlichman on or about February 27, 1973, that concern the assignment of Mr. Dean to work directly with the President on Watergate and Watergate-related matters.

Both Mr. Haldeman and Mr. Ehrlichman have testified that the President decided toward the end of February 1973, that Mr. Dean would work directly with the President on Watergate-related matters and that this decision was discussed with them (Ehrlichman, 7 SSC p. 2739; Haldeman, 7 SSC p. 2891). Mr. Dean has testified that when he met with the President on February 27, 1973, the President told him that Watergate "was taking too much time from Haldeman's and Ehrlichman's normal duties and . . . they were principals in the matter, and I, therefore, could be more objective than they." (Dean, 3 SSC p. 991)

(3) Conversations between the President and Mr. Dean on March 17, 1973, from 1:25 to 2:10 p.m. and March 20, 1973 from 7:29 to 7:43 p.m.

(a) March 17

The President has stated that he first learned at this meeting of the break-in of the office of Daniel Ellsberg's psychiatrist which the White House Special Investigation Unit committed in September 1971 (President's Statement August 15, 1973, Pres. Doc p. 993).

The White House has also stated that Mr. Dean told the President on this date that no White House aides were involved in the Watergate burglary except possibly Mr. Strachan and that the President suggested that Mr. Dean, Mr. Haldeman and Mr. Ehrlichman testify before the Senate Select Committee (Exhibit 70-A, 4 SSC p. 1798—Memorandum of Substance of Dean's Calls and Meetings With the President).

(b) March 20

The White House has said that in the course of this phone call from the President to Mr. Dean, Mr. Dean stated that there was not a "scintilla of evidence of White House involvement" in Watergate (Exhibit 70-A, 4 SSC p. 1798—Memorandum of Substance of Dean's Calls and Meetings with the President). President Nixon confirmed this statement (President's News Conference August 22, 1972, Pres. Doc. p. 1019). Mr. Dean has testified that during this call he scheduled a meeting with the President to discuss the facts of Watergate and the obstruction of the Watergate investigation (Dean, 3 SSC p. 997-98).

(4) Conversations between the President and Mr. Ehrlichman on March 27, 1973, from 11:10 a.m. to 1:30 p.m. and on March 30, 1973 from 12:02 to 12:18 p.m.

(a) March 27

Mr. Ehrlichman has testified that on March 27, 1973, he met with the President and discussed White House involvement in the break-in at the Democratic National Committee Headquarters (Ehrlichman, 7 SSC p. 2747). Mr. Ehrlichman has testified that the President instructed him to inform Attorney General Kleindienst that the President had no information that Mr. Ehrlichman, Mr. Colson, Mr. Dean, Mr. Haldeman or any other White House staff had any prior knowledge of the Watergate burglary (Ehrlichman, 7 SSC p. 2748–49; Exhibit 99 p. 2944–45). Mr. Ehrlichman has also testified that the President asked him to inquire of the Attorney General about the procedures for granting immunity (Ehrlichman, 7 SSC p. 2750).

(b) *March 30*

The President has said that after Mr. Dean's disclosures of March 21 he ordered new investigations. (President's Statements April 17, 1973, Pres. Doc p. 387; President's Statement April 30, 1973, Pres. Doc. p. 434; President's Statement August 15, 1973, Pres. Doc. p. 993). The President has stated that on this date the President asked Mr. Ehrlichman to take over that investigation from Mr. Dean (President's Statement August 15, 1973, Pres. Doc p. 993; Ehrlichman, 7 SSC p. 2747).

(5) All conversations between the President and Mr. Haldeman and the President and Mr. Ehrlichman from April 14 through 17, 1973, inclusive.

(6) All conversations between the President and Mr. Kleindienst and the President and Mr. Petersen from April 15 through 18, 1973, inclusive.

(a) *April 14, 1973*

The President's records indicate that the following meetings and telephone conversations took place between the President and Mr. Haldeman and the President and Mr. Ehrlichman on April 14, 1973:

8:55 to 11:31 a.m.	Meeting between the President and Mr. Ehrlichman in the President's EOB office. (The President's daily diary shows that Mr. Haldeman was present from 9:00 to 11:30 a.m.)
1:55 to 2:13 p.m.	Meeting between the President and Mr. Haldeman
2:24 to 3:55 p.m.	Meeting among the President, Mr. Ehrlichman and Mr. Haldeman in the Oval Office.
5:15 to 6:45 p.m.	Meeting among the President, Mr. Ehrlichman and Mr. Haldeman in the President's EOB office
11:02 to 11:16 p.m.	Telephone conversation between the President and Mr. Haldeman
11:22 to 11:53 p.m.	Telephone conversation between the President and Mr. Ehrlichman

The President has stated that it was on April 14 that Mr. Ehrlichman reported to him the results of the inquiry of the Watergate matter which the President, on March 30, 1973, ordered Mr. Ehrlichman to conduct (President's Statement August 15, 1973, Pres. Doc. p. 993). Mr. Ehrlichman testified that he informed the President that Messrs. Dean, Magruder and Mitchell were involved in the planning of the Watergate break-in (Ehrlichman, 7 SSC p. 2755, 2757–58, 2737; SSC Exhibit 98 at p. 2915–43). The President, according to Mr. Ehrlichman, ordered that the information be turned over to Mr. Kleindienst (Ehrlichman, 7 SSC p. 2758).

It was on April 14 that Mr. Magruder informed Mr. Ehrlichman that he was giving the prosecutors new information with respect to the Watergate break-in and its aftermath. (Magruder, 2 SSC p. 808; Ehrlichman, 7 SSC p. 2765–66). Mr. Ehrlichman and Mr. Haldeman knew that Mr. Dean already had been talking to the prosecutors and on April 14 Mr. Dean told them that Mr. Ehrlichman and Mr. Haldeman were targets of the grand jury investigation (Dean, 3 SSC p. 1014). Thus, when Mr. Ehrlichman telephoned Mr. Kleindienst on the evening of April 14 and was advised by the Attorney General to turn over all information to the Department of Justice to avoid being charged with obstruction of justice, Mr. Ehrlichman stated that "it doesn't really make any difference anymore" since Mr. Dean and Mr. Magruder were talking to the prosecutors (Kleindienst, 9 SSC p. 3577).

(b) April 15, 1973

The President's records indicate that the following meetings and telephone conversations took place among the President, Mr. Haldeman, Mr. Ehrlichman, Mr. Kleindienst and Mr. Petersen:

10:13 to 10:15 a.m.	Telephone conversation between the President and Mr. Kleindienst
10:35 to 11:15 a.m.	Meeting between the President and Mr. Ehrlichman
1:12 to 2:22 p.m.	Meeting between the President and Mr. Kleindienst
2:24 to 3:30 p.m.	Meeting between the President and Mr. Ehrlichman
3:27 to 3:44 p.m.	Telephone conversation between the President and Mr. Haldeman
3:48 to 3:49 p.m.	Telephone conversation between the President and Mr. Kleindienst
4:00 to 5:15 p.m.	Meeting among the President, Mr. Kleindienst and Mr. Petersen
7:50 to 9:15 p.m.	Meeting among the President, Mr. Haldeman and Mr. Ehrlichman
8:14 to 8:18 p.m.	Telephone conversation between the President and Mr. Petersen
8:25 to 8:26 p.m.	Telephone conversation between the President and Mr. Petersen
9:39 to 9:41 p.m.	Telephone conversation between the President and Mr. Petersen
10:16 to 11:15 p.m.	Meeting among the President, Mr. Ehrlichman and Mr. Haldeman
11:45 to 11:53 p.m.	Telephone conversation between the President and Mr. Petersen

It was on April 15 that Mr. Kleindienst and Mr. Petersen directly brought to the attention of the President the new information which was being conveyed to the prosecutors by Mr. Dean and Mr. Magruder. (President's Statement August 15, 1973, Pres. Doc p. 993). April 15 was also the date on which the President, beginning at 9:17 p.m., had an important conversation with Mr. Dean that the President has stated was not recorded because the tape had run out (President's Statement November 12, 1973, Pres. Doc p. 1330; President's News Conference November 17, 1973, Pres. Doc p. 1346–47). According to Mr. Dean the President stated at that conversation that he was joking when he said earlier that it would be no problem to raise $1,000,000 (Dean, 3 SSC p. 1016). Following the conversation with Mr. Dean the President had a meeting with Mr. Ehrlichman and Mr. Haldeman at which Mr. Ehrlichman called Mr. Gray with respect to what happened to documents from Mr. Hunt's safe which were given to Mr. Gray in June 1972. Mr. Gray informed Mr. Ehrlichman that the documents were destroyed (Ehrlichman, 7 SSC p. 2675–76).

As the listing of conversations indicates, immediately following each of his various conversations with Mr. Kleindienst or Mr. Petersen, the President had conversations, some of which were quite lengthy, with Mr. Haldeman or Mr. Ehrlichman or both. It was on April 15 that Mr. Petersen suggested to the President that Mr. Haldeman and Mr. Ehrlichman be fired (Petersen, 9 SSC p. 3628–29). The President stated that he owed an obligation of fairness to Mr. Haldeman and Mr. Ehrlichman (Petersen, 9 SSC p. 3628).

(c) *April 16, 1973*

The President's records indicate that the following meetings and telephone conversations took place among the President, Mr. Haldeman, Mr. Ehrlichman, Mr. Kleindienst and Mr. Petersen:

12:08 to 12:23 a.m	Telephone conversation between the President and Mr. Haldeman
8:18 to 8:22 a.m	Telephone conversation between the President and Mr. Ehrlichman
9:50 to 9:59 a.m	Meeting among the President, Mr. Haldeman and Mr. Ehrlichman
10:50 to 11:04 a.m	Meeting among the President, Mr. Haldeman and Mr. Ehrlichman
12:00 to 12:31 p.m	Meeting among the President, Mr. Ehrlichman and Mr. Haldeman
1:39 to 3:25 p.m	Meeting between the President and Mr. Petersen (Mr. Ziegler present from 2:25 to 2:52 p.m.)
3:27 to 4:02 p.m	Meeting between the President and Mr. Ehrlichman (Mr. Ziegler present from 3:35 to 4:04 p.m.)
8:58 to 9:14 p.m	Telephone conversation between the President and Mr. Petersen
9:27 to 9:49 p.m	Telephone conversation between the President and Mr. Ehrlichman

On April 16, according to Mr. Dean's testimony, the President asked Mr. Dean to sign a letter of resignation, but Mr. Dean said he would not resign unless Mr. Ehrlichman and Mr. Haldeman also resigned (Dean, 3 SSC p. 1017–1018). The President had further discussions with Mr. Petersen about the prosecutors' evidence of Mr. Haldeman and Mr. Ehrlichman's possible involvement in the Watergate matter and the possibility of granting immunity to Mr. Dean (Petersen, 9 SSC p. 3634; President's Statement April 17, 1973 Pres. Doc p. 387). Again, prior to and subsequent to his conversations with Mr. Dean and Mr. Petersen the President had a number of conversations with Mr. Ehrlichman and Mr. Haldeman.

(d) *April 17, 1973*

The President's records indicate that the following meetings and telephone conversations took place among the President, Mr. Haldeman, Mr. Ehrlichman, Mr. Kleindienst and Mr. Petersen:

9:47 to 9:59 a.m	Meeting between the President and Mr. Haldeman
12:35 to 2:30 p.m	Meeting among the President, Mr. Haldeman and Mr. Ehrlichman (Mr. Ziegler present from 2:10 to 2:17 p.m.)

2:39 to 2:40 p.m.	Telephone conversation between the President and Mr. Ehrlichman
2:46 to 3:49 p.m.	Meeting between the President and Mr. Petersen
3:50 to 4:35 p.m.	Meeting among the President, Mr. Haldeman and Mr. Ehrlichman
5:50 to 7:14 p.m.	Meeting among the President, Mr. Haldeman and Mr. Ehrlichman (Mr. Rogers present from 5:20 to 6:19 p.m.)

On April 17 the President issued a statement that there were "major developments" in the Watergate case and that "real progress has been made on finding the truth." The President also stated that "no individual holding, in the past or at present, a position of major importance in the administration should be given immunity from prosecution." (Pres. Doc p. 387) Mr. Dean has testified that by the "no immunity" provision in the April 17 statement, the President was "quite obviously trying to affect any discussion I was having with the government regarding my testimony." Mr. Dean has stated that Mr. Garment, another Presidential Assistant, believed that the "no immunity" provision was inserted into the President's statement by Mr. Ehrlichman (Dean, 3 SSC p. 1020).

Also, on April 17, the pattern of the previous few days is repeated in that prior to and subsequent to conversations between the President and Mr. Petersen there are numerous conversations between the President and Mr. Haldeman and the President and Mr. Ehrlichman.

(e) *April 18, 1973*

The President's records indicate that the following meetings and telephone conversations took place between the President and Mr. Petersen:

2:50 to 2:56 p.m.	Telephone conversation between the President and Mr. Petersen
6:28 to 6:37 p.m.	Telephone conversation between the President and Mr. Petersen

On April 18, the President learned from Mr. Petersen that Mr. Dean had informed the prosecutors of the break-in by Messrs. Hunt and Liddy of the office of Dr. Fielding, Daniel Ellsberg's psychiatrist. (President's News Conference, August 22, 1973, Pres. Doc. p. 1020; Petersen, 9 SSC p. 3631). There was also a continuation of the discussion respecting possible immunity for Mr. Dean during which the President said he had a tape to prove that Mr. Dean had told the President he had received immunity (Petersen, 9 SSC p. 3630, 3654–56). With respect to the Fielding break-in the President has stated that he first learned of it on March 17, 1973, and that on April 18 he instructed Mr. Petersen to stay out of the matter because it involved national security.

* * * * * * *

In calling for the above conversations the Committee is seeking to determine:

Whether any of the conversations in any way bear upon the knowledge or lack of knowledge of, or action or inaction by the President and/or any of his senior administration officials with respect to, the investigation of the Watergate break-in by the Department of Justice, the Senate Select Committee, or any other legislative, judicial, executive or administrative body, including members of the White House staff;

Whether any of the conversations in any way bear upon the President's knowledge or lack of knowledge of, or participation or lack of participation in, the acts of obstruction of justice and conspiracy charged or otherwise referred to in the indictments returned on March 1 in the District Court for the District of Columbia in the case of *U.S.* v. *Haldeman, et al.*; and

Whether any of the conversations in any way bear upon the President's knowledge or lack of knowledge of, or participation or lack of participation in, the acts charged or otherwise referred to in the informations or indictments returned in the District Court for the District of Columbia in the cases of *U.S.* v. *Magruder, U.S.* v. *Dean, U.S.* v. *Chapin* and *U.S.* v. *Ehrlichman*, or other acts which may constitute illegal activities.

244

COPY

BY AUTHORITY OF THE HOUSE OF REPRESENTATIVES OF THE CONGRESS OF THE UNITED STATES OF AMERICA

To Benjamin Marshall, or his duly authorized representative:

You are hereby commanded to summon Richard M. Nixon, President of the United States of America, or any subordinate officer, official or employee with custody or control of the things described in the attached schedule,

to be and appear before the Committee on the Judiciary of the House of Representatives of the United States, of which the Hon. Peter W. Rodino, Jr. is chairman, and to bring with him the things specified in the schedule attached hereto and made a part hereof,

in their chamber in the city of Washington, on or before May 22, 1974, at the hour of 10:00 A.M., then and there to produce and deliver said things to said Committee, or their duly authorized representative, in connection with the Committee's investigation authorized and directed by H. Res. 803, adopted February 6, 1974.

Herein fail not, and make return of this summons.

Witness my hand and the seal of the House of Representatives of the United States, at the city of Washington, this 15th day of May, 1974.

Peter W. Rodino, Jr., Chairman

Attest:

_____ Jennings
Clerk

On behalf of Richard M. Nixon, President of the United States of America, I accept service of the original subpoena, of which the foregoing is a copy.

Dated: May 15, 1974

JAMES D. ST. CLAIR
Special Counsel to the President

SCHEDULE OF THINGS REQUIRED TO BE PRODUCED PURSUANT TO SUBPOENA OF THE COMMITTEE ON THE JUDICIARY

The President's daily diaries (as reflected on U.S. Government Printing Office Form "1972 0-472-086" or any predecessor or successor forms) for the period April through July 1972, February through April 1973, July 12 through July 31, 1973 and October 1973.

COPY

BY AUTHORITY OF THE HOUSE OF REPRESENTATIVES OF THE CONGRESS OF THE UNITED STATES OF AMERICA

To Benjamin Marshall, or his duly authorized representative:

You are hereby commanded to summon Richard M. Nixon, President of the United States of America, or any subordinate officer, official or employee with custody or control of the things described in the attached schedule,

to be and appear before the Committee on the Judiciary of the House of Representatives of the United States, of which the Hon. Peter W. Rodino, Jr. is chairman, and to bring with him the things specified in the schedule attached hereto and made a part hereof,

in their chamber in the city of Washington, on or before May 22, 1974, at the hour of 10:00 A.M., then and there to produce and deliver said things to said Committee, or their duly authorized representative, in connection with the Committee's investigation authorized and directed by H. Res. 803, adopted February 6, 1974.

Herein fail not, and make return of this summons.

Witness my hand and the seal of the House of Representatives of the United States, at the city of Washington, this 15th day of May, 1974.

Peter W. Rodino, Jr.   *Chairman.*

Attest:

_____
Clerk.

On behalf of Richard M. Nixon, President of the United States of America, I accept service of the original subpoena, of which the foregoing is a copy.

Dated: May 15, 1974

JAMES D. ST. CLAIR
Special Counsel to the President

SCHEDULE OF THINGS REQUIRED TO BE PRODUCED PURSUANT TO SUBPOENA OF THE COMMITTEE ON THE JUDICIARY

All tapes, dictabelts, other electronic and mechanical recordings, and transcripts, memoranda, notes or other writings or things relating to the following conversations:

1. Meetings among the President, Mr. Haldeman and Mr. Mitchell on April 4, 1972 from 4:13 to 4:50 p.m. and between the President and Mr. Haldeman from 6:03 to 6:18 p.m.
2. Conversations on June 20, 1972 between the President and Mr. Haldeman, and the President and Mr. Colson, as follows:

2:20 to 3:30 p.m.	Meeting between the President and Mr. Colson
4:35 to 5:25 p.m.	Meeting between the President and Mr. Haldeman
7:52 to 7:59 p.m.	Telephone conversation between the President and Mr. Haldeman
8:04 to 8:21 p.m.	Telephone conversation between the President and Mr. Colson
8:42 to 8:50 p.m.	Telephone conversation between the President and Mr. Haldeman
11:33 p.m. 6/20 to 12:05 a.m. 6/21.	Telephone conversation between the President and Mr. Colson

3. Conversations on June 23, 1972 between the President and Mr. Haldeman, as follows:

10:04 to 10:39 a.m.	Meeting between the President and Mr. Haldeman (Mr. Ziegler present from 10:33–10:39 a.m.)
1:04 to 1:13 p.m.	Meeting between the President and Mr. Haldeman
2:20 to 2:45 p.m.	Meeting between the President and Mr. Haldeman (Mr. Ziegler present from 2:40–2:43 p.m.)

MEMORANDUM SETTING FORTH FACTS AND BASES UNDERLYING APRIL 19, 1974 REQUEST FOR PRESIDENTIAL CONVERSATIONS NECESSARY FOR COMMITTEE'S INQUIRY INTO WATERGATE AND AFTERMATH

The following sets forth the facts and bases underlying the request contained in Mr. Doar's letter to Mr. St. Clair, dated April 19, 1974, for Presidential conversations necessary for the House Judiciary Committee's inquiry into Watergate and its aftermath. An asterisk following a specified conversation indicates that the Special Prosecutor has subpoenaed such conversation for the trial of the indictment in *U.S.* v. *Mitchell, et al.* filed on March 1, 1974 respecting Watergate and its aftermath.

(1) Meetings among the President, Mr. Haldeman, and Mr. Mitchell on April 4, 1972, from 4:13 to 4:50 p.m. and between the President and Mr. Haldeman from 6:03 to 6:18 p.m*

---

* Conversations followed by an asterisk have been subpoenaed by the Watergate Special Prosecution Force.

Mr. Magruder has testified that on March 30, 1972 Mr. Mitchell approved Mr. Liddy's plan for electronic surveillance of the President's political opponents and an entry into the Democratic National Committee Headquarters in Washington. (Magruder, 2 SSC 794–95). Mr. Magruder called Mr. Strachan and indicated the project had been approved, and immediately thereafter, in early April, 1972, Mr. Strachan sent a memorandum to Mr. Haldeman which stated that a sophisticated political intelligence-gathering system for CRP had been approved with a budget of $300,000. (Magruder, 2 SSC 795; Strachan, 6 SSC 2441, 2452). Mr. Strachan has testified that he prepared a talking paper for a meeting between Mr. Haldeman and Mr. Mitchell which took place at 3:00 p.m. on April 4, 1972, and this talking paper included a reference to the sophisticated intelligence-gathering system. (Strachan, 6 SSC 2453–54). Mr. Haldeman has testified that the 3:00 p.m. meeting was "in conjunction with" the meeting commencing at 4:13 p.m. among the President, Mr. Mitchell and Mr. Haldeman during which matters relating to the political campaign and ITT were discussed. (Haldeman, 8 SSC 3180–81). Mr. Haldeman has testified that his notes of the meeting among the President, Mr. Haldeman and Mr. Mitchell do not indicate a discussion of intelligence. (Haldeman, 7 SSC 2881). Not long after the meeting among the President, Mr. Haldeman and Mr. Mitchell ended, the President met with Mr. Haldeman alone.

(2) Specified conversations on June 20, 1972, between the President and Mr. Haldeman, and the President and Mr. Colson.

The President's records set forth that the following meetings and telephone conversations took place between the President and Mr. Haldeman and the President and Mr. Colson on June 20, 1972:

2:20 to 3:30 p.m.*	Meeting between the President and Mr. Colson
4:35 to 5:25 p.m.	Meeting between the President and Mr. Haldeman
7:52 to 7:59 p.m.	Telephone conversation between the President and Mr. Haldeman
8:04 to 8:21 p.m.*	Telephone conversation between the President and Mr. Colson
8:42 to 8:50 p.m.	Telephone conversation between the President and Mr. Haldeman
11:33 p.m., 6/20 * to 12:05 a.m.,	Telephone conversation between the President and Mr. Colson

At an earlier meeting on June 20 between Mr. Haldeman and the President (11:26–11:45 a.m.), the Watergate matter was one of the items discussed. (Haldeman's Notes, Exhibit 61. *In Re Subpoena Duces Tecum* ("SDT"), Misc. No. 47–73). The tape of that conversation contained an 18 minute and 15 second hum which obliterated the conversation. Also on June 20, a meeting among Mr. Ehrlichman, Mr. Mitchell, Mr. Haldeman, Mr. Dean, and Mr. Kleindienst occurred to discuss the Watergate incident and investigation. (Ehrlichman, 7 SSC 2822; Haldeman, 8 SSC 3039–40). Mr. Strachan has testified that on this date, following Mr. Haldeman's instructions, he shredded the Political Matters Memorandum containing the reference to the plan for electronic surveillance formulated by Gordon Liddy. (Strachan, 6 SSC 2458, 2442). On the evening of June 20, 1972, the President spoke by telephone to Mr. Mitchell. A tape of this conversation was subpoenaed by the Special Prosecutor but was not produced as the President stated that it was not recorded. (President's Statement, November 12, 1973; Pres. Doc. 1329). The President's recorded recollection of this conversation was produced. Mr. Mitchell has testified that in this conversation he and the President discussed the Watergate break-in and Mr. Mitchell expressed regret that he had not kept better control over his men. (Mitchell, 4 SSC 1633). After this conversation with Mr. Mitchell, the President had the four telephone conversations specified with Mr. Haldeman and Mr. Colson.

(3) Specified conversations on June 23, 1972 between the President and Mr. Haldeman.

The President's records set forth that the following meetings took place between the President and Mr. Haldeman on June 23, 1972:

10:04 to 10:39 a.m.*	Meeting between the President and Mr. Haldeman (Mr. Ziegler present from 10:33 to 10:39 a.m.)
1:04 to 1:13 p.m.*	Meeting between the President and Mr. Haldeman
2:20 to 2:45 p.m.*	Meeting between the President and Mr. Haldeman (Mr. Ziegler present from 2:40 to 2:43 p.m.)

Mr. Haldeman has testified that on the basis of information supplied by Mr. Dean to the effect that the FBI believed that the CIA might have been involved in the Watergate break-in, he raised the possibility of CIA involvement with the President on June 23, 1972. (Haldeman, 8 SSC 3040–41). Mr. Haldeman also testified that the President ordered Mr. Haldeman and Mr. Ehrlichman to meet with Mr. Helms and Mr. Walters at the CIA to determine the CIA's involvement and interest in the Watergate break-in and to request Mr. Walters to meet with Acting FBI Director Mr. Gray to insure that the FBI's investigation of the Watergate participants not be expanded into unrelated matters which could lead to disclosure of non-Watergate related covert CIA operations or other non-related national security activities that had been undertaken previously by some of the Watergate participants. (Haldeman, 7 SSC 2881–85). The President has stated that he instructed Mr. Haldeman and Mr. Ehrlichman to insure that the FBI investigation of the Watergate break-in did not expose either unrelated covert operations of the CIA or the activities of the White House Special Investigations Unit. (President's Statement, May 22, 1973, Pres. Doc. 696). Mr. Haldeman and Mr. Ehrlichman did meet with Mr. Helms and General Walters of the CIA on June 23, 1972, at 1:35 p.m. The three meetings specified above between the President and Mr. Haldeman preceded and followed the meeting among Mr. Haldeman, Mr. Ehrlichman and the representatives of the CIA. (Ehrlichman, 7 SSC 2712; Walters' Memorandum, SSC Exhibit 101, 7 SSC 2948; Haldeman, 8 SSC 3041). At 2:34 p.m., General Walters met with Mr. Gray of the FBI and stated that the FBI Watergate investigation should not be pursued into Mexico and should be tapered off at the five people arrested on June 17, 1972. (Walters' Memorandum of Meeting with Mr. Gray, SSC Exhibit 129, 9 SSC 3815; Gray 9 SSC 3452). Mr. Gray agreed to postpone two interviews involving funds in the bank account of Bernard Barker, one of the men arrested in the Democratic National Committee headquarters.

COPY

BY AUTHORITY OF THE HOUSE OF REPRESENTATIVES OF THE CONGRESS OF THE UNITED STATES OF AMERICA

To ~~Benjamin Marshall, or his duly authorized representative:~~

You are hereby commanded to summon ~~Richard M. Nixon, President of the United States of America, or any subordinate officer, official or employee with custody or control of the things described in the attached schedule,~~

to be and appear before the Committee on the Judiciary ~~Committee~~ of the House of Representatives of the United States, of which the Hon. Peter W. Rodino, Jr. is chairman, ~~and to bring with him the things specified in the schedule attached hereto and made a part hereof,~~

in their chamber in the city of Washington, on ~~or before~~ June 10, 1974, at the hour of 10:00 A.M., then and there to produce and deliver said things to said Committee, or their duly authorized representative, in connection with the Committee's investigation authorized and directed by H. Res. 803, adopted February 6, 1974.

Herein fail not, and make return of this summons.

Witness my hand and the seal of the House of Representatives of the United States, at the city of Washington, this 30th day of May, 1974.

Peter W. Rodino, Jr. *Chairman.*

Attest:

Clerk.

On behalf of Richard M. Nixon, President on the United States of America, I accept service of the original subpoena, of which the foregoing is a copy.

Dated: 5/31, 1974

JAMES D. ST. CLAIR
Special Counsel to the President

SCHEDULE OF THINGS REQUIRED TO BE PRODUCED PURSUANT TO SUBPOENA OF THE COMMITTEE ON THE JUDICIARY

A. All tapes, dictabelts, other electronic and mechanical recordings, transcripts, memoranda, notes and other writings and things relating to the following conversations:

1. Meeting on the morning of November 15, 1972 among or between Mr. Haldeman, Mr. Ehrlichman and Mr. Dean in the President's office at Camp David.

2. Conversation in which the President participated after December 8, 1972 (the date Mr. Hunt's wife died) during which there was a discussion that a commutation of the sentence for Mr. Hunt could be considered on the basis of Mr. Hunt's wife's death.

3. Meeting and telephone conversation on January 5, 1973 between the President and Mr. Colson from 12:02 to 1:02 p.m. and from 7:38 to 7:58 p.m. respectively.

4. Meetings between the President and Mr. Colson on February 13, 1973 from 9:48 to 10:52 a.m. and on February 14, 1973 from 10:13 to 10:49 a.m.

5. Meeting between the President and Mr. Dean on February 27, 1973 from 3:55 to 4:20 p.m.

6. Conversations on March 1, 1973 between the President and Mr. Dean, as follows:

9:18 to 9:46 a.m.	Meeting between the President and Mr. Dean
10:36 to 10:44 a.m.	Meeting between the President and Mr. Dean (Mr. Kissinger was present until 10:37 a.m.)
1:06 to 1:14 p.m.	Meeting between the President and Mr. Dean

7. Meeting between the President and Mr. Dean on March 6, 1973 from 11:49 a.m. to 12:00 p.m.

8. Telephone conversations between the President and Mr. Colson on March 16, 1973, from 7:53 to 8:12 p.m., and on March 19, 1973, from 8:34 to 8:58 p.m.

9. Conversations on March 20, 1973 among or between the President, Mr. Haldeman and Mr. Ehrlichman, as follows:

10:47 a.m. to 12:10 p.m.	Meeting between the President and Mr. Haldeman (Mr. Ehrlichman present from 11:40 a.m.–12:10 p.m.)
4:26 to 5:39 p.m.	Meeting between the President and Mr. Ehrlichman
6:00 to 7:10 p.m.	Meeting between the President and Mr. Haldeman

10. Conversations on March 21, 1973 between the President and Mr. Ehrlichman and the Prseident and Mr. Colson, as follows:

9:15 to 10:12 a.m.	Meeting between the President and Mr. Ehrlichman
7:53 to 8:24 p.m.	Telephone conversation between the President and Mr. Colson

11. Meeting between the President and Mr. Haldeman on March 22, 1973 from 9:11 to 10:35 a.m.

12. Telephone conversations between the President and Mr. Colson on April 12, 1973 from 7:31 to 7:48 p.m.

13. Two telephone conversations between Mr. Ehrlichman and Mr. Gray on April 15, 1973 between 10:16 and 11:15 p.m.

14. Telephone conversation between the President and Mr. Dean on April 17, 1973 from 9:19 to 9:25 a.m.

15. Conversations on April 18, 1973 among or between the President Mr. Haldeman and Mr. Ehrlichman, as follows:

12:05 to 12:20 a.m.	Telephone conversation between the President and Mr. Haldeman
3:05 to 3:23 p.m.	Meeting between the President and Mr. Ehrlichman
6:30 to 8:05 p.m.	Meeting among the President, Mr. Ehrlichman and Mr. Haldeman

16. Conversations on April 19, 1973 among or between the President, Mr. Haldeman, Mr. Ehrlichman and Mr. Petersen as follows:

9:31 to 10:12 a.m.	Meeting among the President, Mr. Haldeman and Mr. Ehrlichman
10:12 to 11:07 a.m.	Meeting between the President and Mr. Petersen
1:03 to 1:30 p.m.	Meeting between the President and Mr. Ehrlichman
5:15 to 5:45 p.m.	Meeting between the President and Mr. Ehrlichman
9:37 to 9:53 p.m.	Telephone conversation between the President and Mr. Haldeman
10:54 to 11:04 p.m.	Telephone conversation between the President and Mr. Ehrlichman

17. Conversations on April 20, 1973 among or between the President, Mr. Haldeman and Mr. Ehrlichman, as follows:

11:07 to 11:23 a.m.	Meeting between the President and Mr. Haldeman
12:15 to 12:34 p.m.	Meeting among the President, Mr. Haldeman and Mr. Ehrlichman (Mr. Kissinger was present until 12:16 p.m.)

18. Conversations on April 25, 1973 among or between the President. Mr. Haldeman, Mr. Ehrlichman, Mr. Wilson and Mr. Strickler, as follows:

approximately 9:25 to approximately 10:45 a.m.	Meeting among the President, Mr. Wilson and Mr. Strickler
11:06 a.m. to 1:55 p.m.	Meeting among the President, Mr. Haldeman and Mr. Ehrlichman
4:40 to 5:35 p.m.	Meeting between the President and Mr. Haldeman (Mr. Hart present from 5:30 to 5:32 p.m.)
6:57 to 7:14 p.m.	Telephone conversation between the President and Mr. Haldeman
7:17 to 7:19 p.m.	Telephone conversation between the President and Mr. Ehrlichman
7:25 to 7:39 p.m.	Telephone conversation between the President and Mr. Ehrlichman
7:45 to 7:53 p.m.	Telephone conversation between the President and Mr. Haldeman

19. Conversations on April 26, 1973 among or between the President, Mr. Haldeman and Mr. Ehrlichman, as follows:

8:55 to 10:24 a.m.	Meeting between the President and Mr. Haldeman
3:59 to 9:03 p.m.	Meeting between the President and Mr. Haldeman (Mr. Ehrlichman was present from 5:57 to 7:14 p.m.)

20. Telephone conversations on June 4, 1973 between the President and Mr. Haldeman from 10:05 to 10:20 p.m. and from 10:21 to 10:22 p.m.

B. All papers and things (including recordings) prepared by, sent to, received by or at any time contained in the files of, H. R. Haldeman, John D. Ehrlichman, Charles W. Colson, John Dean, III and Gordon Strachan to the extent that such papers or things relate or refer directly or indirectly to the break-in and electronic surveillance of the Democratic National Committee Headquarters in the Watergate office building during May and June of 1972 or the investigations of that break-in by the Department of Justice, the Senate Select Committee on Presidential Campaign Activities, or any other legislative, judicial, executive or administrative body, including members of the White House staff.

MEMORANDUM SETTING FORTH FACTS AND BASES UNDERLYING PROPOSED SUBPOENA FOR PRESIDENTIAL CONVERSATIONS NECESSARY FOR THE COMMITTEE'S INQUIRY INTO WATERGATE AND AFTERMATH

The following sets forth the facts and bases underlying the proposed subpoena dated May 30, 1974 for Presidential conversations necessary for the House Judiciary Committee's inquiry into Watergate and its aftermath. An asterisk following a specified conversation indicates that the Special Prosecutor has subpoenaed such conversation for the trial of the indictment in *United States* v. *Mitchell, et al.*, filed on March 1, 1974, respecting Watergate and its aftermath.

(1) Meeting on the morning of November 15, 1972 among or between Mr. Haldeman, Mr. Ehrlichman and Mr. Dean in the President's office at Camp David.[2]

Dean testified that on November 15 he met at Camp David with Haldeman and Ehrlichman to inform them of the increased demands for money transmitted by Hunt's lawyer through O'Brien to the White House. At that meeting Dean played a tape of a conversation between Colson and Hunt during which Hunt made demands for money. (Dean, 3 SSC 969; Transcript, SSC Exhibit 152, 9 SSC 3888–91). Also at that meeting Dean testified that Ehrlichman and Haldeman said the President had decided that based on information linking Chapin with Segretti's campaign activities, Chapin would have to leave the White House staff (Dean, 3 SSC 966).

(2) Conversation in which the President participated after December 8, 1972 (the date Mr. Hunt's wife died) during which there was a discussion that a commutation of the sentence for Mr. Hunt could be considered on the basis of Mr. Hunt's wife's death.*

---

[2] These conversations have been subpoenaed by the Watergate Special Prosecution Force.

Materials presented to the Committee in executive session indicate that such a conversation took place.

(3) Meeting and telephone conversations on January 5, 1973 between the President and Mr. Colson from 12:02 to 1:02 p.m.* and from 7:38 to 7:58 p.m.* respectively.

On January 3, 1973 in a meeting among Ehrlichman, Colson and Dean, Dean has testified that Colson said he felt it was imperative that Hunt be given some assurances of executive clemency. Ehrlichman said, according to Dean, that he would speak to the President and that Colson should not talk to the President about this matter. Despite Ehrlichman's warning, Dean testified that on January 5, 1973, following a meeting among Ehrlichman, Colson and Dean, Colson told Dean that he did discuss the offer of executive clemency with the President (Dean, 3 SSC 973-74). Dean also testified that in March and April, 1973, the President stated that he previously had discussed with Colson the possibility of executive clemency for Hunt. (Dean, 3 SSC 995, 1017). Ehrlichman has testified that he met with Colson on January 3 and told him that under no circumstances should executive clemency be discussed (Ehrlichman, 7 SSC 2770-71; 2847-48).

(4) Meetings between the President and Mr. Colson on February 13, 1973, from 9:48 to 10:52 a.m.* and on February 14, 1973, from 10:13 to 10:49 a.m.*

Material in the possession of the Committee indicates that in mid-February 1973 Colson and the President discussed the Watergate matter. Also, in a newspaper interview, Colson stated that during a February 14, 1973 meeting he told the President, "you've got to call Mitchell in and have him accept his responsibility" for the Watergate matter. The President replied, according to Colson, that while he wanted to resolve the Watergate matter, he was not willing to do so "at the expense of making an innocent person a scapegoat." (*New York Times*, interview with Mr. Colson, June 10, 1973)

(5) Meeting between the President and Mr. Dean on February 27, 1973, from 3:55 to 4:20 p.m.*

This is the first meeting of Dean with the President since September 15, 1972. Dean has testified that the President told him that Watergate "was taking up too much time from Haldeman's and Ehrlichman's normal duties and . . . they were principals in the matter, and I, therefore, could be more objective than they." Dean also testified that he told the President that he was not sure Watergate could be confined indefinitely, and the President told Dean "we would have to fight back." (Dean, 3 SSC 991-92). The White House has stated that executive privilege and the Senate Select Committee were discussed at this meeting. (Exhibit 70-A, 4 SSC 1796—Memorandum of substance of Dean's calls and meetings with the President).

(6) Specified Conversations on March 1, 1973, between the President and Mr. Dean.

The President's records indicate that the following meetings took place between the President and Dean on March 1, 1973:

9:18 to 9:46 a.m	Meeting between the President and Mr. Dean
10:36 to 10:44 a.m	Meeting between the President and Mr. Dean
1:06 to 1:14 p.m	Meeting between the President and Mr. Dean

Dean testified that on March 1 the President asked him questions about the ongoing confirmation hearings for Gray, and assured him that it was proper for Dean to have received FBI reports about the Watergate investigation. Dean testified the President told him that Gray should not turn over Watergate materials to the Senate Judiciary Committee. Dean told the President that he had met with William Sullivan, a former FBI official, and Sullivan had indicated that the FBI had been used for political purposes in past administrations; the President instructed Dean to get this information about FBI practices from Sullivan. Dean testified also that the President discussed executive privilege during these meetings. (Dean, 3 SSC 993–94). The White House has stated that on March 1 at a meeting with Dean the President prepared for his press conference on March 2, and it was decided that the answer to the question of why Dean was sitting in on FBI interviews during the Watergate investigation was that Dean was conducting an investigation for the President. The President asked Dean to write a report. (Exhibit 70–A, 4 SSC 1796—Memorandum of substance of Dean's calls and meetings with the President).

(7) Meeting between the President and Mr. Dean on March 6, 1973, from 11:49 a.m. to 12:00 p.m.

Dean has testified that at this meeting the President reminded Dean that he should report directly to him and not involve Haldeman and Ehrlichman in Watergate-related matters. (Dean, 3 SSC 994). The White House has stated that executive privilege guidelines were discussed at this meeting, and it was decided that executive privilege would cover former White House personnel as well as present personnel. (Exhibit 70–A, 4 SSC 1796—Memorandum of substance of Dean's calls and meetings with the President).

(8) Telephone conversations between the President and Mr. Colson on March 16, 1973, from 7:53 to 8:12 p.m. and on March 19, 1973, from 8:34 to 8:58 p.m.

On March 16, 1973, David Shapiro, Colson's law partner, met with Hunt. Hunt has testified that he had expected to meet with Colson and not Shapiro. During this meeting, Hunt told Shapiro that he needed money prior to his sentencing. Hunt felt that Shapiro should convey all Hunt had said to Colson. (Hunt, 9 SSC 3705–06). Material in the possession of the Committee indicates that Shapiro reported to Colson on his conversation with Hunt.

(9) Specified conversations on March 20, 1973, among or between the President, Mr. Haldeman and Mr. Ehrlichman.

The President's records set forth that the following meetings took place between the President, Haldeman and Ehrlichman on March 20, 1973:

10:47 a.m. to 12:10 p.m.*	Meeting between the President and Mr. Haldeman (Mr. Ehrlichman present from 11:40 a.m. to 12:10 p.m.)
4:26 to 5:39 p.m.	Meeting between the President and Mr. Ehrlichman
6:00 to 7:10 p.m.*	Meeting between the President and Mr. Haldeman

Materials presented to the Committee in executive session indicate that Haldeman spoke with the President about the Watergate matter on this date, the day prior to Dean's disclosures of White House involvement to the President on March 21, 1973. Also, Dean has testified that on or about March 20, 1973, he informed Ehrlichman of Hunt's threat to tell about the "seamy things" he had done for Ehrlichman unless he received additional money. (Dean, 3 SSC 999). Ehrlichman on March 20 became concerned that Hunt's blackmail attempt might lead to the exposure of the Special Investigations Unit. (Ehrlichman, 6 SSC 2565). Ehrlichman has testified that about this time he had a conversation with the President about the break-in at the office of Dr. Fielding. (Ehrlichman, 6 SSC 2551).

(10) Specified conversations on March 21, 1973, between the President and Mr. Ehrlichman and the President and Mr. Colson.

The President's records indicate that the following meetings and telephone conversations took place between the President and Ehrlichman, and the President and Colson on March 21, 1973:

9:15 to 10:12 a.m.* _ _ _ _ _ _ _ _ _ _ _ Meeting between the President and Mr. Ehrlichman
7:53 to 8:24 p.m.* _ _ _ _ _ _ _ _ _ _ _ Telephone conversation between the President and Mr. Colson

The 9:15 to 10:12 a.m. meeting with Ehrlichman immediately preceded the President's March 21 meeting with Dean (10:12–11:55 a.m.) at which time the President said he first learned of the money payments to the Watergate defendants and the attempt of one of the defendants to blackmail the White House. (President's Statement August 15, 1973, Pres. Doc. 992). As indicated above, it also came shortly after Ehrlichman learned of Hunt's alleged blackmail threat. The telephone conversation between the President and Colson is the first conversation between them after Dean's conversation with the President on March 21, 1973. Materials in the possession of the Committee indicate that Colson and the President discussed the Watergate matter in this conversation. This is also the date on which it is alleged that a delivery of $75,000 for the benefit of Hunt was made by LaRue. (*United States v. Mitchell, et al.*, Indictment, overt act 43).

(11) Meeting between the President and Mr. Haldeman on March 22, 1973 from 9:11 to 10:35 a.m.*

This meeting is Haldeman's first meeting with the President following the $75,000 payment which allegedly was made in the evening of March 21. It immediately precedes a morning meeting among Haldeman, Ehrlichman, Mitchell and Dean, at which Dean testified that Ehrlichman asked Mitchell if Hunt's money problem had been taken care of and Mitchell replied that it was no longer a problem. (Dean, 3 SSC 1000–01; Ehrlichman, 7 SSC 2853). Mitchell has denied making such a statement. (Mitchell, 4 SSC 1650). The second meeting is one of the overt acts alleged in the conspiracy indictment in *United States v. Mitchell, et al.*, (Indictment, overt act 44). The President has stated that he directed this second meeting to take place to determine "the best way to get the whole story out" about the Watergate matter. (President's News Conference, March 6, 1974, Pres. Doc. 293).

(12) Telephone conversation between the President and Mr. Colson on April 12, 1973, from 7:31 to 7:48 p.m.*

Materials in the possession of the Committee indicate that the President called Colson in Boston on April 12, said that he wanted to act promptly on Watergate and asked Colson to prepare a specific set of recommendations. This conversation is the last contact between Colson and the President prior to two meetings which Colson had with Ehrlichman on April 13, 1973 as part of Ehrlichman's inquiry, directed by the President, into the Watergate matter. Ehrlichman has testified that, at Colson's request, they met and Colson told him that Hunt, on April 16, would testify to the grand jury about the payments to the Watergate defendants and that McCord would testify about an attempt to break into the offices of Henry Greenspun, a Las Vegas newspaper publisher. Colson, according to Ehrlichman, said that he had some suggestions to convey to the President. (Ehrlichman, 7 SSC 2800–01; Ehrlichman's notes of this meeting, Exhibit 98, 7 SSC 2933–36).

(13) Two telephone conversations between Mr. Ehrlichman and Mr. Gray on April 15, 1973 between 10:16 and 11:15 p.m.

Ehrlichman has testified that while he was in the presence of the President he, at the President's request, telephoned Gray with respect to the documents that had been taken from Hunt's White House safe shortly after the Watergate break-in and given to Gray. During these conversations, Gray informed Ehrlichman that he had destroyed the documents and Ehrlichman transmitted this information immediately to the President. (Ehrlichman, 7 SSC 2675–76). Gray has confirmed that Ehrlichman made these two telephone calls. (Gray, 9 SSC 3470).

(14) Telephone conversation on April 17, 1973, between the President and Mr. Dean from 9:19 to 9:25 a.m.

On April 17, 1973, the President had a telephone conversation with John Dean. Dean has testified that during this conversation the President stated that he had decided not to request any resignations until after the grand jury took action and that he would issue a statement very shortly. (Dean, 3 SSC 1019).

(15) Specified conversations on April 18, 1973 among or between the President, Mr. Haldeman and Mr. Ehrlichman.

The President's records set forth that the following meeting and telephone conversations took place on April 18, 1973 among the President, Haldeman and Ehrlichman:

12:05 to 12:20 a.m.*	Telephone conversation between the President and Mr. Haldeman
3:05 to 3:23 p.m.*	Meeting between the President and Mr. Ehrlichman
6:30 to 8:05 p.m.*	Meeting among the President, Mr. Ehrlichman and Mr. Haldeman

These conversations occurred the day after the President's statement on April 17, 1973, during which he stated that "there have been major developments in the [Watergate] case." (President's Statement, April 17, 1973, Pres. Doc. 387). During this period, various White House officials were being summoned to testify before the Watergate grand jury. In addition, shortly before his conversation with Ehrlichman, the President had a telephone conversation with Petersen and stated that Dean had told him that the prosecutors had given immunity to Dean and the President had a tape to prove this statement by Dean. Petersen denied that immunity had been granted. (Petersen, 9 SSC 3630, 3654–56). This was also the date on which the President learned that the prosecutors had been told of the break-in of the office of Daniel Ellsberg's phychiatrist by members of the White House Special Investigations Unit. (President's News Conference, August 22, 1973, Pres. Doc. 1020).

(16) Specified conversations on April 19, 1973, among or between the President, Mr. Haldeman, Mr. Petersen and Mr. Ehrlichman.

The President's records set forth that the following meeting and telephone conversations took place on April 19, 1973, among the President, Haldeman, Ehrlichman and Petersen:

9:31 to 10:12 a.m.*	Meeting among the President, Mr. Haldeman and Mr. Ehrlichman
10:12 to 11:07 a.m.	Meeting between the President and Mr. Petersen
1:03 to 1:30 p.m.*	Meeting between the President and Mr. Ehrlichman
5:15 to 5:45 p.m.*	Meeting between the President and Mr. Ehrlichman
9:37 to 9:53 p.m.*	Telephone conversation between the President and Mr. Haldeman
10:54 to 11:04 p.m.*	Telephone conversation between the President and Mr. Ehrlichman

In his meeting on April 19, 1973, the President and Petersen spoke about the Watergate investigation. Petersen gave the President a report on the progress of the investigation. The President met with Ehrlichman and Haldeman both immediately prior to the meeting with Petersen and subsequent to that meeting. Moore has testified that on April 19 he told the President that Dean had said that Ehrlichman would have a problem involving the *Ellsberg* case. (Moore, 5 SSC 1961). Dean, on this date, issued a public statement that he would not be made "a scapegoat" in response to the President's April 17 statement against granting immunity to high White House aides. (Dean, 3 SSC 1020). In the evening, from 8:26 to 9:32 p.m., the President had his first meeting with John Wilson and Frank Strickler, the attorneys who were retained to represent Haldeman and Ehrlichman in the Watergate matter. The President has produced an edited transcript of that conversation. Immediately thereafter, the President spoke by telephone with Haldeman and then with Ehrlichman.

(17) Specified conversations on April 20, 1973 among or between the President, Mr. Haldeman and Mr. Ehrlichman.

The President's records set forth that the following meetings and telephone conversations took place on April 20, 1973 involving the President, Haldeman and Ehrlichman:

11:07 to 11:23 a.m.*	Meeting between the President and Mr. Haldeman
12:15 to 12:34 p.m.*	Meeting among the President, Mr. Haldeman and Mr. Ehrlichman

Materials in the possession of the Committee reflect that on April 20, 1973, Petersen again reported to the President on the progress of the investigation of the Watergate matters and discussed potential conflicts of testimony. Both immediately prior to and subsequent to the conversation between the President and Petersen, there are conversations between the President and Haldeman, with Ehrlichman being present at the second conversation.

(18) Specified conversations on April 25, 1973 among or between the President, Mr. Haldeman, Mr. Ehrlichman, Mr. Wilson and Mr. Strickler.

The President's records set forth that the following meetings and telephone conversations took place among the President, Haldeman, Ehrlichman, Wilson and Strickler on April 25, 1973:

approximately 9:25 a.m. to approximately 10:45 a.m.	Meeting among the President, Mr. Wilson and Mr. Strickler
11:06 a.m. to 1:55 p.m.*	Meeting among the President, Mr. Haldeman and Mr. Ehrlichman
4:40 to 5:35 p.m.*	Meeting between the President and Mr. Haldeman (Mr. Hart present from 5:30 to 5:32 p.m.)
6:57 to 7:14 p.m.*	Telephone conversation between the President and Mr. Haldeman
7:17 to 7:19 p.m.*	Telephone conversation between the President and Mr. Ehrlichman
7:25 to 7:39 p.m.*	Telephone conversation between the President and Mr. Ehrlichman
7:46 to 7:53 p.m.*	Telephone conversation between the President and Mr. Haldeman

On the morning of April 25, after speaking by telephone with Petersen, the President met with Wilson and Strickler, the attorneys for Haldeman and Ehrlichman, and then had a lengthy meeting with Haldeman and Ehrlichman. Secret Service records indicate that at approximately the time this later meeting ended, Stephen Bull, a Presidential assistant, signed out 22 tapes of Presidential conversations. (Exhibit 7, *In Re SDT*, Misc. 47-73). Bull has testified that he turned over these tapes to Haldeman. (Bull, *In re SDT*, Tr. 343-45.) Haldeman has testified that he listened to the tape of the March 21, 1973 conversations between the President and Dean. (Haldeman, *In Re SDT*, Misc. 47-73, Tr. 927, 937-38.) The President has stated that Haldeman listened to this tape at the request of the President. (President's Statement, November 12, 1973, Pres. Doc. 1329.) Also on April 25, Petersen and Kleindienst asked the President to change his decision not to send the information about the Fielding break-in to Judge Byrne in the *Ellsberg* trial. The President did change his decision. (Kleindienst, 9 SSC 3574-75; Petersen, 9 SSC 3631-32; President's Statement, August 15, 1973; Pres. Doc. 993; President's News Conference, August 22, 1973, Pres. Doc. 1020-21).

(19) Specified conversations on April 26, 1973 among or between the President, Mr. Haldeman and Mr. Ehrlichman.

The President's records set forth that the following meetings and telephone conversations took place on April 26, 1973, among the President, Haldeman, and Ehrlichman:

8:55 to 10:24 a.m.*	Meeting between the President and Mr. Haldeman
3:59 to 9:03 p.m.*	Meeting between the President and Mr. Haldeman. (Mr. Ehrlichman was present from 5:57 to 7:14 p.m.)

According to Secret Service logs, on April 26, Bull took out a series of Presidential tapes which were returned on May 2, 1973. (Exhibit 7, *In Re SDT*, Misc. 47-73). Haldeman listened to the tape of March 21, 1973, again at the President's request. (Haldeman, *In Re SDT*, Tr. 937). A lengthy five hour and four minute meeting was held between the President and Haldeman at which Ehrlichman was present for one hour and seventeen minutes. During this meeting, the President called Kleindienst four times (having called him twice earlier in the day) and Petersen twice. Petersen has testified that on this date the President called him to ask if Gray should resign as Acting FBI Director. Gray had acknowledged that he had destroyed documents given to him by Dean in June 1972 from Hunt's White House safe. Petersen also testified that pursuant to the President's instructions, he asked Gray to meet with Kleindienst and him to discuss the situation. (Petersen, 9 SSC 3625). During the course of this meeting in Kleindienst's office, a telephone call was made to the President and the President was advised that Gray did not wish to resign. The President responded that Gray could remain as Acting FBI Director until the situation was analyzed. (Gray, 9 SSC 3591–92; Petersen, 9 SSC 3654; Kleindienst, 9 SSC 3598–99).

(20) Telephone conversations on June 4, 1973 between the President and Mr. Haldeman from 10:05 to 10:20 p.m.* and from 10:21 to 10:22 p.m.*

The President has stated that on June 4, 1973, he listened to tapes of his various conversations with Dean. (President's Statement, November 12, 1973, Pres. Doc. 1329). Haldeman had previously listened to tapes at the President's request. Material in the possession of the Committee indicates the likelihood of the President speaking to Haldeman about certain of the recorded conversations.

*   *   *   *   *   *   *

In calling for the above conversations, the Committee is seeking to determine:

> Whether any of the conversations in any way bear upon the knowledge or lack of knowledge of, or action or inaction by the President and/or any of his senior administration officials with respect to, the investigation of the Watergate break-in by the Department of Justice, the Senate Select Committee, or any other legislative, judicial, executive or administrative body, including members of the White House staff;

> Whether any of the conversations in any way bear upon the President's knowledge or lack of knowledge of, or participation or lack of participation in, the acts of obstruction of justice and conspiracy charged or otherwise referred to in the indictments returned on March 1 in the District Court for the District of Columbia in the case of *United States v. Mitchell*, et al., and

> Whether any of the conversations in any way bear upon the President's knowledge or lack of knowledge of, or participation or lack of participation in, the acts charged or otherwise referred to in the informations or indictments returned in the District Court for the District of Columbia in the case of *United States v. Magruder*; *United States v. Dean*; *United States v. Chapin*; and *United States v. Ehrlichman, et al.*, or any other acts which may constitute illegal activities.

COPY

BY AUTHORITY OF THE HOUSE OF REPRESENTATIVES OF THE CONGRESS OF THE UNITED STATES OF AMERICA

To ~~Benjamin Marshall, or his duly authorized representative~~:

You are hereby commanded to summon ~~.....~~ Richard M. Nixon, President of the United States of America, or any subordinate officer, official or employee with custody or control of the things described in the attached schedule,

to be and appear before the Committee on the Judiciary ~~Committee~~ of the House of Representatives of the United States, of which the Hon. Peter W. Rodino, Jr. is chairman, ~~and to bring with him the things specified in the schedule attached hereto and made a part hereof,~~

in their chamber in the city of Washington, on ~~or before~~ July 2, 1974, at the hour of 10:00 A.M., then and there to ~~xxxxxxxxxxxxxxxxxxxxxxxxxxxxxxxx~~ produce and deliver said things to said Committee, or their duly authorized representative, in connection with the Committee's investi- ~~xxxxxxxxxxxxxxxxxxxxxxxxxxxxxxxxx~~ gation authorized and directed by H. Res. 803, adopted February 6, 1974.

Herein fail not, and make return of this summons.

Witness my hand and the seal of the House of Representatives of the United States, at the city of Washington, this 24th day of June, 1974.

Peter W. Rodino, Jr. Chairman.

Attest: _____ Clerk.

On behalf of Richard M. Nixon, President of the United States of America, I accept service of the original subpoena, of which the foregoing is a copy.

Dated: June 25, 1974.

JAMES D. ST. CLAIR
Special Counsel to the President

SCHEDULE OF THINGS REQUIRED TO BE PRODUCED PURSUANT TO
SUBPOENA OF THE COMMITTEE ON THE JUDICIARY

A. All tapes, dictabelts, other electronic and mechanical recordings, transcripts, memoranda, notes and other writings and things relating to the following conversations:

1. Conversations of the President with Mr. Haldeman and Mr. Ehrlichman, or either of them, between about 12:30 p.m. and about 1:28 p.m., and between about 5:15 p.m. and about 6:32 p.m., March 6, 1972.

2. Conversations between the President and Mr. Haldeman from about 1:40 p.m. to about 2:13 p.m., March 6, 1972.

3. Telephone conversation between the President and Mr. Colson from about 7:36 p.m. to about 8:02 p.m., March 6, 1972.

4. Telephone conversation between the President and Mr. Mitchell beginning about 6:05 p.m., March 14, 1972.

5. Conversation between the President and Mr. Colson from about 1:24 p.m. to about 3:40 p.m., March 18, 1972.

6. Conversations between the President and Mr. Haldeman on March 30, 1972, from about 9:38 a.m. to about 9:58 a.m.; about 10:42 a.m. to about 11:10 a.m.; about 11:50 a.m. to about 12:15 p.m.; and about 5:32 p.m. to about 6:08 p.m.

7. Any conversation of the President with Mr. Haldeman and Mr. Colson, or either of them, between about 12:46 p.m. and about 2:32 p.m., March 30, 1972.

8. Any conversation of the President with Mr. Haldeman and Mr. Colson, or either of them, between about 5:32 p.m. and about 6:11 p.m., March 30, 1972.

9. Telephone conversation between the President and Mr. Colson between about 7:33 p.m. and about 7:45 p.m., March 30, 1972.

10. Conversations between the President and Mr. Haldeman from about 9:44 a.m. to about 10:06 a.m.; about 10:48 a.m. to about 11:45 a.m.; about 2:45 p.m. to about 3:00 p.m.; and 6:03 p.m. to about 6:18 p.m., April 4, 1972.

11. Telephone conversation between the President and Mr. Colson between about 10:46 a.m. and about 11:09 a.m., April 4, 1972.

12. Conversation between the President and Mr. Colson between about 11:45 a.m. and 12:23 p.m., April 5, 1972.

B. The President's copies of daily news summaries (and all his notes and memoranda with respect thereto) which were compiled by White House staff members during the period February 22, 1972 through June 9, 1972, inclusive, summarizing news reports by newspapers, periodicals, wire services, and the broadcast media, to the extent that such news summaries relate, directly or indirectly, to any of the following subjects: (a) the International Telephone and Telegraph Corporation (ITT) or any of its subsidiaries, directors, officers, or employees; (b) litigation or administrative investigations or proceedings, actual or proposed, against or otherwise respecting said corporation, or any subsidiary, director, officer or employee thereof; (c) the nomination of Richard G. Kleindienst to be Attorney General or any proposal, suggestion or consideration of whether to withdraw said nomination; or (d) the hearings before the Senate Judiciary Committee on the nomination of Richard G. Kleindienst to be Attorney General, including the testimony given during such hearings.

MEMORANDUM SETTING FORTH FACTS AND BASES UNDERLYING PROPOSED SUBPOENA FOR RECORDINGS OF PRESIDENTIAL CONVERSATIONS AND OTHER THINGS NECESSARY FOR THE COMMITTEE'S INQUIRY RELATING TO ITT AND THE KLEINDIENST CONFIRMATION HEARINGS

The following sets forth the facts and bases underlying the proposed subpoena dated June 24, 1974 for recordings of Presidential conversations and other things necessary for the House Judiciary Committee's inquiry into the ITT case and the hearings before the Senate Judiciary Committee on the nomination of Richard G. Kleindienst to be Attorney General.

In 1969, three antitrust suits were filed by the United States against the International Telephone and Telegraph Corporation (ITT), each seeking to prevent a corporate acquisition or to require a corporate divestiture. During 1970 and 1971, particularly in August of the former year and April of the latter, officials of ITT made numerous contacts with Administration officials for the purpose of attempting to persuade the Administration that the suits should be settled on a basis consistent with the interests of ITT. (Documents supplied to the Committee by the White House; Memo C. W. Colson to H. R. Haldeman, March 20, 1972, Senate Select Committee (SSC) Exhibit 121, 8 SSC 3372.)

Late in December, 1970, ITT won in the District Court one of the three suits, brought in connection with its acquisition of the Grinnell Corporation. The once-postponed deadline for the United States to file its appeal in the United States Supreme Court in the *ITT-Grinnell* case was April 20, 1971. (Petition of Government filed in Supreme Court on March 19, 1971, and granted by Mr. Justice Harlan on March 20, 1971.)

On April 19, 1971, the President, in the course of a meeting with John D. Ehrlichman and George P. Shultz, telephoned Deputy Attorney General Kleindienst and ordered that the appeal not be filed. The President has said that he took this action because in his opinion the further prosecution by Assistant Attorney General Richard McLaren of the suit was inconsistent with the antitrust policy approved by the President in consultation with his senior economic advisers. During the meeting, the President expressed irritation with McLaren's failure to follow administration policy. (White House "White Paper," *The ITT Anti-Trust Decision*, January 8, 1974, p. 5.) On the following day, the Solicitor General's office obtained from the Supreme Court an extension of the time in which to file the *ITT-Grinnell* appeal. (White House "White Paper," *supra*, p. 5; Griswold testimony, Kleindienst Confirmation Hearings (KCH) 2 KCH 389; Application for Extension of Time filed in the Supreme Court.)

On April 21, 1971, the President met with Attorney General Mitchell. The Attorney General said that in his opinion it was inadvisable for the President to order no appeal in the *Grinnell* case, that there would be adverse repercussions in Congress, and that Solicitor General Griswold might resign. The President agreed to follow the Attorney General's advice. (White House "White Paper," *supra*, p. 5.)

Sometime during the spring of 1971, ITT-Sheraton, an ITT subsidiary, made a pledge to the San Diego Convention and Visitors Bureau in support of a bid by the City of San Diego to attract the 1972 Republican National Convention. (White House "White Paper," *supra*, p. 7.) Evidence indicates that sometime in May or June of 1971, Attorney General Mitchell became aware of the pledge. (Documents supplied to the Committee by the White House; Memo C. W. Colson to H. R. Haldeman, March 30, 1972, SSC Exhibit 121, 8 SSC 3372.)

During June, 1971, the Antitrust Division of the Justice Department decided to try to settle the three ITT antitrust cases. (McLaren, 2 KCH 111–112.) The final settlement was announced on July 31, 1971. (McLaren, 2 KCH 113.) Several authorities have stated that the settlement, calling for the largest antitrust-related corporate divestiture in history, was a good one from the government's standpoint. (See, *e.g.*, Griswold, 2 KCH 374.) It did, however, enable ITT to retain its Hartford Fire Insurance subsidiary, a matter of paramount importance to the company.

On February 15, 1972, the nomination of Richard G. Kleindienst to become Attorney General was forwarded by the President to the Senate for confirmation. (Weekly Compilation of Presidential Documents, Vol. 8, p. 440.) Mr. Kleindienst was to replace John Mitchell, who was leaving the Justice Department to head the Committee for the Re-election of the President. The Senate Judiciary Committee held hearings on this nomination and quickly agreed to recommend confirmation to the Senate. (Report of the Senate Judiciary Committee on the Nomination of Richard G. Kleindienst, 92d Cong., 2d Sess., Executive Rep. No. 92–19, February 29, 1972.)

Before the Senate could act, however, beginning on February 29, 1972, a series of three articles by Jack Anderson was published alleging a link between the ITT-Sheraton pledge and the antitrust settlements and purporting to involve Messrs. Mitchell and Kleindienst. (2 KCH 461–465.) Mr. Kleindienst immediately asked that the Senate Judiciary Committee hearings be reopened so that he could respond to the charges. (2 KCH 95.)

At about the same time, the Securities and Exchange Commission (SEC) demanded that ITT turn over to it documents believed by the SEC to be in the files of ITT's Washington, D.C. office. The documents included several which reflected ITT contacts with the Administration in 1970 and 1971 in connection with attempts to settle the antitrust cases. On March 2, 1972, the first day of the resumed Kleindienst nomination hearings, attorneys for ITT turned copies of one or more of these documents over to White House aide Wallace Johnson. The following week, others of these documents were also furnished to Johnson. Later, during March or April, copies of the documents were provided by ITT to the SEC.

During the course of the hearings, Mr. Kleindienst on several occasions denied having ever received any instructions from the White

House with respect to antitrust suits. (2 KCH 157; 2 KCH 191; 2 KCH 353.) On Friday, March 3, 1972, Senator Kennedy asked Mr. Kleindienst about the extension of time to apeal the *Grinnell* case which had resulted from the President's April 19, 1971 telephone call to him. Mr. Kleindienst responded:

"Senator Kennedy, I do not recollect why that extension was asked." (2 KCH 204.)

The following Tuesday, March 7, 1972, Mr. Kleindienst, in a prepared statement, described the circumstances surrounding the request for an extension, omitting any mention of the President's order to drop the case. (2 KCH 249-250.)

On March 14 and March 15, 1972, John Mitchell appeared before the Senate Judiciary Committee. He testified that there had been no communication between the President and him with respect to the ITT antitrust litigation or any other antitrust litigation. (2 KCH 552; 2 KCH 571.)

In early March, a White House task force, including Messrs. Ehrlichman, Colson, Fielding, Johnson, Mardian and others, was established to keep track of the Kleindienst hearings, and its activities continued throughout the month. Members of the task force met from time to time with Messrs. Mitchell and Kleindienst. Mr. Fielding was given the responsibility of reviewing White House files to collect all documents which related to ITT.

On March 24, 1972, the President held his only press conference during this period. He said that:

". . . as far as the [Senate Judiciary Committee] hearings are concerned, there is nothing that has happened in the hearings to date that has in one way shaken my confidence in Mr. Kleindienst as an able, honest man, fully qualified to be Attorney General of the United States." (Weekly Compilation of Presidential Documents, Vol. 8, No. 8, pp. 673-674.)

He also said that, "In this Administration we moved on ITT. We are proud of that record." He said that administration action had prevented ITT from growing further and quoted Solicitor General Griswold as to the excellence of the ITT settlement. "We moved on [ITT] and moved effectively . . . Mr. McLaren is justifiably very proud of that record . . . [and he] should be." (*Id.* at p. 675.)

On the morning of March 30, 1972, Messrs. Colson, Haldeman and MacGregor met. That afternoon, Mr. Colson sent a memorandum to Mr. Haldeman indicating his disagreement with Mr. Haldeman's view, apparently presented at a meeting that morning, that the White House should continue to support Mr. Kleindienst's nomination. His reasons included the possibility that documents would be revealed suggesting that the President was involved in the ITT situation in 1971 and contradicting statements made by Mr. Mitchell under oath. (SSC Exhibit 121, 8 SSC 3372.)

On April 4, 1972, John Mitchell returned to his office after about two weeks in Florida. (Mitchell logs.) That afternoon, he met with the President and Mr. Haldeman at the White House and, according to Mr. Haldeman's testimony before the Senate Select Committee, they discussed the Kleindienst hearings. (7 SSC 2881.) The Committee has received from the President an edited transcript of the tape of this meeting.

On April 19, 1972, Ed Reinecke, Lt. Governor of California, testified that he had not told then Attorney General Mitchell about the ITT-Sheraton financial pledge until September, 1971. Clark MacGregor and Mr. Mardian had met with Mr. Reinecke the morning he testified. On April 3, 1974, Mr. Reinecke was indicted by a District of Columbia grand jury for perjury in connection with that testimony. (Indictment, April 3, 1974, *U.S.* v. *Reinecke*, Crim. No. 74–155.)

On April 27, 1972, the last day of the hearings, Mr. Kleindienst referred to his earlier testimony about communications with the White House and said:

> I tried to make it clear, Senator Fong, that in view of the posture I put myself in, in this case, I could have had several conversations but I would have had a vivid recollection if someone at the White House had called me up and said, 'Look, Kleindienst, this is the way we are going to handle that case.' People who know me, I don't think would talk to me that way, but if anybody did it would be a very sharp impact on my mind because I believe I know how I would have responded.

No such conversation occurred. (3 KCH 1682.) The Committee needs to examine certain conversations during the period between February 29 and April 5, 1972, to aid in determining the participation or nonparticipation, knowledge or lack of knowledge of the President and his senior advisors with respect to testimony before the Senate in the Kleindienst hearings.

The specific conversations referred to in Part A of the schedule attached to the proposed subpoena are as follows:

A. Items 1, 2 and 3 of Part A refer to conversations between the President and Messrs. Haldeman, Ehrlichman or Colson on Monday, March 6, 1972. This was the day after the President returned from a weekend at Key Biscayne, and four days after the ITT document or documents had been delivered to White House aide Johnson. The Kleindienst hearings had resumed the previous Thursday and were continuing. On the same day Mr. Ehrlichman contacted the Chairman of the SEC to discuss ITT documents.

B. On the evening of March 14, 1972, the President and Mr. Mitchell had a telephone conversation. It was their only phone conversation during the month of March of which we are aware. This was the evening of the first day of Mr. Mitchell's testimony during which he twice denied ever having discussed antitrust litigation with the President. Materials respecting the conversation are requested in Item 4 of Part A of the schedule attached to the proposed subpoena.

C. According to Mr. Colson's calendar, he spent the morning of March 18, 1972, on "ITT" matters. He had three telephone conversations with Mr. Mitchell during the morning. That afternoon, the President and Mr. Colson met over two hours. The Kleindienst hearings were still continuing. Item 5 of Part A of the schedule attached to the proposed subpoena covers this conversation.

D. In a memorandum from Mr. Colson to Mr. Haldeman dated March 30, 1972 (Exhibit 121, 8 SSC 3372), Colson indicated that the subjects of discussion among senior White House aides on that date were the Kleindienst hearings, the possibility of withdrawing his nomination, documents relating to the Senate Judiciary

Committee hearings, and testimony by Mr. Mitchell before the Committee. The President met with Mr. Haldeman and Mr. Colson on March 30. Haldeman during the course of two of his meetings with the President on March 30 talked by telephone with Kleindienst. Items 6, 7, 8 and 9 of Part A of the schedule attached to the proposed subpoena request materials respecting the March 30 conversations involving the President, Haldeman and Colson.

E. On April 4 and 5, 1972, the President had conversations with Mitchell, Haldeman and Colson. At about this time the President apparently made the decision not to withdraw the Kleindienst nomination. Items 10, 11 and 12 of Part A of the schedule attached to the proposed subpoena call for materials relating to these conversations.

Part B of the schedule attached to the proposed subpoena requests news summaries submitted to the President during the period of the hearings on the nomination of Kleindienst before the Senate Judiciary Committee and the debate by the Senate on that nomination. The summaries are compiled from various news media and submitted to the President daily. From time to time the President makes written comments and notations on these news summaries. The President's copies of these summaries would be probative of the President's knowledge or lack of knowledge of the testimony during, and events surrounding, the hearings and debates on the Kleindienst nomination.

COPY

BY AUTHORITY OF THE HOUSE OF REPRESENTATIVES OF THE CONGRESS OF THE UNITED STATES OF AMERICA

To ...Benjamin Marshall, or his duly authorized representative:

You are hereby commanded to summon Richard M. Nixon, President of the United States of America, or any subordinate officer, official or employee with custody or control of the things described in the attached schedule,

to be and appear before the Committee on the Judiciary of the House of Representatives of the United States, of which the Hon. Peter W. Rodino, Jr., is chairman, and to bring with him the things specified in the schedule attached hereto and made a part hereof,

in their chamber in the city of Washington, on or before July 2, 1974, at the hour of 10:00 A.M., then and there to produce and deliver said things to said Committee, or their duly authorized representative, in connection with the Committee's investigation authorized and directed by H. Res. 803, adopted February 6, 1974.

Herein fail not, and make return of this summons.

Witness my hand and the seal of the House of Representatives of the United States, at the city of Washington, this ...24th... day of June, 1974.

(signed) Peter W. Rodino, Jr., Chairman

Attest: *(signed)* Clerk

On behalf of Richard M. Nixon, President of the United States of America, I accept service of the original subpoena, of which the foregoing is a copy.

Dated: June 25, 1974.

(signed) JAMES D. ST. CLAIR
Special Counsel to the President

1061

SCHEDULE OF THINGS REQUIRED TO BE PRODUCED PURSUANT TO SUBPOENA OF THE COMMITTEE ON THE JUDICIARY

A. The President's daily diaries (as reflected on U.S. Government Printing Office Form "1969–0–332–068" or its successor forms) for the period March 19, 1971 to March 25, 1971, both inclusive.

B. All tapes, dictabelts, other electronic and mechanical recordings, transcripts, memoranda, notes and other writings and things relating to the following conversations:

1. Between the President and John Ehrlichman on March 19, 1971 from approximately 8:30 a.m. to approximately 11:00 a.m.; on March 23, 1971, beginning at approximately 12:00 noon and ending at approximately 1:07 p.m.; on March 25, 1971, beginning at approximately 8:30 a.m.; and on March 25, 1971, beginning at approximately 3:00 p.m.

2. Between the President and John B. Connally on March 20, 1971; March 22, 1971; and on March 23, 1971 from 5:35 p.m. to 5:38 p.m.

3. Between the President and Charles W. Colson on March 19, 1971; March 21, 1971; March 22, 1971 (four conversations); March 23, 1971; March 24, 1971 (three conversations); and March 25, 1971.

MEMORANDUM SETTING FORTH FACTS AND BASES UNDERLYING PROPOSED SUBPOENA FOR RECORDINGS OF PRESIDENTIAL CONVERSATIONS AND OTHER THINGS NECESSARY FOR THE COMMITTEE'S INQUIRY INTO THE 1971 MILK PRICE SUPPORT DECISION

The following sets forth certain of the facts and bases underlying the proposed subpoena for materials necessary for the Committee's inquiry into the President's 1971 decision to increase milk price supports. The Committee has received additional evidence with respect to this matter in executive session.

Part A of the schedule attached to the proposed subpoena lists:

The President's daily diaries (as reflected on U.S. Government Printing Office Form "1969–0–332–068" or its successor forms) for the period March 19, 1971, to March 25, 1971, both inclusive.

The President's daily dairy is a log compiled by the Secret Service of the time and duration of the President's meetings and telephone conversations throughout the day. The daily diaries would enable the Committee to ascertain whether the President met or spoke with persons likely to be involved with contributions by the milk producer cooperatives during the period when the White House was considering whether to increase milk price supports above the level fixed by the Secretary of Agriculture.

Part B of the schedule attached to the proposed subpoena lists tapes and other things respecting the following specified presidential conversations:

(1) Between the President and John Ehrlichman on March 19, 1971, from approximately 8:30 a.m. to approximately 11:00 a.m.; on March 23, 1971, beginning at approximately 12:00 noon and ending at approximately 1:07 p.m.; on March 25, 1971, beginning at approximately 8:30 a.m.; and on March 25, 1971, beginning at approximately 3:00 p.m.

As the President's principal advisor on domestic affairs, Mr. Ehrlichman participated in the White House review of the Secretary of Agriculture's milk price support decision and the President's decision to increase the milk price support level.

The Committee has received a copy of Mr. Ehrlichman's office diary which indicates that Mr. Ehrlichman met with the President at the times specified above during the period March 19, 1971–March 25, 1971.

(2) Between the Preisdent and John B. Connally on March 22, 1971, and on March 23, 1971, from 5:35 p.m. to 5:38 p.m.

Beginning in February, 1971, AMPI representatives communicated with Secretary of the Treasury Connally to urge an increase in milk price supports. Secretary Connally discussed the milk price support issue with the President and participated in the decision to increase the milk price support level.

According to a White House compilation of meetings and telephone calls between the President and Connally, the President met or spoke with Connally on the dates and times indicated above.

(3) Between the President and Charles W. Colson on March 19, 1971; March 21, 1971; March 22, 1971 (four conversations); March 23, 1971; March 24, 1971 (three conversations); and March 25, 1971.

As the White House liaison with the milk producer cooperatives, Mr. Colson communicated frequently with AMPI representatives from 1970 through 1971 regarding political contributions to the President's re-election. Mr. Colson met with representatives of the milk producer cooperatives during the period the President determined to increase the milk price support level.

According to a White House compilation of meetings and telephone calls between the President and Colson, Colson met or spoke with the President on the dates indicated above.

COPY

BY AUTHORITY OF THE HOUSE OF REPRESENTATIVES OF THE CONGRESS OF THE UNITED STATES OF AMERICA

To Benjamin Marshall, or his duly authorized representative:

You are hereby commanded to summon Richard M. Nixon, President of the United States of America, or any subordinate officer, official or employee with custody or control of the things described in the attached schedule,

to be and appear before the Committee on the Judiciary of the House of Representatives of the United States, of which the Hon. Peter W. Rodino, Jr. is chairman, and to bring with him the things specified in the schedule attached hereto and made a part hereof,

in their chamber in the city of Washington, on or before July 2, 1974, at the hour of 10:00 A.M. then and there to produce and deliver said things to said Committee, or their duly authorized representative, in connection with the Committee's investigation authorized and directed by H. Res. 803, adopted February 6, 1974.
Herein fail not, and make return of this summons.

Witness my hand and the seal of the House of Representatives of the United States, at the city of Washington, this 24th day of June, 1974.

Peter W. Rodino, Jr., Chairman.

Attest:

_____ Jennings _____
Clerk

On behalf of Richard M. Nixon, President of the United States of America, I accept service of the original subpoena, of which the foregoing is a copy.

Dated: June 25, 1974

JAMES D. ST. CLAIR
Special Counsel to the President

1065

37-777 O - 74 - 18

Schedule of Things Required To Be Produced Pursuant to Subpoena of the Committee on the Judiciary

All tapes, dictabelts, other electronic and mechanical recordings, transcripts, memoranda, notes (including notes of H. R. Haldeman), and other writings and things relating to:

(1) A conversation on September 15, 1972, among the President, H. R. Haldeman and John Dean between approximately 6:00 and approximately 6:13 p.m.

(2) A conversation on September 15, 1972 between the President and H. R. Haldeman between 4:43 and 5:27 p.m. (Ronald Ziegler was present between 4:43 and 4:49 p.m.)

Memorandum Setting Forth Facts and Bases Underlying Proposed Subpoena for Recording of Presidential Conversations and Other Things Necessary for the Committee's Inquiry Into Alleged Abuse of IRS

The following sets forth the facts and bases underlying the proposed subpoena dated June 24, 1974 for recordings of Presidential conversations and other things necessary for the House Judiciary Committee's inquiry into alleged abuse of IRS.

(1) Conversation on September 15, 1972 among the President, H.R. Haldeman and John Dean, from approximately 6:00 p.m. to approximately 6:13 p.m.[1]

According to an affidavit of SSC Minority Counsel Fred Thompson, he was informed in or about early June 1973 by J. Fred Buzhardt, then Special Counsel for the President, that during the September 15, 1972 meeting Dean reported to the President on the IRS investigation of Larry O'Brien. (4 SSC 1794–96)

On May 28, 1974, the Watergate Special Prosecutor moved Judge Sirica for an order that the recording of this portion of the conversation of September 15, 1972, and the notes of Haldeman relating thereto, be turned over for presentation to the appropriate grand juries, on the basis that the recording is relevant to alleged White House attempts to abuse and politicize the IRS. According to the supporting affidavit of Special Prosecutor Leon Jaworski dated May 28, 1974, evidence assembled by his office substantiates allegations that in September 1972 the White House presented lists of "enemies" to the IRS with the direction that they be audited or otherwise harassed, and that in August and September 1972 the White House unlawfully attempted to have the IRS investigate Larry O'Brien. After listening to the tape of the September 15, 1972 conversation,

---

[1] The Committee has in its possession a tape of that portion of the September 15, 1972 conversation among the President, Haldeman and Dean which took place between 5:27 p.m. and approximately 6:00 p.m. It also has in its possession a tape of a portion of a conversation between the President and Haldeman on September 15, 1972 from approximately 5:12 p.m. to 5:27 p.m.

Judge Sirica orally granted the motion of the Special Prosecutor on June 7, 1974. On June 12, 1974, the Court ordered that the recording of the conversation from 6:00 p.m. until approximately 6:13 p.m., and the notes taken during that conversation by H. R. Haldeman, be made available to the Special Prosecutor. The President, through his counsel, filed a notice of appeal of that order on June 14, 1974.

Dean has testified before the SSC that during the meeting on September 15, 1972, with the President and Haldeman, they discussed using the IRS to attack their enemies. According to Dean's testimony, the President said that Democratic administrations used the IRS in the past and that after the election they would get people who would be responsive to White House requirements. Dean testified that at that point in the discussion Haldeman started taking notes. (3 SSC 958; 4 SSC 1479-80, 1535) Haldeman testified that there was discussion about the Democratic orientation of the IRS and the reluctance of the IRS to follow up on complaints of possible violations against people who were supporting opponents of the White House, and of cleaning house after the election. (7 SSC 2889)

In addition, other materials presented to the Committee in Executive Session further support the relevance of the recording of this conversation to the Committee's inquiry.

(2) Conversation on September 15, 1972, between the President and H. R. Haldeman between 4:43 and 5:27 p.m. (Ronald Ziegler was present between 4:43 and 4:49 p.m.)

On September 15, 1972 the indictment of the seven defendants in *United States* v. *Liddy*, charging violations with respect to the break-in at the Democratic National Committee headquarters was announced. The House Judiciary Committee has previously obtained a tape recording of the portion of this conversation from approximately 5:12 to 5:27 p.m. This portion of the conversation relates to the use of the Internal Revenue Service.

COPY

BY AUTHORITY OF THE HOUSE OF REPRESENTATIVES OF THE CONGRESS OF THE UNITED STATES OF AMERICA

To ~~Benjamin Marshall, or his duly authorized representative:~~

You are hereby commanded to summon ~~Richard M. Nixon, President of the United States of America, or any~~ subordinate officer, official or employee with custody or control of ~~the things described in the attached schedule,~~

to be and appear before the Committee on the Judiciary ~~Committee~~ of the House of Representatives of the United States, of which the Hon. Peter W. Rodino, Jr. is chairman, ~~and to bring with him the things specified in the schedule attached hereto and made a part hereof,~~

in their chamber in the city of Washington, on or before July 2, 1974, at the hour of 10:00 A.M., produce and deliver said things to said Committee, or their duly authorized representative, in connection with the Committee's investigation authorized and directed by H. Res. 803, adopted February 6, 1974. Herein fail not, and make return of this summons.

Witness my hand and the seal of the House of Representatives of the United States, at the city of Washington, this 24th day of June, 1974.

(signed) Peter W. Rodino, Jr., Chairman.

Attest: *(signed)* W. Pat Jennings, Clerk.

On behalf of Richard M. Nixon, President of the United States of America, I accept service of the original subpoena, of which the foregoing is a copy.

Dated: June 25, 1974.

(signed) JAMES D. ST. CLAIR
Special Counsel to the President

1070

SCHEDULE OF THINGS REQUIRED TO BE PRODUCED PURSUANT TO
SUBPOENA OF THE COMMITTEE ON THE JUDICIARY

A. All tapes, dictabelts, other electronic and mechanical recordings, transcripts, memoranda, notes and other writings and things relating to the following conversations:
  1. Meeting among the President, Charles Colson and H. R. Haldeman on June 23, 1971, between 11:39 a.m. and 12:41 p.m.
  2. Meeting between the President and Charles Colson on June 28, 1971 between 6:50 and 7:25 p.m.
  3. Meeting among the President, Charles Colson and H. R. Haldeman on July 1, 1971 between 10:28 and 11:49 a.m. (John Ehrlichman was present between 10:58 and 11:49 a.m. and Henry Kissinger was present between 11:22 and 11:24 a.m.)
  4. Meetings between the President and John Ehrlichman on September 7, 1971 between 8:33 and 10:35 a.m.; on September 8, 1971 between 3:26 and 5:10 p.m.; and on September 10, 1971 between 3:03 and 3:51 p.m.
  5. Meeting among the President, H. R. Haldeman and Charles Colson on September 7, 1971 between 10:37 a.m. and 12:00 p.m. and telephone conversation between the President and Charles Colson on September 10, 1971 between 3:53 and 4:17 p.m.
  6. Meeting between the President and Henry Petersen on April 19, 1973 between 10:12 and 11:07 a.m.
  7. Meeting between the President and Richard Kleindienst on April 25, 1973.

B. All memoranda, correspondence, papers and things prepared by, sent to, received by, or at any time contained in, the files of Charles Colson, H. R. Haldeman, John Ehrlichman, Egil Krogh and David Young, to the extent that such memoranda, correspondence, papers and things relate or refer directly or indirectly to the origin or to the activities of the White House Special Investigations Unit. These memoranda, correspondence, papers and things include, but are not limited to, all handwritten notes of John Ehrlichman produced by the White House on June 5 and June 6, 1974 pursuant to an order of Judge Gerhard Gesell in *United States* v. *Ehrlichman* (D.C.D.C. Cr. 74–116).

C. Handwritten notes of John Ehrlichman of a meeting on July 12, 1971 among the President, John Ehrlichman and Robert Mardian.

MEMORANDUM SETTING FORTH FACTS AND BASES UNDERLYING PROPOSED SUBPOENA FOR RECORDINGS OF PRESIDENTIAL CONVERSATIONS AND OTHER THINGS NECESSARY FOR THE COMMITTEE'S INQUIRY INTO DOMESTIC SURVEILLANCE ACTIVITIES

The following sets forth the facts and bases underlying the proposed subpoena dated June 24, 1974 for recordings of Presidential conversations and other things necessary for the House Judiciary

Committee's inquiry into Domestic Surveillance activities and their aftermath.

Part A of the proposed subpoena regards tape recordings and other materials respecting the following specified conversations:

(1) Meeting among the President, Charles Colson and H. R. Haldeman on June 23, 1971, between 11:39 a.m. and 12:41 p.m.

The President met with Colson and Haldeman from 11:39 a.m. to 12:41 p.m. Two days later Colson sent to Haldeman a memorandum detailing the political gains to be derived from the prosecution of Daniel Ellsberg. Charles Colson submitted an affidavit in *United States* v. *Ehrlichman* (D.C. D.C. Cr. 74-116) dated April 29, 1974 in which Colson stated that in meetings during this period the President repeatedly emphasized the gravity of the leaks and his concern about Ellsberg.

(2) Meeting between the President and Charles Colson on June 28, 1971 between 6:50 and 7:25 p.m.

This is the first meeting between the President and Colson following Colson's June 25, 1971 memorandum. Daniel Ellsberg was indicted on this date and surrendered to federal authorities.

(3) Meeting among the President, Charles Colson and H. R. Haldeman on July 1, 1971 between 10:28 and 11:49 a.m. (John Ehrlichman was present between 10:58 and 11:49 a.m. and Henry Kissinger was present between 11:22 and 11:24 a.m.)

Colson's affidavit of April 29, 1974 filed in *United States* v. *Ehrlichman* states that in a meeting between the President, Haldeman and Colson the President issued directions to stop security leaks at all cost. This is also the day that Colson called Howard Hunt to discuss the Pentagon Papers and Daniel Ellsberg and in a memorandum forwarding a transcript of that conversation to Haldeman, Colson referred to a previous discussion between Haldeman and Colson.

(4) Meetings between the President and John Ehrlichman on September 7, 1971 between 8:33 and 10:35 a.m.; on September 8, 1971 between 3:26 and 5:10 p.m.; and on September 10, 1971 between 3:03 and 3:51 p.m.

According to the testimony of John Ehrlichman (John Ehrlichman testimony, Grand Jury, *People* v. *Ehrlichman*, June 8, 1973, 604) and his logs, these are the first meetings between the President and Ehrlichman following the Fielding break-in. On September 8, Ehrlichman met with Egil Krogh and David Young (who headed the Plumbbers unit) at 10:45 a.m. and later in the day, between 3:26 and 5:10 p.m., met with the President. On September 10, Ehrlichman went directly from a meeting with the President between 3:03 and 3:51 p.m. to meet with Krogh and Young. (Meetings and conversations between the President and Ehrlichman, furnished by the White House and John Ehrlichman logs).

(5) Meeting among the President, H. R. Haldeman and Charles Colson on September 7, 1971 between 10:37 a.m. and 12:00 p.m. and telephone conversation between the President and Charles Colson on September 10, 1971 between 3:53 and 4:17 p.m.

According to the log of meetings and conversations between the President and Colson, and Charles Colson's log, these are the first meetings between the President and Colson following the Fielding break-in. The meeting on September 7, 1971 immediately followed a meeting between the President and Ehrlichman. On September 10, 1971 the President talked to Colson immediately following the President's meeting with Ehrlichman. Ehrlichman met at 4:00 p.m. with Krogh and Young and Colson met with Young at 8:00 p.m.

(6) Meeting between the President and Henry Petersen on April 19, 1973 between 10:12 and 11:07 a.m.

The President, by letter of April 29, 1974, forwarded to Judge Gerhard Gesell in *United States* v. *Ehrlichman* a transcript of this conversation between the President and Henry Petersen during which there was a discussion of the Fielding break-in. In his letter the President stated that if the Judge desired to hear the tape itself, arrangements could be made with the President's Counsel. Materials in the possession of the Committee indicate that the President discussed internal security considerations.

(7) Meeting between the President and Richard Kleindienst on April 25, 1973.

Richard Kleindienst has testified that he met with the President on April 25, 1973 at the White House to advise the President to send information about the Fielding break-in to Judge Byrne in the *Ellsberg* case. (Richard Kleindienst testimony, 9 SSC 3574–75, 3607). The President has stated that Kleindienst came to see him and the President instructed that the Justice Department memoranda relating to the break-in be filed with the Court in Los Angeles. (President Nixon's statement, May 22, 1973, 9 Pres. Docs. 696).

Part B of the subpoena requests the following materials:

All memoranda, correspondence, papers and things prepared by, sent to, received by or at any time contained in the files of Charles Colson, H. R. Haldeman, John Ehrlichman, Egil Krogh and David Young to the extent that such memoranda, correspondence, papers and things relate or refer directly or indirectly to the activities of the White House Special Investigations Unit. These memoranda, correspondence, papers and things include, but are not limited to:

(1) All handwritten notes of John Ehrlichman produced by the White House on June 5 and June 6, 1974 pursuant to an order of Judge Gerhard Gesell in *United States* v. *Ehrlichman* (D.C.D.C. Cr. 74–116).

(2) Handwritten notes of John Ehrlichman of a meeting on July 12, 1971 among the President, John Ehrlichman and Robert Mardian.

Part B of the subpoena seeks materials in the files of specified White House staff members relating to the activities of the White House Special Investigations Unit; the White House staff members listed in Item B were involved in activities relating to the Special Investigations Unit.

Item B refers to the handwritten notes of John Ehrlichman with respect to certain specified meetings. They were produced by the White House on June 5 and June 6, 1974, pursuant to the Order of the Court and arrangements with the White House in *United States* v. *Ehrlichman* (D.C.D.C. Cr. 74–116) in which Ehrlichman is charged with perjury and other violations in connection with the Fielding break-in.

In an affidavit dated June 12, 1974, Fred Buzhardt, Counsel to the President, acknowledged that these materials bore on the issues in that trial.

Item C refers to handwritten notes by John Ehrlichman of a meeting on July 12, 1971 among the President, Ehrlichman and Robert Mardian. Ehrlichman has requested these notes in connection with the forthcoming trial in *United States* v. *Ehrlichman*, but the White House has refused to produce them. An index supplied by the White House sets forth that the subject matter on these notes concerns "national security wiretaps." Robert Mardian has testified that on July 12, 1971 the President instructed him to pick up the logs and records of the 1969–71 wiretaps from William Sullivan of the FBI and deliver those documents to John Ehrlichman. (Mardian, 6 SSC 2405–08). Ehrlichman has testified that the President asked him to take custody of the wiretap records (Ehrlichman, 6 SSC 2534).

SUPPLEMENTAL, ADDITIONAL, SEPARATE, DISSENTING, MINORITY, INDIVIDUAL, AND CONCURRING VIEWS

CONCURRING VIEWS OF MESSRS. RAISBACK, FISH, HOGAN, BUTLER, COHEN AND FROEHLICH

For reasons we articulated in debate before the Judiciary Committee, the undersigned voted to recommend Articles I and II to the House. We agree in substance with this Report as it relates to those two articles. However, lest anyone infer that we agree without reservation to every point made, and given the lack of adequate time to prepare a detailed response to such points, suffice it to say that we do not necessarily agree that there is clear and convincing evidence to support every conclusion contained in the Report or that every fact referred to is necessary or relevant to support such articles.

                                      Tom Railsback.
                                      Hamilton Fish, Jr.
                                      Lawrence J. Hogan.
                                      M. Caldwell Butler.
                                      William S. Cohen.
                                      Harold V. Froehlich.

ADDITIONAL VIEWS OF MESSRS. BROOKS, KASTENMEIER, EDWARDS, CONYERS, EILBERG, SEIBERLING, DANIELSON, RANGEL, MS. JORDAN, MS. HOLTZMAN, AND MR. MEZVINSKY

On two occasions, Richard M. Nixon has taken the oath set forth in the Constitution of the United States to which all Presidents must swear. In that oath Richard Nixon promised to "faithfully execute the Office of the President of the United States." He swore to "preserve, protect and defend the Constitution of the United States." He promised to "take care that the laws be faithfully executed."

In each of these areas Richard Nixon has violated his solemn obligation to the American people. The evidence is overwhelming that Richard Nixon has used the Office of President to gain political advantage, to retaliate against those who disagreed with him, and to acquire personal wealth. To achieve these objectives he chose a course designed to obstruct the administration of justice, to misuse the functions of agencies of the Federal government, and to abuse the powers of his office in a manner that threatened the sanctity of our democratic form of government and the constitutional rights and safeguards of every American citizen.

Richard Nixon obstructed the due administration of justice by covering up White House involvement in criminal activities. He attempted to prevent the Federal grand juries, Federal prosecutors, the Department of Justice and the Congress of the United States from fully investigating those criminal activities and taking appropriate action. He concurred in the perjury of witnesses, participated in the payment of money to purchase silence, refused to produce evidence, interfered with the Office of the Special Prosecutor and discharged the Special Prosecutor for pursuing the course of justice too forthrightly.

Richard Nixon attempted to use the Internal Revenue Service to harass his enemies and to favor his friends. He directed the Federal Bureau of Investigation and the Secret Service to engage in illegal wiretapping. He endeavored to use the Central Intelligence Agency to sidetrack the Federal Bureau of Investigation's investigation into the illegal entry of the National Headquarters of the Democratic National Committee. He authorized a domestic intelligence operation that would have suspended the constitutional rights of all Americans.

Richard Nixon has continually refused to cooperate with the Congress of the United States in the exercise of its constitutional responsibilities. He has concealed information legitimately subpoenaed by the Congress and its committees. He has supplied misleading information to the Congress and the American people; and he has knowingly permitted his aides and appointees to testify erroneously and dishonestly before various congressional committees.

For these activities the House Judiciary Committee has recommended three articles of impeachment against Richard M. Nixon. These articles are fully supported by the evidence presented to the Committee. They do not, however, include all of the offenses committed by Richard Nixon for which he might be impeached, tried and removed from office.

There is ample evidence that Richard Nixon has violated the Constitution and the laws of the United States in an effort to enrich himself at the cost of the American taxpayer.

Shortly after his election in 1968, Mr. Nixon purchased three private homes. He then prevailed upon agencies of the Federal government to spend thousands of dollars of public funds at those properties. Intensive investigations by the House Government Operations Committee, the General Accounting Office, the Joint Committee on Internal Revenue Taxation, and the U.S. Internal Revenue Service have concluded that many of these expenditures were for Mr. Nixon's personal benefit and served no proper government function.

To preclude the possibility that a President might, because of personal financial considerations, either misuse the office for his own benefit or be held hostage to a hostile Congress, the drafters of our Constitution provided:

> The President shall, at stated times, receive for his service, a compensation, which shall neither be increased nor diminished during the period for which he shall have been elected, and he shall not receive within that period any other emolument from the United States or any of them of them.

The meaning of this clause is both clear and certain. Alexander Hamilton, writing in the *Federalist Papers No. 73*, succinctly stated its purpose as follows:

> It is impossible to imagine any provision which would have been more eligible than this. The legislature, on the appointment of a President, is once for all to declare what shall be the compensation for his services during the time for which he shall have been elected. This done, they will have no power to alter it, either by increase or diminution, till a new period of service by a new election commences. . . . Neither the Union, nor any of its members, will be at liberty to give, nor will he be at liberty to receive, any other emolument than that which may have been determined by the first act.

During his term of office, Richard Nixon has received a stated compensation for his services as Chief Executive Officer of our government, including a salary of $200,000 each year and an annual expense account of $50,000. Clearly, the payment of thousands of dollars by the Federal government for new heating systems, remodeling den windows, a sewer line, boundary surveys, landscape maintenance, sprinkler systems, and a shuffle board court constitutes additional "emoluments."

In its audit of Mr. Nixon's income tax returns for 1969 through 1972, the Internal Revenue Service concluded that:

> In view of the taxpayer's relationship to the United States Government as its Chief Executive Officer, *the above items constitute additional compensation to him for the performance of his services for the Government.*

In addition to receiving unlawful emoluments while in office, Mr. Nixon has attempted to evade the payment of his lawful taxes. There is substantial evidence that when Mr. Nixon signed his Federal income tax returns for 1969, 1970, 1971 and 1972, he knowingly attested to false information intending to defraud the American people of approximately one-half million dollars. On his tax returns for those years, he claimed an unlawful deduction for a charitable contribution of his pre-presidential papers when, in fact, no such gift had been made. He or his agents manufactured misleading and dishonest documents to support the deduction. As a result of attesting to false information, Mr. Nixon, for two consecutive years, reduced his tax liability to less than $1,000 on income of approximately one-quarter million dollars a year.

The Internal Revenue Service has also established that Mr. Nixon unlawfully reduced his taxes by failing to report certain income from the sale of properties in California, New York and Florida. The Senate Select Committee has documented Mr. Nixon's failure to report as income the receipt of $5,000 of campaign funds used to purchase platinum and diamond earrings for his wife's birthday present. The Senate Select Committee also determined that $45,000 was paid personally by C. G. Rebozo for improvements at Mr. Nixon's Key Biscayne vacation retreat at a time when Rebozo's personal financial records indicate that he did not have that much money available. Mr. Rebozo avoided being served with a subpoena for the information needed to determine the source of those funds by leaving the United States during the final days of the Senate Select Committee's existence.

The refusal of Mr. Nixon and his associates to cooperate with efforts to determine the legality of his tax returns led the Commissioner of Internal Revenue Service to refer the matter to the Special Prosecutor for presentation to a grand jury. The IRS Commissioner said:

> We have been unable to complete the processing of this matter in view of the lack of cooperation of some of the witnesses and because of many inconsistencies in the testimony of individuals presented to the Service. The use of grand jury process should aid in determining all of the facts in this matter. It is our opinion that a grand jury investigation of this matter is warranted, and because this investigation will involve presidential appointees, we believe it would be appropriate for it to be carried forward by your office.

The three articles of impeachment adopted by the House Judiciary Committee provide ample reason for exercise of the impeachment and removal power of Congress. In addition to these, however, the Committee should have adopted an article citing Mr. Nixon for violation of the emoluments provision of the Constitution and violation of the tax laws of the United States.

A number of Members of the Committee agreed that Mr. Nixon had "set a very sorry example," or that he "did knowingly underpay his taxes in the four years in question by taking unauthorized deductions," or that he was "guilty of bad judgment and gross negligence." Those Members, however, for reasons of their own, chose not to view such actions on the level of impeachable offenses. That, of course, is a matter for each Member to determine. For myself, I find that these offenses bring into focus, in a manner every American can understand, the nature and gravity of the abuses that permeate Mr. Nixon's conduct in office.

The integrity of the Office of President cannot be maintained by one who would convert public funds to his own private benefit and who would refuse to abide by the same laws that govern every American taxpayer. All doubt should be removed that any American, even if he be President, can disregard the laws and the Constitution of the United States with impunity.

JACK BROOKS.
BOB KASTENMEIER.
DON EDWARDS.
JOHN CONYERS, JR.
JOSHUA EILBERG.
JOHN F. SEIBERLING.
GEORGE E. DANIELSON.
C. B. RANGEL.
BARBARA JORDAN.
ELIZABETH HOLTZMAN.
EDWARD MEZVINSKY.

SUPPLEMENTAL VIEWS OF MR. EDWARDS

I fully and without reservation concur with the majority views of this report. I add supplementary views only to emphasize that there is a profoundly important aspect to the grievous and sustained misconduct of Mr. Nixon that in my opinion constituted a grave threat to the liberties of the American people.

In his attempts to subvert the processes of representative government and the guarantees of the Bill of Rights, Mr. Nixon and his associates used repeatedly the justification he described as "national security".

It was a familiar theme, referred to by James Madison in a letter to Jefferson in 1786. "Perhaps it is a universal truth", wrote the author of the Bill of Rights, "that the loss of liberty at home is to be charged to the provisions against dangers, real or pretended, from abroad."

Sad episodes in our history reflect that we have not always paid heed to Madison's warning. During World War I U.S. Attorney General Palmer jailed thousands of innocent Americans for conduct and words clearly legal but, in Palmer's view, a threat to "national security". During World War II thousands of loyal Japanese-Americans were illegally incarcerated in concentration camps for the same specious reason. And the era of the Korean War was blighted by Senator Joseph McCarthy, the sedition convictions, and the cruel antics of the House Un-American Activities Committee, all in the name of "national security".

It was less than 4 months after his inauguration that Richard Nixon began to use the notion "dangers from abroad", or "national security" to assault rights of Americans which are protected by the Constitution.

In mid May, 1969, he ordered the first of 17 wiretaps of newsmen, broadcasters, government employees and private citizens. His justification for the first few was "national security", in his view endangered by newspaper accounts of the secret and illegal bombings of Cambodia. Some were instituted for no possible national security reasons and were continued until 1971 for personal and political purposes. No leaks of classified information were ever discovered by these wiretaps.

The majority view of this report relates in frightening detail how this pattern of conduct continued. The Watergate cover-up began with Nixon's direction to the F.B.I. through the C.I.A. to suspend its investigation because of "national security". The F.B.I. was told to "lay off" the Fielding burglary because of "national security". The White House secret police, *The Plumbers*, were established for "national security". The Huston Plan, authorizing the F.B.I. and other Federal agencies to engage in burglary, mail covers, wiretapping and other illegal activities was approved by President Nixon for "national security".

I found it immensely disturbing that the talented and distinguished counsel for Mr. Nixon in the impeachment inquiry supported the view that the mere invocation of the catch phrase "national security" justified illegal wiretaps and personal surveillances. Indeed, he told the Judiciary Committee that in his view a President should be impeached for *not* proceeding as Mr. Nixon did.

So, I am writing these supplementary views to emphasize the urgency of Madison's two-hundred year old warning. Congress, the press, and indeed all of the American people must be vigilant to the perils of the subversive notion that any public official, the President or a policeman, possesses a kind of inherent power to set aside the Constitution whenever he thinks the public interest, or "national security" warrants it. That notion is the essential postulate of tyranny.

Don Edwards.

ADDITIONAL VIEWS OF MR. CONYERS

The Judiciary Committee undertook this impeachment inquiry with a clear recognition of the gravity of its responsibility to the Congress and the Constitution. Our task was unique in modern history and complicated by the sheer weight of the evidence to be evaluated. But the process of impeachment is not, and was never intended to be, familiar, convenient, or comfortable. It was framed with the intention that it be used only as a last constitutional resort against the danger of executive tyranny. The Congress should not lightly interpose its judgment between the President and the people who elect him, but we cannot avoid our duty to protect the people from "a long train of Abuses and Usurpations."

Impeachment has been simply but most accurately described as the great guardian of the purity of the Constitution. As such, the end of impeachment—trial and removal from office—is wholly unlike the end of conviction for a criminal offense, which is punishment. In the latter case, a citizen is stripped of the liberties the Constitution grants him as a matter of right as the price he must pay for wronging society. A removed President, however, may not suffer such loss. He must surrender the powers of the office entrusted to him by the people for using them to undermine the freedoms he swore to protect; only then is he subject to the normal processes of criminal law. This duality puts the roles of the Congress as a constitutional tribunal and the more common tribunals in perspective: the former is to assess his offenses against the Constitution; the latter, his offenses against the laws that execute the Constitution and govern the people.

The articles of impeachment recommended by the Committee, although narrowly drawn, are fully consistent with our constitutional responsibility. There is clear and convincing proof that Richard Nixon violated his oath of office and committed high crimes and misdemeanors which jeopardized the liberties of the people. In calling him to account, we also re-establish the proper parameters of presidential conduct. It is essential, therefore, that the record of our inquiry be complete so that no future president may infer that we have implicitly sanctioned what we have not explicitly condemned.

President Nixon's determination to Vietnamize the Indochina war led him to conclude that the infiltration of men and supplies through Cambodia and Laos had to be interdicted. This could have been done by bombing North Vietnam, but at the cost of destroying the fragile Paris Peace talks, then in progress. His only recourse, given his assumptions, was to bomb the supply routes in Cambodia which led into South Vietnam. At the same time, he apparently realized that public disclosure of such bombing would create a firestorm of Congressional and public protest.

In a desperate attempt, therefore, to achieve what he euphemistically called "peace with honor," he committed the massive destructiveness of American air power to yet another country, and attempted futilely to conceal his actions from the Congress and the American people. When the Cambodian bombing was first reported, he did not respond with a full public disclosure. Instead, he authorized a program of wiretapping, not merely of reporters but of government officials as well.

In retrospect, the logic of the White House becomes clear: Vietnamization required the bombing of Cambodia, which in turn required secrecy at all costs. The pressures of concealment led in turn to a spirit of distrust within the administration which spread as the President and his aides became increasingly enmeshed in the snare of lies and half-truths they had themselves created. Having decided that the people and the Congress could not be trusted with the truth, Mr. Nixon's distrust was soon extended to his own foreign policy advisors and assistants.

The authorization and concealment of the Cambodian bombing, and the means he employed to prevent its disclosure, illustrated in the very first months of his administration that the President was prepared to do anything he considered necessary to achieve his objectives. To defend both the bombing and the subsequent wire-tapping, he invoked the concept of national security, a convenient rationalization to be used whenever the occasion demanded an explanation for some concealed governmental conduct. The imperial presidency of Richard Nixon came to rely on this claim as a cloak for clandestine activity, and as an excuse for consciously and repeatedly deceiving the Congress and the people.

The evidence presented to this Committee demonstrates that the President's invocations of national security were often used as a shield, motivated primarily by a desire to protect himself from personal and political embarrassment. He would have us believe that he could not disclose the existence of the Plumbers, or the break-in of Dr. Fielding's office, or the falsification of State Department cables, or even the Cambodian bombing itself, because to have done so would have jeopardized national security.

Once in the White House, Mr. Nixon turned on his critics with a vengeance, apparently not appreciating that others could strenuously disagree with him without being either subversive or revolutionary. He took full advantage of the FBI's willingness to invade people's private lives without legal justification and without regard for their civil liberties. This willingness was documented during Congressional Black Caucus hearings on governmental lawlessness in June, 1972, which revealed that the files of the FBI and the Secret Service are laden with unverified information, often inaccurate and slanderous, on thousands of citizens, particularly Blacks, who have had the temerity to speak out against racism, injustice, or the Indochina war. This surveillance of government critics by the FBI began, of course, before Mr. Nixon took office, but his administration gave renewed approval to some of the ugliest abuses of governmental power.

Obsessed by the notion that the disruptive activities of the Blacks and students who criticized him were receiving foreign support, he repeatedly demanded that the FBI and CIA conduct extensive investigations to verify this potential conspiracy. But, even with additional authority conferred on these agencies, their reports continually indicated that his fears were unfounded. The inability of the FBI and CIA to substantiate the President's conviction that many of his critics were engaged in subversion or international conspiracy led him to increasingly question their operational efficiency.

Hence, the President's approval of the Huston plan in July, 1970, represented nothing more than an extension of an already demonstrated willingness to harass and spy on his political opponents. Even if the Huston plan itself was subsequently tabled, its spirit lived on in the White House and soon took tangible form with attempts to use the Internal Revenue Service for discriminatory personal and political purposes, and with the activities of the Plumbers unit. The Plumbers put the essence of the Huston plan into practice and provided the President with his own secret intelligence force to investigate his critics and discredit them by any means possible, without even the most elementary regard for individual privacy or public morality.

With the assistance of the President's closest advisors, the Plumbers violated the charter of the Central Intelligence Agency by seeking CIA assistance to impugn the integrity of Senator Edward Kennedy, and to assess the administration's potential vulnerability from ITT's Dita Beard, whose confidential memo implied that a bribe had been offered to settle the ITT antitrust case. They sought to discredit the Democratic party by falsifying State Department cables to implicate President Kennedy in the assassination of South Vietnamese President Diem. They broke into the Los Angeles office of Dr. Fielding in an attempt to gain medical information that would defame Daniel Ellsberg and, through him, the critics of the President's war policies. In these ways, and perhaps in other ways still undisclosed, they violated every canon of morality and legality which stood between them and their goal of discrediting and undermining the President's "enemies."

These activities provide part of the basis for the charge in Article II that President Nixon seriously abused the powers of his office. They also demonstrate that the break-in and bugging of the Democratic National Committee, and the subsequent cover-up specified in Article I, were not inexplicable aberrations from a standing presidential policy of strict adherence to the law. Instead, in proper perspective, the Watergate break-in emerges as only one incident in a continuous course of conduct which had its origins in the first months following President Nixon's inauguration. The subsequent concealment was intended not merely to protect the White House from its complicity in the Watergate incident itself, but to avoid disclosure of the entire train of illegal and abusive conduct that characterized the Nixon presidency: obstruction of justice, perjury and subornation of perjury, offers of executive clemency, attempts to influence a federal judge, destruction of evidence, disclosure of secret grand jury proceedings, withholding information of criminal activity, impoundment of Congressional appropriations, willful tax evasion, possible bribery in connection with the ITT antitrust and milk price support decisions, and interference with the lawful activities of the CIA, FBI, IRS, Special Prosecutor, House Banking and Currency Committee, Senate Select Committee on Presidential Campaign Activities, and finally, the House Judiciary

Committee. In these ways, the President sought to avert disclosure of a seamless web of illegality and impropriety.

That cover-up continued to the end, in that the President attempted to deceive the Congress and the American people by concealing and misrepresenting his knowledge and participation in these activities, and even while resigning, refusing to admit his complicity. Additionally, he withheld necessary information from the Special Prosecutors and fired Special Prosecutor Cox for his efforts to fully discharge his responsibilities. He refused to comply with the legal and proper subpoenas of the Judiciary Committee, as charged in Article III. He mutilated and destroyed evidence in his possession or caused that to happen, and did very nearly everthing in his power to impede, delay, and obstruct the proper course of justice.

In my judgment, this course of presidential conduct, outlined above and specified in Articles I, II, and III, provide irrefutable evidence that Richard Nixon was not fit to enjoy the trust and authority which reposes in the Presidency of the United States.

But of at least equal importance is the uncontroverted evidence that Mr. Nixon authorized an illegal war against the sovereign nation of Cambodia, and sought to protect himself from criticism and possible repudiation by engaging in deliberate policies of concealment, deception, and misrepresentation.

On July 30, 1974, I proposed the following article of impeachment:

In his conduct of the office of President of the United States, Richard M. Nixon, in violation of his constitutional oath faithfully to execute the office of President of the United States and, to the best of his ability, preserve, protect, and defend the Constitution of the United States, and in disregard of his constitutional duty to take care that the laws be faithfully executed, on and subsequent to March 17, 1969, authorized, ordered and ratified the concealment from the Congress of the facts and the submission to the Congress of false and misleading statements concerning the existence, scope and nature of American bombing operations in Cambodia in derogation of the power of the Congress to declare war, to make appropriations, and to raise and support armies, and by such conduct warrants impeachment and trial and removal from office.

Although this article was not recommended by the Committee, it is fully supported by the facts and the Constitution.

The President of the United States must exercise only those powers which are legally and constitutionally his to exercise, and, by his actions, he must demonstrate due respect for the democratic rights of the people and the constitutional responsibilities of the Congress. The manner in which the Cambodian bombing was initiated, conducted, and reported clearly exceeded the constitutional powers of the presidency, and presented indisputable evidence of impeachable conduct.

President Nixon unilaterally initiated and authorized a campaign of bombing against the neutral nation of Cambodia. For the next four years, he continually deceived the Congress and the American people as to when the bombing began and how far it extended. In so doing, he exceeded his constitutional power as commander-in-chief. He usurped the power of the Congress to declare war, and he expended monies for a purpose not authorized or approved by the Congress. In so doing, he also denied the people of the United States their right to be fully informed about the actions and policies of their elected officials.

It is important to note that the facts pertinent to the Cambodian bombing are not in question. On 11 February 1969, General Creighton Abrams, Commander of the United States Military Assistance Command Vietnam, recommended and requested authorization to conduct bombing strikes in Cambodia. Between 12 February and 17 March 1969, this request was considered by the President in meetings of the National Security Council. On 17 March 1969, President Nixon authorized the bombing of Cambodia.

The bombing began on 18 March 1969 and continued unabated until 15 August 1973. From 18 March 1969 to 1 May 1970, when the United States initiated ground combat operations in Cambodia, 3,695 B-52 sorties were conducted, during which a total of 105,837 tons of bombs were dropped on Cambodia. From the beginning to the end of the bombing campaign in August, 1973, more than 150,000 sorties dropped in excess of 500,000 tons of bombs in Cambodia.

The bombing operations took the form of three different operations, code named "Menu Operation", "Patio", and "Freedom Deal". Under the procedures instituted for reporting "Menu Operation" bombing missions, the regular operational reports prepared after each mission indicated that the strikes had taken place in South Vietnam rather than in Cambodia. Most "Patio" bombing missions were not reported at all; forty-eight "special" "Patio" strikes were reported as having occurred in Laos, rather than Cambodia. The "Freedom Deal" tactical air strikes began on 30 June 1970, the date on which the last contingent of American ground forces was withdrawn from Cambodia. These strikes were reported as having taken place in Cambodia, but in many cases, the targets of "Freedom Deal" strikes were not those which were authorized and reported.

Similarly, there is no dispute that the President made a decision to keep the bombing secret. When President Nixon approved the first bombing strikes in Cambodia, he directed General Earle Wheeler, Chairman of the Joint Chiefs of Staff, to inform General Abrams that the bombing operations were not to be discussed with any unauthorized person, even though this meant circumventing the normal chain of command which would otherwise have included the Secretary of the Army, the Vice Chief of Staff for the Air Force, and the Commander of the Seventh Air Force.

The President's policy of concealment, deception, and misrepresentation was consistently reflected in his own public statements and in the Congressional testimony of his military and civilian subordinates.

In a nationally televised address on 14 May 1969, two months after the bombing in Cambodia began, the President stated, "I have tried to present the facts about Vietnam with complete honesty, and I shall continue to do so in my reports to the American people".

At a news conference on 8 December 1969, the President asserted that the people of the United States were entitled to know everything they could with regard to any involvement of the United States abroad.

At another news conference on 21 March 1970, President Nixon declared that the United States would continue to "respect Cambodia's neutrality".

On 30 April 1970, when the President announced the American invasion of Cambodia, he reviewed previous American policy toward Cambodia in the following terms:

> American policy since then has been to scrupulously respect the neutrality of the Cambodian people. We have maintained a skeleton diplomatic mission of fewer than 15 in Cambodia's capitol, and that only since last August. For the previous 4 years, from 1965 to 1969, we did not have any diplomatic mission whatever in Cambodia. And for the past 5 years, we have provided no military assistance whatever and no economic assistance to Cambodia.
>
> For 5 years, neither the United States nor South Vietnam has moved against these enemy sanctuaries because we did not wish to violate the territory of a neutral nation. Even after the Vietnamese Communists began to expand these sanctuaries 4 weeks ago, we counseled patience to our South Vietnamese allies and imposed restraints on our own commanders.

On 30 June, the President released a report entitled "The Cambodian Operation" which stated in part:

> For five years, North Vietnam has used Cambodian territory as a sanctuary from which to attack allied forces in South Vietnam. For five years, American and allied forces—to preserve the concept of Cambodian neutrality and to confine the conflict in Southeast Asia—refrained from moving against these sanctuaries.

The evidence is unmistakable, therefore, that President Nixon personally and directly lied to the American people by repeatedly concealing the fact that the United States had begun to bomb Cambodia in March, 1969.

The President's public assurances were complemented by the erroneous and misleading statements made to the Congress by his civilian and military subordinates. Such statements were made by the Chief of Staff of the Air Force, the Secretary of State, the Secretary of the Army, the Secretary of Defense, and the Secretary of the Air Force in testimony before the Senate Committee on Armed Services, the Senate Committee on Foreign Relations, the Senate Committee on Appropriations, and the House Committee on Appropriations.

For example, on 27 April 1970, Secretary of State Rogers testified before the Senate Foreign Relations Committee, declaring that, "Cambodia is one country where we can say with complete assurance that our hands are clean and our hearts are pure . . . Our best policy is to be as quiet as possible, to avoid any action which appears to violate the neutrality of Cambodia".

For example, on 16 April 1970, Secretary of the Army Resor testified before the Senate Appropriations Committee that there had been no "U.S. Military aid and no Army support for Cambodia" since January, 1964.

For example, on 31 March 1971, Secretary of the Air Force Seamans was requested by the Senate Armed Services Committee to submit a report on American bombing missions in Indochina. Seamans subsequently submitted a classified report which indicated that no bombing strikes had been conducted in Cambodia prior to 1 May 1970, even though bombing strikes had actually begun in March, 1969.

It was not until 16 July 1973 that Secretary of Defense Schlesinger was forced to confirm earlier disclosures to the Senate Armed Services Committee that the United States had bombed Cambodia, a sovereign and neutral nation, before May, 1970.

Richard Nixon authorized the bombing of Cambodia. In a series of subsequent public statements, he deliberately and intentionally lied to the American people. And in their testimony before duly authorized committees of the Congress, his civilian and military subordinates failed to testify fully and accurately. Whether his subordinates deceived the Congress intentionally or unintentionally, the fact remains that the President must have known that they testified inaccurately, and he made no attempt to correct the record.

By his secret bombing of Cambodia, President Nixon unquestionably exceeded his powers as commander-in-chief, for not even the most tortured interpretation of Article II, Section 2 could support a war begun and pursued in secrecy. He also violated Sections 7 and 8 of Article I, which give to the Congress the authority to make appropriations and declare war. For the "power of the purse" to have any meaning, the Congress must know how the money it appropriates is being spent. Yet there is no evidence of any request by this Administration for appropriations for any American military activity in Cambodia between March, 1969, and August, 1973. And by conducting a war without the knowledge of the Congress, President Nixon further eroded whatever remains of the constitutional power of the Congress to decide when and where the United States shall be at war. We cannot sanction such a policy of deliberate deception, intended to nullify the constitutional powers of the Congress to legislate for the people we represent.

By the same policies of secrecy and deception, Richard Nixon also violated a principal tenet of democratic government: that the President, like every other elected official, is accountable to the people. For how can the people hold their President to account if he deliberately and consistently lies to them? The people cannot judge if they do not know, and President Nixon did everything within his power to keep them in ignorance. In all good conscience, we must condemn his deception regarding Cambodia with the same fervor and outrage we condemn his deception regarding Watergate.

The difficult question is not whether the secret bombing of Cambodia constitutes impeachable conduct. That is too obvious to require further argument. Instead, the question we must ponder is why the Congress has not called the President to judgment. The painful answer is that condemning the Cambodian bombing would also have required us to indict previous administrations and to admit that the Congress has failed to fully meet its own constitutional obligations.

Whether intentionally or not, the Congress has participated in the degeneration of its power to declare war. Although a War Powers Act was passed recently, over the veto of President Nixon, no legislation is self-executing. Whatever its limitations and faults, this legislation, and the constitutional provisions on which it is based, will only have meaning to the extent that the Congress invests them with meaning. Instead of merely ratifying the decisions and recommendations of the executive branch, the Congress must demonstrate that it is once again prepared to play an active and constructive role in the formulation of foreign policy—in the creation of policies which will direct this nation toward war or peace.

If this is truly to be a representative government, then the people's representatives in Congress must no longer allow any one person to decide unilaterally when, where, and why Americans shall die violent deaths. The Congress may not be subject to impeachment, but it is subject to emasculation. We must directly confront the fact that the secret bombing of Cambodia is only the most recent and egregious illustration of the disintegration of the war power of Congress, and that the Congress has participated in this process, wittingly or unwittingly. If, during this impeachment proceeding, we have failed to learn this lesson, then we deserve the obloquy, not the gratitude, of the people of the United States. If we do not now fully dedicate ourselves to regaining every bit of constitutional ground we have surrendered, then—to paraphrase one of the President's men—we shall have lost our constitutional and moral compass.

It has frequently been argued during the past weeks that this Committee's inquiry and the President's subsequent resignation demonstrate that "the system works". But such satisfaction or complacency is misguided. We must recognize that we were presented with a seemingly endless series of public revelations and presidential actions which did more to undermine Mr. Nixon's position than any independent investigation undertaken by this Committee or its staff. Our inquiry has been the beneficiary of literally years of work by investigative reporters, the Special Prosecutor's office, and the Senate Select Committee on Presidential Campaign Activities. And most importantly, the President himself documented his words and actions through his secret taping system, without which our inquiry might never have even begun. The President himself did more than anyone or anything to insure his removal from office.

If the system has worked, it has worked by accident and good fortune. It would be gratifying to conclude that this House, charged with the sole power of impeachment, exercised vigilance and acted on its own initiative. However, we would be deluding ourselves if we did not admit that this inquiry was forced on us by an accumulation of disclosures which, finally and after unnecessary delays, could no longer be ignored.

Perhaps ironically, and certainly unintentionally, we have ourselves jeopardized the future of the impeachment process. Before this inquiry, the prospect of impeaching a president was disquieting because it had not been attempted in more than a century. Now with our inquiry as a precedent, future Congresses may recoil from ever again exercising this power. They may read the history of our work and conclude that impeachment can never again succeed unless another President demonstrates the same, almost uncanny ability to impeach himself. If this is our legacy, our future colleagues may well conclude that ours has been a pyrrhic victory, and that impeachment will never again justify the agony we have endured. It is imperative, therefore, that we speak to them clearly: impeachment is difficult and it is painful, but the courage to do what must be done is the price of remaining free.

JOHN CONYERS, Jr., M.C.

SEPARATE COMMENTS OF MR. WALDIE

Impeachment of a President should be undertaken not to punish a President, but to constitutionally redefine and to constitutionally limit the powers of the Presidency when those powers have been dangerously extended and abused.

It is therefore necessary to consider impeachment not in terms of its effects on Richard Nixon but in terms of its effects on the powers of future occupants of the Presidency.

Richard Nixon has committeed impeachable offenses as alleged in Articles I, II, and III. Those offenses constitute serious constitutional abuses of power and warrant impeachment that we might redefine Presidential power in the future.

Clearly, Richard Nixon has sought to obstruct justice in his efforts to prevent his and his associates' roles in Watergate from surfacing.

In that effort, the President has used the great powers of his office to thwart and prevent lawful inquiry into Watergate both from the Judicial and from the Legislative Branches. He has used and abused, in this effort, agencies of the Executive Branch of Government including the CIA and the FBI. He has thereby sought to remove the Presidency from accountability to the institutions of law.

If we do not redefine Executive Power in this instance and by such redefinition, limit that power for future Presidents, we risk all future Presidents claiming immunity from accountability for unlawful conduct in the furtherance of political objectives.

Clearly, Richard Nixon has failed to faithfully execute his oath of office and has abused the powers of his office by authorizing illegal acts and dangerous intrusions into personal privacy to further political objectives.

Wiretapping to obtain information that was used to counter political opponents; illegal entry to obtain information to counter political opponents; secret police not accountable to any authority but the President and whose primary function appears to have been to further political objectives of the President; the use of agencies of our Government such as the IRS to persecute political enemies and reward political friends; the pattern of excessive accumulation of power and of dangerous abuse of power is undeniable.

Impeachment for such activities is clearly warranted that we might redefine executive power and thereby limit it that future Presidents will not so abuse their powers—that future Presidents will understand theirs is a constitutionally limited office and an office as to which accountability is ever present.

Though the Legislative, Judicial, and Executive Branches are co-equal, that "equality" is non-existent when the Legislative Branch is inquiring into impeachable conduct of the Executive. In that limited instance, in the pursuit of that Constitutional obligation, the Legislative Branch is supreme and cannot be thwarted by claims of Executive privilege on the part of the Executive Branch.

Executive privilege is a doctrine dependent on Separation of Powers. Impeachment is a process that assumes an "intrusion" by the Legislative Branch into the Executive and thus the Separation of Powers upon which Executive privilege is premised is absent.

Failure of a President to respond to a lawfully authorized subpoena of the Legislative Branch pursuant to its impeachment authority, constitutes an impeachable offense.

If this President can ignore these subpoenas, all future Presidents will assuredly ignore all future subpoenas of any impeachment inquiry.

We must redefine this Executive power and by impeachment, limit it so future Presidents will ignore lawfully authorized subpoenas in the impeachment process at their own risk.

Finally, I believe we should have approved an Article of Impeachment dealing with the exercise of the War Power.

Though it is undeniable that abuse of the War Power did not begin with President Nixon, that in fact it was severely abused by President Johnson, the truth remains that Richard Nixon, too, seriously abused the War Power by concealing and misrepresenting the facts concerning the massive bombing of neutral Cambodia. A War Power whose exercise is dependent on the deception of the American People is a War Power that is seriously abused. And yet the ability to wage war in recent years has almost seemed dependent on a President deceiving the American People. It is increasingly clear that the Vietnam War was a result of lies and deception on a massive scale, not to confuse or mislead the enemy, but to confuse and mislead the American People, the source from which all powers of the President, including the War Power, must flow.

Therefore, if ever a power of the President desperately needed a Constitutional redefinition and thereby a Constitutional limitation, it is the War Power.

I regret we did not recommend an Article of Impeachment based on the conduct of the President in concealing and deceiving the American People with respect to the exercise of the War Power in the bombing of Cambodia. Failing to do so, we may have unintentionally ratified such conduct for future Presidents. And if we have done that, all the good we might have done in redefining and limiting Presidential power in other fields may be of little avail.

Subsequent to preparing these views, Richard Nixon, facing certain impeachment and conviction, resigned his office.

Gerald Ford, in his first address to Congress as President, described these events as a "National Nightmare."

The "nightmare," as Gerald Ford so aptly described it, is not yet over, but it is undeniable that it is receding. The final admission of complicity in obstruction of justice by Richard Nixon precipitated his forced resignation under the universal perception that his impeachment and conviction were certainties.

It was with mixed feelings that I viewed those events. I desired that the constitutional process of impeachment and trial be carried out that a full and complete record of what Mr. Nixon did to our country might be had. In the long run I believe such a course would have been in the best interest of the Country.

But it was clearly with a great feeling of relief that I saw Richard Nixon leave the Presidency; not relief at the disgrace and dishonor that accompanied his departure, but relief that the great power of that office would no longer be responsive to his whims or decisions.

And so, in the immediate future, the country is clearly well served by Mr. Nixon's departure and, perhaps, in the long term it will have been well served by his not being in position, even for a short time, to wield that massive power dangerously and irresponsibly.

But the certainty that the long run best interests of the Nation will be served only exists if we assure that the lessons of Richard Nixon's "nightmare" are fully understood.

Those lessons would essentially, I believe, distil down to the principle that no man, "be he President or pauper" is above the law.

Mr. Nixon never understood that. The Congress was slow in coming to its comprehension. The people never wavered or doubted in their instinctive belief in that principle.

That all in the future might comprehend that vital lesson, it is necessary that the full extent of Mr. Nixon's abuse of America—that a full record of the "nightmare" he visited upon us, be made.

The process whereby that will occur will include the Congress and the Report of the House Judiciary Committee—now—and additional reports as evidence accumulates. It will also include the Courts of our land. The full extent of Richard Nixon's participation in illegal activities will only unravel as accountability to the institution of justice is accomplished. To deny that process by granting immunity to Mr. Nixon would materially detract from the necessity of a full exposition of the "nightmare."

It would also essentially deny the basic lesson that no man, "be he President or pauper," is above the law. We upheld that principle when we forced the resignation of President Richard Nixon under the certainty of impeachment and conviction. We would shatter that principle, so hard fought and dearly won, if we place Richard Nixon, citizen, above the law; beyond accountability for his conduct.

JEROME R. WALDIE.

ADDITIONAL VIEWS OF MESSRS. SARBANES AND SEIBERLING, JOINED BY MESSRS. DONOHUE, EILBERG, MANN, DANIELSON, THORNTON, SMITH AND HOGAN

While in the majority who voted against the proposed Article concerning President Nixon's concealment from Congress of the bombing of Cambodia, we certainly did not intend our vote to indicate approval of such conduct on his part. In fact, as some of us stated during the debate, we consider his action to have been a usurpation of Congress' power to declare war and to make appropriations.

The issue in the proposed article was the wrongful withholding of information from the Congress and the falsification of reports to the Congress. On March 17, 1969, President Nixon, without consulting or informing the Congress and in spite of the fact that Cambodia was a neutral country, authorized the bombing of Cambodia and ordered that information on these bombing operations be held in the closest secrecy. The President's orders led to the establishment by high ranking military officers of a dual reporting system for Cambodian bombing operations. This reporting system circumvented both the normal chains of command and information within the Defense Department and the normal channels of communication between the Executive Branch and appropriate Congressional committees. A result of this dual reporting system was that Congressional committees were deceived about the existence of American air operations against Cambodian territory prior to the April 1970 "incursion"; official reports were formally submitted to Congress indicating that there had been no such operations when in fact extensive bombing activities in Cambodia had taken place. The policy of the President with respect to the reporting of the bombing thereby deprived Congress of the ability to exercise its constitutional powers.

Despite the grave and deplorable implications of this policy, there are certain reasons why impeachment is not the appropriate remedy in this instance. Although neither the House of Representatives nor the Senate nor any Congressional committee was advised of the bombing prior to May, 1970, when the clandestine air operations had been underway for 14 months, a few key members of the Congress in positions of responsibility had been informally advised of the bombing. Clearly, the informing by the Administration of a few, carefully selected individuals in the Congress is not the same as informing the Congress and cannot be considered proper or adequate notice. Nonetheless, the situation as to executive responsibility is clouded by the fact that certain members of the Congress were made aware of the bombing.

Furthermore, it appears likely that had the President formally consulted the Congress prior to April, 1970, the Congress would have acquiesced in the bombing policy. Although air operations were openly conducted over Cambodian territory from July, 1970 until mid-August,

1973, it should be noted that the Congress took no action, until June, 1973, to stop them. On the contrary, the Congress during this period repeatedly approved major authorizations and appropriations bills which provided authority for the continuation of these bombing operations. These considerations raise doubts about here invoking the impeachment remedy, although they in no sense justify the concealment from Congress of information about the bombing.

It is, moreover, difficult to separate in retrospect the Cambodian bombing operations either from the extensive American military involvement in Southeast Asia or from certain trends in recent years in the conduct of our Nation's foreign policy. Impeachment of a President should not be foreclosed in situations where Congress was forced by events to support a military venture initiated by a President acting in excess of his authority; indeed, such actions go to the very heart of the Constitutional allocation of powers and would require a serious impeachment inquiry. But where—as here—Congress over a considerable period of time had accepted and condoned Presidential encroachments on its powers, Congress' own inaction makes it questionable whether invoking the impeachment remedy in this instance is appropriate.

Finally, it is not necessary for Congress to take such action in this case in order to establish a proper precedent for the future. By enacting, over a Presidential veto, the War Powers Resolution of 1973 (PL 93-148) Congress has laid down specific guidelines requiring the President to report promptly to Congress whenever United States Armed Forces are introduced into hostilities or into the territory, airspace or waters of a foreign nation. Certainly any President who violated the provisions of that Law would invite Congressional action through the impeachment remedy to protect the Constitutional separation of powers against abuse by the Executive.

PAUL S. SARBANES.
JOHN F. SEIBERLING.
HAROLD D. DONOHUE.
JOSHUA EILBERG.
JAMES R. MANN.
GEORGE E. DANIELSON.
RAY THORNTON.
HENRY P. SMITH III
LAWRENCE J. HOGAN.

ADDITIONAL VIEWS OF MR. DANIELSON

IMPEACHABLE CONDUCT

Precisely what constitutes impeachable conduct, or an impeachable offense, is the subject of endless debate. I concur in the definition included in the discourse contained in the Committee's report of February 21, 1974, set forth above. I submit, however, that there probably can be no single answer which is suitable for all cases and for all times and the term had best be defined in the context of the events and the times in which the controversy has arisen.

I am convinced, however, that impeachable conduct need not be criminal conduct. It is enough to support impeachment that the conduct complained of be conduct which is grossly incompatible with the office held and which is subversive of that office and of our Constitutional system of government. With respect to a President of the United States it is clear, in my mind, that conduct which constitutes a substantial breach of his oath of office, is impeachable conduct.

ROLE OF PRESIDENT'S COUNSEL IN IMPEACHMENT INQUIRY

In the Nixon inquiry, the President's counsel participated actively and to a degree that is without precedent in our history. His participation was provided for by the rules adopted by the Committee at the outset of the inquiry, but was expanded considerably as the inquiry progressed, to the point where the President's counsel filled the role of an advocate for the President and was permitted to examine and cross-examine at length. In my opinion, this expanded role of the President's counsel was improvidently permitted, for it gravely threatened to transform the proceeding from its constitutional role of the "Grand Inquest of the Nation" to that of an adversary proceeding similar to a judicial trial. I would urge that in any future impeachment inquiries the role of the counsel of the person subject to the impeachment process not be extended beyond that of an observer and auditor. In the Nixon hearings, the extensive participation was permitted out of an overabundance of caution that the hearings be conducted with fairness and that due process be observed. Those goals were not only achieved, but surpassed, and because of excessive participation by President's counsel, both fairness and due process were threatened.

THE SUFFICIENCY OF PLEADING THE ARTICLES OF IMPEACHMENT

A careful reading of the three articles of impeachment returned by the Committee clearly demonstrates that they are finely drawn and sufficient to meet fully any objections or demands as to whether the person impeached would be adequately informed of the charges against him. Impeachment is neither a civil nor a criminal judicial procedure. It is a parliamentary procedure. Impeachment is not governed by either civil or criminal procedural rules or rules of pleading. Nevertheless, both civil and criminal rules and procedures serve as useful analogies and guidelines in the preparation of articles of impeachment. In the Nixon inquiry, much debate centered on whether the articles contained sufficient specificity. That was a false issue. It is submitted that each of the articles returned by the Committee was drawn with sufficient specificity to inform the person accused fully of the charges placed against him, thus enabling him adequately to prepare his defense. In addition, the President was furnished, through his counsel, with a full and complete copy of every item of evidence in the possession of the Committee.

ALLEGED IMMUNITY OF PRESIDENTS FROM CRIMINAL PROSECUTION

During the hearings, Members of the Committee commented in passing, on three occasions, that an incumbent President of the United States cannot be indicted and tried for a criminal charge until after he is impeached and removed from office.

Many Members of the Committee, including myself, do not agree with that statement. I am convinced that it has no basis in our Constitution, our statutes or the decisions of our courts.

The argument that the President is immune from criminal process is based upon a misreading of *Mississippi* v. *Johnson*, 71 U.S. (4 Wall.) 475. That case did not involve the question of whether or not a President was subject to judicial process for a criminal offense. It had to do with a request for an injunction against President Andrew Johnson to prevent him from executing a law. It is not authority for the contention that an incumbent President cannot be prosecuted for a criminal offense prior to impeachment.

The language of the Constitution which is sometimes misinterpreted as to the indictability of a President is Article I, Section 3, Clause 7, which proves that "Judgment in Cases of Impeachment shall not extend further than to removal from Office, and disqualification to hold and enjoy any Office of honor, Trust or Profit under the United States: but the Party convicted shall nevertheless be liable and subject to Indictment, Trial, Judgment and Punishment, according to Law." There is nothing in that language providing an exemption from criminal prosecution for Presidents. The framers of the Constitution were mindful of exemptions, and knew how to provide for them. In fact, they did so in providing for a limited immunity from arrest for Senators and Representatives under Article I, Section 6 of the Constitution. They provided no exemption for the President.

The Constitutional remedy of impeachment is available against the President, Vice President, and all civil officers of the United States, which includes judges. In our history, there have been a number of instances when an incumbent judge or cabinet officer has been indicted, and even tried, judged and punished without first being impeached. Judge Kerner was a recent example of this process. It would strain common sense to hold that the words of the Constitution have one meaning for Presidents, but another meaning for other officials who are also subject to the impeachment process.

THE CONDUCT CHARGED IN ARTICLE II CONSTITUTES IMPEACHABLE CONDUCT

As I argued in committee, in opposition to a point of order against Article II, on Monday, July 29, 1974, in my opinion, this is the most important article being considered by the committee.

The offenses charged in this Article II are truly high crimes and misdemeanors within the purest meaning of those words as established in Anglo-American parliamentary law over a period of now some 600 years. The offenses charged against the President in this article are uniquely Presidential offenses. No one else can commit them. Anyone, the most lowly citizen, can obstruct justice. Anyone, the most lowly citizen, can violate any of the laws in our criminal code. But only the President can violate the oath of office of the President. Only the President can abuse the powers of the Office of the President.

When our Founding Fathers put our Constitution together, it was no accident that they separated the powers and it was no accident that they included the impeachment clause. Against the backdrop of 400 years of English constitutional history they realized the need to have a device, a constitutional means, of removing from office a chief magistrate who had violated his solemn oath of office. And I respectfully submit that the impeachment clause of our Constitution which we use now for only the second time against a President, is that means.

These are high crimes and misdemeanors, in that they are crimes and offenses against the very structure of the state, against the system of government, the system that has brought to the American people and has preserved for the American people the freedoms and liberties which we so cherish. This is uniquely a Presidential offense and the most important subject of these hearings.

There are many conscientious, dedicated, Americans who harbored a feeling of fear and apprehension at this proceeding. Some of them believed that the inquiry should not be held because it might harm the Presidency. There is no reason for that fear.

Only the President can harm the Presidency. No one but the President can destroy the Presidency. It is our responsibility, acting under the impeachment clause, to preserve and protect the Presidency as we preserve and protect every other part of our marvelous structure of government, and we do it through this impeachment process.

The American people want a government which they can honor and respect. They are entitled to a government which they can honor and respect. The American people want a President whom they can revere. They are entitled to a President whom they can revere.

I ask "Is not the violation of the solemn oath of office an impeachable offense?" It is not found in our criminal code. It is implicit in our Constitution. It is necessarily implicit in the Constitution for otherwise why would there be an oath of office?

EMOLUMENTS RECEIVED BY THE PRESIDENT

Article II, Section 1, Clause 6 of the U.S. Constitution forbids the receipt by the President, during his term of office, of "any other emolument from the United States,"—other than his fixed compensation.

"Emolument" is defined as "the profit arising from employment, usually in the form of compensation or perquisites."

The investigations by the House Committee on Government Operations, the General Accounting Office, the Internal Revenue Service, and the Joint Congressional Committee on Internal Revenue Taxation have all concluded that many of the expenditures on Mr. Nixon's private homes were for his personal benefit. They were paid for by agencies of the United States Government. I submit that, therefore, the money value of those expenditures constituted "other emolument from the United States" during Mr. Nixon's term of office, and are unconstitutional under the provisions of Article II, Section 1, Clause 6 of the Constitution. It follows that since they are unconstitutional, and *a fortiori*, unlawful, they cannot constitute "income" to Mr. Nixon received from the Federal government, and the problem is not disposed of by having the money value included as added "income" to Mr. Nixon with "income tax" paid thereon, for that would leave a "net after taxes", which itself would be an unconstitutional emolument.

There is no way under the U.S. Constitution that Mr. Nixon can receive and retain such emoluments. Therefore, it necessarily follows that he is holding the full money value of those expenditures as a constructive trustee for the United States, and that the matter cannot be resolved until he has paid the full money value thereof to the United States.

GEORGE E. DANIELSON.

SUPPLEMENTAL VIEWS OF MR. DRINAN

INTRODUCTION

Contemporary commentators and future historians will have reason, it seems to me, to raise the most serious questions as to why the House Judiciary Committee did not more adequately investigate the deliberate and persistent cover-up by President Nixon of the clandestine bombing which he personally authorized over the neutral nation of Cambodia between March 18, 1969 and May 1, 1970. From the beginning of the impeachment inquiry I persistently raised with the members and with the staff of the Committee the possibility of an impeachable offense based upon the usurpation of the power of Congress as well as the deception of Congress involved in the Cambodian bombing and the subsequent falsification of military records submitted to the U.S. Senate.

CAMBODIAN ISSUE ACCORDED LOW PRIORITY

The fact is that the House Judiciary Committee made its decision against the Cambodian bombing as an impeachable offense upon inadequate evidence. The concurring statement contained in this report by Congresswoman Holtzman, joined in by myself and several other members of the Committee, indicates that "the statistical information regarding [Cambodia] is incomplete because the inquiry staff declined to obtain it." Congresswoman Holtzman continues by stating that "unfortunately, the investigation in general of the secret Cambodian bombing was not pursued as fully by the staff as its seriousness required."

The fact of the matter is that not a single subpoena was issued in connection with the Cambodia question, not a single witness was summoned and no apparent attempt was made to compel the declassification of those documents essential to an investigation of the reasons why the air war in Cambodia was concealed from the American people until it was discovered quite by accident in July 1973.

I am not minimizing the seriousness and the gravity of the three articles of impeachment set forth and justified in this report. I have concurred in the judgment that all of them constitute impeachable offenses. At the same time is seems paradoxical that a bipartisan majority emerged for votes to impeach the President on the basis of strictly domestic offenses whereas a bipartisan majority did not emerge with respect to the presumably bipartisan role which the President fulfilled as Commander-in-Chief. Only history will be able to decide the reasons for this phenomenon. I feel compelled to state at this time, however, that I find it incongruous that a President be impeached for unlawful wiretapping but not for unlawful war making. Similarly, I find it disturbing that the Committee voted to impeach a President for concealing a burglary but not for concealing a massive bombing.

In the scant material in the Committee Report on the Cambodian question there is reference in a footnote to "the detailed findings of the Inquiry Staff concerning the bombing of Cambodia." Not everyone will agree that those findings are "detailed". The origins of those findings are described in this footnote as based on "all available sources of material". This contention is also open to question. A careful review of the written record of the debate in the Judiciary Committee on the Cambodian question indicates that many of the members did not have answers to the questions which in their judgment were essential to a decision on the impeachability of the President's conduct in ordering that information concerning bombing in Cambodia be withheld from Congress and the American people.

Members did not have that information because from the beginning of the impeachment inquiry the Cambodian question was given a very low priority. The members of the Judiciary Committee did not establish that low priority. Clearly the inherent seriousness of the matter could not justify the paucity of staff assigned to the Cambodian issue. Only history will be able to decide whether a Congress which funded a war in Indo-China even after it had repealed the Gulf of Tonkin Resolution in December, 1970, was so confused about its own role in the Vietnam War that it was unable or unwilling to delve into presidential conduct more shocking and more unbelievable than the conduct of any president in any war in all of American history.

THE PROPOSED ARTICLE ON IMPEACHMENT ON CAMBODIA

The proposed article of impeachment which was rejected by the Judiciary Committee on July 30, 1974, by a vote of 26 to 12 reads as follows:

> In his conduct of the office of President of the United States, Richard M. Nixon, in violation of his constitutional oath faithfully to execute the office of President of the United States and, to the best of his ability, preserve, protect, and defend the Constitution of the United States, and in disregard of his constitutional duty to take care that the laws be faithfully executed, on and subsequent to March 17, 1969, authorized, ordered and ratified the concealment from the Congress of the facts and the submission to the Congress of false and misleading statements concerning the existence, scope and nature of American bombing operations in Cambodia in derogation of the power of the Congress to declare war, to make appropriations and to raise and support armies, and by such conduct warrants impeachment and trial and removal from office.

The gravamen of this proposed article of impeachment is not the bombing itself nor even the secrecy of the bombing, but, rather, its concealment from the Congress. The concealment was carried out in a course of conduct by President Nixon which was a clear usurpation of the right of Congress to declare war.

It is overwhelmingly clear that the Framers of the Constitution granted to Congress exclusively "the power of the sword". Alexander Hamilton pointed out that the Constitution provides that it is "the exclusive province of Congress, when the nation is at peace, to change that state into a state of war." Similarly in the *Federalist Papers*, James Madison states:

> The power to declare war, including the power of judging the causes of war is fully and exclusively vested in the legislature; but the Executive has no right, in any case, to decide that question, whether or not there is a cause of declaring war.

One need not approach the ultimate scope of congressional power in the area of declaring war in order to recognize the unconstitutional conduct of the President in carrying out a policy of deception from March, 1969 until July 16, 1973,—more than four years after the bombing commenced. That deception included a violation of Article I, Section 9 of the Constitution which declares that "a regular statement and account of the receipts and expenditures of all public money shall be published from time to time." One of the delegates to the Constitutional Convention, Colonel Mason, stated during the Virginia ratifying convention of 1787 that he could not conceive of any situation in which the receipts and expenditures of public money ought to be concealed. "The people," he affirmed, "had a right to know the expenditures of their money." The President violated both the letter and spirit of that constitutional mandate by misrepresenting the expenditure of 145 million dollars for the bombing of Cambodia as having been spent in South Vietnam.

The article of impeachment reproduced above refers directly and exclusively to the massive cover-up of the facts during and after the secret bombing raids of 3,695 B52's over Cambodia carried on over a period of 14 months. Although the evidence suggests that these bombings were not successful in eliminating the alleged sanctuaries of the North Vietnamese in Cambodia, one need not dispute the claimed merits of these bombings in order to condemn their concealment. The proposed article of impeachment based on the secret bombing in Cambodia takes no position on the war in Indo-China. The resolution was not designed to separate those who approved of the war from those who disapproved. Indeed one can hold that the 3700 B52 sorties actually saved American lives in South Vietnam and still recognize that the cover-up of these bombings is such a serious offense against Congress and the Constitution that it reaches the level of impeachability.

PROPOSED JUSTIFICATIONS FOR CONCEALMENT

Those who would justify the withholding of information from the Congress and the country on the basis that the bombing of Cambodia was necessary to preserve the lives of American troops in South Vietnam cannot use that justification for the policy of deception which was continued until July 16, 1973,—more than four years after the bombing began. Indeed President Nixon never asserted any military justification for the secrecy and deception. The alleged justification of protecting Prince Sihanouk from embarrassment clearly ceased when Sihanouk was overthrown on March 18, 1970.

There was no military justification for maintaining secrecy about the Cambodian bombings. There was no diplomatic reason, at least after the overthrow of Sihanouk on March 18, 1970. The only reason for the deception of Congress and of the country was President Nixon's political objective of deceiving and quieting the anti-war movement. The President orchestrated a conspiracy to keep the lid on Cambodia until at least after the elections of November, 1972.

Those who would justify the deception of Congress on the grounds of national security contend that the alleged communication of the bombing in Cambodia to a handful of members of Congress satisfies the requirements of the Constitution. No one has ever revealed who communicated what information to the alleged 13 members of Congress who were reported to be advised about the secret bombing. In direct contradiction to the claim that some members of Congress knew about the bombing, there stands the testimony of General Wheeler on July 30, 1973 before the Senate Armed Services Committee in which the general reported that President Nixon had ordered him personally never to disclose the bombing of Cambodia to any member of Congress.

THE UNRAVELLING OF THE COVER-UP

The calculated cover-up of Cambodia like the cover-up of Watergate, unravelled by accident. According to Senator Symington, the acting Chairman of the Armed Services Committee, during the hearings in July and August 1973, he and other members of Congress heard of the secret bombings of Cambodia because of the circumstances he describes in these words.

> I would like to point out that the knowledge of this whole bombing of B52's in Cambodia resulted from a foreign correspondent in a small airplane going from Phnom Penh to Saigon seeing the craters that the B52's had made in Cambodia. If it had not been for that, there would have been no knowledge of the subject on the part of the American people . . .

This accidental unravelling of a calculated deception revealed the falsity of testimony given on a regular basis over a four year period by the highest military and civilian officials of the government. It is clear, moreover, that all of the persistent testimony on behalf of the cover-up of the bombing in Cambodia is directly traceable to the decree of the President that there should be absolute and abiding secrecy about the bombing in Cambodia. No other motivation except a presidential directive can explain the testimony of Secretary of the Army Stanley Resor on April 16, 1970, the testimony of General Earle Wheeler in May, 1970, and the report of Secretary of the Air Force Seamans in May, 1970, all of whom reported that no bombing strikes had occurred in Cambodia prior to May 1, 1970.

Unfortunately the staff of the House Judiciary Committee declined to investigate the unprecedented and indefensible falsification of military documents by Pentagon officials. All of the documents related to the 3,695 raids were altered to indicate that these attacks had occurred in South Vietnam rather than in Cambodia. Pentagon officials testified falsely to the Senate regularly and persistently. The Pentagon spokesman, Jerry Friedheim, distributed falsehoods to the press knowing them to be falsehoods. When confronted later, Mr. Friedheim said: "I knew at the time that it was wrong and I am sorry." The President never urged that Mr. Friedheim be fired and he was not. Mr. Friedheim's summary judgment of the long series of lies came to this: "We were not smart enough to foresee" that the secret bombing and falsification would inevitably be disclosed.

THE PRESIDENT'S RESPONSIBILITY

No plausible explanation of this deception is sustainable except the conclusion that it originated in a Presidential command that no disclosure ever be made of the clandestine Cambodian bombings. When the falsification of records became known in July, 1973, Dr. Kissinger deplored it. General Wheeler, the former chairman of the Joint Chiefs of Staff, expressed horror at the falsification of records but stated that if the President had ordered him to falsify them, "I would have done it." If all of the lying was done originally to diminish domestic opposition to the war in Vietnam it was indefensible. If Prince Sihanouk had agreed to the bombing and the lies were to protect him from the wrath of his own people, the deception was still indefensible.

One can come only to a single and inescapable conclusion: the deception and falsification was ordered by the President so that he could pursue the bombing without objection from anyone in the Congress or in the country. Independent of whether one approves of that massive bombing, the conduct of President Nixon simply cannot be said to satisfy the requirement of the Constitution that Congress appropriate all funds necessary for the waging of war.

The unconstitutionality of the conduct of President Nixon was cogently stated by Senator Symington in these words:

> I have been on this committee, this is my 21st year. I knew nothing whatsoever about this (the secret bombing of Cambodia). I put up the money. Apparently nobody knew about this except two or three Senators at the most. If we are asked to appropriate money for one thing and it is used for another, regardless of its effectiveness, that puts us in a pretty difficult position.
>
> I personally think it is unconstitutional, because you dropped over a hundred thousand tons on this country, and I had no idea you dropped one ton, nor did other members of the committee except those chosen few, all of whom, I might add, supported the war, which I once did and later changed in 1967.

Senator Harold E. Hughes, reflecting on the persistent deception engaged in by Pentagon officials about the Cambodian bombing came to these conclusions in a speech on the Senate floor:

> I deeply believe that the peril to our free institutions created by these official practices of official deceit and secret warfare are more ominous than any problem confronting our country.
>
> No group within our society, however well-intentioned, can be permitted to make the momentous decision to wage secret warfare while officially deceiving the Congress and the public.

CONCLUSION

The Framers of the Constitution came together in Philadelphia from May to September in 1787 in order to create a government where no one ever again would have to enter into an armed rebellion to vindicate his right to be free of tyranny. The framers of the Constitution deemed the ultimate tyranny to be war carried on illegally by the executive. Mr. Randolph of Virginia noted that the President would have great opportunities in the American system of abusing his power,—particularly in time of war. In order to prevent the Executive from engaging the entire nation in war, the Framers of the Constitution carefully diffused that power among both bodies of the Congress. The authors of the Constitution, after an extensive debate, gave the power to "declare" war to Congress and the power to "make" that war to the Executive. The Framers of the Constitution devised the remedy of impeachment for those members of the executive branch of government who would bring the ultimate tyranny of war on the people of America without the Congress officially and formally declaring that war.

The manner in which President Nixon unilaterally conducted an air war in Cambodia and the subsequent course of conduct in which he covered up that period of massive bombing in a neutral country cannot be justified by the Constitution, by the relevant laws, or by any traditional relationship between the Congress and the President in a period of war. The fact is that President Nixon, in the concealment and cover-up of the war in Cambodia, violated the most fundamental right of the Congress and usurped the most basic constitutional privileges of the people of America. He committed offenses for which the remedy of impeachment is uniquely suited and for which that extraordinary remedy was placed in the Constitution. Nothing in the exalted powers of the President as Commander-in-Chief can justify the manner in which President Nixon treated the Congress and the country when he entered into a course of conduct that began in March, 1969, two months after he became President, and terminated in July, 1973, to the embarrassment of the Pentagon and the White House. The dark series of events during that period and the habitual deceptions of the American people by the President constitute conduct, as outlined in the proposed Article IV of Impeachment, which rivals, if not surpasses, the lawless activity set forth in the first three articles of impeachment as outlined in this report.

It is exceedingly regrettable that the unconscionable and unconstitutional conduct of Richard Nixon with respect to the neutral nation of Cambodia was not also deemed by the Committee to be an impeachable offense. I can only hope that future generations will not interpret this decision of the Judiciary Committee as implied consent and sanction of such conduct.

ROBERT F. DRINAN.

SEPARATE AND ADDITIONAL VIEWS OF MR. RANGEL, CONCERNING ARTICLES OF IMPEACHMENT AGAINST THE PRESIDENT OF THE UNITED STATES, RICHARD M. NIXON

INTRODUCTION

These separate and additional views are submitted in an effort to establish the historical record of the facts and circumstances surrounding the resignation of the 37th President of the United States. The 38 members of the Judiciary Committee have recorded their support for Article I of the three articles of impeachment voted by the Committee clearly established the existence of clear and convincing evidence of the President's involvement in impeachable crimes; had not the President resigned, it is clear that he would have been impeached by the House of Representatives and convicted in the Senate for his criminal activities.

This record needs to be established for the sake of historical accuracy in view of the fact that even on the day of his resignation President Nixon attempted to convey to the American people the impression that his resignation was caused by erosion of his political base as a result of some poor judgments he made during his term of office. The record, as set forth in the Committee report makes it abundantly clear that Richard M. Nixon violated his oath of office as President of the United States, that he committed impeachable crimes, and that on the available evidence he would have been impeached by the House of Representatives.

For only the second time in the one hundred and ninety-eight years of our Constitutional history the House of Representatives is presented with articles of impeachment against the President of the United States. After seven months of staff preparation, ten weeks of concentrated presentation of the evidence to the members of the Committee, and a week of debate, the Committee on the Judiciary by majority vote has recommended three articles of impeachment to the House. I voted in Committee for these three articles and associate myself with the majority report setting forth the recommended articles of impeachment and the evidence underlying them. I wish, however, to set forth my separate views supporting the articles of impeachment voted by the Committee and my dessenting views concerning the two articles of impeachment that were presented to the Committee, but rejected, and another possible article of impeachment that was not voted upon by the Committee.

SUPPORT OF THE ARTICLES OF IMPEACHMENT VOTED BY THE COMMITTEE

The articles of impeachment which the Committee on the Judiciary presents to the House of Representatives charge Richard M. Nixon with the following high crimes and misdemeanors against the Presidency and against the people of the United States: obstruction of justice in his participation in an effort to impede the investigation of the Watergate burglary and related crimes; abuse of power and misuse of the Office of the Presidency to achieve political and personal gain; and contempt of the Congress by his refusal to cooperate with the Constitutionally based and lawfully mandated investigation of the Committee on the Judiciary. We are asking the members of the House of Representatives to examine the evidence and find, as we did, that these offenses are sufficiently proven to mandate the impeachment of the President and his trial in the Senate to determine whether he should be removed from office.

I also want to ask the members of the House to consider a responsibility which weighed upon us on the Committee on the Judiciary as we went through the great mass of evidence gathered by the impeachment inquiry staff—a responsibility to act to protect the Constitution, and with it our democratic system of government, from the type of usurpation of power which would have successfully occurred under this President if it had not been for the conscientious performance of his job by Frank Wills, a black, poorly paid night watchman at the Watergate on the night of June 17, 1972.

As a black American, I have been especially struck by the poetic justice of the discovery of the Watergate burglars by a black man. Black people were not considered by the Founding Fathers of this nation when they undertook to issue the Declaration of Independence in the name of freedom. Although a black man was among the first to fall in the American revolution and blacks fought alongside the revolutionary heroes for freedom, we were not included when citizenship was defined in the Constitution. We have spent the one hundred and ninety-eight year history of this nation trying to become covered by the guarantees of freedom and equality contained in the Constitution. Despite the ending of legal slavery with the Emancipation Proclamation, for which we had to wait eighty-seven years, black Americans have had to win their social and economic freedom in a revolutionary struggle which has characterized our American experience and which continues to the present day. It is only in the last two decades that black Americans have made significant progress in extending the coverage of Constitutional guarantees to us. We therefore value, perhaps to a greater extent than most Americans, the guarantees of freedom and equality expressed in the Constitution and the structure of government which provides, through democratic participation, for the will of the people to prevail.

The crimes to which Richard M. Nixon was a willing accessory threatened the system of law and justice, and for this alone they are impeachable offenses; but more fundamentally, this President has undermined the very basis of our government. If we do not impeach him for this, then we will be accessories to his crime and jointly responsible for raising the Presidency above the law.

What Richard Nixon has done is to substitute power for law, to define and attempt to impose a standard of amorality upon our government that gives full rein to the rich and powerful to prey upon the poor and weak. What Richard Nixon has done is to demean the importance of national security by using it as a handy alibi to protect common burglars. What Richard Nixon has done is attempt to stain the reputation of the agencies of our government by using them to obstruct justice, harass political enemies, illegally spy upon citizens, and cover-up crimes. What Richard Nixon has done is show contempt for the Congress by refusing to provide information necessary for the Constitutionally legitimate conduct of an inquiry into the question of impeachment by the Committee on the Judiciary of the House of Representatives. What Richard Nixon has done is threaten the Constitution by declaring himself and the Office of the Presidency beyond the reach of law, the Congress, and the courts.

To a large extent he has succeeded. We have reached a state in our national life where responsible members of Congress argue that the President does not have to account for his actions to anyone or recognize any higher authority. Thus we stand on the brink of total subversion of our Constitutional government and dictatorship. A few weeks ago the Supreme Court of the United States ruled unanimously that the President's claim of executive privilege could not justify his refusal to provide the United States District Court for the District of Columbia and the Special Prosecutor with evidence necessary for the successful completion of the investigation and trial of charges of the involvement of White House and other high Administration officials in the Watergate cover-up The contempt in which the law is held by Richard Nixon was never more evident than in his persistent refusal to state that he would abide by the decision of the Supreme Court. On the day of the decision the American people had to wait for hours for the announcement that the President would comply with the unanimous decision of the United States Supreme Court. Some of the President's defenders were even heard to praise the President for his decision to comply with the Supreme Court decision, as if Richard Nixon was not subject to the Supreme Court, and the law of the land, unless he wanted to be. If we do not act to impeach this President, will we still have a democracy?

We all have a large stake in preserving our democracy, but I maintain that those without power in our society, the black, the brown, the poor of all colors, have the largest stake—not because we have the most to lose, but because we have worked the hardest, and given the most, for what we have achieved. The framers of the Constitution perhaps never conceived that the Republic they created would be defended by the underprivileged, but this has happened in every war in which this nation has been involved. The sons of slaves have joined the sons of poor immigrants on the front lines in disproportionate numbers to defend our democracy. I went to Korea from the streets of Harlem and fought, although I had no understanding of what that socalled "police action" was all about. But I had sworn on oath to defend the Constitution, and I went and fought to do so. Richard M. Nixon swore that oath on two inauguration days, but he had dishonored it. We have all sworn that same oath and we must live up to it by voting the articles of impeachment of Richard M. Nixon voted by the Committee on the Judiciary.

DISSENTING VIEWS CONCERNING THE TWO ARTICLES PRESENTED TO, BUT NOT VOTED BY THE COMMITTEE

I do not believe, however, that we will have fulfilled our Constitutional duty if we vote impeachment solely on the basis of the three articles recommended by the Committee. The very nature of the impeachment process, we have recognized in the Judiciary Committee, infuses our decision on the grounds for impeachment with the weight of historical precedent. We are not merely making a judgment on the conduct of the Richard M. Nixon Presidency, we are making judgments that will determine the limits of Presidential, legislative, and judicial power. For this reason I supported the two articles of impeachment which were recommended to the Committee on the Judiciary, but which have not been recommended by the Committee to the House. These two articles, based upon the President's authorization of the secret bombing of Cambodia without the lawful direction of the Congress and the President's use of his office for his self-enrichment in derogation of the Constitutional provision forbidding the taking of emoluments, are as equally indicative of the President's contempt for the law as the three articles recommended by the Committee. The Presidential conduct to which these articles are addressed is as potentially destructive of the Constitution as the President's obstruction of justice, abuse of power and contempt of Congress even though the particular activity involved did not appear to offend as large a number of members of the Judiciary Committee as the activity addressed in the first three articles.

In the last twenty-five years we have become accustomed, it appears, to national involvement in undeclared war. The Korean police action, the invasion of Lebanon, the Bay of Pigs, the intervention in the Dominican Republic, and the Indochina war were all instances of American military involvement initiated by an American President without the Constitutionally required declaration of war by the Congress. In each of these instances the Congress acquiesced in the Presidential action, thus becoming a party to the erosion of the Congressional power to declare war. We in the Congress must share the blame for the taking on to the Presidency of a power to involve our nation militarily that is not contemplated by the Constitution. Yet the secret bombing of Cambodia authorized by President Nixon during 1969 and 1970 is different from these earlier examples of Presidential war making. Instead of the traditional notification of and consultation with Congressional leadership, President Nixon moved unilaterally to authorize the bombing of a neutral country. The evidence that has been presented of Congressional notification is not convincing. Selected members of the House and Senate were allegedly told that the bombing was going on, yet none of the men supposedly informed clearly remembers the notification. Whatever notice was given, it was certainly inadequate to provide the Congress as a whole with the information that was needed to articulate a judgment of the military and diplomatic wisdom of the President's action. The information was insufficient, and its dissemination so controlled, that it was impossible for a position in opposition to be developed. This is Presidential war making, and if we are to preserve the integrity of the Constitution's reservation of the war-making power to the Congress, if we are to prevent future Presidents from committing the lives of American youth to adventurous forays, we have a duty to seriously consider President Nixon's authorization of the secret bombing of Cambodia as an abuse of Presidential power constituting an impeachable offense.

Similarly, to check the potential excesses of future Presidents, the members of the House of Representatives should move to impeach Richard M. Nixon for willful taking of government property for his self-enrichment and his evasion of his lawful tax liability.

Article II, Section I, clause 7 of the Constitution provides that the President shall not receive "any . . . emolument from the United States" during his term of office other than a stated compensation for his services. This explicit Constitutional prohibition applies solely to the President. The Founding Fathers recognized the potential for self-enrichment in the Presidency and provided this language to prevent "powers delegated for the purpose of promoting the happiness of a community" from being "perverted to the advancement of the personal emoluments of the agents of the people".[1] From the wealth of evidence gathered by the investigation of the Government Operations Committee into unlawful expenditures of government funds on President Nixon's private properties at Key Biscayne, Florida and San Clemente, California and presented to the Committee on the Judiciary, an article of impeachment was drawn charging Richard M. Nixon with violating the emoluments clause of the Constitution by knowingly receiving the benefits of expenditures on this personal properties. Although the Judiciary Committee did not recommend this Article to the House, I urge its consideration by the full House.

Summarizing from the staff report on the evidence on the question of the President's violation of the emoluments clause, the evidence presented to the Committee on the Judiciary shows that since Richard M. Nixon became President the General Services Administration (GSA) has spent approximately $701,000 directly on his San Clemente property and $575,000 directly on his Key Biscayne property for capital expenses, equipment, and maintenance. The evidence before the Committee further establishes that substantial expenditures for improvements and maintenance services on the President's properties were made by GSA that are unrelated to the lawful duty of the GSA to make expenditures at the direction of the Secret Service for the installation of security devices and equipment on the private property of the President or others to protect the President. Some of these expenditures were made by the GSA at the direction of the President or his representatives, with no Secret Service request. Others were made after Secret Service requests, but included substantial amounts to meet aesthetic or personal preferences of the President and his family. Yet others, while they served security purposes, involved items that are normally paid for by a homeowner, such as the replacement of worn-out or obsolete equipment or fixtures and routine landscape maintenance. The staff of the Joint Committee on Internal Revenue Taxation concluded that more than $92,000 of expenditures on the

---

[1] III Elliott, *The Debates on the Adoption of the Federal Constitution,* 117 (reprint of 2d edition) (Randolph).

President's properties was for his personal benefit and constituted income to him (Joint Committee Report, p. 201). The Internal Revenue Service concluded that the President had realized $62,000 in such imputed income (HJC Tax Report, Appendix 10).

The evidence presented to the Committee on the Judiciary shows that President Nixon participated in an effort to evade his full income tax liability in 1969 by claiming a huge deduction for a gift of Presidential papers that was actually not made until after the date of final eligibility for claiming a deduction for such a gift.

On December 30, 1969 President Nixon signed the Tax Reform Act of 1969 into law. That Act included a provision eliminating the tax deduction for contributions of collection of private papers made to the government or to charitable organizations after July 25, 1969. On April 10, 1970 the President, who is an attorney who in the past has engaged in tax practice, signed his income tax return for 1969, claiming a deduction for the donation to the National Archives of pre-Presidential personal papers allegedly worth $576,000. The President and his attorney went over the return page by page and discussed the tax consequences of the gift of papers deduction. (Kalmbach testimony, 3 HJC 671) An appraisal valuing the donated papers at that amount and a sheet describing the gift were attached to the return. These documents, which constitute part of the return signed by the President assert that the gift had been made on March 27, 1969.

There can be no doubt, the impeachment inquiry staff report on this matter concludes, that the President knew that the Tax Reform Act required that, for the claim of deduction to be valid, a gift must be completed by July 25, 1969. It is also clear that the President knew that his return indicated that the gift had been made on March 27, 1969. The Internal Revenue Service has disallowed this deduction. The IRS found that, as a matter of fact, the gift of papers was not made on or before July 25, 1969. On the basis of its investigation, the IRS concluded that the President was negligent in the preparation of its taxes and assessed a negligence penalty of 5%. Because the IRS did not assess a civil penalty for fraud, those members of the Judiciary Committee who opposed this article during debate declared that the IRS had reached a definitive conclusion that no civil fraud was involved, thus exonerating the President. It is clear, however, that the IRS investigation of the President's negligence was less than complete out of that agency's deference to his office. The President was never interviewed, nor were others with important information concerning the preparation of the return such as John Ehrlichman. Thus the IRS was unable to make a determination on the question of fraud. Similarly, the Joint Committee on Internal Revenue Taxation's investigation of the 1969 return, after concluding that the gift of papers had not been made by July 25, 1969 as claimed in the report, stopped short of addressing the question of fraud out of deference to the Judiciary Committee's impeachment inquiry.

The Judiciary Committee's impeachment inquiry staff did address the question of criminal tax fraud in its investigation and, in my opinion, found evidence that the President did not file a false tax return for 1969 through mistake or negligence, but knowingly participated in a scheme to defraud the United States Government by claiming falsely that he had made his gift of papers prior to July 25, 1969, the date of expiration of the eligibility for valid tax deductions for such gifts.

The Judiciary Committee heard the expert testimony of Fred Folsom, a consultant to the Committee who for 24 years was an attorney in the Criminal Section of the Justice Department's Tax Division and chief of that section for 12 years. Considering all the circumstances surrounding the alleged gift of papers and its inclusion as a deduction on the President's 1969 return, including the lack of a satisfactory response from the taxpayer, it was the judgment of Folsom that in this case "the case of an ordinary taxpayer, on the facts as we know them in this instance, the case would be referred out for presentation to a Grand Jury for prosecution." (Folsom testimony, June 21, 1974, Tr. 1976).

It is clear to me from the evidence that President Nixon directed or knowingly received the benefit of improper expenditures on his San Clemente and Key Biscayne properties in violation of the law and the emoluments clause of the Constitution. It is equally clear that Richard Nixon had knowledge of and bears full responsibility for the willful evasion of his income tax obligation.

Richard M. Nixon did this while preaching economy in government and imposing devastating cuts on vital social programs in his budgets and through the impoundment of Congressionally appropriated funds. He enriched himself at the taxpayers' expense while children were going hungry and uncared for, the poor and elderly were being denied adequate housing, and growing hope was being turned into despair as Federal assistance to help people out of the bondage of poverty was being brutally terminated in the name of economy. Perhaps the greatest indictment against Richard Nixon that can be voted by the House is that by his actions he created a moral vacuum in the Office of the Presidency and turned that great office away from the service of the people toward the service of his own narrow, selfish interests.

CONCLUSION

As I stated in my opening statement in the Judiciary Committee's debate on the Articles of Impeachment which are now before the House, I do not approach the impeachment of Richard M. Nixon with a heavy heart. I regard the impeachment of this President, the impeachment of any President, as a grave Constitutional responsibility that cannot be taken lightly. I am saddened by the many personal tragedies that are the legacy of Watergate. A number of otherwise honorable and decent men let their hunger for power and their devotion to a leader overcome their integrity, judgment, and sense of responsibility to the law and the national interest. Because of this, their careers lie in ruin. Yet at the same time I am heartened, and my faith in the Constitution and in our democracy is strengthened by the now irrefutable proof that the Constitution is not a dead instrument, that truly no man is above the law, and that if a President acts unlawfully he can be inpeached and sent to the Senate for a trial to determine whether he should be removed from office. I am encouraged that our Constitution works, for I am especially dependent upon its protection. I am encouraged that the American system permits a black nightwatchman and the son of an Italian immigrant family sitting as a District Court judge, each through applying the law, to be the instruments of uncovering the most extensive and highly placed corruption in our national history and the bringing to justice of the most powerful men in our society. I am encouraged that what the Judiciary Committee has done, and what the full House must now do, in voting Articles of Impeachment against Richard M. Nixon, will begin a process of restoring the faith of the American people in our government.

CHARLES B. RANGEL.

ADDITIONAL VIEWS OF MS. HOLTZMAN

In view of President Nixon's resignation on August 9, 1974, several footnotes should be added to the Judiciary Committee report.

First, Richard Nixon's resignation was in response to the certainty of his impeachment, conviction and removal from office. The evidence was overwhelming.

Second, the Watergate break-in—which precipitated his downfall—was not an accident. It was the logical outgrowth of President Nixon's repeated condonation of wiretapping and break-ins for political purposes. That pattern of lawlessness began only four months after President Nixon first took office when he authorized a program of illegal wire-taps and permitted them to be used for political purposes. It continued with his adoption of the Huston Plan calling for routine use of criminal methods—wire-tapping, break-ins and mail openings—for political intelligence gathering. It continued with his creation of an extra-legal investigations unit in the White House (the Plumbers) whose members engaged in covert political surveillance and an illegal break-in, later condoned by Richard Nixon, to obtain political information.

Given President Nixon's long-standing approval of unlawful action for political purposes in a non-campaign context, his men had every reason to believe that when the election campaign began they would be allowed, even expected, to resort to illegal methods to obtain political information—and they did. In this sense, at the very least, President Nixon authorized the Watergate break-in and was responsible for it.

Third, the Watergate break-in was not an isolated abuse of Richard Nixon's re-election campaign; it was but one element in a pervasive pattern of immoral, unethical and criminal conduct. Contempt for the electoral process spawned Segretti's activities (libelous campaign materials distributed on opponents' stationery), Sedan Chairs I and II (spies in opponents' campaigns), "black advance" operations (disruption of opponents' campaigns), illegal corporate contributions, and offers of ambassadorships and high milk price supports in return for political contributions.

Nor was President Nixon's abuse of his powers restricted to attacks on the Constitutional freedoms of the American citizens and his political opponents. He also systematically arrogated to himself the powers of Congress; he waged a secret war in the neutral country of Cambodia; he unlawfully impounded funds appropriated by Congress; he attempted to dismantle social programs mandated by law.

The conclusion is inescapable that Richard Nixon engaged personally in wrongful acts, allowed and encouraged his subordinates to do the same, and indeed stretched the Constitution beyond its breaking point, because he felt he would not have to answer for his conduct. Concealment, deception, and cover-up became a way of life in the Oval Office.

This impeachment proceeding—in the thoroughness, fairness and gravity of its approach, as well as the strength of its findings—stands as a warning to all future Presidents that they will be held accountable to their oaths of office. Nonetheless, it will be an empty warning unless the American public and the Congress continue to demand from their Presidents and other public officials respect for the Constitution, acknowledgment of the supremacy of law and commitment to decency and honesty.

ELIZABETH HOLTZMAN.

DISSENTING VIEWS OF MS. HOLTZMAN, JOINED BY MESSRS. KASTENMEIER, EDWARDS, HUNGATE, CONYERS, WALDIE, DRINAN, RANGEL, OWENS AND MEZVINSKY

PROPOSED ARTICLE IV: SECRET BOMBING OF CAMBODIA

We believe that Richard Nixon committed a high crime and misdemeanor when, as President, he unilaterally ordered the bombing of Cambodia and deliberately concealed this bombing from Congress and the American public, through a series of false and deceptive statements, for more than four years. Proposed Article IV—which would impeach Mr. Nixon for these acts—is one of the most serious the Committee on the Judiciary considered during the course of its inquiry.

It is difficult to imagine Presidential misconduct more dangerously in violation of our constitutional form of government than Mr. Nixon's decision, secretly and unilaterally, to order the use of American military power against another nation, and to deceive and mislead the Congress about this action. By depriving Congress of its constitutional role in the war-making and appropriations processes, the President denied to the American people the most basic right of self-government: the right to participate, through their elected representatives, in the decisions that gravely affect their lives.

The framers of our Constitution were well aware of the horrors of war. They knew it could impoverish a country; they knew the toll it could take in death and ruined lives; they knew the destruction it could wreak. They were therefore careful to construct checks and balances so that a decision to go to war would never be made casually or lightly, without a national consensus. As Jefferson put it, to check the "dog of war," it was necessary to take the war-making power out of the hands of a single person, the President, and place it in the hands of Congress where a majority vote—arrived at after debate and deliberation—would be required.

The decision to make war has enormous human, economic and ethical implications. It is intolerable in a constitutional democracy to permit that decision to be made in secret by a President and to be hidden through deception from the law-making bodies and the public.

For that reason the Committee should have found that President Nixon, in waging a secret war in Cambodia, committed a high crime and misdemeanor.

THE PRESIDENT'S ROLE

The central facts with regard to Richard Nixon's role in the concealment of the bombing of Cambodia are undisputed.

On March 17, 1969—less than 2 months after he took office—President Nixon authorized a series of B-52 bombing strikes in Cambodia.

The bombing began on March 18, and in the succeeding 14 months, 3,695 B-52 sorties were flown, dropping 105,837 tons of bombs, at a cost of more than 150 million dollars.

President Nixon's decision to conceal the Cambodia bombing operations from the Congress was an integral part of the decision to bomb, made at the same time. On several occasions thereafter he ordered the highest secrecy for the raids and forbade their disclosure.

In accordance with President Nixon's instructions, the top officials in his administration, including the Secretaries of Defense and State, two Chairmen of the Joint Chiefs of Staff and the Chief of Staff for the Air Force, made false and misleading statements to the Congress, even though their testimony was usually given under the cloak of top secret communications. In order to carry out President Nixon's directions, the Defense Department falsified its own classified records and submitted false reports to Congress based on these records.

President Nixon personally misrepresented to the Congress the facts concerning the bombing of Cambodia when, on February 25, 1971, he stated in his Foreign Policy Report to Congress:

> In Cambodia we pursued the policy of the previous administration until North Vietnamese actions after Prince Sihanouk was deposed made this impossible.

This policy of deception continued until July 16, 1973, more than four years after the bombing began.[1]

When the secret Cambodia bombing was finally exposed, President Nixon told the American people, in his August, 1973, press conference, that the secrecy had been necessary. He thus ratified and approved the policy of concealment and deception, a policy which he had earlier ordered.

PURPORTED JUSTIFICATION FOR SECRECY

The bombing of Cambodia was initiated only two months after Richard Nixon became President in 1969. The concealment of that bombing and deception of the Congress continued uninterrupted for more than *four* years—and persisted even after all American troops had been withdrawn from Vietnam and our prisoners had been returned.

President Nixon has attempted to justify this deceit on diplomatic grounds: that without the secrecy, Prince Sihanouk, the ruler of Cambodia, would have been compelled to abandon his position of "affirmative acquiescence" and publicly protest the bombing strikes. No military justification for the secrecy and deception has been asserted. The V.C. and North Vietnamese knew they were being bombed. The only people who did not know about the bombing operations were Members of Congress and the American people.

Assuming, for the moment, that protecting Prince Sihanouk was a legitimate justification for the deception of Congress and the American people, that justification ceased when Sihanouk was overthrown on March 18, 1970. After that date there was no justification for secrecy or deception. Nonetheless, for three years *after* the fall of Sihanouk, Mr. Nixon persistently lied about the bombing.

---

[1] In fact, absent persistent efforts in the Senate to uncover the full truth about American military activities in Southeast Asia, the facts regarding American bombing operations in Cambodia might still be secret.

Thus, on April 30, 1970 (two months after Sihanouk's overthrow and 13 months after the bombing had commenced), in announcing the invasion of Cambodia by American ground troops, President Nixon told the following lie to the American public in a televised address:

> American policy . . . has been to scrupulously respect the neutrality of the Cambodian people.

*   *   *   *   *   *   *

> For five years, neither the United States nor South Vietnam has moved against these enemy sanctuaries because we did not wish to violate the territory of a neutral nation.

Again, on June 30, 1970, President Nixon repeated the lie:

> For five years, American and allied forces—to preserve the concept of Cambodian neturality and to confine the conflict in Southeast Asia—refrained from moving against those sanctuaries.

Because Prince Sihanouk was no longer in office at the time of these Presidential statements, there was no justification for these or subsequent falsehoods.

The fact that the deception went on for years after any purported justification ceased to exist substantially impeaches what little validity that justification may have had for the period prior to March 18, 1970, when Sihanouk was still ruler.[2]

In any event, no authority exists for the proposition that the explicit provisions of the Constitution regarding the war-making and appropriations powers of Congress may be overridden by a President in the interest of protecting a foreign prince.

ARGUMENTS OFFERED AGAINST THE ARTICLE

In the course of debate on this Article, many Members of the Judiciary Committee conceded that President Nixon's deception was improper. The majority of those who voted against the Article, however, appeared to do so for reasons not directly related to the offense charged. Rather, they referred in the debate to assertions that Congress had acquiesced in the bombing or would have if it had been disclosed, that some Members of Congress had been notified of the secret bombing, that former Presidents had acted similarly, and that the recently enacted War Powers Resolution somehow alleviated the problem of future offenses. Examination of these arguments, however, demonstrates that they do not provide a viable defense to impeachment under Article IV.

1. The President's defenders contended that Congress ratified the secret bombing operations in Cambodia through the passage of various appropriations measures.

In fact, there was *no* ratification of this bombing. Congress passed on the Indochina war for the last time on June 29, 1973, when it ordered an August 15th cut-off date for all bombing. The secret bombing of Cambodia did not become known until July 16th—two weeks later. There is no way in which Congress could have ratified actions of which it was unaware.

---

[2] The evidence concerning Sihanouk's alleged acquiescence in the bombing is inconclusive at best.

2. Other Members opposed to Article IV argued that the disclosure of the Cambodia bombing operations to selected Members of Congress constituted sufficient notification to Congress and satisfied the Constitutional requirement.

This position is not supported by the facts or the law. According to the Department of Defense, President Nixon, and newspaper reports, thirteen Members of Congress were allegedly advised about the secret bombing. Of this number, three are deceased, three have denied being informed, and only four definitely recall being told. No record has been found of these briefings. There is no evidence that any Representative or Senator was fully informed of the nature, extent and purpose of the secret bombing or the reasons for its secrecy. In fact, the evidence suggests otherwise. Thus, Senator Stennis, Chairman of the Senate Armed Services Committee and the only Member who has spoken to the issue, specifically stated that he was given "no indication of the massiveness of the bombing."

It is significant, too, that whatever procedures for notification were used in this case, they were not those established and regularly followed for the handling of the most highly secret matters such as the CIA budget and its intelligence activities, nuclear research and new weapons development.[3]

In any event, selective notification to persons who supported President Nixon's war policy hardly satisfied the Constitutional requirement of Congressional participation in appropriations and war-making. That mandate of the Constitution—to require legislative debate and decision on grave matters such as the bombing of a neutral country—was frustrated by the concealment of the Cambodia bombing from the Congress regardless of the knowledge, or even consent, of a few members.

3. It was also argued that the Cambodia bombing aided President Nixon's efforts to end American involvement in the Vietnam War, and that, therefore, Congress would have approved it.

We do not question whether the Congress would have approved the bombing had it been informed. It might well have done so. On the other hand, Congress might have chosen to impose limitations on such actions, as it did with regard to American ground operations in Cambodia, and later, with regard to all other bombing in Cambodia.

The question is not what Congress would have decided had it not been deceived, but whether Mr. Nixon had the right to order that deception. He clearly did not.

4. Another argument advanced on behalf of President Nixon is that other Chief Executives, notably President Johnson, deceived the American people about the Vietnam War, and, thus, President Nixon should not be made to answer for wrongs that others have also committed.

The simple answer to this proposition is that the existence of prior misconduct does not justify its continuation or repetition, and that the

---

[3] Under such procedures, secret matters are treated as "classified line items," hidden in the Federal budget, but accessible to the appropriate committees of Congress. These procedures would certainly have been adequate to meet whatever legitimate need for secrecy existed. For example, these procedures were used to report secret ground operations in Laos, begun under President Johnson, providing full disclosure to all the Members of the relevant House and Senate committees.

unsanctioned wrongdoings of some do not justify the misdeeds of others. This Committee has firmly rejected the notion that because other Presidents may have abused their powers, the abuses of President Nixon are acceptable.

Moreover, the deception in prior administrations was not related to the very fact of U.S. involvement as in the case of Cambodia, but to the purposes and motives of the disclosed involvement. When the Congress is misled about the purpose of governmental conduct, it can, at least, review the facts independently and adopt or change that conduct. If, however, Congress is unaware of military action, it has no way to decide whether that action should be allowed to continue.

In addition, in this inquiry we are engaged in setting standards of conduct for Presidents. We should make it clear that Presidential lying and deception, in derogation of the Constitutional powers of Congress, are intolerable. James Iredell, one of the first Supreme Court Justices, made this point in the course of debate on the impeachment clause of the Constitution when he said:

The President must certainly be punishable for giving false information to the Senate.

5. The final opposing argument advanced in the Committee debate was that the War Powers Resolution enacted by Congress in November, 1973, is a sufficient deterrent against repetition of such activity in the future and that, therefore, impeachment of President Nixon on this ground was unnecessary.

This argument is a thin reed. Do its proponents believe, analogously, that the fact Congress is considering a bill to increase the penalties for obstruction of justice bars impeachment of President Nixon under the obstruction count of Article I?

The War Powers Resolution cannot and does not provide any deterrent to secret decisions by a President to institute war in a neutral nation. If a President would violate the clear mandate of the Constitution, the passage of a mere statute reasserting those Constitutional proscriptions can add nothing further in the way of deterrence.

The sole remedy which Congress can employ to bring a President to account for usurpation of the war-making and appropriations powers is impeachment. Only the use of that power is an effective deterrent; and, failure to employ it, when necessary, sets a dangerous precedent.

CONCLUSION

In these proceedings we have sought to return to the fundamental limitations on Presidential power contained in the Constitution and to reassert the right of the people to self-government through their elected representatives within that Constitutional framework.

The Constitution does not permit the President to nullify the war-making and appropriations powers given to the Congress. Secrecy and deception which deny to the Congress its lawful role are destructive of the basic right of the American people to participate in their government's life-and-death decisions. Adoption of Article IV would give notice to all future Presidents that the American people and the Congress may not be excluded from those decisions.

By failing to recommend the impeachment of President Nixon for the deception of Congress and the American public as to an issue as grave as the systematic bombing of a neutral country, we implicitly accept the argument that any ends—even those a President believes are legitimate—justify unconstitutional means. We cannot permit a President to sidestep constitutional processes simply because he finds them cumbersome.

This Committee has refused to accept that argument elsewhere in the course of our inquiry; we should not do so here. It is inherent in any government committed to democracy that the representatives of the people must be permitted a voice in the great decisions of state, even if a President believes in good faith that the course of the democratic process itself will make it more difficult or even impossible to achieve the desired goal.

ELIZABETH HOLTZMAN.
BOB KASTENMEIER.
DON EDWARDS.
WILLIAM L. HUNGATE.
JOHN CONYERS, Jr.
JEROME R. WALDIE.
ROBERT F. DRINAN.
CHARLES B. RANGEL.
WAYNE OWENS.
EDWARD MEZVINSKY.

ADDITIONAL SEPARATE VIEWS OF MR. HUNGATE

I have joined in the foregoing dissenting views on proposed Article IV because I think they lay down the guidelines to which the Congress should adhere, and the statement is generally consonant with my views. I do not mean to indicate that President Nixon is the first or only Chief Executive to exceed what I consider the appropriate boundaries of the war-making powers. Nor would I assert that the Congress has circumspectly met its responsibilities and opportunities to checkrein the Executive in his use of these powers.

When the question is directly presented to us, as here, the problem as I see it is that if we do not condemn it, we may be seen to have condoned it, and I fear the ultimate consequences of this to the Republic.

WILLIAM L. HUNGATE.

ADDITIONAL VIEWS OF MR. OWENS

I concur with the majority views expressed in this Report and support the Judiciary Committee's recommendation to the House of Representatives that it vote to impeach the President and send him to trial in the Senate on the basis of the findings reflected in the three Articles of Impeachment.

These Articles of Impeachment are the product of eight months of deliberation and intense work by the Committee. During this period of time I have studied the evidence before the Committee very carefully. I have participated in every single presentation of evidence. I have listened to every single witness.

As a result of this study, I have concluded that impeachment of a president is a grave act, to be undertaken only in the most extreme of circumstances. In my view, impeachable conduct is presidential action which seriously violates the trust and responsibilities of that high Constitutional office. It need not be conduct prohibited by criminal statute, though it must be clearly offensive—that is, known to be wrong by the person who commits it at the time it was committed. It could be a substantial abuse of power, blatantly unethical conduct, or a flagrant violation of Constitutional duties. But it must not be a simple matter of disagreement over policies or politics. In the final analysis must be a violation of a principle of conduct which members of th.. House determine should be applied to all future presidents and established as a Constitutional precedent.

Each member of Congress must determine for himself whether the evidence is sufficient to call the President to account before the United States Senate, whose Constitutional role is that of the final judge. I believe that we *must* vote to impeach if we believe the evidence that the President committed an impeachable offense is clear and convincing and would support conviction of the President during a Senate trial.

Our Committee's task during these hearings has been made easier because we have had the benefit of the views of the President's attorney on the sufficiency and meaning of the evidence, and we have had a partial presentation of the President's legal and evidentiary defense both by Mr. St. Clair and by the acting minority counsel to the Committee. This assistance has been scholarly and helpful.

However, much of the relevant evidence has been wrongfully and unconstitutionally withheld from this Committee by the President, preventing it and the House of Representatives from making a judgment on all of the facts. To a very great extent, the President has chosen the evidence which we shall see. We thus can assume for purposes of this decision, that all of the evidence which is favorable to the President is now before us. We can also reasonably infer, as any civil court would instruct its jury, that the additional evidence we have sought has been denied because it is detrimental to the President's case.

On the basis of all the evidence, I am persuaded that the President has knowingly engaged in conduct which constitutes impeachable offenses under the requirements of the Constitution, and that he should now be called to account before the United States Senate.

I support each of the three Articles of Impeachment as agreed upon by the House Judiciary Committee.

ARTICLE I: THE WATERGATE COVER-UP

I find the evidence convincing that the President knowingly and willfully directed and participated in a cover-up of the Watergate break-in. There is clear proof that the President made false statements to investigators; withheld evidence from the authorities; counseled witnesses to make false statements; interfered with the investigations of the FBI, the Justice Department, and the Special Prosecutor; approved the payment of money and attempted to offer clemency and other favorable treatment to buy the silence or procure false testimony of witnesses; tried to misuse the CIA to aid the cover-up; disseminated secret Grand Jury testimony to suspects; and made false statements to the Nation. I have listened to the tape recordings of the President's own words as he discussed the cover-up, and in particular, I have listened repeatedly to the tape of the morning of March 21, 1973. I do not find any ambiguity in the President's decision to allow payment of hush money to Howard Hunt.

ARTICLE II: ABUSE OF POWER

The evidence in this area demonstrates that the President repeatedly abused the powers of his office, violated the Constitutional rights of citizens, misused government agencies, and broke his oath of office. He tried to use the Internal Revenue Service as a tool of partisan, political intimidation and punishment; he directed unlawful and illegitimate wiretapping and other secret surveillance to gather political intelligence, unrelated to any national security or law enforcement purposes; and he created the Plumbers Unit which engaged in covert, unlawful activities.

ARTICLE III: REFUSAL TO OBEY LAWFUL SUBPOENAS

The President's refusal to respond to our Committee's legal subpoenas constitutes, in itself, an obstruction of the impeachment process which, in my view, is an extremely grave Constitutional offense. The Committee subpoenaed only carefully justified and relevant evidence relating to serious charges of impeachable conduct for which there already existed substantial evidence. By so acting, the Committee accepted a conservative reading of its subpoena powers, which I think go far beyond those which we have tried to assert. The Committee has been forced to compile its case from bits and pieces of evidence extracted from other investigations and from tape recordings furnished by the District Court. The President's refusal to comply with House subpoenas would make a nullity of the impeachment power if the House were not to judge this offense impeachable.

The Committee rejected two additional Articles of Impeachment, the first of which I supported.

ARTICLE IV: THE CAMBODIAN WAR

The Constitution grants Congress the sole power to declare war. Congress must know from the Commander in Chief what actions the armed forces of our nation are taking, so that Congress can act, if it so chooses, to exercise this power. In spite of this clear constitutional duty given to Congress, the President directed that false reports be submitted to Congress over four years of bombing of Cambodia, while the Administration publicly and in reports to Congress, claimed it was not engaged in hostilities with that country. The purpose of this secrecy could only have been to hide the Cambodian bombing from the Congress and the American people, since our adversaries knew about it. I believe that such conscious misleading of Congress in order to prevent us from exercising our Constitutional responsibilities is an impeachable offense, which Congress must enforce if it is to regain its proper Constitutional role.

I fully realize that this matter involves the expansion of a war begun by Democratic Presidents, and at times one of those Presidents, Lyndon B. Johnson himself misled the Congress and the public about the course of that war. But past transgressions of this gravity, even if accepted or ratified by a Congress victimized by deceit, do not make a later repetition Constitutionally acceptable.

I believe the Committee should have supported this article of impeachment, in addition to the three voted by the Committee, to set a precedent for the future. In this time of growing nuclear capability around the world, Congress must make clear to future presidents that which we have tried to set forward this Congress with passage over the President's veto of the War Powers Act: No more wars of any nature must be started without the consent of the people's elected representatives, exactly as set forth in the Constitution.

ARTICLE V: THE PRESIDENT'S TAXES

The evidence before the Congress demonstrates that the President engaged in unethical, shabby, and disgraceful conduct by grossly underpaying his income taxes while in office. There is, however, no clear and convincing evidence available to the Committee to show the two elements necessary to make this offense impeachable.

To become an impeachable offense here, in my opinion, there must be clear proof of fraud by the President himself, coupled with clear indications that he used the power of his presidential office to avoid being audited by the IRS.

This test is not met by evidence available to us. Although I do not find that they rise to the level of impeachability, I do join other Americans in condemning these unconscionable acts which indicate serious violations of Richard Nixon's obligation as a taxpayer.

But there are other remedies for these abuses. Prosecution by the IRS for civil or criminal fraud are still available, even if President Nixon were allowed to serve out his full term. The unique power of impeachment is not needed here. The people of the United States have other remedies. The other impeachable offenses voted by the Committee have only one method of correction—the ultimate weapon of impeachment—which should be used only when it is the sole adequate response.

The report of this historic impeachment proceeding would not be complete without a record of how each member voted on the five proposed Articles of Impeachment. Because regular House procedures do not provide that such votes should be printed in the body of the report, I am here submitting that material to be printed as a part of my additional views.

COMMITTEE ON THE JUDICIARY
HOUSE OF REPRESENTATIVES
93D CONGRESS

ROLL CALL

No. .... DATE July 27, 1974

H. .... S. ....

	COMMITTEE	\multicolumn{5}{c}{Article I}
Present		Ayes	Nays	Present	Ayes	Nays
	MR. DONOHUE	X				
	MR. BROOKS	X				
	MR. KASTENMEIER	X				
	MR. EDWARDS	X				
	MR. HUNGATE	X				
	MR. CONYERS	X				
	MR. EILBERG	X				
	MR. WALDIE	X				
	MR. FLOWERS	X				
	MR. MANN	X				
	MR. SARBANES	X				
	MR. SEIBERLING	X				
	MR. DANIELSON	X				
	MR. DRINAN	X				
	MR. RANGEL	X				
	MS. JORDAN	X				
	MR. THORNTON	X				
	MS. HOLTZMAN	X				
	MR. OWENS	X				
	MR. MEZVINSKY	X				
	MR. HUTCHINSON		X			
	MR. McCLORY		X			
	MR. SMITH		X			
	MR. SANDMAN		X			
	MR. RAILSBACK	X				
	MR. WIGGINS		X			
	MR. DENNIS		X			
	MR. FISH	X				
	MR. MAYNE		X			
	MR. HOGAN	X				
	MR. BUTLER	X				
	MR. COHEN	X				
	MR. LOTT		X			
	MR. FROEHLICH	X				
	MR. MOORHEAD		X			
	MR. MARAZITI		X			
	MR. LATTA		X			
	MR. RODINO, Chairman	X				
	Total					

336

COMMITTEE ON THE JUDICIARY
HOUSE OF REPRESENTATIVES
93D CONGRESS

ROLL CALL

No. ....   DATE July 29, 1974

H. ....   S. ....

	COMMITTEE	Article II				
Present		Ayes	Nays	Present	Ayes	Nays
	MR. DONOHUE	X				
	MR. BROOKS	X				
	MR. KASTENMEIER	X				
	MR. EDWARDS	X				
	MR. HUNGATE	X				
	MR. CONYERS	X				
	MR. EILBERG	X				
	MR. WALDIE	X				
	MR. FLOWERS	X				
	MR. MANN	X				
	MR. SARBANES	X				
	MR. SEIBERLING	X				
	MR. DANIELSON	X				
	MR. DRINAN	X				
	MR. RANGEL	X				
	MS. JORDAN	X				
	MR. THORNTON	X				
	MS. HOLTZMAN	X				
	MR. OWENS	X				
	MR. MEZVINSKY	X				
	MR. HUTCHINSON		X			
	MR. McCLORY	X				
	MR. SMITH		X			
	MR. SANDMAN		X			
	MR. RAILSBACK	X				
	MR. WIGGINS		X			
	MR. DENNIS		X			
	MR. FISH	X				
	MR. MAYNE		X			
	MR. HOGAN	X				
	MR. BUTLER	X				
	MR. COHEN	X				
	MR. LOTT		X			
	MR. FROEHLICH	X				
	MR. MOORHEAD		X			
	MR. MARAZITI		X			
	MR. LATTA		X			
	MR. RODINO, *Chairman*	X				
	TOTAL					

COMMITTEE ON THE JUDICIARY
HOUSE OF REPRESENTATIVES
93D CONGRESS

ROLL CALL

No. ....   DATE July 30, 1974

H. ....   S. ....

	COMMITTEE	Article III				
Present		Ayes	Nays	Present	Ayes	Nays
	MR. DONOHUE	X				
	MR. BROOKS	X				
	MR. KASTENMEIER	X				
	MR. EDWARDS	X				
	MR. HUNGATE	X				
	MR. CONYERS	X				
	MR. EILBERG	X				
	MR. WALDIE	X				
	MR. FLOWERS		X			
	MR. MANN		X			
	MR. SARBANES	X				
	MR. SEIBERLING	X				
	MR. DANIELSON	X				
	MR. DRINAN	X				
	MR. RANGEL	X				
	MS. JORDAN	X				
	MR. THORNTON	X				
	MS. HOLTZMAN	X				
	MR. OWENS	X				
	MR. MEZVINSKY	X				
	MR. HUTCHINSON		X			
	MR. McCLORY	X				
	MR. SMITH		X			
	MR. SANDMAN		X			
	MR. RAILSBACK		X			
	MR. WIGGINS		X			
	MR. DENNIS		X			
	MR. FISH		X			
	MR. MAYNE		X			
	MR. HOGAN	X				
	MR. BUTLER		X			
	MR. COHEN		X			
	MR. LOTT		X			
	MR. FROEHLICH		X			
	MR. MOORHEAD		X			
	MR. MARAZITI		X			
	MR. LATTA		X			
	MR. RODINO, Chairman	X				
	TOTAL					

COMMITTEE ON THE JUDICIARY
HOUSE OF REPRESENTATIVES
93D CONGRESS

ROLL CALL

No. ....   DATE July 30, 1974

H. ....   S. ....

Article IV

Present	COMMITTEE	Ayes	Nays	Present	Ayes	Nays
	MR. DONOHUE		X			
	MR. BROOKS	X				
	MR. KASTENMEIER	X				
	MR. EDWARDS	X				
	MR. HUNGATE	X				
	MR. CONYERS	X				
	MR. EILBERG		X			
	MR. WALDIE	X				
	MR. FLOWERS		X			
	MR. MANN		X			
	MR. SARBANES		X			
	MR. SEIBERLING		X			
	MR. DANIELSON		X			
	MR. DRINAN	X				
	MR. RANGEL	X				
	MS. JORDAN	X				
	MR. THORNTON		X			
	MS. HOLTZMAN	X				
	MR. OWENS	X				
	MR. MEZVINSKY	X				
	MR. HUTCHINSON		X			
	MR. McCLORY		X			
	MR. SMITH		X			
	MR. SANDMAN		X			
	MR. RAILSBACK		X			
	MR. WIGGINS		X			
	MR. DENNIS		X			
	MR. FISH		X			
	MR. MAYNE		X			
	MR. HOGAN		X			
	MR. BUTLER		X			
	MR. COHEN		X			
	MR. LOTT		X			
	MR. FROEHLICH		X			
	MR. MOORHEAD		X			
	MR. MARAZITI		X			
	MR. LATTA		X			
	MR. RODINO, Chairman		X			
	TOTAL					

COMMITTEE ON THE JUDICIARY
HOUSE OF REPRESENTATIVES
93D CONGRESS

ROLL CALL

No. ....   DATE July 30, 1974

H. ....   S. ....

Present	COMMITTEE	Article V		Present		
		Ayes	Nays	Present	Ayes	Nays
	MR. DONOHUE		X			
	MR. BROOKS	X				
	MR. KASTENMEIER	X				
	MR. EDWARDS	X				
	MR. HUNGATE		X			
	MR. CONYERS	X				
	MR. EILBERG	X				
	MR. WALDIE		X			
	MR. FLOWERS		X			
	MR. MANN		X			
	MR. SARBANES		X			
	MR. SEIBERLING	X				
	MR. DANIELSON	X				
	MR. DRINAN		X			
	MR. RANGEL	X				
	MS. JORDAN	X				
	MR. THORNTON		X			
	MS. HOLTZMAN	X				
	MR. OWENS		X			
	MR. MEZVINSKY	X				
	MR. HUTCHINSON		X			
	MR. McCLORY		X			
	MR. SMITH		X			
	MR. SANDMAN		X			
	MR. RAILSBACK		X			
	MR. WIGGINS		X			
	MR. DENNIS		X			
	MR. FISH		X			
	MR. MAYNE		X			
	MR. HOGAN		X			
	MR. BUTLER		X			
	MR. COHEN		X			
	MR. LOTT		X			
	MR. FROEHLICH		X			
	MR. MOORHEAD		X			
	MR. MARAZITI		X			
	MR. LATTA		X			
	MR. RODINO, Chairman	X				
	TOTAL					

CONCLUSION

The Committee's responsibility was perhaps more sobering and awesome than that faced by any Committee of Congress in the past century. I believe that the Committee fulfilled its responsibilities in a way that brought credit to the Congress and to our nation. The durability of our institutions of government has proven adequate to these difficult times. The Committee has moved to reinstate the rule of law as supreme, even in the Oval Office. Our democracy and our constitution have not only survived; they have been strengthened by this ordeal.

Millions of Americans were able to see the Committee during the final week of its deliberations. I had the honor of authoring the House Resolution which made this public participation possible. In an historical innovation, America saw, through television, a panel of serious, responsible, and non-partisan Members of Congress wrestle with grave matters of evidence and reach sober judgments.

In the end, the Committee supported three Articles of Impeachment because of overwhelming, undeniable evidence of grave Presidential misfeasance adjusted to be impeachable in nature and gravity. For months prior to our televised proceedings, the Committee painstakingly examined the mass of evidence which was before it. This evidence was applied carefully and selectively, and there was great debate over what acts, if proven, were serious enough to warrant impeachment. The Committee acted with restraint, ultimately rejecting two Articles of Impeachment.

It was the overwhelming cumulative effect of the evidence, viewed in its entirely, which persuaded so many members of the Committee—both liberal and conservative, Republican and Democratic—that Articles of Impeachment were required. Any member of Congress, or any citizen who carefully examines this evidence would, I believe, support the Committee's actions.

I feel it incumbent to express my reservations concerning the decision to cite as supporting evidence in this report, transcripts of Presidential conversations which were released by President Nixon following completion of the Committee's deliberations. The Committee carefully reviewed a massive amount of materials for an intensive twelve-week period, and a large majority of the Committee found the evidence in support of three Articles of Impeachment to be clear and convincing. The members made their decisions based solely on this evidence, which was, in my view, overwhelming and conclusive. The Committee report should reflect these salient facts upon which the members based their judgment, and should not, in my opinion, show supporting evidence which the Committee did not have available at the time of decision.

The edited transcripts submitted by Mr. Nixon on August 5, 1974 had been subpoenaed by the Committee, and refused to us by him. They were highly incriminating and reinforced the Committee's decision and, in fact, were the catalyst for subsequent expressed support of Article I by the ten Committee members who had earlier voted against reporting that Article. But this new information should be segregated and appear as an addendum to the body of the report, not intermixed with the evidence which led to the Committee's action detailed in this report.

By acting so responsible and by submerging their political allegiances and fortunes for this difficult process, the members of the Committee have strengthened the Congress. By voting to impeach the President for conduct which violated our guarantees of liberty, the Committee has strengthened the Constitution and the Bill of Rights. And by creating clear precedents for future Presidential conduct, it will strengthen the Presidency.

Awesome as the impeachment and removal of a President can be, the framers of our Constitution provided for this power, expecting it to be used rarely, but to be used, nevertheless, when necessary to maintain the rule of law. There should be no fear, if Congress finds the evidence sufficiently strong, that impeachment and conviction will damage the presidency. The framers created a government of laws, not a government of men. And impeachment is the only tool the Constitution provides to control a President who has refused to obey the laws or his Constitutional obligations.

I believe the significance of what this Committee has done will endure for many years to come. If our standards of impeachment had been too low or insubstantial, we would have seriously weakened the presidency and created a precedent for future use of the impeachment power when charges may be trivial or partisan. We have avoided this mistake. On the other hand, if we had rejected these Articles of Impeachment with this clear and convincing evidence of serious wrongdoing before us, no president would ever have been impeached, and the impeachment power, which the Constitution vested in Congress as the last resort to prevent serious abuses of power by a president, would be rendered impotent.

WAYNE OWENS.

ADDITIONAL VIEWS OF MR. MEZVINSKY, JOINED BY MESSRS. BROOKS, KASTENMEIER, EDWARDS, CONYERS, EILBERG, DANIELSON, RANGEL, AND MS. HOLTZMAN CONCERNING INCOME TAX EVASION BY THE PRESIDENT

We support the three Articles of Impeachment approved by the Committee for reporting to the House.

The Committee had before it clear and convincing proof that President Nixon committed the offenses described in those Articles. We believe that the Committee also was presented with clear and convincing proof that the President willfully evaded the payment of his federal income taxes. In fact, the proof was such that the Committee was told by a criminal tax fraud expert that on the evidence presented to the Committee, if the President were an ordinary taxpayer, the government would seek to send him to jail.

The President, however, is not an ordinary taxpayer; his willful tax evasion affects the very integrity of our government. Such conduct calls for the constitutional remedy of impeachment.

The facts lead to no other conclusion.

The Internal Revenue Service ruled on April 2, 1974 that Mr. Nixon had underpaid his federal income taxes by nearly $420,000 during his first term in office. (Book X, 410–11) The IRS found that, on his tax returns for 1969 through 1972, the President had claimed over $565,000 in improper deductions and had failed to report more than $230,000 in taxable income, a total error in excess of $795,000 for those years.

The key to the gross underpayment of taxes was his unlawful claim of a charitable deduction for an alleged gift of his personal papers (stated to be worth $576,000)[1] to the National Archives in 1969. The IRS and the Joint Committee on Internal Revenue Taxation, which, at the President's request, also reviewed his taxes, found that deduction to be improper because:

> (a) the gift was not made on or before July 25, 1969, the last date on which such gifts could be made to qualify for a tax deduction; and
>
> (b) restrictions placed on the gift by President Nixon made the papers a gift of a "future interest" and therefore ineligible for tax benefits, even if the gift had been made prior to the change in the tax law.

On his tax return for 1969, the President stated that the gift was made "free and clear with no rights remaining in the taxpayer." (Book X, 348) In fact, the deed of gift retained for Mr. Nixon substantial rights in the papers.

---

[1] During the audit of the President's returns for the years 1969 through 1972, the IRS had a private independent appraiser value the papers claimed by the President on his returns to be worth $576,000. The conclusion of the independent appraiser was that the papers were worth $270,000.

On his tax return, the President also claimed that the gift was made before the July 25, 1969 cut-off date. (Book X, 348.) The deed of gift transferring those papers stated on its face that it was executed on April 21, 1969. In fact, that deed was executed on April 10, 1970 and backdated to make it appear that it was signed a year earlier. (Book X, 14–15) The National Archives, the recipient of this alleged half-million dollar gift, did not know until April 1970 that the President's "1969" gift had been made. (Book X, 297)

Considering the solid documentary evidence of the illegality of the gift of papers deduction, which was the key element of the President's gross underpayment of his lawful taxes, the responsibility of the Committee was to determine whether the President was aware of—and either acquiesced or actively participated in—this attempt to defraud the government.

While the IRS assessed only a negligence penalty against the President, and not a fraud penalty, IRS Commissioner Donald Alexander recommended to the Special Prosecutor that he conduct a grand jury investigation into the matter of the President's 1969 tax return. Alexander noted that the lack of cooperation of some witnesses and inconsistencies in testimony prevented the IRS from completing its processing of the case. (Book X, 404)

When the Joint Committee staff issued its report on the President's taxes, it specifically noted that it had not attempted to determine the President's culpability for the irregularities on his tax returns. Instead, that question was referred to this Committee for resolution through the impeachment process.

The Joint Committee staff did formulate and send to President Nixon a series of questions concerning the President's knowledge and participation in the preparation of his tax returns. (Book X, 416–22) The President failed to respond to those questions during the Joint Committee investigation, and later ignored a request that he respond to the inquiries for the benefit of this Committee.

An analysis of the undisputed facts and circumstances makes it abundantly clear that the President knew that the gift of papers was not made on or before July 25, 1969 and did not legally qualify for the tax deductions he claimed on his tax returns.

Mr. Nixon is a lawyer who has prided himself on his knowledge of tax law. The $576,000 gift was by far the largest gift ever made by Mr. Nixon in his lifetime. It was more than twice his statutory annual income as President.

He was personally familiar with the procedures which had to be followed in order to make a valid gift of his papers so as to be entitled to the tax deduction. A much smaller gift of papers—amounting to approximately $80,000—was made by the President in December 1968. He was an active and interested participant at that time. He discussed the gift and its tax benefits with his attorneys, chose between alternate deeds of gift, and personally executed a deed which was co-signed by a representative of the GSA accepting the gift for the United States. The President also knew that the papers constituting the 1968 gift were selected prior to the end of 1968. (Book X, 41–61) Although the President claimed that less than 3 months later he made a gift six times as large, the record shows that none of these procedures was observed.

No contemporary written evidence has been produced to support the claim that the President intended on or before July 25, 1969 that a large gift be made or that he authorized anyone to sign a deed of gift on his behalf. Rather, the Committee was shown a February 1969 memorandum—which the President received and endorsed—contemplating not a large gift of papers which would use up all the President's charitable deductions for 1969 and the five succeeding years, but, instead, small periodic gifts of papers plus other charitable contributions. (Book X, 64–65)

Two June 1969 memoranda show that the President was an individual interested in the minute details of his tax deductions. Neither these memoranda nor any other writings in 1969 refer to a gift of papers so large as to eliminate all other charitable deductions for six years. (Book X, 177–79)

While the President's papers were delivered to the Archives on March 27, 1969, they were part of and intermingled with a much larger group of papers. The documentary evidence is overwhelming that the Archives did not consider that any of these papers had been given to the United States, but that it was routinely holding all of them in storage. The papers that ultimately were stated to constitute the "1969" gift were not finally selected until late March 1970. They were not even preliminarily valued until early November 1969, and then only as part of the larger group of papers delivered for storage on March 27. The preliminary appraisal was promptly sent to the President on November 7, 1969 who acknowledged to the appraiser, Ralph Newman, on November 16 that he knew of the appraisal. (Book X, 190–98)

The backdated deed was executed on April 10, 1970, in the Executive Office Building by White House attorney Edward Morgan in the presence of Frank DeMarco, the President's tax attorney. (Book X, 319–27) A few hours later, DeMarco met with the President for the execution of the President's tax return. The Committee has heard testimony that the President went over his tax return with his attorneys page by page, and discussed the tax consequences of the gift of papers deduction. (Kalmbach testimony, 3 HJC 670–71)

Finally, logic compels the conclusion that the President knew he made no gift of papers in March 1969. This is true because unless one could know in March 1969 that there would be a July 25, 1969 cut-off date, it would be contrary to rational tax planning for the President: (a) to make a gift of papers in March 1969, which would eliminate the opportunity to take other charitable deductions for six years (especially when he appeared to approve a contrary plan a month before); and (b) to make a gift that early in the year, when many of his financial matters were unsettled, instead of waiting until the end of the year when his income and deductions could be accurately estimated.

The fact is that neither President Nixon nor anyone else could know in March 1969 of a July 25, 1969 cut-off date. Not until May 27, 1969 was there any indication that Congress might consider passing legislation eliminating the gift of papers deduction. And it was not until November 21, 1969 (when the Senate Finance Committee reported its bill to the Senate with a December 31, 1968 cut-off date) that it became a serious possibility that individuals might not have until the end of 1969 to make a gift of papers and take the deduction. On December 22, 1969, Congress finally fixed July 25, 1969 as the cut-off date for the gift of papers deduction. (Book X, 149–51)

It is noteworthy that once officials outside of the White House began investigating the gift of papers deduction, the President's attorneys, DeMarco and Morgan, and his appraiser, Newman, began to tell conflicting versions of events which they had previously agreed upon. Also, documents central to the President's deduction (including a deed allegedly executed in 1969) were found to be missing, and others (such as the affidavit of appraisal which was part of the President's return) proved to be erroneous.

The President's failure to respond to the questions submitted to him by the Joint Committee staff adds an additional inculpatory circumstance to a record which points to intentional wrongdoing in connection with the gift of papers deduction.

The facts and circumstances noted above demonstrate that when President Nixon signed his tax return on April 10, 1970 he knew that he did not make a gift of papers on or before July 25, 1969 valued at $576,000. With respect to how any other taxpayer would be treated under these facts and circumstances, this Committee has heard the expert opinion of Fred Folsom, an attorney who spent 24 years in, and who for 12 years was Chief of, the Justice Department's criminal tax section. Mr. Folsom stated that "in the case of an ordinary taxpayer, on the facts as we know them in this instance, the case would be referred out for presentation to a Grand Jury for prosecution." (Folsom testimony, HJC 6/21/74, TR. 1976) To state it more bluntly, under these facts and circumstances, the government would seek to send any other taxpayer to jail.

The facts set forth above show that the Committee had before it evidence of tax evasion by the President which met the most stringent standards of proof. The use of tape recordings and similar documentary evidence to prove the charges set forth in the Articles recommended by the Committee perhaps led some to expect that type of evidence for all of the Articles. Most cases, however, whether criminal or civil, do not turn on the availability of tape recordings. They are decided on an evaluation of all the proven facts and circumstances and the logical inferences to be drawn from those facts and circumstances. Whatever the applicable standard of proof, the evidence presented to the Committee demonstrated that the President of the United States was guilty of willful income tax evasion for the years 1969 through 1972. He should have been impeached for such conduct.

TAX EVASION AS AN IMPEACHABLE OFFENSE

Some question whether willful tax evasion by a President should be considered an impeachable offense. The President, who is obligated by the Constitution to faithfully execute the laws, is perforce constrained to live within the statutes and regulations which govern all citizens. As with any other citizen, the President's evasion of taxes constituted a serious felony—which, even under the "criminality" standards urged on the Committee by the President, constitutes an impeachable offense. But because of his position, the President's acts went beyond criminal wrongdoing; they necessarily involved taking advantage of the power and prestige of the Presidency.

As Chief Executive, President Nixon could expect that his tax returns would not be subject to the same scrutiny as those of other taxpayers. The superficial examination of his 1971 and 1972 returns conducted in May, 1973, which caused the IRS to write the President commending him (instead of sending him a bill for the more than $180,000 by which he had underpaid his taxes for those two years) bears out this expectation of favoritism.

The President had a special obligation to scrutinize his own returns—especially when those returns showed that he was paying only a nominal amount of tax on a very high income. Rather than so doing, he took advantage of his office to avoid paying his proper taxes. Had his entire Presidency not been subjected to public scrutiny—for the reasons contained in Articles I and II—Mr. Nixon's tax evasion would have succeeded.

A President's noncompliance with the revenue laws does not merely deprive the Treasury of funds from one taxpayer; it affects the very foundation of our voluntary system of tax collection. Allowing such conduct to go unchecked threatens to damage seriously the ability of the government to efficiently raise from all the citizens of the Nation the funds necessary to govern our society. If a President commits willful tax evasion and is not brought to account by the Congress, then not only the tax system, but our entire structure of government risks corrosion. For this most fundamental reason we believe that the willful tax evasion by President Nixon should have been considered an impeachable offense by the Committee, and that the Article charging this offense should have been reported to the House.

EDWARD MEZVINSKY.
JACK BROOKS.
BOB KASTENMEIER.
DON EDWARDS.
JOHN CONYERS, JR.
JOSHUA EILBERG.
GEORGE E. DANIELSON.
C. B. RANGEL.
ELIZABETH HOLTZMAN.

ADDITIONAL VIEWS OF MR. McCLORY ON ARTICLE III CONCURRED IN BY MR. DANIELSON AND MR. FISH

The power of impeachment is the Constitution's paramount power of self-preservation. This power is textually committed by the Constitution solely to the House of Representatives. The power to impeach includes within it the power to inquire. Without the corollary power to inquire, the power to impeach would be meaningless—and dangerous.

The power of impeachment is made necessary by the allocation of jurisdiction among three separate branches. The Articles of Confederation which reposed all powers in Congress found no need of an impeachment process. For there was no "other" branch whose excesses had to be checked by Congress. But the Constitution dispersed the powers among three separate branches to protect the liberties of the people and hold distant the spectre of tyranny. However, this protection against tyranny raised the question of how Congress could make the executive—who under the Constitution would have the greatest potential for tyranny—answer for wrongs committed against the people.

It was that question that led the framers to adapt the impeachment process to their new government. In addressing the question of possible Presidential misconduct at the Constitutional Convention, George Mason said: "No point is of more importance than that the right of impeachment should be continued." And in *The Federalist* No. 66, Alexander Hamilton made clear that the purpose of the impeachment process was to serve as "an essential check in the hands of [the legislature] upon the encroachments of the executive."

In the same passage and in others in *The Federalist*, it is explained that the doctrine of separation of powers is modified by the system of checks and balances. In explaining the "true meaning" of the doctrine of separation of powers, Madison states that "it is not possible to give each department an equal power of self defense. In republican government, the legislative authority necessarily predominates. The remedy for this inconveniency is to divide the legislature into different branches. . . ." *The Federalist*, No. 51.

Moreover, the doctrine of separation of powers does not mean that in a given instance no branch may have "control" over the acts of another; rather, all that is meant by the doctrine is that at no time may the whole power of one branch be exercised by another entity that possesses the whole power of a second branch. *The Federalist*, No. 47, (Madison).

Hamilton refers to Madison's explanation of the doctrine with approval and adds that in the context of the impeachment process the check on the arbitrary action of the House is the requirement of "concurrence of two-thirds of the Senate." *The Federalist*, No. 66. Thus, it is the Senate—not the President—that is the check on the House's power to impeach and its corollary power to inquire.

The doctrine of separation of powers does not mean that no branch can tell another branch what to do. Separation of powers is not the creation of three sovereign governments, but one government of three branches, each with an assigned role. Each branch within its assigned role may "control" another. Thus, for example, a President may "control" a judicial decision by granting a pardon, or he may "control" a legislative act by vetoing it.

The framers not only foresaw but intended that there exist a tension between branches. But the question in each case must be which branch has been, under the Constitution, assigned the role of checking and which branch has been deprived of its "self defense."

If the power of impeachment is assigned solely to the House and if its fundamental purpose is to check encroachments by the executive, it is clear that the separation of powers doctrine does not grant to the executive an institutional privilege which he may assert against either the power to impeach or the corollary power to inquire. For the framers to have granted such a defense to a President would have been a contradictory, irrational act.

The power of impeachment, as stated above, is the Constitution's paramount power of self-preservation. Thus, it has been recognized through our history by every President, every legislator, and every judge that has ever spoken on the question that the impeachment power was sufficient to require of everyone, including the President, all necessary evidence—recognized, that is, until the exigencies of the present inquiry have forced the incumbent President and his defenders to assert an institutional privilege against the House's power to inquire. This assertion is not only legally mistaken but, upon analysis, frivolous. Whatever success such an assertion may have appears attributable to the fact that it plays to commonly mistaken notions that no branch can tell another branch what to do—a notion which in the everyday workings of our government is regularly disproved.

The principle that is the subject of this discussion is clear and simple: the Constitution does not give to the House of Representatives, exercising its power to impeach, a power to ask while giving to the President—as President—an equal power to refuse. It is respectfully submitted that our Constitution makes more sense than that. The Constitution does not give to the President a privilege to refuse *by virtue of his office* when his use or abuse of that office is at issue.

When the trustee of the highest office in the land is called upon by the representatives of the people to make an accounting of his performance, his assertion that Presidents need not answer is contemptuous of his trust and of the people who have placed their trust in him.

In talking to my colleagues I am greatly disturbed that the issue in Article III is so misunderstood. All that Article III says is that Richard M. Nixon did not present a "lawful cause or excuse" for failing to comply with subpoenas for evidence critically necessary to an impeachment inquiry. The President's basic answer to the subpoenas was that Presidents do not have to comply with such subpoenas by virtue of the office and that if the power to impeach included within it the power to inquire, then no President ever again would be safe.

All that I ask of my colleagues is to think through the ramifications of the President's position. For me, I do not wish to have a Presidency that is safe from the power of the people's representatives to demand an accounting. And that is precisely what is at stake in Article III.

In discussions with my colleagues I am frequently beset with many hypothetical questions—questions that have not occurred. I am asked whether the President could assert "national security" or "diplomatic secrecy" or some such excuse against impeachment inquiry subpoenas.

The only answer is that Article III does not treat those questions because the President offered no such excuses. We need not decide those questions at this time. Those special circumstances differ substantially from the excuse offered by this President that Presidents *as such* need not comply. And it is that excuse which Article III holds invalid.

To be complete, I must also note that other excuses were offered by the President, but they appear secondary to his basic assertion. In his letter of June 9, 1974, to Chairman Rodino, the President complained that our requests were "unlimited" and suggested that each branch must be immune from unlimited searches by other branches. That excuse is factually without foundation. The facts set forth in this Report make clear that our subpoenas were modest in scope and thoroughly justified.

Additionally, the President said in that letter that the Committee had "the full story of Watergate." That answer had two defects: first, it was not true; second, even if true, it was no answer to outstanding Committee requests for materials in other areas under investigation, such as ITT, the dairy contributions, and misuse of the Internal Revenue Service. When such materials were later subpoenaed, the President offered *no* excuse for his failure to comply. Presumably, we were to try to fashion one for him.

Finally, the President said that "the Executive must remain the final arbiter of demands on its confidentiality." However, it should be noted that no special circumstances were offered as an excuse. Rather, the President was asserting a flat privilege not to comply based on general operational needs of his office lest "the Presidency itself ... be fatally compromised." He was asserting, in other words, an executive privilege against the House's power to inquire.

Such a privilege was asserted in *United States* v. *Nixon* against the functions of the judicial branch. The Supreme Court unanimously rejected such a flat privilege as one that would make our government unworkable and would impair the role of the courts. That conclusion applies with even stronger force in an impeachment proceeding against the President, the occurrence of which is so rare and the needs of which relate so fundamentally to the welfare of society itself.

Therefore, in sum, Richard M. Nixon has not offered any "lawful cause or excuse." His offer of excuses on behalf of future Presidents is untenable when he has, in truth, no valid excuse of his own.

It has been suggested we should interpolate an excuse on his behalf because he may have been reluctant to state it. That excuse is the constitutional privilege against self-incrimination which Richard M. Nixon possesses as private citizen. For purposes of Article III, it is sufficient to answer that he did not offer this excuse. But if he had, the Committee could have granted him "use" immunity and ordered him to produce the subpoenaed materials, and thereafter the House could have impeached him for high crimes or misdemeanors on the basis of the produced materials because removal from office is not a criminal sanction.

But it appears that for some of my colleagues laying out an impeachable offense on the basis of undisputed facts and clear law is not enough. For some unstated reasons unknown to me, special preconditions are postulated for Article III which were not applied to any other article.

First, it is argued that the presence of a disagreement over an important constitutional issue between the President and the Committee requires that we test our position in court before impeachment. What is incongruous is that this principle is applied only to Article III. Yet there are important constitutional questions relating to Article I and Article II over which the President and the Committee disagree. For example, do either Article I or Article II comply with due process requirements of fair notice of the charges? Why don't we go to court to find out? Is obstruction of justice an impeachable offense? The President's statement on August 5, 1974, appears to say no. So why don't we go to court to find out? Is misuse of executive agencies an impeachable offense? Since it is not an indictable offense, the President's position is no. So why don't we go to court to find out?

In deciding on *any* article of impeachment, one must determine the facts and whether those facts constitute impeachable conduct. The latter is always a construction of the phrase "treason, bribery, or other high crimes and misdemeanors," always a constitutional question. If all constitutional questions should be sent to a court first, not only Article III but all three of the Articles of impeachment must fall.

It is also suggested that simply because two branches have disagreed over their respective roles, the third branch should be called on to referee. But is this how our government works? If the Congress and the Supreme Court disagree on the constitutionality of a bill, does the President act as referee, or does the Court's view prevail because of its assigned role under the Constitution? If the Congress and the President disagree over whether our armed forces should act or continue to act against some foreign land and Congress cuts off appropriations, does the Supreme Court act as referee, or does the Congressional view prevail because of its assigned role under the Constitution? And when the President and the Supreme Court disagreed on the question of whether the President was obligated to produce subpoenaed material, did Congress act as referee, or did the Court's view prevail because of its assigned role under the Constitution?

In short, the asserted principle does not explain how our government actually works. The worth of this assertion can be analyzed by hypothecating an inquiry into the conduct of a Justice of the Supreme Court or of the entire Supreme Court wherein a "judicial privilege" is asserted against Congressional subpoenas. Would the President be the proper referee in that case? The question answers itself.

It should not go without comment that the Constitution grants no such "referee power" to any branch in any of its provisions. The only approximation of such a grant is the "case or controversy" jurisdiction of the judicial branch. And, as the Report demonstrates, the history of that phrase rejects any notion that the doors of the courts are open to resolve constitutional confrontations between the two other branches.

It is also commonly argued that no branch can decide its own role under the Constitution, citing a sentence to that effect from *The Federalist*, No. 49. Unfortunately, what is not explained is that the sentence is a paraphrase by Madison of an argument that Thomas Jefferson made on behalf of a provision written for a Virginia constitution which the framers rejected in drafting our Constitution. Jefferson argued that disputes between branches should be referred to the people, assembled in convention. Madison answered that this would be unworkable as a general proposition and that the best that could be done was to establish a system of checks and balances, *The Federalist*, No. 51. Under such a system, each branch is supreme within its assigned role. It is this truth to which *United States* v. *Nixon* is living testament.

So why didn't we go to court to be sure? (1) Because the federal district courts can only exercise jurisdiction granted by Congress and none has been granted to cover such a case. (2) Because both the President and the Committee agreed that such questions were not justiciable. (3) Because the House has the sole power of impeachment, which includes the duty of deciding whether certain facts constitute impeachable conduct. (4) Finally, because these constitutional questions are tried in a court specially set aside by the Constitution for this very purpose. It is the Senate, "the court of impeachment," and it exercises judicial power, as Hamilton made clear in *The Federalist*, No. 66. And, as is the case in all trials of Presidents, the Chief Justice of the United States presides.

Second, it is argued that the Committee should have initiated contempt proceedings as a precondition to recommending Article III to the House. However, it should be noted that Article III does not charge contempt. Article III does not charge the President merely with refusal to obey the subpoenas of a Congressional Committee. Rather it charges that the President violated the doctrine of separation of powers by arrogating to himself the functions of the House in an impeachment inquiry and thereby attempted to nullify the Constitution's ultimate check on what Hamilton referred to as the "misconduct of public men." Of course, the Committee itself does not charge but only recommends that the House make the charge, just as in a statutory contempt proceeding pursuant to 2 U.S.C. § 192. The difference is that in a contempt proceeding initiated by the House the defendant is heard in a district court whereas in an impeachment proceeding the respondent is heard in the Senate. But in terms of due process requirements, there is no difference. In neither case is a sanction imposed before the opportunity to be heard. If the House's voting impeachment were viewed as a sanction, then all three articles would fall equally. And the House could never impeach without previously conducting its own trial to determine the facts.

For those who still press that contempt proceedings should have been completed as a precondition to charging an impeachable offense, it should be noted that the Supreme Court in *United States* v. *Nixon*, when confronted with the question of whether contempt proceedings should have been initiated against the President as a procedural precondition for determining the obligatory character of the subpoenas, said that such a precondition would be inappropriate against a President since it would force an additional constitutional confrontation and delay resolution of the merits of the case. The same is true for us.

I trust that those who contend that contempt proceedings should have been completed as a precondition believe that it is legally possible to hold an incumbent President in contempt. If that is so, it would follow that an incumbent President may be indicted for other crimes as well. In which case, it might be asked why the Committee has not urged that charges against the President be filed by the Special Prosecutor as a precondition to recommending Article I.

Again, it seems peculiar that the doctrine of "failure to exhaust other remedies" should be raised against Article III alone. Moreover, those other remedies are, in fact, unavailable. As that doctrine is applied in courts of law, that fact makes the doctrine inapplicable.

Article III compares favorably with the other articles reported by the Committee. Its underlying facts are undisputed. It is the most specific and least duplicitous of the three articles. It is the only article wherein the President was put on notice before he acted that his conduct could result in impeachment. And as a matter of law, since the charge is that the President, in effect, attempted to nullify the constitutional procedure whereby he is made accountable for his conduct to the people he serves, there can be no higher crime against the people with the possible exception of treason.

Article III is no make-weight article. For posterity, it is the most important article. It preserves for future generations the power to hold their public servants accountable.

When we began this inquiry many months ago, no one would have denied that the House of Representatives had the power to impeach a President. In the absence of our recommendation of Article III, serious doubts about this power would have persisted. Indeed, this impeachment will have been made possible by circumstances extraneous to our inquiry. It was not our subpoena that brought to light the additional evidence on August 5, 1974. The same sadly can be said of much of the substantial evidence which we possess. Our subpoenas still stand unanswered. It was only by the coincidence of an investigation into the conduct of private citizens who formerly worked at the White House that evidence necessary to our inquiry into Presidential conduct fell into our hands. By experiencing that coincidence, have we acquitted ourselves of our responsibility to preserve for our grandchildren a workable government wherein even the highest remain accountable to the people through their representatives? Shall we protect the people's rights and prevent the crippling of the Constitution's essential check against unconstitutional government?

In recommending Article III to the House the Committee has sought to answer these questions in the affirmative.

The concur in full with the foregoing views on Article III.

ROBERT McCLORY.
GEORGE E. DANIELSON.
HAMILTON FISH, JR.

CONCURRING VIEWS OF MR. FISH

AND THE PRESIDENT "SHALL TAKE CARE . . ."

In reviewing the solemn proceeding in which we have been engaged, every Member of the Committee on the Judiciary, every other Member of Congress, and every other American must evaluate the evidence in the light of adherence to law, devotion to the Constitution and to the institutions of this land. Article II of the United States Constitution sets forth the power and the responsibilities of the President. It opens with majestic simplicity: "The executive Power shall be vested in a President of the United States of America." The standard of conduct required of all Presidents appears in Section 3 of that Article which commands that the President "shall take Care that the Laws be faithfully executed." Section I of the same Article requires that the President acknowledge the "take Care" duty when assuming office by affirming under oath that he will "preserve, protect and defend the Constitution of the United States."

The "take Care" clause "is a comprehensive description of the duty of the executive to watch with vigilance over all the public interests." *Field v. People*, 2 Scan. 79 (Ill. 1839) (quoting a contemporary treatise on American law). President Benjamin Harrison described the duty to "take Care that the Laws are faithfully executed" as "the central idea of the office." Justice Frankfurter observed that apart from the responsibility for conducting foreign affairs, "the embracing function of the President is that 'he shall take Care that the Laws be faithfully executed.'" The Supreme Court has made it clear that the "Laws" to which the "take Care" clause refers are not limited solely to "the . . . Acts of Congress or treaties of the United States;" rather, the "Laws" also include those "rights, duties and obligations growing out of the Constitution itself . . . and all the protections implied by the nature of the government under the Constitution." *In re Neagle*, 135 U.S. 1, 64 (1890).

The Impeachment Clause is the sole exception to the system of separation of governmental powers provided by the Constitution. It is the ultimate check on a President's abuse of the powers of his office. The duty to "take Care that the Laws be faithfully executed" circumscribes the President's authority with respect to overall conduct of the Executive Department and the administration of justice and is central to the exercise of the impeachment power.

The three Articles of Impeachment recommended to the full House of Representatives charge that the great powers of the presidential office have been seriously abused. In words repeated in the preamble to each Article it is charged that the President, "in violation of his constitutional oath faithfully to execute the office of President of the United States and to the best of his ability preserve, protect and defend the Constitution of the United States, and in violation (or 'disregard,' in Article II) of his constitutional duty to take care that the laws be faithfully executed," performed acts therein specified. All three Articles thus frame the issue in constitutional terms.

Much attention has been given, and properly, to the specific charges against the President; but there are also larger considerations involved. The issue for history is the constitutional standard by which this President, or any future President, shall be held to account for his own acts or omissions and those of his immediate subordinates.

The clear and understandable thrust of the "take Care" clause imposes on a President the affirmative duty to take care that the laws are carried out fully, fairly, and justly.

The "take Care" clause imposes on a President a personal obligation faithfully to honor, respect, obey and execute the laws. At the very least he is bound not to violate the law; not to order others to violate the law; and not to participate in the concealment of evidence respecting violations of law of which he is made aware. This is scarcely novel: the same could be said of any citizen, whether or not bound by oath of office. Unlike the misconduct of an ordinary citizen, of course, presidential actions which contravene an Act of Congress may raise fundamental constitutional issues involving the overreach of the President's powers, e.g., *Youngstown Sheet and Tube Co. v. Sawyer*, 343 U.S. 579 (1952) (steel seizure); *United States v. United States District Court*, 407 U.S. 297 (1917) (warrantless wiretapping); *United States v. Nixon*, ——— U.S. ——— (1974) (executive privilege). In such case, since the President's action can be effectively tested in the courts, resort to the extraordinary remedy of impeachment is not necessary. Impeachment is appropriate only where the President's action involves an undermining of the integrity of office, an arrogation of power, a disregard of constitutional duties, or otherwise has a substantial adverse impact on the system of government.

The President's constitutional duties extend beyond his personal obligation. The "take Care" clause includes the President's superintendency of the vast bureaucracy of the executive branch, including all departments, agencies, commissions, and of course the immediate White House staff. The President's general obligation in this regard was described by Attorney General William Wirt in advice he gave in 1823 to President John Quincy Adams: "[The President] is not to perform the duty but to see that the officer assigned by law performs his duty faithfully—that is, honestly; not with perfect correctness of judgement, but honestly." 1 Ops. Atty. Gen. 624 (1823).

The President's duty to supervise his principal subordinates is further emphasized by other provisions of the Constitution. Considered in conjunction with the President's constitutional power to "require the opinion in writing, of the principal officer in each of the Executive Departments, upon any subject relating to the duties of their respective offices," Article II, Section 2, the "take Care" clause implies an affirmative duty to be informed about the conduct of executive officers. Likewise, when considered in the light of the President's power to appoint and remove executive officers, the intention of the Framers of the Constitution that there be a single, responsible executive, and the provision of Article II, Section 1 vesting the executive power solely in the President, the "take Care" clause imposes a duty to oversee the conduct of executive officers.

This general duty of supervision is necessarily subject to certain practical limitations. The President's constitutional duty does not require that he personally execute the laws. As Gouverneur Morris pointed out at the Constitutional Convention, "Without . . . ministers the Executive can do nothing of consequence." II *The Records of the Federal Convention* 54 (M. Farrand ed.). Clearly he cannot exercise direct supervision over any substantial segment of the executive branch. He should not be held responsible under the "take Care" clause for acts of individual wrongdoing by executive officers in the performance of their duties, in which he is not in any way involved. He and his party may have to respond to the electorate for instances of revealed corruption at any level of the executive establishment, but unless the corruption serves to subvert the system of government, impeachment is not warranted.

Under the "take Care" clause, however, the President may not knowingly countenance—let alone authorize or direct—serious unlawful conduct in an official capacity on the part of any agency or executive official within the executive establishment. Furthermore, whatever may be the responsibility of the President for the conduct of those executive officers in the various agencies of government, his responsibility for the conduct of his immediate subordinates in the White House is even more compelling. All members of the White House staff are selected by the President and are directly responsible to him alone. No member of the White House staff is subject to Senate scrutiny or approval on appointment; and of course discharge is also within the sole discretion of the President. It is not unreasonable to suggest that the closer the relationship to the President, the greater is his responsibility for the misconduct of a particular subordinate in the discharge of his duties.

Although the clause does not require day-to-day supervisory responsibility for each executive department or agency, neither does the size and complexity of the executive branch excuse the President's failure to take reasonable steps calculated to ensure that his subordinates have faithfully carried out his responsibility of faithful execution of the laws. The President must exercise due diligence in overseeing the acts of his immediate subordinates. He can neither mislead them by offering ambiguous instructions and then fail to police their actions, nor can he with impunity simply ignore available facts bearing on their wrongful official conduct. He must remain always alert for any hint or suggestion of improper official conduct on their part. If a President has knowledge that the laws are being violated or improperly executed, he is under a duty to take appropriate steps to remedy these wrongs. Among other things, he must bring the matter to the attention of authorized law enforcement officials. Furthermore, a President may not deliberately position or arrange to screen himself with intent to avoid such knowledge, or notice of such actions. And if a President permits or directly or indirectly stimulates a course of activity on the part of his immediate subordinates which amounts to serious abridgement of the "take Care" clause, he is accountable for that conduct in an impeachment proceeding directed against him, whether or not he had knowldege of its actual occurrence.

The failure of a President to discharge his duty by disregarding or knowingly tolerating official dishonesty in the executive department or the faithless execution of the laws by his subordinates or executive department officials, may well, as President Andrew Jackson stated, subject a President to the same liability as his subordinates—removal from office. 3 *Messages of the President* 1352.

The President, in short, may *not* use any department of the executive branch, or any person within the executive establishment, to subvert the Constitution or the laws, or to serve the President's personal or political advantage in an unlawful manner. This is what Article II of the Constitution is all about. It puts the President upon his oath to preserve, protect and defend the Constitution and to take care that the laws will be faithfully executed.

This is also what Impeachment Articles I and II are all about. Article I charges obstruction of justice by interfering with federal investigating agencies and concealing from them critical information. Paragraphs 1, 2 and 5 of Article II charge abuse of office by directing unlawful activities to be undertaken by the Internal Revenue Service, the Federal Bureau of Investigation, the Secret Service, the Criminal Division of the Department of Justice, the office of Watergate Special Prosecutor, and the Central Intelligence Agency. Paragraphs 3 and 4 charge other illegal acts of the President, done "personally and through his subordinates and agents," in subversion of the political process; in derogation of individual liberty; and in the development of a plan to prevent discovery of illegal activities. Furthermore, the offenses charged in Article II are peculiarly presidential offenses, for the President is in a unique position to subvert and abuse the federal investigative and law enforcement agencies. Under the Constitution the President may properly exercise broad discretionary powers to see that the Department of Justice and other agencies serve the needs of law enforcement, but those powers are circumscribed by his corresponding duty to uphold the integrity of the administration of justice. The President has special obligations in the even-handed enforcement of the criminal laws of the land. Article II charges at the very least a gross disregard for those special obligations, and a total dereliction of the duty to take care that the laws be faithfully executed.

HAMILTON FISH, Jr.

MINORITY VIEWS OF MESSRS. HUTCHINSON, SMITH, SANDMAN, WIGGINS, DENNIS, MAYNE, LOTT, MOORHEAD, MARAZITI AND LATTA

Preliminary Statement

A. General

It is true, as President Gerald R. Ford said in his inaugural remarks, that "our long national nightmare is over," at least in the sense that anxiety over the impact of a raging Watergate controversy on the ability of the country's Chief Executive to govern effectively, or even to remain in office, abruptly ended upon the resignation of Richard Nixon from the Presidency. That resignation also rendered moot, in our view, the sole question to which this Committee's impeachment inquiry was addressed, namely, whether sufficient grounds exist for the House of Representatives to exercise its constitutional power to impeach Mr. Nixon. We see no need for the Members of the House to take any action whatsoever with respect to the filing of this Committee Report, other than to read it and the individual and minority views included herein.

It is perhaps less *urgent*, but it is surely no less *necessary*, that we record our views respecting the more significant questions of law and fact which we perceive to be posed by the record compiled by the Committee in the course of its Impeachment Inquiry. This remains important, not because whatever we in the minority or our colleagues who constituted the Committee's majority on these issues now say about them will affect the tenure in office of any particular President, but because we have an obligation, both to our contemporaries and to posterity, not to perpetuate, unchallenged, certain theories of the evidence, and of law, which are propounded by the majority but which we believe to be erroneous.

It is essential that, as the emotional and intellectual tensions of the pre-resignation period subside, neither Members of the Committee nor other Americans so relax their efforts to analyze and understand the evidence accumulated by the Committee that they become indiscriminate in their approach to the various allegations of misconduct which we examined. Our gratitude for his having by his resignation spared the Nation additional agony should not obscure for history our judgment that Richard Nixon, as President, committed certain acts for which he should have been impeached and removed from office. Likewise, having effectively admitted guilt of one impeachable offense—obstruction of justice in connection with the Watergate investigation—Richard Nixon is not consequently to be presumed guilty of all other offenses with which he was charged by the majority of the Committee that approved recommending to the full House three Articles of Impeachment against him. Indeed, it remains our view that, for the most part, he was not guilty of those offenses and that history should so record.

Our views respecting the merits of each of the major allegations made by the majority of the Committee against President Nixon are set out more fully in the separate discussions of the three proposed Articles which follow. To summarize:

(1) With respect to proposed Article I, we believe that the charges of conspiracy to obstruct justice, and obstruction of justice, which are contained in the Article in essence, if not in terms, may be taken as substantially confessed by Mr. Nixon on August 5, 1974, and corroborated by ample other evidence in the record. Prior to Mr. Nixon's revelation of the contents of three conversations between him and his former Chief of Staff, H. R. Haldeman, that took place on June 23, 1972, we did not, and still do not, believe that the evidence of presidential involvement in the Watergate cover-up conspiracy, as developed at that time, was sufficient to warrant Members of the House, or dispassionate jurors in the Senate, in finding Mr. Nixon guilty of an impeachable offense beyond a reasonable doubt, which we believe to be the appropriate standard.

(2) With respect to proposed Article II, we find sufficient evidence to warrant a belief that isolated instances of unlawful conduct by presidential aides and subordinates did occur during the five-and-one-half years of the Nixon Administration, with varying degrees of direct personal knowledge or involvement of the President in these respective illegal episodes. We roundly condemn such abuses and unreservedly favor the invocation of existing legal sanctions, or the creation of new ones, where needed, to deter such reprehensible official conduct in the future, no matter in whose Administration, or by what brand or partisan, it might be perpetrated.

Nevertheless, we cannot join with those who claim to perceive an invidious, pervasive "pattern" of illegality in the conduct of official government business generally by President Nixon. In some instances, as noted below, we disagree with the majority's interpretation of the evidence regarding either the intrinsic illegality of the conduct studied or the linkage of Mr. Nixon personally to it. Moreover, even as to those acts which we would concur in characterizing as abusive and which the President appeared to direct or countenance, neither singly nor in the aggregate do they impress us as being offenses for which Richard Nixon, or any President, should be impeached or removed from office, when considered, *as they must be*, on their own footing, apart from the obstruction of justice charge under proposed Article I which we believe to be sustained by the evidence.

(3) Likewise, with respect to proposed Article III, we believe that this charge, standing alone, affords insufficient grounds for impeachment. Our concern here, as explicated in the discussion below, is that the Congressional subpoena power itself not be too easily abused as a means of achieving the impeachment and removal of a President against whom no other substantive impeachable offense has been proved by sufficient evidence derived from sources other than the President himself. We believe it is particularly important for the House to refrain from impeachment on the sole basis of noncompliance with subpoenas where, as here, colorable claims of privilege have been

asserted in defense of non-production of the subpoenaed materials, and the validity of those claims has not been adjudicated in any established, lawful adversary proceeding before the House is called upon to decide whether to impeach a President on grounds of noncompliance with subpoenas issued by a Committee inquiring into the existence of sufficient grounds for impeachment.

Richard Nixon served his country in elective office for the better part of three decades and, in the main, he served it well. Each of the undersigned voted for him, worked for and with him in election campaigns, and supported the major portion of his legislative program during his tenure as President. Even at the risk of seeming paradoxical, since we were prepared to vote for his impeachment on proposed Article I had he not resigned his office, we hope that in the fullness of time it is his accomplishments—and they were many and significant—rather than the conduct to which this Report is addressed for which Richard Nixon is primarily remembered in history.

We know that it has been said, and perhaps some will continue to say, that Richard Nixon was "hounded from office" by his political opponents and media critics. We feel constrained to point out, however, that it was Richard Nixon who impeded the FBI's investigation of the Watergate affair by wrongfully attempting to implicate the Central Intelligence Agency; it was Richard Nixon, who created and preserved the evidence of that transgression and who, *knowing that it had been subpoenaed by this Committee and the Special Prosecutor*, concealed its terrible import, even from his own counsel, until he could do so no longer. And it was a unanimous Supreme Court of the United States which, in an opinion authored by the Chief Justice whom he appointed, ordered Richard Nixon to surrender that evidence to the Special Prosecutor, to further the ends of justice.

The tragedy that finally engulfed Richard Nixon had many facets. One was the very self-inflicted nature of the harm. It is striking that such an able, experienced and perceptive man, whose ability to grasp the global implications of events little noticed by others may well have been unsurpassed by any of his predecessors, should fail to comprehend the damage that accrued daily to himself, his Administration, and to the Nation, as day after day, month after month, he imprisoned the truth about his role in the Watergate cover-up so long and so tightly within the solitude of his Oval Office that it could not be unleashed without destroying his Presidency.

We submit these Minority Views in the hope that we might thereby help provide to our colleagues in the House, and to the public at large, a broader perspective than might otherwise be available on these events which have come to play such a surprisingly large part in all of our lives. Joined, we are confident, by our colleagues on the majority of the Committee who, through these past nine months, struggled as we did to find the truth, we conclude by expressing a final, earnest hope: that these observations and all that we have said and done during the course of this Inquiry will prove to have served, as they were intended to serve, the security, liberty and general welfare of the American people.

B. Meaning of "Treason, Bribery or other high Crimes and Misdemeanors"

The Constitution of the United States provides that the President "shall be removed from Office on Impeachment for, and Conviction of, Treason, Bribery, or other high Crimes and Misdemeanors." Upon impeachment and conviction, removal of the President from office is mandatory. The offenses for which a President may be impeached are limited to those enumerated in the Constitution, namely "Treason, Bribery, or other high Crimes and Misdemeanors." We do not believe that a President or any other civil officer of the United States government may constitutionally be impeached and convicted for errors in the administration of his office.

1. ADOPTION OF "TREASON, BRIBERY, OR OTHER HIGH CRIMES AND MISDEMEANORS" AT CONSTITUTIONAL CONVENTION

The original version of the impeachment clause at the Constitutional Convention of 1787 had made "mal-practice or neglect of duty" the grounds for impeachment. On July 20, 1787, the Framers debated whether to retain this clause, and decided to do so.

Gouverneur Morris, who had moved to strike the impeachment clause altogether, began by arguing that it was unnecessary because the executive "can do no *criminal act* without Coadjutors who may be punished." [1] George Mason disagreed, arguing that "When great *crimes* were committed he [favored] punishing the principal as well as the Coadjutors." [2] Fearing recourse to assassinations, Benjamin Franklin favored impeachment "to provide in the Constitution for the regular *punishment* of the executive when his misconduct should deserve it, and for his honorable acquittal when he should be unjustly accused." [3] Gouverneur Morris then admitted that "corruption & some few other offenses" should be impeachable, but thought "the case ought to be enumerated & defined." [4]

Rufus King, a co-sponsor of the motion to strike the impeachment clause, pointed out that the executive, unlike the judiciary, did not hold his office during good behavior, but during a fixed, elective term; and accordingly ought not to be impeachable, like the judiciary, for "misbehaviour:" this would be "destructive of his independence and of the principles of the Constitution." [5] Edmund Randolph, however, made a strong statement in favor of retaining the impeachment clause:

> Guilt wherever found ought to be *punished*. The Executive will have great opportunitys of abusing his power, particularly in time of war when the military force, and in some respects the public money will be in his hands.
>
> ... He is aware of the necessity of proceeding with a cautious hand, and of excluding as much as possible the influence of the Legislature from the business. He suggested for consideration ... requiring some preliminary inquest of whether just grounds for impeachment existed.[6]

---

[1] *The Records of the Federal Convention of 1787* (M. Farrand ed., 1911) 64 (emphasis added).
[2] *Id.*, at 64 (emphasis added).
[3] *Id.*, at 65 (emphasis added).
[4] *Id.*, (emphasis added).
[5] *Id.*, at 67.
[6] *Id.*, at 67 (emphasis added).

Benjamin Franklin again suggested the role of impeachments in releasing tensions, using an example from international affairs involving a secret plot to cause the failure of a rendezvous between the French and Dutch fleets—an example suggestive of treason.[7] Gouverneur Morris, his opinion now changed by the discussion, closed the debate on a note echoing the position of Randolph:

> Our Executive . . . may be bribed by a greater interest to betray his trust; and no one would say that we ought to expose ourselves to the danger of seeing the first Magistrate in foreign pay without being able to guard agst. it by displacing him. . . . The Executive ought therefore to be impeachable for treachery; Corrupting his electors, and incapacity were other causes of impeachment. For the latter he should be punished not as a man, but as an officer, and punished only by degradation from his office. . . . When we make him amenable to Justice however we should take care to provide some mode that will not make him dependent on the Legislature.[8]

On the question. "Shall the Executive be removable on impeachments," the proposition then carried by a vote of eight states to two.[9]

A review of this debate hardly leaves the impression that the Framers intended the grounds for impeachment to be left to the discretion, even the "sound" discretion, of the legislature. On a fair reading, Madison's notes reveal the Framers' fear that the impeachment power would render the executive dependent on the legislature. The concrete examples used in the debate all refer not only to crimes,[10] but to extremely grave crimes. George Mason mentioned the possibility that the President would corrupt his own electors and then "repeat his guilt," and described grounds for impeachment as "the most extensive injustice." Franklin alluded to the beheading of Charles I, the possibility of assassination, and the example of the French and Dutch fleets, which connoted betrayal of a national interest. Madison mentioned the "perversion" of an "administration into a scheme of peculation or oppression," [11] or the "betrayal" of the executive's "trust to foreign powers." Edmund Randolph mentioned the great opportunities for abuse of the executive power, "particularly in time of war when the military force, and in some respects the public money will be in his hands." He cautioned against "tumults & insurrections." Gouveneur Morris similarly contemplated that the executive might corrupt his own electors, or "be bribed by a greater interest to betray his trust"— just as the King of England had been bribed by Louis XIV—and felt he should therefore be impeachable for "treachery."

After the July 20 vote to retain the impeachment clause, the resolution containing it was referred to the Committee on Detail, which substituted "treason, bribery or corruption" for "mal-practice or neglect of duty." No surviving records explain the reasons for the change, but they are not difficult to understand, in light of the floor discussion just summarized. The change fairly captured the sense of the July 20 debate, in which the grounds for impeachment seem to have been such acts as would either cause danger to the very existence

---

[7] *Id.*, at 68.
[8] *Id.*, at 68–69.
[9] *Id.*, at 69.
[10] The frequent use of the terms "punish," "punishment," and "guilt" in this debate indicates the tenor of the proceedings, and seems to have occasioned Morris' suggestion that the "offenses" cognizable in an impeachment proceeding be "enumerated & defined."
[11] "Peculation" and "oppression" were both technical words of law, and constituted indictable crimes at common law. 4 W. Blackstone *Commentaries on the Laws of England* (1771) 122 (peculation), 140 (oppression).

of the United States, or involve the purchase and sale of the "Chief of Magistracy," which would tend to the same result. It is *not* a fair summary of this debate—which is the only surviving discussion of any length by the Framers as to the grounds for impeachment—to say that the Framers were principally concerned with reaching a course of conduct, whether or not criminal, generally inconsistent with the proper and effective exercise of the office of the presidency. They were concerned with preserving the government from being overthrown by the treachery or corruption of one man. Even in the context of that purpose, they steadfastly reiterated the importance of putting a check on the legislature's use of power and refused to expand the narrow definition they had given to treason in the Constitution. They saw punishment as a significant purpose of impeachment. The changes in language made by the Committee on Detail can be taken to reflect a consensus of the debate that (1) impeachment would be the proper remedy where grave crimes had been committed, and (2) adherence to this standard would satisfy the widely recognized need for a check on potential excesses of the impeachment power itself.

The impeachment clause, as amended by the Committee on Detail to refer to "treason, bribery or corruption," was reported to the full Convention on August 6, 1787, as part of the draft constitution. Together with other sections, it was referred to the Committee of Eleven on August 31. This Committee further narrowed the grounds to "treason or bribery," while at the same time substituting trial by the Senate for trial by the Supreme Court, and requiring a two-thirds vote to convict. No surviving records explain the purpose of this change. The mention of "corruption" may have been thought redundant, in view of the provision for bribery. Or, corruption might have been regarded by the Committee as too broad, because not a well-defined crime. In any case, the change limited the grounds for impeachment to two clearly understood and enumerated crimes.

The revised clause, containing the grounds "treason and bribery," came before the full body again on "September 8, late in the Convention. George Mason moved to add to the enumerated grounds for impeachment. Madison's Journal reflects the following exchange:

Col. MASON. Why is the provision restrained to Treason & bribery only? Treason as defined in the Constitution will not reach many great and dangerous offenses. Hastings is not guilty of Treason. Attempts to subvert the Constitution may not be Treason as above defined—as bills of attainder which have saved the British Constitution are forbidden, it is the more necessary to extend: the power of impeachments. He movd. to add after "bribery" "or maladministration." Mr. Gerry seconded him—

Mr. MADISON. So vague a term will be equivalent to a tenure during pleasure of the Senate.

Mr. GOVR. MORRIS., it will not be put in force & can do no harm—An election of every four years will prevent maladministration.

Col. Mason withdrew "maladministration" & substitutes "other high crimes and misdemeanors" agst. the State." [12]

On the question thus altered, the motion of Colonel Mason passed by a vote of eight states to three.

Madison's notes reveal no debate as to the meaning of the phrase "other high Crimes and Misdemeanors." All that appears is that

---
[12] 2 Farrand 550.

Mason was concerned with the narrowness of the definition of treason; that his purpose in proposing "maladministration" was to reach *great* and *dangerous* offenses; and that Madison felt that "maladministration," which was included as a ground for impeachment of public officials in the constitutions of six states, including his own,[13] would be too "vague" and would imperil the independence of the President.

It is our judgment, based upon this constitutional history, that the Framers of the United States Constitution intended that the President should be removable by the legislative branch only for serious misconduct dangerous to the system of government established by the Constitution. Absent the element of danger to the State, we believe the Delegates to the Federal Convention of 1787, in providing that the President should serve for a fixed elective term rather than during good behavior or popularity, struck the balance in favor of stability in the executive branch. We have never had a British parliamentary system in this country, and we have never adopted the device of a parliamentary vote of no-confidence in the chief executive. If it is thought desirable to adopt such a system of government, the proper way to do so is by amending our written Constitution—not by removing the President.

2. ARE "HIGH CRIMES AND MISDEMEANORS" NON-CRIMINAL?

a. *Language of the Constitution*

The language of the Constitution indicates that impeachment can lie only for serious criminal offenses.

First, of course, treason and bribery were indictable offenses in 1787, as they are now. The words "crime" and "misdemeanor", as well, both had an accepted meaning in the English law of the day, and referred to criminal acts. Sir William Blackstone's *Commentaries on the Laws of England*, (1771), which enjoyed a wide circulation in the American colonies, defined the terms as follows:

> I. A crime, or misdemeanor is an act committed, or omitted, in violation of a public law, either forbidding or commanding it. This general definition comprehends both crimes and misdemeanors; which, properly speaking, are mere synonymous in terms: though, in common usage, the word "crimes" is made to denote such offenses as are of a deeper and more atrocious dye; while smaller faults, and omissions of less consequence, are comprised under the gentler name of "misdemeanors" only.[14]

Thus, it appears that the word "misdemeanor" was used at the time Blackstone wrote, as it is today, to refer to less serious crimes.

Second, the use of the word "other" in the phrase "Treason, Bribery or other high Crimes and Misdemeanors" seems to indicate that high Crimes and Misdemeanors had something in common with Treason and Bribery—both of which are, of course, serious *criminal* offenses threatening the integrity of government.

Third, the extradition clause of the Articles of Confederation (1781), the governing instrument of the United States prior to the

---

[13] The six were Virginia ("maladministration, corruption, or other means by which the safety of the State may be endangered"), Delaware (same), North Carolina ("violating any part of the Constitution, maladministration, or corruption"), Pennsylvania ("maladministration"), Massachusetts ("misconduct and maladministration"). We believe it is significant that with such models before them, the Framers elected to define the grounds for impeachment under the Federal Constitution in narrow and seemingly criminal terms.
[14] 4 Blackstone 1, 5.

adoption of the Constitution, had provided for extradition from one state to another of any person charged with "treason, felony or *other high misdemeanor.*" [15] If "high misdemeanor" had something in common with treason and felony in this clause, so as to warrant the use of the word "other," it is hard to see what it could have been except that all were regarded as serious crimes. Certainly it would not have been contemplated that a person could be extradited for an offense which was non-criminal.

Finally, the references to impeachment in the Constitution use the langauge of the criminal law. Removal from office follows "conviction," when the Senate has "tried" the impeachment. The party convicted is "nevertheless . . . liable and subject to Indictment, Trial, Judgment and Punishment, according to Law." The trial of all Crimes is by Jury, "except in cases of Impeachment." The President is given power to grant "Pardons for Offenses against the United States, except in Cases of Impeachment."

This constitutional usage, in its totality, strengthens the notion that the words "Crime" and "Misdemeanor" in the impeachment clause are to be understood in their ordinary sense, i.e., as importing criminality. At the very least, this terminology strongly suggests the criminal or quasi-criminal nature of the impeachment process.

b. English impeachment practice

It is sometimes argued that officers may be impeached for non-criminal conduct, because the origins of impeachment in England in the fourteenth and seventeenth centuries show that the procedure was not limited to criminal conduct in that country.

Early English impeachment practice, however, often involved a straight power struggle between the Parliament and the King. After parliamentary supremacy had been established, the practice was not no open-ended as it had been previously.[16] Blackstone wrote (between 1765 and 1769) that

> [A]n impeachment before the Lords by the commons of Great Britain, in parliament, is a prosecution of *the already known and established law.* . . .[17]

The development of English impeachment practice in the eigtheenth century is illustrated by the result of the first major nineteenth century impeachment in that country—that of Lord Melville, Treasurer of the Navy, in 1805–1806. Melville was charged with wrongful use of public moneys. Before passing judgment, the House of Lords requested the formal opinion of the judges upon the following question:

> Whether it was lawful for the Treasurer of the Navy, before the passing of the Act 25 Geo. 3rd, c. 31, to apply any sum of money [impressed] to him for navy [sumpsimus] services to any other use whatsoever, public or private, without express authority for so doing; *and whether such application by such treasurer would have been a misdemeanor, or punishable by information or indictment?*[18]

---

[15] Articles of Confederation, Art. IV (emphasis added); printed in *Documents Illustrative of the Formation of the Union of the American States,* 69th Cong., 1st Sess., H. Doc. No. 398 (1927), p. 28.

[16] For example, the House of Lords in the thirteenth century had not thought itself bound by the common law as used in the inferior courts, but it reversed that position in 1709, when it decided that cases of impeachment would thenceforth be tried "according to the Law of the Land." Feerick, *Impeaching Federal Judges: A Study of the Constitutional Provisions,* 39 Fordham L. Rev. 1, 6, citing Hatsell, *Precedents of Proceedings in the House of Commons.*

[17] 4 Blackstone 256 (emphasis added).

[18] A. Simpson, *Federal Impeachments,* 64 Univ. Pa. L. Rev. 651, 685 (1916) (emphasis added).

The judges replied:

> It was *not unlawful* for the Treasurer of the Navy before the Act 25 Geo. 3rd, c 31, ... to apply any sum of money imprested to him for navy services, to other uses, ... without express authority for so doing, *so as to constitute a misdemeanor punishable by information or indictment.*[19]

Upon this ruling by the judges that Melville had committed no crime, he was acquitted. The case thus strongly suggests that the Lords in 1805 believed an impeachment conviction to require a "misdemeanor punishable by information or indictment." The case may be taken to cast doubt on the vitality of precedents from an earlier, more turbid political era and to point the way to the Framers' conception of a valid exercise of the impeachment power in the future. As a matter of policy, as well, it is an appropriate precedent to follow in the latter twentieth century.

The argument that the President should be impeachable for general misbehavior, because some English impeachments do not appear to have involved criminal charges, also takes too little account of the historical fact that the Framers, mindful of the turbulence of parliamentary uses of the impeachment power,[20] cut back on that power in several respects in adapting it to an American context. Congressional bills of attainder and *ex post facto* laws,[21] which had supplemented the impeachment power in England, were expressly forbidden. Treason was defined in the Constitution[22]—and defined narrowly—so that Congress acting alone could not change the definition, as Parliament had been able to do. The consequences of impeachment and conviction, which in England had frequently meant death, were limited to removal from office and disqualification to hold further federal office.[23] Whereas a majority vote of the Lords had sufficed for conviction,[24] in America a two-thirds vote of the Senate would be required.[25] Whereas Parliament had had the power to impeach private citizens, the American procedure could be directed only against civil officers of the national government.[26] The grounds for impeachment—unlike the grounds for impeachment in England—were stated in the Constitution.[27]

In the light of these modifications, it is misreading history to say that the Framers intended, by the mere approval of Mason's substitute

---

[19] *Id.* at 685 (emphasis added); 29 *Howell's State Trials* 1468–1471.

[20] The most egregious example was probably the case of Lord Strafford, who after the result of his impeachment seemed in doubt in the House of Lords, was executed in 1641 pursuant to the parliamentary bill of attainder. The bill of attainder was repealed (too late for Strafford) by the Act 13 and 14 Charles II, ch. 29, which stated, "That he [Strafford] was condemned upon accumulative treason, none of the pretended crimes being treason apart; that he was adjudged guilty of constructive treason; that the bill was forced through both houses by mobs of armed and tumultuous persons." 4 Hatsell, *Precedents of Proceedings in the House of Commons* 239 (1796). The execution of Strafford for "accumulative treason," whatever its role in the establishment of parliamentary power, illustrates the potential dangers of abandonment of a criminal standard. So too, perhaps, does the conviction of Judge Halsted Ritter in 1936 upon a seventh Article incorporating the substantive charges of the first six Articles. The opinion of Senator Austin, who voted Not Guilty on Article VII, urged that "six legal naughts cannot become a legal unit of general misbehavior." *Proceedings of the Senate in the Trial of Impeachment of Halsted L. Ritter*, 74th Cong., 2d sess., Sen. Doc. No. 200, p. 655.

[21] U.S. Const. art. I, sec. 9, cl. 3.

[22] *Id.* art. III. sec. 3.

[23] *Id.* art. I, sec. 3, cl. 7.

[24] Feerick, *Impeaching Federal Judges: A Study of the Constitutional Provisions*, 39 Fordham L. Rev. 1, 6 (1970).

[25] U.S. Const. art. I, sec. 3, cl. 6.

[26] *Id.* art. II, sec. 4.

[27] *Id.* art. II, sec. 4. The power of either House of Congress to expel a Member by a two-thirds vote, by contrast, contains no such limiting statement of grounds. *Id.* art. I, sec. 5, cl. 2.

amendment, to adopt *in toto* the British grounds for impeachment. Having carefully narrowed the definition of treason, for example, they could scarcely have intended that British treason precedents would guide ours.

c. American impeachment practice

The impeachment of President Andrew Johnson is the most important precedent for a consideration of what constitutes grounds for impeachment of a President, even if it has been historically regarded (and probably fairly so) as an excessively partisan exercise of the impeachment power.

The Johnson impeachment was the product of a fundamental and bitter split between the President and the Congress as to Reconstruction policy in the Southern states following the Civil War. Johnson's vetoes of legislation, his use of pardons, and his choice of appointees in the South all made it impossible for the Reconstruction Acts to be enforced in the manner which Congress not only desired, but thought urgently necessary.

On March 7, 1867, the House referred to the Judiciary Committee a resolution authorizing it

> to inquire into the *official conduct of* Andrew Johnson . . . and to report to this House whether, in their opinion, the said Andrew Johnson, while in said office, has been guilty of acts which were *designed or calculated to overthrow or corrupt the government of the United States* . . . ; and whether the said Andrew Johnson has been guilty of any act, or has conspired with others to do acts, which, in contemplation of the Constitution, are high crimes and misdemeanors, requiring the interposition of the constitutional powers of this House.[28]

On November 25, 1867, the Committee reported to the full House a resolution recommending impeachment, by a vote of 5 to 4.[29] A minority of the Committee, led by Rep. James F. Wilson of Iowa, took the position that there could be no impeachment because the President had committed no crime:

> In approaching a conclusion, we do not fail to recognize two stand-points from which this case can be viewed—the legal and the political.
> . . . Judge him politically, we must condemn him. But the day of political impeachments would be a sad one for this country. Political unfitness and incapacity must be tried at the ballot-box, not in the high court of impeachment. A contrary rule might leave to Congress but little time for other business than the trial of impeachments.
> . . . [C]rimes and misdemeanors are now demanding our attention. Do these, within the meaning of the Constitution, appear? Rest the case upon political offenses, and we are prepared to pronounce against the President, for such offenses are numerous and grave . . . [yet] we still affirm that the conclusion awhich we have arrived is correct.[30]

The resolution recommending impeachment was debated in the House on December 5 and 6, 1867. Rep. George S. Boutwell of Massachusetts speaking for the Committee majority in favor of impeachment, and Rep. Wilson speaking in the negative. Aside from characterization of undisputed facts discovered by the Committee, the only point debated was whether the commission of a crime was an essential element of impeachable conduct by the President. Rep. Boutwell began by saying, "If the theory of the law submitted by the minority of the

---
[28] H. R. Rep. No. 7, 40th Cong., 1st Sess., p. 1 (emphasis added).
[29] *Id.*, at 59.
[30] *Id.*, at 105.

committee be in the judgment of this House a true theory, then the majority have no case whatsoever."[31] "The country was disappointed, no doubt, in the report of the committee," he continued, "and very likely this House participated in the disappointment, that there was no specific, heinous, novel offense charged upon and proved against the President of the United States."[32] And again, "It may not be possible, by specific charge, to arraign him for this great crime, but is he therefore to escape?"[33]

The House of Representatives answered this question the next day, when the majority resolution recommending, impeachment was defeated by a vote of 57 to 108.[34] The issue of impeachment was thus laid to rest for the time being.

Earlier in 1867, the Congress had passed the Tenure-of-Office Act,[35] which took away the President's authority to remove members of his own Cabinet, and provided that violation of the Act should be punishable by imprisonment of up to five years and a fine of up to ten thousand dollars and "shall be deemed a high misdemeanor"[36]—fair notice that Congress would consider violation of the statute an impeachable, as well as a criminal, offense. It was generally known that Johnson's policy toward Reconstruction was not shared by his Secretary of War, Edwin M. Stanton. Although Johnson believed the Tenure-of-Office Act to be unconstitutional, he had not infringed its provisions at the time the 1867 impeachment attempt against him failed by such a decisive margin.

Two and a half months later, however, Johnson removed Stanton from office, in apparent disregard of the Tenure-of-Office Act.[37] The response of Congress was immediate: Johnson was impeached three days later, on February 24, 1868, by a vote of 128 to 47—an even greater margin than that by which the first impeachment vote had failed.

The reversal is a dramatic demonstration that the House of Representatives believed it had to find the President guilty of a crime before impeaching him. The nine articles of impeachment which were adopted against Johnson, on March 2, 1868, all related to his removal of Secretary Stanton, allegedly in deliberate violation of the Tenure-of-Office Act, the Constitution, and certain other related statutes. The vote had failed less than three months before; and except for Stanton's removal and related matters, nothing in the new Articles charged Johnson with any act committed subsequent to the previous vote.[38]

The only other case of impeachment of an officer of the executive branch is that of Secretary of War William W. Belknap in 1876. All five articles alleged that Belknap "corruptly" accepted and received considerable sums of money in exchange for exercising his authority to

---

[31] *Cong. Globe,* 40th Cong., 2d Sess., Appendix. p. 55.
[32] *Id.,* at 60.
[33] *Id.,* at 61.
[34] *Id.,* at 68.
[35] Act of March 2, 1867, 14 *Stat. L.,* p. 430.
[36] *Id.,* sec. 6; U.S. *Rev. Stat.* (1878), p. 315.
[37] There was some question whether Stanton was actually covered by the Tenure-of-Office Act, but this technical issue did not receive thorough consideration at the time.
[38] The House later added a Tenth Article, charging Johnson with making an inflamatory speech impugning the authority of Congress. However, since that speech had been made on August 18, 1866, if the House had thought its delivery to have been an impeachable offense, it would have been at liberty to impeach the President on that ground when it voted in December of 1867.
The Tenth Article received the lowest margin of House approval of any of the Articles. *Cong. Globe,* 40th Cong., 2d Sess. 1641. The Senate never voted on it.

appoint a certain person as a military post trader.[39] The facts alleged would have sufficed to constitute the crime of bribery. Belknap resigned before the adoption of the Articles and was subsequently indicted for the conduct alleged.

It may be acknowledged that in the impeachment of federal judges, as opposed to executive officers, the actual commission of a crime does not appear always to have been thought essential. However, the debates in the House [40] and opinions filed by Senators [41] have made it clear that in the impeachments of federal judges, Congress has placed great reliance upon the "good behavior" clause. The distinction between officers tenured during good behavior and elected officers, for purposes of grounds for impeachment, was stressed by Rufus King at the Constitutional Convention of 1787.[42] A judge's impeachment or conviction resting upon "general misbehavior," [43] in whatever degree, cannot be an appropriate guide for the impeachment or conviction of an elected officer serving for a fixed term.

The impeachments of federal judges are also different from the case of a President for other reasons: (1) Some of the President's duties, *e.g.*, as chief of a political party, are sufficiently dissimilar to those of the judiciary that conduct perfectly appropriate for him, such as making a partisan political speech, would be grossly improper for a judge. An officer charged with the continual adjudication of disputes labors under a more stringent injunction against the appearance of partisanship than an officer directly charged with the formulation and negotiation of public policy in the political arena—a fact reflected in the adoption of Canons of Judicial Ethics. (2) The phrase "and all civil Officers" was not added until after the debates on the impeachment clause had taken place. The words "high crimes and misdemeanors" were added while the Framers were debating a clause concerned exclusively with the impeachment of the President. There was no discussion during the Convention as to what would constitute impeachable conduct for judges. (3) Finally, the removal of a President from office would obviously have a far greater impact upon the equilibrium of our system of government than the removal of a single federal judge.

d. The need for a standard: criminal intent

When the Framers included the power to impeach the President in our Constitution, they desired to "provide some mode that will not make him dependent on the Legislature." [44] To this end, they withheld

---

[39] 15 *Cong. Rec.* 2160 (1876). Commenting upon the possibility that a certain investigation might have been directed toward impeachment of an executive officer, the United States Supreme Court stated in *Kilbourn v. Thompson*, 103 U.S. 168, 193 (1881), "[T]he absence of any words implying suspicion of criminality repel the idea of such purpose, for the Secretary could only be impeached for 'high crimes and misdemeanors.'"

[40] See, *e.g.*, remarks of Rep. Sumners, 76 *Cong. Rec.* 4924 (Louderback case; "good behavior" tenure expressly contrasted with fixed term of President).

[41] See, *e.g.*, *Proceedings of the Senate in the Trial of Impeachment of Harold Louderback*, 73rd Cong., 1st Sess., pp.837 (opinion of Senator Bailey), 841 (opinion of Senator Thomas).

[42] 2 Farrand 67. It was the more necessary to establish some system for the trial of "bad behavior" in judges, because the Framers had rejected the English system of removal of judges by address, provided by the Act of Settlement (1700), whereby the King could remove a judge upon a formal request by both Houses of Parliament.

[43] The charges upon which Judge Ritter was convicted in the Senate were characterized by the Chair, in overruling a point of order, as "general misbehavior." *Proceedings of the Senate in the Trial of Impeachment of Halsted L. Ritter*, 74th Cong., 2d Sess., Doc. No. 200, at p. 638.

[44] 2 Farrand 69 (remarks of Gouverneur Morris.)

from the Congress many of the powers enjoyed by Parliament in England; and they defined the grounds for impeachment in their written Constitution.[45] It is hardly conceivable that the Framers wished the new Congress to adopt as a starting point the record of all the excesses to which desperate struggles for power had driven Parliament, or to use the impeachment power freely whenever Congress might deem it desirable. The whole tenor of the Framers' discussions, the whole purpose of their many careful departures from English impeachment practice, was in the direction of limits and of standards.[46] An impeachment power exercised without extrinsic and objective standards would be tantamount to the use of bills of attainder and *ex post facto* laws, which are expressly forbidden by the Constitution and are contrary to the American spirit of justice.

It is beyond argument that a violation of the President's oath or a violation of his duty to take care that the laws be faithfully executed, must be impeachable conduct or there would be no means of enforcing the Constitution. However, this elementary proposition is inadequate to define the impeachment power. It remains to determine what kind of conduct constitutes a violation of the oath or the duty. Furthermore, reliance on the summary phrase, "violation of the Constitution," would not always be appropriate as a standard, because actions constituting an apparent violation of one provision of the Constitution may be justified or even required by other provisions of the Constitution.

There are types of misconduct by public officials—for example, ineptitude, or unintentional or "technical" violations of rules or statutes, or "maladministration"—which would not be criminal; nor could they be made criminal, consonant with the Constitution, because the element of criminal intent or *mens rea* would be lacking. Without a requirement of criminal acts or at least criminal intent, Congress would be free to impeach these officials. The loss of this freedom should not be mourned; such a use of the impeachment power was never intended by the Framers, is not supported by the language of our Constitution, and, if history is to guide us, would be seriously unwise as well.

As Alexander Simpson stated in his *Treatise on Federal Impeachments* (1916):

The Senate must find an intent to do wrong. It is, of course, admitted that a party will be presumed to intend the natural and necessary results of his voluntary acts, but that is a presumption only, and it is not always inferable from the act done. So ancient is this principle, and so universal is its application, that it has long since ripened into the maxim, *Actus non facit reum, [nisi] mens sit rea,* and has come to be regarded as one of the fundamental legal principles of our system of jurisprudence. (p. 29).

The point was thus stated by James Iredell in the North Carolina ratifying convention: "I beg leave to observe that, when any man is impeached, it must be for an error of the heart, and not of the head.

---

[45] See above, p. 367.
[46] A thoughtful historian has assessed the Chase impeachment as follows: "Its gravest aspect lay in the theory which the Republican leaders in the House had adopted, that impeachment was not a criminal proceeding but only a method of removal, the ground for which need not be a crime or misdemeanor as those terms were commonly understood." 1 Charles Warren, *The Supreme Court in United States History,* 293 (1922).
It has also been argued that impeachment of federal judges has been used as a partisan weapon in more recent cases. Ten Broek, *Partisan Politics and Federal Judgeship Impeachments Since 1903,* 23 Minn. L. Rev. 185 (1939); Thompson and Pollitt, *Impeachment of Federal Judges: An Historical Overview,* 49 N. Car. L. Rev. 37 (1970).

God forbid that a man, in any country in the world, should be liable to be punished for want of judgment. This is not the case here.[47]

C. The evidence before the Committee on the Judiciary

On August 5, 1974, the President released to the Committee and to the public the transcripts of three conversations between himself and H. R. Haldeman on June 23, 1972. Suffice it to say that these transcripts, together with the circumstances of their belated disclosure, foreclosed further debate with respect to the sufficiency of proof of the charges embodied in proposed Article I and led inevitably to the President's resignation three days later.

In the wake of these sudden and decisive events it may seem academic to discuss the character of the evidence which, prior to August 5, 1974, had been adduced in support of the allegations against the President. We are nevertheless constrained to make some general observations about that evidence, for two reasons. First, the disclosure of the June 23, 1972 transcripts, though dispositive of the case under proposed Article I, did not substantially affect the nature of the evidence in support of proposed Article II. Second, the fact that this disclosure cured the evidentiary defects earlier associated with proposed Article I must not be allowed to obscure the fact that a majority of the Members of the Committee had previously, and in our view wrongly, voted to recommend to the House the adoption of that Article on the basis of information then at their disposal.

1. RELIANCE ON HEARSAY EVIDENCE

The "evidence" relied on in the committee report is based essentially on the Summary of Information prepared by the majority staff. The facts and inferences contained in this one-sided document were drawn selectively from Statements of Information also prepared by the inquiry staff. The Statements of Information comprise a compilation of documentary materials already produced by other proceedings and investigations, for the impeachment inquiry staff initiated surprisingly little investigative work of its own. The source most frequently cited in the Statements of Information is the record of the 1973 proceedings of the Senate Select Committee on Presidential Campaign Activities.

The testimony before that Committee by John Dean, H. R. Haldeman, John Ehrlichman, and John Mitchell, was not limited to the actions of the persons testifying, but concerned statements made to them by others, motives supposed by them to have been shared by others, assumptions regarding the purposes of others, opinions of the guilt or innocence, truthfulness or perjury, of others. The witnesses before the Senate Select Committee were not always in agreement as to what had happened.

In the face of the sharply conflicting testimony and hotly contested issues of fact, the Committee's staff, unfortunately in our view, relied upon the printed record of proceedings held in another forum, for another purpose. The Committee staff was not able to interview H. R.

---

[47] 4 J. Elliot, Debates in the Several State Conventions on the Adoption of the Federal Constitution 125–126.

Haldeman, nor did he give testimony before this Committee. The Committee staff was not able to interview John Ehrlichman, nor did he give testimony before this Committee. Despite a public invitation to do so, the Chairman and Ranking Minority Member of the Committee did not interview the President of the United States under oath, nor, despite a public invitation to do so, did the Committee submit written interrogatories to the President to be answered under oath. The staff did, of course, interview a number of witnesses, such as John Dean, and nine of them gave testimony before this Committee.

Much has been made of the voluminousness of the "evidence" which was accumulated in support of impeachment, and upon which the majority of the Members of the Committee has relied in reporting out three proposed Articles of Impeachment. However, a fair examination of the character of that "evidence" reveals that it is comprised of layer upon layer of hearsay. We venture to say that ninety per cent of the "evidence" against the President would have been inadmissible in any court of law in the United States. We do not regard this as a legal quibble. Multiple hearsay evidence is inadmissible in our system of justice, not for some arcane and technical reason, but *because it is considered unreliable.*

Hearsay evidence is not subject to the test of cross-examination—described by the preeminent American scholar of the law of evidence as "beyond any doubt the greatest legal engine ever invented for the discovery of truth."[48] Our courts have been particularly sensitive to government proceedings which affect an individual's employment, and have required that an individual be afforded an opportunity to cross-examine his accusers before such governmental action can be taken. In *Greene v. McElroy*, 360 U.S. 474 (1959), for example, the United States Supreme Court held that the Government could not revoke an individual's security clearance on the basis of written records of testimony and reports by persons whom the individual had no opportunity to cross-examine. This result was reached even though the individual had been able to take several appeals from the action complained of.

In *Greene v. McElroy* the Court explained the basis of its holding as follows:

> Certain principles have remained relatively immutable in our jurisprudence. One of these is that where governmental action seriously injures an individual, and the reasonableness of the action depends on fact findings, the evidence used to prove the Government's case must be disclosed to the individual so that he has an opportunity to show that it is untrue. While this is important in the case of documentary evidence, it is even more important where the evidence consists of the testimony of individuals whose memory might be faulty or who, in fact, might be perjurers or persons motivated by malice, vindictiveness, intolerance, prejudice or jealousy. We have formalized these protections in the requirements of confrontation and cross-examination. They have ancient roots. . . . This court has been zealous to protect these rights from erosion. It has spoken out not only in criminal cases . . . but also in all types of cases where administrative and regulatory actions were under scrutiny. (360 U.S. at 496–97)

It might be argued that the rights of confrontation and cross-examination have less vitality in an impeachment proceeding than in other

---

[48] 5 Wigmore, *Evidence*, § 1367. Dean Wigmore further states:
"For two centuries past, the policy of the Anglo-American system of Evidence has been to regard the necessity of testing by cross-examination as a vital feature of the law. The belief that no safe-guard for testing the value of human statements is comparable to that furnished by cross-examination, and the conviction that no statement (unless by special exception) should be used as testimony until it has been probed and submitted by that test, has found increasing strength in lengthening experience." (*Id.*)

contexts, because the occupancy of public office is not an individual right of the respondent. But this is precisely the reason why the Committee's reliance on hearsay evidence, untested by cross-examination, is so disturbing. For it is not the personal rights of the President which were at stake, but rather the collective rights of the electorate which chose him to serve as the Chief Executive for a fixed term of four years.

To emphasize the importance of cross-examination and the deficiencies of hearsay evidence is not to say that the Committee should have declined to take cognizance of any evidence which could not meet the formal tests of admissibility. Surely it was appropriate for the impeachment inquiry to conduct a wide-ranging search for all information relevant to allegations of presidential misconduct. In this respect the Committee may be thought to resemble a grand jury, whose investigation is not circumscribed by narrow rules of admissibility. However, in fulfilling its role in the impeachment process the Committee should equally have been influenced by the House's potential prosecutorial function. In our view it would have been irresponsible to recommend to the House any Article of Impeachment grounded upon charges which could not be proved at trial, to whatever standard of proof and under whatever rules of evidence the Senate might reasonably be expected to apply. Because of the Committee's excessive reliance on hearsay and multiple hearsay evidence, we were obliged to conclude—like the subcommittee which investigated the conduct of Judge Emory Speer in 1914—"that the competent legal evidence at hand is not sufficient to procure a conviction at the hand of the Senate." [49]

Furthermore, even if liberal latitude were properly accorded by the House in considering certain types of inadmissible evidence, it does not follow that any other procedural or evidentiary rule need be relaxed. As the United States Supreme Court has stated, in describing the function and procedures of an administrative agency:

> The Commission is an administrative body and, even where it acts in a quasi-judicial capacity, is not limited by the strict rules, as to the admissibility of evidence, which prevail in suits between private parties. . . . But the more liberal practice in admitting testimony, the more imperative the obligations to preserve the essential rules ... by which rights are asserted or defended. ... All parties must be fully apprised of the evidence submitted or to be considered, and must be given opportunity to cross-examine witnesses, to inspect documents and to offer evidence in explanation or rebuttal. In no other way can a party maintain its rights or make its defense. In no other way can it test the sufficiency of the facts to support the findings.[50]

2. RELIANCE ON ADVERSE INFERENCES

Again putting aside the President's disclosures on August 5, 1974, we would draw attention to a second defect of the approach which the majority of the Committee has taken with respect to the evidence. Seemingly recognizing that even if every fact asserted in hearsay evidence were taken to be true, the case against the President might still have failed, the majority relied further upon inferences from inadmissible evidence, and upon the legal doctrine known as the "adverse inference" rule.

---

[49] VI *Cannon Precedents of the House of Representatives* § 527.
[50] *Interstate Commerce Commission v. Louisville & Nashville R. Co.*, 227 U.S. 88, 93 (1913).

The drawing of an inference is a process whereby a fact not directly established by the evidence is deduced as a logical consequence of some other fact, or state of facts, which is directly established by the evidence. The process is never mandatory; indeed, the same set of facts may give rise to conflicting inferences. However, an inference must lie within the range of reasonable probability, and some courts have held that it is the duty of the judge "to withdraw the case from the jury when the necessary inference is so tenuous that it rests merely upon speculation and conjecture." [51]

It has long been accepted in both civil and criminal cases that an inference may be drawn from a party's withholding or destruction of relevant evidence. The inference which may be drawn is that the unavailable evidence, if produced, would be adverse to the party who has not produced it. This rule is stated by Wigmore as follows:

> The opponent's spoliation (destruction) or suppressions of evidential facts ... and particularly of a document ... has always been conceded to be a circumstance against him, and in the case of a document, to be some evidence that its contents are as alleged by the first party. But that a rule of presumption can be predicated is doubtful.[52]

The operation of the adverse inference rule may be illustrated by the following language from a Supreme Court antitrust decision:

> The failure under the circumstances to call as witness those officers who did have authority to act for the distributors and who were in a position to know whether they had acted in pursuance of agreement is itself persuasive that their testimony, if given, would have been unfavorable to appellants.[53]

The operation of the adverse inference rule is subject to several restrictions. First, the party who has the burden of persuasion as to an issue cannot avail himself of the inference until he has produced sufficient evidence to shift the burden of going forward to his opponent.[54] Second, an adverse inference cannot arise against a person for failing to produce evidence which is merely corroborative or cumulative.[55] Third, the adverse inference rule cannot be applied where the evidence sought is the subject of a privilege [56] or where the party has a constitutional right to withhold the evidence.[57]

---

[51] *Wratchford v. S. J. Groves and Sons Co.*, 405 F. 2d 1061, 1066 (4th Cir. 1969).
[52] 9 Wigmore, *Evidence* (3d ed.) § 2524.
[53] *Interstate Circuit, Inc. v. United States*, 306 U.S. 208, 225–26 (1939).
[54] *Vanity Fair Paper Mills, Inc. v. Federal Trade Commission*, 311 F. 2d 480 (2d Cir. 1962).
[55] *Gafford v. Trans-Texas Airways*, 299 F. 2d 60 (5th Cir. 1962).
[56] 2 Wigmore, *Evidence* (3d ed). § 291.
In *Griffin v. California*, 380 U.S. 609 (1965), a case involving the privilege against self-incrimination, the Supreme Court held that it was constitutionally forbidden for the prosecution to make any comment upon the failure of a defendant to take the stand, or for a judge to instruct a jury that such failure constitutes evidence of guilt.
The proposed Federal Rules of Evidence provide as follows:

RULE 513

COMMENT UPON OR INFERENCE FROM CLAIM OF PRIVILEGE: INSTRUCTION

"(a) *Comment on inference not permitted*. The claim of a privilege, whether in the present proceeding or upon a prior occasion, is not a proper subject of comment by judge or counsel. No inference may be drawn therefrom.
". . . (c) *Jury instruction*. Upon request, any party against whom the jury might draw an adverse inference from a claim of privilege is entitled to an instruction that no inference may be drawn therefrom."
The Advisory Committee's Note to Rule 513 states,
"Destruction of the privilege by innuendo can and should be avoided. *Tallo v. United States*, 344 F. 2d 467 (1st Cir. 1965); *United States v. Tomaiolo*, 249 F. 2d 683 (2d Cir. 1957); *San Fratello v. United States*, 343 F. 2d 711 (5th Cir. 1965); *Courtney v. United States*, 390 F. 2d 521 (9th Cir. 1968)."
56 F.R.D. 183, 260–61 (1973). The proposed Rules are not yet effective, but Rule 513 is intended to be declarative of existing law.
[57] *International Union (U.A.W.) v. National Labor Relations Board*, 459 F. 2d 1329 (D.C. Cir. 1972).

As the statement of the adverse inference rule by Dean Wigmore indicates, the most familiar application of the rule is in a situation where one party to a suit demands a specific document from another party, and the other party refuses to produce it. Frequently, that document will have operative legal significance—e.g., in a contract dispute, or, in a criminal case, where the document sought might constitute a means or instrumentality of crime (written threat, attempt to bribe, etc.).

In the present case, the Committee has issued subpoenas for tapes, transcripts, dictabelts, memoranda, or other writings or materials relating to 147 presidential conversations, as well as for the President's daily diaries for an aggregate period of many months, and for various other materials and documents. It is true that these subpoenas have been issued only after the Committee's staff submitted to the Committee memoranda justifying each set of requests, in terms of their necessity to the Committee's inquiry. But in most cases, what these justifications tend to show is that given the chronology of facts known to the Committee, the President was, at a certain point in time, in a position where he could receive certain information, or have discussions with his aides on certain topics. In other words, in many cases the Committee lacks any independent evidence as to the content of the conversations and other materials subpoenaed.

Despite this tenuous basis for the operation of the adverse inference rule, on May 30, 1974, the Committee informed the President by letter:

> The Committee on the Judiciary regards your refusal to comply with its lawful subpoenas as a grave matter . . . Committee members will be free to consider whether your refusals warrant the drawing of adverse inferences concerning the substance of the materials.

Upon examination, however, this portentous statement does little to advance the analysis of the evidence. For even if it were proper to apply the adverse inference rule here, what inferences could plausibly be drawn? The inferences presumably would suggest that the material withheld was in some way damaging to the President; but there is no way of knowing why the material would be damaging. The President might have been reluctant to disclose conversations in which he had used abusive or indelicate language; or had engaged in frank discussions of his political opposition, or of his personal and family life; or had discussed campaign strategy and revealed an interest in raising a great deal of money for his re-election campaign. In short, there are a myriad of reasons why materials withheld from the Committee might have been embarrassing or harmful to the President if disclosed, without in any way constituting evidence of grounds for impeachment. In the absence of extrinsic evidence as to the particular content of a given presidential conversation or memorandum, the application of the adverse inference rule would be a futile exercise.

Finally, the justification for applying the adverse inference rule in the first instance is severely undercut, if not eliminated, by the presidential assertion of executive privilege. The President claimed that disclosure of the subpoenaed materials would destroy the confidentiality of the executive decision-making process—a reasonable and presumptively valid argument. The Committee might have challenged this argument in court, but instead voted 32 to 6 in late May 1974, not to seek the assistance of the federal judiciary in enforcing its subpoenas. The Committee also consistently declined to seek an "adjudication" of the validity of its demands upon the President for evidence, or potential evidence, by resort to formal contempt proceedings, whereby the President would have been afforded the opportunity to show cause before the full House why his invocation of executive privilege rendered non-contemptuous his failure to produce subpoenaed materials.

Having thus declined to take some action better calculated to secure the production of the evidence sought, if the Committee was entitled to it, the majority of the Committee can scarcely be heard to argue that the evidence is superfluous because its non-production gives rise to adverse inferences as to its contents.

D. Standard of Proof

The foregoing discussion of the character of the evidence which was adduced in support of impeachment would not be complete without reference to the standard of proof which that evidence was expected to satisfy.

In this context a threshold distinction must be drawn between the sufficiency of the allegation and the sufficiency of the proof. In deciding whether to vote for or against an article of impeachment, each Member of the Committee was obliged to make two separate judgments. First, it was necessary to consider whether a particular offense charged to the President, if proved, would constitute a ground for impeachment and removal. For example, certain Members intimated in debate that even if it were established to a certainty that the President had been guilty of tax fraud, this offense was too peripheral to the performance of his official duties to warrant removal from office. Second, where the charge was deemed sufficiently serious to justify removal, it was necessary to judge whether the evidence was compelling enough to "prove" the case. Prior to the disclosure of the June 23, 1972 conversations between the President and H.R. Haldeman, for instance, we believed that the evidence adduced in support of Article I did not constitute adequate proof of presidential involvement in the Watergate cover-up.

Neither the House nor the Committee on the Judiciary has ever undertaken to fix by rule the appropriate standard of proof for a vote of impeachment, nor would we advocate such a rule. The question is properly left to the discretion of individual Members. The discussion which follows is intended only to outline the process of reasoning which has persuaded us that the standard of proof must be no less rigorous than proof by "clear and convincing evidence."

1. STANDARD OF PROOF FOR CONVICTION BY THE SENATE

Our jurisprudence has developed a number of formulaic phrases which comprise a spectrum of the various standards of proof applicable in different types of legal proceeding. A Member of the House might most easily resolve his dilemma by simply choosing one of these standards, basing his judgment on some perception of the impeachment process. For example, a Member might require a very strict standard, such as proof beyond a reasonable doubt, on the ground that the drastic step of impeaching a President should not be undertaken except on the most compelling proof of misconduct.

This approach, however, is insensitive to the express terms of the Constitution, which provides that "the House of Representatives shall have the sole Power of Impeachment" [58] but that "the Senate shall have the sole Power to try all Impeachments." [59] The Members of the House might best give effect to this distinction by adopting a standard of proof which reflects the reservation of the ultimate decision of factual issues to the Senate. In other words, Members would be required to make a judgment as to whether the Senate could reasonably convict the respondent on the evidence before the House. That judgment would of course necessitate a prior judgment as to the appropriate standard of proof to be applied in the Senate.

Because the Senate proceeding *is* a trial, the inquiry may sensibly be narrowed to focus on trial-type standards of proof. In general, the courts recognize three types of burden of persuasion which must be borne by litigants in civil actions and in criminal prosecutions.[60] In most civil actions the party who has the burden of proof must adduce evidence which will sustain his claim by a "preponderance of the evidence." In a certain limited class of civil actions the facts must be proved by "clear and convincing evidence," which is a more exacting standard of proof than is "preponderance of the evidence." In criminal prosecutions the burden is on the prosecutor to prove all elements of the crime "beyond a reasonable doubt." These familiar formulas are not particularly susceptible to meaningful elaboration. One commentator has suggested that the three standards respectively denote proof that a fact is probably true; highly probably true; and almost certainly true.[61]

The Senate has never promulgated a rule fixing the standard of proof for conviction, but the overwhelming weight of opinion from past impeachment trials favors the criminal standard of proof beyond a reasonable doubt.[62] Similarly, during the pendency of the present impeachment inquiry at least three Senators have stated on the record that proof of guilt beyond a reasonable doubt would be required.[63]

This view finds strong support in the Constitution, whose provisions pertaining to impeachment are couched in the language of the criminal law. The respondent is to be "tried," and the trial of "all Crimes except . . . Impeachment" shall be by jury. The offenses cognizable in an impeachment trial are "Treason, Bribery, or other high Crimes

---

[58] U.S. Const., art. I, sec. 2, cl. 5.
[59] *Id.*, art. I, sec. 3, cl. 6.
[60] 9 Wigmore, *Evidence* (3d ed. 1940) §§ 2497, 2498; McCormick, *Evidence* (2d ed. 1972) § 339.
[61] McBaine, *Burden of Proof: Degrees of Belief*, 32 Calif. L. Rev. 244, 246–47 (1944); cited with approval in McCormick, *Evidence* (2d ed. 1972) § 339, n. 47.
[62] A typical example is the following excerpt from the memorandum opinion of Senator Pittman, filed in protest to the conviction of Judge Ritter in 1936:
"The Senate, sitting as a Court, is required to conduct its proceedings and reach its decision in accordance with the customs of our law. In all criminal cases the defendant comes into court enjoying the presumption of innocence, which presumption continues until he is proven guilty beyond a reasonable doubt." *Proceedings of the United States Senate in the Trial of Impeachment of Halsted L. Ritter* 642.
[63] See remarks of Senator Biden, 120 Cong. Rec. S5574 (April 10, 1974); Senator Stennis, *id.* S5738 (April 11, 1974); Senator Ervin, *id.* S5737 (April 11, 1974).

and Misdemeanors." The Senators are asked to vote Guilty or Not Guilty on each article of impeachment, and if two-thirds vote Guilty the respondent is "convicted."

Even if it were admitted that the Senate impeachment proceeding is a criminal trial, and that the grounds for impeachment are limited to criminal offenses, the argument might still be made that the traditional criminal standard of proof should not necessarily apply. Adherents of this view point out that the requirement of a more exacting standard of proof in criminal cases was introduced to mitigate the rigors of the criminal code in Eighteenth Century England, where nearly all crimes were punishable by death.[64] The use of capital punishment has virtually disappeared; but though his life is no longer at stake, the criminal defendant still stands to be deprived of his liberty. The purpose of the rigorous standard of proof in criminal cases is to guard against the possibility that an innocent man might be wrongly convicted and subjected to this severe punitive sanction. By contrast, it is argued, the primary purpose of impeachment is not punitive but remedial. Since removal from office is not punishment, there is no reason to apply the strict criminal standard of proof.

This argument is refuted by reference to the intentions of the Framers, who clearly conceived of removal from office as a punishment.[65] Thus, Mason favored "*punishing* the principal" for "great crimes"; Franklin thought that the Constitution should provide for "the regular *punishment* of the executive"; Randolph stated that "guilt wherever found ought to be *punished*"; and Mason said that the executive should be "*punished* only by degradation from his office." No one who has witnessed the recent agony and humiliation of President Nixon can seriously doubt that removal from office is a punishment.[66]

Because of the fundamental similarity between an impeachment trial and an ordinary criminal trial, therefore, the standard of proof beyond a reasonable doubt is appropriate in both proceedings. Moreover, the gravity of an impeachment trial and its potentially drastic consequences are additional reasons for requiring a rigorous standard of proof. This is especially true in the case of a presidential impeachment. Unlike a federal judge, an appointed officer who enjoys lifetime tenure during good behavior, the President is elected to office for a fixed term. The proper remedy for many instances of presidential misbehavior is the ballot box. The removal of a President by impeachment in mid-term, however, should not be too easy of accomplishment, for it contravenes the will of the electorate. In providing for a fixed four-year term, not subject to interim votes of No Confidence, the Framers indicated their preference for stability in the executive. That

---

[64] May, *Some Rules of Evidence: Reasonable Doubt in Civil and Criminal Cases*, 10 Am. L. Rev. 642, 656 (1876).

[65] See pp. 7–12, *supra*. Article I, Section 3, Clause 7 of the Constitution, which provides that the party convicted at an impeachment trial "shall nevertheless be liable and subject to Indictment, Trial, Judgment and Punishment," is often cited as evidence that the Framers meant to distinguish removal from punishment. But the clause may also fairly be read to mean that after the respondent has been punished by removal from office, he remains subject to the *additional* punishment provided by the criminal laws.

[66] Representative Weaver's remarks during the debate over the impeachment of Judge English in 1926 have a poignant application to the present case:

"Why, gentlemen, it is true the punishment does not go to his life or his liberty or his property. It does not touch those things. It does not reach the physical man, but, gentlemen, it goes to the destruction of his soul, the very essence of the man . . ." 67 Cong. Rec. 6706 (1926).

stability should not be jeopardized except on the strongest possible proof of presidential wrongdoing.

2. STANDARD OF PROOF FOR IMPEACHMENT BY THE HOUSE

In the light of the foregoing considerations, the temptation is great to insist that the standard of proof for impeachment by the House should also be proof beyond a reasonable doubt. It might be objected that if the House and the Senate were to adopt the same standard, the trial in the Senate would lose all of its significance since the House would have already adjudicated the case. This conclusion does not necessarily follow, however, because conviction in the Senate requires a two-thirds majority as against the simple majority of the House required for impeachment. Furthermore, as a logical proposition there is no intrinsic reason why the respondent should not be separately tried in each House and removed from office only after an effective vote in both—a procedure which would reflect the equal importance of the two Houses as in the exercise of their legislative functions.

The principal defect in applying the criminal standard of proof in both Houses of Congress is that this approach is not contemplated in the Constitution, which gives to the Senate the sole power to try all impeachments. If the vote on impeachment in the House required proof beyond a reasonable doubt, the House would effectively become the trier of fact. Instead, the Constitution intends that the House should frame the accusation but without adjudicating the ultimate guilt or innocence of the respondent.

The proper function of the House in an impeachment inquiry has often been described as analogous to the function of the grand jury. Both conduct an investigation which is not limited to evidence admissible at trial. Both are charged with determining whether that evidence warrants binding the case over for trial by another body, in which the standard of proof beyond a reasonable doubt is applied. In both cases the operative question is whether the trier of fact could reasonably convict the defendant.

The House differs from a grand jury, however, in that after returning the "indictment" it has an ongoing responsibility to bring the case to trial. In this respect the House more nearly resembles a public prosecutor. Like the grand jury, the prosecutor must also ask whether the trier of fact could reasonably convict. But his decision of whether or not to prosecute is typically founded on a greater mass of evidence than was available to the grand jury; and his perspective may involve an analysis of certain pragmatic factors, such as the availability or admissibility at trial of key testimony or evidence, with which the grand jury need not concern itself. These pragmatic factors must also affect the judgment of the House whether or not to impeach, particularly in a case like this one where so much of the evidence is multiple hearsay which might be ruled inadmissible at the Senate trial.

In order to justify bringing a case to trial, the prosecutor must personally believe in the guilt of the accused. It is not necessary, however, that he personally believe the accused to be guilty beyond a reasonable doubt; to impose such a requirement would in effect preempt the role of the trier of fact. Rather, the prosecutor should allow for the possibility that the trier of fact may find the evidence to be even more convincing than he does. Conversely, the prosecutor's mere belief that the accused is more likely guilty than not (i.e., proof by a preponderance of the evidence), would not be a sufficient basis on which to bring the case to trial. On balance, it appears that prosecution is warranted if the prosecutor believes that the guilt of the accused is demonstrated by clear and convincing evidence.

Without unduly overemphasizing the aptness of the analogy to a public prosecutor, we therefore take the position that a vote of impeachment is justified if, and only if, the charges embodied in the articles are proved by clear and convincing evidence. Our confidence in this proposition is enhanced by the fact that both the President's Special Counsel and the Special Counsel to the Committee independently reached the same conclusion.

ARTICLE I

INTRODUCTION

On February 25, 1974, the Federal grand jury that investigated the circumstances surrounding the June, 1972 unlawful entry into the Democratic National Committee headquarters in the Watergate Office Building voted to name Richard M. Nixon, President of the United States, as an unindicted member of the conspiracy to defraud the United States and to obstruct justice charged in Count One of the indictment that it subsequently returned in the case of *United States* v. *Mitchell et al.*, Cr. No. 74-110, United States District Court for the District of Columbia.[1]

Simultaneously with the issuance of that indictment, on March 1, 1974 the grand jury filed with the court a Report and Recommendation requesting that certain evidentiary materials bearing upon the President's involvement in the alleged conspiracy which the grand jury had accumulated in the course of its investigation be forwarded to this Committee for such consideration as we might deem proper. On March 26, 1974, by order of Chief Judge John J. Sirica, the Report and Recommendation and accompanying evidentiary materials were delivered to the Committee in accordance with the grand jury's request.

We view proposed Article I as the analogue of Count One of the indictment in *United States* v. *Mitchell et al.*, believing that it substantially charges President Nixon with conspiracy to obstruct justice, and obstruction of justice, in connection with the official investigation of the Watergate offenses.

We recognize that the majority of the Committee, as well as its Special Counsel, apparently do not consider it necessary or appropriate to charge impeachable offenses in terms of the violation of specific Federal criminal statutes, such as Title 18 U. S. C. § 371 (conspiracy), § 1001 (false statements to a government agency) or §§ 1503, 1505 and 1510 (obstruction of justice). The Special Counsel, indeed, has expressly disclaimed viewing the case as one of conspiracy, stating: "I don't believe that it is possible to have a conspiracy involving the President of the United States." (Summary of Information, 10)

We disagree. To the contrary, we believe the evidence warrants the conclusion that the President did conspire with a number of his aides and subordinates to delay, impede and obstruct the investigation of the Watergate affair by the Department of Justice. The Special Counsel's thesis that the President cannot be treated as a co-conspirator because "[y]ou don't have co-equals when you are dealing with the President of the United States" (Summary of Information, 11) seems to be not so much a proposition of law as a rhetorical device to bridge

---

[1] See Opinion of the Court in *United States* v. *Nixon*, No. 73-1766, Supreme Court of the United States, July 24, 1974, reprinted in "Criminal Cases," 163-64.

a number of gaps in the evidence relating to Presidential knowledge or direction of specific acts performed by his subordinates and associates, and thus to magnify Presidential culpability in the cover-up.

Simply as a matter of sound legal analysis, we think it more consonant with the Constitutional scheme [2] to determine Presidential *liability* for the acts of his subordinates in accordance with established rules of vicarious liability derived from the ordinary criminal law, and to assess the *seriousness* of Presidential misconduct on the basis of the evidence bearing upon his actual knowledge of, and involvement in, particular acts performed in furtherance of the aims of the conspiracy. It is not only of doubtful Constitutionality to resort to exotic theories of Presidential accountability for the Watergate cover-up in order to arrive at a proper disposition of proposed Article I, but on the record before us it is patently unnecessary to do so.

WATERGATE AND THE PRESIDENT'S "POLICY"

In the Summary of Information which he presented to the Committee before our debate on proposed Articles of Impeachment, the Special Counsel dealt with the question of Presidential responsibiliy for the two unlawful entries and wiretapping of the Democratic National Committee headquarters in a manner which continues to disturb us:

> The evidence available to the Committee establishes that on May 27 and June 17, 1972, agents of CRP, acting pursuant to a political intelligence plan (which included use of illegal electronic surveillance), authorized in advance by John Mitchell, head of CRP, and H. R. Haldeman, the President's chief of staff, broke into the DNC Headquarters at the Watergate for the purpose of effecting electronic surveillance; *and that this was part of the President's policy of gathering political intelligence to be used as part of his campaign for re-election.* (Summary of Information, 29; emphasis added)

We consider this to be a careless and unfair characterization of the weight of the evidence then before the Committee. The quoted paragraph assumes (1) that H.R. Haldeman authorized in advance a political intelligence plan that he knew contemplated the use of illegal electronic surveillance; (2) that he knew that implementation of that plan would or reasonably could involve the commission of unlawful entries; and (3) that, in approving such planned or foreseeable activities, Haldeman was carrying out the President's wishes. The point is made more explicit elsewhere on the same page of the Summary of Information: "It is a fair inference that Haldeman was implementing the President's policy with respect to the tactics he wanted used in his re-election campaign."

This sweeping allegation will not withstand close scrutiny in the light of the available evidence. In support of the statement last quoted above, the only purported citation of direct evidence that the President approved of illegal electronic surveillance and burglary as campaign techniques is as follows:

> The President endorsed the belief that in politics everybody bugs everybody else, and said that he could understand the desire for electronic surveillance, prior to the Democratic Convention. (House Judiciary Committee, "Transcripts of Eight Recorded Presidential Conversations," 4, hereinafter cited as HJCT.)

---

[2] See discussion of Article II, Paragraph (4), below.

However, if one examines the material on page 4 of the Committee's publication "Transcripts of Eight Recorded Presidential Conversations," upon which the Special Counsel relies to support his allegation that the President evidenced, after the fact, approval of the kind of activities represented by the Watergate offenses, he quickly observes how very misplaced that reliance was.

The pertinent Presidential remarks were made during the course of a discussion among Dean, Haldeman and the President on September 15, 1972 concerning the apparent finding of a second "bug" in the offices of the Democratic National Committee. The statements by which the President supposedly "endorsed the belief that in politics everybody bugs everybody else" consist of the President's *quoting* Senator Barry Goldwater as saying that "everybody bugs everybody else" and the President himself responding:

The PRESIDENT. Well, it's true. It happens to be totally true.
DEAN. [Unintelligible.]
The PRESIDENT. We were bugged in '68 on the plane and bugged in '62, uh, even running for Governor. God damnedest thing you ever saw. (HJCT, 4)

Thus, the President supported Senator Goldwater's view of the prevalence of "bugging" as a campaign practice by reference to instances in which he felt that *he*, Nixon, had been "bugged" by *his* political opponents. There was no reference to the President ever having approved the electronic surveillance of his own political opponents, nor was there any reference by any participant in the conversation to the commission of unlawful entries by partisans of any political persuasion.

In contrast to the "inference"—which we feel should more accurately be labelled as "suspicion"—that the President's wishes with regard to electronic surveillance were implemented by his close aides and associates, such as Haldeman and Mitchell, we cite our colleagues to the recently released transcripts of the earliest of three conversations between the President and Haldeman on June 23, 1972. However damaging this transcript may have been to the President for other reasons, it nevertheless supplies convincing evidence that the Watergate burglars were not acting in furtherance of any "policy" adopted by Richard Nixon.

Alone with Haldeman in the Oval Office, nearly a year before the existence of the White House taping system was publicly disclosed, the President's motive to speak less than candidly "for the record" would seem logically to have been minimal. The incriminating nature of what he *did* say on that occasion should suffice to prove that point. Yet in his dialogue with Haldeman, the President appears quite clearly to be chagrined and upset with those who "masterminded"—a malapropism?—the break-ins:

The PRESIDENT. . . . Well what the hell, did Mitchell know about this?
HALDEMAN. I think so. I don't think he knew the details, but I think he knew.
The PRESIDENT. He didn't know how it was going to be handled through—with Dahlberg and the Texans and so forth? Well who was the asshole that did? Is it Liddy? Is that the fellow? He must be a little nuts?
HALDEMAN. He is.
The PRESIDENT. I mean he just isn't well screwed on is he? Is that the problem?
HALDEMAN. No, but he was under pressure, apparently, to get more information, and as he got more pressure, he pushed the people harder to move harder—
The PRESIDENT. Pressure from Mitchell?

HALDEMAN. Apparently.
The PRESIDENT. Oh, Mitchell, Mitchell was at the point (unintelligible).
HALDEMAN. Yeah. (WHT, June 23, 1972, 10:09—11:39 a.m., 6)

Concededly, the Summary of Information was prepared before the release of the transcript from which the foregoing excerpt was taken, and we recognize that the view of the Special Counsel and the majority of the Committee regarding presidential responsibility for the unlawful entries and wiretapping of the Democratic National Committee headquarters may well have been modified as a result of this new evidence.

In all candor, however, we believe that the insubstantiality of the "Presidential policy" thesis was apparent long before President Nixon made his last, fateful disclosure of evidence.

The President's unfamiliarity with the various political intelligence schemes devised by some of his aides and associates was well illustrated, we think, by his response to Ehrlichman on April 14, 1973, after the latter told him in some detail how Mitchell blamed the White House for having originated the "grandfather" of the Watergate break-in plan, "Operation Sandwedge." The President replied simply, "What is Operation Sandwedge?" (WHT 526)

Evidence supporting the very linchpin of the thesis, that Haldeman knew or anticipated that illegal electronic surveillance and burglaries would be committed as part of the intelligence gathering program of the Committee to Re-elect the President, is sparse. The first evidence of Haldeman's knowledge of the general nature of the "Liddy Plan" arises from a conversation which he had with Dean in the spring of 1972, in which Dean told him essentially what Liddy had proposed to Mitchell. On that occasion, Haldeman agreed with Dean that Liddy's elaborate plan for muggings, buggings, prostitutes and the like was not necessary and that Dean should have no part of it. (Book I, 66) On March 21, 1973, Dean described this conversation to the President:

The PRESIDENT. Who else was present? Besides you—
DEAN. It was Magruder, Magruder.
The PRESIDENT. Magruder.
DEAN. uh, Mitchell, Liddy and myself. I came back right after the meeting and told Bob, I said, "Bob, we've got a growing disaster on our hands if they're thinking this way," and I said, "The White House has got to stay out of this and I, frankly, am not going to be involved in it." He said, "I agree John." And, I thought, at that point, the thing was turned off. That's the last I heard of it, when I thought it was turned off, because it was an absurd proposal.
The PRESIDENT. Yeah. (HJCT, 83)

The extent of Haldeman's appreciation of the true nature of Liddy's political intelligence gathering program as it later evolved is also uncertain. On March 31, 1972 Gordon Strachan sent Haldeman a "political matters memorandum" relaying Magruder's report that CRP then had a "sophisticated political intelligence gathering system." Strachan illustrated the operation of the system with samples of reports from "Sedan Chain II" which could not fairly put the reader of the memorandum on notice that the commission of criminal offenses was contemplated by the intelligence-gathering operatives.[3] Further, it is not even established that Haldeman read or knew the contents of

---
[3] "Sedan Chair II" was the code name of Michael McMinoway, who operated as an "undercover" political intelligence agent for CRP during the 1972 primary season.

the entire memorandum when he first received it. Three days after the arrest of the Watergate burglars, when Strachan reminded Haldeman about the March 30th memorandum and showed it to him again, Haldeman acknowledged that he had probably read part of it when it was first given to him but denied that he had ever read the tab concerning "Sedan Chair II." Haldeman then did read the tab and remarked to Strachan, "Maybe I should have been reading these, these are quite interesting." (Book I, 165)

Although Strachan prepared a "talking paper" for Haldeman's meeting with Mitchell on April 4, 1972 which included a reference to the CRP political intelligence plan, Haldeman neither recalls nor denies having discussed the subject with Mitchell on that occasion. Immediately after the meeting for which the "talking paper" was prepared, Haldeman and Mitchell both met with the President. The White House has furnished the Committee with an edited transcript of a tape recording of that conversation, and it reflects no mention of the subject of political intelligence whatsoever.

At several points during their conversation on March 13, 1973 the President and Dean speculated about the extent of Haldeman's advance knowledge of the DNC entries or his knowledge of the wiretapping while it was in progress:

The PRESIDENT. Ultimately, uh, Haldeman, uh, Haldeman's problem is Chapin, isn't it?
DEAN. Bob's problem is, is circumstantial.
The PRESIDENT. What I meant is, looking at the circumstantial. I don't know that [unintelligible]. On top of that, Bob had nothing—didn't know any of those people—like the Hunt's and all that bunch. Colson did. But, uh, Bob, Bob did know Chapin.
DEAN. That's right.
The PRESIDENT. Now, what—Now however the hell much Chapin knew I'll be God damned. I don't know.
DEAN. Well, Chapin didn't know anything about the Watergate, and—
The PRESIDENT. You don't think so?
DEAN. No. Absolutely not.
The PRESIDENT. Did Strachan?
DEAN. Yes.
The PRESIDENT. He knew?
DEAN. Yes.
The PRESIDENT. About the Watergate?
DEAN. Yes.
The PRESIDENT. Well, then, Bob knew. He probably told Bob, then. He may not have. He may not have.
DEAN. He was, he was judicious in what he, in what he relayed, and, uh, but Strachan is as tough as nails. I—
The PRESIDENT. What'll he say? Just go in and say he didn't know?
DEAN. He'll go in and stonewall it and say, "I don't know anything about what you are talking about." He has already done it twice, as you know, in interviews.
The PRESIDENT. Yeah. I guess he should, shouldn't he, in the interests of—Why? I suppose we can't call that justice, can we? We can't call it [unintelligible]
DEAN. Well, it, it—
The PRESIDENT. The point is, how do you justify that?
DEAN. It's a, it's a personal loyalty with him. He doesn't want it any other way. He didn't have to be told. He didn't have to be asked. It just is something that he found is the way he wanted to handle the situation.
The PRESIDENT. But he knew? He knew about Watergate? Strachan did?
DEAN. Uh huh.
The PRESIDENT. I'll be damned. Well, that's the problem in Bob's case, isn't it. It's not Chapin then, but Strachan. 'Cause Stratchan worked for him.

DEAN. Uh huh. They would have one hell of a time proving that Strachan had knowledge of it, though. (HJCT, 70–71)

* * * * * * *

DEAN. . . . I think that Chuck had knowledge that something was going on over there. A lot of people around here had knowledge that something was going on over there. They didn't have any knowledge of the details of the specifics of, of the whole thing.

The PRESIDENT. You know, that must, must be an indication, though, of the fact that, that they had God damn poor pickings. Because naturally anybody, either Chuck or Bob, uh, was always reporting to me about what was going on. If they ever got any information they would certainly have told me that we got some information, but they never had a God damn [laughs] thing to report. What was the matter? Did they never get anything out of the damn thing?

DEAN. No. I don't think they ever got anything.

The PRESIDENT. It was a dry hole. huh?

DEAN. That's right.

The PRESIDENT. Jesus Christ.

DEAN. Well, they were just really getting started.

The PRESIDENT. Yeah. Yeah. But, uh. Bob one time said something about the fact we got some information about this or that or the other, but, I, think it was about the Convention, what they were planning. I said [unintelligible]. So I assume that must have been MacGregor, I mean not MacGregor, but Segretti. (HJCT, 72)

* * * * * * *

The PRESIDENT. Who is "they"? The press?

DEAN. The press—

The PRESIDENT. The Democrats?

DEAN. —the Democrats, the intellectuals—

The PRESIDENT. The Packwoods?

DEAN. Right. Right. "They" would never buy it, uh, as far as (1) White House involvement in the Watergate which I think there is just none, uh, for that incident that occurred over in the Democratic National Committee Headquarters. People just, here, would—did not know that that was going to be done. I think there are some people who saw the fruits of it, but that's another story. I am talking about the criminal conspiracy to, to go in there. The other thing is that, uh. the Segretti thing. You hang that out. uh. they wouldn't believe that. They wouldn't believe that, that. uh. Chapin acted on his own to put his old friend, friend [unintelligible] Segretti in to be a Dick Tuck on somebody else's campaign. They would, they would have to paint it into something more sinister, something more involved, a part of a general plan. (HJCT, 74–75)

These passages indicate not only that, in Dean's mind, Haldeman's connection with the Watergate offenses was tenuous at most, but even more significantly, that Haldeman had apparently never told the President what he did or did not know prior to June 17, 1972 about Liddy's political espionage program.

On the morning of March 21, 1973, Dean reiterated his belief that Haldeman had no specific advance knowledge of the Watergate break-in:

The PRESIDENT. Did Colson—had he talked to anybody here?

DEAN. No. I think this was an independent—

The PRESIDENT. Did he talk to Haldeman?

DEAN. No. I don't think so. Now, but here's the other the thing where the next thing comes in the chain. I think that Bob was assuming that they had something that was proper over there, some intelligence gathering operation that Liddy was operating. And through Strachan, uh, who was his tickler, uh, he started pushing them.

The PRESIDENT. [Sighs] Yeah.

DEAN. To get something, to get some information and they took that as a signal—Magruder took that as a signal—to probably go to Mitchell and say, "They are pushing us like crazy for this from the White House." And so Mitchell probably puffed on his pipe and said, "Go ahead," and never really re—, reflected on what it was all about. So, they had some plan that obviously had, I gather, different targets they were going to go after. They were going to infiltrate, and bug, and do all this sort of thing to a lot of these targets. This is knowledge I have after the fact. [Coughs] And, apparently, they, uh, they, they had, they had after they had initially broken in and bugged the Democratic National Committee, they were getting information. The information was coming over here to Strachan. Some of it was given to Haldeman, uh, there is no doubt about it. Uh—

The PRESIDENT. Did he know what it was coming from?
DEAN. I don't really know if he would.
The PRESIDENT. Not necessarily.
DEAN. Not necessarily. That's not necessarily. Uh—
The PRESIDENT. Strachan knew what it was from.
DEAN. Strachan knew what it was from. No doubt about it, and whether Strachan—I had never come to press these people on these points because it,
The PRESIDENT. Yeah.
DEAN. It hurts them to, to give up that next inch, so I had to piece things together. All right, so Strachan was aware of receiving information, reporting to Bob. At one point Bob even gave instructions to change their capabilities from Muskie to McGovern, and had passed this back through Strachan to Magruder and, apparently to Liddy. And Liddy was starting to make arrangements to go in and bug the, uh, uh, McGovern operation. They had done prelim—
The PRESIDENT. They had never bugged Muskie, though, did they?
DEAN. No, they hadn't but they had a, they had, uh, they'd
The PRESIDENT. [Unintelligible]
DEAN. infiltrated by a, a, they had
The PRESIDENT. A secretary.
DEAN. a secretary and a chauffeur. Nothing illegal about that. (HJCT, 84–85)

*　　*　　*　　*　　*　　*　　*

DEAN. and Liddy was charged with doing this. We had no knowledge that he was going to bug the DNC. Uh—
The PRESIDENT. Well, the point is, that's not true.
DEAN. That's right.
The PRESIDENT. Magruder did know that—
DEAN. Magruder specifically instructed him to go back in the DNC.
The PRESIDENT. He did?
DEAN. Yes.
The PRESIDENT. You know that? Yeah. I see. Okay.
DEAN. Uh. I honestly believe that no one over here knew that. I know, uh, as God is my maker. I had no knowledge that they were going to do this.
The PRESIDENT. Bob didn't either [unintelligble]
DEAN. Uh. But—
The PRESIDENT. They know you're not the issue. Bob, Bob, now—he wouldn't know.
DEAN. Bob—I don't believe specifically knew they were going in there.
The PRESIDENT. I don't think so.
DEAN. I don't think he did. I think he knew there was a capacity to do this but he wouldn't, wasn't giving it specific direction.
The PRESIDENT. Strachan, did he know?
DEAN. I think Strachan did know. (HJCT, 87–88)

INVOLVEMENT OF PRESIDENT IN COVER-UP

We will not belabor the abundant evidence tending to establish the *existence* of a conspiracy to obstruct and impede the official investigation of the Watergate break-in. We do question, however, any suggestion that the evidence shows Presidential knowledge and involvement from the very beginning. That beginning, as John Dean has testified, occurred literally within hours after the arrest of the burglars inside the Democratic National Committee headquarters:

Mr. ST. CLAIR. ... Now, sir, I would like to go way back to the break-in at the DNC, if I may. You were actually in Hawaii, as I understand it?

Mr. DEAN. No sir, I was in Manila.
Mr. ST. CLAIR. In Manila. When you returned to the United States, I think you have testified that you became involved in the coverup almost from the very beginning, or words to that effect?
Mr. DEAN. That is correct.
Mr. ST. CLAIR. I think at one point, you said it just sort of happened, it grew like Topsy, or words to that effect?
Mr. DEAN. It made me wish I had stayed in Manila.
Mr. ST. CLAIR. I am sure in retrospect, that is so. But is it true that you testified that this was not any set policy of any kind, it just sort of grew, and you just sort of fell into it, or words to that effect?
Mr. DEAN. That is correct.
Mr. ST. CLAIR. All right. And that state of affairs commenced almost immediately upon your return to the United States?
Mr. DEAN. Correct. (Dean testimony, 2 HJC 282)

In his earlier testimony before the Senate Select Committee on Presidential Campaign Activities, Dean had described the inception of the cover-up in similar terms:

Senator MONTOYA. When was the first real meeting to organize the coverup and who was present at that first meeting?
Mr. DEAN. I think that the coverup is somewhat similar to the planning of this whole thing, that just sort of happened. I know that when I came back from out of the country there had already been significant events which had occurred. The coverup was already—it had begun and was, in fact, in place and was going. (Dean testimony 3 SSC 1091)

* * * * * * *

Mr. DEAN. . . . When I came back to the office on the 18th and talked to Mr. Strachan, I realized that the coverup was already in effect, in being, and I realized that when Mr. Strachan told me of the documents that he had destroyed and Mr. Haldeman's instruction, that there certainly wasn't going to be a revelation of the White House involvement in the matter. I didn't at that point in time know the potentials of the White House involvement.

* * * * * * *

Senator GURNEY. Who set the policy on the coverup?
Mr. DEAN. I would say the policy was just—I do not think it was a policy set. There was just no alternative at that point in time.
Senator GURNEY. It sort of grew like Topsy, and you were a part of it, is that not right?
Mr. DEAN. That is correct.
Senator GURNEY. Now, since this thing started out with such a flurry and a spate of phone calls and meetings between everybody, did you advise the President of what was going on?
Mr. DEAN. Senator, the first time I ever talked to the President was on September 15. (Dean testimony, 4 SSC 1357)

POINTERS IN THE WRONG DIRECTION

Without in any way suggesting that the President himself was not fully and genuinely responsible for his decision to join the cover-up conspiracy no later than June 23, 1972, we must point out, admittedly only in slight mitigation, that when the President desperately needed sound advice from good men, he was surrounded by aides and advisers who were themselves inclined by the circumstances to give him the worst possible advice. Haldeman, Ehrlichman, Mitchell, Colson and Dean each had selfish, personal reasons for wanting the full story of Watergate concealed from official investigators, the general public, indeed, in varying degrees, from the President himself. In addition, they shared a misguided desire to shield the President, as much as possible, from the need to assume personal responsibility for such a sorry episode in the middle of his re-election drive.

Haldeman

Whatever Haldeman did or did not know about the precise nature of the Liddy Plan as it finally evolved (see discussion on pp. ——— above), it was his job to oversee, through Gordon Strachan, on behalf of the White House the operations of the Committee for the Re-election of the President. At the very least, Haldeman had obviously failed to take adequate steps to control Liddy and his bizarre surveillance schemes, and this failure had made possible an incident of great potential embarassment to the President, namely, the Watergate fiasco.

The majority relies heavily upon the testimony before the Committee of Alexander P. Butterfield, former Deputy Assistant to the President and aide to Haldeman, to lend credence to the proposition that anything Haldeman knew, the President knew. That very concept is, on its face, inconsistent with Haldeman's role as Chief of Staff, necessarily the filterer and organizer of the flow of information to the President. A more accurate description of the matter, it seems to us, would be "anything Haldeman thought the President ought to know, the President knew."

Moreover, the majority ignores testimony by former Special Counsel to the President Charles W. Colson which is more plausible and more clearly probative of the likelihood that Haldeman would have told the President all he knew about the Watergate break-in:

> Mr. HOGAN. There has been some testimony before the committee about what got to the President through Haldeman. On the basis of your knowledge of White House operations, if Mr. Haldeman had made a mistake or fouled up on some activity, would he likely admit that and bring that to the President's attention, or would he likely try to isolate the President from that?
> Mr. COLSON. Well, it's the kind of speculation that I really don't like to engage in. But, there were some other instances, and *I think Bob was very reluctant to admit he made a mistake to anyone. He's by nature the kind of guy who doesn't like to acknowledge any errors, and I think he would be unlikely to do so.*
> Mr. HOGAN. Could you tell the committee what some of those instances were?
> Mr. COLSON. Oh, I can remember some mistakes in scheduling and Bob said, don't, you know, this wasn't a mistake. We did it and don't go into this with the President. There were some things that I from time to time that I knew he had made mistakes with. He asked me not to talk about it. Bob just didn't like to admit that kind of a thing. I don't think anybody does.
> Mr. HOGAN. Well, is it conceivable then that he and other White House staff people might have been engaged in certain activities following the Watergate break-in that the President had no knowledge of?
> Mr. COLSON. Well, let me give you an illustration that I gave to the staff, Mr. Hogan.
> We had a thing in the campaign called Chapman report, which was a very useless document. It would come 3 days after you had read the same stuff in the newspapers, and Murray Chotiner's galfriend who was a reporter was sending this back from the campaign. I asked Mr. Haldeman if I could receive copies of that and he said yes, but under one strict instruction. And I said what's that. And he said, you don't tell the President where the information comes from if you ever discuss it with him, and I said that this is silly, this stuff is not that hot to begin with, and he said, that's the condition, if you discuss the Chapman report with the President, you don't identify it as the Chapman report or identify from where it came from. (Colson testimony, 3 HJC 478; emphasis added)

In any event, from the dialogue between Haldeman and the President on the morning of June 23, 1972, quoted above, regarding the extent of John Mitchell's role in authorizing the Watergate folly, it is obvious that either (1) Haldeman did not actually know a great deal about the involvement of senior CRP officials in the instigation of the DNC break-ins and wiretapping, or else (2) he did not impart to the President on that occasion the full benefit of his knowledge on the subject.

Ehrlichman

On the day of the second Watergate entry, John Ehrlichman was the senior White House staff member in Washington, since Haldeman was in Key Biscayne with the President. That afternoon, Ehrlichman was informed by Secret Service Agent Boggs that the White House telephone number of Howard Hunt had been found among the effects of the Watergate burglars. (Book II, 118) Through Haldeman, the President placed Ehrlichman in charge of learning what had happened at the Watergate, and on June 19th, Ehrlichman turned the matter over to John Dean to look into the question of possible White House involvement. ("Presidential Statements," 8/22/73, 46; Book II, 150) That afternoon, Dean told Ehrlichman that Liddy had personally confirmed to Dean an earlier report by Magruder that the break-in had been a CRP operation which Liddy directed. (Book II, 144–45)

During 1971, Ehrlichman himself had been overall supervisor of the White House Special Investigations Unit—the "Plumbers"—of which both Hunt and Liddy were members. Ehrlichman had never told the President about the "Plumbers" September, 1971 burglary of the office of Dr. Lewis Fielding, Daniel Ellsberg's psychiatrist. (In fact, Ehrlichman never did tell the President about that; John Dean did, on March 17, 1973.) (WHT, 157–58) Thus, Ehrlichman would have been motivated to discourage official investigation of Hunt's and Liddy's previous activities, not only to preserve the secrecy of legitimate "Plumbers" national security investigations, but also to prevent the revelation of his and other White House staff members' roles in an enterprise of such questionable legality as the Fielding break-in, of which the President remained totally unaware for nine more months.

We readily acknowledge that one statement by the President on the morning of June 23, 1972 gives rise to the possibility—at the most it is no more than a suspicion—that the President may on that date have been aware of the Fielding break-in. The President remarked to Haldeman:

The PRESIDENT. Of course, this Hunt, that will uncover a lot of things. You open that scab there's a hell of a lot of things and we just feel that it would be very detrimental to have this thing go any further. This involves these Cubans, Hunt, and a lot of hanky-panky that we have nothing to do with ourselves. . . . (WHT, June 23, 1972, 10:09–11:39 a.m., 6)

It is more likely, however, that the President is simply "rehearsing" with Haldeman what kind of remark might be dropped with C.I.A. Director Helms or Deputy Director Walters to alert them to the potential for embarrassment to the Agency if Hunt's comings and goings were too closely scrutinized by the F.B.I. Even if the President was addressing a specific concern of his to Haldeman, the reference is obviously too vague and general to permit an inference that it was the Fielding break-in, rather than some other covert activity of Hunt as a member of the Special Investigations Unit, about which the President was concerned.

Mitchell

The weight of the evidence is that John Mitchell had indeed authorized Liddy to undertake some form of intelligence-gathering operation for CRP of which the Watergate break-ins and bugging were the disastrous upshot. Even if he did not, Mitchell acknowledges that after the break-in he learned of both Magruder's involvement as overseer of the Liddy operation and of certain so-called "White House horrors," but he did not tell the President about these things for fear that

> he would lower the boom on all of this matter and it would come back to hurt him and it would affect him in his re-election. (Mitchell testimony, 4 SSC 1666)

Upon learning of the arrest of the burglars in the Watergate office building, the thought of his own possible criminal liability as an accessory before the fact or co-conspirator to the Watergate offenses must have crossed Mitchell's mind; it could reasonably have influenced his actions as well. In any event, the President did not learn the truth about Watergate from his former Attorney General and political confidant who, among his other motives for concealment, may genuinely not have wished to put the President in a position of *having* to take some action by telling him how the Watergate crimes were instigated.

It is clear from all the transcripts of tape recorded presidential conversations available to the Committee that even by March of 1973, Mitchell had not acknowledged to the President his role in approving the "Liddy Plan." Specifically, the President's question to Haldeman in their morning conversation on June 23, 1972—"Well what the hell, did Mitchell know about this?"—should establish beyond doubt that Mitchell did not, during his telephone conversation with the President on the evening of June 20, 1972 (which was not recorded because the President placed the call from a residence telephone not connected to the recording system) tell the President that the Watergate burglars were carrying out an "official" CRP assignment.

Colson

Like Ehrlichman, Colson had reason to be concerned about where an exhaustive investigation of Hunt and Liddy might lead. Colson had recommended Hunt's hiring as a White House consultant the previous summer and had raised the money to pay for Hunt's and Liddy's 1971 Labor Day weekend excursion to California during which the Fielding break-in was committed. (Book VII, Part 3, 1248–49)

Moreover, in February of 1972, in response to a complaint from Hunt and Liddy, Colson called Magruder and, without specifically mentioning anything relating to wiretapping or espionage, urged him to "get off the stick and get the budget approved for Mr. Liddy's plans." (Book I, 105, 110–14) In the aftermath of the DNC arrests, Colson may well have worried about how his February call to Magruder might *appear* to the President, as well as to investigators, in view of his relationship with Hunt. Dean and the President considered the very point on March 21, 1973:

> DEAN. . . . They came up with, apparently, another plan, uh, but they couldn't get it approved by anybody over there. So Liddy and Hunt apparently came to see Chuck Colson, and Chuck Colson picked up the telephone and called Magruder and said, "You all either fish or cut bait. Uh, this is absurd to have these

guys over there and not using them, and if you're not going to use them, I may use them." Things of this nature.

The PRESIDENT. When was this?

DEAN. This was apparently in February of '72.

The PRESIDENT. That could be—Colson know what they were talking about?

DEAN. I can only assume, because of his close relationship with

The PRESIDENT. Hunt.

DEAN. Hunt, he had a damn good idea of what they were talking about, a damn good idea. He would probably deny it, deny it today and probably get away with denying it. But I, uh, I still—

The PRESIDENT. Unless Hunt—

DEAN. Unless Hunt, uh, blows on him—

The PRESIDENT. But then Hunt isn't enough. It takes two doesn't it?

DEAN. Probably. Probably. But Liddy was there also and if, if Liddy were to blow—

The PRESIDENT. Then you've got a problem—I was saying as to the criminal liability in the

DEAN. Yeah.

The PRESIDENT. White House· Okay.

DEAN. I will go back over that, and tell

The PRESIDENT. Was that Colson?

DEAN. You where I think the, the soft spots are.

The PRESIDENT. Colson—that, that, that Colson, uh, you think was the, uh, was the person who

DEAN. I think he.

The PRESIDENT. pushed?

DEAN. I think he helped to get the push, get the thing off the dime. Now something else occurred, though—(HJCT, 84)

*   *   *   *   *   *   *

The PRESIDENT· The absurdity of the whole damned thing,

DEAN. But it—

The PRESIDENT. bugging and so on. Well, let me say I am keenly aware of the fact that, uh, Colson, et al., and so forth, were doing their best to get information and so forth and so on. But they all knew very well they were supposed to comply with the law.

DEAN. That's right.

The PRESIDENT. No question.

DEAN. Uh—

The PRESIDENT· [Unintelligible] you think—you feel that really the man, the trigger man was Colson on this then?

DEAN. Well, no, he was one of s—, he was just in the chain. He was, he helped push the thing.

The PRESIDENT. Called [unintelligible] and said, "We've got a, we've got a good plan." I don't know what the Christ he would be doing. Oh, I'll bet you. I know why. That was at the time of ITT. He was trying to get something going there because ITT, they were bugging us. I mean they were

DEAN. Right.

The PRESIDENT. giving us hell.

DEAN. Well, I know, I know he used, uh,

The PRESIDENT. Hunt to go out there?

DEAN. Hunt. (HJCT, 100)

Colson had better reason than most to know how the President would react to news that one of his own White House aides had played a part in spurring Liddy on. On Sunday, June 18th, the day after the Watergate arrests, the President had displayed his anger over the publicized involvement of McCord, the CRP security consultant:

Mr. JENNER. All right. You had two conversations with him on that day?

Mr. COLSON. Yes, sir.

Mr. JENNER. Were they in person or by telephone?

Mr. COLSON. The President was calling me from Key Biscayne both times.

Mr. JENNER. Now, tell us to the best of your recollection that conversation, and any benchmark you might have to refresh your recollection.

Mr. COLSON. Well, I had no recollection of those two calls at all, but a former assistant of mine——
Mr. JENNER. Please name him.
Mr. COLSON. Mr. Desmond Barker said that he came into my office on that Monday or Tuesday following the DNC break-in and that we were talking about it and I was describing to Mr. Barker, no relation to the Barker who was involved in the break-in, I was describing to Mr. Barker how incensed I was and how stupid I thought the whole thing was. And he asked me what the President's reaction was and I told him that the President had called me a couple of times on Sunday and he was so furious that he had thrown an ashtray across the room at Key Biscayne and thought it was the dumbest thing he had ever heard of and was just outraged over the fact that anybody even remotely connected with the campaign organization would have anything to do, anything to do with something like Watergate. At that point we knew, of course, from the newspaper accounts that Mr. McCord, whom I had never heard of before that day, nor had the President, we knew that Mr. McCord was one of those that had been caught at the Watergate and was a consultant or on the payroll in some way of the Republican National Committee and the Committee for the Re-Election.
Mr. JENNER. You used the expression "we knew." Are you referring to knowing as of, knowing that fact or those facts respecting Mr. McCord as of June 18, 1972?
Mr. COLSON. I remember, I think I remember it being on the front page of the newspapers on Sunday morning. (Colson testimony, 3 HJC 259)

Dean

Dean had been instrumental in getting Gordon Liddy hired as General Counsel of the Committee to Re-Elect the President at a higher salary than he had been receiving as a member of the White House Domestic Counsel staff, contrary to an established CRP policy against such raises. (Book I, 50) Moreover, Dean had been involved in discussions pertaining to the abortive "Sandwedge" political intelligence plan during the latter half of 1971 (Book I, 44), had undertaken some relatively tame political intelligence himself at the request of Haldeman (Dean testimony, 2 HJC 221, 347–48), and had participated in meetings in Attorney General Mitchell's office on January 27 and February 4, 1972 at which Liddy had presented his proposals for an elaborate political intelligence operation—a fact known to Haldeman as well as to the other participants in the meetings. (Book I, 59–60) Mitchell, indeed, looked to Dean for assistance in developing a political intelligence capability after "Sandwedge" was scrapped. (Book I, 34)

Obviously, from Dean's standpoint, the less said to anyone who did not already know about his relationship with Liddy and his knowledge of the pre-Liddy and early Liddy political espionage plans, the better.

In any event, it is undisputed that Dean did not personally disclose to the President any information he had or suspicions he may have harbored concerning the involvement of White House or top CRP officials in the advance planning of the Watergate crimes until some time in March 1973.

Just how much Dean had to fear from complete disclosure of the facts surrounding the Watergate offenses remains to this day unclear. Honoring a claim of attorney-client privilege, the Committee chose not to explore the tantalizing remark made by William O. Bittman, former attorney for Howard Hunt, during his testimony before the Committee:

Mr. COHEN. Now, as I recall your testimony earlier this morning, you had a conversation with Mr. Colson during which time you were discussing Mr. Hunt's

safe or the safe of the U.S. Government in the Executive Office Building, and Colson told you to talk to Mr. Dean, as I recall, and correct me if I am wrong, and you said that you didn't want to talk to Dean because he was involved?
Mr. BITTMAN. Yes, sir.
Mr. COHEN. Now, when was that conversation that you had with Mr. Colson?
Mr. BITTMAN. January 3, 1973.
Mr. COHEN. What do you mean, Mr. Dean was involved in what?
Mr. BITTMAN. In the initial Watergate planning and break-in.
Mr. COHEN. And you knew this, I take it, as a result of your conversations with your client?
Mr. BITTMAN. Well, based on the hearsay information of my client. Mr. Hunt never had any personal knowledge of anything. It is all hearsay. (Bittman testimony, 2 HJC 89–90)

Whether Hunt had reference only to Dean's presence at the two meetings in Mitchell's office when the Liddy plans was discussed, we may never know.

THE PRESIDENT ENTERS THE CONSPIRACY

Given the varied motives of these principal actors to suppress the facts in their own interests, as well as in what they jointly, but mistakenly, perceived to be the best interests of the President, it is wholly plausible that the cover-up conspiracy arose immediately and spontaneously as word of the arrest of McCord *et al.* spread, just as Dean suggested (see above). Since there is no logical need to hypothesize an all-knowing, all-powerful President at the center of the conspiracy from its beginning, organizing and directing the cover-up activities of each of his aides and subordinates (at least in general outline), in order adequately to explain the events that transpired in the first several days following the discovery of the burglars, we consider it our Constitutional mandate not to do so unless and until specific evidence convinces us that it is *at least* more probable than not that the President had become involved.

The edited transcripts of three conversations between the President and H. R. Haldeman on June 23, 1972 which were submitted to the Committee on August 5, 1974 provide, in our view, the first direct and persuasive evidence of Presidential knowledge and intent to participate in an ongoing conspiracy to obstruct justice in 1972.

In the morning conversation, after telling the President that the FBI had been able to trace the source of cash in the possession of Bernard Barker, one of the arrested burglars, Haldeman recommended as a solution:

HALDEMAN. . . . Mitchell came up with yesterday, and John Dean analyzed very carefully last night and concludes, concurs now with Mitchell's recommendation that the only way to solve this, and we're set up beautifully to do it. . .

* * * * * * *

That the way to handle this now is for us to have [CIA Deputy Director L. Vernon] Walters call Pat Gray and just say, 'Stay to hell out of this—this ah, business here we don't want you to go any further on it.' That's not an unusual development, and ah, that would take care of it. ("Submission of Recorded Presidential Conversations to the Committee on the Judiciary of the House of Representatives by President Richard Nixon, August 5, 1974," hereinafter cited as WHT) (WHT, June 23, 1972, 10:09–11:39 a.m., 3)

The President inquired as to the source of the funds and was told that Minnesota industrialist Kenneth Dahlberg's $25,000 contribution check had gone directly to Barker. Then the following dialogue ensued:

The PRESIDENT. It isn't from the Committee though, from Stans?
HALDEMAN. Yeah. It is. It's directly traceable and there's some more through some Texas people that went to the Mexican bank which can also be traced to the Mexican bank—they'll get their names today.
HALDEMAN. —And (pause)
The PRESIDENT. Well, I mean, there's no way—I'm just thinking if they don't cooperate, what do they say? That they were approached by the Cubans. That's what Dahlberg has to say, the Texans too, that they—
HALDEMAN. Well, if they will. But then we're relying on more and more people all the time. That's the problem and they'll stop if we could take this other route.
The PRESIDENT. All right.
HALDEMAN. And you seem to think the thing to do is get them to stop?
The PRESIDENT. Right, fine.
HALDEMAN. They say the only way to do that is from White House instructions. And it's got to be to Helms and to—ah, what's his name . . . ? Walters.
The PRESIDENT. Walters.
HALDEMAN. And the proposal would be that Ehrlichman and I call them in, and say, ah—
The PRESIDENT. All right, fine. How do you call him in—I mean you just—well, we protected Helms from one hell of a lot of things.
HALDEMAN. That's what Ehrlichman says. (*Id.*, 4–5)

While there are references to the belief of FBI agents investigating the break-in that the affair was a CIA operation, nowhere in the transcript does there appear any indication that either Haldeman or the President believed or suspected that the Democratic National Committee headquarters entry was in fact a CIA operation.

The President was clearly put on notice during the conversation that the break-in was both sponsored and financed by the Committee to Re-elect the President:

The PRESIDENT. . . . Well what the hell, did Mitchell know about this?
HALDEMAN. I think so. I don't think he knew the details, but I think he knew.
The PRESIDENT. He didn't know how it was going to be handled though—with Dahlberg and the Texans and so forth? Well who was the asshole that did? Is it Liddy? Is that the fellow? He must be a little nuts!
HALDEMAN. He is.
The PRESIDENT. I mean he just isn't well screwed on is he? Is that the problem?
HALDEMAN. No, but he was under pressure, apparently, to get more information, and as he got more pressure, he pushed the people harder to move harder—
The PRESIDENT. Pressure from Mitchell?
HALDEMAN. Apparently.
The PRESIDENT. Oh, Mitchell. Mitchell was at the point (unintelligible).
HALDEMAN. Yeah.
The PRESIDENT. All right, fine, I understand it all. We won't second-guess Mitchell and the rest. Thank God it wasn't Colson. (*Id.*, 6–7)

The manner in which Haldeman broached the subject suggests that he and the President had discussed at least some aspect of the Watergate investigation previously:

HALDEMAN. Now, on the investigation, you know the Democratic break-in thing, *we're back in the problem area* because the FBI is not under control, because Gray doesn't exactly know how to control it and they have—their investigation is now leading into some productive areas—because they've been able to trace the money—not through the money itself—but through the bank sources—the banker. And, and it goes in some directions we don't want it to go. (*Id.*, 2–3; emphasis added)

Even though the burglars had been in custody since their arrest six days earlier, Haldeman told the President that certain "things" had begun "filtering in" to the FBI:

> HALDEMAN. Ah, also there have been some things—like an informant came in off the street to the FBI in Miami who was a photographer or has a friend who is a photographer who developed some films through this guy Barker and the films had pictures of Democratic National Committee letterhead documents and things. (*Id.*, 3)

And the President himself, in the materal quoted above, asked whether Liddy had been responsible for the arrangements. According to the evidence available to the Committee, Liddy's participation in the break-in had not been learned by the FBI on June 23rd, meaning that someone on the White House staff or in CRP who was knowledgeable as to the facts must have discussed the matter with the President prior to this conversation with Haldeman. Likewise, Haldeman's remark about the photographer/informant in Miami appears to presume knowledge on the part of the President that CRP agents had some opportunity to photograph DNC documents prior to the night of the arrests—a fact not known publicly or to official investigators until a few days later when Alfred Baldwin became an FBI informant.

INTERPRETING EVENTS IN LIGHT OF THE JUNE 23, 1972 TRANSCRIPTS

We do not consider it nit-picking to suggest that, even with the benefit of the additional evidence produced by the President on August 5, 1974, some of the specific allegations made against him in the majority report are not well founded. It is still important—perhaps even more important, now that Mr. Nixon is not able to mount a formal defense to the Committee's accusations in an appropriate forum—for us to caution against the indiscriminate adoption of each and every adverse interpretation that could be placed upon specific presidential actions and statements, merely because the President has been shown to be culpable *to some extent* at an early stage of the cover-up.

False or Misleading Public Statements

Paragraph (8) of Article I, for example, charges President Nixon with "making false or misleading public statements" in order to deceive the public as to the adequacy of his investigation into allegations of misconduct on the part of White House and CRP personnel. While the Paragraph itself does not specify which presidential statements material to the subject matter of the Committee's inquiry were false, or which of them were misleading, the Introduction to the discussion of evidence relating to proposed Article I found above in this Committee report does contain a list of sixteen public utterances and three comments made by the President in published writings, which, by virtue of their enumeration there, are allegedly false or misleading and part of a "pattern of concealment, deception and cover-up."

We are satisfied that most of these statements were actually false or misleading when made. In some cases, however, it remains to be seen whether the President knew of their false or misleading character when he made them.

June 22, 1972

The first example given is the President's statement in a news conference on June 22, 1972 that his Press Secretary, Ronald Ziegler, had spoken "accurately" when he had said of the Watergate break-in, "the White House has had no involvement whatever in this particular incident." There is, however, no evidence that prior to his making that statement facts had come to his attention, from any source, giving him reason to believe that the statement was untrue. We now know that on the following morning, June 23, 1972, the President appeared already to have received some information regarding Hunt and Liddy's role in the Watergate offense, but we are left only to speculate whether he received that information before or after his June 22 news conference, and whether he was given any reason to believe that the involvement of either Hunt or Liddy amounted to "White House involvement."

It should be noted that nothing in the White House edited transcripts of that conversation between Haldeman and the President on the morning of June 23, 1972 suggests that the President was told at that time, or was conscious of having been previously told, that anyone at the White House had been involved in the Watergate matter.

In the Conclusion of the Committee report's discussion of proposed Article I, the same presidential statement of June 22, 1972, appears to be listed as the third in a pattern of thirty "undisputed acts" in which the President was involved after the break-in which the majority asserts cannot be "rationally explained" except in terms of the President's guilt as charged in Article I. Curiously, at that point in the report it is alleged that the President publicly denied on June 22, 1972 that members of the Committee for the Re-election of the President were involved in the Watergate break-in. We have been unable to find any evidence in the record showing clearly that the President's denial of involvement was intended by him to extend beyond members of the White House staff.

While the President appeared to adopt, by general reference, the denials of either White House or official CRP involvement made earlier in the week by both Mitchell and Ziegler, the President's specific reference was more narrow:

> ... And, as Mr. Ziegler has stated, the White House has no involvement whatever in this particular incident. ("Presidential Statements," 6/22/72, 2)

In view of McCord's arrest inside the Watergate office building, surely any presidential statement asserting the non-involvement of CRP personnel would have to have been as carefully qualified as were the press releases made by Mitchell on June 18 and 20, 1972. (LaRue testimony, 1 HJC 212; Book II, 29)

August 29, 1972

The second false or misleading public statement listed in the Introduction to the Committee report on Article I is one about which there has been controversy since the Senate Select Committee conducted its public hearings into the Watergate affair in 1973, namely, the President's statement in his news conference of August 29, 1972 that

> ... within our own staff, under my direction, Counsel to the President, Mr. Dean, has conducted a complete investigation of all leads which might involve

any present members of the White House staff or anybody in the Government. I can say categorically that his investigation indicates that no one in the White House Staff, no one in this Administration, presently employed, was involved in this very bizzare incident. ("Presidential Statements," 8/29/72, 3)

The quoted statement refers, of course, to the so-called "Dean investigation" during the summer of 1972, which Dean himself has denied ever having conducted.

Soon after the arrest of the Watergate burglars, the President instructed Ehrlichman to investigate possible White House involvement in the incident. ("Presidential Statements," 8/22/73, 46) On June 19, 1972 Ehrlichman delegated this responsibility to Dean, who was Counsel to the President. (Book II, 144–46, 152) Colson testified that in August, 1972 Dean "was handling the Watergate matter and handling the investigation and acting as Counsel for all of us...." (Colson testimony, 3 HJC 275) On June 21, 1972, Ehrlichman told Acting FBI Director Pat Gray that Dean would be handling an inquiry into Watergate for the White House. (Book II, 314) On the same day, Dean informed Gray that he would sit in on any F. B. I. interviews of White House staff personnel, and that he would do so in his official capacity as counsel to the President. (Book II, 314)

According to Attorney General Richard Kleindienst, Dean unsuccessfully requested permission from him to receive raw F. B. I. investigative reports, representing to Kleindienst and Assistant Attorney General Henry Petersen that he was dealing strictly with the President. (Kleindienst testimony, 9 SSC 3564, 3575–76) To induce Gray to permit him access to the raw F. B. I. files, Dean on at least two occasions assured Gray that he was reporting directly to the President on the Watergate matter. (Gray testimony, 9 SSC 3450–51, 3482)

Despite these representations to Kleindienst, Petersen and Gray, Dean in fact never saw the President during June or July of 1972, and he met with him only once, briefly and in a group, that August. (Book III, 598)

On the morning of April 16, 1973, Dean and the President met and discussed, among other things, the applicability of the attorney-client privilege to various activities of Dean on behalf of the President. In that connection, the subject of the 1972 "Dean investigation" came up:

The PRESIDENT. Let me say, on this point, I would, uh, would not waive. You could say, "I reported to the President." Uh, that "The President called me in." I mean. "The President has authorized me to say—He called me in, and, uh, and, uh, asked me—"
DEAN. Uh huh.
The PRESIDENT. Uh, make that, that before, that when the event first occurred, you conducted an investigation and passed to the President the message: "No White House personnel, according to your investigation, was involved." You did do that, didn't you?
DEAN. I did that through Ehrlichman and Haldeman.
The PRESIDENT. That's it. You did do that.
DEAN. If I'm under oath, now, I'm, I'm going to have to say I did that through Ehrlichman and Haldeman.
The PRESIDENT. No. But I know you did that. I didn't see you.
DEAN. That's right. (HJCT 195)

The fact that Dean did not meet personally with the President to discuss the progress of his "investigation" casts no more doubt on whether, from the President's standpoint, he was actually conducting an investigation under the President's direction, than does the same absence of private, personal contact call into question whether during that period Dean was really serving as "Counsel to the President."

The sixth item on the list of thirty presidential acts set out in the Conclusion of the Committee report on proposed Article I is described as: "The President's public statement on August 29, 1972, *a statement later shown to be untrue,* that an investigation by John Dean 'indicates that no one in the White House staff, no one in the Administration, presently employed, was involved in this very bizarre incident.'" (Emphasis added.)

It is not clear precisely what the majority there alleges to have been untrue: the assertion that Dean had conducted an investigation? the implication that any such investigation was legitimate? the assertion that the investigation indicated that no one then employed at the White House or elsewhere in the Administration had been involved in the Watergate incident? or the fact that no one then employed at the White House or elsewhere in the Administration had actually been involved in the Watergate incident?

As late as April 16. 1973 Dean assured the President that no one at the White House had been involved in the original Watergate offenses:

DEAN. It's unfortunate that I, you know. I'm hoping that the ultimate resolution of this thing is that no one has any problems. And that's possible,
The PRESIDENT. Legally.
DEAN. legally.
The PRESIDENT. That's right. Which I hope is your case, too. In other words, when I say no one, nobody at the White House staff—not you, not Colson, not Ehrlichman, not Haldeman, because God damn it—Let me, let me, let me summarize this specific point again, because I need to, uh, you know, they, we know there was no—on the Dean report. Ziegler has always said it was oral.
DEAN. That's right.
The PRESIDENT. Right. But you remember when you came in, I asked you the specific question: "Is anybody on the White House staff involved?" You told me "No."
Dean. That's right. And I have no knowledge—
The PRESIDENT. You still believe that?
DEAN. Yes sir, I do. (HJCT 192)

In view of the above dialogue, Dean's professed uncertainty in March, 1973 about Haldeman's knowledge of the Watergate operation prior to the arrests, and the tenor of the Nixon-Haldeman conversation on the morning of June 23, 1972, it should come as no surprise if Dean's investigation in the summer of 1972 had actually revealed no White House involvement in the DNC entries and wiretapping, in the sense apparently meant by both Dean and the President in their discussion on April 16. 1973, just quoted above. There would be no reason, of course, why Dean could not convey such a conclusion to the President "through channels" in August, 1972, just as there is no reason why the "channels" themselves could not exaggerate to the President the good faith and vigor with which the "Dean investigation" had been pursued, particularly if any of the "channels" had a motive to minimize the extent of Dean's own awareness, before or during the fact, of Liddy's Watergate operation.

If the President had no reason to doubt the truth of his August 29, 1972 statement *when he made it,* no subsequent revelations could vitiate its essential truthfulness for purposes of our inquiry.

Obviously, the statement at issue was still defective, but because it was misleading, not because the evidence demonstrates that it was false. Several weeks earlier, the President had been put squarely on notice by Haldeman that the highest officials in his re-election committee were probably behind the Watergate break-ins. It is *that* which the President chose not to acknowledge publicly in a press conference that took place two-and-one-half months before the 1972 Presidential election. His statement was probably substantially true, as far as it went, but it carefully avoided going far enough either to be untrue or to damage the President in the heat of his re-election campaign.

President Nixon's seeming obsession with the narrow question whether any of his White House aides had in some fashion been involved in the planning or execution of the actual entries and wiretapping of the Democratic National Committee headquarters, as contrasted with their obvious involvement in the cover-up of the CRP connection with the crimes, is paradoxical. It is both an aggravating and a mitigating factor, when considered for different purposes.

On the one hand, the President's "tunnel vision" on this question, if genuine, tends to negate the existence of a *mens rea* with respect to "covering up the cover-up." It may help explain the President's apparent slowness to appreciate the import of what Dean told him on the morning of March 21, 1973, about the details of the cover-up:

DEAN. . . . Uh, but some people are going to have to go to jail. That's the long and short of it, also.
The PRESIDENT. Who? Let's talk about that.
DEAN. All right. Uh, I think I could, for one.
The PRESIDENT. You go to jail?
DEAN. That's right.
The PRESIDENT. Oh, hell no. I can't see how you can. But I—no,
DEAN. Well, because—
The PRESIDENT. I can't see how, that—Let me say I can't see how a legal case could be made against you, J—, uh, John.
DEAN. It'd be, it'd be tough but, you know, uh,
The PRESIDENT. Well.
DEAN. I can see people pointing fingers, you know, to get it out of their own, put me in the impossible position, disproving too many negatives.
The PRESIDENT. Oh, no. Uh let me say I—not because you're here—But just looking at it from a cold legal standpoint: you are a lawyer, you were a counsel—you were doing what you were doing as a counsel, and you were not, uh,
DEAN. [Clears throat.]
The PRESIDENT. doing anything like that. You mean—What would you go to jail on [unintelligible]?
DEAN. The obstruc—, the obstruction of justice.
The PRESIDENT. The obstruction of justice?
DEAN. That's the only one that bothers me.
The PRESIDENT. Well, I don't know. I think that one. I think that, I feel, could be cut off at the pass. Maybe the obstruction of justice—(HJCT 102–03)

Even if the President failed to appreciate the gravity of the situation from the standpoint of individual criminal liabilities because, in part, he was looking at the crux of the matter in the wrong focus, we would concede that this, in itself, would suggest a certain insensitivity to the demands of his high office for the exposure, rather than the concealment, of serious misconduct on the part of his subordinates and close political associates acting to further his personal political interests.

CLEMENCY

Paragraph (9) of proposed Article I alleges that the President sought to induce criminal defendants and convicts to remain silent about their knowledge of the criminal involvement of others, in exchange for the expectation of some favorable treatment or consideration which presumably the President would be in a position to grant. The Members of the Committee know full well, however, that the gist of this allegation is that the President offered or authorized the offering of executive clemency to those who were or might be convicted of the original Watergate offenses.

We earnestly submit that, taken as a whole, the evidence simply does not fairly permit the inference that the President ever offered or authorized the offer of clemency to any person in exchange for his silence or false testimony.

When the subject was first broached to him in July, 1972, the President firmly and categorically rejected even the idea of discussing it. Later, in January, 1973, in an unguarded moment the President did tell his Special Counsel, Charles Colson, who was seeking some assurance of help for his friend Howard Hunt, that clemency was a possibility only because of Hunt's tragic family circumstances. Then, on March 21, 1973, the President firmly and unhesitatingly rejected the possibility of offering clemency to Hunt in order to maintain his silence with regard to "seamy things" he had done for the White House. It does not appear from the evidence that the President ever considered the use of clemency as an enticement to the hapless Watergate defendants.

The first time clemency was discussed with the President by anyone in the White House was on or about July 8, 1972 when the President met with John Ehrlichman. (Book III, 181–97) In the course of a long, rambling discussion on the beach about different matters, Ehrlichman raised the point that, because of the political nature of the Watergate case, the question of presidential pardons would inevitably become a problem for the White House. After a brief discussion, the President expressed his "firm view" that he would never be in a position to grant these particular individuals any form of clemency. The two men agreed that clemency for the Watergate suspects was the kind of subject which should be excluded forever from the President's consideration. (Book III, 183)

As a result of his wife's death in an airplane crash on December 8, 1972, Howard Hunt decided to plead guilty. (Bittman testimony, 2 HJC 21) Hunt and Charles Colson were close personal friends. (Colson testimony, 3 HJC 275, 416–17) On December 31, 1972, Hunt wrote to Colson asking him to see Hunt's attorney, William Bittman. (Book III 458) Colson forwarded the letter to Dean, since Dean was responsible for Watergate matters within the White House, with a covering memo stating, "[n]ow, about what the hell do I do?" (Colson testimony, 3 HJC 457.)

On January 3, 1973, Colson, Dean and Ehrlichman discussed Hunt's letter. (Book III, 460, 463–64, 466–68) Colson was anxious to assure Hunt of his continued friendship and willingness to help. Ehrlichman told Colson he could see Bittman, but that there could be no commitments regarding clemency. Ehrlichman restated the President's position of July, 1972. (Book III, 463–64) Colson, however, wanted to see the President about clemency but Ehrlichman forbade it. (Book III, 460; WHT 419–21)

Dean has testified that Ehrlichman told him he would see the President on the matter and that the next day Ehrlichman told him that he had given Colson "an affirmative" regarding clemency for Hunt. (Book III, 460–61) Erlichman denies discussing anything concerning Hunt with the President at that time. (Book III, 464)

On both January 3 and 4, 1973, Colson met with Bittman. Bittman has testified:

> We went into much more detail [than on January 3], or I did, with respect to Howard Hunt's plea of guilty, and the fact that Howard Hunt was very concerned about his children when he would go to jail, and he was very concerned about the possibility of Judge Sirica giving him a substantial sentence.
> In view of the fact that his wife had been killed less than a month earlier, he was terrified with the prospect of receiving a substantial sentence. Mr. Colson indicated that he was a very close, dear friend of Howard Hunt, that if necessary he would take Howard Hunt's children into his own home, that in his opinion it would be outrageous if Judge Sirica would give him a substantial sentence because of his own health problems, his family's health problems and his service to the country, and because of the nature of the offense.
> And he told me to go back to Howard Hunt to indicate to him that he would always be a close friend of Howard Hunt's and that he would do anything whatsoever to assist Howard Hunt as a friend, whether he was in or out of the White House. (Bittman testimony, 2 HJC 23)

Bittman testified that he conveyed Hunt's desire to know whether Colson could help him if he received a substantial sentence. (Bittman testimony, 2 HJC 24) Colson has substantiated Bittman's testimony by his own testimony, an affidavit to the Special Prosecutor and a memo of the conversations he wrote on January 5, 1973. (Book III, 469, 472–74; Colson testimony, 3 HJC 303–04) Colson has also stated:

> In addition, I may well have told Bittman that I had made "people" aware that, if it were necessary, I was going to come back to the White House to speak for Hunt. Indeed, since I wanted to do all I could to comfort Hunt, it is most probable that I did say this. I do not know how Bittman evaluated my position and influence at the White House, but despite my insistence that I could do no more than try to help Hunt as a friend, Bittman might have inferred that if Hunt received an unreasonably long sentence, my willingness to go to bat for Hunt would result in Hunt's sentence being reduced by executive action of some sort. (Colson testimony, 3 HJC 311)

Dean has testified that after January 5th Colson told him that he had spoken to the President about clemency despite Ehrlichman's instructions. (Book III, 461) Colson, however, has testified that he discussed the matter with the President in late January. (Colson testimony, 3 HJC 311, 318)

Tapes or transcripts of recorded presidential conversations twice reflect mention by the President of a conversation with Colson about possible clemency for Hunt. On the morning of March 21, 1973 he told Dean:

> . . . there was some discussion over there with somebody about, uh, Hunt's problems after his wife died and I said, of course, commutation could be considered on the basis of his wife, and that is the only discussion I ever had in that light. (HJCT 93)

On April 14, the President told Haldeman and Ehrlichman:

> ... As I remember a conversation this day was about five thirty or six o'clock that Colson only dropped in in sort of parenthetically, said I had a little problem today, talking about Hunt, and said I sought to reassure him, you know, and so forth. And I said, well. Told me about Hunt's wife. I said obviously we will do just, we will take that into consideration. That was the total of the conversation. (WHT 419)

It seems beyond question that whatever assurances Colson may have made to Bittman, they were given before he had talked to the President. (Summary of Information, 78)

It is important to distinguish between what the President said to Colson and his knowledge, if any, of commitments already made by Colson before he talked to the President. There is no evidence that the President was aware of any specific assurances given by Colson until April 14, 1973. On February 28, the President inquired of Dean whether the defendants had any expectation of clemency:

> The PRESIDENT. *What the hell do they expect, though? Do they expect that they will get clemency within a reasonable time?*
> DEAN. I think they do. [Unintelligible] going to do.
> The PRESIDENT. *What would you say? What would you advise on that?*
> DEAN. Uh, I think it's one of those things we'll have to watch very closely. For example—
> The PRESIDENT. You couldn't do it, you couldn't do it, say in six months?
> DEAN. No.
> The PRESIDENT. No.
> DEAN. No, you couldn't. This thing may become so political as a result of these
> The PRESIDENT. Yeah.
> DEAN. hearings that it is, it, it, is more—
> The PRESIDENT. A vendetta?
> DEAN. Yeah, it's a vendetta. This judge may, may go off the deep end in sentencing, and make it so absurd that, uh, it's clearly an injustice, uh—
> (HJCT 40; emphasis added)

On March 21, 1973 the President showed awareness of Colson's having talked to Hunt about the possibility of clemency but not of what assurances had been made:

> The President. . . . But the second thing is, we're not going to be able to deliver on, on any kind of a, of a clemency thing. You know Colson has gone around on this clemency thing with Hunt and the rest.
> DEAN. Hunt, Hunt is now talking in terms of being out by Christmas.
> HALDEMAN. This year?
> DEAN. This year. Uh, he was told by O'Brien, who is my conveyor of doom back and forth.
> HALDEMAN. Yeah.
> DEAN. uh, that, uh, hell, he'd be lucky if he were out a year from now, after the Ervin hearings were, uh, you know, over. He said, "How in the Lord's name could you be commuted that quickly?" He said, "Well, that's my commitment from Colson."
> HALDEMAN. By Christmas of this year?
> DEAN. Yeah.
> HALDEMAN. See that, that really, that's very believeable 'cause Colson,
> The PRESIDENT. Do you think Colson could have told him—
> HALDEMAN. Colson is an, is an—that's, that's your fatal flaw, really, in Chuck, is he is an operator in expediency, and he will pay at the time and where he is
> The PRESIDENT. Yeah (HJCT 115)

Finally, on April 14, 1973, Ehrlichman explained to the President his understanding of the events surrounding Colson's January meetings with Bittman:

> EHRLICHMAN. Well, I had, we had had a couple of conversations in my office—

The PRESIDENT. With Colson?
EHRLICHMAN. I had with Colson. Yeah.
The PRESIDENT. Well how was, who was getting, was Bittman getting to Colson? Was that the point? Who—
EHRLICHMAN. Hunt had written to Colson.
The PRESIDENT. Oh?
EHRLICHMAN. Hunt wrote Colson a very, I think a I've been abandoned kind of letter.
The PRESIDENT. When was this, John?
EHRLICHMAN. I am sorry—
The PRESIDENT. After the election?
EHRLICHMAN. Oh yes. Yeah.
The PRESIDENT. Oh. And Colson, you knew about this letter?
EHRLICHMAN. Colson came in to tell me about it. And he said, "What shall I do?" And I said, "Well, better talk to him." I thought somebody had better talk to him, the guy is obviously very distraught.
The PRESIDENT. Right.
EHRLICHMAN. And has a feeling abandoned.
The PRESIDENT. Right.
EHRLICHMAN. And he said, "What can I tell him about clemency or pardon." And I said, "You can't tell him anything about clemency or pardon." And I said, "Under no circumstances should this ever be raised with the President."
The PRESIDENT. (Unintelligible). Well, he raised it, I must say, in a tangential way. Now he denies that, as I understand it, that he said they'd be out by Christmas. He says—
EHRLICHMAN. I've never talked to Chuck about that, have you?
The PRESIDENT. What did he say he said? Well, I'll tell you what I, what Dean, or somebody, tells me he said he said. He said that he didn't. He just talked or saw Bittman causally—were off on (unintelligible) or something of that sort. (WHT 419–21)

Later that same day Haldeman and Ehrlichman discussed with the President the possible criminal liability of Colson for having offered Hunt clemency.

EHRLICHMAN. My guess is that a fellow like Bittman [sic] has probably negotiated immunity for himself, and has—
HALDEMAN. Dean strongly feels they wouldn't give it to him.
The PRESIDENT. They would.
HALDEMAN. Will not—
EHRLICHMAN. He is going to tell them about a lot of conversations he had with a lot of people.
The PRESIDENT. Bitman is?
EHRLICHMAN. Yeah.
The PRESIDENT. Do we know that?
EHRLICHMAN. I don't know that but I know, for instance, that Bitman had a conversation with Colson that was a Watergate conversation. And I know what Colson says about it—that he was brilliant and adroit, avoided any—
HALDEMAN. And he says Bitman's recollection of it would be exactly the same as Colson's—his recollection of the specific conversation—but he says Bitman may draw conclusions from it.
The PRESIDENT. This is the clemency conversation? And his conclusion would be that he felt the President had offered clemency?
HALDEMAN. No. His conclusion he, Colson, will have Hunt out by Christmas. He says you know what kind of pull I have at the White House. I will be able to to work that. That's what he would have thought. That by saying—
The PRESIDENT. How does Colson handle that?
EHRLICHMAN. He says he has a paper or a memo or something that says exactly what he said.
The PRESIDENT. Just a minute.
HALDEMAN. He wrote a memorandum of the conversation immediately after the conversation. That's all it is—his side of the story.
The PRESIDENT. You don't think this would lead to an indictment of Colson do you?
EHRLICHMAN. I don't know. Dean thinks everybody in the place is going to get indicted.

HALDEMAN. They're all doing the same thing. Look, Dean said just looking at the worst possible side of the coin that you could make a list of everybody who in some way is technically indictable in the cover-up operation. And that list includes, in addition to Mitchell, Haldeman, Ehrlichman, Colson, Dean—
The PRESIDENT. Because they all discussed it?
HALDEMAN. Strachan, Kalmbach, Kalmbach's go-between, Kalmbach's source, LaRue, Mardian, O'Brien, Parkinson, Bittman, Hunt and you know just to keep wandering through the impossibles, maybe for everybody on that list to take a guilty plea and get immediate—what do you call it—
EHRLICHMAN. Clemency.
HALDEMAN. Clemency. That shows you the somewhat incredible way of some of John Dean's analytical thinking.
EHRLICHMAN. No way.
The PRESIDENT. It's a shame. There could be clemency in this case and at the proper time having in mind the extraordinary sentences of Magruder, etc. etc., *but you know damn well it is ridiculous to talk about clemency. They all knew that. Colson knew that, I mean when you talked to Colson and he talked to me.* (WHT 542–44; emphasis added)

Two days later, on April 16, 1973, the President brought up the problem of the criminal liability of others for offering clemency and expressed a desire to know what had been offered and what the legal considerations thereof would be:

The PRESIDENT. Yeah. Well, you take, for example, the clemency stuff. That's solely Mitchell, apparently, and Colson's talk with, uh. Bittman where he says, "I'll do everything I can because as a, as a friend—"[1]
DEAN. No, that was with Ehrlichman.
The PRESIDENT. Huh?
DEAN. That was Ehrlichman.
The PRESIDENT. Ehrlichman with who?
DEAN. Ehrlichman and Colson and I sat up there, and Colson presented his story to Ehrlichman
The PRESIDENT. I know.
DEAN. regarding it and, and then John gave Chuck very clear instructions on going back and telling him that it, you know. "Give him the inference he's got clemency but don't give him any commitments."
The PRESIDENT. No commitment?
DEAN. Right.
The PRESIDENT. Now that's all right. But first, if an individual, *if it's no commitment—I've got a right to sit here—Take a fellow like Hunt, or, uh, or, or a Cuban whose wife is sick and something—that's what clemency's about.*
DEAN. That's right.
The PRESIDENT. Correct?
DEAN. That's right.
The PRESIDENT. But, uh, but John specifically said, "No commitment," did he? He—
DEAN. Yeah.
The PRESIDENT. No commitment. Then, then Colson then went on to, apparently—
DEAN. I don't know how Colson delivered it, uh—
The PRESIDENT. Apparently to Bittman—
DEAN. for—
The PRESIDENT. Bittman. It that your understanding?
DEAN. Yes, but I don't know what his, you know, specific—
The PRESIDENT. Where did this business of the Christmas thing get out, John? What the hell was that?
DEAN. Well, that's, a, that's a—
The PRESIDENT. That must have been Mitchell, huh?
DEAN. No, that was Chuck, again. I think that, uh—
The PRESIDENT. That they all, that they'd all be out by Christmas?

---

[1] Two days earlier, on April 14th, Ehrlichman had told the President that Colson and his attorney, David Shapiro, had said that Mitchell had promised Hunt a pardon. (WHT 412; see also WHT 485)

DEAN. No, I think he said something to the effect that Christmas is the time that clemency generally occurs.
The PRESIDENT. Oh, yeah.
DEAN. Uh—
The PRESIDENT. Well, that doesn't—I, I, I don't think that is going to hurt him.
DEAN. No.
The PRESIDENT. Do you?
DEAN. No.
The PRESIDENT. *"Clemency," he says—One* [unintelligible] *he's a friend of Hunt's. I'm just trying to put the best face on it. If it's the wrong—if it is—I've got to know.* (HJCT 204–05; emphasis added.)

In his March 21, 1973 morning conversation with Dean, after Dean had recited the facts of the cover-up as he saw them, the President brought up the subject of clemency and, after a brief discussion, decisively rejected the idea:

The PRESIDENT. One problem: you've got a problem here. You have the problem of Hunt and, uh, his, uh, his clemency.
DEAN. That's right. And you're going to have the clemency problem for the others. They all would expect to be out and that may put you in a position that's just
The PRESIDENT. Right.
DEAN. untenable at some point. You know, the Watergate Hearings just over, Hunt now demanding clemency or he is going to blow. And politically, it'd be impossible for, you know, you to do it. You know, after everybody—
The PRESIDENT. That's right.
DEAN. I am not sure that you will ever be able to deliver on the clemency. It may be just too hot.
The PRESIDENT. You can't do it till after the '74 elections, that's for sure. But even then
DEAN. [clears throat]
The PRESIDENT. your point is that even then you couldn't do it.
DEAN. That's right. It may further involve you in a way you shouldn't be involved in this.
The PRESIDENT. No it's wrong; that's for sure. (HJCT, 103–04.

For our present purposes, of course, it is wholly immaterial whether the President rejected the possibility of granting clemency because it was morally "wrong" or because it was "wrong" as a practical matter. The essential point is that once again the President appears quite firmly opposed to the granting of clemency; thereafter, he consistently put down any notion of awarding clemency to any of the Watergate defendants:

. . . we're not going to be able to give them clemency. (HJCT 107)
. . . we're not going to be able to deliver on, on any kind of clemency thing. (*Id.* 115)
. . . you couldn't provide clemency. (*Id.* 116)
We can't provide clemency. (*Id.*)
. . . you know damn well it is ridiculous to talk about clemency. (WHT 544)

The allegation contained in Paragraph (9) is without substantial support in the evidence, whether viewed according to the state of the record when the Committee voted to recommend the adoption of Article I to the full House, or according to the state of the record as we file these views. Paragraph (9) is a bad charge; it should never have been lodged against President Nixon.

THE MARCH 21, 1973 PAYMENT TO HOWARD HUNT

When the June 1972 grand jury of the United States District Court for the District of Columbia returned its now famous indictment in the case of *United States* v. *Mitchell, et al.* on March 1, 1974 there began a five-month period of intense public preoccupation with the events of a single day—March 21, 1973—such as has seldom been seen in the history of this country. This occurred because the content and sequence of the overt acts alleged to have been perpetrated in furtherance of the aims of the Watergate cover-up conspiracy charged in Count One of the indictment appeared to allege, in essence, that the final payment of "hush money" to Howard Hunt was set in motion by a direct order of the President, conveyed by Haldeman to Mitchell, then by Mitchell to LaRue, who actually saw to the execution of the order.

The central thrust of this allegation was reiterated when the same grand jury forwarded to this Committee its Report and Recommendation and supporting evidentiary materials relating to the possible involvement of the President in the criminal conspiracy charged in Count One of the Mitchell indictment.

When we voted in Committee against recommending to the House the adoption of proposed Article I, we were already convinced that the President's criminal liability as a co-conspirator in the Watergate cover-up did not turn upon whether the payment of $75,000 made to Hunt on the evening of March 21, 1973 was the result of a direct Presidential order, as the Watergate grand jury apparently felt was the fact, or even upon whether the payment was one of "hush money." Rather, it seemed to us, the question of the President's *criminal liability* turned upon whether the President had, during his conversation with John Dean on the morning of the 21st, acted affirmatively and intentionally in some fashion to associate himself with the ongoing conspiracy.

From the standpoint of Presidential *liability to impeachment*, we thought it to be relevant, but not controlling, whether the President had knowingly ordered the payment of "hush money" to Hunt, to "buy time" or for whatever purpose. Even this question was overshadowed, in our estimate, by another, more critical one: if the President ever did become criminally liable for participating in the Watergate cover-up conspiracy, did he do so early in the course of the conspiracy, and was his role active and leading, or did he first join the conspiracy long after it was underway, such as in March of 1973, by virtue of his imprudent and unlawful response to having, to put it colloquially, the entire mess dumped suddenly in his lap as a result of the Dean disclosures of March 13 and 21, 1973.

While the President's revelation of new evidence on August 5, 1974 effectively resolved this latter question for us, as it seems to have done for the rest of the Nation as well, the enormous amount of public attention focused upon this issue during most of 1974 persuades us that it is still important that we set down our analysis of the evidence bearing upon the manner in which the final payment of CRP funds to Hunt came to be made. Our view of the evidence on this point differs substantially from that of the grand jury, as well as from that set out in the Committee report.

The majority of the Committee has, we believe, rendered a version of the facts relating to the March 21, 1973 payment to Hunt that flies in the face of a considerable amount of evidence in the record. One who reads the "Payments" section of the discussion of proposed Article I in the Committee report is led to believe that Dean met with the President and Haldeman on the morning of the 21st; that following that meeting Dean telephoned LaRue to arrange the making of the payment to Hunt; that LaRue and Mitchell then conferred by telephone, whereupon Mitchell authorized the payment to go forward; and that later that day LaRue effectuated the delivery of the money to Hunt.

We think this construction of the facts is mistaken. The evidence clearly shows that Dean talked to both LaRue and Mitchell before meeting with the President on the morning of March 21st, that arrangements for the delivery of the money were made independently of that meeting or any of its results, and that in all probability the delivery of the money to Hunt would have taken place even if Dean had not talked with the President that day.

On or about March 16, 1973, Howard Hunt met with Paul O'Brien, a CRP attorney. Hunt informed O'Brien that commitments had been made to him but not met; that he had done "seamy" things for the White House; and that, unless his commitments were met (including $130,000 for attorney's fees and support), he might be forced to review his options. (Book III, 902, 906, 915; Bittman testimony, 2 HJC 25). On March 16th, Hunt also met with Colson's attorney, David Shapiro. According to Colson, Hunt requested of Shapiro that Colson act as Hunt's liaison with the White House, but was told that this was impossible. (Book III, 924; Colson testimony, 3 HJC 323, 331).

Colson has testified that Shapiro informed his after Shapiro's meeting with Hunt that Colson should have no further contact with either Hunt or anyone in the White House concerning Hunt. Shapiro also told Colson that the situation in the White House was getting serious. Shapiro said, "for God's sake, the President has to get the facts. Who knows what's going on in that place. The fox may be guarding the chickens." Colson reminded Shapiro that Colson had earlier voiced to the President suspicions about Mitchell, but the President had responded that Mitchell swore he was innocent. Colson told Shapiro that it was impossible to know what advice the President was getting, or from whom he was getting it, and that Colson suspected the President would not know whom to believe. (Book III, 926)

O'Brien has testified that he went immediately from his meeting with Hunt to see Dean at his office in the Executive Office Building. (O'Brien testimony, 2 HJC 125–28; Dean testimony, 2 HJC 238–240)

Paul O'Brien's name appears on Dean's telephone logs for March 20, March 21, and March 23, 1973. Dean's logs for the period January 3 through April 30, 1973 reflect almost daily contact with both O'Brien and Mitchell until March 22, 1973, when contact with Mitchell dropped off sharply. (Dean testimony, 2HJC 314–16; Dean logs, impeachment inquiry files) Dean has testified, and the White House appointment records verify, that O'Brien met with Dean on March 19th in the Executive Office Building. Because of the frequency of contacts between the two men, however, it is unclear whether this meeting was the one that O'Brien contended took place on Friday, March 16th, immediately following his meeting with Hunt.

Dean, in any event, testified that it was on the 19th that O'Brien conveyed to him Hunt's grim message suggesting that commitments made to him were not kept, and that if money for his attorney's fees and family support was not forthcoming he might have to reconsider his options, in which case he might have some very "seamy" things to say about Ehrlichman. (Book III, 946-49) Dean testified that he told O'Brien that he was "out of the money business."

On March 20, 1973, Ehrlichman met with Dean at the White House. They discussed Hunt's demand for money, and the possibility that Hunt might reveal the "seamy" things he had done for Ehrlichman if the money was not forthcoming. Ehrlichman has said that he thought Hunt was referring to his previous activities as a member of the White House "Plumbers" unit when he mentioned "seamy" things. (Book III, 952-59) According to Dean, Ehrlichman said he wondered what Hunt meant and suggested that Dean discuss the matter with Mitchell. Ehrlichman, on the other hand, claims that he suggested Dean talk to Colson. (Book III, 955, 957)

That same afternoon Ehrlichman had a telephone conversation with Egil Krogh in which he told Krogh that Hunt was asking for a lot of money. Krogh has testified that Ehrlichman told him that Hunt might "blow the lid off" and that Mitchell was responsible for " the care and feeding of Howard Hunt." (Book III, 961-62)

Also on March 20th, Dean had a conversation with Richard Moore, a Special Counsel to the President, before they met with the President to discuss a draft of a proposed public statement relating to possible appearance of White House personnel before the Senate Select Committee. Dean told Moore that Hunt was demanding a large sum of money before his sentencing, then scheduled for that Friday, March 23rd, and that if the demand was not met, Hunt was threatening to say things that would be serious for the White House. (Book III, 966-68)

Dean has testified that after their meeting with the President that day he told Moore that he did not think the President understood all the facts involved in Watergate, and particularly the implications of those facts, and that he felt he had to lay the facts and implications out for the President. Moore, however, has testified that it was he who told Dean of his own feeling "that the President had no knowledge of the things that were worrying Dean" and that Dean should tell the President what he knew. The next day, according to Moore, Dean told him that he talked with the President and told him "everything," and that the President had been surprised. (Book III, 966-68)

Dean has testified that he and LaRue met in Dean's office on either the afternoon of March 20th or the morning of March 21st, and that he told LaRue of Hunt's latest demand for money. LaRue then asked Dean if he was planning to do anything about Hunt's demand, and Dean said no, he was out of the money business. LaRue asked Dean what he (LaRue) should do, and Dean suggested that he contact Mitchell. (Dean testimony, 2 HJC 250)

Whether this meeting occurred on the early morning of March 21st or on the previous afternoon, it is Dean's "best recollection" that it took place some time before Dean met with the President on the morning of the 21st. (Dean testimony, 2 HJC 260)

During the afternoon of the 20th, Dean was visited by Krogh who, as a result of his conversation with Ehrlichman about Hunt, had become alarmed as to his potential liability for perjury in connection with his knowledge of the activities of Hunt and Liddy. Dean told Krogh about Hunt's demands and told him that the President was being ill-served, that something had to be done. (Dean testimony, 2 HJC 248)

On the evening of March 20, 1973, Dean talked with the President by telephone and in the course of the conversation he arranged to see the President the next day. (WHT 164)

Apparently Dean also spoke by telephone with John Mitchell at his home in New York that evening and told him of Hunt's demand for money. (Dean testimony, 2 HJC 248) During his conversation with the President the next morning, Dean described the conversation as follows:

> DEAN. . . . Apparently, Mitchell has talked to Pappas, and I called him last—John asked me to call him last night after our discussion and after you'd met with John to see where that was. And I, I said, "Have you talked to, to Pappas?" He was at home, and Martha picked up the phone so it was all in code. "Did you talk to the Greek?" And he said, uh, "Yes, I have." and I said, "Is the Greek bearing gifts?" He said, "Well, I want to call you tomorrow on that." (HJCT 122)

Dean did not, however, tell the President at any point during this conversation that he had also already spoken with LaRue about the Hunt situation, even though by advising Mitchell of the problem and by urging LaRue to talk with Mitchell about it, Dean had already taken all the steps which would be necessary to set in motion a payment of cash to Hunt in response to his demand.

Notwithstanding the extensive discussion among Dean, Haldeman and the President on the morning of March 21st about the desirability of taking some action to "buy time" lest Hunt begin talking and eliminate all of the conspirators' "options," the content of the conversation taken as a whole and the subsequent behavior of the three participants in it suggests that the only firm conclusion that can be drawn regarding the President's attitude toward meeting Hunt's immediate demand is that *he considered it.*

While at several other points in the conversation the President appeared favorably disposed toward making a payment to Hunt as a temporary expedient, there are indications near the end of the conversation that the President had not actually settled on that course:

> The PRESIDENT. That's right. Try to look around the track. We have no choice on Hunt but to try to keep him—
> DEAN. Right now, we have no choice.
> The PRESIDENT. But, but my point is, do you ever have any choice on Hunt? That's the point.
> DEAN. [Sighs]
> The PRESIDENT. No matter what we do here now, John,
> DEAN. Well, if we—
> The PRESIDENT. Hunt eventually, if he isn't going to get commuted and so forth, he's going to blow the whistle. (HJCT 125).

The conversation concludes on a distinctly indecisive note:

> The PRESIDENT. All right. Fine. And, up, my point is that, uh, we can, uh, you may well come—I think it is good, frankly to consider these various options. And then, once you, once you decide on the plan—John—and you had the right plan, let me say, I have no doubts about the right plan before the election. And you handled it just right. You contained it. Now after the election we've got to

have another plan, because we can't have, for four years, we can't have this thing—you're going to be eaten away. We can't do it. (HJCT 129–30)

The only evidence of contact between either Mitchell or LaRue and anyone at the White House following the morning conversation among Dean, Haldeman and the President is the telephone call placed to Mitchell by Haldeman at 12:30 p.m. During the morning conversation, the President had ordered that Mitchell be brought to Washington to meet with Haldeman, Ehrlichman and Dean to discuss alternative means of extricating the group from the cover-up:

> The PRESIDENT. . . . Second, you've got to get Mitchell down here. And you and Ehrlichman and Mitchell and let's—and—by tomorrow.
> HALDEMAN. Why don't we do that tonight?
> The PRESIDENT. I don't think you can get him that soon, can you?
> HALDEMAN. John?
> The PRESIDENT. It would be helpful if you could.
> DEAN. I think it would be.
> The PRESIDENT. You need—
> DEAN. Get him to come down this afternoon. (HJCT 129)

Haldeman has testified that his only purpose in calling Mitchell was to arrange for him to come to Washington. (Book III, 1121) Mitchell testified before this Committee that he has a definite recollection of Haldeman's having called him shortly after noon asking him to come to Washington. Moreover, he recalls that this conversation took place *after* he had talked with LaRue about whether Hunt's demand should be met. (Mitchell testimony, 2 HJC 179–87) In his June, 1973 testimony before the Senate Select Committee, Dean indicated that it came to his attention in some fashion that, after the morning meeting with the President broke up, Haldeman "called Mitchell and asked him to come down the next day for a meeting with the President on the Watergate matter." (3 SSC 1000)

During a conversation among Haldeman, Ehrlichman, Dean and the President in the late afternoon of March 21st, an ambiguous remark by Dean may give rise to a suspicion—but only a suspicion—that someone in the group there assembled had discussed the Hunt problem with either Mitchell or LaRue since Dean's morning meeting with the President:

> The PRESIDENT. So then now—so the point we have to, the bridge you have to cut, uh, cross there is, uh, which you've got to cross, I understand, quite soon, is whether, uh, we, uh, what you do about, uh, his present demand. Now, what, what, uh, what [unintelligble] about that?
> DEAN. *Well, apparently Mitchell and*, and, uh, uh,
> UNIDENTIFIED. LaRue.
> DEAN. *LaRue are now aware of it*, so they know what he is feeling.
> The PRESIDENT. True. [Unintelligible] do something.
> DEAN. I, I have, *I have not talked with either*. I think they are in a position to do something, though. (HJCT 133; emphasis added)

Since that very morning Dean had told the President that he had talked with Mitchell the previous evening about Pappas and the money situation generally, it is reasonable to infer that Dean meant he had not talked with either Mitchell or LaRue since meeting with the President earlier that day. Dean's comment that Mitchell and LaRue "are *now* aware of it" suggests that someone other than Dean had talked with one of the two and told Dean about it, but the remark is still puzzling, since Dean had known when he talked with the

President in the morning that both Mitchell and LaRue were well aware of the situation—Dean himself had informed both of them. The most likely explanation, then, it seems to us, is that Dean was covering the fact that he had earlier withheld from the President the fact that he had already spoken with both Mitchell and LaRue *specifically about meeting the Hunt demand* but had allowed the President to think that he was being presented with a problem which Dean had not yet taken concrete steps to address.

The evidence is highly persuasive that none of the participants in the March 21st morning conversation seems to have formed the impression that the President had affirmatively sought to insure that the payment to Hunt would be made. This in itself is probative of the fact that the President's role in arranging for the making of that payment was, at most, quite passive and certainly not instrumental.

In testifying before the Senate Select Committee in June of 1973, only three months after the events in question, Dean evidenced no belief that the President had authorized or directed "hush money" to be paid to Hunt. Nowhere in his lengthy testimony did he make such an allegation. To the contrary, although Dean seems erroneously to have recalled that some aspects of raising "hush money" over a long period of time were discussed with the President on March 13, 1973, Dean makes it clear throughout his SSC testimony that at the conclusion of his discussions of "hush money" with the President,

> the money matter was left very much hanging at that [March 13th] meeting. Nothing was resolved. (Dean testimony, 4 SSC 1423)
>
> ... The conversations then turned back to a question from the President regarding the money that was being paid to the defendants. He asked me how this was done. I told him I didn't know much about it other than the fact that the money was laundered so it could not be traced and then there were secret deliveries. I told him I was learning about things I had never known before, but the next time I would certainly be more knowledgeable. This comment got a laugh out of Haldeman [who did not, in fact, attend the March 13th meeting]. The meeting ended on this note and there was no further discussion of the matter and it was left hanging just as I have described it. (Dean testimony, 3 SSC 996)

Likewise, in his recitation of the content of his March 21, 1973 morning conversation with the President, Dean did not in any way suggest that a presidential decision to order or encourage the payment of "hush money" to Hunt or any other Watergate defendant had been made. (Dean testimony, 3 SSC 998–1000)

What perplexes us is this: if Hunt's demand for cash alarmed Dean enough to precipitate his going in to see the President and lay out the "full" story about the cover-up, is it reasonable to believe that he left that momentous meeting with the President without *knowing* what was to be done about Hunt's demand? Dean, of course, had a very personal interest in the maintenance of Hunt's silence, at least until the cover-up might be unravelled in some orderly, tolerable manner, because of Dean's own potential criminal liabilities which he so vividly described to the President during the course of their conversations on March 21st.

It is truly remarkable, therefore, that in the course of reading his veritable litany of charges levelled by him against President Nixon during five days of testimony before the Senate Select Committee Dean did not once allege that the President authorized, directed or even expressly approved the payment of $75,000 in "hush money" to Howard

Hunt—unless, of course, the President took no such action and made no such decision.

According to remarks made during their conversation with Ehrlichman and Ziegler in the Oval Office on April 17, 1973, it appears that neither Haldeman nor the President had any recollection that the President had manifested on the morning of March 21st a desire that Hunt be paid:

> HALDEMAN. You explored in that conversation the possibility of whether such kinds of money could be raised. You said, "Well, we ought to be able to raise—"
> The PRESIDENT. That's right.
> HALDEMAN. "How much money is involved?" and he said, "Well it could be a million dollars." You said, 'That's ridiculous. You can't say a million. Maybe you say a million, it may be 2 or 10, and 11"
> The PRESIDENT. But then we got into the blackmail.
> HALDEMAN. You said,' 'Once you start down the path with blackmail it's constant escalation."
> The PRESIDENT. Yep. That's my only conversation with regard to that.
> HALDEMAN. They could jump and then say, "Yes, well that was morally wrong. What you should have said is that blackmail is wrong not that it's too costly." (WHT 1034)

This last remark by Haldeman bespeaks a recollection that it was the amoral appearance of the President's reason for refusing to go along with the payment of "blackmail" which might pose a political or public relations problem, not that the President was vulnerable on the more serious count that he had actually approved the payment of "hush money" to Hunt. It should be noted, parenthetically, that there is no evidence that either Haldeman or the President had listened to a tape recording of the March 21st morning conversation as of the date on which Haldeman spoke the lines quoted above, April 17, 1973.

Indeed, as of March 22, 1973 there was evidence that the President had rejected, not approved, the payment of money to maintain Hunt's silence. The White House edited transcript of his conversation with Haldeman between 9:11 and 10:35 a.m. that day shows the President saying:

> Damn it—when people are in jail there is every right for people to raise money for them. (inaudible) and that's all there is to it. I don't think we ought to (inaudible)—there's got to be funds—I'm not being—*I don't mean to be blackmailed by Hunt—that goes too far*, but for taking care of these people that are in jail—my God they did this for—we are sorry for them—we did it out of compassion, yet I don't (inaudible) about that—people have contributed (inaudible) report on that damn thing—there's no report required (inaudible) what happens. . . . (WHT, March 22, 1973; 9:11—10:35 a.m., 1—2; emphasis added)

WHITE HOUSE RELATIONSHIP WITH THE OFFICE OF THE WATERGATE SPECIAL PROSECUTOR

The President felt that putting a special prosecutor on the Watergate case would be a negative reflection on the efficacy and the integrity of the Department of Justice. (WHT, April 15, 1973, 712.) The President felt that the U.S. Attorney's Office was doing a fine job and he was inclined to let them stay in charge of the case, especially since a special prosecutor would have to familiarize himself with the facts.

> PRESIDENT. Oh, they're [Mitchell et al] all going to be indicted. Well, that's my point. I thought, I think if the course just goes like it is they're going to be indicted. You mean you'd [Kleindienst] have a special prosecutor immediately?

Here's my point, if they're going to indict anyway that sort of—that shows that . . . the thing does work. . . . . These guys are crowding in—Silbert and the rest—they aren't taking any program—we're not giving them any—

I could call in Titus and Silbert I'd say, look—you are totally independent here and you ought . . . to tear this case up. Now go to it. See my point is, you call in a special prosecutor, he's got to learn the whole damn thing. . . . (WHT 716–17).

KLEINDIENST. No, the special prosecutor would not try the case, Mr. President. What he would do is substitute himself for the Attorney General. Silbert would try the case. What he would do would have overview with respect to what they were doing and participating in the prosecuting decisions that are made from time to time. (WHT 737)

The President did not initially envision a completely independent special prosecutor. The concept as explained by Kleindienst would be that of an independent overseer.

On April 15, 1973 the President told Haldeman he had concluded that he would have to have a special prosecutor. The President then explained to Haldeman his concept of a special prosecutor.

PRESIDENT. This is not to prosecute the case. A special prosecutor, to look at the indictments to see that the indictments run to everybody they need to run to, so that it isn't just the President's men, you see.

HALDEMAN. In other words, he is above Silbert rather than replacing Silbert?

PRESIDENT. Oh no, Silbert runs the case and that's all. But he is just in there for the purpose of examining all this to see that the indictment covers everybody. (Telephone conversation between the President and Haldeman, April 15, 1973, (WHT 752–53)

On April 30, 1973 the President announced that Elliot Richardson would be the new Attorney General and would have absolute authority to make all decisions bearing upon the prosecution of the Watergate case. He also stated that Richardson would have the authority to name a *special supervising prosecutor* for matters arising out of the case. The President still regarded the special prosecutor to be in the role of a general supervising attorney who would provide a careful overview. (Book IX, 134–135)

On May 21, 1973 Richardson announced his selection of Archibald Cox as Special Prosecutor. (Book IX, 146) Richardson also presented the Senate Judiciary Committee with guidelines created by the Attorney General's Office, giving Cox a great degree of independence and an extensive jurisdiction. Cox became the Special Prosecutor officially on May 25, 1973. (Book IX, 150) The President was caught by surprise. He was definitely not committed to the terms of that charter. Richardson has testified:

[T]he President was not personally committed to the terms of the charter. He approved of it. At least he acquiesced in it. But he was not consulted in any way during the course of the development of the so-called guidelines under which Mr. Cox worked, and he was never in a position where he was called upon directly to say "I personally stand back of and will adhere to these terms and conditions."

The second problem was that the charter itself could not and did not purport to guarantee access by the Special Prosecutor to Presidential papers, memoranda or notes and, of course, there was no reason at that point to foresee the potential availability or existence of tape recordings. (Richardson testimony, Special Prosecutor Hearings, 238)

Richardson never defined what he meant by the fact that the President acquiesced or approved of the charter. The clear inference is that the President only "acquiesced and approved" of Richardson's having the right to draw up a charter and to negotiate this charter with the Senate Judiciary Committee and with the new Special Prosecutor and not to the charter itself. (Special Prosecutor Hearings, 250)

On May 25, 1973 the President told Richardson that although he had waived executive privilege as to testimony referred to, he was not waiving executive privilege as to documentary evidence. (Book IX, 15) The President had specifically given Richardson authority for all decisions with regard to Watergate. However, the then Attorney General never informed Cox of President Nixon's stated intention not to waive executive privilege with regard to non-testimonial evidence, although Richardson had created the office of the Special Prosecutor and was Cox's superior. The President never communicated directly to Cox, but always through Richardson or some other intermediary. It can be inferred that the President believed that Cox was aware of his intention and could therefore only regard his constant requests for non-testimonial evidence as being subject to the President's discretion.

In an interview with the inquiry staff, Cox stated that it never occurred to him that the White House would make a distinction between testimony and documents. Cox stated specifically that "nobody in May" thought that executive privilege was limited to oral testimony. (Staff Interview with Cox, May 10, 1974)

As Richardson was to testify later:

> Senator McCLELLAN. In other words, the right to executive privilege has not yet been waived?
> Mr. RICHARDSON. That is correct.
> Senator McCLELLAN. It is still reserved?
> Mr. RICHARDSON. It is still reserved. When I appeared here originally, and Mr. Cox appeared with me after he had been selected, neither of us thought . . . of asking in effect for a waiver of executive privilege by the President. (1 Special Prosecutor Hearings 243)

Cox accepted the position of Special Prosecutor on May 18, 1973. The staff which he immediately began to assemble included in the top positions a number of Democratic attorneys who had served in the Department of Justice during the Kennedy Administration. This caused great alarm at the White House and set a tone of White House mistrust and hostility toward the Special Prosecutor.

On June 19, 1973 Haig complained to Richardson about Cox. Haig stated "The President was upset about references to subpenaing the President or indicting the President or what he interpreted as references to that general effect"; that "the Republicans were shocked by this, it was indicative of an unlimited hunting license to Cox, that the whole thing was blatantly partisan, or to that effect." (Richardson testimony, 2 Special Prosecutor Hearings 405)

From June 25 through June 29, 1973 John Dean testified extensively about the Watergate affair and made many charges against the President. On June 27, 1973 Cox wrote J. Fred Buzhardt, the President's lawyer, and formally requested that the President furnish a detailed narrative answering the allegations mentioned in Dean's testimony before the Senate Select Committee. (Book IX, 314, 316, 318)

On or about July 3, the Los Angeles Times reported that the Special Prosecutor's office was investigating expenditures relating to the

"Western White House" at San Clemente. The President was very upset about this and demanded to know if, in fact, he was being investigated. Cox later issued a statement that the Western White House was not under investigation by the Office of the Special Prosecutor. Haig complained to Richardson that it could not be part of the Special Prosecutor's charter directly to investigate the President of the United States. Haig commented that the President might fire Cox. (Book IX, 330)

On July 23, 1973 General Haig again contacted Richardson and complained that "the boss" was very "uptight" about Cox because the Office of the Special Prosecutor was seeking information from the IRS and the Secret Service including guidelines for electronic surveillance. The President apparently felt that the information which the Office of the Special Prosecutor was seeking from these agencies was overbroad, and Haig told Richardson, "if we have to have a confrontation we will have it." He added that the President wanted "a tight line drawn with no further mistakes" and that "if Cox does not agree we will get rid of Cox." Richardson communicated the President's displeasure to the Office of the Special Prosecutor and Cox agreed that the request for information contained in the letter sent by his office to the Treasury Department agencies had been overbroad. (Book IX, 404)

On August 22, at a hearing on the Grand Jury tapes subpoena of July 23, 1973 issued to the President, Charles Alan Wright argued that one of the reasons the President was not obliged to turn over the tapes was that of presidential privilege. He stated, "there are, in the United States today, 400 district judgeships authorized by law. A holding that the court has power to pass on a President's claim of privilege as to his most private papers and to compel him to give up those papers would be a precedent for all 400 of those district judges." (*In re Grand Jury*, Misc. No. 47-73, 5)

During this same hearing before Judge Sirica, Cox argued against the applicability of presidential privilege in the instant case:

> They tell us that the privilege is needed to keep secret conversations, in which corruption like the Teapot Dome might be planned, to hide a businessman's discussion with the President of violations of the Sherman Act, or to protect against charges of perjury a general who may bomb a country secretly with which we are at peace or who may then lie to a Senate committee and the general public, and discuss his perjury with the President. (*In re Grand Jury*, Misc. No. 47-73, 34-35)

Cox, in arguing that executive privilege must fall when there is an overriding reason to challenge it, states, "There is not merely accusation, but strong reason to believe that the integrity of the Executive offices has been corrupted, although the extent of the rot is not yet clear." (*Id.* 28) Cox stated that "the case is one that weighs heavily upon me. At some points I may have pressed the arguments too sharply in an effort to make the nature of the point. I certainly intended no disrespect to either the Presidency or to respondent." (*Id.* 48)

During this same hearing, Cox alluded to the President's power to dismiss both the case and the prosecutor.

> I think the executive can't have it both ways. If he wishes to leave the matter to the courts, then he must leave the matter to the courts to be decided in

accordance with rules of law, and counsel should not bring in the back door the mention of this ultimate power to dismiss the case. If he wishes to dismiss the case, if he has the power, then he should exercise it and people know where the responsibility lies.

But it is unfair to the court to put it in the position of saying, I think, we rule as a matter of law that these papers may be withheld, when in fact, what is influencing it is the executive ultimate power of dismissal. That, if I may venture without any disrespect, would seem to me to be almost a deceit which would undermine confidence in the processes of justice. (*In re Grand Jury*, Misc. No. 47-73, 52)

The COURT. One final question. Are you presently empowered to make the final decision or not to pursue further prosecutions in the Watergate matter, and, if so, are you committed to pursue such prosecutions, provided the evidence in your opinion warrants and a grand jury votes the indictment?

Mr. Cox. I am unquestionably committed to pursue it. And, as I understand it, I have the final authority by delegation from the Attorney General, who has the authority under the statutes. The only conceivable way to putting an end to it would be to exercise the power that the President interjects and exercises when he several times dismissed his Secretary of the Treasury until he got one who would proceed as he wished. But short of that, I think I have such authority, Your Honor. Yes, I certainly am so committed. (*Id.* 53-54)

In late September or early October, 1973 after one of the final meetings regarding the Agnew matter, the President stated to Richardson that now that they had disposed of this problem, they could go ahead and get rid of Cox. (Book IX, 332)

On October 12, 1973 the United States Court of Appeals for the District of Columbia ordered the President to turn over recordings for *in camera* inspection by Judge Sirica. (Book IX, 748)

On October 15, 1973 Richardson attended a meeting at the White House, which was not attended by the President, to discuss the tapes litigation and the appellate court decision. The President's aides discussed the possibility of producing a version of the tapes and then firing Cox. Richardson stated that this was unacceptable to him, and he then agreed to try to persuade Cox to accept the "Stennis proposal." (Book IX, 756, 757, 759, 762)

On October 17, 1973 Richardson submitted to Cox a proposal of the Stennis compromise which dealt only with the tapes covered by the subpoena. Richardson's explanation to Cox did not refer to Cox being unable to seek access to future documents. (Book IX, 766)

On October 18, 1973 Cox replied that he was not unalterably opposed to the essential idea of providing an impartial but non-judicial means for reviewing the tapes, so that an accurate version thereof could be obtained. However, he did submit certain distinct comments on the proposal, among which was a provision that, should the transcripts prepared by "special masters" not be acceptable for use at trial, the relevant portions of the tapes must be furnished. This of course left the door open for the tapes themselves to come into evidence and in a sense nullified the ultimate objectives of the President's Stennis compromise. It was Cox who brought up the question of access to other documents by his comment No. 9: "The narrow scope of the proposal is a grave defect, because it would not serve the function of a court decision in establishing the Special Prosecutor's entitlement to other evidence. We have long-pending requests for many specific documents. The proposal also leaves half a law suit hanging (i.e., the subpoenaed papers). Some method of resolving these problems is required." (Book IX, 774)

On October 19, 1973 Cox wrote to the President's attorney, Charles Alan Wright, to say that he could not accept a number of proposals by the White House, notably that he agree not to subpoena any other White House tapes, papers or documents. Cox felt that to agree to waive his right to go to court would violate the promises which he had made to the Senate Judiciary Committee at the time of the confirmation of Attorney General Richardson. (Book IX, 791)

On October 19, 1973 Wright replied to Cox's letter of that same date, explaining that "categorically agreeing not to subpoena any other White House tape, paper or document" referred only to "private Presidential papers and meetings;" a category that Wright regarded as "much, much smaller than the great mass of White House documents with which the President has not personally been involved." Charles Alan Wright stated that in his professional opinion the Stennis compromise was "very reasonable—indeed an unprecedentedly generous—proposal that the Attorney General put to you in an effort, in the national interest, to resolve our disputes by mutual agreement at a time when the country would be particularly well served by such an agreement." (Book IX, 795)

On October 19, 1973 the President wrote to Richardson commanding him to direct the Special Prosecutor to make no further attempts by judicial process to obtain tapes, notes or memoranda or presidential conversations. The President had stated earlier in the letter that he reluctantly had agreed to a limited breach of presidential confidentiality (the Stennis proposal) "in order that our country might be spared the agony of further indecision and litigation about these tapes at a time when we are confronted with other issues of much greater moment to the country and the world." (Book IX, 798)

At this time the President was dealing with the Mideast crisis precipitated by the October War.

On October 20, 1973 Richardson wrote the President and stated, *inter alia*, that "of course you have every right as President to withdraw or modify any understanding on which I hold office under you." Richardson then went on to state that, although the President could tell the Attorney General what to do, he could not dictate to the Special Prosecutor, who in effect was a creature of the Attorney General's office; and that Richardson had made many promises to the Senate Judiciary Committee regarding the independence of the Spcial Prosecutor and had reaffirmed his "intention to assure the independence of the Special Prosecutor." Richardson described the Stennis compromise as "reasonable and constructive" and stated that he had done his best "to persuade Mr. Cox of the desirability of the solution of the issue." Richardson did balk at the concept of precluding Cox from seeking further access to presidential documents. (Book IX, 812)

On October 20, 1973 Cox held a press conference at 1:00 p.m. and asserted that "there was clearly *prima facie* evidence of serious wrongdoing on the part of high government officials." (Cox Press Conference, October 20, 1973, 3) In making his case public before the nation, Cox elaborated on his reasons for rejecting the Stennis proposal. He complained, "I would be instructed not to use the judicial process in order to obtain tapes or documents, memoranda relating to other Presidential conversations . . . and I think the instructions are inconsistent with pledges that were made to the United States Senate, and through the Senate to the American people before I was appointed and before Attorney General Richardson's nomination was confirmed." (*Id.*, 6-7) Cox catalogued all of the logs and documents he had requested, and explained how he had been frustrated by the White House. (*Id.*, 9-15) He stated his intention to continue his duties and to pursue the mandate of the court of appeals in seeking the tapes. (*Id.*, p. 16) He intimated that he might seek an order to show cause why the President should not be held in contempt of court. (*Id.* 17)

On September 29, 1973 an article had been published by the noted constitutional scholar Alexander M. Bickel. The central point of the article was that Special Prosecutor Cox was "not only the President's adversary, he is also the President's subordinate". Bickel elaborated on this proposition as follows:

> Mr. Cox has no constitutional or otherwise legal existence except as he is a creature of the Attorney General who is a creature of the President. Both exercise on behalf of the President and subject to his direction the President's constitutional responsibility and authority to take care that the laws be faithfully executed. To the extent therefore that the President's adversary is Mr. Cox, the President is litigating with himself .... The President is in fact litigating with himself and has it in his lawful power to nullify the result of litigation in the end by collapsing his creature Mr. Cox into his creature Mr. Wright—if this is so, then this law suit is no law suit, it is an internal controversy between the President and one of his subordinates, which the President at the moment: but only for the moment, is unwilling to conclude by discharging Mr. Cox .... the Federal courts have no jurisdiction to hear such contrived controversies. They do not sit to resolve the executive's family quarrels. It is not their function to render advisory opinions. Hence, the case must be dismissed."

Bickel's point is that the President could destroy the lawsuit by discharging Cox. (New Republic, September 29, 1973, 13-14.) According to Cox, Charles Wright also initially assured the President that he did not have to surrender the tapes. Wright apparently maintained a strong position on this point until shortly before Cox was fired. (Cox interview, May 10, 1974)

On October 20, 1973, after the press conference of the Special Prosecutor, President Nixon discharged Cox and abolished the Office of the Special Prosecutor. (Book IX, 816, 818, 821-25)

In the eyes of the President and his advisors, he had made a monumental concession of executive privilege in acceding to the Stennis compromise. At that point in time, it was not at all clear that the President would ever have had to surrender the tapes. Charles Wright, Alexander Bickel and Archibald Cox, all eminent constitutional scholars, had indicated in diverse ways that the President could legally end present tapes litigation by discharging Special Prosecutor Cox. Instead, in acceding to the Stennis compromise President Nixon had agreed to what in his eyes was an unprecedented breach of presidential privilege. It was the President's opinion, as expressed in his press conference of October 26, 1973, that Cox had rejected the Stennis compromise, a compromise which President Nixon believed had been accepted by Attorney General Richardson, Senator Baker, Senator Irvin and others. This obstinacy on the part of Cox was regarded by the President as a severe breach of etiquette and loyalty at a time of grave national crisis (the Mideast situation), and the President felt that he could not govern effective with Cox as Special Prosecutor.

There is strong reason to believe that President Nixon dismissed Cox as Special Prosecutor because he regarded Cox as a disaffected employee and disagreed with his methodology of prosecution.

There is absolutely no evidence that President Nixon discharged the Special Prosecutor in an attempt to obstruct justice.

In this testimony before the Senate Judiciary Committee during the Special Prosecutor Hearings, Richardson summed up the situation as follows:

> All I can testify to is what I know about what happened, and while there was this chronic sense of friction and strain arising out of the very existence of the Cox role, and that feeling erupted from time to time in some reaction, nevertheless, the ultimate firing of Cox is proximately related to the attempt to negotiate an arrangement whereby he would be shut off from further access to presidential documents and so on. You can, if you choose, draw inferences with respect to the history as a whole. I am saying to you that while that is a possible inference, then one could well conclude that these frustrations and irritations to a degree had been cumulative; nevertheless, I think it would be going beyond the evidence as I know it to conclude that the only explanation of all this was a determination to get rid of Cox going back to July as distinguished from a combination of concern with the exercise of his role, the character of his staff, impressions of that staff, coupled with the frustration arising out of the failure to get an agreement on what the President thought was a major concession. (2 Special Prosecutor Hearings 420, 421)

On October 23, 1973 the President authorized Special Counsel Wright to inform Judge Sirica that the subpoenaed tapes would be turned over to the court. (Book IX, 828) On October 26, 1973, the President stated that the new Special Prosecutor would have total independence and cooperation from the executive branch. (Book IX, 833) The President immediately made provisions for a new Special Prosecutor less than one week after Cox had been dismissed. The Special Prosecutor's office continued to function at full strength and efficiency. On October 31, 1973 new Special Prosecutor Leon Jaworski met with General Haig and received assurances of complete independence both jurisdictionally and in the sense of being able to take the President to court. This independence was guaranteed to Jaworski personally by Haig after immediate consultation with the President. (Book IX, 838-843)

On November 19, 1973 Acting Attorney General Bork filed an amendment to the Special Prosecutor's charter which provided that the jurisdiction of a Special Prosecutor would not be limited, nor would the Special Prosecutor be fired unless the President first consulted with the Majority and Minority leaders in the Congress and the Chairman and Ranking Minority Members of the Judiciary Committees of the Senate and House of Representatives, and ascertained that their consensus was in accord with his proposed action. Jaworski was made aware of these assurances and commitments. (Book IX, 862-866)

On November 20, 1973, while testifying before the Senate Judiciary Committee during the Special Prosecutor Hearings Jaworski was questioned by Senator Hruska regarding the obtaining of evidence from the White House. Hruska was interested in Jaworski's concept of what presidential non-cooperation might constitute. The following colloquy occurred:

> Senator HRUSKA. So that by the charter, by your agreement and your discussions you are not to be denied access to the courts. Would you consider that

at that point where General Haig would assert, on behalf of the President, a privileged character to public documents, ... he was acting for or on behalf of the President beyond the law or above the law?

Mr. JAWORSKI. No; if he has a right to take that position—I have to recognize that I am not infallible—it may be that I am in error. It may be that my construction of what our rights are is in error. This is why we have the right to go to court and let the court determine who is correct.

Senator HRUSKA. So that it would be a difference in judgment on a particular document, or a particular line of documents, but it would not be construed at that point that the President or somebody on his behalf was proceeding in defiance of law?

Mr. JAWORSKI. Certainly I agree with that. And I do not intend to leave any impression to the contrary. (2 Special Prosecutor Hearings, 600)

On January 31, 1974 Jaworski was quoted by the *Washington Star News* as having stated "So far I've gotten what I insisted we were entitled to" (referring to the materials he requested from the White House). (*Washington Star News*, January 13, 1974, p. 12.) On January 18, 1974 Jaworski appeared on the *Today* show, and the following exchange took place:

INTERVIEWER. A few weeks ago you said the White House was being quite open and cooperative in furnishing you all the information that you wanted. Is this still the case? Do you have any reservations about the cooperation you are getting from the White House?

JAWORSKI. I have none at this point because the things I have asked for have either been furnished or have not yet been refused. I'm not saying that everything has been found that I have asked for. That's another question. But I have not been refused the matters I have asked for. . . . Now, there are some requests outstanding." January 18, 1974. *Today* show interview with Jaworski.

On February 4, Jaworski's public attitude changed a bit toward the President and he stated on Issues and Answers, "Any idea that this material has been spoon fed to me is an error . . . I've had to go after it . . . There was not one occasion when something was handed to me that I hadn't asked for." (*Washington Star News*, February 4, 1974.

On February 14, 1974 Jaworski sent a letter to Senator Eastland, Chairman of the Senate Judiciary Committee, stating that full compliance and cooperation regarding information from the White House had not been forthcoming. Jaworski itemized the disputed areas and stated that he was sending this letter in response to a promise he had made to the Committee during the Saxbe confirmation hearings that he would inform them of the cooperation he received from the White House. Jaworski stated that he had experienced difficulty getting materials of the Watergate investigation, the dairy industry investigation, and the Plumbers investigation. However, he stated that he had received a great amount of information from the White House and that the White House had allowed him to examine some files in the custody of the White House on various occasions. The Office of the Special Prosecutor was provided with documents from those files which were relevant to their investigations. Furthermore, the White House had provided the Office of the Special Prosecutor with four additional presidential conversations not subpoenaed and had allowed Jaworski access to six other conversations which were also not subpoenaed. Jaworski went on to state that in his opinion the grand jury would be able to return indictments without the benefit of some of the tapes requested of the White House. However, he stated that the materials sought and not turned over to date were "important to a complete and thorough investigation and may contain the evidence necessary for any future trials." (Jaworski's letter to the Senate Judiciary Committee of February 14, 1974, reprinted verbatim in the *New York Times*, February 15, 1974, 12; Book IX, 936)

On February 20, 1974 the Office of the Special Prosecutor sent a grand jury subpoena to President Nixon requesting, *inter alia*, communications containing recommendations to the President with respect to personnel selections and nominations, telephone logs, appointment calendars; and other documents pertaining to Mr. Maurice Stans. On May 31, 1974 the White House filed a formal claim of privilege to this subpoena and the matter is presently in litigation. (Book IX, 1045–1052)

On March 6, 1974 President Nixon announced at a press conference that in addition to the tapes which were subpoenaed by the Office of the Special Prosecutor on July 23, 1973, he had turned over eleven additional tapes bringing the total to 19 tapes that he had surrendered. The President stated further that he had turned over 700 documents, in addition to case loads of documents from five executive departments and two agencies, enough material to enable Jaworski to state that the Special Prosecutor and the grand jury had enough evidence for indictments. ("Presidential Statements," March 6, 1974, 71.) On March 15, 1974 the Special Prosecutor served a grand jury subpoena on the White House calling for materials needed for investigation independent of both the Watergate cover-up and the Fielding break-in. On March 29, 1974 the White House agreed to comply with the subpoena. (Book IX, 970–72)

On April 1, 1974 Jaworski publicly stated that he owed his survival as Special Prosecutor to an agreement between himself and Richard Nixon. He is quoted as saying "When I took this job one of the things that the President and I agreed on was my right to sue and to get whatever testimony I needed, and he has respected that." (*Washington Post*, April 2, 1974, B3)

On April 12, 1974 Special Prosecutor Jaworski wrote Senator Percy and stated that he still needed evidentiary material from the White House in order adequately to prepare for trial and to provide the defendants with possible Jencks Act material. (Book IX, 984–985)

On April 18, 1974 Judge Sirica issued a trial subpoena requested by the Special Prosecutor for 64 presidential conversations. It is this subpoena which was the subject of the recent Supreme Court decision in *United States* v. *Nixon* (U.S. S. Ct. July 24, 1974) "Criminal Cases," 159–92). The Court held in a unanimous 8–0 decision that under the particular circumstances of the case, the President's assertion of executive privilege on the ground of a generalized interest in confidentiality must yield to the demonstrated, specific need for evidence in a pending criminal trial. Accordingly, the President promptly complied with the Court's ruling by turning over to the district court all of the subpoenaed materials with the exception of nine tapes which were subsequently discovered not to exist.

In conclusion, the charge that the President deliberately obstructed the Office of the Special Prosecutor is principally grounded on two facts: his discharge of Special Prosecutor Cox, and his resistance to certain subpoenas issued on behalf of the Special Prosecutor. Both presidential actions, however, can be explained in terms of proper motives and need not give rise to any inference of an intention to obstruct justice.

A fair reading of the evidence suggests that the discharge of Cox was motivated at least in part by the President's perception of Cox as a long-term member of the "Kennedy clique", and therefore a political opponent whose impartiality was subject to question. Whether or not this perception was accurate is immaterial; the point remains that the President may have feared that he would not receive fair treatment from the Office of the Special Prosecutor while Cox was in charge. Significantly, the President was able to maintain a satisfactory relationship with Jaworski right to the end.

It is true that the President stoutly resisted compliance with certain subpoenas, notably the April 18, 1974 trial subpoena. His resistance was consistently premised on the ground of executive privilege, a doctrine whose general validity the Supreme Court reaffirmed in *United States v. Nixon* even while holding that in the instant case it was outweighed by the demands of due process in the fair administration of criminal justice. Indeed, the Court specifically remarked on the propriety of the President's course of action:

> If a president concludes that compliance with a subpoena would be injurious to the public interest he may properly, as was done here, invoke a claim of privilege on the return of the subpoena. (U.S. v. Nixon, slip opinion at 28)

The same principle was enunciated over a hundred years ago by Representative James Beck of Kentucky, in the course of House debate during the impeachment of President Andrew Johnson:

> I maintain that the President of the United States in duty bound to test the legality of every law which he thinks interferes with his rights and powers as the Chief Magistrate of this nation. Whenever he has powers conferred upon him by the Constitution of the United States, and an act of Congress undertakes to deprive him of those powers or any of them, he would be false to his trust as the Chief Executive of this nation, false to the interests of the people whom he represents, if he did not by every means in his power seek to test the constitutionality of that law, and to take whatever steps were necessary and proper to have it tested by the highest tribunal in the land, and to ascertain whether he has a right under the Constitution to do what he claims the right to do, or whether Congress has the right to deprive him of the powers which he claims have been vested in him by the Constitution of the United States.
> ... The humblest citizen has the undoubted right to try judicially his constitutitional rights. (Congressional Globe (1868), 1349–51)

"MISSING" OR INCOMPLETE TAPES

18½ Minute Gap

On September 29, 1973, Alexander Haig called Rose Mary Woods and informed her that the President's conversation with Haldeman on the June 20, 1972 tape was not covered by the subpoena. (Transcript, *In re Grand Jury Misc.* 47–73, Tr. 1231, 1938–40). Haig received this information from J. Fred Buzhardt, who confirms advising Haig and President Nixon that the Haldeman portions of the June 20 tape referred to in the subpoena were not required. (T 1470–71)

On November 26, 1973, Rose Mary Woods testified that she did not transcribe the Haldeman portion of the conversation at Camp David and did not begin doing so until she returned to the White House because she did not believe it was required by the subpoena.

(T 1228-30.) Since the Haldeman conversation was never fully transcribed because neither Miss Woods nor the President believed it was subpoenaed, there would have been no reason for it to have been delivered to the President or for him to have known what was on the Haldeman portion of the tape. Therefore, he would have had no reason to have ordered its destruction.

There is absolutely no evidence that President Nixon was ever in actual personal possession of the June 20 tape or the Uher 5000 tape recorder. Indeed, all the evidence is to the contrary. The tape and the recorder were stored in a safe in the office of Rose Mary Woods and Rose Mary Woods has testified that she is the only person with the combination to that safe.

The notes of H.R. Haldeman taken on June 20, 1972, in no way suggest that the President received incriminating knowledge regarding the Watergate break-in. The notes refer entirely to a possible public relations counter-offensive. Since President Nixon and H.R. Haldeman were both known to be conscious of public relations, this would have been a completely normal subject for them to have discussed in response to a potential problem during the presidential campaign. There is nothing in these notes to suggest that any illegal activity was discussed:

be sure EOB office is *thoroly* ckd re bugs at all times—etc.
what is our counter-attack?
   PR offensive to tip this—
     hit the opposition w/ their activities
pt. out libertarians have created public [unreadable]
   do they justify this less that
      stealing Pentagon papers, Anderson file etc.?
we shld be on the attack—for diversion—(Book II, 246.)

Judge Sirica conducted 15 days of hearings over a 3-month period in an effort to determine the cause and significance, if any, of this and other missing tape segments.

The Grand Jury supplemented an FBI probe of this matter and called numerous witnesses in its investigation of the tapes. To date, no indictment has resulted from this investigation.

Should the President be expected personally to solve the mystery of the 18½ minute gap when the Office of the Special Prosecutor, Judge Sirica, the FBI, and the Grand Jury have been unable thus far to do so?

Should he discharge his personal secretary or any other employee when no charges have been placed?

President Nixon in his public address on April 29, 1974, has denied any knowledge of how the 18½ minute gap occurred. There has not been any direct evidence produced by anyone to show that the President ever listened to the original June 20th tape with the Uher 5000 machine. The only time the President listened to this tape, according to the evidence, is on September 29 at Camp David while Rose Mary Woods was using the 800B Sony machine.

Other "Missing" Tapes

There has been no evidence introduced to contradict the explanations given by the White House for the absence of the June 20, 1972 telephone call between the President and Mr. Mitchell and the non-recording of the April 15, 1973, conversation between the President and John Dean.

The telephone call was made from a phone which was not equipped to record conversations. This phone was in the private residence of the White House. The presidential log shows that at the time the call was made, the President was in fact in the residential wing of the White House.

Technical experts have testified regarding the procedures for changing reels on the Executive Office Building tape recorder. They have testified that one reel was usually left on over weekends in order to avoid necessitating a Technical Division officer's coming in to change it; that, due to the unusually heavy traffic in the Executive Office Building over the particular weekend in question, this reel of tape ran out in the early afternoon, long before the conversation between Dean and the President.

Moreover, in oral argument, the Minority Counsel offered a detailed explanation for his view that Henry Petersen's report that a recording of the April 15th conversation between Dean and the President existed was mistaken. (Minority Memorandum on Facts and Law, argument of Minority Counsel)

There has been no testimony that the gaps on the June 20, 1972, dictabelt and on the March 21, 1973, cassette were caused by erasures, deliberate or accidental. These were personal recordings in which the President expressed his private thoughts. He may simply have hesitated or paused during the recording process.

Article II

A. Legal Considerations

1. *Duplicity*

Five proposed Articles were considered by the Committee on the Judiciary. Four of these were structured according to a common-sense classification by factual subject matter: Watergate; noncompliance with subpoenas; Cambodian bombing; and personal finances. Article II, by contrast, is a catch-all repository for other miscellaneous and unrelated presidential offenses which were thought to have sufficient support among Committee Members to warrant inclusion. If this Article has any organizing principle at all, it is not a common factual basis but rather a common legal theory supposedly applicable to each specified offense.

The charge encompassed by Article II is that the President "repeatedly engaged in conduct" which constituted grounds for impeachment on one or more of the following three legal theories.

(1) "Violating the constitutional rights of citizens," or
(2) "Impairing the due and proper administration of justice and the conduct of lawful inquiries," or
(3) "Contravening the laws governing agencies of the executive branch and the purposes of these agencies."

The Article then states, "This conduct has included one or more of the following," whereupon five completely disparate types of activity are alleged:

(1) Attempt to misuse the Internal Revenue Service to harass political opponents.
(2) Warrantless wiretapping.
(3) Authorization and maintenance of the "Plumbers."
(4) Failure to prevent subordinates from impeding inquiries.
(5) Interference with agencies of executive branch.

Our opposition to the adoption of Article II should not be misunderstood as condonation of the presidential conduct alleged therein. On the contrary, we deplore in strongest terms the aspects of presidential wrongdoing to which the Article is addressed. However, we could not in conscience recommend that the House impeach and the Senate try the President on the basis of Article II in its form as proposed, because in our view the Article is duplicitous in both the ordinary and the legal senses of the word. In common usage, duplicity means belying one's true intentions by deceptive words; as a legal term of art, duplicity denotes the technical fault of uniting two or more offenses in the same count of an indictment.[1] We submit that the implications of a vote

---

[1] In criminal law, an indictment is void for duplicity if it joins two or more separable charges in the same count, and the jury does not come to a unanimous verdict *as to each offense*. *United States* v. *Warner*, 400 F. 2d 130, 735 (8th Cir.) *cert. denied*, 4-0 U.S. 930 (1970); *United States* v. *Bachman*, 164 F. Supp. 898, 900 (D.D.C. 1958).

for or against Article II are ambiguous and that the Committee debate did not resolve the ambiguities so as to enable the Members to vote intelligently. Indeed, this defect is symptomatic of a generic problem inherent in the process of drafting Articles of impeachment, and its significance for posterity may be far greater than the substantive merits of the particular charges embodied in Article II.

As a starting point for discussion, one might wonder why the five specifications of this Article were lumped together rather than being expressed in five separate Articles. The specifications are not bottomed in the same operative set of facts, nor were the presidential actions in question related to one another as part of a common scheme or plan. Of course, it could be argued that any separate actions taken by a President are elements of the overall administration of his office and are thus loosely related. As a realistic organizing principle, however, it does not aid analysis to combine such widely disparate events as the wiretapping of National Security Council staff members in 1969 and the testimony of Richard Kleindienst during his 1972 confirmation hearings. Nor does the Article even suggest that there is a factual subject-matter connection between the five specifications. It merely states that the President "repeatedly engaged" in certain "conduct."

One must therefore look for an organizing principle in the three legal theories advanced in Article II. Parenthetically, it may be observed that if the Article had been restricted to the first three specifications (discriminatory use of the IRS; warrantless wiretapping; the Plumbers), a specific and possibly useful legal theory could have been established as a framework for analysis. These three alleged offenses all potentially involve violations of individual rights guaranteed under the First Amendment, the Fourth Amendment, or both. The fourth and fifth specifications, however, do not fit within that framework. Consequently the legal theories applicable to the charges had to be so broadened that they are not useful as an organizing principle. For example, it is hard to understand why the fourth specification (failure to prevent subordinates from impeding inquiries) is included in this Article at all, since it seems much more germane to Article I.

We submit that the recitation of legal theories, far from being an organizing principle, was in fact a disingenous rationalization added as an afterthought in an effort to bind together the five unrelated specifications. The real reason for collecting those specifications in a single Article was purely pragmatic. It was correctly perceived that each of the five charges, standing alone in a separate Article, might be unable to command a majority vote. The strategy was therefore adopted of grouping the various charges together under a single umbrella, in the hope that enough Members of the Committee, the House, and ultimately the Senate would be persuaded by one or another specification that the aggregate vote for Article II would be sufficient for impeachment and conviction. The superimposition of the three legal theories was a secondary stratagem designed to make it more difficult for the Article to be split, by subsequent amendment, into separate Articles.

We do not take the position that the grouping of charges in a single Article is necessarily always invalid. To the contrary, it would make good sense if the alleged offenses together comprised a common scheme or plan, or even if they were united by a specific legal theory. Indeed, even if there were no logical reason at all for so grouping the charges (as is true of Article II), the Article might still be acceptable if its ambiguous aspects had been satisfactorily resolved. For the chief vice of this Article is that it is unclear from its language whether a Member should vote for its adoption if he believes any one of the five charges to be supported by the evidence; or whether he must believe in the sufficiency of all five; or whether it is enough if he believes in the sufficiency of more than half of the charges. The only clue is the sentence which states, "This conduct has included one or more of the following [five specificatoions]". This sentence implies that a Member may—indeed, must—vote to impeach or to convict if he believes in the sufficiency of a single specification, even though he believes that the accusations made under the other four specifications have not been proved, or do not even constitute grounds for impeachment. Thus Article II would have unfairly accumulated all guilty votes against the President, on whatever charge.[2] The President could have been removed from office even though no more than fourteen Senators believed him guilty of the acts charged in any one of the five specifications.

Nor could the President have defended himself against the ambiguous charges embodied in Article II. Inasmuch as five specifications are included in support of three legal theories, and all eight elements are phrased in the alternative, Article II actually contains no fewer than fifteen separate counts, any one of which might be deemed to constitute grounds for impeachment and removal. In addition, if the President were not informed which matters included in Article II were thought to constitute "high Crimes and Misdemeanors," he would have been deprived of his right under the Sixth Amendment to "be informed of the nature and cause of the accusation" against him.

This defect of Article II calls to mind the impeachment trial of Judge Halsted Ritter in 1936. Ritter was narrowly acquitted of specific charges of bribery and related offenses set forth in the first six Articles. He was convicted by an exact two-thirds majority, however, under Article VII. That Article charged that because of the specific offenses embodied in the other six Articles, Ritter had "[brought] his court into scandal and disrepute, to the prejudice of said court and public confidence in the administration of justice . . . ."[3] The propriety of convicting him on the basis of this vaque charge, after he had been acquitted on all of the specific charges, will long be debated.[4] Suffice it to say that the putative defect of Article VII is entirely different from that of Article II in the present case, and the two should not be confused.

---

[2] The failure of the Committee to vote separately on each specification did a disservice not only to the President, but also to Members of the Committee. The undifferentiated vote for or against Article II obscured the Members' views with respect to particular specifications, and conveyed the impression that each Member was convinced by all five specifications or by none of them. Similarly, if the Senate had convicted the President under Article II without voting separately on each specification, it would be impossible to know upon what basis and for what offenses the President was removed from office.
[3] *Proceedings of the United States Senate in the Trial of Impeachment of Halsted L. Ritter*, 74th Cong., 2d Sess. at 637 (1936).
[4] In the impeachment of Judge Robert Archbald in 1912, Article XIII reiterated in general terms the charges specified in the other twelve Articles. Archbald's conviction under this omnibus charge was less controversial, however, because he had already been found guilty on several of the specific charges.

A more relevant precedent may be found in the House debates during the impeachment of Judge Charles Swayne in 1905. In that case the House had followed the earlier practice of voting first on the general question of whether or not to impeach, and then drafting the Articles. Swayne was impeached in December 1904, by a vote of 198–61, on the basis of five instances of misconduct.[5] During January 1905 these five grounds for impeachment were articulated in twelve Articles. In the course of debate prior to the adoption of the Articles, it was discovered that although the general proposition to impeach had commanded a majority, individual Members had reached that conclusion for different reasons. This gave rise to the embarrassing possibility that none of the Articles would be able to command a majority vote. Representative Parker regretted that the House had not voted on each charge separately before voting on impeachment:

> [W]here different crimes and misdemeanors were alleged it was the duty of the House to have voted whether each class of matter reported was impeachable before debating that resolution of impeachment, and that the committee was entitled to the vote of a majority on each branch, and that now for the first time the real question of impeachment has come before this House to be determined—not by five men on one charge, fifteen on another, and twenty on another coming in generally and saying that for one or another of the charges Judge Swayne should be impeached, but on each particular branch of the case.[6]
>
> When we were asked to vote upon ten charges at once, that there was something impeachable contained in one or another of those charges, we have already perhaps stultified ourselves in the mode of our procedure....[7]

In order to extricate the House from its quandary, Representative Powers urged that the earlier vote to impeach should be construed to imply that a majority of the House felt that each of the separate charges had been proved;

> At that time the committee urged the impeachment upon five grounds, and those are the only grounds which are covered by the articles, ... and we had assumed that when the House voted the impeachment they practically said that a probable cause was made out in these five subject-matters which were discussed before the House.[8]

Powers' retrospective theory was ultimately vindicated when the House approved all twelve Articles.

If this episode from the Swayne impeachment is accorded any precedential value in the present controversy over Article II, it might be argued by analogy that the Committee's vote to adopt that Article must be construed to imply that a majority believed that all five specifications had been proved. Because the Committee did not vote separately on each specification, however, it is impossible to know whether those Members who voted for Article II would be willing to accept that construction. If so, then one of our major objections to the Article would vanish. However, it would still be necessary to amend the Article by removing the sentence "This has included one or more of the following," and substituting language which would make it plain that no Member of the House or Senate could vote for the Article unless

---

[5] The five grounds were: false certification of expenses; private use of railroad car in possession of receiver; failure to reside in judicial district; and two cases of maliciously punishing a lawyer for contempt of court. Like the five specifications in Article II, these charges were quite unrelated to each other. Therefore it is not surprising that Members varied widely with respect to which charges they considered to make out a case for impeachment.
[6] 39 Cong. Rec. 810 (1905).
[7] *Id.* 813.
[8] *Id.* 810.

he was convinced of the independent sufficiency of each of the five specifications.

However, there remains another and more subtle objection to the lumping together of unrelated charges in Article II:

> There is indeed always a danger when several crimes are tied together, that the jury will use the evidence cumulatively; that is, that although so much as would be admissible upon any one of the charges might not have persuaded them of the accused's guilt, the sum of it will convince them as to all.[9]

It is thus not enough protection for an accused that the Senate may choose to vote separately upon each section of an omnibus article of impeachment: the prejudicial effect of grouping a diverse mass of factual material under one heading, some of it adduced to prove one proposition and another to prove a proposition entirely unrelated, would still remain.

2. *"Abuse of Power" as a Theory of Impeachment of a President*

Just as Article I is drawn from Section I of the Majority staff's Summary of Information, entitled "Watergate," so the allegations of Article II are drawn from Section II of the Summary of Information, entitled "Abuse of Presidential Powers." Section II of the Summary of Information lists six Watergate-related and seven non-Watergate-related instances of alleged misuse of Presidential powers. According to the Summary of Information, "The issue in each of these areas is whether the President used the powers of his office in an illegal *or improper* manner to serve his personal, *political* or financial interests." [4] The sponsor of the proposed form of Article II which was adopted by the Committee stated during the Committee debate that the Article was not a criminal charge, but that it recognized the President was subject to a "higher standard" than the criminal law.[5] Another Member supporting Article II stated that it would apply to an undertaking "to do something legal for political or improper purposes." [6]

It is respectfully submitted that allegations of "abuse of power" fail to state a "high Crime and Misdemeanor" within the meaning of the Constitution. Abuses of power in general terms may have been the occasion for the exercise of the impeachment power in England in the Fourteenth and Seventeenth Centuries, during the great struggles for Parliamentary supremacy; but "abuse of power" is no more a high crime or misdemeanor in this country than "maladministration"—which was explicitly rejected by the Framers of our Constitution because it was too "vague." [7]

It is a far-reaching and dangerous proposition, that conduct *which is in violation of no known law*, but which is considered by a temporary majority of the Congress to be "improper" because undertaken for "political" purposes, can constitute grounds for impeachment. We wonder whether the Majority have fully considered the implications of this concept in terms of the liability to impeachment of an elected official, or a political appointee, or for that matter, by analogy, in terms of the liability of an elected Member of Congress to expulsion.

---

[5] HJC Debates, 7/29/74, TR. 809.
[6] HJC Debates, 7/29/74, TR. 1063.
[7] See discussion above.
[9] *United States* v. *Lotsch*, 102 F. 2d 35, 36 (2d Cir.), *cert. denied,* 307 U.S. 622 (1939).
[4] Summary of Information, p. 123 (emphasis added).

For Congress to impeach a President for an act which could not reasonably be known to be punishable when it was committed, however much Congress may disagree with that act, would meet the textbook definition of a bill of attainder or *ex post facto* law—both so hated by the Framers of our Constitution that they were prohibited not only to the Congress but also to the States. (U.S. Constitution, Article I, Section 9, clause 3; Article I, Section 10, clause 1.)

Have we slipped so far since the Eighteenth Century that we can no longer rely on our laws to tell us what is right and wrong? Why is it now, suddenly, necessary to go outside those laws? Blackstone wrote between 1765 and 1769:

> An impeachment before the Lords by the Common of Great Britain, in Parliament, is a *prosecution of the already known and established law*, . . . being a presentment to the most high and supreme court of criminal jurisdiction by the most solemn grand inquest of the whole kingdom.[8]

Woddeson wrote in 1777:

> [Impeachments] are founded and proceed upon the *law in being*.[9]

Joseph Story wrote in 1833, in this country:

> Impeachments are not framed to alter the law; but to carry it into more effectual execution.[10]

Why is it now necessary to impeach the President for conduct which is thought "improper"? We submit it is a violation of history and of our Constitution to do so.

Entirely apart from the requirement of "high Crimes and Misdemeanors" contained in the Impeachment Clause of the Constitution, demands of fundamental fairness are also imposed by the Due Process Clause of the Fifth Amendment, which provides, "No person shall . . . be deprived of life, liberty, or property, without due process of law." It is settled law that governmental action having an impact upon an individual's employment or employment prospects affects not only "property" interests, but also the individual's "liberty" as well.[11]

Under the due process clause, the vice of a formulation like "abuse of power" as the gravamen of allegedly impeachable offenses is its elasticity—it would be completely unmanageable as a standard even if the charge contained only one specification. It appears from the Summary of Information that to use power "improperly" for "political" purposes is an "abuse" of power, but what is the test for impropriety? Does an action, otherwise lawful or proper, become *per se* illegal or improper if it is motivated by a desire to discredit members of the opposition party, by a desire to conceal politically embarrassing information, by "political" considerations?

Like members of Congressional staffs, White House staff members are exempt from the prohibition on certain forms of political activity by federal employees imposed by the Hatch Act.[12] This fact ought to

---

[8] 4 W. Blackstone *Commentaries on the Laws of England* (1771) 256–57. (Emphasis added.)
[9] 2 R. Wooddeson *Laws of England* 611, 612. (Emphasis added.)
[10] 1 J. Story, *Commentaries on the Constitution* (3d ed. 1858) § 798.
[11] *Greene* v. *McElroy*, 360 U.S. 474, 496–97 (1959); *McNeill* v. *Butz*, 480 F.2d 314, 320 (4th Cir. 1973); *Perry* v. *Sindermann*, 408 U.S. 593, 597, 601 (1972); *Willner* v. *Committee on Character and Fitness*, 373 U.S. 96, 103 (1963); *In re Ming*, 469 F.2d 1352 (7th Cir. 1972); *Bottcher* v. *State of Florida Dept. of Agric. and Consumer Services*, 361 F. Supp. 1123, 1129 (N. D. Fla., 1973); *Joint Anti-Fascist Refugee Committee* v. *McGrath*, 341 U.S. 123, 185 (1951) (Jackson, J., concurring).
[12] 5 U.S.C. § 7324(d)(1).

shed some light on the difficulty that Congress has perceived in the past in separating the political from the governmental functions of elected officials and those who serve directly under them. As approved by the Committee, moreover Article II leaves unclear the Committee's view as to whether the President's action, in order to be impeachable, must be motivated by a criminal intent, as argued above, by only an "improper" intent, or with particular reference to Paragraph (4), by any intent at all.

Finally, it is difficult to understand how content can be given to terms such as "abuse of power," or "improper" use of power, unless some attempt is made to determine the historical practice in prior Administrations in the areas described by Article II—efforts to prevent leaks of national security information, for example, or the general scope of activities conducted by the Central Intelligence Agency. No such meaningful comparisons were undertaken by either the Committee or its staff during this impeachment inquiry. If the Congress may remove an elected President for conduct which is violative of no known law, but is merely in its view "improper", and if the Congress refuses to consider what has been thought "proper" or "improper' in the past, but will address only the question of what now seems "improper" in the subjective view of a temporary majority of legislators, we will have traded in the Constitution for new Articles of Confederation. We will have established a government essentially by one branch, not three.

B. HISTORICAL CONTEXT

Proposed Article II represents an unwieldy agglomeration of alleged abuses of power by President Nixon: efforts to procure discriminatory income tax audits, warrantless wiretapping, covert activities of the "Plumbers", etc. In order to evaluate the gravity of these allegations, it is instructive to compare them with certain historical incidents illustrative of the alarming growth of executive power during the past forty years.

Frustrated by the intransigent opposition of the Supreme Court to his New Deal legislation in 1937, President Roosevelt attempted, under color of the most transparently specious rationalization, to pack the court with additional Justices who would be more sympathetic to his political ideology. Later in his Administration the wartime emergency was invoked to justify the suspension of the constitutional rights of thousands of Japanese-Americans who were interned in detention camps. It was also Roosevelt who, in 1940, initiated the practice of warrantless "national security" wiretapping which has been carried on by each of his successors.

President Truman took the law into his own hands with his unconstitutional seizure of the nation's steel mills in 1952. His successors in office were responsible for the involvement of the United States in a protracted but undeclared war in Southeast Asia.

During his first year in office, President Kennedy also indulged in an irresponsible military adventure in Cuba. Later in his Administration, the Department of Justice was used, many feel, for the improper purpose of discriminatory harrassment both of certain labor union leaders and of steel company executives who thwarted the President's economic policies.

This eclectic catalogue of arguable abuses of power by recent Presidents is not intended to suggest necessarily that there are precedents for each of the specific instances of misconduct charged against President Nixon in proposed Article II. If President Nixon was guilty of misconduct justifying removal from office, no one would argue that he should have been spared simply because previous Presidents were not impeached for their similar excesses. Rather, these historical incidents are mentioned only to illustrate a point which is all too easily lost in the current preoccupation with President Nixon's alleged offenses: no President who attempts to make full use of the lawful powers of his office is likely to complete his term without having committed, even in good faith, a constitutional violation. The President's duties and responsibilities frequently expose him to conflicting constitutional demands. In these situations he must choose either to act, knowing that any action may prove to involve a violation of the Constitution, or to refrain from acting, knowing that inaction—though technically not a violation of his oath of office—may be the worst policy of all.

To constitute an impeachable offense, therefore, it is not enough merely to show a presidential violation of the Constitution (or, in the jargon of proposed Article II, an "abuse of power" or failure to "take care that the laws be faithfully executed"). The critical question is whether the President's action was undertaken in good faith: whether he acted under color of law and in furtherance of his constitutional duties as he honestly saw them.

The phrase "national security" is presently in bad odor because of a widespread intuition that it has been too often unnecessarily invoked as a talisman to justify otherwise indefensible exercises of executive power. Yet each of the presidential actions listed above, like many of those specified in proposed Article II, was undertaken for the avowed purpose of protecting the national security, in response to what the President perceived to be a legitimate military, economic or diplomatic imperative.

C. FACTUAL ALLEGATIONS

Paragraph (1)

This paragraph charges the President with having endeavored to violate the constitutional rights of citizens in relation to the official governmental activities of the Internal Revenue Service in two principal ways: by obtaining confidential information from income tax returns, and by instigating tax audits and investigations on a politically discriminatory basis.

Ineffectual attempts

This paragraph does not charge the President with actual misuse of the IRS. Indeed, no evidence before this Committee could support such a charge. Instead the President is charged with responsibility for the unsuccessful attempts by his subordinates to achieve allegedly improper or unlawful goals.

We think, however, that the majority gives too little thought to the potential implications in an impeachment proceeding of ineffectual efforts by presidential staff to execute presidential wishes. Because such efforts were unsuccessful, certainly the conclusion that the President was seriously intent on, or interested in the misuse of the IRS is negated. Given the plenary powers of a President to manage, direct and control the operations of the executive branch of government, if he had desired an illegitimate goal to be accomplished, it would have been accomplished. As in pulling or pushing on a string, the ability of a President to succeed in accomplishing some affirmative objective is quite different from his ability to prevent or correct subordinate conduct of which he is actually unaware.

The case of John Dean's September, 1972 attempt to initiate IRS audits of 575 people named on a list of McGovern staff and contributors illustrates the point. After John Dean had given IRS Commissioner Walters the list on September 11, 1972, and after Dean's alleged discussion with the President about the IRS on September 15, Dean did not make his second effort to influence IRS Commissioner Johnnie Walters to order the audits until September 25, ten days after his conversation with the President. The majority argues that Dean's second approach to Walters was a result of his conversation with the President. However, the record fails to disclose any evidence that the President at any time followed up the matter with Dean, either directly or through Haldeman or Ehrlichman.

To us, this raises at the very least a serious question as to the degree of the President's true interest in the matter, one aspect of his *mens rea*. Such a factor would be considered relevant in possible mitigation of punishment in an ordinary criminal proceeding. Since fitness for office is the ultimate question in all impeachment cases, the depth of the President's personal commitment to the achievement of some specific improper objective must likewise be held relevant to a determination of the *impeachability* of his conduct relative to such impropriety. The evidence of the President's interest and involvement in the "Enemies List" case is therefore exceedingly weak, and the majority is faced merely with John Dean's unsuccessful attempts to misuse the IRS.

There is, of course, no question that Dean's attempts were unsuccessful. The Joint Committee on Internal Revenue taxation conducted a detailed and thorough investigation of the whole matter of the enemies list. The conclusion of that Committee's staff was as follows:

The staff has found absolutely no evidence that audits of people on the political opponents lists were on the average conducted more harshly than normal. (Joint Committee Report, 11)

Established practice or custom

We also believe that the Committee's inquiry pertaining to the allegations of this Paragraph was fatally flawed by our failure to develop substantial evidence concerning the routine practices of the IRS, over a period of years spanning several previous Administrations, with respect to the impingement of political or other "extraneous" considerations upon the interpretation and implementation of pertinent regulations and statutory provisions.

Since the point we now make is one easily misunderstood, it bears some elaboration. We do not suggest as a general proposition that the commission of clear-cut violations of law by any President can or should be excused on the sole ground that similar offenses can be shown to have been committed by his predecessors. We do suggest that where the presidential conduct embodied in some enactment of positive law, it is helpful, if not absolutely essential, to consider whether such conduct is rare or commonplace in attempting to place the conduct outside the parameters of permissible "use" of presidential power.

There is evidence in the record indicating that the operations of the IRS have not traditionally been held aloof from political considerations. For example, in his affidavit to this Committee former IRS Commissioner Randolph Thrower referred to the existence of a "Sensitive Case Report" which for years had been circulated within the Commissioner's staff and also delivered to the Secretary of the Treasury. Thrower stated:

> I understand that customarily the Secretary of the Treasury would advise the President of any matters in the sensitive case report about which the President, *by reason of his official duties and responsibilities*, should be advised. (Book VIII, 40; emphasis added)

The emphasized phrase, in context, strikes us as being patently euphemistic.

During 1972 it was IRS policy to postpone investigations involving sensitive cases until after the November elections whenever possible. (Book VIII, 233) John Ehrlichman testified in executive session before the Senate Select Committee that it was because he suspected IRS favoritism for Democratic National Chairman Lawrence O'Brien, as contrasted with the pre-election audit policy toward Republicans, that he tried to move the O'Brien audit along. (Book VIII, 224-25)

In the light of the foregoing indications that IRS policy-makers were traditionally sensitive to political considerations, we think the Committee was under an obligation to make inquiry into the customary or routine practices of the Service in situations comparable to those with which this Paragraph is concerned. Had the Committee found—and we categorically do not assert it to be the fact—that the specific instances of alleged attempted abuse of the IRS by White House personnel in this Administration typical conduct of presidential aides in other administrations, the House might perceive a need for appropriate remedial legislation to deal with the problem prospectively without concluding that the President should be *impeached* for failing to put a stop to practices that had sprung up during the tenure of his predecessors.

Repeated conduct

Article II charges that President Nixon "repeatedly engaged in conduct violating the constitutional rights of citizens." We must point out, therefore, that with respect to only one of the specific allegations made under this Paragraph—that involving the McGovern supporters list—is there any competent, credible evidence from which the Committee could infer that the President actually knew of the nature of his aides' dealings with the IRS. We reject the notion that one such instance in five-and-one-half years can fairly be viewed as "repeated" misconduct, rather than as a genuinely isolated incident. We concede that if the President were aware and approved of all of the questionable contacts of, say, Caulfield and Dean with IRS officials during the 1971–72 period, it would then be reasonable to argue that, through his subordinates and agents, the President had "repeatedly" sought to misuse the facilities of the IRS for purposes not sanctioned by Congress. As a matter of fact, however, we are satisfied that the evidence simply does not support any such conclusion.

The President's state of mind that government agencies had been neither "repeatedly" abused nor abused at all during his first term was strongly evidenced during his conversation with Dean and Haldeman on the late afternoon of September 15, 1972:

> The PRESIDENT. We, we have not used the power in this first four years, as you know.
> DEAN. That's right.
> The PRESIDENT. We have never used it. We haven't used the Bureau and we haven't used the Justice Department, but things are going to change now. And they're going to change, and, and they're going to get it right—
> DEAN. That's an exciting prospect.
> The PRESIDENT. It's got to be done. It's the only thing to do.
> HALDEMAN. We've got to.
> The PRESIDENT. Oh, oh, well, we've just been, we've been just God damn fools. For us to come into this election campaign and not do anything with regard to the Democratic senators who are running, and so forth. [Characterizations deleted] That'd be ridiculous. Absolutely ridiculous. It's not going, going to be that way any more, and, uh—
> HALDEMAN. Really, it's ironic, you know, because we've gone to such extremes to do every—You know, you, you and your damn regulations with—
> The PRESIDENT. Right.
> HALDEMAN. Everybody worries about,
> The PRESIDENT. That's right.
> HALDEMAN. about picking up a hotel bill or anything.
> DEAN. Well, I think, we can, I think, I think we can be proud of the White House staff. It really has,
> The PRESIDENT. That's right.
> DEAN. had no problems of that—
> The PRESIDENT. Well, that's right. (HJCT 10–11)

This statement by the President indicates to us that at that moment he was considering an effort to make the agencies more politically responsive than they had been. Musing over the question could not in itself constitute an impeachable offense, however, absent clear and convincing evidence of his effort to implement the idea in concrete terms.

We note also that in this comment the President did not refer specifically to the IRS.

a. Endeavoring to Obtain Confidential Tax Information

(i) *The President's authority to obtain information.*—While we believe the evidence shows no extensive presidential involvement in Dean's and Caulfield's activities with respect to the IRS, it should be noted that the President himself has an absolute right of access to tax returns and data of the Internal Revenue Service. Article II, Section 2 of the Constitution provides:

> The President . . . may require the Opinion, in writing, of the principal officer in each of the executive Departments, upon any subject relating to the Duties of their respective offices, ...

More specifically, Section 6103(a)(1) of the Internal Revenue Code of 1954 provides:

(a) PUBLIC RECORD AND INSPECTION.—
(1) Returns made with respect to taxes imposed by chapters 1, 2, 3 and 6 upon which the tax had been determined by the Secretary or his delegate shall constitute public records; but, except as hereinafter provided in this section, they shall be open to inspection only upon order of the President and under rules and regulations prescribed by the Secretary or his delegate and approved by the President.

An opinion dated April 22, 1970 from the Chief Counsel of the IRS to Commissioner Randolph W. Thrower stated:

... It is inconceivable that the President should be bound by rules and regulations [under Section 6103] in prescribing the circumstances or manner in which returns are to be disclosed to a member of his staff for his use. Since any such rules and regulations are subject to revision or modification by the Secretary at any time with the approval of the President, and the Secretary is the subordinate of the President appointed to serve at the pleasure of the President, it cannot be believed that he should be limited by the requirements of any such rules and regulations or that Congress so intended.

* * * * * * *

... To assume that a 'presidential request' must comply with such regulations assumes that the Secretary of the Treasury or the Commissioner of Internal Revenue could frustrate a request of the President for returns—in the face of the fact that the statutory provision says that they should be open for inspection on his order.

The statute as I interpret it, and as interpreted by my predecessors, is not the source of the right of the President to inspect returns, but merely sets forth the manner in which returns may be made available to other persons without Presidential order.

This opinion concludes as follows:

... Thus, there would seem to be no question about the President's right of access to these returns through a designated member of his staff. While ... there is no legal requirement that such requests be written, the procedure you have followed requiring that all requests be detailed in writing is procedurally preferable to accepting oral requests.[1]

The general question of access to by a member of the President's staff apparently first arose in 1961 in regard to Carmine Bellino, who was then Special Consultant to President Kennedy. In a memorandum of March 23, 1961 to the General Counsel of the Department of the Treasury from then IRS Commissioner Mortimer M. Caplin, the following statement concerning the legality of Bellino's inspection of returns was set forth:

On January 26, Mr. Bellino, Special Consultant to the President, called at my office and requested permission to inspect our files on _____ and others. Although we had no precedent to guide us, we decided that Mr. Bellino, in his capacity as a representative of the President, could inspect our files without a written request. This reflects the view that Section 6103 of the Code specifically provides that returns shall be open to inspection upon order of the President, and since Mr. Bellino's official capacity constitutes him the representative of the President, the action taken is regarded as conforming to law. Based on this decision, we permitted Mr. Bellino to inspect the files relating to _____ _____. Since that time we have also permitted him to inspect tax returns and related documents pertaining to other persons.[2]

---

[1] Definitive opinion of K. Martin Worthy, Chief Counsel to Randolph W. Thrower, Commissioner, dated April 22, 1970.
[2] Compare this opinion with the conclusion reached in a legal opinion dated April 9, 1970, rendered to Mr. Lawrence F. O'Brien by former Commissioner Caplin, which appears in the [*Congressional Record*, April 16, 1970, S 5911–12].

Again in 1964 the office of the Chief Counsel of IRS concluded that the Warren Commission was entitled to access to IRS returns on the basis of Executive Order 11130, which generally indicated that all agencies and departments should furnish the Commission with such facilities, service, and cooperation as might be requested. The IRS opinion stated:

> ... [I] is axiomatic that in the exercise of power of his office the President is not required to personally take care of day to day details but may, in his discretion, delegate certain functions to others.... Manifestly, Sec. 6103(a)(1) could not have been designed to require the Secretary or his delegate and the President to prescribe and approve rules and regulations regarding a personal inspection of returns by the President. Such construction should apply equally to an inspection by the Commission acting for the President.

Thereafter a question arose as to whether the Warren Commission could publish the returns disclosed to it. This resulted in a request by Sheldon S. Cohen (then IRS Chief Counsel) to the Director of the Legislation and Regulations Division of IRS for his opinion as to whether the Commission had authority to inspect returns. The Legislation and Regulations Division advised Cohen by opinion of September 24, 1964 that it concurred in the January 6, 1964 opinion of the Enforcement Division, reiterating that:

> ... [T]he Commission is the "alter ego" of the President, and since there is no restriction on the President's authority to inspect tax returns, likewise there is no restriction on the right of the Commission as his "alter ego", to inspect tax returns within the scope of the Executive order.

In light of the strong stand the IRS has consistently taken regarding the right of access of the President and his authorized representatives to tax returns and other data of the service, it is obvious that there is no illegality or impropriety involved in the receipt of such information by authorized White House staff members *per se*. If the receipts were not authorized, of course, we would not view those actions by presidential subordinates as constituting grounds for impeachment of President Nixon.

(*ii*) *Gerald Wallace report.*—The Majority Report charges the President with responsibility for the unlawful disclosure to a Washington newsman of confidential IRS information concerning a 1970 tax investigation of the brother of Alabama Governor George Wallace.[3] It is conceded that the unauthorized disclosure occurred and that the information may have been disclosed by someone in the White House. Nevertheless, there is no competent credible evidence connecting the President to this "news leak."

The only suggestion of presidential involvement in this matter is a hearsay statement by the ex-White House employee who obtained the information from the IRS that Haldeman had said that the Wallace tax information was to be obtained at the request of the President. (Book VIII, 38). There is no evidence to indicate that the President was involved in the disclosure of the information to the newsman.

Even if the hearsay statement of the aide is credited, it is an established principle of IRS law and procedure that the disclosure of tax information to White House aides is proper. Both the White House

---

[3] Under 26 U.S.C. § 7213, the unauthorized disclosure of tax information by any officer or employee of the United States is prohibited.

staff member who obtained the information, and IRS Commissioner Randolph Thrower, who authorized releases of the information to him, have stated in affidavits given to this Committee that the disclosure of the information to the White House was legal and proper. (Book VIII, 38, 40)

There is no evidence that the President received the report. There is no evidence that the President knew of, approved, or had anything to do with the transmission of information to the newsman.

There is no evidence of any interference by anyone at the White House with the IRS investigation, or of any request with respect thereto by any White House staff member, certainly not by the President.

(*iii*) *Other tax information.*—The majority also charges the President with culpability for the acts of a member of John Dean's staff, John Caulfield, who, from time to time in 1971 and 1972 obtained confidential tax information about various individuals from the IRS and on occasion attempted to have audits conducted. There is no evidence that the President knew anything about the activities of Caulfield.

b. *Endeavoring to Instigate Tax Audits*

(*i*) *Lawrence O'Brien.*—The evidence establishes that during the summer of 1972, John Ehrlichman attempted to get the IRS to investigate the possibility that Democratic National Committee Chairman Lawrence O'Brien had received large amounts of income which had not been reported properly. (Book VIII, 217–35) After IRS agents had interviewed O'Brien and his returns were found to be in order, Commissioner Walters and his assistant met with Shultz and agreed that the investigation should be closed, and they so informed Ehrlichman. No other action was taken in the O'Brien case by the IRS.

Evidence of presidential involvement in this episode is virtually nonexistent. An affidavit by the Minority Counsel to the Senate Select Committee states that he was told over the telephone by J. Fred Buzhardt, a White House Special Counsel, that during the meeting between the President and John Dean on September 15, 1972 Dean reported on the IRS investigation of O'Brien. It is on this third-hand hearsay alone that the Majority would connect the President to the case. However, when Dean was interviewed by this Committee's staff, he said that he had no recollection of having discussed the O'Brien tax audit with the President on that or any other occasion. Dean also stated that he would have had no reason to report on the O'Brien case since he was not involved in it and knew nothing of its details. (Dean interview, HJC files.) Thus, there is no competent evidence to connect the President to the O'Brien tax investigation.

(*ii*) *List of McGovern Supporters.*—The record before the Committee suggests that on September 11, 1972 John Dean gave IRS Commissioner Johnnie Walters a list of McGovern supporters and requested that the IRS begin tax investigations of the individuals named on the list. Pursuant to Ehrlichman's instructions, Dean told Walters that he had not been asked by the President to have this done and that he did not know whether the President had asked the action to be undertaken. (Book VIII, 240) Walters told Dean that compliance with the request would be disastrous. Two days later, Walters met with Shultz and they agreed they should not comply with Dean's request. Shultz told Walters to do nothing with respect to the list and Walters put it in his office safe. (Book VIII, 275-79)

On September 15, 1972, the President and Haldeman were discussing Dean:

HALDEMAN. Between times, he's doing, he's moving ruthlessly on the investigation of McGovern people, Kennedy stuff, and all that too. I just don't know how much progress he's making, 'cause I—
The PRESIDENT. The problem is that's kind of hard to find.
HALDEMAN. Chuck, Chuck has gone through, you know, has worked on the list, and Dean's working the, the thing through IRS and, uh, in some cases, I think, some other [unintelligible] things. He's—He turned out to be tougher than I thought he would ... (HJCT1)

Shortly thereafter, Dean entered the room, and the conversation turned to a number of topics, chiefly matters related to the Watergate area. There is no mention of the IRS during the portion of the tape which was available to the Committee, but Dean has testified that during the last seventeen minutes of that meeting he, Haldeman and the President discussed the use of the IRS. (Dean testimony, 2 HJC 229) As Dean recalled the conversation, Dean told the President and Haldeman of his difficulty in getting Walters to commence audits, and the President complained that Shultz had not been sufficiently responsive to White House requirements. (Dean testimony, 2 HJC 229; Book VIII, 334-36)

Dean has testified that because of this conversation with the President, he [Dean] again contacted ten days later Walters, but Walters still refused to co-operate. (Dean testimony, 2 HJC 250)

In his testimony before this Committee, Dean was unable to recall precisely what he and the President discussed on September 15th regarding Dean's meeting with Commissioner Walters four days earlier:

Mr. FISH. It was my understanding that this morning, in response to Mr. Doar, you said that at the time you met the President on the 15th, you told the President about your meeting with Mr. Walters and, as I had you down here, you say "I related this to the President."
My question to you is, Did you relate to him the specifics of why you went to Mr. Walters and of the meeting with Mr. Walters?
Mr. DEAN. *I cannot recall with specificity how much of that matter was raised.* I just have this vivid recollection of the discussion about Mr. Shultz' role and the fact that the IRS was not performing and I think that the best evidence of that is obviously the tape. (Dean testimony, 2 HJC 311; emphasis added)

Apparently, when Dean returned to see Commissioner Walters on September 25, 1972 he did not indicate to Walters that it was the President's wish that Dean make another attempt at getting the McGovern list audits underway, even though on other occasions Dean had represented himself to be acting under direct presidential supervision when that was not actually the case. (Kleindienst testimony, 9 SSC 3564, 3575-76) Even if Dean felt that he was this time genuinely following presidential instructions, he may have continued to heed Ehrlichman's earlier pointed admonition that he should not tell Walters that the President had anything to do with his visit.

(*iii*) *Segment of September 15, 1972 tape.*—On May 28, 1974 the Special Prosecutor moved the United States District Court for the District of Columbia to turn over to the appropriate grand jury the last seventeen minutes of the tape recording of the conversation among

Haldeman, Dean and the President on September 15, 1972. The Special Prosecutor alleged, in support of his motion, that that portion of the recording—which Judge John J. Sirica had earlier withheld from the grand jury after sustaining a particularized claim of executive privilege by the President—was relevant to alleged White House efforts to abuse and politicize the IRS, including the unlawful attempt in August and September of 1972 to instigate an IRS investigation of Lawrence O'Brien.

On July 12, 1974 Judge Sirica granted the motion as to that portion of the conversation occurring between approximately 6:00 and 6:13 p.m., but his order was stayed pending appeal by the President. [So far as we are presently informed, the grand jury and the Special Prosecutor have not yet received this segment of the tape recording.] On June 24, 1974 this Committee issued a subpoena to the President for tapes, dictabelts, memoranda and other records of this portion of the conversation, but President did not furnish any such materials to the Committee before leaving office.

Standing alone, Dean's testimony before this Committee that the President told him on September 15, 1972 to come back to the President if Dean had any problems with Shultz over the IRS audits, so that the President could "get it straightened out" (Dean testimony, 2 HJC 229) could, if true, be taken as evidence only of some "tough talk" among copartisans during an election campaign, taking place in the privacy of an office where such talk is cheap. The late Stewart Alsop once, with characteristic insight, commented upon the abundant evidence produced during the 1973 hearings of the Senate Select Committee that CRP and the White House were inhabited by a personality type which Alsop labelled—without benefit of the White House transcripts—the "phony tough:" people like Dean who were given to displays of bravado, arrogance and insensitivity to the rights of others because they seemed to feel that such attitudes were expected of them.[4]

The Haldeman comment to the President at the beginning of the recorded September 15th conversation—"Chuck, Chuck has gone through, you know, has worked on the list, and Dean's working the, the thing through IRS . . ." (HJCT 1)—provides evidence of Presidential knowledge that *some* political use of the IRS was contemplated by his aides, however, which simply cannot be ignored. Taken together, the Haldeman remark and the Dean testimony before this Committee make it reasonable to infer that the thirteen-minute segment of the September 15, 1972 tape recording which both we and the Special Prosecutor have been seeking to obtain from either the White House or Judge Sirica *may*, indeed, contain additional evidence damaging to Mr. Nixon.

We think, however, that the appropriate response of the Committee under these circumstances was not to accept the word of a witness—Dean—who has been demonstrated to be of doubtful credibility (See, for example, the evidence in Book III, 415–26, relating to Dean's possible perjury concerning his disposition of certain notebooks taken from Howard Hunt's White House safe on the evening of June 19, 1972.) Rather, we believe that the President should have been ac-

---

[4] *Newsweek,* September 10, 1973, p. 94.

corded a presumption of innocence as to each and every allegation against him and that, lacking evidence to corroborate Dean's assertion that the President had instructed him to go back to Commissioner Walters in an effort to get the McGovern list audits instituted, the Committee should not have voted to recommend impeachment on the basis of this allegation under Paragraph (1).

Our view, of course, is readily subject to change if additional relevant evidence, such as is suspected to be contained on the thirteen-minute September 15, 1972 tape segment, should come to light. Whether or not Dean's efforts to procure audits of the McGovern supporters violated positive law, they were reprehensible. If the President did, in fact, countenance such activity on the part of his own White House counsel, it might then be appropriate for the House, and the American people, to consider him liable to censure, even if such conduct, as an isolated event, did not render the President liable to impeachment.

Paragraph (2)

The gravamen of the charge in Paragraph (2) is that the President misused the Federal Bureau of Investigation, the Secret Service, and other personnel from the executive branch, to carry out at his direction the unlawful electronic surveillance of citizens. Paragraph (2) refers in particular to the authorization, execution and concealment of the so-called 1969-71 wiretaps; the surveillance of Joseph Kraft in 1969; the surveillance of Donald Nixon in 1970; the investigation of Daniel Schorr in 1971; and the Huston plan. These incidents are individually analyzed below, except for the Schorr investigation which does not appear even colorably to have constituted an unlawful or otherwise improper action.

a. *The 1969–71 Wiretaps.*

The 1969-71 wiretapping program, and the applicable statutory and constitutional law, are treated at great length in the Minority Memorandum of Law and the Evidence. Because the facts of the case are presented in detail in that document,[5] no factual summary will be reiterated here. With respect to the allegation that 1969-71 wiretaps constituted grounds for impeachment, we believe that the following points have not received the attention they deserve.

(*i*) *"Leaks" as a Justification for Wiretapping.*—Not every leak of classified information, to be sure, represents a *bona fide* threat to the national security. The 1969-71 wiretapping program, though triggered by William Beecher's article of May 9, 1969 about the Cambodian bombing, was really a response to a whole series of news articles based on leaks during the spring of 1969. Kissinger has described the effect of these leaks as follows:

> During this period, policies were being considered which would establish the fundamental approach to major foreign policy issues such as the United States' strategic posture, Strategic Arms Limitation Talks (SALT), Vietnam and many other national security issues. Because of the sensitive nature of these matters, the secrecy of each was of vital importance and the success or failure of each program turned in many instances upon the maintenance of the necessary security. These leaks included discussions of National Security Council deliberations,

---

[5] Minority Memorandum on Facts and Law, "Abuse of Presidential Powers, Wiretaps."

intelligence information, negotiating positions and specific military operations. In several cases, significant consequences resulted from these premature releases of internal policy deliberations. In addition, the release of such classified information had obvious benefit for the potential enemies of this country. Of particular concern to the President were news leaks which occurred from early April until June 1969, involving Vietnam policy, strategic arms and the Okinawa reversion.[6]

The first leak was reflected in articles published in the *New York Times* on April 1 and April 6, 1969 indicating that the United States was considering unilateral withdrawal from Vietnam. Kissinger stated that these disclosures were "extremely damaging" in that they "raised a serious question as to our reliability and credibility as an ally" and "impaired our ability to carry on private discussions with the North Vietnamese."[7]

The second leak was the basis for an article of May 1, 1969 in the *New York Times* reporting the five strategic options under study for the SALT negotiations; these options were published before they were considered by the NSC. Kissinger said that this disclosure was "of the most extreme gravity" because it revealed the apparent inability of U.S. intelligence to assess accurately the Soviet missile capability; and because it "raised serious questions as to the integrity of the USIB and created severe doubts about our ability to maintain security . . ."[8]

The third leak allegedly resulted in Beecher's May 9, 1969 article revealing the air strikes in Cambodia. This article had "obvious adverse diplomatic repercussions," according to Kissinger, and raised "a serious question in the mind of the President as to . . . whether in the future he could make critical foreign policy decisions on the basis of full and frank discussions."[9]

The fourth leak produced a *New York Times* article of June 3, 1969 reporting that the President had determined to remove nuclear weapons from Okinawi in the upcoming negotiations with Japan over the reversion of the island. This decision had not yet been formally communicated to Japan. Kissinger stated that this article compromised negotiating tactics, prejudiced the government's interests, and complicated our relations with Japan; and that it "clearly preempted any opportunity we might have had for obtaining a more favorable outcome" from the negotiations.[10]

The fifth leak was the foundation for articles on June 3 and 4, 1969 in the *Washington Evening Star* and the *New York Times* reporting the President's decision to begin withdrawing troops from Vietnam before this decision had been communicated to the South Vietnamese. Kissinger characterized these disclosures as "extremely damaging with respect to this Government's relationship and credibility with its allies."[11]

(*ii*) *Historical Precedent.*—The argument has been advanced that no reliance can be placed on the warrantless wiretapping carried on by the Department of Justice between 1940 and 1968, because these wiretaps were in violation of § 605 of the Federal Communications

---
[6] *Statement of Information Submitted on Behalf of President Nixon*, Book IV, 143–44.
[7] *Id.* 145.
[8] *Id.* 171–72.
[9] *Id.* 165.
[10] *Id.* 182.
[11] *Id.* 159.

Act of 1934.[12] In a sense, though, whether or not the prior practice of the Department of Justice was technically legal is academic. The practice was continued uninterruptedly and virtually unchallenged for nearly thirty years, under five Presidents and their Attorneys General. Under these circumstances it would be too much to expect President Nixon to challenge the legality of the investigative technique he believed proper and necessary. Moreover, Title III of the Omnibus Crime Control and Safe Streets Act of 1968 had recently been enacted and on its face appeared to represent a relaxation of the earlier statutory prohibition of wiretapping.

(*iii*) *Title III.*—The majority opinion in the *Keith* case clearly rejects the proposition that a warrantless national security wiretap must first satisfy the criteria of 18 U.S.C. § 2511(3) and then be judged according to Fourth Amendment standards. Rather, when the President or the Attorney General deems electronic surveillance to be necessary for one of the reasons listed in § 2511(3), Title III no longer has any application at all. Nothing in Justice Powell's opinion suggests that judicial review is or should be available to inquire into the soundness of the President's determination.

> If we could accept the Government's characterization of § 2511(3) as a congressionally prescribed exception to the general requirement of a warrant, it would be necessary to consider the question of whether the surveillance in this case came within the exception. . . . But . . . we hold that the statute is not the measure of the executive authority asserted in this case. Rather, we must look to the constitutional powers of the President.[13]

Justice Powell quite properly assumed that the President would not abuse his power thus to withdraw from the ambit of Title III cases which bore no relation to national or domestic security; and if an abuse of this sort ever took place, the Fourth Amendment would render unconstitutional what the statute could not touch.

Nor can it be argued that § 2517 applies to warrantless wiretaps, and thus governs the uses which were made of the 1969–71 wiretaps. The phrase, "by any means authorized by this chapter" clearly does not contemplate warrantless wiretaps as an authorized means. It could be argued, of course, that even a warrantless wiretap was "authorized" by § 2511(3). That section also states, however, that *"nothing* contained in this chapter . . . shall limit the constitutional power of the President to take such measures as he deems necessary . . ." (emphasis supplied).

---

[12] However, the more modern view reaches a contrary interpretation of § 605 in cases which involve the national security. *United States* v. *Butenko,* 494 F. 2d 593 (3d Cir. 1974), for example, the court held that not only the interception but also the divulgence was permissible under § 605, where the wiretap was conducted in the foreign affairs field pursuant to Executive order. (494 F. 2d at 598). *Nardone* was distinguished because it involved the routine investigation of domestic criminals as opposed to foreign intelligence gathering. *Coplon,* a celebrated espionage case, was rejected as authority because the court in that case (Judge Learned Hand wrote the opinion) never addressed the precise question raised in *Butenko.* The court drew attention to the fact that there was virtually no discussion in Congress of such a situation under § 605.

The absence of legislative consideration of the issue does suggest that Congress may not have intended § 605 to reach the situation presented in the present case. (Id. 601).

The opinion concluded that the legislators simply did not consider the possible effect of § 605 in the foreign affairs field, and that the statute must therefore be read so as not to interfere with the President's various foreign powers.

[13] *United States* v. *United States District Court,* 407 U.S. 297, 308 (1972). As the court observed in *United Staes* v. *Butenko,* 494 F. 2d 593, 600 n. 25 (3d Cir. 1974):

With the passage of the Omnibus Crime Control and Safe Streets Act of 1968, it appears that the only limitations on the President's authority to engage in some forms of electronic surveillance are those set forth in the Constitution.

(iv) Exception to Fourth Amendment Warrant Requirement.—
The decision of the Supreme Court in *Keith* does not apply to the
1969-71 wiretaps, because that case was not decided until 1972. During the period in question there was very little applicable case law to
which the President could look for guidance. Indeed, as of May 1969
none of the lower courts had addressed the question whether the
Fourth Amendment permitted an exception to the warrant requirement in wiretap cases involving national or domestic security.[14] The
first case which dealt with this issue was *United States* v. *Brown*,
317 F. Supp. 531 (E.D. La. July 1970) *aff'd*, 484 F. 2d 418 (5th Cir.
1973), which upheld the validity of the warrantless wiretaps:

> The surveillance as here in question should be declared lawful on the ground that they were authorized by the President or the Attorney General for the purpose of national security.[15]

This proposition laid down in *Brown* has not been affected by subsequent decision except to the extent that *Keith* limited the scope of
"national security" matters to those which have a "significant connection with a foreign power, its agents or agencies." [16]

Even if that limitation were retrospectively applied to the case
of the 1969-71 wiretaps, they would meet the test of a "significant
connection." For the effect of disclosure of classified information in
the news media and its transmittal to some foreign power for subsequent use against this country is clearly equivalent to the effect of the
operations of a foreign intelligence service. Whether the information
is leaked to the newspapers or covertly transmitted to a foreign agent
is immaterial, since the result is the same in both cases.

In any event, as of 1969-71 the *Keith* distinction between national
and domestic security had not been authoritatively formulated. The
wiretapping program initiated by the President may have raised constitutional issues, but in that event he deserved to have his actions
tested in the Supreme Court. It would be an abuse of the impeachment power to impeach the President for a decision made in good
faith, where circumstances of compelling urgency favored a program
whose constitutionality was not questioned by clear authority.

Reliance on the principles which justify warrantless searches can
be misleading if those principles are applied indiscriminately to the
case of national security wiretaps. In the 1969-71 wiretaps there was
admittedly no urgent immediacy, such as exists in a search incident
to an arrest; the delay involved in obtaining a court order was not a
factor in the President's decision. In view of the fact that the need
for electronic surveillance arose because of leaks of confidential information by government officials, it is understandable that the President was anxious lest the effectiveness of the wiretapping program
itself should be compromised by further leaks. His decision not to
apply for court orders was therefore justified by his realistic fear that
the purpose of the wiretaps would be frustrated unless their very

---

[14] *United States* v. *Stone*, 305 F. Supp. 75 (D.D.C. September 1969) and *United States* v. *Clay*, 430 F. 2d 165 (5th Cir. July 1970) are admittedly not on point because in both cases the wiretaps antedated *Katz*, so the Fourth Amendment was inapplicable.
[15] 317 F. Supp. at 535.
[16] *United States* v. *United States District Court*, 407 U.S. 297, 309 n. 3 (1972). *Cf. United States* v. *Butenko*, 318 F. Supp. 66 (D.N.J. 1970), *aff'd*, 494 F. 2d 593 (1974); *United States* v. *Hoffman*, 334 F. Supp. 504 (D.D.C. 1971); *United States* v. *Dellinger*, 472 F. 2d 340 (7th Cir. 1972); *Zweibon* v. *Mitchell*, 363 F. Supp. 936 (D.D.C.1973).

existence was known only to a handful of trusted subordinates: Mitchell, Kissinger, Haldeman and his administrative assistant, Ehrlichman, Hoover and a few other top F.B.I. officers.

(v) *Reasonableness of the "Search": Probable Cause.*—A wiretap cannot be initiated, with or without a warrant unless there is "probable cause." In the ordinary criminal context this phrase means probable cause to believe that the suspect has committed, is committing, or is about to commit a crime. We would call attention to 18 U.S.C. § 793, entitled "Gathering, transmitting, or losing defense information." Section 793(d) provides heavy criminal penalties for anyone who, "lawfully having possession of . . . any . . . information relating to the national defense, which information the possessor has reason to believe could be used to the injury of the United States or to the advantage of any foreign nation, willfully communicates . . . the same to any person not entitled to receive it . . ." Section 793(e) refers to any one who, "having unauthorized possession of . . . any . . . information relating to the national defense," etc. Daniel Ellsberg was indicted under both subsections, and both subsections are relevant here.

Furthermore, in the case of a search which is not undertaken for purposes of criminal prosecution, the probable cause requirement need not be the same as the criminal context:

> The standard [of probable cause] may be modified when the government interest compels an intrusion based on something other than a reasonable belief of criminal activity.[17]

In the case of non-criminal administrative searches, for example, specific probable cause is often not determinable, and no warrants for this type of search could issue if the traditional showing of probable cause were required.[18] Likewise, in the case of wiretaps initiated for the purpose of intelligence gathering rather than criminal prosecution, it is reasonable to take into account the function of the "search" in applying a standard of probable cause.

During the course of the 1969-71 wiretaps seventeen persons were placed under electronic surveillance. Seven of these persons were employees of the National Security Council (Halperin, B, O, C, I, L, and K); two were State Department officials (A and H); and one was at the Department of Defense (General Pursley). All ten had access to the classified information which was leaked, and it is therefore beyond argument that sufficient probable cause existed to justify the surveillance of these persons.

Four were newsmen, at least two of whom (Beecher and D) were known to have published newspaper articles, based on leaks, which were extremely damaging to the effectiveness of U.S. foreign policy initiatives. The other two newsmen (M and P) were known to have frequent contact with Soviet-bloc personnel; though perhaps not in itself a sufficient reason to justify wiretapping, this fact must be considered as an aggravating factor under the circumstances.

With respect to the three remaining persons who were wiretapped (White House staff members E, F, and J), it is true that none of

---

[17] *United States* v. *Butenko*, 494 F. 2d 593, 606 (3d Cir. 1974).
[18] *E.g., Adams* v. *Williams*, 407 U.S. 143 (1972); *Camara* v. *Municipal Court*, 387 U.S. 523 (1967).

them had direct access to classified foreign policy information. It is possible, however, that any one of these persons might have inadvertently come into possession of this type of information simply by virtue of their close contact with other White House personnel. For example, E was an aide to John Ehrlichman, one of the President's closest confidantes. In any event, even if there was not a sufficient showing of probable cause to justify wiretapping these three persons, the entire wiretapping program cannot be condemned simply because of an inadvertent and good faith error in judgment with respect to two or three of the seventeen persons who were placed under surveillance. It is appropriate to keep in mind that the decisions as to which persons should be wiretapped were made, for the most part, in the context of an emergency situation.

It should also be recalled that in each of the seventeen cases the decision to place a wiretap was reviewed by F.B.I. Director Hoover and specifically authorized by Attorney General Mitchell. Both of these men were better qualified than the President to judge the legality of a particular wiretap, and the President properly relied on them to warn him if there was not a sufficient legal basis for one of the surveillances.

(*vi*) *Reasonableness of the "Search": Duration of Wiretaps.*— There is no denying that the 1969–71 wiretaps, by and large, were maintained for longer periods of time than is customary in the case of ordinary criminal investigations. However, the wiretapping program was no ordinary criminal investigation; it was undertaken in response to a serious and ongoing threat to the national security. When a Title III wiretap is used as a weapon against organized crime, because of the inherent nature of the activity being monitored the wiretap will usually achieve its objective or prove unsuccessful within a relatively short time. The opposite is apt to be true of intelligence surveillance, whose purpose is not simply to accumulate a critical mass of incriminating evidence sufficient to obtain an indictment. One of the major purposes of the 1969–71 wiretaps, in President Nixon's words, was to "tighten the security of highly sensitive materials." [19] This is an objective which can never be completely achieved; rather its is a continuous process. Viewed in this light, the lengthy duration of the wiretaps may be regarded as a rational and justifiable means toward that end.

(*vii*) *Reasonableness of the "Search": Interception of Innocent Conversations.*—It may also be true that the 1969–71 wiretaps intercepted a number of conversations which turned out to be irrelevant or innocent. Again, this was not an ordinary criminal investigation. For example, a typical Title III wiretap might have to do with gambling or narcotics activities. In cases of that sort, it can be determined without great difficulty whether a particular conversation does or does not involve the criminal conduct under investigation. By contrast, a surveillance whose purpose is to gather intelligence must be attentive to many details of conversation which, on their face, have nothing to do with the subject of the "search". Subtle nuances of meaning or inflection which would not constitute admissible evidence at a criminal trial

---

[19] *Statement of Information*, Book VII, 147.

may provide vital clues toward the resolution of a national security problem.

Furthermore, even in criminal cases the courts have differed widely as to the seriousness of a failure to minimize the interception of irrelevant conversations. Some courts have held that it requires the exclusion of all the wiretap evidence, whether relevant or not; [20] other courts have excluded only the wrongfully seized conversations.[21] While the excessive interception of irrelevant conversations is unconstitutional under *Berger* v. *New York*, it may be doubted whether this abuse is of comparable gravity to the failure to obtain a warrant. In short, this defect of the 1969–71 wiretapping program is not sufficiently important to warrant the removal of a President from office.

(*viii*) *Use of Wiretap Information.*—Much has been made of the fact that in a handful of isolated instances the wiretaps yielded information which was of incidental political usefulness to the President. This has not been shown to be anything more than an accidental by-product of surveillance undertaken for a different and proper purpose, nor can such a showing be supported by the facts.

The wiretapping program has also been criticized because the identity of the source of the leaks was not discovered, and because no prosecutions or personnel actions were taken as a result of information generated by the wiretaps. But these conclusions do not necessarily follow from the facts, nor do they hold any significance even if true. The objective of the wiretapping program was not to provide the basis for criminal prosecutions nor even to bring about the removal of untrustworthy government employees, but rather to tighten the security of classified information. Three NSC staff members (Halperin, L, and O) resigned while they were under surveillance; one or more of these persons may have been the source of the leaks, in which case an objective of the wiretaps would have been accomplished without any visible governmental action.[22] Similarly, information yielded by the wiretaps may have resulted in the institution of new procedures designed to improve security; this result would not be highly visible either, but would nonetheless vindicate the usefulness of the surveillance.

It has been asserted that there could have been no proper purpose for wiretapping Halperin and L after May, 1970, since the government would not have been able after that date to take personnel action or to bring criminal prosecution against them. It is not necessarily true, however, that these ex-NSC employees could not have been prosecuted on the basis of evidence obtained through the warrantless wiretaps. If the wiretap was justifiable for the purpose of protecting classified information against foreign intelligence operations (if, for example, even after leaving the NSC Halperin and L still possessed certain secret information), then some courts have suggested that incriminating evidence obtained incidentally in the course of the surveillance is admissible at a criminal trial:

Since the primary purpose of these searches is to secure foreign intelligence information, a judge, when reviewing a particular search must, above all, be

---

[20] *E.g., United States* v. *Scott*, 331 F. Supp. 233 (D.D.C. 1971).
[21] *E.g., United States* v. *King*, 335 F. Supp. 523 (S.D. Cal. 1971).
[22] Indeed, there is substantial evidence that O did not voluntarily resign, but was dismissed. For example, in an intercepted conversation he mentioned that his employment on the NSC staff was being terminated because he had been seeing reporters. (*Statement of Information*, Book VII, ¶7.1, unpublished).

assured that this was in fact its primary purpose and that the accumulation of evidence of criminal activity was incidental.[23]

(*ix*) *Concealment of the Wiretap Records.*—The allegation that President Nixon ordered the records of the 1969–71 wiretaps not to be entered in the FBI indices is based on the following excerpt from an internal FBI memorandum of May 11, 1969:

> Haig came to my office Saturday to advise me the request [for wiretaps on Halperin, Pursley, B, and O] was being made on the highest authority and involves a matter of most grave and serious consequence to our national security. He stressed that it is so sensitive it demands handling on a need-to-know basis, with no record maintained.[24]

As evidence of what the President may have ordered, this statement is hearsay upon hearsay. Furthermore, it is wholly ambiguous. First, it is not clear whether "the highest authority," which may be understood to refer to the President, is meant to govern the second sentence as well as the first. Second, even if the President had directly ordered the FBI "to handle the case on a need-to-know basis, with no record maintained," this would not justify the conclusion that he intended the FBI to act in dereliction of its legal duty to maintain such wiretap indices as are necessary to supply logs of conversations to the courts in *Alderman* "taint" hearings. The President may not even have been aware of this duty, much less what specific procedures (the ELSUR index) were customarily employed by the FBI to discharge the duty. These are the responsibilities of the Director of the FBI, on whom the President properly relied to carry out his orders in an appropriate and legal manner.

The failure to maintain records of the wiretaps on the FBI indices, and the subsequent retrieval of all the 1969–71 wiretap records from the FBI, have been cited as evidence of the President's awareness that the wiretapping program might be illegal. This inference is rebutted, however, by a more compelling inference that the President's actions had an innocent motivation. Whatever his precise instructions to Haig may have been the President was understandably anxious to take all appropriate measures which would ensure that the existence of the wiretaps would not, through leaks, become known to the very persons on whom the surveillance had been placed. The recovery of the wiretap records from the FBI in July 1971 was motivated by the allegation of William Sullivan, Assistant to the Director, that Director Hoover intended to use those records for an improper purpose.[25] No doubt the President was skeptical about this allegation, but felt that no harm would be done by taking prophylactic action.

(*x*) *Termination of the Wiretaps.*—All of the wiretaps still in force, of which there were nine, were terminated on February 10, 1971. There is no apparent reason for this abrupt and total discontinuation of the wiretapping program. It may be noted, however, that in January 1971 two separate district courts held, for the first time, that there is no exception to the warrant requirement of the Fourth Amendment in the case of domestic security wiretaps.[26] Prior to *Smith* and

---

[23] *United States* v. *Butenko*, 494 F. 2d 573, 606 (3d Cir. 1974).
[24] Book VII, 189.
[25] Book VII, 757.
[26] *United States* v. *Smith*, 321 F. Supp. 424 (C.D. Cal. January 8, 1971); *United States* v. *Sinclair*, 321 F. Supp. 1074 (E.D. Mich. January 26, 1971). *Sinclair* was decided by Judge Keith and became popularly known as the *Keith* case.

Sinclair, the lower courts had uniformly upheld warrantless "national security" wiretapping, but the earlier cases had all involved wiretaps for the gathering of foreign intelligence so that there had been no need to draw the distinction between domestic and national security. If the President's opinion as to the legality of the wiretapping program had previously been influenced by the decisions of the lower courts, the termination of the wiretaps shortly after the decisions in *Smith* and *Sinclair* might be considered evidence of his willingness to abide by developing law in the area.

b. *Wiretap and Surveillance of Joseph Kraft*

The surveillance of Washington newspaper columnist Joseph Kraft took four forms, each of which must be analyzed separately in order to determine whether any wrongful actions were taken, and if so, whether the President may properly be held responsible for them.

First, in June, 1969 John Ehrlichman directed his assistant, John Caulfield, to have a wiretap installed on the office telephone in Kraft's residence in Washington, D.C. (Book VII, 314). According to Ehrlichman, there was a national security justification for this wiretap (Book VII, 317, 323). Caulfield enlisted the aid of John Ragan, former Security Chief for the Republican National Committee, in installing the wiretap. The telephone was wiretapped for one week during which time Kraft was out of the country, so that none of his conversations was intercepted. (Book VII, 314–19, 324). At the end of that short period, Ehrlichman directed the removal of the wiretap for the reason that the operation was going to be turned over to the FBI. (Book VII, 315). Despite its short duration and unproductive yield, this wiretap might be argued to constitute a violation of Kraft's constitutional rights. The question is academic, however, since there is no evidence that the President authorized or even retrospectively approved the wiretap. Testifying before the Senate Select Committee, Ehrlichman stated only that he had at some point "discussed" the Kraft wiretap with the President. (Book VII, 323). There is no indication of presidential approval; indeed, Ehrlichman himself claimed not to have been aware that the wiretap actually took place. (Book VII, 323).

Second, after the discontinuation of the Caulfield wiretap, the FBI considered placing Kraft under electronic surveillance. No wiretap was ever installed on Kraft's telephone by the FBI, however, because the Attorney General never authorized it. (Book VII, 356; unpublished material from Book VII, ¶ 14.3, p. 2.)

Third, in June 1969 the FBI arranged to have a microphone installed in Kraft's hotel room in a European country. William Sullivan, Assistant to the Director of the FBI, *apparently* with the knowledge and consent of Director J. Edgar Hoover, traveled to the foreign country and supervised the installation of the microphone. (Book VII, 356; unpublished material from Book VII, ¶ 14.3, p. 1.) In this case the evidence does not even clearly establish that Hoover knew about and approved the surveillance, let alone that it was performed on the President's authority.

Fourth, from November 5 to December 12, 1969, the FBI placed Kraft under "spot physical surveillance" in Washington, D.C. This entailed no more than agent following Kraft to report on his evening social activities. (Book VII, 356–57; unpublished material from Book VII, ¶ 14.3, pp. 2–3.) It may be doubted that this surveillance constituted a violation of law or of Kraft's constitutional rights (under the Fourth Amendment or any other provision of the Constitution). In any event, there is no evidence at all to suggest that the President authorized or approved this spot physical surveillance.

c. Wiretap and Surveillance of Donald Nixon

In 1969 H. R. Haldeman and John Ehrlichman asked the Central Intelligence Agency to conduct physical surveillance of Donald Nixon, the President's brother, who was moving to Las Vegas and who, it was feared, might come into contact with criminal elements. (Report of CIA Inspector General and Deputy Director Robert Cushman, June 29, 1973.) The CIA refused, since it has no jurisdiction under 50 U.S.C. § 403(d)(3) to engage in domestic law enforcement activities.

In the latter part of 1970, Ehrlichman contacted his assistant John Caulfield and asked him to monitor a project which involved a wiretap which had been placed by the Secret Service on the telephone of Donald Nixon at his residence in Newport Beach, California. (Book VII, 508–09.) The apparent reason for this wiretap had to do with the fact that in 1969 Donald Nixon had visited the Dominican Republic where he had been a guest of President Balaguer; there is a suggestion that Mr. Nixon's traveling companions may have been "unsavory". (Book VII, 509–20.) The wiretap was conducted with the knowledge of Mr. Nixon, and was terminated after only three weeks. (Book VII, 510, 522.) During that period the Secret Service also kept Mr. Nixon under physical surveillance. (Book VII, 512–15.)

There are several reasons why the surveillance of Donald Nixon does not constitute an offense, let alone an offense for which the President should be removed from office. First, there is no evidence that the surveillance was ordered by the President or even known to him until after the fact. Second, the Secret Service is responsible for protecting the physical safety of the President and his immediate family. While the primary concern in the case of Donald Nixon may have been that his associations would cause embarrassment to him and therefore to the President, in view of the criminal elements and unsavory characters with whom he was thought to have had contact it is not unreasonable to suppose that the Secret Service was concerned as well for his physical safety. In this regard it is appropriate to concede to the Secret Service a certain latitude of discretion to err on the side of caution. Third, the surveillance was conducted with Donald Nixon's knowledge and consent. Technically, under 18 U.S.C. § 2511(2)(b) such consent must be obtained in advance of the installation of the wiretap; but since Mr. Nixon subsequently approved of the surveillance, it would be preposterous to suggest that the President should be removed from office because of this technicality.

d. The "Huston Plan"

(i) *Facts.*—On June 5, 1970, the President held a meeting with FBI Director J. Edgar Hoover, Defense Intelligence Agency Director Donald Bennett, National Security Agency Director Noel Gayler, and Central Intelligence Agency Director Richard Helms. (Book VII, 375.) Also present were H. R. Haldeman, John Ehrlichman, and

Presidential Staff Assistant Tom Huston. (Book VII, 375.) The President discussed the need for better domestic intelligence operations in light of an escalating level of bombings and other acts of domestic violence. (Book VII, 377) The President asked the Intelligence Agency Directors for their recommendations on whether the government's intelligence services were being hampered by restraints on intelligence gathering methods. Huston has testified that it was the opinion of the Directors that they were in fact being hampered. (Book VII, 378.) The President appointed Hoover, General Bennett, Admiral Gayler, and Helms to be an ad hoc committee to study intelligence needs and cooperation among the Intelligence Agencies, and to make recommendations. Hoover was designated Chairman and Huston served as White House liaison. (Book VII, 377–78, 382)

On June 25, 1970 this ad hoc committee completed its report, entitled "Special Report Interagency Committee on Intelligence (Ad Hoc)" (hereafter "Special Report").

The first page of the Special Report, immediately following the title page, bore the following notation:

"June 25, 1970

This report, prepared for the President, is approved by all members of this committee and their signatures are affixed hereto.

/s/ J. EDGAR HOOVER,
Director, Federal Bureau of Investigation, Chairman.
/s/ RICHARD HELMS,
Director, Central Intelligence Agency.
/s/ LT. GENERAL D. V. BENNETT, USA,
Director, Defense Intelligence Agency.
/s/ VICE ADMIRAL NOEL GAYLER, USN,
Director, National Security Agency."

(Book VII, 385)

Part One of the Special Report, entitled "Summary of Internal Security Threat," was a lengthy threat assessment, including assessments of the current internal security threat of various domestic groups, of the intelligence services of communist countries, and of other revolutionary groups. (Book VII, 389–410)

Part Two, entitled "Restraints on Intelligence Collection," was a discussion of official restraints under which six types of United States intelligence collection procedures operated, and of the advantages and disadvantages of continuing or lifting such restraints. (Book VII, 411–29)

Part Three, entitled "Evaluation of Interagency Coordination," assessed the degree of coordination between the Intelligence Agencies and recommended means to improve it. (Book VII, 430–31)

Although the Special Report took no position with respect to the alternative decisions listed, it included statements in footnotes that the FBI objected to lifting the restraints discussed, except those on legal mail coverage (keeping a record of the return address of communications addressed to an individual) and National Security Agency communications intelligence. (Book VII, 416, 419, 421, 424, 427)

During the first week of July, 1970, Huston sent the Special Report, together with a memorandum entitled "Operational Restraints On Intelligence Collection," to Haldeman. In the memorandum Huston recommended that most, although not all, of the present procedures imposing restraints on intelligence collection activities should be changed. Huston's recommendation included the following:

"Electronic Surveillances and Penetrations.
Recommendation:
Present procedures should be changed to permit intensification of coverage of individuals and groups in the United States who pose a major threat to the internal security.
  . . . *Mail Coverage.*
Recommendation:
Restrictions on legal coverage should be removed.
ALSO, present restrictions on covert coverage should be relaxed on selected targets of priority foreign intelligence and internal security interest.
  Rationale: . . . Covert coverage is illegal and there are serious risks involved. However, the advantages to be derived from its use outweigh the risks. This technique is particularly valuable in identifying espionage agents and other contacts of foreign intelligence services.
  . . . *Surreptitious Entry.*
Recommendation:
Present restrictions should be modified to permit procurement of vitally needed foreign cryptographic material.
ALSO, present restrictions should be modified to permit selective use of this technique against other urgent and high priority internal security targets.
  Rationale:
Use of this technique is clearly illegal: it amounts to burglary. It is also highly risky and could result in great embarrassment if exposed. However, it is also the most fruitful tool and can produce the type of intelligence which cannot be obtained in any other fashion.
  The FBI, in Mr. Hoover's younger days, used to conduct such operations with great success and with no exposure. The information secured was invaluable." (Book VII, 438–40)

On July 14, 1970, Haldeman sent a memorandum to Huston stating, "The recommendations you have proposed as a result of the review have been approved by the President. . . . The formal official memorandum should, of course, be prepared and that should be the device by which to carry it out." (Book VII, 447)

On July 23, 1970 Huston sent a "decision memorandum" entitled "Domestic Intelligence" to each of the Directors of the four Intelligence Agencies, informing them of the options approved by the President. (Book VII, 454)

Shortly after the decision memorandum of July 23, 1970 had been received by Mr. Hoover, Huston received a telephone call from Assistant FBI Director William Sullivan indicating that Hoover had been very upset by the decision memorandum, and that Hoover either had talked or intended to talk to the Attorney General to undertake steps to have the decisions reflected in the memorandum reversed. (Book VII, 470) On or before July 27, 1970, Director Hoover met with Attorney General Mitchell, who joined with Hoover in opposing the recommendations contained in the memorandum of July 23, 1970. (Book VII, 463)

Shortly after his telephone conversation with Sullivan, Huston received a call from Haldeman indicating that the Attorney General had talked to the President, or that Haldeman had talked to the Attorney General and then to the President, but that, in any event, Huston was instructed to recall the decision memorandum; that the President desired to reconsider the matter, and that Haldeman, Hoover, and the Attorney General would have a meeting in the near future to discuss the matter. (Book VII, 470)

Huston arranged for the recall of the document through the White House Situation Room. (Book VII, 470) Copies of the decision memorandum on "Domestic Intelligence" were returned by each of the four Intelligence Agencies to the White House Situation Room on or about July 28, 1970. (Book VII, 472, 474) Although Huston continued to press for adoption of his recommendations (Book VII, 480–85), the plans for lifting operational restraints on intelligence collection activities were not reinstituted.[27]

(ii) *Discussion.*—(a) With respect to electronic surveillance and penetrations, the Special Report of the Interagency Committee stated, "The President historically has had the authority to act in matters of national security. In addition, Title III of the Omnibus Crime Control and Safe Streets Act of 1968 provides a statutory basis." (Book VII, 415) The Special Report also stated that routine mail coverage was legal. (Book VII, 417) Other intelligence collection activities, such as development of campus sources, appeared to present political rather than legal questions.

However, with respect to both covert mail coverage and surreptitious entry, both the Interagency Committee's Special Report and the "Operational Restraints" memorandum prepared by Huston stated that such intelligence collection activities were illegal. (Book VII, 418, 420, 439 and 440) The President's approval of Huston's recommendations in these areas may consequently be viewed as approval of otherwise illegal actions by government agencies.

(b) The Special Report was prepared by a committee consisting of intelligence professionals from each of the four Intelligence Agencies. Although it did not make recommendations, it listed as options the relaxation or removal of restrictions on all categories of intelligence collection activities. The recommendations made by Huston in the "Operational Restraints" memorandum are taken verbatim from among the options listed by the Special Report of the Interagency Committee; they do not go beyond options listed by the Committee. The Special Report was approved by all members of the Committee, consisting of the Directors of the four Intelligence Agencies, and their signatures were affixed to the first page. This approval might have been taken by Haldeman or by the President to indicate that the options listed were not regarded as improper by the professional United States intelligence community, despite the footnoted objections of Mr. Hoover contained in the body of Part Two of the Special Report.

(c) The options of lifting restraints on intelligence gathering activities, listed in Part Two of the Special Report, were intended to be taken in the context of the threat assessment contained in Part One of the Special Report. There had been a substantial number of bombings and riots in the spring and summer of 1970. (Book VII, Part 1, p. 377) Part One stated that communist intelligence services possessed a capability for actively fomenting domestic unrest, although it also

---

[27] In or before December, 1970, when John Dean had assumed responsibility for matters of domestic intelligence for internal security purposes, an Intelligence Evaluation Committee was created to improve coordination among the intelligence community and to prepare evaluations and estimates of domestic intelligence. (Book VII, 487, 497) This step may be seen as an outgrowth of the recommendations in Part Three of the Special Report, entitled "Evaluation of Interagency Coordination." (Book VII, 430–31)

stated that there had been no substantial indications that this had yet occurred. (Book VII, 402)

(d) The recommendations by Huston contained in the memorandum entitled "Operational Restraints on Intelligence Collection" are cast in general terms, e.g., "present procedures should be changed" (electronic surveillance), or "relaxed" (mail coverage), or "modified" (surreptitious entry). (Book VII, 438-39) Much might have depended upon how the modifications might have been implemented.

(e) The President's approval in principle of modifying some operational restraints which had been in existence since 1966 was withdrawn within five days after the circulation of Huston's decision memorandum, which was the device for carrying out the recommendations. (Book VII, 447, 472, 474) There is no evidence before the Committee that any illegal mail coverage, surreptitious entry, or electronic surveillance or penetration was ever undertaken, during these five days, under the authority of the decision memorandum.

(f) It has occasionally been urged that the formation and operation of the "Plumbers" group is evidence that the Huston Plan was not actually rescinded. This is untenable. The two matters were handled by entirely different groups of White House staff members and they arose a year apart. The problem to which the Huston Plan was directed was, essentially, domestic violence, whereas the "Plumbers" were concerned with news leaks and the theft of the Pentagon Papers. It strains the facts to find any connection between the two.

Paragraph (3)

Paragraph (3) of proposed Article II charges that President Nixon, "acting personally and through his subordinates and agents," authorized the maintenance of a "secret investigative unit" within the White House, which (1) unlawfully utilized the resources of the Central Intelligence Agency, (2) engaged in covert and unlawful activities, and (3) attempted to prejudice the constitutional right of an accused to a fair trial. Paragraph (3) also alleges that the Special Investigations Unit was financed in part with money derived from campaign contributions.

The language employed by the majority of the Committee to frame these charges stops short—but just barely—of echoing the near-hysterical cry of some that the President established in the White House a personal "secret police" force that gravely threatened the civil liberties of the entire population. We think it helps to place the matter in better perspective to note at the outset that the "secret investigative unit" mentioned in the Paragraph appears never to have numbered more than four persons at any one time; its members received no special training for their work; they carried no weapons; they made no arrests nor otherwise asserted any power or authority to engage in either general or localized law enforcement.

Any willful violation of an individual's civil liberties by government employees acting at the direction of the President, if proved, would be a matter of deep concern to us all, but we frankly feel that much of the discussion of the White House Special Investigations Unit is characterized by rank hyperbole. All of the evidence before the Committee bears out the truth of President Nixon's description of the group's mission:

> This was a small group at the White House whose principal purpose was to *stop security leaks* and to investigate other *sensitive security matters*. (Book VII, 593; emphasis added)

Thus, the now-popular nickname "Plumbers."

a. Establishment of Special Investigations Unit in June, 1971.—On June 13, 1971 the *New York Times* began publication of a top secret Defense Department study of American involvement in the Vietnam war—the so-called "Pentagon Papers," which had been removed from Defense Department files. (Book VII, 593) On July 23, 1971 the *New York Times* published details of the United States negotiating position on the Strategic Arms Limitations Talks. (Brief on Behalf of the President, 95)

These two unauthorized disclosures of sensitive government information in quick succession were not the first such instances to plague the President and his top foreign policy planners. Earlier in his first Administration on April 6, 1969, the President had directed that the possibility of unilateral troop withdrawals from Vietnam be studied. On April 6, 1969 the *New York Times* reported that the United States was considering unilateral troop withdrawal from Vietnam. (Brief on Behalf of the President, 83) In early June of the same year, the United States Intelligence Board issued a report setting forth its estimates of the Soviet Union's strategic strength and possible first-strike capability. On June 18, 1969 the *New York Times* published this official estimate of the first-strike capabilities of the Soviet Union. (Brief on Behalf of the President, 85)

The evidence before the Committee establishes that the President was genuinely concerned about the leaks of national security that had occurred. During the first week following the publication of the Pentagon Papers by the *New York Times*, the President ordered an FBI investigation of the leaks, and ordered a security clearance review by each department and agency of the government having responsibility for the classification of information affecting the national defense. In addition the President ordered that a legal action be instituted to prevent further publication of the Papers which ultimately resulted in the Supreme Court's 6 to 3 decision in the case of *New York Times* v. *United States*. Finally, he authorized the establishment of a small "special investigations" unit within the White House for the purpose of investigating and preventing leaks of national security information. (Brief on Behalf of the President, 91, and authorities cited; Book VII, 619–32)

In the two weeks following the publication of the Pentagon Papers, the President called a series of meetings with senior advisors to discuss the adverse effect of the publication of the Pentagon Papers upon national security and foreign policy. (Book VII, 619) The participants at these meetings discussed the possibility that Daniel Ellsberg, who had been identified as the person who stole the Pentagon Papers from the Defense Department, possessed additional sensitive information which he might disclose. (Book VII, 619) At one of the meetings, the Assistant Attorney General in charge of the Internal Security Division told the White House staff members present that some or all of the

Pentagon Papers had been delivered to the Soviet Embassy on June 17, 1971. (Book VII, 619) At a meeting between the President, his National Security Advisor Henry Kissinger, and John Ehrlichman, Dr. Kissinger told the President that Ellsberg was a "fanatic" and that he had "knowledge of very critical defense secrets of current validity, such as nuclear deterrent targeting." (Book VII, 621)

The President stated on a number of occasions closely following the publication of the Pentagon Papers that if the leaks continued, there could be no "credible U. S. foreign policy," and that the damage to the government and to the national security at a very sensitive time would be severe. (Book VII, 626) The President referred in these discussions to many of the sensitive matters which were then either being negotiated or considered by the Administration, e.g., the Strategic Arms Limitations Talks, Soviet Détente, the Paris Peace Negotiations, and his plan for ending the war in Vietnam. In addition, the President had already formed a desire to visit the Peoples Republic of China. (Book VII, 625)

With respect to the purpose of the Special Investigations Unit, it is the sworn testimony of Egil Krogh that on or about July 15, 1971 he was given oral instructions by Mr. John Ehrlichman "to begin a special national security project to coordinate a government effort to determine the causes, sources, and ramifications of the unauthorized disclosure of classified documents known as the Pentagon Papers." (Book VII, 796).

Under all the circumstances, we believe that if the President had not acted decisively against epidemic leaks of national security material, that would have been a breach of his responsibilities for the protection of the nation's security.

b. President's knowledge of the Ellsberg break-in.—The evidence before the Committee is that Egil Krogh and David Young received authorizaton from John Ehrlichman for Liddy and Hunt to fly to California over Labor Day weekend, 1971, to complete an investigation of Daniel Ellsberg. It is alleged that the trip to California was financed with funds solicited by Charles Colson from the dairy industry. Assuming that this was the case, there is no evidence whatsoever to indicate that the President was aware of any part of the transaction. In the memorandum on which John Ehrlichman initialed his approval, the project was described as a "covert operation." Interestingly, Patrick Buchanan's memorandum to Ehrlichman dated July 8, 1971 stating that the political dividends would not justify the magnitude of the investigation recommended for "Project Ellsberg," referred to the investment of personnel resources in a "covert operation" over a *3-month period*, timed to undercut the McGovern-Hatfield opposition by linking the theft of the Pentagon Papers with "Ex-NSC types." "leftist writers" and "left-wing papers." (Book VII, 708–11; 1024) It seems unlikely that Mr. Buchanan was referring to a three-month burglary.

After the fact, Egil Krogh reported to Ehrlichman that there had been a break-in in California. The sworn testimony of Mr. Krogh is that Ehrlichman's response "was one of surprise, that he considered what had been done to be in excess of what he contemplated was going to be carried out." (Book VII, 1315) Ehrlichman, however, was recently convicted of conspiring with Krogh and others to violate the civil rights of Dr. Fielding.

The weight of the evidence before the Committee is that the President neither authorized the Fielding break-in nor was even aware of its occurrence until March 17, 1973. It is true that the President was deeply concerned about the leaks of national security information. Ehrlichman has testified that the President stated to him that Krogh "should, of course, do whatever he considered necessary to get to the bottom of the matter—to learn what Ellsberg's motives and potential further harmful action might be." (Book VII, 1001) We do not believe that this can reasonably be interpreted to mean that the President intended to authorize an unlawful act.

The President has stated:
Because of the extreme gravity of the situation, and not then knowing what additonal national secrets Mr. Ellsberg might disclose, I did impress upon Mr. Krogh the vital importance to the national security of his assignment. I did not authorize and had no knowledge of any illegal means to be used to achieve this goal. ("Presidential Statements," 5/22/73, 23)

We think it is relevant here to consider the President's remarks made in a different but analogous context. During a conversation with John Dean on March 21, 1973 speaking of Colson's possible role in the Watergate matter the President said:

The PRESIDENT. The absurdity of the whole damned thing.
DEAN. But it—
The PRESIDENT. bugging and so on. Well, let me say I am keenly aware of the fact that, uh, Colson et al., and so forth, were doing their best to get information and so forth and so on. But they all knew very well they were supposed to comply with the law. (HJCT 100)

The evidence is virtually undisputed that the President did not know in advance about the break-in at Dr. Fielding's office. Ehrlichman has testified that he did not inform President Nixon of the break-in after Ehrlichman learned of it from Krogh. (Book VII, 1334) Charles Colson testified before this Committee that not only did he not have any evidence that the President authorized the Fielding entry, but also that Ehrlichman had told Colson that he, Ehrlichman, had not discussed the Ellsberg entry with the President. (Colson testimony, 3 HJC 450) Ehrlichman allegedly made this statement to Colson in connection with preparing for his recent trial in the District of Columbia, and it would have been greatly to Ehrlichman's advantage, in establishing his defense on national security grounds, to disclose any discussions he had had with the President regarding the entry into Dr. Fielding's office which might tend to prove Presidential authorization of the "covert operation."

David Young has testified that he "had no discussions with the President about the ... Ellsberg-Fielding matter." [David Young testimony; *United States v. Ehrlichman*, Cr. 74–116 (D. D. C. 1974), 1120–21; Brief on Behalf of the President, 99.]

The President's sworn answers to interrogatories submitted to him in connection with the Ehrlichman trial state that he first learned of the Ellsberg break-in on March 17, 1973. The White House edited transcript of the conversation between the President and Dean on March 17, 1973 reveals that Dean told the President that Hunt and Liddy had worked for Ehrlichman, stating "These fellows had to be some idiots as we've learned after the fact. They went out and went into Dr. Fielding's office and they had, they were geared up with all this CIA equipment—cameras and the like." The President stated:

PRESIDENT. What in the world—what in the name of God was Ehrlichman having something (unintelligible) in the Ellsberg (unintelligible)?

DEAN. They were trying—this was part of an operation that—in connection with the Pentagon papers. They were—the whole thing—they wanted to get Ellsberg's psychiatric records for some reason. I dont know.

PRESIDENT. This is the first I ever heard of this. (WHT 158)

Upon hearing of the Fielding operation, and having knowledge of all the other unrelated national security work carried on by the Special Investigation Unit, the President was concerned that disclosure of the Fielding break-in would lead to exposure of all the Unit's efforts to determine the source of various national security leaks. The first reaction of the Justice Department was that it was not necessary to disclose the Fielding operation to the judge presiding over the Ellsberg trial since it appeared that the operation had not provided any information which could have tainted the evidence being offered by the government. Henry Petersen has testified as follows:

And I consulted with Mr. Maroney, in whom I had confided, and with the chief of my appellate section to whom I put it in a hypothetical case as to whether or not the disclosure for this information was mandated by *Brady* v. *Maryland* [373 U.S. 83(1963)], which, in effect, holds that material in the hands of the prosecution which touches on guilt or innocence needs to be disclosed.

Mr. Maroney and some of his associates suggested that since this information did not go to guilt or innocence, that nothing had been obtained, and that since at most it would lead to a motion to suppress, which if granted would have meant there was nothing to suppress, we were under no obligation to disclose to the court. (Petersen testimony, 3 HJC 98)

Notwithstanding the view of these Justice Department officials, when Petersen and Kleindienst concluded that the information should be transmitted to the judge trying the Ellsberg matter, as a matter of good practice, they so informed the President, the President agreed, and the information was disclosed to Judge Byrne on April 25, 1973.

In considering whether the President failed in a duty to inform law enforcement officials, either federal or state, about the Fielding break-in when he learned of it, we think the conduct of Assistant Attorney General Petersen is illuminating. When he was informed that the United States Attorneys for the District of Columbia had been told about the break-in by "an informant"—Dean—it appears that Petersen's sole concern was with the impact of this revelation upon the course of the Russo-Ellsberg trial then underway. In both his conversations with the President and those with associates within the Department of Justice, Petersen did not manifest a concern about disclosing the facts about the break-in to California authorities, or *about the conduct of an FBI investigation of the break-in.*

We think this was essentially the focus of the President's concern as well. While Ehrlichman had indicated to the President on March 22, 1973 that revelation of the Fielding break-in might result in a mistrial in the Ellsberg case, it is entirely possible that Ehrlichman, Dean or one of Dean's assistants in the office of the White House Counsel researched the question of the duty of the government to disclose unlawful government acts from which no evidence is gained. The same legal conclusion may have been reached and conveyed to the President as was reached within the Department of Justice, namely, that disclosure was probably not legally required. Unfortunately, our record is completely silent on whether the President asked for or received from any of his legal advisors (other than Henry Petersen) an opinion on the legal duty to disclose to Judge Byrne the fact of the Fielding break-in.

There are many reasons why it may not have occurred to Henry Petersen to suggest to the President that he advise the local California authorities of an apparent violation of state law. We think, however, that Petersen's concentration on the Russo-Ellsberg implications of the crime, rather than the need for a criminal investigation of it, is probative of what would constitute a reasonable reaction by the President himself upon learning of the break-in from Dean on March 17th. If it is urged by the majority that President Nixon is impeachable for what essentially was a misprision of federal and state felonies, the apparent parallel between the focus of the President's concern and that of Petersen would argue strongly against the existence of any *mens rea* on the part of the President when he remained silent about his knowledge of the offense.

c. Alleged Public Relations Campaign to Discredit Ellsberg.—The majority believes that the President's concern with the Ellsberg case was not with espionage or national security, but with politics and public relations. The Special Counsel has argued that the "primary purpose [of the "Plumbers" was] to discredit Daniel Ellsberg for the President's political advantage." (Summary of Information, 133) As the Summary of Information indicates, John Ehrlichman's handwritten notes of a meeting with the President on July 6, 1971, three weeks after the publication of the Pentagon Papers, indicate that the President said to John Mitchell, "Get conspiracy smoked out through the papers. Hiss and Bently cracked that way." (Summary of Information, 130.) However, the notes also state. "*No Ellsberg (since already indicted).*" (Ehrlichman notes, July 7, 1971, 39; emphasis added) It is thus clear that President Nixon did not contemplate a public relations campaign *against Dr. Ellsberg*, who was already under indictment.

The testimony of Charles Colson before this Committee was that the President never asked Colson to disseminate any information that was not true. (Colson testimony, 3 HJC 414) Colson also testified that he was assigned the responsibility of working with Congress in an effort to have a Congressional hearing on the problem of security leaks. (Colson testimony, 3 HJC 197–98)

Even if the President did wish to conduct a public relations campaign to smoke out the persons who were leaking national security information, it must be remembered that a public relations campaign is not illegal. Public relations campaigns, in fact, are not uncommon in either politics or government.

d. Assistance given by the Central Intelligence Agency to the Special Investigations Unit.—The majority argues that the President interfered with the lawful functioning of the Central Intelligence Agency by requiring it to provide assistance for the Special Investigations Unit (the "Plumbers").

Ehrlichman got in touch with CIA Deputy Director Cushman on July 6, 1971 notifying him that Hunt was working on security problems for the President and might be requesting assistance of Cushman. On July 22, 1971, Hunt requested Cushman to provide disguise material and alias identification which the CIA provided the next day. The complaint is that this action by the CIA violated a provision of a 1947 statute, which states that the CIA has no "internal security" functions. The CIA's jurisdiction extends to foreign matters only.

On any reasonable interpretation of the events of June and July, 1971 the involvement of the CIA was altogether proper. The top secret Defense Department study of American policy in the Vietnam War had been published on the front page of the New York Times on June 13, 1971. Robert C. Mardian, the Assistant Attorney General for Internal Security had told a meeting of White House staff members that a copy of this top scecret document, which had been, in effect, stolen from the Defense Department files, had been delivered to the Soviet Embassy on June 17, 1971. The *New York Times* had published the details of the United States' negotiating position in the Strategic Arms Limitation Talks. Earlier leaks had led to newspaper publication of the Administration's decision to study the possibility of unilateral troop withdrawal from Vietnam, and publication of the United States' intelligence board's official assessment of the nuclear first-strike capacity of the Soviet Union. The President had been told by his Chief National Security Advisor, Henry Kissinger, that Ellsberg had "knowledge of very critical defense secrets of current validity, such as nuclear deterrent targeting."

We find it simply beyond reason to argue that, in these circumstances, the leaks of national security information had no relation to foreign intelligence information or foreign affairs. The point is not whether Dr. Ellsberg was or was not an American citizen. The point is not whether Howard Hunt would travel abroad in connection with his assignments with the Special Investigations Unit—although he had certainly done so for the CIA in the past. The point is, that if top secret defense documents are published on page 1 of the *New York Times*, that constitutes an effective publication and delivery of the information to foreign intelligence sources. An action which jeopardizes the success of American policy in a foreign war or in talks with the Soviet Union to limit the spread of nuclear weapons, is clearly the proper concern of the Central Intelligence Agency. The President's action, which was limited to authorizing CIA assistance to a legitimate national security project, was entirely proper.

Paragraph (4)

Paragraph (4) of Article II charges that the President "has failed to take care that the laws were faithfully executed by failing to act when he knew or had reason to know that his close subordinates endeavored to impede and frustrate lawful inquiries." These inquiries concerned the Watergate break-in and cover-up, and "other unlawful activities" including those relating to electronic surveillance, the Fielding break-in, the campaign financing practices of the Committee to Re-elect the President, and the confirmation of Richard Kleindienst as Attorney General.

a. Legal theory

The theory upon which Paragraph (4) is based deserves careful examination. The President is charged with violation of the "take care" duty, and specifically with violation of his duty of supervision, in that he failed to exercise his authority when he should have done so in order to prevent his close subordinates from interfering with investigations into criminal or improper conduct.

(i) *The "take care" duty.*—Article I, Section 3 of the Constitution commands that the President "shall take care that the Laws be faithfully executed." Since he cannot execute the laws alone and unaided, he must rely on his subordinates: the vast bureaucracy of the executive branch, including all departments, agencies, commissions, and of course the immediate White House staff. As Gouverneur Morris pointed out at the Constitutional Convention, "Without . . . ministers the Executive can do nothing of consequence." [1]

The "take care" clause therefore imposes on the President the implied duty of supervising his subordinates in the discharge of their delegated responsibilities.

This supervisory responsibility is further emphasized by other provisions of the Constitution. For example, Article II, Section 2 authorizes the President to "require the Opinion, in writing, of the principal Officer in each of the executive Departments, upon any Subject relating to the Duties of their respective Offices." Read in conjunction with the "take care" clause, this provision implies an affirmative duty to be informed about the official conduct of executive officers. Article II, Section 1 vests the executive power exclusively in the President, which reflects the intention of the Framers that there be a single, responsible executive answerable for the conduct of his subordinates. The President's duty of supervision is also implicit in his power to appoint and remove executive officers.[2] Two years after adoption of the Constitution, James Madison argued in the First Congress that the President's power to remove subordinates would

> subject him to impeachment himself, if he suffers them to perpetrate with impunity high crimes or misdemeanors against the United States, or neglect to superintend their conduct, so as to check their excesses.[3]

The general duty of supervision is necessarily subject, however, to significant practical limitations. First, with respect to the particular persons whom the President is expected to supervise, common sense dictates that he cannot exercise direct personal supervision over more than a fraction of the enormous executive establishment. He is immediately responsible for the official acts of the Cabinet Secretaries, the Joint Chiefs of Staff, the Attorney General, and his close subordinates on the White House staff. These officers are all hand-picked by the President and serve at his pleasure; members of the White House staff are not even subject to Senate approval on appointment. Beyond this inner circle, however, the President's supervisory responsibility is much more attenuated. He and his political party are accountable to

---

[1] II *The Records of the Federal Convention* 54 (M. Farrand ed.).
[2] *Myers v. United States*, 272 U.S. 117 (1926).
[3] 1 Annals of Congress 372-73 (1789). The reliability of this statement is called into question, however, by the fact that in the course of the same debate Madison stated that the President would be removable for "maladministration"—although this ground for impeachment had been explicitly rejected at the Federal Convention. *Id.* 498.

the electorate for widespread official misconduct in the lower echelons of the executive branch, but this would not ordinarily be grounds for impeachment.

Second, with respect to the nature of the President's duty to supervise his immediate subordinates, no one would contend that he is strictly liable to removal on account of the actions of these subordinates. The responsibility to see to the execution of the laws has been interpreted by the Supreme Court to mean a general superintendence of administration, rather than day-to-day supervision with attention to every detail.[4] The President must exercise due diligence in overseeing the official conduct of his immediate subordinates. Mere negligence in failing to discover official misconduct, however, is not in our opinion sufficient to justify removal from office unless the President becomes so habitually and egregiously negligent in this regard that his failure to supervise his subordinates assumes the character of a willful abdication of responsibility.

Needless to say, the President may be removed for directing a subordinate to perform a serious illegal act; and this proposition would not be limited to his inner circle of immediate subordinates. By the same token, when he obtains actual knowledge of official misconduct he must make an appropriate response, which means that at the very least he must bring the matter to the attention of law enforcement officials. The difficult question arises in a situation where he did not in fact know, but arguably should have known, that an immediate subordinate had committed an unlawful act. We submit that the President should not be removed from office for the act of a subordinate, unless he took some step to make that act his own—by knowingly assisting or approving it, or knowingly failing to exercise his control over a subordinate to prevent the commission of the act. The requirement of *mens rea* is a basic principle of Anglo-American jurisprudence.[5] As a matter of common sense, it serves no purpose to impose sanctions on a person for that of which he has no knowledge. This simple proposition is abundantly supported by the hostility of our jurisprudence toward strict criminal liability and criminal liability for the acts of others.

For example, in *Burkhardt v. United States*, 13 F. 841, 842 (6th Cir. 1926), the court dismissed the indictment of a sheriff, one of whose deputies had participated in a criminal conspiracy. The court found the evidence insufficient to demonstrate that the defendant had knowledge of the criminal violations, and stated the applicable legal test to be as follows:

> ... [L]ack of vigilance ... is not enough; there must also be proof of knowledge of facts, coupled with an intention to aid in the unlawful act by refraining from doing that which he was duty bound to do. These essential elements cannot be inferred from inaction alone.

To similar effect is *Jezewski v. United States*, 13 F. 2d 599, 603 (6th Cir. 1926), where convictions of public officials were upheld because the facts established that

> the refusal of these officers to perform their sworn duty *was not attributable to neglect and indifference only*, but rather that it was part and parcel of the

---

[4] *Williams v. United States*, 1 How. (42 U.S.) 29 (1843).
[5] *E.g., Dennis v. United States*, 341 U.S. 494, 500 (1951), *reh. denied*, 342 U.S. 842 (1951). See discussion of the requirement of criminal intent as an element of "High Crimes and Misdemeanors;" Preliminary Statement.

plan of the conspiracy . . . and practically essential to its perpetuity and success. (Emphasis added).

The rule of these cases, which we believe sound, is that a public official may be found guilty of a criminal conspiracy whose object he has a duty to prevent, only if the evidence proves that he had actual knowledge of the crime but failed to enforce the law, with the result that the crime was promoted or furthered.

The legal theory underlying Paragraph (4) is potentially a dangerous principle, unless the President's supervisory responsibility is limited to cases where he actually knew that a subordinate had committed or was about to commit an unlawful act.[6] If he is also made liable in impeachment for subordinates' misconduct of which he "should have known", by what standard could his failure to discover be judged? We reiterate our strong conviction that the President should not be removed from office for failure to meet the standard of care of ordinary civil negligence (the "reasonable man" standard). But if that standard were applied, let it be observed that the President's acts or omissions would properly be judged with reference to a reasonable man *in his position*. The President labors under the most extraordinary pressures and responsibilities. Particularly in a time of complex problems in both domestic and foreign affairs, as an efficient administrator he must so delegate the mechanical details of his supervisory function as to reserve to himself the greatest possible amount of time for making the decisions which he alone may make. In effecting that delegation, the President must place his trust somewhere; and who shall say that if he is deceived, he must be removed?

(*ii*) *Misprision of felony.*—In the context of Paragraph (4), the standard of conduct required of a President by the "take care" clause may reasonably be expressed in terms of the federal criminal offense of misprision of felony.

Title 18 U.S.C. § 4, entitled "Misprision of felony," provides:

Whoever, having knowledge of the actual commission of a felony cognizable by a court of the United States conceals and does not as soon as possible make known the same to some judge or other person in civil or military authority under the United States, shall be fined not more than $500 or imprisoned not more than three years, or both.

The statutory offense of misprision of felony has four elements:

To sustain a conviction . . . for misprision of felony it (is) incumbent upon the government to prove beyond a reasonable doubt
(1) That . . . the principal had committed and completed the felony alleged prior to (the date of the alleged misprision);
(2) That the defendant had full knowledge of that fact;
(3) That he failed to notify the authorities; and
(4) That he took (an) affirmative step to conceal the crime of the principal.[7]

(*a*) *Affirmative act of concealment.*—As the Supreme Court has pointed out, 18 U.S.C. § 4 "has been construed . . . to require both knowledge of a crime and some affirmative act of concealment or

---
[6] Of course, the President may not avoid actual knowledge by deliberately isolating himself from the normal channels of communication. Nor may he escape responsibility by deliberately issuing ambiguous instructions to his subordinates and then failing to police their actions.
[7] *Neal v. United States*, 102 F. 2d 643, 646 (8th Cir. 1939); *Lancey v. United States*, 356 F. 2d 407, 409 (9th Cir. 1966), cert. den. 385 U.S. 922; *United States v. King*, 402 F. 2d 694, 695 (9th Cir. 1968).

participation." [8] The basic reason for the affirmative act requirement is that to punish mere nondisclosure would impose an undue burden on the citizen:

> To suppose that Congress reached every failure to disclose a known federal crime, in this day of myriad federal tax statutes and regulatory laws, would impose a vast and unmeasurable obligation. It would do violence to the unspoken principle of the criminal law that "as far as possible privacy should be respected." *United States* v. *Worcester*, 190 F. Supp. 548, 565–67, (D. Mass. 1960) (*dictum*) (Wyzanski, J.).

Another reason for the affirmative act requirement is to afford some basis for an inference of evil intent. It has been held that "the motive prompting the neglect of a misprision must be in some form evil as respects the administration of justice." [9]

In *State* v. *Michaud*, 114 A. 2d 352, 355 (Me., 1955) the court similarly suggested that the requirement of an affirmative act was necessary to prevent overbroad application of the statute:

> The act of concealment must be alleged. Otherwise, a person could be tried and erroneously convicted on slight evidence that was only to the effect that he was in the vicinity of where a felony was "actually" committed, and from that improperly argue (sic) that he must have "known," and that he concealed because he knew and did "not disclose." He might not have seen. He might not have known or understood all the facts.

A dictum of Chief Justice Marshall also reflects the reluctance of the Judiciary to construe misprision statutes so as to punish bare nondisclosure of information:

> It may be the duty of a citizen to accuse every offender, and to proclaim every offense which comes to his knowledge; but the law which would punish him in every case, for not performing this duty, is too harsh for man. *Marbury* v. *Brooks*, 7 Wheat. 556, 575–76 (1822).

(b) *Degree of knowledge required.*—Several federal cases state that in order to support a conviction for misprision, it is necessary to prove that the defendant had "full knowledge" of the commission of the crime by the principal.[10] In *Commonwealth* v. *Lopes*, 318 Mass. 453, 458–59 (1945), the court intimated that mere "suspicion" that a felony had been committed could not render the defendant's silence criminal.

(c) *Duty of a President of the United States under the Misprision statute.*—The federal misprision statute requires that felonies be reported to "some judge or other person in civil or military authority under the United States." The President of the United States is the chief officer of the executive branch of the federal government.[11] He is the commander in chief of the Army and Navy of the United States.[12]

In view of the unambiguous language of the statute, it is difficult to resist the conclusion that the President is a "person in civil or military

---

[8] *Branzburg* v. *Hayes*, 408 U.S. 665, 696 n. 36 (1972) (*dictum*) ; and see cases cited in note 6, *supra*.
[9] *State* v. *Wilson*, 80 Vt. 249, 67A, 533, 534 (1907). Accord, *Commonwealth* v. *Lopes*, 318 Mass. 453, 458, 61 N.E. 2d 849 (1945) ; *State* v. *Michaud*, 114 A. 2d 352, 357–58 (Me., 1955) (concurring opinion).
[10] *Neal* v. *United States*, 102 F. 2d 643, 646 (8th Cir. 1939) ; *Launcey* v. *United States*, 356 F. 2d 407, 409 (9th Cir. 1966), cert. den. 385 U.S. 922 ; *United States* v. *King*, 402 F. 2d 694, 695 (9th Cir. 1968).
[11] U.S. Const. art. II, sec. 2, cl. 1.
[12] *Id*.

authority under the United States," within the meaning of the statute.[13]

Under our Constitution, the President is situated differently from any other person of authority in the government. He appoints the Attorney General of the United States, and in this sense stands at the apex of the system of law enforcement.[14] The President commissions all officers of the United States.[15] The President can pardon any person for any felony, before or after the initiation of prosecution.[16] The President is responsible for the national security.[17] In view of all these constitutional duties and responsibilities, which may, after all, with each other in a given case, the President is properly entitled to balance considerations of national security and the public interest in the punishment of persons who infringe the provisions of a criminal statute.

b. *Factual allegations.*

(*i*) *Concealment of electronic surveillance as an obstruction of the Ellsberg trial.*—During the period from May 1969 to February 1971, the FBI wiretapped the home telephone of Morton Halperin and thereby incidentally intercepted a number of conversations to which Daniel Ellsberg was a party. The subsequent failure of the Department of Justice to produce logs of these conversations at Ellsberg's trial was due to the fact that the FBI had not, in the case of the 1969–71 wiretaps, followed its usual procedure of entering records of the wiretapped conversations in a data retrieval bank (the ELSUR index).[18] This action does not constitute a ground for impeachment of President Nixon, for reasons which have been previously discussed.[19]

The principal reason is that while the President *may* have expressed to then Colonel Haig, in May 1969, a general desire that the wiretap program be handled by the FBI on a particularly confidential basis, there is no evidence at all that he specifically directed the FBI not to

---

[13] In England, the offense of misprision could be avoided by making a report to the King. Concerning the punishment for concealment of felonies, Lord Coke wrote:
"From which punishment if any will save himself he must follow the advice of Bracton, to discover it to the King, or to some judge or magistrate that for the administration of justice supplieth his place, with all speed that he can."
3 *Inst. Cop.* 65.

[14] 28 U.S.C. § 503. The discretionary power exercised by a prosecuting attorney in initiation and discontinuance of a prosecution is universally recognized as being very extensive. The Federal courts have no power to control or compel the initiation of criminal proceedings, that being the prerogative and duty of the U.S. Attorney. *Smith* v. *United States*, 375 F. 2d 243, 247 (1967); *United States* v. *Brakow*, 60 F. Supp. 100 (1945); *United States* v. *Thompson*, 251 U.S. 407 (1920); 28 U.S.C.A. § 507. Mandamus will not lie to control the exercise of this prosecutorial discretion. *Confiscation Cases*, 74 U.S. (7 Wall.) 454 (1868); *Moses* v. *Katzenbach*, 359 F. 2d 234 (1965); *Goldberg* v. *Hoffman*, 225 F. 2d 464 (1955). A United States Attorney cannot be required or forced to sign an indictment. *United States* v. *Cox*, 342 F. 2d 167 (1965). The discretionary power of the attorney for the United States, in determining whether or not a prosecution shall be commenced or maintained, may well depend upon matters of policy wholly apart from the question of probable cause. *United States* v *Cox, supra.*

[15] U.S. Const. art II, sec. 3.

[16] *Id.* art. II, sec. 2, cl. 1: *ex parte Grossman*, 267 U.S. 87, 118–20 (1925).

[17] U.S. Const. art. II, sec. 2, cl. 1.

[18] The function of the ELSUR index is to provide a cross-referencing system containing the names of all persons who are overheard in conversations intercepted by the FBI, so that if one of those persons should be indicted, the logs of his overhears can be quickly produced from the files. In July 1971 all logs, summaries and other records of the 1969–71 wiretaps were removed from the FBI to the White House, where they ended up in John Ehrlichman's safe. Thus, it might be argued that even if Ellsberg's name had been properly entered in the ELSUR index, the Department of Justice would still have been unable to produce the logs. In that event, however, knowledge of the fact that Ellsberg had been overheard would have directed the court's attention to the White House to explain why the logs had been removed from the FBI.

[19] See discussion of Article II, paragraph (2), *supra.*

enter the wiretap records on the ELSUR index. First, there is no reason to suppose that the President was familiar with the responsibility of the FBI to produce wiretap logs at "taint" hearings, as required by *Alderman* v. *United States* (which had been decided by the Supreme Court only two months before). Second, even if the President was aware of the *Alderman* holding in May 1969, it seems very improbable that he would also have known precisely what procedure (the ELSUR index) had been established by the FBI to enable the Bureau to discharge its duty of furnishing wiretap logs. Third, even in the unlikely event that the President was familiar with the ELSUR index, there is no evidence that he intended—let alone directed—that in adopting special security procedures for the 1969-71 wiretaps, the FBI should go so far as to ignore its legal duty of maintaining records so that wiretap logs could be produced in court when necessary. A reasonable man in the President's position would surely have relied on the vast experience and discretion of FBI Director Hoover to ensure that appropriate and legal measures were taken to provide extra security for the wiretapping program.

If the failure of the Department of Justice to produce the wiretap logs at Ellsberg's trial was an obstruction of justice, therefore, the FBI itself should be held accountable—not the President. Furthermore, regardless of whether that failure was technically an obstruction of justice, its only effect was to cause Judge Byrne to dismiss the case against Ellsberg. Since the President could have ordered the prosecution of Ellsberg to be dropped anyway, as a valid exercise of prosecutorial discretion, the actual result hardly justifies his impeachment.

(*ii*) *Obstruction of Watergate inquiries.*—The belated disclosure of the June 23, 1972 conversations between the President and H.R. Haldeman made it clear for the first time that the President did indeed conspire to obstruct justice, and did obstruct justice, by impeding the lawful inquiries into the Watergate break-in and cover-up. Since this obstruction of justice represents the gravamen of the charge under Article I and has been treated at length in the discussion of that Article, it requires no further comment here.

(*iii*) *Obstruction of inquiries into campaign financing practices and use of campaign funds.*—Paragraph (4) alleges that the President, after learning that his subordinates were trying to obstruct lawful investigations into allegedly illegal campaign financing practices of the Committee to Re-elect the President, failed to take action to inform the appropriate authorities of his subordinates' conduct. The Majority Report offers four examples in support of this proposition. We submit that in at least three of these cases, a further elaboration of the facts is necessary in order to reach an intelligent judgment as to whether the President is properly accused of wrongdoing.

First, it is charged that the President failed to inform the authorities after learning on March 13, 1973 from John Dean the method used by Allen and Ogarrio to make "illegal campaign contributions." In fact, on February 28, 1973, the President had told Dean that he expected the Watergate investigation to explore the financing transaction through Mexico; to which Dean had replied that it could be explained and that "When they get the facts, they are going to be disappointed." (HJCT 43). In the conversation on March 13, the

President raised the question again: "What happened to this Texas guy that took his money back?" Dean replied that "All hell broke loose for Allen" because "The money apparently originally came out of a subsidiary . . . down in Mexico." Dean briefly described the problems Allen had but then went on to explain that the money was not used for the Watergate break-in. (HJCT 65) These conversations scarcely seem to corroborate the allegation that the President was made aware of illegal acts. Indeed, the characterization of the transactions in question as "illegal campaign contributions" is rather misleading in view of the fact that Allen had been called before a grand jury on September 7, 1972 in connection with these contributions, and no indictment had issued. (FBI memorandum from Mr. Bolz to Mr. Bates, September 15, 1972) As of March 1973, therefore, the President would have been justified in concluding that, insofar as the contributions had been subjected to judicial scrutiny, their legality had been vindicated. In any event, there was no reason for him to have brought to the attention of a prosecutor a matter which had been resolved six months earlier by a grand jury's refusal to indict.

Second, it is charged that the President failed to stop plans, of which he was informed on September 15, 1972, to interfere with proposed hearings of the House Banking and Currency Committee on campaign financing practices of the Committee to Re-elect the President. Whether or not this statement is technically correct, it omits pertinent information. The Chairman of the House Banking and Currency Committee, Representative Patman, announced in September, 1972 that his Committee intended to conduct an investigation into the campaign financing practices of CRP. In point of fact, Mr. Patman ordered the investigation on his own initiative, without first submitting the proposal to his Committee for a vote. Indeed, it is questionable whether the Banking Committee even had jurisdiction to inquire into campaign financing practices, and the Committee subsequently decided not to hold any hearings. With all due respect to Mr. Patman, we suggest that his rather precipitous action may have been motivated in part by political considerations—such as a desire to make public, before election day, the facts respecting CRP practices. While there is nothing at all improper about a political motive of this sort, neither does an attempt to impede such an investigation necessarily rise to the level of an obstruction of justice.

Third, we would draw attention to the conversation on the afternoon of March 21, 1973 between the President, Haldeman, and Ehrlichman. Ehrlichman stated that he thought that Strachan was "an accessory in . . . a undeclared campaign fund." Haldeman disputed this opinion, but Ehrlichman replied that the law included Strachan. The President was unconvinced and said, "well that was . . . undeclared for a while I think it was '70, '68." (This is clearly a reference to the funds under Kalmbach's control from 1969 to early 1972.) Ehrlichman agreed with the President but went on to indicate his belief that Strachan's control of unreported political funds after April 7, 1972 was a violation of law: "Yeah. But then it got back into the coffers and, uh, was used in this campaign." (HJCT 142). It would be fair to say that the participants in this conversation did not reach a consensus that Strachan had in fact violated the law. Furthermore, it was known that Strachan would soon be called to testify before the grand jury. Under these circumstances, the President might reasonably have believed that the demands of the orderly administration of justice did not require him to rush to the prosecutor with news of a possible violation of law, particularly when he was personally unconvinced that it was in fact a violation.

(iv) *Kleindienst confirmation hearings.*—(a) *Facts.*—On February 15, 1972, the President nominated Deputy Attorney General Richard Kleindienst to be Attorney General of the United States to succeed John Mitchell, who was leaving the Department of Justice to participate in the President's re-election campaign.

The Senate Committee on the Judiciary held brief hearings on the nomination and quickly voted to recommend that the nomination be confirmed. (Book V, 605)

On February 29, 1972, Jack Anderson, a newpaper columnist, published the first of three articles alleging that three antitrust cases, commenced by the Department of Justice in 1969, had been settled favorably to the defendant, the International Telephone & Telegraph Corporation (ITT), in 1971 in return for a large financial contribution to the 1972 Republican National Convention in San Diego. Kleindienst immediately asked that the Senate Judiciary Hearings be reconvened in order that he might answer these allegations. (Book V, 633)

On March 2, 1972, pursuant to Kleindienst's request, the hearings reconvened. The purpose of the hearings was to determine what connection, if any, existed between the settlement of the ITT antitrust cases and the ITT convention contributions. In connection with the investigation, the Senate Committee on the Judiciary inquired into several areas including: (1) the extent of involvement of the White House in the filing, handling and settling of the ITT antitrust cases; (2) the circumstances under which the ITT convention pledge was obtained; and (3) the actions of the Department of Justice personnel in the ITT antitrust cases. (Book V, 677–904, *passim*)

Richard Kleindienst testified that he had never been interfered with by anyone at the White House in the exercise of his responsibilities in the ITT antitrust cases. (Book V, 677–80, 729–34, 755–58, 849–53) In fact, on April 19, 1971, the day before an appeal was due to be filed in the Supreme Court in the *ITT-Grinnell* case, the President telephoned Kleindienst and ordered that the appeal not be filed. (Book V, 311) In his Senate testimony, Kleindienst also described the circumstances of the decision to delay this appeal without mentioning the President's phone call. (Book V, 729–34, 751–54)

On May 16, 1974 Kleindienst pleaded guilty to an information charging a failure to answer accurately and fully questions pertinent to the Senate Judiciary Committee's inquiry, in violation of 2 U.S.C. § 192. (Book V, 965)

John N. Mitchell testified in part as to his involvement in the handling of the ITT antitrust cases. Mitchell testified that he had recused himself in the ITT cases. (Book V, 771) In fact, Mitchell had been involved in contacts with ITT officials concerning the cases during 1970 and had various discussions with White House staff members about the ITT antitrust cases. (Book V, 143) In his Senate testimony, Mitchell denied that he had ever discussed the ITT antitrust cases with the President, although he had discussed the *ITT-Grinnell* appeal with the President on April 21, 1971, two days after the President's order to Kleindienst. (Book V, 371-76; 771-75) In that discussion Mitchell had persuaded the President not to interfere with the appeal of *ITT-Grinnell* to the Supreme Court. (Book V, 371)

(b) *Evidence relating to President's knowledge*

The evidence of Presidential knowledge of this testimony given by Mr. Kleindienst and Mr. Mitchell in March and April, 1972 is circumstantial.

The President returned from China on the evening of February 28, 1972. After spending a few days in Key Biscayne the President began his first full day in the White House on Monday, March 6. (Book V, 141-42) Three days earlier, on March 3, Richard Kleindienst had testified about the circumstances surrounding the delay of the appeal of the *ITT-Grinnell* case a year earlier. (Book V, 729-34)

On Monday, March 6, the President met, and talked by telephone, with three of his top aides, Haldeman, Ehrlichman and Colson. (Book V, 735) Also on March 6, Richard Kleindienst's diary reflects the fact that he was at the White House for a Cabinet meeting with the President. (Richard Kleindienst diary, submitted to the Inquiry staff after the initial presentation to the Committee of information regarding the ITT matter.) The next day Kleindienst in a detailed statement to the Senate Committee described the events of April 19, 1971 without mentioning the President's order to him not to file the *ITT-Grinnell* appeal. (Book V, 751)

On March 14, 1972, John Mitchell appeared before the Senate Judiciary Committee and twice testified that there had been no communications between the President and with him with respect to the ITT antitrust litigation or any other antitrust litigation. That evening the President and Mr. Mitchell had their only telephone conversation during March of which the Committee staff is aware. (Book V, 771) Mr. Mitchell has denied in an unsworn interview with the inquiry staff that he discussed his testimony, or the testimony of any other witness before the Senate Committee with the President, with Mr. Kleindienst, or with any members of the President's staff.

According to Charles Colson's calendar, he spent the morning of March 18, 1972 on "ITT" matters. He had three telephone conversations with Mr. Mitchell during the morning. That afternoon the President and Colson met for over two hours.

On March 24, 1972, the President held his only press conference of this period. He said that:

> ... as far as the [Senate Judiciary Committee] hearings are concerned, there is nothing that has happened in the hearings to date that has in one way shaken my confidence in Mr. Kleindienst as an able, honest man, fully qualified to be Attorney General of the United States. (Book V, 801)

In this press conference, the President also said that, "we moved on it [ITT] and moved effectively. . . . Mr. McLaren is justifiably very proud of that record . . . [and he] should be." (Book V, 802) He said that Administration action had prevented ITT from growing further and quoted Solicitor General Griswold as to the excellence of the ITT settlement. (Book V, 799)

Charles Colson testified before the Committee as to a meeting during this time period that he attended with the President and Haldeman. Colson testified that the President recalled that he had made a telephone call to Kleindienst:

Mr. COLSON. I recall one instance when the President was basically talking to Haldeman, but I was in the room and obviously the question of his involvement in the ITT settlement had somehow come up.
Mr. JENNER. When you say his you are referring to who?
Mr. COLSON. The President.
Mr. JENNER. All right.
Mr. COLSON. Because he said do you, he said to Haldeman, he said do you remember the time I called Kleindienst and got very agitated or very excited with Dick and did I discuss the *ITT* case or was I talking about policy. And Bob said no you were talking about policy, you weren't discussing the case.
And the President said are you sure?
And Haldeman said yes, either I was there while you called or Ehrlichman was there and heard your call and the President said thank God I didn't discuss the case.
Mr. JENNER. Do you have a recollection with better certainty that this conversation you have now described took place during the span of the ITT-Kleindienst hearings?
Mr. COLSON. Yes, I think it did. I can't imagine why it would come up at another time. I think it must have—I know it is the first time I ever knew the President talked to Kleindienst about this matter at all. And I don't think I learned about it until late in the month and I remember learning about it in that fashion, that the President was trying to recall what he had said to Kleindienst hearings?

Colson also testified that on March 27 and 28, 1972 he and Clark MacGregor met with the President and presented to him the reasons why they felt the nomination of Kleindienst should be withdrawn. Colson testified that he left that meeting feeling that the President was inclined to agree that the nomination should be withdrawn. (Colson testimony, 3 HJC 384–85)

On March 29, Colson and MacGregor met with H. R. Haldeman who informed them that the President was going to meet with Kleindienst that afternoon to determine whether or not Kleindienst would withdraw his name from consideration. (Colson testimony, 3 HJC 385) Colson also testified that on the morning of March 30, he and MacGregor met with Haldeman who described the President's meeting with Kleindienst in which Kleindienst convinced the President that the nomination should not be withdrawn. (Colson testimony, 3 HJC 386)

Colson took notes of his meeting with Haldeman and MacGregor (Colson Exhibit No. 22, 3 HJC 387–91) and later returned to his office to dictate a memorandum to Haldeman that argued that the nomination should be withdrawn. (Colson testimony, 3 HJC 393–97) His reasons included the fact that he had reviewed documents that would tend to contradict Mitchell's testimony to the Senate Committee. (Book V, 805–09) Later that day Colson met with the President and informed him that he had written such a memorandum. After meeting with the President, Colson sent the memorandum to H. R. Haldeman. Colson testified that by normal practice the memorandum would be given by Mr. Haldeman to the President. (Colson testimony, 3 HJC 397)

Mr. Mitchell has told the inquiry staff that, near the end of March, he recalls generally that he conveyed to the President, either directly, or through Mr. Haldeman, his view that the Kleindienst nomination should not be withdrawn but that he recalls no specific conversations.

On April 4, 1972 the President met four times with Haldeman and talked once by telephone with Colson. During the afternoon the President met with Haldeman and Mitchell and discussed, among other things, changing the convention site from San Diego to Miami. An edited transcript of this conversation has been supplied to the Committee. The transcript indicates no evidence of Presidential knowledge of the testimony of Kleindienst or Mitchell, and indeed shows that there was very little discussion of the hearings.

On June 8, 1972, Kleindienst was confirmed by the Senate. On June 12, 1974, Kleindienst was appointed to the office of the Attorney General, and was sworn in at a ceremony at the White House attended by the President. (Book V, 901)

During the period that the Kleindienst nomination was pending before the Senate, the press provided extensive coverage of the hearings, the debates and the final vote. (Book V, 855) This press coverage was reflected in the news summaries prepared daily by the White House staff for the President.

On January 8, 1974 the office of the White House Press Secretary issued a "White Paper" entitled, "The ITT Antitrust Decision", describing the President's role in the ITT antitrust cases and their settlement. The White Paper denied that the President had any involvement in the ITT settlement and denied that the settlement was made in exchange for an ITT convention pledge, but admitted the telephone call to Kleindienst. (Book V, 956)

(c) *Was the testimony of Kleindienst or Mitchell perjury?*

In the course of their testimony before the Senate Committee on the Judiciary, Kleindienst and Mitchell appear to have given incorrect or misleading testimony several times. Kleindienst apparently misled the Committee about the nature of his contacts with the White House in the filing, handling and settlement of the ITT antitrust cases. Mitchell apparently misled the Committee about his contact with the White House and with ITT officials regarding the ITT cases, and he further was evasive about his involvement in the Administration's decision to select San Diego as the site of the 1972 Republican National Convention. Certain statements by Kleindienst and Mitchell appear to be clearly incorrect. On March 7, 1972, Kleindienst described the reasons for the decision to delay the *ITT-Grinnell* appeal on April 19, 1971, without mentioning the President's telephone call of that day in which the President ordered the appeal to be dropped. On March 14, 1972, Mitchell stated that he never discussed the ITT antitrust cases with the President, whereas actually he had discussed the appeal with the President on April 21, 1971.[20]

A factual issue may be raised as to the intent of Mitchell in his misstatements. In his interview with the inquiry staff, for example, Mr. Mitchell indicated that what he meant when he denied talking to

---

[20] To date, neither Kleindienst nor Mitchell has been prosecuted for perjury in connection with the ITT hearings. Kleindienst has pleaded to the lesser offense of failure to fully respond under 2 U.S.C. § 192. Mitchell has not been prosecuted for any act relating to the ITT/Kleindienst hearings.

the President about the ITT cases was that he had never talked to the President about the *merits* of those cases. In such a case his testimony would not be perjury.

The alleged misstatements by Kleindienst concerning the *ITT-Grinnell* appeal to the Supreme Court in April 1971 are subject to the defense of "literal truth." For example, the lengthy statement which Kleindienst read to the Committee on March 7, 1972, omitting any mention of the President's telephone call, may be misleading but not in fact false. Kleindienst's statement related only actual events of April 19, minus the telephone call, and therefore it may be literally true but incomplete. Therefore, under the recent Supreme Court decision in *Branston* v. *United States*, 409 U.S. 352 (1973), in which the Court held that testimony that is literally true but arguably misleading by negative implication is not perjury. Kleindienst's remarks on March 7 would not constitute perjury.

The alleged misstatements of both Mitchell and Kleindienst were not perjurious because they were not material to the Senate Inquiry. The test of materiality is whether the testimony has a natural effect or tendency to influence, impede or dissuade the investigative body from pursuing its investigation.[21] The Senate Committee on the Judiciary was charged with evaluating the qualifications of Richard Kleindienst to be Attorney General. In the exercise of this constitutional responsibility the Senate Committee was investigating the connection between the ITT antitrust cases and the ITT convention pledge. The Senate Committee's investigation into the ITT scandal was focused properly only on the settlement of the ITT cases and the reasons for the settlement. Thus an alleged misstatement about an appeal in the *ITT-Grinnell* case would not be material to the Committee's inquiry.

It may be questioned, furthermore, whether disclosure of the President's telephone call to Kleindienst and the latter's successful resistance would have had any adverse impact upon the Committee's judgment as to Mr. Kleindienst's qualifications. In omitting to mention the telephone call Kleindienst also omitted to mention that his response to the call was to threaten to resign. In part because of that threat, the President rescinded his order two days later. Kleindienst's strong resistance to presidential intervention could only have reflected favorably on his integrity and qualifications for the office of Attorney General. In such a case it makes no sense to attempt to impeach a President because his nominee withheld information that would have markedly enhanced the nominee's chances of confirmation.

(*d*) *Was the President aware of the false testimony of his subordinates?*

To charge the President with knowledge that his close subordinates had endeavored to frustrate the Senate inquiry, two facts must be proven. First, it must be shown that the President had knowledge of the specific testimony of Kleindienst and Mitchell. Second, it must be shown that the President knew that testimony to be false.

The Majority Report offers several facts to prove that the President had knowledge of the testimony. First, the "extensive press coverage"

---

[21] *United States* v. *Morgan*, 194 F. 2d 623 (2d Cir. 1952), *cert. denied*, 343 U.S. 965 (1952).

of the Kleindienst hearings supposedly reflected in the President's daily news summaries is suggested as a source of information from which the President is presumed to have learned about the testimony. Second, the President had a telephone conversation with Mitchell on the evening of March 14, the day of Mitchell's allegedly perjured testimony. The inference is drawn that during this telephone call Mitchell informed the President of his testimony that day. Third, the President indicated in his March 24 press conference that he was familiar with the hearings and testimony of the witnesses. Because the President quoted the general statements about the ITT settlements by then Solicitor General Griswold, the majority charges the President with knowledge of the testimony of other witnesses about the appeal. Fourth, Colson testified to the Committee that Haldeman informed him on March 29 and 30 that the President intended to meet, and did in fact meet, with Kleindienst on the afternoon of March 29. It is inferred from this meeting that the President learned of and discussed Kleindienst's misleading testimony. Fifth, Colson's March 30 memorandum to Haldeman cites certain documents in White House files that contradicted Mitchell's testimony about his role in the settlement and tended to show that the President was involved in the ITT case in 1971. It is argued that if the President read this memorandum, he would have realized that evidence existed that contradicted the testimony of Mitchell about the *ITT-Grinnell* appeal.

Under close scrutiny, however, this evidence does not persuasively establish presidential knowledge. First, no direct evidence of actual presidential knowledge exists. Except for the President's general statement in his press conference of March 24, the evidence is   irely inferential. Nor does the press conference itself indicate specifi .nowledge of the actual testimony of either Kleindienst or Mitchell. Colson and other witnesses have informed the inquiry staff that the President does not prepare for news briefings by studying primary news sources. Instead he utilizes a briefing book prepared by his staff. There is no evidence before the Committee as to what the briefing book for the President's March 24 press conference contained, nor has the Committee requested production of this briefing book. An inference of presidential knowledge of testimony from the press conference is therefore wholly unwarranted.

Second, although the Majority Report attaches great significance to the "extensive press coverage," the specific testimony by Kleindienst concerning the appeal was actually *not* reported. The focus of the news media was on the allegations concerning the settlement of the ITT cases, not the appeal of the *ITT-Grinnell* case. Thus by reading the newspaper or the news summaries the President could not have learned of the critical testimony of either Kleindienst or Mitchell.

Third, although Haldeman may have told Colson that Kleindienst and the President met on the afternoon of March 29, Kleindienst has specifically denied this to the inquiry staff. Kleindienst said that he had no conversations with anyone at the White House during March, April and May of 1972. As uncorroborated hearsay, Colson's testimony is not entitled to much weight.

Fourth, although Colson's memo of March 30 does indicate that documents contradicted Mitchell's testimony, the testimony concerned the settlement and *not* the appeal. In any event, Colson testified that he does not know whether the President received or read the memo. In fact, Colson has testified to the Committee that he did not discuss with the President either his memo, the documents describe therein, or the testimony of Mitchell or Kleindienst. Nor did the President ever indicate to Colson any awareness that Kleindienst had not told the truth to the Senate Committee. (Colson testimony, 3 HJC 401) Finally, Colson has said that he did not follow the testimony of any of the witnesses before the Senate Judiciary Committee. Because Colson was the White House staff man in charge of the Kleindienst confirmation fight, if he never followed the testimony and never talked about the testimony with the President, it is difficult to see how the President could have learned of the testimony.

Even if the evidence established that the President was aware of the testimony of Kleindienst and Mitchell—which we believe it does not—the allegation of wrongdoing on the President's part further depends on proof that he also would have known the testimony to be false. This conclusion is urged by the majority because the President had participated in the events of April, 1971 about which Kleindienst and Mitchell testified falsely. But those events can hardly be said to have been of critical importance to the Nixon Presidency. The President's telephone call to Kleindienst on April 19, 1971 in which he ordered Kleindienst to drop the *ITT-Grinnell* appeal, lasted no more than three minutes. The President's discussion two days later with Mitchell about the appeal lasted less than five minutes. One is scarcely compelled to conclude that, after the passage of ten and a half months filled with events of the order of importance of his trip to China, the President would advert to and recall those comparatively trivial conversations.

Moreover, the evidence supports the conclusion that in fact the President inaccurately recalled the substance of the telephone call to Kleindienst. Colson has testified that sometime in March, 1972, the President was assured by Haldeman that the call was not about the ITT case but rather was about the antitrust policies of McLaren. According to Colson, the President responded, ". . . thank God I didn't discuss the case." (Colson testimony, 3 HJC 383)

In conclusion, the evidence establishes that the testimony of Kleindienst and Mitchell, though perhaps misleading, was not perjurious; that the President was probably not aware of the substance of their testimony; and that even if he had been aware of it, he would not have recognized it as false. This fair reading of the evidence does not even make out a case of negligence against the President, let alone support the charge that he knowingly failed to take care that the laws be faithfully executed.

Paragraph (5)

Paragraph (5) charges that the President "knowingly misused the executive power by interfering" with the Federal Bureau of Investigation, the Criminal Division of the Department of Justice, the Watergate Special Prosecutor, and the Central Intelligence Agency. This charge is essentially a repetition of allegations which are encompassed by Article I, Paragraphs (4) and (6).

If the allegations in Article II, Paragraph (5) are regarded as having an independent significance apart from the Watergate conspiracy, then they are reduced to describing a few isolated incidents which do not, in our opinion, rise to the level of a ground for impeachment. Conversely, if the allegations *are* concerned with the Watergate conspiracy, then Paragraph (5) merely duplicates Article I and is redundant.

Article III

Article III charges that the President, "without lawful cause or excuse," failed to produce papers and things subpoenaed by the Committee on the Judiciary, which were deemed necessary by the Committee in order to resolve questions relating to Presidential knowledge or approval of certain actions "demonstrated by other evidence to be substantial grounds for impeachment of the President." Proponents of the Article urged that its adoption was necessary to establish, as a matter of law, that no President may resist a duly authorized impeachment inquiry by the House of Representatives. It was suggested in the Committee's debate on this Article that impeachment should be "automatic" if a President refuses to surrender evidence in a legitimate impeachment inquiry.[1]

We believe that adoption of Article III would have unnecessarily introduced an element of brittleness at the heart of our system of Constitutional checks and balances, and for this reason would have been unwise. Furthermore there may appear to be an element of unfairness, or even circularity, in removing a President from office for failure to cooperate in his own impeachment—for failure to furnish information to his accusers, as it were—particularly where other grounds for impeachment are thought to exist.

If this were nevertheless to be done, certainly it should be done only after a formal adjudication by the House of Representatives as to the relevance of the material sought, the adequacy of the President's response, and the applicability of any privilege or other "lawful cause or excuse" claimed by the President. Such is the time-honored procedure of the House, and to abandon it in this, of all cases, could only cause grave doubts as to the fairness of a vote to impeach on this ground.

FACTUAL BACKGROUND

The question of the limits of the President's obligation to waive claims of confidentiality and make available, to investigators and to the public, information and records pertaining to the work of the Executive Branch, has perplexed the Government for more than a year. On May 22, 1973, the President formally waived Executive privilege "as to any testimony concerning possible criminal conduct or discussions of possible criminal conduct in the matters presently under investigation, including the Watergate affair and the alleged cover-up."[2] The Senate Select Committee on Presidential Campaign Activities issued subpoenas for various taped conversations and documentary materials, and eventually brought suit to enforce its subpoenas pursuant to specially enacted legislation conferring jurisdiction on the United States District Court for the District of Columbia. The

---
[1] HJC Debates, July 30, 1974, TR. 1105.
[2] "Presidential Statements," May 22, 1973, p. 25.

President successfully resisted these demands for information, and prevailed in the suit brought against him.[3]

Also in 1973, the Federal grand jury investigating the Watergate matter issued its own subpoenas for tapes and other materials which it declared to be necessary to its investigation. Its subpoenas were eventually upheld in the courts,[4] and the President released the tapes in question.

More recently, the Office of the Watergate Special Prosecutor issued trial subpoenas for tapes and other documentary material, for use in the upcoming trials in the case of *United States* v. *Mitchell et al.*, now pending in the United States District Court for the District of Columbia.[5] The President's challenge to the validity of these subpoenas resulted in a recent decision of the United States Supreme Court, reaffirming the doctrine of Executive privilege but holding that, under the circumstances of that case, the President was obliged to turn over the material.[6] The President stated that he would comply with this decision, and accordingly surrendered the tapes in question to the Special Prosecutor in compliance with this decision.

The authority for the subpoenas issued by this Committee derives from the adoption, on February 6, 1974, of H. Res. 803, which conferred subpoena power on the Committee for the purposes of its impeachment inquiry.

We believe that the following matters have some bearing upon whether the President should be impeached because of his responses to the Committee's subpoenas:

On February 25, 1974, following initial discussions between the Special Counsel to this Committee, John Doar, and the Special Counsel to the President, James D. St. Clair, Mr. Doar wrote to Mr. St. Clair, stating in part as follows:

> We believe the next logical step is to have you outline for us how the White House files are indexed, how Presidential papers are indexed, and how Presidential conversations and memoranda are indexed. We are particularly interested in knowing how the files of Mr. Haldeman, Mr. Ehrlichman, Mr. Colson and Mr. Dean are indexed. If we could work out a way whereby members of the Inquiry staff may examine these files for the purpose of selecting materials which, in our opinion, are necessary for the investigation, I believe that the inquiry would be expedited.

On April 4, 1974, following further discussions, Mr. Doar sent another letter to Mr. St. Clair, stating in part as follows:

> Of course, if any of the conversations requested in our letter of February 25, concerns a subject entirely unrelated to the matters that I have outlined, the Committee would have no interest therein. In the final analysis, however, the Committee itself would have to make that determination. I am sure it would give careful initial consideration to your response in making its determination as to a particular conversation which you might believe to be totally unrelated to the matters that I have outlined .

On April 19, 1974 Mr. Doar wrote to Mr. St. Clair requesting, in part, the following material:

> All papers and things prepared by, sent to, received by, or at any time contained in the files of, H. R. Haldeman, John D. Ehrlichman, Charles W. Colson,

---

[3] *Senate Select Committee* v. *Nixon*, D.C. Cir. Civ. No. 74-1258 (May 23, 1974).
[4] *Nixon* v. *Sirica*, 487 F. 2d 700 (D.C. Cir., 1973).
[5] Cr. No. 74-110.
[6] *United States* v. *Nixon*, (U.S.S.Ct., July 24, 1974).

John Dean 3d, Gordon C. Strachan, Egil Krogh, David Young, E. Howard Hunt, G. Gordon Liddy and John Caulfield to the extent that such papers or things relate or refer directly or indirectly to one or more of the following subjects:

1. The break-in and electronic surveillance of the Democratic National Committee Headquarters in the Watergate office building during May and June of 1972, or the investigations of that break-in by the Department of Justice, the Senate Select Committee on Presidential Campaign Activities, or any other legislative, judicial, executive or administrative body, including members of the White House staff;
2. The . . . Huston Plan;
3. The activities of the White House Special Investigation Unit.

On April 11, May 15, May 30, and June 24, 1974, the Committee, after considering factual memoranda prepared by the Inquiry staff outlining the need for the materials sought, issued eight subpoenas for (i) tape recordings and other materials related to 147 Presidential conversations, 98 related to Watergate and 49 related to the dairy inquiry, the ITT matter, the domestic surveillance area, and the alleged misuse of the IRS; (ii) all documents in the files of Messrs. Haldeman, Ehrlichman, Colson, Dean and Strachan relating to the Watergate matter;[7] (iii) all documents from the files of Haldeman, Ehrlichman, Colson, Krogh and Young relating to the White House Special Investigations Unit; (iv) all Presidential daily diaries for the months of April, May, June and July, 1972, February, March, April, October, and part of July, 1973; and (v) certain other Presidential daily diaries and daily news summaries delivered to the President. Of the 147 conversations for which the Committee has subpoenaed tape recordings, dictabelts, memoranda and other related documents, it is known that 126 cover a period of approximately 90 hours (5,361 minutes). The duration of the remaining 21 conversations has not been ascertained by the Committee.

On March 6, 1974, the President's Special Counsel announced that the President would give to the Committee all material which he had previously submitted to the Watergate Special Prosecutor, including nineteen tape recordings relating to Watergate, ITT, "Plumbers," and the dairy areas of the inquiry, and over 700 documents.[8]

On April 29, 1974, the President announced that he would submit to the Committee the transcripts of subpoenaed conversations dealing with Watergate, as well as transcripts of some other taped conversations dealing with Watergate which had not been subpoenaed. These transcripts were delivered to the Committee the next day in a docu-

---

[7] The subpoena of May 30, 1974 required the production of:
"All papers and things (including recordings) prepared by, sent to, received by or at any time contained in the files of H. R. Haldeman, John D. Ehrlichman, Charles W. Colson, John Dean III, and Gordon Strachan to the extent that such papers or things relate or refer directly or indirectly to the break-in and election surveillance of the Democratic National Committee Headquarters in the Watergate office building during May and June of 1972 or the investigations of that break-in by the Department of Justice, the Senate Select Committee on Presidential Campaign Activities, or any other legislative, judicial, executive or administrative body, including members of the White House staff."

[8] The materials entitled "Facts Respecting Defense of Subpoenas," prepared by the Inquiry staff and submitted to the members of the Committee before the vote on Article III states that "the twelve Watergate tape recordings were already on their way to the Committee as part of the Grand Jury submission." (pp. 2, 6) Actually, the hearing at which the President's Special Counsel announced that the material would be turned over was held by Judge John J. Sirica for the purpose of determining *whether* the Grand Jury submission would or would not be turned over to this Committee. It is only in retrospect that it appears that the materials "were already on their way" to this Committee; there is no reason to think that the hearing and decision by Judge Sirica were empty formalities, mere "window-dressing" to ratify a course of action already chosen by the Special Prosecutor.

ment of 1,308 pages entitled, "Submission of Recorded Presidential Conversations to the Committee on the Judiciary of the House of Representatives by President Richard Nixon" hereinafter cited as WHT.[9]

On August 5, 1974, the President released to the Committee and to the public the transcripts of three conversations between himself and H. R. Haldeman on June 23, 1972, together with a formal statement. The President said:

> On April 29, in announcing my decision to make public the original set of White House transcripts, I stated that "as far as what the President personally knew and did with regard to Watergate and the cover-up is concerned, these materials—together with those already made available—will tell it all."
>
> Shortly after that, in May, I made a preliminary review of some of the 64 taped conversations subpoenaed by the Special Prosecutor.
>
> Among the conversations I listened to at that time were two of those of June 23. Although I recognized that these presented potential problems, I did not inform my staff or my Counsel of it, or those arguing my case, nor did I amend my submission to the Judiciary Committee in order to include and reflect it. At the time, I did not realize the extent of the implications which these conversations might now appear to have. As a result, those arguing my case, as well as those passing judgment on the case, did so with information that was incomplete and in some respects erroneous. This was a serious act of omission for which I take full responsibility and which I deeply regret.
>
> Since the Supreme Court's decision twelve days ago, I have ordered my Counsel to analyze the 64 tapes, and I have listened to a number of them myself. This process has made it clear that portions of the tapes of these June 23 conversations are at variance with certain of my previous statements. Therefore, I have ordered the transcripts made available immediately to the Judiciary Committee so that they can be reflected in the Committee's report, and included in the record to be considered by the House and Senate.

This submission was later supplemented by the delivery to the Committee of an edited transcript of a conversation which took place between the President, H. R. Haldeman and John Mitchell on April 11, 1972, for which tapes and other materials have been subpoenaed by the Committee.

MATERIALS TURNED OVER TO THE COMMITTEE

In addition to the edited transcripts mentioned above, the White House submitted to the Committee the materials listed in the Committee's "Index to Investigative Files—Materials Received from the White House," given to the Members of the Committee on May 9, 1974. These materials included the following:

1. Handwritten Notes of the President and H. R. Haldeman (5 items)
2. Memoranda, Daily Diaries and Other Material. (11 items)
3. White House Political Matters Memoranda, 8/13/71–9/18/72, to H. R. Haldeman from Gordon Strachan. (21 items)
4. Documents regarding the Special Investigations Unit ("Plumbers"). (38 categories or items)
5. Documents regarding ITT. (73 categories or items)
6. Documents regarding the Dairy Industry. (20 categories or items)

---

[9] As to the adequacy of this submission for the Committee's purposes, see discussion under heading "Substantial Compliance" below.

7. Documents from the files of the Federal Home Loan Bank Board. (98 documents and 8 sets of documents)

8. Documents from the files of the Environmental Protection Agency. (12 files)

9. Documents from the files of the Interior Department. (5 files)

10. Tape recordings of Presidential conversations. (19 recordings)

The Committee was also subsequently furnished copies of certain of the President's daily news summaries and notes of John D. Ehrlichman previously supplied to the Special Prosecutor.

ARGUMENTS ADVANCED BY THE PRESIDENT

The unsigned memorandum accompanying the President's submission of edited White House transcripts to the Committee on April 30, 1974 stated:

[The Committee's] subpoena called for the production of tapes and other materials relating to 42 presidential conversations. With respect to all but three of these conversations, the subpoena called for the production of the tapes and related materials without regard to the subject matter, or matters, dealt with in these conversations. In the President's view, such a broad scale subpoena is unwarranted. . . . As the President has repeatedly stated, he will not participate in the destruction of the office of the Presidency of the United States by permitting unlimited access to Presidential conversations and documents.

. . . In order that the Committee may be satisfied that he has in fact disclosed this pertinent material to the Committee, *the President has invited the Chairman and Ranking Minority Member to review the subpoenaed tapes to satisfy themselves that a full and complete disclosure of the pertinent contents of these tapes has, indeed, been made.* If, after such review they have any questions regarding his conduct, *the President has stated that he stands ready to respond under oath to written interrogatories and to meet with the Chairman and Ranking Minority Member of the Committee at the White House to discuss these matters if they so desire.* (Emphasis added.)

Prior to the Committee's issuance of the subpoena of May 15, the President's Special Counsel submitted "Responses on Behalf of the President to Requests of Special Staff" that a subpoena issue for tapes of Presidential conversations of April 4, 1972 and June 23, 1972. These Responses argued that the evidence then before the Committee demonstrated that these tapes were unnecessary to the Committee's inquiry, and that therefore subpoenas should not be issued for them "to satisfy curiosity or to seek confirmation of undisputed facts."

The letter of May 22, 1974, from the President to the Chairman Rodino, referring to the two subpoenas dated May 15, 1974, stated:

. . . It is clear that the continued succession of demands for additional Presidential conversations has become a never-ending process, and that to continue providing these conversations in response to the constantly escalating requests would constitute such a massive invasion into the confidentiality of Presidential conversation that the institution of the Presidency itself would be fatally compromised.

. . . Continuing ad infinitum the process of yielding up additional conversations in response to an endless series of demands would fatally weaken this office not only in this administration but for future Presidencies as well.

Accordingly, I respectfully decline to produce the [documents subpoenaed].

However, I again remind you that if the Committee desires further information from me about any of these conversations or other matters related to its inquiry,

I stand ready to answer, under oath, pertinent written interrogatories, and to be interviewed under oath by you and the ranking minority member at the White House. (Emphasis added.)

The President's letter of June 9, 1974, to the Chairman of the Committee stated as follows:

The question at issue is not who conducts the inquiry, but where the line is to be drawn on the apparently endlessly escalating spiral of demands for confidential Presidential tapes and documents. The Committee asserts that it should be the sole judge of Presidential confidentiality. I cannot accept such a doctrine. . . .

What is commonly referred to now as 'executive privilege' is part and parcel of the basic doctrine of separation of powers—the establishment, by the Constitution, of three separate and co-equal branches of Government.

While many functions of Government require the concurrence or interaction of two or more branches, each branch historically has been steadfast in maintaining its own independence by turning back attempts of the others, whenever made, to assert an authority to invade without consent, the privacy of its own deliberations.

. . . If the institution of an impeachment inquiry against the President were permitted to override all restraints of separation of powers, this would spell the end of the doctrine of the separation of powers; it would be an open invitation to future Congresses to use an impeachment inquiry, however frivolously, as a device to assert their own supremacy over the Executive, and to reduce executive confidentiality to a nullity.

My refusal to comply with further subpoenas with respect to Watergate is based essentially on two considerations.

First, preserving the principle of separation of powers—and the Executive as a co-equal branch—requires that the Executive, no less than the Legislative or Judicial branches must be immune from unlimited search and seizure by the other co-equal branches.

Second, the voluminous body of materials that the Committee already has—and which I have voluntarily provided, partly in response to Committee requests and partly in an effort to round out the record—does give the full story of Watergate, insofar as it relates to Presidential knowledge and Presidential actions.

. . . The Executive must remain the final arbiter of demands on its confidentiality, just as the Legislative and Judicial branches must remain the final arbiters of demands on their confidentiality.

SUBPOENA POWER OF THE HOUSE OF REPRESENTATIVES IN AN IMPEACHMENT INQUIRY

Each House of Congress possesses an implied Constitutional power to compel the production of documents and the testimony of witnesses, as an aid to the intelligent exercise of its Constitutional functions. The power was first judicially recognized in the context of a legislative investigation,[10] but it applies *"a fortiori*, where [a House of Congress] is exercising a judicial function,"[11] such as impeachment.

The power of the Houses of Congress to compel the production of evidence, however, like all their other powers under our Constitution, is not unlimited.

Limits on the Power

A. Subject Matter of Investigation

All Congressional powers of inquiry exist to be exercised not as ends in themselves, but only as a means of providing Congress information

---
[10] *McGrain* v. *Daugherty*, 273 U.S. 135, 174 (1927).
[11] *Barry* v. *United States ex rel. Cunningham*, 279 U.S. 587, 616 (1929). A House of Congress may punish a person for contempt either through its own process or through the judicial process established by 2 U.S.C. §§ 192–194.

on which to found actions and decisions which it is charged by the Constitution to make.¹² Accordingly, the power cannot be exercised to compel the production of information which is not related to a decision or action entrusted to Congress by the Constitution. As the Supreme Court has stated,

> Congressional investigating Committees . . . are restricted to the missions delegated to them, i.e., to acquire certain data to be used by the House or the Senate in coping with a problem that falls within its . . . sphere. No witnesses can be compelled to make disclosures on matters outside that area. This is a jurisdictional concept of pertinency drawn from the nature of a Congressional Committee's source of authority.¹³

President Nixon consistently took the position that the Committee's subpoenas were overbroad in failing to specify the subject matter of many conversations sought. This raised the issue of the relevance of the information sought to any proper subject matter of the Committee's inquiry.¹⁴ Ordinarily the recipient of a subpoena *duces tecum* in a judicial proceeding may not himself judge the relevance of the subpoenaed materials to the subject matter of the case. It is equally true, however, that the decision as to relevance is not left solely to the party demanding production of the evidence. In a judicial proceeding the final determination of relevance is for the Court.

Even though the Committee never formally acknowledged its inquiry to be an adversary proceeding, the Committee's position was not strictly analogous to that of the Court in a judicial proceeding: the Committee was also the party seeking to compel the production of the material in question. Under these circumstances, if the Committee were to act as the final arbiter of the legality of its own demand, the result would seldom be in doubt.

1. Adjudication before full House of Representatives.—It is for the reason just stated that, when a witness before a Congressional Committee refuses to give testimony or produce documents, the Committee cannot itself hold the witness in contempt. Rather, the established procedure is for the witness to be given an opportunity to appear before the full House or Senate, as the case may be, and give reasons, if he can, why he should not be held in contempt. For example, he might argue that his refusal was justified, or excusable, or based on some mistake. The Supreme Court has held that this kind of notice and opportunity for hearing are constitutionally required, under the Fifth and Fourteenth Amendments, before a legislative body may punish a person for contempt of its prerogatives.¹⁵

It may be argued that the President had an opportunity to "show cause" before the Committee why his response was satisfactory. (The brief dated July 19, 1974, and submitted to the Committee on

---

¹² See *Marshall* v. *Gordon*, 243 U.S. 52, 547 (1927), indicating that even in an impeachment inquiry, the House would not have the power to punish for contempt of its prerogatives unless the exercise of that power were in aid of its impeachment function under the Constitution.
¹³ *Watkins* v. *United States*, 354 U.S. 178, 187, 198, 206 (1957).
¹⁴ The Committee is authorized under H. Res. 803 to compel the production of all items it deems "necessary" to its Inquiry. The alternative of limiting the Committee's authority to securing items necessary and relevant, or reasonably calculated to lead to the production of relevant evidence, was considered, but not adopted by the House.
¹⁵ *Groppi* v. *Leslie*, 404 U.S. 496, 500 (1972). As the Supreme Court there noted, Congress had long followed these procedures as a matter of policy, in order to ensure fairness to witnesses and persons summoned to produce evidence, rather than as a matter of Constitutional command.

behalf of the President, did not address this issue, although it stated that the President's Special Counsel would welcome the opportunity to respond to any Committee requests for further submissions.) However, there was no opportunity to make this showing before the full House, as is the traditional practice.

Arguably the President's statement of August 5, 1974 (see above) and the transcripts of the three conversations of June 23, 1972, recently released make clear that, in fact, the President did withhold relevant evidence from the Committee, so that a hearing would have been unnecessary. However, we believe the answer is still the same: the merits of the question of compliance must be determined by the full House.

A confession of error by the President does not predetermine the result of a hearing before the House, nor foreclose the possibility that the House would decide the President did not stand in contempt. For one thing, even if the President's withholding of the June 23, 1972 conversations was in contempt of the House, it might have been found that the President had purged himself of contempt by turning over the transcripts on August 5, 1974. Alternatively, the House might have found, as the President's statement of August 5 suggested, that the President had not earlier realized the significance of the June 23 conversations, so that his withholding of them was originally based upon a mistake on his part.

If a Member of the House or Senate believed that the President withheld the tapes or transcripts of the June 23, 1972 conversations from the Judiciary Committee for the purpose of concealing his own involvement in a criminal conspiracy to obstruct justice in the Watergate matter, this would have been relevant to a determination of the President's guilt or innocence under proposed Article I, whether or not the withholding of the materials was technically lawful. As noted above, even an act lawful in itself but directed toward an unlawful end may be proved as an overt act in furtherance of a criminal conspiracy.[16]

It seems somewhat strained to rely upon a trial of the President in the Senate to "arbitrate" the initial dispute between the President and the House as to whether the Presidential response to all Committee subpoenas was satisfactory. Impeachment by the House is a sufficiently important step so that every reasonable effort should have been made to ensure the integrity and accuracy of the result reached in the House. Due process cannot be held in abeyance until Senate proceedings commence.

2. Judicial Determination.—Some of us * believe that the Committee failed to pursue the most obvious means of securing an adjudication of its entitlement to the subpoenaed materials, namely, the institution of a court action seeking a declaration of the validity of our subpoenas and an order to compel compliance with them.

Congress can authorize judicial enforcement of its subpoenas through appropriate legislation, and there is recent precedent for

---

[16] *Braverman v. United States*, 317 U.S. 49, 53 (1942).
* Subsection 2, "Judicial Determination," sets out the views of Messrs. Smith, Railsback, Dennis, Mayne, Froehlich, Moorhead, Maraziti, Latta and Flowers; the remaining undersigned Members do not necesarily concur in the opinions expressed in this subsection.

taking such a step. On October 17, 1973, Chief Judge John J. Sirica dismissed a suit brought against the President in the United States District Court for the District of Columbia by the Senate Select Committee on Presidential Campaign Activities to enforce that Committee's subpoenas for certain tape recordings then in the possession of the President, on the grounds that the court could find no jurisdictional statute supporting the action. Judge Sirica stated in his opinion:

The Court has here been requested to invoke a jurisdiction which only Congress can grant but which Congress has heretofore withheld. *Senate Select Committee v. Nixon*, 366 F. Supp. 51 (D.C. D.C. 1973)

While the case was pending on appeal, Congress enacted S. 2641 (Pub. Law 93-160), conferring jurisdiction upon the United States District Court for the District of Columbia to entertain the committee's suit. S. 2641 was passed by the Senate by unanimous consent shortly after Judge Sirica's dismissal of the Senate Select Committee's suit. On November 13, 1973, Senator Sam Ervin wrote to Chairman Rodino requesting expedited consideration of S. 2641 by this Committee. This request was granted, and the bill was passed by the full House less than three weeks later.

Now pending before the Committee is H.R. 13708, a bill similar in purpose and effect to S. 2641. Under this proposed legislation, the Committee would have authority to prosecute such civil actions as it might deem necessary to secure a declaration of the validity of its subpoenas to the President, or to seek judicial enforcement of them. H.R. 13708 also provides for expediting such proceedings in the courts.

It is plain that the Constitution does not expressly state whether the Congress has an absolute right to demand information of the President or the President has an absolute discretion to refuse to supply such information. Essentially this is a dispute about the scope of intersecting powers. In Federalist No. 49, Madison said: "One branch cannot finally decide the reach of its own power when the result is to curtail that claimed by another. Neither of the two departments can pretend to an exclusive or superior right of settling the boundaries between their respective powers."

In *Marbury v. Madison*, 5 U.S. (1 Cranch) 137 (1803), at 177, the Supreme Court stated that "It is emphatically the province and duty of the judicial department to say what the law is." Moreover, the Supreme Court proceeds from the premise that it has the authority to interpret claims with respect to powers alleged to derive from powers enumerated in the Constitution.[17]

In late May, 1974, the Committee voted 32 to 6 not to seek the assistance of the Federal judiciary in enforcing its subpoenas.

We recognize that most of our colleagues who joined with us in opposing the adoption of Article III also opposed the Committee's seeking judicial assistance in enforcing our subpoenas.

Whatever may have been his true motives, in withholding any portion of the materials sought by the Committee, we do not believe that this or any President should be impeached for acts based on his colorable claim of important Constitutional rights, absent a prior judicial determination that such claim was ill-founded. Where, as here, the

---

[17] *United States v. Nixon*, (U.S.S.Ct., July 24, 1974), printed in ("Criminal Cases," 180.)

situation seemed literally to cry out for an arbiter, we believe that the Committee should have sought an early resolution of the Controversy by invoking the aid of the Federal judiciary, the branch of government which tradition and the Constitution have deemed the best suited to undertake the arbiter's role.

We recognize that some of our colleagues who joined with us in opposing the adoption of Article III also sided with the majority on May 30, 1974 when the Committee voted 32 to 6 not to seek the aid of the Federal judiciary in enforcing our subpoenas to the President. The issue before us now is different from that which confronted the Committee in May, however, for some Members then felt that it was already too late to begin the process of enacting necessary legislation and instituting litigation with any reasonable prospect of reaching a final adjudication of the matter in time for the Committee to conclude its inquiry with the dispatch that the people of the Nation had every right to demand of us.

Frankly, we presume that the President would have complied with any final judicial decree that he must honor our subpoenas, just as he had complied whenever the courts ordered him to surrender evidence subpoenaed by the Special Prosecutor, however damaging that evidence proved to be. If a favorable court ruling had been obtained early enough to produce additional evidence for the Committee's impeachment inquiry that was not otherwise available, then obviously the public interest in knowing the truth of the allegations being investigated by the Committee would have been better served.

On the other hand—and we consider this to be of vital importance—had the President chosen to disobey a final court order for the production of materials subpoenaed by this Committee, he would have thereby become liable to citation for contempt of court, itself a punishable offense. We are satisfied that any wilful disobedience of lawful judicial process which was duly adjudicated to be a contempt of the court would also have constituted an impeachable offense.

B. *Privileges to Withhold Information*

Despite the public interest in Congress securing of necessary information, sometimes our law recognizes a countervailing public interest in permitting a person who is subpoenaed to withhold information. For example, the Fifth Amendment privilege against self-incrimination has been held applicable in an impeachment inquiry.[18] Similarly, the privilege for confidential communications between attorney and client has been recognized and honored as a matter of policy by

---

[18] In 1879, impeachment proceedings were brought against George Seward, Consul-General and Minister of the United States in China during the administration of President Hayes. The report of the House Judiciary Committee in that case stated:

"The Committee procured a subpoena . . . Mr. Seward appeared in obedience to the subpoena, but declined to be sworn as a witness in a case where crime was alleged against him, and where articles of impeachment might be found against him, claiming, through his counsel, his constitutional privilege of not being obliged to produce evidence in a criminal case tending to criminate himself.

". . . If these books of Mr. Seward's are his private books . . . or whether they contain records of his action as a public officer intermixed or otherwise with his private transactions, it is believed he cannot be compelled to produce them."
H.R. Rep. No. 141, 45th Cong., 3d Sess. (1879).

Dean Wigmore also states that the Fifth Amendment is applicable in impeachment proceedings. 8 Wigmore, *Evidence* (McNaughton rev., 1961) § 2257, p. 357, citing *United States v. Collins*, 25 Fed. Cas. 545, 549 (No. 14, 837) (C.C.S.C. Ga. 1873); *Thruston v. Clark*, 107 Cal. 285, 40 P. 435 (1895); *Daugherty v. Nagel*, 28 Idaho 302, 154 P. 375 (1915); *Nye v. Daniels*, 75 Vt. 81, 53 Atl. 150 (1902).

committees of Congress in both legislative and impeachment investigations.[19]

Presidential privilege

In the present case, the President claimed a privilege to withhold information based upon the need to maintain confidentiality between the President and his advisers, so as to promote the candid exchange of advice and views among them and ensure efficient and fully-informed decision-making at the Presidential level. The President argued that, despite a felt Congressional need for access to his conversations to support and assist a Congressional decision, it is essential that a President be able to maintain the privacy of those conversations, when he deems it essential, in order to preserve the unfettered character of his conversations with his aides, and hence the integrity of all the decisions which he makes as head of the co-equal Executive branch. Conversely, the Committee asserted the directly contrary proposition "that the sole power of impeachment" vests with it the sole authority to determine which documents shall be produced and which withheld. The result is a direct Constitutional clash.

In its recent decision in *United States* v. *Nixon*, holding that a Presidential claim of privilege did not, in the circumstances of that case, prevail over the Special Prosecutor's need for materials subpoenaed for criminal trials,[20] the Supreme Court of the United States nevertheless recognized "the valid need for protection of communications between high government officials and those who advise and assist them in the performance of their manifold duties," and stated that "the importance of this confidentiality is too plain to require further discussion." [21]

The Court's opinion also stated:

> Human experience teaches that those who expect public dissemination of their remarks may well temper candor with a concern for appearances and for their own interests to the detriment of the decision-making process. . . . The privilege can be said to derive from the supremacy of each branch within its own assigned area of constitutional duties. ('Statement of Information, Appendix II,' p. 181.)
>
> The expectation of a President as to the confidentiality of his conversations and correspondence, like the claim of confidentiality of judicial deliberations, for example, has all the values to which we accord deference for the privacy of all citizens and added to those values the necessity for protection of the public interest in candid, objective, and even blunt or harsh opinions in presidential decision-making. A President and those who assist him must be free to explore alternatives in the process of shaping policies and making decision and to do so in a way many would be unwilling to express except privately. These are the considerations justifying a presumptive privilege for presidential communications. The privilege is fundamental to the operation of government and in-

---

[19] Impeachment inquiries: see *Proceedings of the House of Representatives* in the following impeachment investigations: Marshall, pp. 687, 688, 693 ("The Committee will enforce the rule, as long as counsel raises the question of privilege. Even if the counsel were disposed to testify about a privileged matter, the Committee would not permit him to do so.")

During the course of this Inquiry, the Committee chose to respect a claim of attorney-client privilege asserted on behalf of E. Howard Hunt by his former attorney, William O. Bittman. On the other hand, a claim asserted by John N. Mitchell with respect to proposed testimony by Paul L. O'Brien, counsel to the Committee for the Re-election of the President when Mr. Mitchell was its Director, was not honored by this Committee during our hearings, for reasons which do not clearly appear from the record. See O'Brien testimony, 1, HJC 129–34.

[20] The Court stated, "We are not here concerned with the balance between . . . the confidentiality interest and Congressional demands for information." "Criminal Cases," 188, fn 19.

[21] "Criminal Cases," 181

extricably rooted in the separation of powers under the Constitution. ("Criminal Cases," 184.)

... [A] President's communications and activities encompass a vastly wider range of sensitive material than would be true of any 'ordinary individual.' It is therefore necessary in the public interest to afford presidential confidentiality the greatest protection consistent with the fair administration of justice. The need for confidentiality even as to idle conversations with associates in which casual reference might be made concerning political leaders within the country or foreign statesmen is to obvious to call for further treatment. ("Criminal Cases," 191.)

It has been contended by some that there can never be a valid claim of privilege by a President in an impeachment inquiry, because impeachment is an exception to the separation of powers.[22] We believe, however, that the values referred to in the Supreme Court's opinion, quoted above, compel the rejection of a flat "no-privilege" rule for impeachment inquiries.

The fact that the power of "impeachment" is an exception to the separation of powers does not answer the question of how far the exception was meant to extend, and how far the impeachment power was meant to cut across Presidential powers (other than the underlying "power" to remain in office.) For example, in cases of impeachment the President loses his pardoning power—but the Framers thought it necessary to spell this out in the Constitution. (Article II, Section 2, clause 1) It seems highly plausible that the "exception" represented by the impeachment clause is limited to Congress' power to bring the President to trial in the Senate and to remove him from office if he is convicted, and that it does not extend to requiring him to spread his records before the Congress as a condition of his remaining in office.

It may also be argued that the public interest in maintaining the confidentiality of the Presidential decision-making process, when the President deems it necessary to do so, supports a privilege independently of the separation of powers. Counsel to the President argued that the need for confidentiality is both broader and deeper than the Constitutional separation of the three branches. For those who hold this view, it may make little difference that the impeachment power represents an exception to the doctrine of separation of powers.

Some have urged that an incumbent President should obviously have no privilege in a proceeding designed to test his incumbency. It should be pointed out, though, that the President consistently bottomed his argument not upon his interest in the privacy of his own conversations, but upon the undesirability of a no-privilege rule which would apply to all Presidents, present and future. His argument, in other words, did not rest upon the fact of his incumbency, but upon the requirements of the Presidential decision-making process.

---

[22] It is probably for this reason that many past Presidents have stated that their power to withhold information from Congress would cease to apply in an impeachment proceeding. The statement of President Polk, that in an impeachment situation the House's power of inquiry "would penetrate into the most secret recesses of the Executive Departments," is perhaps the best known. It should be noted, however, that these statements by past Presidents arose in the context of Congressional investigations which were *not* impeachment inquiries. Often they represented a harmless nod in the direction of Congress' inquisitorial power, in the context of a Presidential refusal to turn over documents. It may therefore seem less appropriate to view these statements as settling the "law" of Presidential privilege in an impeachment situation. The limit of Congress' subpoena power was not an issue in the only prior Presidential impeachment investigations, those involving Andrew Johnson in 1867 and 1868.

It is also asserted by some that the power of impeachment would be rendered completely nugatory if it did not include the power to compel the production of documents. (The power to compel the testimony of witnesses is not at issue, since the President waived Executive privilege as to the testimony of all White House personnel and offered to be interviewed and answer interrogatories under oath.)[23] The power of impeachment plainly was not rendered nugatory in the present case, however, even if its exercise was little assisted by the President, since the majority of the Committee believed it had already secured sufficient information to warrant a recommendation of impeachment of the President, even before his submission of additional edited transcripts on August 5, 1974.

The President never suggested that the Committee and the House could do nothing more than vote on the impeachment proposal. He denied not the power of Congress to conduct an inquiry, which this Committee has done in any event, but its power to compel production of Presidential documents as against a Presidential assertion that their production would not be in the public interest.

Finally, a flat no-privilege rule for impeachment investigations would almost necessarily foster unfortunate developments. The President raised the possibility, in his letter of June 9, 1974, that such a rule "would be an open invitation to future Congresses to use an impeachment inquiry, however frivolously, as a device to assert their own supremacy over the Executive, and to reduce Executive confidentiality to a nullity." (10 Presidential Documents, 592–93) While the mere possibility of abuse of a power of inquiry is no conclusive argument against its exitence,[24] we are not concerned here with the existence of a power of inquiry but with the existence of a *limit* to that power. It "will not do to say that the argument is drawn from extremes. Constitutional provisions are based on the possibilities of extremes."[25]

The occasion for misuse of the impeachment power by unduly encroaching upon Executive confidentiality is not the greatest potential abuse which can be foreseen. An even more disturbing possibility would be the removal of a President for no other grievance than his refusal to comply with an impeachment committee's subpoena.[26]

Did the President's overall response to the inquiry demands for information *standing alone*, warrant his impeachment?—that is the question which Article III would have posed for the House.

Relations between Congressional investigating committees and the Executive have not always been so tranquil in our history as to indicate that the possibility of abuse of an "automatic impeachment" rule is fanciful.[27] One might well pause before encouraging a bare major-

---

[23] The argument sometimes advanced that in waiving his privilege with respect to testimony, the President should be deemed to have waived it with respect to other forms of evidence of "related" Presidential conversations, appears not to have been taken as a serious point by the tribunals which have adjudicated the various demands for production of the White House tapes, for the question has been raised and briefed.
[24] *McGrain v. Daugherty*, 273 U.S. 135, 175 (1927).
[25] *General Oil Co. v. Crain*, 209 U.S. 211, 226–27 (1908).
[26] It should be borne in mind that the question whether a refusal to comply with a subpoena in itself constitutes an impeachable offense is distinct from the question whether a refusal to produce evidence can give rise to an "adverse inference" regarding other, independent substantive charges.
[27] The relations between President Lincoln and the Committee on the Conduct of the War come to mind.
It has been suggested that the operation of Presidential privilege may be more limited during a trial in the Senate, when the issues have been narrowed, than during the initial stages of an inquiry by a House Committee, whose investigation will of necessity be more broad-ranging than that of the Senate. C. Black, *Impeachment: A Handbook* (1974) 22.

ity of any committee looking into a civil officer's performance to recommend that he stand trial for his office because it was not fully satisfied with the completeness of the information he produced. Yet if the rule is laid down that, as a matter of Constitutional law, a President can under no circumstances enjoy any privilege to withhold documents or testimony from a duly designated impeachment committee which considers such evidence "necessary" to the conduct of an impeachment inquiry, then the mere attempt to exert such a privilege would afford sufficient grounds for his removal—a sort of default judgment, in the most grave proceeding contemplated by our Constitution. Such a rule would severely and excessively weaken the office of the Presidency. Adherence to such a proposition reflects a dangerous rigidity in Constitutional interpretation seldom contemplated by the Framers.

SUBSTANTIAL COMPLIANCE

Much was made of the inadequacy of the White House edited transcripts as a substitute for the original tapes and other materials subpoenaed. It may be noted, however, that on October 18, 1973, Special Prosecutor Archibald Cox, in commenting upon a proposal by the Attorney General, stated that for the purposes of his and the grand jury's investigation he would be satisfied with transcripts of tapes of Presidential conversations, prepared without the participation of the Special Prosecutor's office, omitting national security material and material not pertinent, and paraphrasing material embarrassing to the President, if certain conditions were observed to guarantee the integrity and accuracy of the transcripts, including court appointment of Special Masters to undertake the work. (Book IX, 774)

It should also be noted that the Committee did not accept the offer of the President to have the Chairman and Ranking Minority Member of the Committee verify the accuracy of the transcripts submitted by the President to the Committee.

The Committee published a comparison of the White House edited transcripts with the transcripts prepared by the Inquiry staff. The "Materials Respecting Proposed Article III" submitted by the staff to the Members of the Committee before the vote on Article III was taken included a section entitled "Comparison: HJC Transcripts with White House Transcripts," containing 10 instances in which the Committee transcript and the White House transcript of the same conversation differ and the White House transcript appeared to omit matter unfavorable to the President, or to state it differently. These examples, however, were selected from hundreds of instances in which the Committee transcripts and the White House transcripts varied. Furthermore, the Committee transcripts represent the product of several months' continuous work by members of the Inquiry staff. Even so, members of the Committee who listened to the Committee's tapes during the 10-week initial evidentiary presentation will recall that some transcripts, notably those of March 21, p.m., and March 22, 1973, appeared to contain inaccuracies and misattributions when they were first heard by the Committee Members. Eventually, entirely new transcripts of these conversations were prepared by the Inquiry staff, in some cases many pages longer than the transcripts first prepared by the staff. Inquiry staff personnel have estimated unofficially that they listened to each minute of taped conversation at least sixty times in attempting to verify the words spoken.

The circumstances under which the White House transcripts were prepared, by way of contrast, are not known. Absent an awareness of the personnel and staff resources available to prepare the White House transcripts which were released on April 30, 1974, it may be an error to attribute the great number of omissions, apparent misattributions of statements, careless punctuation and the like, to any willful effort to obscure the meaning of the tapes. A more likely explanation seems to be the White House staff simply did not spend as much time in preparing its transcripts as the Inquiry staff did in preparing our own.

CONCLUSION

The adoption of proposed Article III by the full House would have set an unwise and potentially mischievous precedent. No President should be impeached for failing to comply with subpoenas issued by an impeachment inquiry Committee for materials which were subject to a colorable claim of Executive or other privilege, unless his noncompliance amounted to contempt of the House, adjudicated in the customary manner, after notice and opportunity for him to appear personally or by counsel before the House and show cause why his failure to comply was not contemptuous.

To those Members who may believe that in this case the claim of Executive privilege was asserted by the President in bad faith, at least as to some materials, we would reiterate our view that this alone should not have deprived the President of an opportunity to make his defense before the full House, like any putative contemnor. Even so, the House would not have been without recourse, inasmuch as a willful refusal to furnish relevant subpoenaed material based on a bad faith claim of privilege, if proved or admitted, would have been relevant to the obstruction of justice charge contained in Article I. It is in that context that we believe the President's response to the Committee's subpoenas should have been examined.

We, the undersigned Members of the Committee on the Judiciary, hereby subscribe to the "Minority Views" respecting Articles I, II and III of the proposed Bill of Impeachment ordered reported to the House on July 30, 1974, which views, together with a "Preliminary Statement," are to be filed with the Committee Report on said Bill of Impeachment:

EDWARD HUTCHINSON.
HENRY P. SMITH, III.
CHARLES W. SANDMAN, Jr.
CHARLES E. WIGGINS.
DAVID W. DENNIS.
WILEY MAYNE.
TRENT LOTT.
CARLOS J. MOORHEAD.
JOSEPH MARAZITI.
DELBERT L. LATTA.

I concur in the views of the minority with respect to Articles I and III but not Article II.

WILEY MAYNE.

We, the undersigned Members of the Committee on the Judiciary, hereby subscribe to the "Minority Views" respecting Article III of the proposed Bill of Impeachment ordered reported to the House on July 30, 1974, which views are to be filed with the Committee Report on said Bill of Impeachment:

TOM RAILSBACK.
WALTER FLOWERS.
M. CALDWELL BUTLER.
HAROLD V. FROEHLICH.

INDIVIDUAL VIEWS OF MR. HUTCHINSON

I joined in the minority report of the ten Members of the Judiciary Committee who voted against all articles of impeachment and I subscribe to that report. I set forth here those considerations, persuasive to me, which led me to oppose impeachment of the President in the Committee and the subsequent developments which brought me to a decision that a case for impeachment had been made on one count.

GENERAL

Impeachment of a President is a drastic remedy and should be resorted to only in cases where the offenses committed by him are so grave as to make his continuance in office intolerable. Unlike criminal jurisprudence, where the sentencing judge has large discretion as to the punishment to be inflicted, the conviction of an impeached President removes him from office, nothing less. The charges against him should be so serious as to fit removal. The three articles of impeachment, when measured against this standard, fall short in all but a single count in my opinion.

I reject the proposition that the impeachment function of the House is nothing more than the indictment function of a grand jury, and that a Member who votes to impeach is merely sending the case to the Senate for trial. When the House votes a bill of impeachment, the House has the burden of proving its case. It becomes the prosecutor before the Senate. It represents that it believes the President is guilty of the offenses charged; that it has legally admissible evidence to prove that guilt; and that it believes the President should be removed from office because of those offenses. This is a much greater burden than that of a grand jury which represents only that there is probable cause to believe a particular offense was committed and that the indicted person committed it. The grand jury has no burden to maintain its cause before any court.

In my judgment, a Member who votes to impeach is recommending to the Senate the removal of the President from office, nothing less. In order to warrant such drastic action, the offenses charged should be serious and grievous violations by the President of his Constitutional duties. They should be described in the articles of impeachment with the particularity required in criminal law. The evidence supportive of each overt act charged should be proof of guilt beyond a reasonable doubt. The lowliest person in the land, charged with wrong-doing, is accorded no less.

If the strict standards of criminal jurisprudence are not required in cases of Presidential impeachment, the issue falls away from the high plane of law and becomes political. In a divided government, with the Congress in control by one political party and the President of another, impeachment becomes a threatening political tool, if one group of politicians can decide over another what is an abuse of power.

In weighing the evidence, if an inference or conclusion favorable to the President can be drawn as well as an inference or conclusion unfavorable to him, I believe the President should be given the benefit of the doubt.

In my judgment, not any of the three articles of impeachment are drawn with the particularity which is required to give the House information of the precise offenses charged and the overt acts claimed to be supportive of them; nor to give the President the notice which constitutional process accorded him, had he chosen to defend against those charges in the Senate.

ARTICLE I

The first article charges the President with conspiracy to obstruct justice: in the words of the article, that the President "engaged personally and through his close subordinates and agents in a course of conduct or plan designed to delay, impede and obstruct the investigation of (the Watergate break-in); to cover up, conceal and protect those responsible; and to conceal the existence and scope of other unlawful covert activities."

Until the August 5th release of conversations held between the President and Mr. Haldeman on June 23, 1972, there was no direct evidence of complicity by the President in the cover-up. The President said he knew nothing about any cover-up until his conversations with John Dean in mid-March, 1973; there was no direct evidence to the contrary and he was entitled to the benefit of the doubt.

It is now evident that the President knew as early as June 23, 1972, six days following the Watergate break-in, of a plan to obstruct the FBI investigation into that event, and that he authorized the plan. Here are the words spoken:

HALDEMAN. Now, on the investigation, you know the Democratic break-in thing, we're back in the problem area because the FBI is not under control, because Gray doesn't exactly know how to control it and they have—their investigation is now leading into some productive areas—because they've been able to trace the money—not through the money itself—but through the bank sources—the banker. And it goes in some directions we don't want it to go. Also there have been some things—like an informant came in off the street to the FBI in Miami who was a photographer or has a friend who is a photographer who developed some films through this guy Barker and the films had pictures of Democratic National Committee letter head documents and things. So it's things like that that are filtering in. Mitchell came up with yesterday, and John Dean analysed very carefully last night and concludes, concurs now with Mitchell's recommendation that the only way to solve this, and we're set up beautifully to do it . . . is for us to have Walters call Pat Gray and just say, "Stay to hell out of this—this is business we don't want you to go any further on it." That's not an unusual development, and that would take care of it.

PRESIDENT. What about Pat Gray—you mean Pat Gray doesn't want to?

HALDEMAN. Pat does want to. He doesn't know how to, and he doesn't have any basis for doing it. Given this, he will have the basis. He'll call Mark Felt in and the two of them—and Mark Felt wants to cooperate because he's ambitious—he'll call him in and say, "We've got the signal foam across the river to put the hold on this" and that will fit rather well because the FBI agents who are working on the case, at this point feel that's what it is.

PRESIDENT. This is CIA? They've traced the money? Who'd they trace it to?

HALDEMAN. Well, they've traced it to a name, but they haven't gotten to the guy yet.

PRESIDENT. Would it be somebody here?
HALDEMAN. Ken Dahlberg.
PRESIDENT. Who the hell is Ken Dahlberg?
HALDEMAN. He gave $25,000 in Minnesota and the check went directly to this guy Barker.
PRESIDENT. It isn't from the Committee though, from Stans?
HALDEMAN. Yeah, it is. It's directly traceable and there's some more through some Texas people that went to the Mexican bank—which can be traced to the Mexican bank—they'll get their names today.
PRESIDENT. Well, I mean, there's no way—I'm just thinking if they don't cooperate what do they say? That they were approached by the Cubans. That's what Dahlberg has to say, the Texans too, that they——
HALDEMAN. Well, if they will. But then we're relying on more and more people all the time. That's the problem and they'll stop it if we take this other route.
PRESIDENT. All right.
HALDEMAN. And you seem to think the thing to do is to get them to stop?
PRESIDENT. Right. Fine.

The Watergate burglary occurred in the early hours of Saturday, June 17, 1972. The Committee to Re-elect the President was already organized and functioning. By the time the pieces of the Watergate event were put together the Democrats had nominated their candidates. If in July President Nixon had disclosed the excesses of the Committee to Re-elect and denounced their foolhardy and illegal performance, that's all there ever would have been to Watergate. Those who broke the law would have been punished in the Courts.

Even the evidence set forth above would not have greatly disturbed the Congress or the country had it been disclosed in the spring of 1973. The damage was done by the apparent policy of the President to withhold until he finally was forced to yield information which because of the timing of disclosure put him in the worst possible light.

But without the evidence of the June 23, 1972, conversation I was prepared to defend the President against the charge of obstructing justice on the basis that he had no knowledge of it until March 1973. At that time he moved to purge his administration of those involved in the conspiracy and had accomplished that by April 30. Until the disclosures of August 5, 1974, which set forth the June 23, 1972, conversations, proponents for impeachment pinned their case for complicity of the President in the cover-up largely on eight taped conversations between the President and John Dean et al, running from September 15, 1972, to April 16, 1973. The Committee published these conversations in a separate volume entitled *Transcripts of Eight Recorded Presidential Conversations.*

If one assumed that the President had knowledge of the conspiracy and was directing it, these conversations are damaging indeed to his claim of innocence. But if one assumed he didn't know, as he said he didn't, these conversations are filled with statements of supportive of his cause. And without the evidence on the June 23, 1972, conversations I felt justified in making the assumption that he didn't know, giving him the benefit of doubt.

Through all of these conversations, the President's position was that there should be no withholding from a grand jury. He urged everyone in his administration who was implicated to testify freely and truthfully. He waived the doctrine of Executive privilege and even the attorney-client relation, before a grand jury.

In fact, it is clear that when the implications of the whole mess were laid out to him on March 21, 1973, he proposed that it all be presented to a grand jury. This would not be the position of a man engaged in a plan to obstruct justice. That he was dissuaded from that immediate course by his advisors, who were so engaged would not make him part of the conspiracy himself.

The President's position regarding the Senate Watergate Committee was different. He viewed that legislative investigating committee for what it was, a political attack against him and his administration. Resistance to the demands of the Senate committee was not an obstruction of justice, since that committee was no part of the system of justice. Its legitimate function was to inquire into the need for changes in statute law. The timing of its investigation, publicly exposing the scandal at the same time the grand jury was inquiring under the strictures of secrecy, probably delayed the work of the grand jury, and in the opinion of many people, constituted a political intrusion into an arena which should have been left to law enforcement agencies and the courts. The President may have viewed the Senate committee as a political move to embarrass him and his administration, and he reacted to it politically. Certainly his initial assertion of executive privilege, and his discussions with his aides as to how to deal with the Senate committee are not relevant to an obstruction of justice charge. Such discussions were had with a view to public relations and political response, not at all with a view to law enforcement and the administration of justice. Those conversations should be considered in that light.

The taped conversations clearly exhibit the President's instructions to his subordinates to talk freely with the prosecutors and to tell the truth, and to appear willingly before the grand jury.

In the face of his personal policy of cooperation with law enforcement agencies, and his expressions to his subordinates that they do likewise, why did the President resist delivery of taped conversations to the Special Prosecutor, even until the Supreme Court directed his compliance? Drawing an inference in the President's favor, perhaps he did not think of a taped conversation as essential evidence of that conversation, since the parties to them were available as witnesses. At the time of the conversations, most of the parties to them were unaware they were being recorded and they might not have spoken exactly as they did had they been so aware. Perhaps the President was concerned about the possible constitutional rights of those participants. Obviously, the taping system was not installed for evidentiary purposes, but for historical purposes, to enable the President to refresh his memory in writing his memoirs. Since the witnesses were available for questioning, the President did not think of the tapes as evidence; he thought of them as his personal papers. And since he never thought of himself as a party in any wrong-doing, his personal papers, in his view, were not properly to be brought into question.

But even more importantly, the President felt that he was constitutionally bound to defend the doctrine of executive privilege, a doctrine as old as the Presidency itself. All of his predecessors had stubbornly defended their office against the intrusion of either the

Congress or the Courts. The doctrine of executive privilege runs back to the administration of George Washington. It is based on the principle of the separation of powers between three co-equal branches of government; legislative, executive, and judicial. Just as this House asserts its privileges and will not answer the subpoena of any court without its consent, and would tolerate no order of any President directing any action by the House, so the President asserts the privileges of his office under the same constitutional right.

His reluctance in surrendering tapes must be viewed as an assertion by the President of constitutional privileges as against the other co-equal branches of government. It is based upon a claim of constitutional duty to preserve the character of his office in a struggle to keep that office co-equal. It cannot fairly be evidentiary of any attempt to obstruct justice, and no inferences of wrong-doing by the President can properly be drawn from that reluctance.

The conversation in the morning of March 21, 1973, must be commented upon under this article of impeachment. At that time Dean revealed to the President the full extent of the mess his subordinates had gotten themselves into. They had even stooped to yielding to Hunt's blackmail. During that conversation, the President fell into his practice of examining all of the options. The majority staff of the impeachment inquiry apparently concluded that the President came to two resolutions: That in the long run Hunt's demands were wrong and intolerable, but that Hunt's immediate demand for $120,000 must be met. The grand jury named the President an unindicted co-conspirator on the theory that following this conversation Haldeman called Mitchell at the President's suggestion, that Mitchell called LaRue, and that LaRue caused $75,000 to be delivered to Hunt's lawyer, Bittman, before that day was out.

But Dean says he talked with LaRue on that morning before he saw the President and LaRue corroborates this. Their conversation was that LaRue told Dean of Hunt's demands and that Dean said he was out of the money business. When LaRue asked what to do, Dean suggested that LaRue might call Mitchell. LaRue did call Mitchell in New York but told Mitchell only about the $75,000 Hunt needed for lawyer's fees, not about an additional $60,000 Hunt was demanding for family support during his incarceration. Mitchell apparently said that if it were for attorney's fees, he would probably pay it if he were LaRue, and LaRue did so.

The President had no input into the matter, and knew nothing about the payment until mid-April. So the hush money charge against the President has been demolished by the facts and the testimony of Mitchell and LaRue before the Committee.

There remains the question whether the evidence making the President part of a conspiracy to obstruct justice rises to the magnitude of an impeachable offense. In my opinion, standing by itself, it probably would not have provoked the House to exercise its impeachment powers. The timing of the disclosure, which for the first time tied the President to the conspiracy, was his undoing. Those who had been defending the President were left without a defense and without time to build a new defense. Under the circumstances impeachment became a certainty and resignation the only viable alternative.

ARTICLE II

This article accuses the President of abusing the powers of his office, in that he "has repeatedly engaged in conduct violating the constitutional rights of citizens, impairing the due and proper administration of justice and the conduct of lawful inquiries, or contravening the laws governing agencies in the Executive branch." During the inquiry this area was called agency practices. It was apparent that Watergate and its aftermath had been the events which provoked the inquiry, especially the dismissal of Special Prosecutor Archibald Cox by the Acting Attorney General at the orders of the President, and the searching for occasional excesses in the attempt to exercise power by the White House over the agencies of government was at the outset a mere adjunct. Yet, this article gained the largest affirmative vote of the three articles reported by the Judiciary Committee. In my opinion, Article II is as weak a basis for removing a President from office as is Article III.

Article II is a catch-all. Culling from tens of thousands of transactions between the White House and the agencies of the Executive branch a few isolated instances of conceived pressure described as abuses of power, and with no evidence of the President's personal involvement, the proponents allege repeated engagement, that is time after time, by the White House in such a course of action.

Would you remove a President from office because one of his subordinates asked for some income tax audits, which requests were denied out of hand by the Commissioner of Internal Revenue whom the President had appointed? Would you remove a President because on a single occasion another of his subordinates did succeed in obtaining income tax information on a political candidate's brother, which information was leaked to a newspaper columnist? Would you remove a President because some wiretaps were installed in the name of national security, at a time when such installations were clearly legal, and there were serious leaks in the confidentiality of negotiations with foreign nations?

Article II next charges that the President should be removed from office because the so-called plumbers unit was set up in the White House. How many times have modern Presidents set up operating units within the White House? If Congress thinks they ought not to do so, then Congress should forbid it by law, not impeach a President who does so with a great number of precedents behind him. But perhaps the evil here is not the creation of the unit, but rather the secret creation of an investigative unit. Was not the CIA secretly organized by another administration? And even today can a Member of Congress find out what that agency is doing or how it is funded, or what its budget is? A Member cannot. There is no evidence the President ever armed the plumbers with any pretended power to operate outside the law, and if the plumbers did that on one or more occasions, those guilty of breaking the laws should be held accountable, as they are, and not the President.

In considering this abuse of power article, whether it be the IRS, the FBI, the CIA or the Justice Department or any other agency of the government which might have been asked by the subordinates of the President for special action in the name of the President, the House should be reminded of what has gone on in other administrations. The House is entitled to a standard by which to measure this administration. In the absence of proof, I believe the public generally believes that most administrations have been about alike, and that this one is no different. If the inquiry had researched prior administrations it is a fair assumpton such research would have turned upon several so-called abuses of power, perhaps as many on the average as are now alleged. That is why, in my judgment, it is manifestly unfair to attack the present President for these things.

Early in this impeachment inquiry the minority requested that a qualified individual be employed to undertake the research of how prior administrations dealt with agencies of government. But we were denied our request. We are thus without a standard of past performance to measure this one, and the abuse of power charge is therefore not fairly sustainable.

The proponents for impeachment rely on the conversation of September 15, 1972, to connect the President with the use of some agencies for political purposes. It must be remembered that the September 15 conversation was the mere talk, without action, of partisans in a political campaign. How many times in their experience have not Members talked to their campaign directors about the opposition? There is absolutely no evidence that anything ever came of any of the mere talk at that September 15 meeting.

Paragraph (4) of Article II alleges that the President has "failed to take care that the laws were faithfully executed" because of the unlawful activity carried on by his close subordinates, when he "had reason to know" of such activities.

The President's duty to take care that the laws be faithfully executed does not impose a liability upon him for the misdeeds of others, but to discharge them. Unquestionably, when serious charges were brought to his attention, he should be permitted a reasonable time in which to satisfy himself of the probability of the truth of them, and in this case the period of examination ran for about six weeks, during which he worked with the Criminal Division of the Department of Justice, and delayed the discharge of Dean at the request of the chief of the Criminal Division. This cannot be fairly said to amount to failure of his constitutional duty.

ARTICLE III

The idea that a President should be removed from office because he does not comply with a subpoena of a committee of the House, even if the precedent be limited to impeachment cases, is frightening. The committee issues its subpoena under the constitutional power of the House to impeach. The President refuses to comply with a subpoena because the constitutional separation of powers demands of him that he maintain the office of President as a co-equal with the House; that to yield to its mandate would make the office of President subservient to the House. How can the House determine that the President should be removed from office, when his failure to comply is based on a constitutional principle as strong as the one on which the House relies?

I opposed issuance of subpoenas by the Committee to the President because such subpoenas would be unenforceable; and because I do not believe the House can order presidential action any more than the President can order the House. The President and the House are co-equal in our system. Neither is above or below the other.

I think Article III does not state an impeachable offense.

CONCLUSION

History will deal more kindly with Richard Nixon than did his contemporaries. As the Watergate affair moves into the past it may be seen for what a little thing a President was forced to resign from office when compared with the accomplishments of his administration. A legal case of obstruction of justice was made against him. But instructions by other Presidents have undoubtedly altered the course of other investigations without controversy. The abuses of power charged against the President were probably no greater than have occurred in some other administrations. What to one man seems an abuse of power appears to another to be strong executive discretion. The President should not have been impeached under Article II. And I believe the House would have rejected Article III.

EDWARD HUTCHINSON.

ADDITIONAL VIEWS OF MR. RAILSBACK, JOINED BY MESSRS. SMITH, SANDMAN, DENNIS, MAYNE, BUTLER, FROEHLICH, MOORHEAD, MARAZITI AND LATTA, IN OPPOSITION TO ARTICLE III

Refusal to fully comply with a Congressional subpoena in and of itself without further action on the part of the Congress is not a ground upon which an impeachment can be based. The House has neither exhausted available remedies on this issue nor can the House in this instance be the ultimate judge of the scope of its own power.

Presently, Congress has two methods of enforcing compliance with its subpoenas. First, is its inherent common law authority and second, is its statutory authority under Title 2, United States Code 192–94. Both methods are forms of criminal contempt. Under its common law power, the House may conduct its own trial for contempt of Congress. By a majority vote, the House may find a person in contempt of Congress. A person adjudged in contempt under this procedure may, under an order of the House, be subjected to one of the three enforcement procedures:

(1) containment in close custody by the Sergeant-at-Arms;
(2) commitment to a common jail in the District of Columbia; or
(3) commitment by the Sergeant-at-Arms to the guardroom of the Capitol Police.

Confinement under the common law procedure cannot extend beyond a particular Congress. In recent times the Congress has not chosen to utilize its common law power but has turned to its statutory provisions contained in Title 2, United State Code 192.

Under Title 2, United States Code 194, when a witness refuses to comply with an order of a Committee that fact is reported to the House of Representatives and if the House agrees by a majority vote the Speaker is required to certify to a U.S. Attorney the question of contempt. The U.S. Attorney will present the matter to a grand jury. If the grand jury should return an indictment, then there would have to be a regular criminal trial before a judge and jury. If the individual subpoenaed should be found guilty of the misdemeanor, it is mandatory under 2 United States Code 192 that the defendant be punished by a fine of not more than $1,000 nor less than $100 and that the defendant be imprisoned in a common jail for not more than 12 months nor less than one month.

A third method available to the Congress for enforcing compliance with its subpoenas would be through legislation. On November 9, 1973, the Other Body passed by unanimous consent S. 2641, conferring jurisdiction upon the District Court of the U.S. for the District of Columbia of civil actions brought by the Senate Select Committee to enforce or secure a declaration concerning the validity of any subpoena or order issued by it. Prior to its enactment, on October 17, 1973, an action of the Senate Select Committee to enforce its subpoenas requesting certain tape recordings which were in the possession of the President was dismissed by the U.S. District Court for the District of Columbia because the court found that there was no jurisdictional statute upon which the action could be based. Judge John J. Sirica stated in his opinion,

The Court has here been requested to invoke a jurisdiction which only Congress can grant but which Congress has heretofore withheld. (*Senate Select Committee v. Nixon*, 366 Fed. Supp. 51)

On November 13, Senator Ervin sent a letter to Chairman Rodino requesting that S. 2641 be expedited by the House Judiciary Committee. In less than three weeks following Senator Ervin's letter the House enacted S. 2641. This Act became law December 18, 1973, without the President's signature (P. Law 93-190).

The Senate Select Committee investigating "Watergate" chose not to attempt an adjudication of the matter by resort to a contempt proceeding under Title 2, United States Code 192, or via congressional commonlaw powers which permit the Sergeant-at-Arms to forcibly secure attendance of the offending party. Either method, the Select Committee stated, "would be inappropriate and unseemly" when the offending party is the President.

Pending before the House Judiciary Committee is a bill similar to S. 2641, H.R. 13708. The purpose of H.R. 13708 is to confer upon the U.S. District Court for the District of Columbia jurisdiction over civil actions brought by the House Judiciary Committee to enforce any subpoena or order issued by it for the production of information relevant to the Committee's constitutional inquiry. Under this legislation the House Judiciary Committee would have authority to prosecute such civil actions to enforce or secure a declaration concerning the validity of such subpoenas. The Committee may be represented by such attorneys as it may designate in any action brought under the bill. H.R. 13708 also contains a provision that would expedite such civil proceedings through the courts.

Irving Younger in a study of separation of powers stated that:

We should not forget that the Supreme Court has decided disputes between Congress and the President under its general power to hold the other two departments within the ambit of the Constitution. (20 U. Pitt. L. Rev. 755, 777 N. 100, 1959; Raoul Berger, "Executive Privilege" *Harvard Univ. Press*, 1974, p. 332)

Alexander M. Bickel, an eminent constitutional lawyer, also supported the Committee's use of the Courts to enforce its subpoenas. In his article that appeared in *The New Republic*, June 8, 1974, pp. 11–14, Mr. Bickel wrote that:

There is no way open to Congress other than a lawsuit of actually getting its hands on the evidence it wants. . . . To be sure if it does not go to Court, and does not run the risk of a court's refusal to enforce a subpoena, the House might cite the President for contempt and base a separate Article of impeachment on his refusal to honor the subpoena. But these are gestures. The contempt citation by itself is pure gesture. An additional Article of impeachment based on it is a makeweight. It is difficult to imagine that the House would vote it without also approving other Articles, or that the Senate would convict on it without convicting on other Articles. So what is gained?

The Supreme Court proceeds from the premise that it is the "ultimate interpreter of the Constitution" vested with the responsibility to decide "whether the action of another branch . . . exceeds whatever authority has been committed." (*United States* v. *Nixon*, decided July 24, 1974, Slip Opinion, Page 18: *Powell* v. *McCormack*, 395 U.S. 486 at 521). In *Marbury* v. *Madison*, 5 U.S. (1 Cranch) 137, 177 (1803), the Court stated that "It is emphatically the province and duty of the judicial department to say what the law is."

Whether the Congress has an absolute right to demand information or the President the absolute discretion to refuse such information is plainly not stated in the Constitution. Essentially this is a dispute about the scope of intersection powers. "One branch cannot finally decide the reach of its own power when the result is to curtail that claimed by another. Neither of the two departments, said Madison in Federalist No. 49, 'can pretend to an exclusive or superior right of settling the boundaries between their respective powers. Some arbiter, said Justice Jackson, is almost indispensable when power is . . . balanced between branches, as the legislative and executive . . . Each unit cannot be left to judge the limits of its own power . . .'" (Raoul Berger, "Executive Privilege" *Harvard Univ. Press*, (1974) pp. 330–31).

In late May, 1974, the Judiciary Committee by a vote of 32–6 chose not to seek the assistance of the courts in enforcing compliance with its subpoenas. The Committee also chose not to utilize its common law power or its contempt of Congress power under Title 2, United States Code 192–94. The President does have certain inherent constitutional rights and privileges. What the President's true motives are in withholding information only history may know but this President or any President should not be impeached for acts based on his assertion of certain constitutional rights. The Supreme Court is the ultimate judge of the boundaries of conflicting constitutional powers, not the Congress.

The enactment of Article III would seriously weaken the Presidency. Such enactment would be dangerous, and a pure exercise of raw legislative power. Article III should be rejected by the House of Representatives.

Thomas F. Railsback.
Henry P. Smith III.
Charles W. Sandman, Jr.
David W. Dennis.
Wiley Mayne.
M. Caldwell Butler.
Harold V. Froehlich.
Carlos J. Moorhead.
Joseph J. Maraziti.
Delbert Latta.

ADDITIONAL VIEWS OF MR. DENNIS

I concur generally in the Minority Views which I have signed in company with my colleagues Messrs. Hutchinson, Smith, Sandman, Wiggins, Mayne, Lott, Moorhead, Maraziti, and Latta, and I commend particularly the discussion of the evidence contained in Part C of the Preliminary Statement of those Minority Views. I desire, however, to add some additional observations of my own, which I set out below.

I was one of the ten members of the Committee on the Judiciary who voted in the Committee against all three Articles of Impeachment.

While the revelation—after the Committee vote—of the taped conversation of June 23, 1972 between President Nixon and H.R. Haldeman, and the President's statement on that subject dated August 5, 1974, led me to change my view as to Article I, so that I would have voted for impeachment on that Article had it been put to a vote of the House, it is my view that my nine colleagues and I were correct on the state of the evidence and the record as it stood before the Judiciary Committee at the time of the Committee vote; and I remain of the opinion that we are still correct today in respect to our opposition to Articles II and III.

On July 25, 1974 I stated my views in formal debate in the Judiciary Committee. That statement still reflects, as well as I can do it in a brief compass, my general position as to Articles II and III (taking them in reverse order) and I therefore report here what I then said:

Article III—Failure To Comply With Committee Subpoenas

Turning first to the matter of failure to observe or to comply with the subpoenas of the Committee on the Judiciary:

We have, of course, had a landmark decision of the Supreme Court of the United States just yesterday which decided, for the first time, that a generalized and unlimited executive privilege cannot be exercised to over-ride specific subpoenas issued by a Special Prosecuting Attorney in furtherance of the prosecution of a criminal case.

This decision does not bear directly on nor, as a matter of law, does it enhance the power of this Committee to issue subpoenas in these impeachment proceedings against the President of the United States, because, very unfortunately, as I believe, this Committee has declined and refused to test and to determine its Constitutional powers in the Courts of this country, despite the well-known statement of Chief Justice Marshall in *Marbury* v. *Madison* that "it is emphatically the province and duty of the Judicial Department to say what the law is."

I believe, however, that the power of this Committee in respect to the issuance of subpoenas in impeachment proceedings is at least equal to—and is, in all probability, the superior of—the power of the Special Prosecuting Attorney.

This decision, therefore, although we are not a party to the litigation, and derive no actual rights therefrom, very well may—and in my judgment in all probability will—result in the furnishing to this Committee of additional relevant and highly material evidence which, up to this time, we do not have.

It is my judgment that should it appear that such evidence will be available to us within a reasonably short period of time, then it will become our positive duty to delay a final vote in these important proceedings until we have examined this additional evidence.

In assessing the President's past treatment of the subpoenas of this Committee, however, we have no right whatever to consider yesterday's decision of the United States Supreme Court because, in addition to the fact that we are not a party to the cause, this decision, of course, had not been handed down when our subpoenas were served, or when the President took his stand in respect thereto.

At that point the President simply asserted what he stoutly maintained to be a Constitutional right—and which he is, in fact, still legally free to assert to be a Constitutional right so far as this Committee is concerned; and we, on the contrary, asserted a Constitutional right in opposition to the Presidential claim.

Such a conflict is properly one for resolution by the Courts, and absent a binding and definitive decision between the parties by the Judicial branch, it escapes me on what ground it can properly be asserted that a claim of Constitutional right is, in any sense, an abuse of power.

It will be observed that I noted at that time that the Committee had *not* obtained—nor had it taken the obvious legal steps to obtain—*all the relevent evidence;* that it was probable, due to the decision of the Supreme Court in *United States* v. *Nixon,* that such evidence would shortly be forthcoming; and that I suggested that we should defer our final vote pending that event.

Ten days later that evidence—the tape of June 23, 1972 which made all the difference—was indeed produced.

As to *Article II*, on July 25 I spoke as follows:

Turning to further alleged *abuses of power,* I look to the proposed articles which we have before us.

In proposed Article II these abuses of power are alleged to be:

1. *Illegal Surveillance,* but the 17 wire-taps chiefly complained of under this heading were all instituted before the *Keith* decision, and were not only presumptively legal at that time, but are probably legal in large part also today since many, if not all of them, had international aspects, a situation in which the need for a court order was specifically not passed upon in the *Keith* decision.

2. Use of the executive power to *unlawfully* establish a special investigative unit "—to engage in *unlawful covert activities—*". But it was *not* unlawful, so far as I am advised, to establish the plumbers' unit; and I suggest that proof is lacking that the President intended for it to, or authorized it to, engage in *unlawful* covert activities. In like manner it is certainly not established as a fact that the purpose of the Fielding burglary was "to obtain information to be used by Richard M. Nixon in public defamation of Daniel Ellsberg", nor is there any substantial evidence that the President knew of or authorized this burglary before it took place. In fact when Dean told the President about the Fielding break-in on March 17, 1973, the President said, "What in the world—what in the name of God was Ehrlichman having—in the Ellsberg . . . This is the first I ever heard of this."

3. *Alleged Abuse of the IRS.* Without going into detail I suggest that the evidence here—so far as the President is concerned—is one of talk only, and not of action; that the independent attempted actions of Dean, Haldeman, and Ehrlichman were unsuccessful and ineffective; and that the only direct evidence of an alleged Presidential order (in the Wallace case) is a hearsay statement of Clark Mollenhoff that Mr. Haldeman *said* to him that the President requested him to obtain a report—which is, of course, not competent proof of anything.

Other allegations of alleged misuse and abuse of the FBI and the CIA can, in the interests of time, be best considered under the heading of alleged obstruction of justice; and the matter of refusing to honor Judiciary Committee subpoenas has already been discussed.

I will add that I consider it improper to seek to multiply offenses by making the identical acts regarding the CIA and the FBI which establish the case under Article I, serve also as the basis for a separate offense called an "Abuse of Power" under Article II.

As to *Article I—Obstruction of Justice*, I then said, in part:

> Whether the President had a design to, or attempted to, interfere with or obstruct the Watergate investigation conducted by the FBI, by a phony attempt to enlist the possibility of CIA involvement, or whether he genuinely believed—due to the personnel concerned, the Mexican connection, and other circumstances—that there might well be a CIA or national security involvement, appears to me to be a debatable proposition.

It is, of course, the subsequently produced tape of the conversation of June 23, 1972 between Haldeman and the President which makes this proposition no longer debatable.

At that time, I also said:

> And where cover-up is considered we need to remember that, after all, the President became fully aware and took charge on March 21 and by April 30 Haldeman, Ehrlichman, Kleindienst and Dean had all left the government for good, and now are dealing as they should with the strictures of the criminal law.

The conversation of June 23, 1972 and the President's statement of August 5, 1974, of course, knock the props out from under this argument because we now know that President Nixon, so far from first becoming aware of the Watergate cover-up on March 21, 1973, was in fact actively and personally engaged therein from at least June 23, 1972, just six days after the Watergate break-in took place.

During our investigation of this case the Committee made no effort to call H. R. Haldeman or John Ehrlichman as witnesses (with some excuse due to their personal legal entanglements) and neither—without any clearly established excuse—did we make any effort to call E. Howard Hunt, the purported blackmailer to whom "hush money" is alleged to have been paid. As to this particular, and important, phase of the cover-up I said in my remarks to the Committee on July 25th:

> * * * the March 21 payment to Hunt was the last in a long series of such payments, engineered by Mitchell, Haldeman, Dean and Kalmbach, and later on LaRue, all so far as appears, without the President's knowledge or complicity. And as to the payment of March 21 the evidence appears to establish that it was set up and arranged for by conversations between Dean and LaRue and LaRue and Mitchell, *before* Dean talked to the President on the morning of the 21st of March. So that even if the President was willing, and even had he ordered it (as to which the proof falls short) it would appear that this payment was *in train* and would have gone forward, had Dean never talked to the President on March 21 at all.

And, while Presidential participation in the over-all cover-up plan is now conceded to be established, I see no reason, on the basis of the record, to change my statement as to this specific matter.

In addition—despite an invitation to do so—no effort was made to address either oral questions or written interrogations to President Nixon. These omissions as to the procurement of evidence all contributed—quite legitimately as I think—to my reluctance to resolve doubtful points against the President of the United States. The now self-revealed concealment of the facts on the President's part from all concerned, including not only the Committee but even his own Counsel, make such doubts easier to resolve.

This case is an American tragedy, in which a fatal decision to conceal the facts, made early in the game and—so far as I can see—without any prior implication on the part of the President, led inexorably to one shift and stratagem after another, and finally to the shattering events of the recent past.

Other matters in the voluminous record, which are referred to and relied upon by the majority, show, in some cases, shoddy practices inconsistent with the better spirit of America, but fail, in my judgment, to establish by any clear and convincing proof the existence of an impeachable offense.

It is the Watergate cover-up which gave birth to this inquiry—and it is that and that alone which has finally been susceptible of proof.

This is proof not as to all of the alleged details, nor need we, nor do we, accept each adverse inference so glibly drawn by the majority. Over-all, adequate legal proof is now available to establish the offense, and on the record we can say of the evidence, in the words of Mercutio,

"No, 'tis not so deep as a well, nor so wide as a church-door; but 'tis enough, 'twill serve . . ."

So be it.

We must follow the facts, and we must vindicate the law. But we must do this without vindictiveness; and we ought not further pursue or harass a man who, whatever his mistakes or his faults, has nevertheless served his country and all of humanity well, as probably the foremost international statesman and the most able architect of world order who has occupied the Presidency during our time.

DAVID W. DENNIS.

ADDITIONAL AND SEPARATE VIEWS OF MR. MAYNE

I join in the minority views of my colleagues insofar as Articles I and III are concerned. I do not join the minority views as to Article II because I believe the admissions made by the President on August 5, 1974, when added to the evidence previously submitted to the Committee, make a case for impeachment under Paragraphs 1, 4 and 5 of that Article.

ARTICLE I

I support the result reached by my colleagues in the minority views discussion of Article I but wish to add the following additional views:

I voted against Article I on July 27, 1974, after carefully considering such evidence as was available to the Committee at that time. It was my conscientious best judgment that no direct evidence had been presented to prove the President was personally involved in the Watergate cover-up or any obstruction of justice in connection with it. I was particularly impressed by the testimony of witnesses who appeared to testify before our Committee in person on this subject. Some stated their strong conviction that the President was in no way involved in the cover-up. Others expressed a complete lack of any information connecting him to it although they were in a position to know if he had been implicated. Only John Dean indicated an impression that the President had any knowledge of the cover-up prior to March 21, 1973. I did not feel his testimony and the inferences drawn from purely circumstantial evidence constituted the clear and convincing proof necessary to link the President personally to a high crime or misdemeanor sufficient to impeach under constitutional standards.

The state of the evidence changed completely on August 5, 1974, when the President made his statement admitting he knew at least as early as June 23, 1972, that the break-in was directed by employees of his re-election committee for political purposes. He not only withheld this important relevant information from the American people and the investigating authorities but obstructed the investigation by having his subordinates tell the FBI it should stop the investigation because it was exposing important undercover operations of the CIA.

The President also admitted on August 5 that he had continued to conceal these important facts and to deceive and mislead the American people and our Committee right up until that date when he made the transcripts of three conversations with H. R. Haldeman on June 23, 1972, available to the public and the Committee. These transcripts and the presidential admissions contained in his two-page statement of August 5 supply the direct evidence of personal involvement of the President in the cover-up which had previously been lacking. They furnish clear and convincing evidence that the President committed an obstruction of justice sufficient to constitute grounds for impeachment under the Constitution. I would, therefore, vote in the full House to impeach on Article I.

Article II

I file views separate from those of my minority colleagues for the following reasons:

1. I would vote in the House to impeach under Article II because I believe a case for impeachment has now been made under Paragraphs 1, 4 and 5 of that Article.

2. The minority views do not give sufficient treatment to the evidence in support of the grave allegations of Paragraph 1, Article II that the President tried to obtain income tax audits or other income tax investigations to be initiated or conducted in a discriminatory manner, i.e. to harass political opponents. During the debate I voted against an amendment to this Paragraph offered by the gentleman from California Mr. Wiggins which in my opinion would have seriously diluted the President's responsibility to prevent the improper use of the Internal Revenue Service for political purposes. The amendment would have stricken the words "acting personally and through his subordinates and agents" and added the following words "personally and through his subordinates and agents *acting with his knowldege or pursuant to his instructions*". (italics added) page 819, Report of Proceedings.

I spoke in opposition to this amendment stating that I certainly did "not want to do anything to dilute or limit in any way whatever responsibility the President may have for the very outrageous attempts to use the Internal Revenue Service for political purposes." I further stated "I consider the evidence shows that the approaches that were made by Mr. Dean and Mr. Ehrlichman to Commissioner Randolph Thrower and Commissioner Johnnie Walters to be absolutely indefensible. Our tax collection system in this country is based on a voluntary contribution assessed and paid by people on a voluntary basis and it will certainly be destroyed if people can not have confidence that it is not being used to reward political friends and to harass political opponents.

"I think that not only does the President have a responsibility not to directly approve such indefensible action but he has a responsibility not to ratify it after it has occurred and has a responsibility over and above that to have enough idea of what is going on in his Administration to be very sure that this kind of political prostitution of the Internal Revenue Service does not occur. There is nothing in this record which to me is more disappointing or more cause for concern for the continuation of free government than the way in which the Internal Revenue Service was attempted to be used for this base purpose."

The minority views fail to give sufficient attention to the following significant evidence:

(a) The affidavit of former IRS Commissioner Johnnie Walters that on September 11, 1972, John W. Dean gave him a list of persons on the 1972 Presidential campaign staff of George McGovern and of contributors to that campaign and requested that IRS undertake examinations or investigations of those on the list. Mr. Walters replied this would be disastrous for the IRS and the Administration and he would recommend to Secretary of the Treasury Shultz that nothing be done on the request. On September 25, 1972, Mr. Dean telephoned Mr. Walters inquiring "as to what progress I had made with the list. I told him that no progress had been made. He asked if it might be possible to develop information on fifty-sixty-seventy of the names. I again told him, that although I would reconsider the matter with Secretary Shultz, any activity of this type would be inviting disaster." Mr. Walters' affidavit states that he discussed these requests with Secretary Shultz on September 13 and September 29 and on both occasions was told to do nothing with the list. At no time did he furnish any name from the list to anyone or request any IRS employee or official to take any action with respect to the list. ("Statement of Information," Book VIII, 238-240)

(b) The conversation between the President and Haldeman on September 15, 1972, four days after Dean had delivered the list to Walters. Dean's activities were discussed by the President and Haldeman in the following recorded conversation:

HALDEMAN. Between times, he's doing, he's moving ruthlessly on the investigation of McGovern people, Kennedy stuff, and all that too. I just don't know how much progress he's making, 'cause I—
PRESIDENT. The problem is that's kind of hard to find.
HALDEMAN. Chuck, Chuck has gone through, you know, has worked on the list, and Dean's working the, the thing through IRS and, uh, in some cases, I think, some other (unintelligible) things. (HJCT 1)

(c) The following testimony by Dean describing his taking the list of McGovern contributors drawn by Murray Chotiner to Walters and discussing it subsequently with the President:

Mr. DOAR. What was the purpose of that meeting?
Mr. DEAN. I had then received the Chotiner list, and my assignment was to ask Mr. Walters if it was possible to have audits conducted on all or any of these people.
Mr. DOAR. Did you discuss your assignment with respect to the IRS with the President during your meeting on September 15?
Mr. DEAN. I am not sure how directly or specifically it came up, but there was a, indeed, a rather extended discussion with the President on the use of IRS. He made some rather specific comments to me, which in turn resulted in me going back to Mr. Walters again.
Mr. DOAR. When you say the use of IRS, what are you talking about?
Mr. DEAN. Well, as I recall the conversation, we were talking about the problems of having IRS conduct audits, and I told him that we hadn't been very successful at this because Mr. Walters had told me that he just didn't want to do it. I did—I did not push him. As far as I was concerned I was off the hook. I had done what I had been asked, and I related this to the President.
And he said something to the effect, well, if Shultz thinks he's been put over there to be some sort of (expletive), he is mistaken, and if you have got any problems, you just come tell me, and I will get it straightened out. (HJCT 229)
Mr. ST. CLAIR. Well, on September 15, 1972, you did meet with the President?
Mr. DEAN. Yes, I did.
Mr. ST. CLAIR. And you say that during the course of that conversation, among other things, you discussed a list being prepared for submission to the IRS?
Mr. DEAN. I am not sure we got into the so-called list of 500 at that time. It may well have come up. I recall general discussions by IRS and the fact that the President—telling the President that I had been less than successful in dealing with IRS and the President became quite annoyed at it. And then that he got very explicit about his thinking about IRS being responsive to the White House. (Dean testimony, 2 HJC 285)

The above affidavit and testimony clearly established that Dean and Haldeman were guilty of trying to use the IRS for illegal purposes and gave rise to strong inferences that the President was personally involved. In weighing whether a sufficient case had been made against the President under Araticle II, I had to consider the fact that Paragraph 1 alleging abuse of the Internal Revenue Service had unfortunately been lumped together with 4 other Paragraphs, which had little if any connection with each other and were supported by less proof than Paragraph 1. Pargraph 3 relative to a special investigative unit set up in the White House to identify and plug national security leaks struck me as especially weak. I could not accept the argument based on inferences alone that a President who had been advised by his closest foreign policy and national defense advisers that it was necessary to take decisive action to stop leaks which were threatening the security of the United States, could be subject to impeachment for taking such action, even though he did not implement it in the best way and it would have been much wiser to rely on the FBI which is the established agency responsible for National Security investigations. My argument in opposition to Paragraph 3 appears at pages 1016–1018 of the Report of Proceedings.

Faced with the choice of voting for a 5 paragraph Article in which there did not seem to me to be clear and convincing evidence sufficient to impeach on 4 of the 5 Paragraphs. I voted against Article II on July 29.

Thereafter the President's admissions of August 5 made available direct evidence sufficient to make a case for impeachment on Paragraphs 4 and 5. It is now clear that he did indeed fail to take care that the laws were faithfully executed and failed to exercise his authority to adequately supervise his close subordinates when he should have done so to prevent their obstructing and interfering with investigations into criminal or improper actions as stated in Paragraph 4.

When the presidential admissions of August 5, 1974, are viewed against the background of the evidence already considered by the Committee with reference to Paragraph 5, I must conclude that the President did in fact misuse his executive power in the manner in which he interfered with the Federal Bureau of Investigation, the Criminal Division of the Department of Justice and the Central Intelligence Agency.

His admissions of August 5 also further strengthen the evidence that he violated the constitutional rights of citizens as alleged in Paragraph 1 relating to abuse of the Internal Revenue Service.

Three of the 5 Paragraphs of Article II having now been proved by clear and convincing evidence I would vote to impeach on this Article in the full House.

Article III

I join in and support the minority views of my colleagues on Article III. No case for impeachment has been made on this Article.

WILEY MAYNE.

ADDITIONAL VIEWS OF MR. COHEN ON ARTICLE III

It is the opinion of this member that neither the President of the United States nor any other official of the United States can lawfully refuse to comply with subpoenas issued by the House Judiciary Committee relevant to issues raised in the course of an impeachment investigation. As the United States Supreme Court held in 1882, "All officers of the Government, from the highest to the lowest, are creatures of the law and are bound to obey it; no officer of the law may set that law at defiance with impunity."

In the case of subpoenas issued by this Committee in the course of its impeachment investigation, the powers of the Committee under the law are clear. The Constitution gives to the House of Representatives the sole power of impeachment. Acting under this provision, the House of Representatives, on February 6, 1974, adopted H. Res. 803. This resolution directed the House Judiciary Committee to consider the possible impeachment of Richard M. Nixon, President of the United States, and conferred subpoena power upon this Committee for purposes of its impeachment inquiry.

Acting under that power, the Committee subsequently voted more than 40 separate subpoenas for tapes, documents, and other materials relevant to its investigation. The President failed to comply with those subpoenas.

In his refusal to comply, the President repeatedly asserted that he was carrying out a Constitutional responsibility to uphold the separation of powers among the branches of government by protecting the confidentiality of communications within the executive branch. It has been suggested that the protection of confidential communications, which appears to have been used synonymously with executive privilege, may, as a doctrine, have taken on mythical proportions. (See Berger, *Executive Privilege: A Constitutional Myth*). But, while not necessarily rising to the level of a Constitutionally conceived and protected doctrine, executive privilege nonetheless serves a valuable purpose in protecting the confidentiality of the decision-making process in the executive branch. Indeed, the Supreme Court recently acknowledged importance of this privilege in its decision, The *United States* v. *Nixon*, (House Judiciary Committee "Statement of Information," Appendix II). Although holding that a Presidential claim of privilege did not, under the specific circumstances of that case, prevail over the Special Prosecutor's need for subpoenaed materials for criminal trials, the Court recognized "the valid need for protection of communications between high government officials and those who advise and assist them." Noting that "Human experience teaches that those who expect public dissemination of their remarks will temper candor with a concern for appearances . . . to the detriment of the decision-making process," the Court further asserted that "the importance of this confidentiality is too plain to require further discussion."

In voting to issue subpoenas to the President, this Committee made no concession to the doctrine of executive privilege. It asserted the absolute right to subpoena whatever materials it deemed relevant to its inquiry. In short, the Committee's subpoenas, coupled with the President's refusal to comply, presented a constitutional confrontation: the President's judicially recognized interest in maintaining the confidentiality of private tapes, papers, and documents, stood in direct conflict with the Constitutional power of the Congress to compel the production of evidence for an impeachment proceeding.

Several courses of action were available to the Committee to resolve the confrontation. It could have sought a judicial review and determination of the scope and power of the Committee's process, or sought a citation of contempt before the full House of Representatives. In addition, in reaching a final decision on articles of impeachment the Committee could have drawn negative or adverse inferences from the President's refusal to comply with its subpoenas.

While I am not satisfied that it is essential or desirable to have the judicial branch pass final judgment on the merits of the respective positions of the President and the Committee, I believe the Supreme Court would have reached a result similar to that in *United States* v. *Nixon, supra*—namely, that the need of the Congress for subpoenaed materials for an impeachment inquiry would have prevailed over the President's claim of privilege.

Although I do not believe it was essential to seek a judicial resolution of the Judiciary Committee's powers, I do not suggest the Committee should be the final arbiter in disputes arising from the issuance of subpoenas. Under accepted Congressional procedure, when a witness before a Congressional Committee refuses to give testimony or produce documents, the Committee itself cannot hold the witness in contempt. Rather, the established procedure is for the witness to be given an opportunity to appeal before the full House or Senate, as the case may be, and give reasons, if he can, why he should not be held in contempt. For example, he might argue that his refusal was justified, or excusable, or based on some mistake. The Supreme Court has held that this kind of notice and opportunity for hearing are constitutionally required, under the Fifth and Fourteenth Amendments, before a legislative body may punish a person for contempt of its prerogatives. (Minority Views of Honorable Edward Hutchinson, et. al., "Article III: President's Response to Committee Subpoenas.")

Before Presidential refusal to comply with Committee subpoenas can be raised to the level of an impeachable offense, the Committee, at a minimum, should wait until the House of Representatives has found the non-compliance to be willful, contemptuous, and illegitimate. Since the Committee did not pursue this course of action, it should not now seek to raise non-compliance to the level of a separate and independent impeachable act.

While the President's stated reasons for his refusal to comply with our Committee's subpoenas may have had a colorable claim or basis, the evidence before the Committee (even before the release of the June 23, 1972, transcript) was more than sufficient to find that the claim of executive privilege was illegitimately and improperly invoked, not to protect the Office of the President, but to protect a particular President from the disclosure of his personal participation in the obstruction of justice. Accordingly, the President's non-compliance with the subpoenas formed an integral part of Article I (and possibly Article II) and rests more soundly and solidly within that factual framework.

Concern for setting a precedent for history's review or need must take into account the need not to arrive at an unnecessary, and in my opinion, unwise conclusion, such as that set forth as Article III. Hopefully, the sword of impeachment will never have to be withdrawn from its scabbard again. But should events summon forth so drastic a constitutional weapon in future years, let the sword be wielded by the guardians of our Constitutional system with a sharp but not overhoned edge.

WILLIAM S. COHEN.

ADDITIONAL VIEWS OF MR. FROEHLICH IN OPPOSITION TO ARTICLE III

Article III charges that Richard M. Nixon "failed without lawful cause or excuse to produce papers and things as directed by duly authorized subpoenas issued by the Committee on the Judiciary of the House of Representatives on April 11, 1974, May 15, 1974, May 30, 1974, and June 24, 1974, and willfully disobeyed such subpoenas." On July 30, 1974, the Committee voted to send this third article of impeachment to the full House for consideration. The vote was 21 to 17. Because I believe this article represents a wholly inadequate and improper basis upon which to impeach, try, and remove a President from office, I opposed the article in committee and now respectfully urge its rejection.

A

The Constitution of the United States, in Article I, Section 2, Clause 5, provides that "The House of Representatives . . . shall have the sole Power of Impeachment." This clause contains a clear, exclusive grant of power. Inherent in this grant of power is the authority to conduct a comprehensive inquiry into alleged grounds for impeachment and to employ all reasonable means, including subpoenas, to secure evidence for that inquiry.

There is no question that the House of Representatives is empowered to confer upon its "impeachment committee" an *expansive* subpoena power; and there is no question that the House properly conferred that power in this matter by approving House Resolution 803, on February 6, 1974.

It does not follow, however, that the Committee's power to secure evidence is unlimited. The impeachment power of the House, like every other power possessed by Congress, must be read together with at least some of the other provisions in the Constitution. If this were not the case, the Impeachment Committee could degenerate into a lawless inquisition, a kangaroo court, wholly at odds with our legal traditions.

Surely, the clause in the Constitution that gives the House of Representatives "the sole Power of Impeachment" does not imply that *any* procedure is acceptable in an impeachment inquiry.[1] Suppose, for instance, that in this inquiry the Committee had insisted that H. R. Haldeman appear to testify, despite his forewarning that he would assert his Fifth Amendment privilege against self-incrimination. Suppose, further, that if Mr. Haldeman failed to testify without a grant of

---

[1] The principal thrust of the clause is to confine the power of impeachment to the House of Representatives. What this plainly means is that no other institution of government has the power to impeach: not the Senate, not the Judiciary, and not the President. For example, non-compliance with a Senate subpoena is not grounds for impeachment in the Senate, even if the subpoena is fully litigated and approved by the courts, *unless* the House of Representatives first cites such non-compliance in an article of impeachment.

immunity, he was confined to a room in the basement of the Rayburn Building and held there incommunicado without adequate sleep or nourishment in an effort to coerce his testimony. Is there any doubt that the House's "sole Power of Impeachment" does not carry with it the right to employ these kinds of improper tactics to secure evidence? Is there any doubt that a court could have intervened to protect Mr. Haldeman's constitutional rights, even in an impeachment inquiry?

It should be self-evident then that there are limitations upon the power of the House of Representatives, and its Impeachment Committee to secure evidence; and hence it becomes highly important to consider what those limitations are and how they are determined.

B

The Committee on the Judiciary issued a total of eight subpoenas to the President. Although the President supplied partial transcripts of many of the items requested in the first subpoena, he clearly failed to comply with the Committee's demands. But that is not the real issue. The real issue is whether the President failed to comply with the subpoenas *"without lawful cause or excuse"*, as charged in the Article. This issue was never litigated, and it was never settled, unless one assumes that the Committee has *unlimited, unreviewable* authority to demand and receive evidence from a witness in an impeachment inquiry.

Some Members asserted at the outset of these proceedings that the House did possess unlimited subpoena power. Against this background, President Nixon had a rational reason for resisting the Committee's demands. Almost any president would have resisted subpoenas issued under such sweeping claims of authority. To have complied fully with all eight subpoenas, without testing the subpoenas in relation to the Committee's constitutional authority, would have been to abandon privileges, and establish precedents that could radically alter the balance of power between the Executive and Legislative branches of government.

The argument is made that if President Nixon honestly believed that the Committee's subpoenas improperly encroached upon the province of the Executive, he would have moved to quash the subpoenas in court. To do that, however, the President would have had to argue that the courts possessed the jurisdiction to intervene in this dispute and to rule on his claim of executive privilege—a position that would have seriously undermined his legal posture in the then pending case of *United States* v. *Nixon*, U.S. (1974). It is entirely possible that had the circumstances been somewhat different, President Nixon would have gone to court in an effort to quash the subpoenas, for there appear to be a number of arguable bases upon which the subpoenas might successfully have been resisted.

Several Members of the Committee urged the Committee to seek court approval of the subpoenas. But this suggestion was rejected on May 30, 1974, by a vote of 32 to 6. At that same meeting, the Committee directed the Chairman to write the President, advising him that "it is not within the power of the President to conduct an inquiry into his own impeachment, to determine which evidence, and what version or portion of that evidence, is relevant and necessary to such an inquiry. These are matters which, under the Constitution, the House has the sole power to determine."

What this means is that the Committee claims the sole power to determine what evidence is relevant and what evidence is necessary in an impeachment inquiry. It asserts that the courts have no jurisdiction to review a Committee determination in this regard. Any objections raised by a witness to the scope or content of a subpoena *duces tecum* will be recognized, if at all, in the sole discretion of the Committee.[2] The witness has no option to *enforce* any of his normal "rights" before a neutral court. The potential penalty for non-compliance with the Committee's demand for evidence is impeachment, and non-compliance with a Committee subpoena, *by itself*, is sufficient grounds for impeaching the President and removing him from office.

This is the real meaning of Article III, and this is why Article III is not only an improper basis for impeachment but also a dangerous precedent for our constitutional system. If the Committee had sought to enforce its subpoenas before a neutral arbiter and given the President the opportunity to litigate his objections to the Committee's demands, I would have no difficulty in supporting an article of impeachment based on non-compliance. But that did not happen. In these proceedings, the Committee rejected court review of its legal process. It refused to seek court enforcement, and it even declined to subpoena the exact same material from Judge John Sirica that it had previously subpoenaed from the President.[3] Under these circumstances, it would be a travesty of justice to impeach President Nixon on the basis of the third article voted by the Committee.

C

There appear to be a number of arguable bases upon which the Committee's eight subpoenas to the President might have been quashed or limited, had they been litigated in a court. A review of these bases is relevant to the question whether President Nixon failed to comply with the subpoenas "without lawful cause or excuse," and it is relevant in considering whether Article III, as it was developed, represents a legitimate and proper basis upon which to impeach, try, and remove a President of the United States.

1. *Executive Privilege.*—In *United States* v. *Nixon*—U.S.—(1974), the Supreme Court ruled on the nature of executive privilege, saying: "If a President concludes that compliance with a subpoena would be

---

[2] Compare *Tumey* v. *Ohio*, 273 U.S. 510 (1927). In this case a defendant accused of violating the Prohibition Act was tried and sentenced by a judge who benefited financially from his conviction. The Court, speaking through Chief Justice Taft, declared: ". . . [I]t certainly violates the Fourteenth Amendment, and deprives a defendant in a criminal case of due process, to subject his liberty or property to the judgment of a court the judge of which has a direct, personal, substantial, pecuniary interest in reaching a conclusion against him in his case." 273 U.S. at 523. The parallel in this situation is obvious. The Committee members would have a direct, personal, substantial, political interest in reaching conclusions adverse to the objectives raised by the subpoenaed party. It is hard to conceive a more clear-cut, obvious conflict of interest.

[3] On June 24, 1974, the Committee tabled my motion to subpoena from United States District Judge John J. Sirica the exact same tape recording of a September 15, 1972, conversation between President Nixon, H. R. Haldeman, and John W. Dean that hours earlier it had subpoenaed from the President. The vote to table was 23 to 15. In response to questions, both John Doar and Albert Jenner agreed that the tape recording in question was "necessary and relevant" to the Committee's inquiry.

injurious to the public interest he may properly ... invoke a claim of privilege on the return of the subpoena. Upon receiving a claim of privilege from the Chief Executive, it became the further duty of the District Court to treat the subpoenaed material as presumptively privileged and to require the Special Prosecutor to demonstrate that the presidential material was 'essential to the justice of the [pending criminal] case.' ... Here ... the Special Prosecutor ... made a sufficient showing to rebut the presumption and [the Court] ordered an *in camera* examination of the subpoenaed material."

In the court's *in camera* review of subpoenaed presidential materials:

"Statements that meet the test of admissibility and relevance must be isolated; all other material must be excised."

"... (T)he District Court has a very heavy responsibility to see to it that presidential conversations, which are either not relevant or not admissible, are accorded that high degree to respect due to the President of the United States."

"It is ... necessary in the public interest to afford presidential confidentiality the greatest protection consistent with the fair administration of justice."

The Court's assessment of the claim of executive privilege is substantially different from the Committee's assessment. One Member of the Committee even declared: "I will state that I do not think we are compelled to set forth ... reasons" for the evidence we subpoena. Clearly, the question whether executive privilege has any place in an impeachment inquiry is a substantial question, and it should not be decided arbitrarily by either of the two contending branches of government.

2. Fifth Amendment Right Against Self-Incrimination.—In *United States v. Onassis,* 125 F. Supp. 190 (D.C. 1954), the court, citing the Fifth Amendment, said that a person has cause to refuse the production of his personal papers whenever he thinks that the production might reasonably tend to incriminate him. "The sole question is whether the subpoenaed documents were Augenthaler's personal records. If so, then compulsory production certainly offended his constitutional rights. As was said in *Boyd* v. *United States,* 1886, 116 U.S. 616, 633, ... it is impossible 'to perceive that the seizure of a man's private books and papers to be used in evidence against him is substantially different from compelling him to be a witness against himself.'" 125 F. Supp. at 206. If this is a correct statement of law, a court might well have suppressed incriminating tape recordings of the President's private conversations as well as his personal memoranda of his thoughts and actions.

3. Unreasonable Search and Seizure.—"The Constitution requires that the forced production of documents by subpoena be not unreasonable." *Application of Harry Alexander,* 8 F.R.D. 559, 560 (S.D.N.Y. 1949). Whether a particular subpoena duces tecum is "reasonable" is clearly a legal question that ought to be decided in each instance on the basis of the facts arising from the subpoena itself.

4. Attorney-Client Privilege.—In *Colton* v. *United States,* 306 F.2d 633, 637 (2d Cir. 1962), the court noted that the policy underlying the attorney-client privilege does not justify "any member of the bar from refusing to testify as to all transactions he may have had with any person whom he chooses to designate a 'client.'" *But*, "It is self-evident that individual documents and files may still be withheld insofar as they thus are or report confidential communications between Colton and his clients . . ." 306 F.2d at 639. That the President's private conversations with the White House Counsel were at least partly covered by the attorney-client privilege is not so outlandish a proposition that it can be dismissed out of hand.

5. *Competent, Relevant, Material Evidence.*—"Generally speaking, a subpoena duces tecum may be used to compel the production of any proper documentary evidence, such as books, papers, documents, accounts, and the like, which is desired for the proof of an alleged fact relevant to the issue before the Court or office issuing the subpoena, *provided that the evidence which it is thus sought to be obtained is competent, relevant, and material.*" 97 C.J.S. § 25 Witnesses, at 381–382 (1957) (Emphasis supplied). Items demanded do not become competent, relevant, and material merely because they are included in a committee subpoena. If there is no test of the worthiness and relevance of the materials subpoenaed, then the subpoena power may be used to conduct a "fishing expedition" that could seriously breach the independence of the Executive Branch.

6. *Discovery.*—"A subpoena *duces tecum* may not be used for the purpose of discovery, either to ascertain the existence of documentary evidence, or to pry into the case of the prosecution." *United States* v. *Carter*, 15 F.R.D. 367, 369 (D.C. 1954). It can certainly be argued that some of the items demanded in the Committee's eight subpoenas were included therein principally as a means of discovering other evidence.

In view of the strength and number of arguments the President might have raised to quash or limit the Committee's subpoenas, it is not surprising that the Committee avoided court review. However, inasmuch as court review was not only avoided but also specifically rejected, it is unseemly for the Committee to insist that the President's non-compliance was "without lawful cause or excuse."

D

An impeachment inquiry—the Grand Inquest of the Nation—is an extraordinary political process. Though quasi-judicial in nature, impeachment is inevitably a political undertaking in which the leading actors are political figures. As a consequence, it is vitally important that impeachment proceedings be fair, both in fact and in appearance, so that they merit the confidence of the American people.

The impeachment of a President of the United States on the grounds stated in Article III is fundamentally unfair in fact and highly political in appearance. To impeach a President and thereby attempt to overturn the mandate of the American people on grounds as suspect and insubstantial as these, would, in any circumstances, engender distrust and jeopardize the legitimacy of the entire impeachment proceedings.

The House must assure the integrity of its impeachment process. But this does not mean that the House must uphold the Committee's action on Article III in order to preserve its constitutional prerogatives. The House always had and always will have the option of seeking enforcement of its subpoenas in court. Subpoenas from a House Committee in an impeachment inquiry are entitled to great respect, and we can safely assume that the courts would require the production of at least as much evidence as could be obtained by a party in a court proceeding.

For all these reasons, Article III should not be approved as grounds for impeaching the President of the United States.

HAROLD V. FROEHLICH.

ADDITIONAL SUPPLEMENTAL VIEWS OF MR. LATTA

Article I charges Richard Nixon with obstruction of justice in connection with the Watergate affair. Obstruction of justice is a federal crime under Title 18 of the United States Code, Sections 1503 and 1510, punishable by a fine of not more than $5,000 or imprisonment for not more than five years, or both. On the sixth day of March, 1974, then President Nixon, in answer to a question at a news conference as to whether or not he considered an obstruction of justice to be an impeachable offense, replied, "the crime of obstruction of justice is a serious crime and would be an impeachable offense." [1]

Paragraph 4 of Article I charges Richard Nixon with "interfering or endeavoring to interfere with the conduct of investigations by the Department of Justice of the United States, the Federal Bureau of Investigation, the Office of Watergate Special Prosecution Force, and Congressional Committees."

Paragraph 6 of Article I charges Richard Nixon with "endeavoring to misuse the Central Intelligence Agency, an agency of the United States."

On August 5, 1974, then President Nixon admitted that he had given certain incomplete and erroneous information to his staff, his attorney, and to the House Judiciary Committee and, thereupon, released transcripts showing that he in fact had used the Central Intelligence Agency to thwart the investigation by the Federal Bureau of Investigation of the Watergate break-in as early as six days after it had occurred, to wit, on June 23, 1972. By so doing, the then President was in effect admitting to the charges of obstruction of justice as contained in Paragraphs 4 and 6 of Article I. This admission coupled with Mr. Nixon's own statement of March 6, 1974, that an obstruction of justice would be an impeachable offense would have been sufficient evidence to cause me to vote affirmatively on these two Paragraphs. However, at the time the vote was taken in the Judiciary Committee in this matter, this evidence of direct presidential involvement had not been revealed and was not before us.

DELBERT L. LATTA.

---

[1] "Presidential Statements," 71, 73.

ABBREVIATIONS

CIA	Central Intelligence Agency
CRP	3/71–9/71 Citizens for the Re-election of the President
	9/71–1973 Committee for the Re-election of the President
DNC	Democratic National Committee
FBI	Federal Bureau of Investigation
FCRP	10/71–2/72 Finance Committee for the Re-election of President Nixon
	2/72–4/72 Finance Committee for the Re-election of the President
	4/72–present Finance Committee to Re-elect the President
GAO	General Accounting Office
GSA	General Services Administration
ICC	International Controls Corporation
IRS	Internal Revenue Service
ITT	International Telephone and Telegraph Corporation
OMB	Office of Management and Budget
OMBE	Office of Minority Business Enterprise (Department of Commerce)
RNC	Republican National Committee
SEC	Securities and Exchange Commission
SSC	Senate Select Committee on Presidential Campaign Activities

CITATIONS

Form	Source
1. Book I, 34–35	House Judiciary Committee, "Statement of Information," Books I–XII.
Book I	Events Prior to the Watergate Break-In December 2, 1971–June 17, 1972
Book II	Events Following the Watergate Break-In June 17, 1972–February 9, 1973
Book III	Events Following the Watergate Break-In June 20, 1972–March 22, 1973
Book IV	Events Following the Watergate Break-In March 22, 1973–April 30, 1973
Book V	Department of Justice/ITT Litigation-Richard Kleindienst Nomination Hearings
Book VI	Political Contributions by Milk Producers Cooperatives: The 1971 Milk Price Support Decision
Book VII	White House Surveillance Activities and Campaign Activities
Book VIII	Internal Revenue Service
Book IX	Watergate Special Prosecutors Judiciary Committee's Impeachment Inquiry April 30, 1973–July 1, 1974
Book X	Tax Deduction for Gift of Papers (includes materials submitted on behalf of President Nixon)
Book XI	Bombing of Cambodia
Book XII	Impoundment of Funds; Government Expenditures on President Nixon's Private Properties at San Clemente and Key Biscayne
2. WHT 586	"Submission of Recorded Presidential Conversations to the Committee on the Judiciary of the House of Representatives by President Richard Nixon, April 30, 1974."
3. HJCT 85	House Judiciary Committee, "Transcripts of Eight Recorded Presidential Conversations."
4. Butterfield testimony, 1 HJC 9–10.	House Judiciary Committee, "Testimony of Witnesses." Books 1–3.
5. Political Matters Memorandum, 12/6/71, 51.	Series of memoranda prepared by Gordon Strachan for H. R. Haldeman in 1971 and 1972 and submitted to the House Judiciary Committee by President Nixon.
6. HJC, Background — White House/CRP, 6.	House Judiciary Committee, "Background Memorandum: White House Staff and President Nixon's Campaign Organizations."
7. "Presidential Statements," 8/15/73, 24–25.	House Judiciary Committee, "Presidential Statements on the Watergate Break-In and Its Investigation."
8. President's Submission, Book I, 14–16.	Counsel for the President, Statement of Information Submitted on Behalf of President Nixon, Books I–IV.
Book I	Events Following the Watergate Break-in June 19, 1972–March 1, 1974

(527)

Book II	Department of Justice—ITT Litigation
Book III	Political Contributions by Milk Producers Cooperatives: The 1971 Milk Price Support Decision
Book IV	White House Surveillance Activities
9. Haldeman testimony, 7 SSC 2871.	Senate Select Committee on Presidential Campaign Activities, Hearings, Books 1–15.
10. Gray logs, 6/21/72	L. Patrick Gray, Appointment Logs, received by the House Judiciary Committee from the Senate Select Committee on Presidential Campaign Activities.
11. Meetings and Conversations between the President and John Ehrlichman, 4/18/73.	Document submitted to the House Judiciary Committee by President Nixon.
12. Report of conversation between CIA Inspector General and Robert Cushman, 6/29/73.	Document received by the House Judiciary Committee from the CIA.
13. Ehrlichman notes	John Ehrlichman handwritten notes of meetings with the President, received by the House Judiciary Committee from the Watergate Special Prosecution Force.
14. Joint Committee Report, 94	Joint Committee on Internal Revenue Taxation, "Staff Report—Examination of President Nixon's Tax Returns for 1969 through 1972."
15. WHT, June 23, 1972, 10:04–11:39 a.m., 19–30	Edited transcripts of three recorded Presidential conversations submitted to the House Judiciary Committee by President Nixon on August 5, 1974.
16. "Criminal Cases," 17	House Judiciary Committee, "Papers in Criminal Cases Initiated by the Watergate Special Prosecution Force—June 27, 1973–August 2, 1974."
17. Kehrli affidavit, 3	Bruce Kehrli, Affidavit submitted to the House Judiciary Committee, July 25, 1974.
18. Roger Barth testimony, SSC Executive Session, June 6, 1974, 3–6	Senate Select Committee on Presidential Campaign Activities, Executive Session testimony, received by the House Judiciary Committee from the Senate Select Committee.
19. May 1974 Tape Report	"The EOB Tape of June 20, 1972: Report on a Technical Investigation Conducted for the U.S. District Court for the District of Columbia by the Advisory Panel on White House Tapes, May 31, 1974."
20. Stanford Research Institute (SRI) Report.	"Review of a Report Submitted to the U.S. District Court for the District of Columbia Entitled 'The Tape of June 20, 1974, May 31, 1974.'"
21. HJC Debates, July 27, 1974, TR. 288.	House Judiciary Committee, Debates on Proposed Articles of Impeachment, July 24–30, 1974.
22. Memorandum from Director, FBI, to Attorney General, June 24, 1974.	Documents received by the House Judiciary Committee from the FBI.

www.ingramcontent.com/pod-product-compliance
Lightning Source LLC
Chambersburg PA
CBHW022005300426
44117CB00005B/44